Abraham
The Story of a Journey

Michael Scharf Publication Trust
Yeshiva University Press

Jonathan Grossman

Abraham

The Story of a Journey

The Noam Series

The Michael Scharf Publication Trust of
Yeshiva University Press

Maggid Books

Abraham
The Story of a Journey

First English Edition, 2023

Maggid Books
An imprint of Koren Publishers Jerusalem Ltd.

POB 8531, New Milford, CT 06776-8531, USA
& POB 4044, Jerusalem 9104001, Israel
www.maggidbooks.com

The publication of this book was made possible through the generous support of *The Jewish Book Trust*.

ISBN 978-1-59264-504-6, *hardcover*

Printed and bound in the United States

The Noam Series
is dedicated to the memory of

Dr. Noam Shudofsky *z"l*

by his family and friends

Noam loved the study of Tanakh
and enabled generations of students to
"Understand and discern, to listen, learn and teach, to observe, perform and fulfill all the teachings of the Torah with love."

Contents

Preface and Acknowledgments

History has seen few revolutionaries like Abraham, who left his home and crossed over to the "other side" of the Euphrates to found a new culture, changing the face of history. One man's journey, at a specific point in time, was a giant leap for humanity. Religious and cultural history as we know it today was unquestionably shaped by the call to "go forth," which marked the first step of a national, ethical saga.

Often, exploration of origin awakens fundamental questions that touch upon the very question of existence. Abraham's narrative cycle grapples with the essential definition of the Israelite nation – or, to be more true to the spirit of the Genesis stories – the definition of "the Israelite family." Other raw, profound issues touch upon the tension between morality and nationality, and the tension between taking an autonomous stand against God and total, unquestioning submission to divine authority.

This book was written in memory of Dr. Noam Shudofsky (1933–2005), an accomplished man whose entire life was devoted to the world of education, both formal and informal. Noam began his career as a Bible teacher, and from there, he advanced along the administrative path until he became the principal of the Ramaz Yeshiva of Manhattan, serving in that capacity for forty dedicated years. He was extraordinarily devoted to his students and staff. His love for the Bible did not wane even after he was no longer actively teaching, and he was especially drawn to the literary approach of Bible study, an approach embraced by the present work. Jewish identity was an inextricable part of his identity, and he held that every person must fulfill himself not only in an intellectual sense, but in life itself. And indeed, Noam was deeply involved in the international Jewish community. His intense efforts – both overt and covert – for the Jews of Russia, who were persecuted solely because of their Judaism, is especially worth mentioning. Writing this book in his memory was a special privilege for me, and I was also privileged to become acquainted with his entire family, people whose lives are deeply rooted in love of Torah and love of humanity, and colored with humility and devotion.

During Hanukkah 2017, Dr. Shudofsky's beloved wife, Nechi, also passed away, and I would like to dedicate this book to her memory as well. Her warmth and generosity enveloped me from our first encounter.

With great pleasure, I wish to thank everyone who helped bring this book to light, from its first conception to its final design. First and foremost, from the depths of my heart, I wish to thank my dear friend Binny Shalev, who made this journey together with me, a journey that taught me so much about humility and kindness. I hope we will always continue reenacting the verse, "And the two of them walked together." We were accompanied on our journey by Rabbi Dr. Itamar Eldar, whose contributions to the ideas expressed in this work were indispensable.

As English is not my mother tongue, Atara Snowbell took on the formidable task of translating the manuscript into English, in the research edition of this book, published in 2016 by Peter Lang. Her love for the words of Genesis translated technical grammatical discussions into precise, sincere explorations of the text's meaning. The work of processing the manuscript and re-editing it for the edition before us was undertaken by Ms. Emily Silverman, who with her literary sensitivity and her love of the Bible led some of the ideas in the book to new heights.

I am privileged to send The Noam Series out into the world through Maggid Books, as part of their Maggid Tanakh Companions series. Matthew Miller and Rabbi Reuven Ziegler have brought about a revolution in Tanakh study, setting new standards for the rare, often incompatible combination of accessibility and caliber in the world of

Jewish publishing. I thank them both for their dedication and ambition, and I hope Maggid Books will continue to soar.

This book has been published through the cooperation of Maggid Books and the Michael Scharf Publication Trust of Yeshiva University Press. This reflects the work's ambition to speak in two dialects, appealing to scholars and *Ohavei Torah* alike. These do not contradict each other; on the contrary, at their best they enrich each other.

Special thanks go to Rabbi Dr. Stu Halpern, the Senior Advisor to the Provost of Yeshiva University, who oversaw this book's publication from Yeshiva University's end. His expertise and broad experience made every consultation a creative, original learning experience, and I thank him for his friendship and partnership. My sincere thanks also go to Maggid's dedicated publication team, Caryn Meltz, Shira Finson, Aryeh Sklar, Debbie Ismailoff, and Nechama Unterman, who worked diligently and thoroughly on the book's language editing – I am indebted to them for their careful attention to detail.

Last but not least, of course, thanks are due to my wife and children, who accompany me on every journey into the world of reading, writing, and study, who so patiently and so fruitfully hear out every thought and dilemma, who color every ordinary day with joy.

יבואו כולם על הברכה
Jonathan Grossman
Tishrei 5783

Introduction

Abraham Was But One Man

"Abraham was but one man, yet he was given possession of the land," declare the people of Jerusalem to the Babylonian exiles (Ezek. 33:24). And in many ways, the Jerusalemites were right in praising Abraham for his accomplishments despite him being "but one man." Abraham is not only the founder of the Israelite nation, he is also largely considered to be the originator of the revolutionary religious philosophy of ethical monotheism.

As a protagonist, Abraham is fascinating. Literary scholars tend to define characters according to the dynamics of their actions and the complexities of their personas. There are "flat characters" and "round characters," "static characters" and "dynamic characters," and other types of literary character profiles. Abraham contains within him complexities that make it difficult to define him according to these classifications. True, Abraham maintains a certain literary consistency throughout the narrative. However, within Abraham there are internal paradoxes that we rarely see coexisting in the same person. The same Abraham who builds altars in the name of God (see, for example, Gen. 12:7) gathers his legions and goes out to battle in order to save Lot (14:14–16). The same Abraham who silently follows God's command to leave his homeland (12:1), who says nothing when God asks him to sacrifice his only son (ch. 22) – this is the same man who stands adamantly in front of God and claims that the Judge of all creation was defying His own value of fair justice when it came to the destruction of Sodom (18:25). Abraham, who in one narrative tells his wife, "She is your maid, do with her what you will" (15:6), later refuses to heed his wife's guidance to expel the maid and her son until God commands him to listen to her (Gen. 21:11–12). It would seem that although Abraham's character is cohesive on the whole, it contains a multitude of complexities and paradoxes. Abraham's story is far more nuanced than a mere description of the founder of institutionalized monotheistic thought; his character, like his journey, is complex and paradoxical.

The Historical Period of the Abraham Narrative

When did Abraham live? Many would claim that this type of question is inconsequential when trying to understand the purpose and messages of the stories of the forefathers. To them, it makes no difference in what time period Abraham lived, because at the end of the day, the narrative remains the same. In many ways, this perspective is correct; any reader who follows the stories of Abraham, Isaac, and Jacob can sense that these stories are not intended to build a precise biographical history. For example, although the stories are rooted in a sequential narrative throughout the characters' lives, the text makes gigantic chronological leaps over long periods of time; it presents details of great personal significance as parenthetical (such as Abraham's marriage to Keturah and the birth of their six children in Genesis 25:1–4); and it engages in a clear methodology by which it builds recurring themes and ideas within the narrative. These literary devices clearly demonstrate that the Abraham narrative is not so much a biographical-historical account as a narrative intended to highlight the moral ideals within the stories. Thus, to paraphrase Martin Buber, Abraham could be defined as a "figure of history," rather than a "figure of archaeology."[1]

1. See Martin Buber, *Koenigtum Gottes, Moses, and The Prophetic Faith*. Using a similar methodological approach, William W. Hallo claims ("Biblical History in Its Near Eastern Setting: The Contextual Approach," in *Scripture in Context: Essays on the Comparative Method*, ed. C. D. Evans [Pittsburg, 1980], 16) that "Israelite history" in the Bible only begins with the Egyptian oppression, whereas the patriarchal narratives do not purport to deliver a historical sequence relating to the nation. Hallo

Despite this characterization, it is important to emphasize the historical realism of the Abraham, Isaac, and Jacob narratives; meaning to say, despite the underlying moral lessons of the stories, the narrative itself does not read as folklore. As Nahum Sarna aptly points out, the stories do not depict mythical figures.[2] In fact, the opposite is true: the characters fail repeatedly, they are subject to criticism, and their stories are well anchored in a historically authentic setting of Mesopotamia and Canaan. Indeed, knowledge of the social and legal norms of Abraham's time leads the reader to a deeper layer of understanding of the stories in which he appears. Ephraim Avigdor Speiser, in his analysis of the forefathers, notes that while early contemporary scholars doubted the historical accuracy of the biblical narrative, today – with the many discoveries of Ancient Near East manuscripts – "these chapters are generally a true reflection of prevalent traditions and customs in the relevant era."[3] In the half-century since Speiser wrote those words, our historical and archaeological understanding of the period has expanded significantly, and it is difficult to imagine that there is any doubt regarding the accuracy of the Abraham narrative's overall historical setting among scholars today, although modern scholars are cautious not to date the occurrences too precisely. Either way, Speiser, along with his colleagues of the "archaeological" school of thought, is correct in his analysis that highlighting Abraham and his progeny's literal place in history only serves to deepen our understanding of their narratives and the lessons they embody.

---

writes that this proposal "does not imply that all that preceded the oppressions is utterly devoid of historicity...only that it has a different character."

2. Nahum Sarna, *Understanding Genesis* (The Heritage of Biblical Israel Series 1: New York, 1966), 81–85.
3. Ephraim A. Speiser, "The Forefathers and their Social Context," in *The Forefathers and the Judges: The History of Israel from Its Beginnings Until the Establishment of the Monarchy*, ed. Benjamin Mazar (Jerusalem and Ramat Gan, 1967), 80 (Hebrew). Kenneth A. Kitchen ("Genesis 12–50 in the Near Eastern World," in *He Swore an Oath: Biblical Themes from Genesis 12–50*, ed. R. S. Hess, G. J. Wenham, and P. E. Satterthwaite [Grand Rapids, MI, 1994], 67–92) reached a similar conclusion after examining various perspectives of links between the patriarchal narratives and literature from the end of the second millennium BCE. See also Yehoshua M. Grintz, *The Book of Genesis: Its Uniqueness and Antiquity* (Jerusalem, 1983); Umberto Cassuto, "Abraham," *Entziklopedya Mikra'it*, 1:64–65.

Those who wish to point to a specific time period in which Abraham, Isaac, and Jacob lived generally refer to the beginning of the second millennium BCE (2200–1550).[4] This is supported by, among other details, the correlation of names and places mentioned in the text;[5]

4. This position is not as broadly accepted as it once was. Many now believe that the ancestral period more likely took place during the fourteen to twelfth centuries BCE: Tertius Chandler ("When Was Abraham?" *Bibbia e Oriente* 50 [2008]: 95–101) proposes from 1396 to 1321 BCE; Andre Lemaire ("La Haute Mésopotamie et l'origine des Benê Jacob," *VT* 34 [1984]: 95–101) suggests the first half of the thirteenth century BCE; and P. Kyle McCarter Jr. ("The Historical Abraham," *Interpretation* 42[4] [1988]: 341–352) believes it is the year 1200 BCE. However, Israel Finkelstein and Thomas Römer suggest ("Comments on the Historical Background of the Abraham Narrative: Between 'Realia' and 'Exegetica,'" *Hebrew Bible and Ancient Israel* 3 [2014]: 3–23) that the early Abraham material represents traditions about the eponymous hero of the population of the southern highlands in the later phases of the Iron Age. Some scholars calculate the date based on the biblical text: Abraham has Isaac at the age of one hundred (Gen. 21:5), and Isaac had Jacob at the age of sixty (Gen. 25:26). Jacob descended to Egypt when he was 130 (Gen. 47:9). Thus, there were 290 years between the birth of Abraham and Jacob's journey to Egypt. According to Exodus 12:40, the Israelites dwelt in Egypt for 430 years. Some 480 years elapsed from the Exodus to the inauguration of the Temple (I Kings 6:1). The Temple was inaugurated in the fourth year of Solomon's reign, around 967 BCE. According to this chronology (290+430+480+967) Abraham was born in 2167 BCE, and departed for Canaan in 2092 BCE. Yehezkel Kaufmann (*The Religion of Israel* [Jerusalem, 1953], vol. 1, 111) notes correctly that this calculation is pure speculation. On this position and additional refutations, see Sarna, *Understanding Genesis*, 81–85. Sarna demonstrates the symbolic significance of the numbers in the story cycle. See also Kenneth A. Mathews, *Genesis* (NAC: Nashville, 2005), vol. 2, 37.
5. See, for example, John Bright, *A History of Israel* (Philadelphia, 1972), 70–71, and Douglas Frayne, "In Abraham's Footsteps," in *The World of the Aramaeans: Studies in Honour of Paul-Eugène Dion*, ed. P. M. M. Daviau, J. Wevers, and M. Weigl (Sheffield, 2001), 216–236, specifically concerning the names mentioned in Genesis 11:27–32; but also see the critique in John van Seters, *Abraham in History and Tradition* (New Haven, CT, 1975), 39–64. The main location that challenges this claim is Beersheba, which, based on archaeological surveys, was "uninhabited until the settlement of the Israelite tribes" (Nadav Ne'eman, "Israel in the Canaanite Era: Middle Bronze Age and Late Bronze Age," in *The History of the Land of Israel*, ed. Yisrael Efal [Jerusalem, 1992], vol. 1, 265 [in the bibliographical notes]). However, the Negev and the Beersheba valley were certainly settled earlier, and it should be noted that the biblical text is unclear regarding whether Abraham lived in an actual city. Abraham might have lived his entire life in a tent as a nomad (as we see in Gen. 18:1); he might have settled in Beersheba before it became a city, while the text uses the known name

by the prevalence of wandering from land to land, as Terah and Abraham do; by the patriarchal lifestyle, which correlates with documents found at Mari (which was destroyed by Hammurabi in the seventeenth century BCE); and by the use of the title "El" as a private name. Some of these indications have been criticized, demonstrating that confining the stories to too narrow a historical timeline can be problematic.[6]

For our purposes, the most important element is the recognition that the lifestyle and common customs depicted in the Abraham narrative coincide with the depiction of ancient life found in the Mari and Hammurabi texts. The legal and social norms reflected in these records correlate with many aspects of the Abraham narratives, which "supports the authenticity of the background circumstances described in the Bible."[7] This connection also sheds light on a number of events and episodes in the Abraham narrative that are otherwise quite perplexing.

However, the enthusiasm that characterized the research of Speiser and his peers in the twentieth century is not shared by current biblical scholarship, which now sees the legal correlation between these sources and the Bible as less convincing than previously believed. That said, regarding social norms and lifestyle, the similarities continue to be most impressive.

For example, details that arise from the Abraham narrative which stand out as not in keeping with the familiar biblical code of conduct find their place in light of these Mesopotamian texts of Mari and Hammurabi.

---

from a later period of settlement (cf. Shemuel Yeivin, "Patriarchs in the Land," in *The History of the People of Israel: The Patriarchs and the Judges*, ed. Benjamin Mazar [Jerusalem, 1967], 107). Based on the geographical locations mentioned in the narrative, John J. Bimson ("Archaeological Data and the Dating of the Patriarchs," in *Essays on the Patriarchal Narratives*, ed. A. R. Millard and D. J. Wiseman [Leicester, 1980], 68–80) divided the patriarchal narratives into two periods: the Abraham narratives in Middle Bronze I, and the Jacob narratives are in Middle Bronze II.

6. Based on the correlation with the Nuzi documents, Cyrus H. Gordon, "Biblical Customs and the Nuzu Tablets," *The Biblical Archaeologist* 3, no. 1 (1940): 1–12, suggests dating the Patriarchal era between the fifteenth and fourteenth centuries. However, based on links with Aramaic literature, Siegfried Herrmann, *A History of Israel in the Old Testament Times*, trans. J. Bowden (Philadelphia, 1975), 450, suggests the twelfth century BCE.
7. Speiser, "The Forefathers and their Social Context," 79.

For example, in Genesis 48:5, Jacob is tasked with choosing an heir, a tradition common to the ancient orient. Similarly, Abraham implies in Genesis 15:3 that in the absence of a son, the steward of his household, Damascus-Eliezer, will be his heir, a norm which is reflected in adoption documents from Nuzi.[8] The Hammurabi Code includes articles regulating the obligations and privileges of a barren woman who has given her maidservant to her husband, which are relevant to the Abraham/Sarah/Hagar drama of Genesis chapter 16. Ishmael's expulsion from Abraham's house (21:10) is also clarified in light of the Hammurabi Code (articles 170–171), which dictates that a master who fails to recognize the heir born of his maidservant is obligated to set the maid and her son free.

Additionally, the role of the family patriarch as described in Genesis also correlates with the period in question, particularly the father's authority over his sons and daughters as reflected in the narrative of Judah and Tamar (Gen. 38:24), and Reuben's statement about his sons (42:37). Interestingly, Manfred R. Lehmann has suggested that Ephron the Hittite gave Abraham not only the cave he requested, but also the field (23:11), because of Hittite tax law – the Hittite Code dictates that even partial ownership of a piece of land would obligate the owner to pay taxes for the entire area, and the owner can only be exempt from taxation by selling the entire land.[9] The presence of the military general at a treaty signing (21:22, 26:26) is also explained by Mesopotamian documents of the era. Similarly, religious ceremonies such as planting trees (21:33) and building altars (28:18, 22) are issues that, though later biblical texts balked at, were commonly accepted in the ancient world.

This work is not concerned with issues of historical accuracy, with the exception of those that touch upon social or legal questions which inform our understanding of the plot. The analysis in this book

8. See, for example, André Parrot, *Abraham and His Times* (Philadelphia, 1968), 103; but see also Thomas L. Thompson's criticism in *The Historicity of the Patriarchal Narrative: The Quest for Historical Abraham* (BZAW 133: Berlin/New York, 1974), 203–230.
9. Manfred R. Lehmann, "Abraham's Purchase of Machpelah and Hittite Law," *BASOR* 129 (1953): 15–18. On additional encounters between the Abraham narrative and Hittite culture and literature, see Itamar Singer, *The Hittites and Their Civilization* (Jerusalem, 2009), 241 (specifically on the phrase "*El-Elyon*, Creator of Heaven and Earth"), and see there, 106–107.

will therefore tentatively rely on documented social and legal customs from the second millennium BCE which can illuminate various details in the Abraham cycle.

The Literary Structure of the Abraham Narrative

The definition of a collection of stories as a "narrative cycle" necessitates two basic assumptions: (a) the units that create the cycle are each independent literary units, yet (b) these units can be read as part of a continuous overall plot. While the central component that creates internal cohesion in the Abraham cycle is clearly the presence of Abraham as the protagonist, major themes can be identified consistently throughout the cycle, such as God's promise of land and offspring, and Sarah's barrenness. There is also an underlying assumption that the order of the stories is just as significant as their content. The larger literary context in which a story appears elucidates new elements of the story's significance that are not apparent when analyzing the story by itself, and the same can be said of a story's juxtaposition to the narrative preceding or following it. Throughout the analysis of the Abraham cycle, we will encounter numerous examples demonstrating the existence of a "dialogue" that exists between each narrative that comprises the cycle. With this in mind, I would like to examine the structure of the narrative cycle.

The Narrative and Artistic Structure of the Abraham Cycle

The stories that comprise the foundation of the Abraham narrative are (loosely): Abraham's journey to Canaan (Gen. 12); his descent to Egypt (ch. 12); his separation from Lot (ch. 13); the War of the Kings (ch. 14); the Covenant Between the Pieces (ch. 15); Hagar's escape (ch. 16); the Covenant of Circumcision (ch. 17); the tidings of Isaac's birth (ch. 18); Sodom's destruction (ch. 19); the birth of Ammon and Moab (ch. 19); Abraham and Sarah in Gerar (ch. 20); the birth of Isaac and expulsion of Ishmael (ch. 22); Sarah's burial (ch. 23); the search for a wife for Isaac (ch. 24); the expulsion of the concubine's children (ch. 25); Abraham's death (ch. 25); the generations of Ishmael (ch. 25).

Two types of links are apparent between the stories tracking Abraham's life: one type creates continuity between the smaller units – like links in a chain – while the other links the stories through a more complex overall structure. The "chain link"-type emphasizes that each individual story relates to the surrounding units. For example, Lot's settlement in Sodom in Genesis 13 provides the necessary background for his captivity in chapter 14. And despite the diverse themes between the War of the Kings (ch. 14) and the Covenant Between the Pieces (ch. 15), the stories are linked by parallels in the language, as well as the continuity indicated by the phrase in Genesis 15:1, "After these things." Moving on, the motifs of suffering and liberation, which are so prominent in the Covenant Between the Pieces (ch. 15), reappear in the Hagar narrative that follows it (ch. 16). The angels' visit to Abraham (ch. 18) opens with a verse that neglects to introduce Abraham by name: "And the Lord appeared to *him* by the terebinths of Mamre; *he* was sitting at the entrance of the tent," relying on the previous narrative of chapter 17 for this information. The narrative relating the story of Sarah in the house of Abimelech (ch. 20) ends with the resolution of the temporary infertility that afflicted the women of Gerar because of Sarah, while the following narrative (ch. 21) resolves the infertility of Sarah herself. There are many more examples of this. These links will be discussed throughout the analysis of the text.

The general literary structure of the cycle contains two perspectives: the plot, and the artistic/creative structure. The narrative element that unites the cycle is God's promises. These promises accompany Abraham throughout the narratives, as does Sarah's infertility, something which represents a constant hindrance to the fulfillment of those promises. The cycle includes six narratives about God's promise to Abraham: three promises/blessings (in Ur of the Chaldeans, Shechem, and Bethel), followed by two covenants between God and Abraham, in which Abraham is promised the land and offspring (the Covenant Between the Pieces and the Covenant of Circumcision), and lastly, God's oath at the binding of Isaac. The other narratives placed between these revelations serve to clarify the fulfillment (or lack of fulfillment) of these promises. Therefore, the promises are the connecting links of the entire cycle. The question at the heart of the cycle is whether God will fulfill His promises of land and offspring to Abraham, and in what way.[10]

---

10. See, for example, Gordon J. Wenham, *Genesis 1–15* (WBC: Waco, Texas, 1987), 259–262, and see Walter Vogels, *Abraham et sa legend: Genèse 12.1–25.11* (Lire la Bible 110: Paris, 1996).

Despite the obvious nationalistic tone of these themes, the narrative is presented as the elaboration of "the line of Terah" (Gen. 11:27). As many have noted, the basic internal division of the book of Genesis is with genealogical "lines."[11] According to this division, the Abraham narrative is presented to the reader as part of Terah's genealogy: Terah had twelve grandsons by Nahor (22:20–24) and two nations by Haran, through Lot (19:30–38). However, Abraham's line is more complex. For one, his wife Sarai is barren, and in addition to her infertility, she is taken twice from Abraham by foreign kings. For another, the alternative heirs – Lot and Ishmael – become inapplicable due to their separation from Abraham, and even Isaac, Abraham's true heir, is nearly sacrificed on an altar. Despite these trials and tribulations, Abraham, too, contributes to the genealogy of Terah by way of Isaac, who survives to be his father's heir and to maintain God's covenant with Abraham.[12]

Presenting Terah's line as the general theme of the narrative highlights the underlying tension that exists in the narrative. On the one hand, Abraham is required to disengage from his family (Gen. 12:1–3), which seems to support an exclusionary approach to the Abraham narrative. We also find this exclusionary approach expressed in the purchase of the Machpelah cave (ch. 23), as well as the search for a wife for Isaac in the appendix of the narrative cycle (ch. 24).[13] On the other

11. See, for example, Karl Friedrich Keil and Franz Delitzsch, *Biblical Commentary on the Old Testament: Volume I: The Pentateuch*, trans. J. Martin (Grand Rapids, MI, 1980), 35–37; Thomas Desmond Alexander, "A Literary Analysis of the Abraham Narrative in Genesis" (PhD diss., The Queen's University of Belfast, 1982), 255–258; Thomas L. Thompson, *The Origin Tradition of Ancient Israel: The Literary Formation of Genesis and Exodus 1–23* (JSOTSup 55: Sheffield, 1987), 167–172; David M. Carr, "'Biblos Geneseos' Revisited: A Synchronic Analysis of Patterns in Genesis as Part of the Torah," *ZAW* 110, 2 (1998): 159–172, 3: 327–347; Klaus Koch, "Die Toledot-Formeln als Strukturprinzip des Buches Genesis," in *Recht und Ethos im Alten Testament – Gestalt und Wirkung*, ed. S. Beyerle, G. Mayer, and H. Strauss (Neukirchen-Vluyn, 1999), 183–191.
12. This is apparent in the frame of the cycle, which opens with the genealogy of Abraham and ends with the genealogy of Nahor. See discussion below regarding the artistic structure of the narrative.
13. The idea of isolationism is emphasized in various studies on the Abraham narrative, such as in Peter Machinist, "Outsiders and Insiders: The Biblical View of Emergent Israel and Its Contexts," in *The Other in Jewish Thought and History: Constructions*

hand, Abraham marries his son to a member of his own family, a practice that will later be adopted by his grandson as well. Arguably, despite Abraham's disengagement from his family, the approach of the text is not truly exclusionary. Furthermore, even alongside the demand to separate from his family, Abraham is told that his blessings will affect "all the families of the land" (12:3), and, in the Covenant of Circumcision, Abraham is informed that God will make him "the father of a multitude of nations" (17:5).[14] The fact that the stories of Abraham are set in the context of the line of Terah also points to the integrative approach of the text, despite the commandments which distinguish Abraham and temporarily separate him from his family.

Aside from this literary structure that connects the plot-driven links between the stories, there is also an artistic structure that arises from the narrative cycle that links the internal messaging of the episodes. Many scholars have pointed to the design of the cycle as two halves surrounding the stories of Hagar's flight and the birth of Ishmael in Genesis 16.[15] However, considering the fact that Ishmael was ultimately rejected from maintaining the covenant, the birth of Ishmael seems an unlikely focus for the structure. It is far more likely that Abraham and Sarah's name change in chapter 17 serves as the fulcrum upon which the narratives divide in two: while the first part describes the events of the

---

of Jewish Culture and Identity, ed. L. J. Silberstein and R. L. Cohn (New York, 1994), 35–60, and see Meir Malul, "The Origins of Israelite Self-Perception – the Motif of the Other and the Foundling," *Zion* 67 (2002): 5–18; Shamai Gelander, *Studies in the Book of Genesis* (Raanana: The Open University of Israel, 2009), 371–372. As stated above, while some elements of the narrative encourage this reading, the narrative also includes elements to the contrary, and this indicates that the isolationism approach is more balanced with the universal approach.

14. Uriel Simon emphasized: "Abraham is not the father of mankind, but the father of a nation; in contrast with Adam and Eve, Abraham was not created by God, but rather selected by God. The significance of this fact is that Abraham's choice is not genetic; it is designated" (Simon, "Biblical Abraham: The Blessing of Contrasts," in *The Faith of Abraham: In the Light of Interpretation Throughout the Ages*, ed. M. Hallamish, H. Kasher, and Y. Silman [Ramat Gan, 2002], 42).
15. See, for example, Robert Crotty, "The Literary Structure of the Binding of Isaac in Genesis 22," *ABR* 53 (2005): 31–41; Gordon J. Wenham, *Genesis 16–50* (WBC: Waco, Texas, 1994), 263; David W. Cotter, *Genesis* (Collegeville, MN, Berit Olam, 2003), 87.

life of Abram and Sarai, the second focuses on the life of Abraham and Sarah.[16] Therefore, the central axis of the cycle is the name change in the Covenant of Circumcision in Genesis 17.

I believe the following is a more accurate reflection of the cycle structure:

A: The line of Terah: Abram, Nahor, and Haran (Gen. 11:27–32).

- **B:** Abram's separation from his father's house: "Go forth…to the land" (11:27–32).
  - **C:** Abram journeys through the land and invokes the name of God (12:1–5).
    - **D:** Abram's separation from family members: Sarai is taken by Pharaoh, but returned to Abram (12:10–20); Lot departs for Sodom and does not return (13:1–18).
      - **E:** Lot is rescued from captivity (14:1–24).
        - **F:** The promise of offspring and land (15:1–21). Abram complains (15:2: "What can You give me") and the word *tzedaka* ("righteousness") is used in the context of his belief in God (15:6).[17]
          - **G:** The angel's tidings to Hagar regarding the birth of Ishmael (16:1–16).
            - **H:** The Covenant of Circumcision: Abram and Sarai's names are changed (17:1–27).

16. A name in the biblical narrative is symbolic of the nature of the character, and often of the situation in which the name was given (see, among others, Yehuda Dvir, *Biblical Proper Names and Their Mission* [Tel Aviv, 1969]; Isaac Heinemann, *The Methods of the Aggadah* [Jerusalem, 1954], 110–111; Moshe Garsiel, *Biblical Names: A Literary Study of Midrashic Derivations and Puns*, trans. Phyllis Hacket [Ramat Gan, 1991], 16–19).
17. The analysis of this narrative will clarify why the tidings of offspring (Gen. 15:1–6) and the tidings of land (15:7–21) should be viewed as one story that includes two separate units.

G': The angel's tidings to Sarah regarding the birth of Isaac (18:1–15).[18]

F': Debate over the destruction of land (18:16–33). Abraham complains (18:25: "Far be it from You to do such a thing!") and the word *tzedaka* is used in the context of God's decision to reveal His plan to Abraham (18:19).[19]

E': Lot is rescued from the destruction of Sodom (19:1–37).

D': Abraham's separation from family members: Sarah is taken by Abimelech but returned to Abraham (20:1–18); Ishmael is expelled to the desert of Paran, and does not return (21:1–21).[20]

C': The covenant of Abraham and Abimelech: Abraham invokes the name of God (21:22–34).[21]

B': Abraham's separation from his son: "Go forth to the land of Moriah" (22:1–19).

A': The line of Nahor (22:20–24).

Transitional Narratives and Conclusion: Sarah's burial and purchasing the cave of Machpelah (ch. 23); finding a wife for Isaac (ch. 24); conclusion

18. The analysis of Gen. 18 will demonstrate that this message is intended for Sarah (and not Abraham).
19. The term *tzedaka* is mentioned only in chs. 15 and 18 out of the entire narrative cycle. The borders of the unit depicting Abraham's argument with God over the destruction of Sodom are complex; Gen. 18:16 deliberately links the episode of Abraham's hospitality with the destruction of Sodom by overlapping the conclusion of the first story and the beginning of the next in the same verse.
20. The reason behind the inclusion of the two parts of the narrative (the birth of Isaac and the expulsion of Ishmael) in one literary unit is discussed in the analysis of Gen. 21.
21. The analysis of these narratives will demonstrate that by journeying through the land and by creating a pact with Abimelech, Abraham in fact assumes ownership of the land.

of Abraham's life and the burial of Abraham (25:1–11); [the line of Ishmael (25:12–18)].

Some of the titles suggested above are debatable, as are the exact definitions of where one story ends and another begins. Furthermore, we must remember that the order of the narratives first and foremost reflects the general chronology of events, and so one cannot expect the overall literary structure to be as tightly constructed as one would find in the artistic structure of an individual story. Nevertheless, this structure contributes to the clarification of the stories in the cycle by following the sequence of the protagonist's life and indicating the thematic links between the various sections.

I would like to justify the omission of the final stories from the overall story cycle. The transitional narratives and conclusions (the deaths of Abraham and Sarah and the appointment of their successors, Isaac and Rebecca), which do not focus on Abraham himself but on the next generation, remain outside the literary structure, and have no parallel in the structure's first section. Moreover, these stories lack one of the major characteristics of the cycle, namely, God's involvement. There are also several literary indications that the binding of Isaac is the climax of the entire narrative, and God's promise to Abraham concludes the theme of blessings and promises throughout the cycle.[22] Instead, the concluding narratives should be categorized as "transitional narratives."[23] The founding generation makes way for the next generation; the unit begins with Sarah's death and ends with the death of Abraham, and between the two deaths the narrative describes the quest for Sarah's replacement and the marriage of the successors. As they are not concerned with our protagonist, but rather with his descendants, a discussion of these episodes is outside the scope of this work.[24]

---

22. Robert D. Bergen, "The Role of Genesis 22:1–19 in the Abraham Cycle: A Computer-Assisted Textual Interpretation," *Criswell Theological Review* 4 (1990): 313–326.
23. Gary A. Rendsburg, *The Redaction of Genesis* (Winona Lake, IN, 1986), 50–51.
24. See also Dixon Sutherland, "The Organization of the Abraham Promise Narratives," *ZAW* 95 (1983): 337–343, and Byron Wheaton's discussion regarding chapters 23–25 in "Focus and Structure in the Abraham Narratives," *Trinity Journal* 27 (2006): 143–162.

The Context of the Narrative Cycle

The cycle opens with a report of Terah's genealogy (A) and culminates with a review of Nahor's line (A'). The reader is therefore drawn into the plot from the perspective of Abraham's past, his father's family, which he will ultimately reconnect with when creating his future, since Abraham's son will marry a woman from the family of Nahor. "Terah's son" – Abraham – disengages from his land and the house of his father and goes to Canaan (A), while a daughter of the line of Nahor disengages from her land and family to marry into Abraham's family in Canaan (A'). The cycle is framed by Abraham's dichotomous relationship with his family, which emphasizes the consistent tension we mentioned above between the universal and separatist approaches expressed in the text. The theme of God's promises emphasizes the separation of Abraham's future nation from his surroundings, while the frame of the cycle accentuates the relationship between Abraham and his family. While God unequivocally commands Abraham to disengage from his family, Abraham ultimately reconnects with his family through the marriage of his son.

In addition to the linking of the individual literary units, the structure attests to the unity of the story cycle. The creation of such a solid elaborate structure for so complex a unit proves the cohesion of the Abraham narrative cycle.

The Interchangeability of God's Names

A fascinating phenomenon, discussed widely among the commentators, is the interchangeability of God's names, both in the Abraham narrative, and in Genesis as a whole. Throughout the narrative, God is sometimes referred to as *Elohim*, and other times as *YHWH*. These changes contribute greatly to a conscientious literary reading that considers the design of the biblical narrative. This has been extensively debated by modern commentators. However, the working hypothesis underlying this book focuses on the literary significance of the use of each of God's names in various contexts.[25]

25. See also Erhard Blum, "Der vermeintliche Gottesname 'Elohim,'" in *Gott Nennen: Gottes Namen und Gott als Name*, ed. I. U. Dalferth and Ph. Stoellger (Tübingen,

It is noteworthy that the interchangeability of God's names is also found outside the Pentateuch, in the books of Joshua, Judges, Samuel, Kings, Chronicles, Jonah, in the frame narrative of Job, and in Daniel 1. The name used to describe God in specific biblical narratives was selected according to the content and atmosphere of the text. In many narratives, the interchangeability of a character's titles in the text has literary significance.[26] One narrative will often refer to a character by several titles, which reflect various perspectives in the narrative: In Genesis chapter 12, Sarai is sometimes referred to by name, and sometimes as the "wife"; in chapter 14, Lot is generally referred to as Lot, but also as Abraham's "brother" or "kin"; Hagar is referred to by name throughout the text, but also by her title as a "maidservant" or "slave";

2008), 97–119; Norbert Clemens Baumgart, "Gottesbild, Schöpfungstheologie und die Völker in der Genesis," in *Schöpfung, Monotheismus und fremde Religionen* (BTS 95), ed. L. Borman (Neukirchen-Vluyn, 2008), 63–98; Eckart Otto, "Abraham zwischen JHWH und Elohim. Zur narrativen Logik des Wechsels der Gottesbezeichnungen in den Abrahamerzählungen," in *Die Erzväter in der biblischen Tradition, Festschrift für Matthias Köckert*, ed. A. C. Hagedorn and H. Pfeiffer (Berlin and New York, 2009), 49–65; Bertin Kalumba, "L'emploi programmatique du nom divin YHWH: Ex 6,3 et son context," *Estudios Bíblicos* 67 (2009): 537–581; Evert Van den Berg, "Van elohim tot JHWH: het boek Job als zoektocht naar het monotheïsme," *Nederlands Theologisch Tijdschrift* 66 (2012): 266–282. Concerning the phrase "*YHWH Elohim*," see Temba L. J. Mafico, "The Divine Compound Name Yhwh Elohim and Israel's Monotheistic Polytheism," *Journal of Northwest Semitic Languages* 22 (1996): 155–173; David Noel Freedman, "The Real Formal Full Personal Name of the God of Israel," in *Sacred History, Sacred Literature: Essays on Ancient Israel, the Bible, and Religion in Honor of R. E. Friedman on His 60th Birthday*, ed. S. Dolansky (Winona Lake, IN, 2008), 81–89; Bruce J. Harvey, *Yhwh Elohim: A Survey of Occurrences in the Leningrad Codex and Their Corresponding Septuagintal Renderings* (New York and London, 2011).

26. See, for example, Nechama Leibowitz, "How to Read a Chapter of the Bible," *Reflections on the Bible* 1 (1973): 99–104; Meir Sternberg, "The Structure of Repetition in Biblical Narratives: Strategies of Informational Redundancy," *Hasifrut* 25 (1977): 109–150; Robert Alter, *The Art of Biblical Narrative* (New York, 1981), 182–184; Meir Weiss, *Scriptures in Their Own Light: Collected Essays* (Jerusalem, 1987), 303–306; Shamai Gelander, *Art and Idea in Biblical Narrative* (Tel Aviv: Hakibbutz Hameuchad, 1997), 52–55; Frank H. Polak, *Biblical Narrative Aspects of Art and Design* (Jerusalem, 1999), 329–330. The idea is prevalent outside biblical literature as well. See Boris Uspensky, *A Poetics of Composition: The Structure of the Artistic Text and Typology of a Compositional Form*, trans. V. Zavarin and S. Wittig (Berkeley and Los Angeles, 1973), 20–32.

the angels who visit Abraham and Lot are referred to both as "people" and "angels"; Ishmael in chapter 21 is the "son" of Abraham, the "son" of the maidservant, the "boy" and the "child"; Abraham's servant in chapter 24 is referred to as the "servant" and the "man"; and so forth. These changes are viewed as part of the figurative design of the narrative, which contributes to the reading process and develops the purpose of the narrative. In each instance, the text may use a different name for a character in order to draw the reader's attention to a certain personality trait or plot point. While the examples above relate to changes in titles and not in names, the Jacob narratives will introduce interchangeability in the names Jacob and Israel.[27]

These names of God might also be viewed as titles instead of names. "*YHWH*" is used as a personal name, while "*Elohim*" is essentially a title describing divine power.[28] Syntactically, the title functions as a common noun, even when the name is integrated into the text as a proper noun. This is evident from the inflections of the noun and the use of the definite article (e.g., "*HaElohim*" in Gen. 17:18, 20:6, 20:17, 22:3, and 22:9).[29] Additionally, the name *Elohim* often functions as an adjective as well as a noun (e.g., "*Elohei hashamayim veElohei haaretz*" in Gen. 24:3).[30] Therefore, the interchangeability of God's titles is no

27. Scholars debate whether the interchangeability of the names Jacob and Israel should be attributed to different sources, or whether they serve a literary purpose. See Umberto Cassuto, "Jacob," *Entziklopedya Mikra'it* 3:718–719. See also Zeev Weisman, *From Jacob to Israel: The Cycle of Jacob's Stories and Its Incorporation within the History of the Patriarchs* (Jerusalem, 1986), 50–51 (regarding the repetition of reasons for naming). In Greek and Roman periods, a double-naming was a common phenomenon (Greg H. R. Horsley, "Name, Double," in *The Anchor Bible Dictionary*, ed. by D. N. Freedman et al. [New York, 1992], vol. 4, 1011–1017), and might have been so in the biblical era as well.
28. Frank M. Cross, "אל," *TDOT* 1:242–261.
29. This was noticed by Rabbi Judah Halevi in *Kuzari* IV:3.
30. See a comprehensive discussion by Friedrich Baumgärtel, *Elohim außerhalb des Pentateuch: Grundlegung zu einer Untersuchung über die Gottesnamen im Pentateuch*, BWAT 19 (Leipzig, 1914). Baumgärtel examined the appearances of God's name outside the Pentateuch, and concluded that the name *Elohim* is usually used as a general noun. His study did not relate to the names of God in the Pentateuch.

different from the changing titles of the biblical characters, which are at times referred to by name and at others by various descriptive titles.

What, then, is the essential difference between the names *Elohim* and *YHWH*, and in which stories can we expect to find each one? As we mentioned, the name *Elohim* is used as a common noun, referring to an entity with divine power ("*El*," the word that "*Elohim*" derives from, means "power"). The stories in which God is presented as the Maker of history all utilize the name *Elohim* to emphasize His omniscience and omnipotence. *YHWH*, on the other hand, personifies God as an entity with characteristics that interact directly with the characters. *YHWH* interacts intimately with our heroes, displaying kindness to those who deserve it (for example in Genesis 18), or, alternatively, anger when necessary (for example, the destruction of Sodom in Genesis 19).

The Abraham narrative cycle plays out on these parallel storylines throughout each of the individual stories it contains. The story of Abraham is the story of a hero, alongside a cast of characters who interact with him, in order to impart important moral lessons to the reader. It is also the story of the birth of a nation, and each event, decision, and moral join to comprise a chronicle with immense historical significance.

Family and Nationality

The story of Abraham also marks the beginning of the story of the nation of Israel. A unique worldview of nationalism is reflected throughout his narrative cycle, touching upon questions raised within classical political philosophy, and greatly discussed in modern political science.[31] Despite the fundamental difference between the biblical notion of a nation and the modern concept of nationalism, which I will discuss shortly, the Abraham cycle presents a view of nationalism that harmonizes elements which modern discourse generally perceives as conflicting.

I wish to begin by addressing a basic question pertaining to the definition of a nation: Should a nation be defined "politically" – that is,

31. See, for example, the collection of articles in John Hutchinson and Anthony Smith, *Nationalism* (New York: Oxford University Press, 1994), and the survey of Assaf Malach, "The Bases for the Legitimacy of a Jewish Nation-state in a Postmodern Era" (Diss., Bar Ilan University, 2009), 15–98.

national-political cooperation is what renders a group of people into a nation – or "culturally" – according to common cultural factors? Hans Kohn already proposed a division between political nationalism as the product of civil society, and cultural-ethnic nationalism, evaluating the former as rational, humane nationalism, associated with Western Europe, while the latter form of nationalism as romantic and anti-rational, more prevalent in Eastern Europe, though notably found in Germany.[32] Many in his wake adopted this division, either directly or indirectly, to the point of establishing that an entity may be defined as a nation either from a "political" point of view, or from a "cultural" point of view.[33]

In modern political science, this question is accompanied by another controversy: Is a "nation" the product of a human decision, of a group of people's declaration that they wish to govern their lives together for a common purpose – whether that be pragmatic or ethical – or should this concept be perceived as a framework imposed upon human society, one that people are involuntarily born into?[34]

Notable members of the former approach are Thomas Hobbes, John Locke, and Jean-Jacques Rousseau. Despite their differences of opinion, they agree that the nation and state are founded upon the free, voluntary union of its members.[35] Locke, for example, argues that a person's natural state is one of freedom to do as he wishes, and that he

32. Hans Kohn, *The Idea of Nationalism* (New York, 1944), 329–331.

33. According to Friedrich Meinecke. See also Anthony D. Smith's discussion in *The Nation in History: Historiographical Debates about Ethnicity and Nationalism* (Hanover, 2000), 22–23. Smith is a leading advocate of the fusion of ethnic nationalism in the ancient world and modern nationalism. He himself called this school of thought "ethno-symbolism" (ibid., ch. 3). Concerning this division and the problems it poses, see also Seymour et al., "Introduction: Questioning the Ethnic/Civic Dichotomy," in *Rethinking Nationalism*, ed. J. Couture et al. (Calgary, 1996), 7–28.

34. In a certain sense, there is a connection between the two issues, and indeed, some have established this connection, such as Malach in "The Bases for the Legitimacy of a Jewish Nation-state in a Postmodern Era."

35. Many scholars use "nation" and "state" interchangeably, even though Walker Connor is correct in stating that more room should be given to ethnic identification within the study of nationalism, and nationalism should not be identified with the state. He opposes Carl Deutsch and the school of "Nation-Building" (Connor, "Nation-Building or Nation-Destroying?" *World Politics* 24 [1972]: 319–355).

has "natural rights" (these assumptions oppose Hobbes' beliefs), but he freely chooses to forfeit these rights in order to form a single community:

> Men being, as has been said, by nature, all free, equal, and independent, no one can be put out of this estate, and subjected to the political power of another, without his own consent. The only way whereby any one divests himself of his natural liberty, and puts on the bonds of civil society, is by agreeing with other men to join and unite into a community for their comfortable, safe, and peaceable living one amongst another, in a secure enjoyment of their properties, and a greater security against any, that are not of it.... For when any number of men have, by the consent of every individual, made a community, they have thereby made that community one body.[36]

According to Locke, a person's choice to forfeit his natural rights and hand them over to a greater entity stems from the unremitting, inevitable fears and dangers integral to the most basic form of freedom.[37]

Proponents of the social contract theory are usually associated with the concept of a "nation state" whose members come together for the sake of a more convenient lifestyle. Essentially, however, the matter is more complicated. The political philosophy of Rousseau, for example, illustrates this complexity. On one hand, he is the most salient advocate of the social contract theory, which is based on the individuals' free consent to form a political body. His work *The Social Contract* (published in 1762) is entirely based on the notion of "the general will" as a fundamental basis for a legitimate political community and government. However, Rousseau is not merely concerned with a technical declaration of a way of life: "Unlike Hobbes and Locke, who justify the social contract through its regulation of existing interests, Rousseau holds that the citizens who sign the contract undergo an immediate process of change and generate a new form of society – a 'moral collective body, composed of as many

---

36. John Locke, *Two Treatises of Government,* ch. 8.
37. Ibid., ch. 9.

members as there are votes in the assembly.'"[38] Rousseau believes that the decision to become a member of a political group is a triumph of the collective good over the individual's narrow personal interests, and therefore, despite the fact that a state's existence depends on its citizens' free will, it should not be considered a mere facilitator of technical needs:

> This passage from the state of nature to the civil state produces a very remarkable change in man: the role that instinct used to play in his conduct is now taken over by a sense of justice, and his actions now have a moral aspect that they formerly lacked. The voice of duty has taken over from physical impulses and a sense of what is right has taken over from appetite; and now – only now – the man who has until now considered only himself finds himself forced to act on different principles and to consult his reason before listening to his inclinations. In this "civil" state he is deprived of many advantages that he got from nature, but he gets enormous benefits in return – his faculties are so stimulated and developed, his ideas are extended, his feelings ennobled, and his whole soul uplifted. All this happens to such an extent that if the abuses of this new condition didn't often pull him down to something lower than he was in the state of nature, he would be bound to bless continually the happy moment that took him from it forever, and out of a dull and limited animal made a thinking being, a man.[39]

As Anthony D. Smith shows, although Rousseau emphasized that consent is the fundamental basis of a nation, he also perceives a nation as a naturally occurring entity, and in several places he relates to various traits that characterize different nations.[40] Therefore, Rousseau also saw importance in allowing each nation the independence to express its cultural nature: "The first rule that we must follow is that of national

38. A. Hoffman, "Between Absolutism and Revolution: Rousseau and the 'Social Contract' in Historical Context," in *Jean-Jacques Rousseau's The Social Contract*, trans. Ido Bassok (Tel Aviv, 2006), 23–24.
39. Jean-Jacques Rousseau, *The Social Contract*, ed. Jonathan Bennett (2010), 9.
40. Anthony D. Smith, *The Nation in History*, 8–9.

character. Every people has, or must have, a character; if it lacks one, we must begin by endowing it with one."[41]

We will explore the attempt to reconcile the notion that a nation has distinguishing traits with the idea that a nation is founded upon free will when we discuss the biblical model.

There are many other proponents of the approach that a nation is the product of its citizens' free will. Some, like Rousseau, propose intriguing analyses of this type of nation.[42] Ernest Renan wrote a famous essay in 1882 entitled "What is a Nation?" and it is considered a classic example of the voluntary approach in political thought. Renan opposed the ethnic criterion of defining a nation, claiming that many dominant nations, such as Britain, France, and Italy, are ethnically diverse. Renan also devoted a separate essay to the subject of Jewish nationalism, claiming that it is also problematic to claim common ethnicity in the context of the Hebrew nation, as many have joined the Jewish nation over time. The problem with equating ethnicity with nationality, Renan argued, is not only technical; a nation should not be considered "natural" from a cultural or linguistic perspective. He opposes the approach that a nation is a collection of individuals who have gathered merely for the sake of common interests, but he does emphasize that "a nation's existence is, if you will pardon the metaphor, a daily plebiscite, just as an individual's existence is a perpetual affirmation of life."[43] Indeed, those who object to any natural definitions of nationalism usually base their theory upon the unceasing consent of the individuals who comprise a nation.

In contrast to this approach, some perceive the formation of a nation as a natural trait of human society. Rousseau's contemporary,

---

41. As quoted in Smith, ibid., 8.
42. For example, John Stuart Mill claimed that the definitive basis of a nation is the sense of solidarity and brotherhood that generates desire for political union. He believed that consciousness of a common past is a central factor in national unity. However, he does not perceive nationalism as an objective unto itself, or a supreme value, nor does he consider a nation a natural form of human existence, but rather something to be acquired (see further in Malach, "The Bases for the Legitimacy of a Jewish Nation-state in a Postmodern Era," 17–18).
43. Cited and discussed in Smith, *The Nation in History*, 26–27, and in Malach, "The Bases for the Legitimacy of a Jewish Nation-state in a Postmodern Era," 19–20.

Johann Gottfried Herder claimed that cultural diversity is a fundamental human characteristic. He argued that the variety of human cultures in areas of different climates and other natural conditions result from the divine intention that humanity will not be uniform, but will fulfill the wide range of possibilities encoded within it. Every nation expresses a unique culture, and it is morally bound to do so.[44] Herder explicitly referred to language as the central means of national expression, claiming that each language determines the speakers' form of thought, and thus every person becomes a product of the nation he belongs to.[45]

Johann Gottlieb Fichte also claimed that a person's affiliation with his nation is natural, and not merely the result of social consent. In Herder's wake, he underscored that each nation must prudently preserve the purity of its own language, and preached that the German nation must zealously prevent the German language from becoming contaminated with foreign words, particularly those of Latin or French origins, because such words, he believed, reflect the corrupt world of the Romans.[46] According to Fichte, not only does a nation's defining language demand that it preserve its culture, its language is what grants a nation the privilege of its own state, in order to freely express its culture and maintain its own language.[47] These theories clearly reflect the connection between the two aforementioned issues: that a nation is "natural," and that this is fundamentally related to the perception of the nation as a "nation of culture," as a community with its own unique way of life.

Nowadays, the inherent danger of extreme nationalism is well known, and in the wake of the trauma of the twentieth century's wars, many perceive nationalism as contradictory to liberal thinking. This danger was already manifest in the philosophy of Heinrich von Treitschke,

---

44. See Elie Kedourie, *Nationalism* (Oxford and Cambridge, MA, 1993), 4, and Malach, "The Bases for the Legitimacy of a Jewish Nation-state in a Postmodern Era," 8–10.
45. Kedourie, *Nationalism*, ch. 5.
46. These ideas are discussed in the series of lectures Fichte gave in Berlin in 1807–1808, called "Addresses to the German Nation" (J. G. Fichte, *Addresses to the German Nation*, trans. R. F. Jones and G. H. Turnbull [Chicago: Open Court, 1922]. Reprint by Westport, CT: Greenwood Press, Inc., 1979).
47. Concerning Fichte's philosophy, see Umut Ozkirimli, *Theories of Nationalism: A Critical Introduction* (New York, 2000), 17–19.

who developed the idea of political nationalism in violent, antisemitic directions. For the sake of this discussion, it is important to mention his position that a nation's power is a supreme, even sacred, value, that war is an expression of the participating nations' virility, and that this virility is what renders a people into a nation and binds its citizens together.[48]

For our discussion, it suffices to present these two extreme positions, whose confrontation escalated with the development of modern political philosophy, and is still a key component of global discourse. Some argue that the two approaches represent two different models of society that developed at different times over the course of history. This is the premise of Elie Kedourie, who argues that modern nationalism is based on common collective objectives, in contrast to ancient tribalism, which formed naturally and spontaneously, and was the agent of cultural expression:

> Nationalism is also sometimes described as a new tribalism. The analogy is meant to indicate that like the tribe, the nation excludes and is intolerant of outsiders. But such characteristics, as has been said, are common to all human groups, and cannot serve to define either tribe or nation. But the analogy is not only unable to shed light on the matter, it can also mislead. A tribesman's relation to his tribe is usually regulated in minute detail by custom which is followed unquestioningly and considered part of the natural or the divine order. Tribal custom is neither a decree of the General Will, nor an edict of legislative Reason. The tribesman is such by virtue of his birth, not by virtue of self-determination. He is usually unaware that the destiny of man is progressive, and that he can fulfil this destiny by merging his will into the will of the tribe. Nationalism and tribalism, then, are not interchangeable terms, nor do they describe related phenomena.[49]

---

48. Zvi Batscha and Avraham Yassour, *The Great Modern Political Theories* (Jerusalem and Tel Aviv, 1975), vol. 1, 365. Nonetheless, it is worth mentioning that some favor the model of the "natural nation" and envision universal peace and harmony (such as Giuseppe Mazzini and Adam Mickiewicz).
49. Kedourie, *Nationalism*, 69.

Kedourie's words are one example of a prevalent position, which dictates that perception of the nation as stemming from natural necessity ("tribal nationalism," to use his terms) considerably reduces the discourse about a nation's purpose and progression, while those who argue that a nation's formation is based upon its members' free will seek to establish the ideological and objective platform of this collective gathering. As we will see, the story of Abraham attempts to reconcile these two apparently polar positions.

The Abraham Cycle: Between "Nation" and "People"

Exploring the Abraham narrative cycle through these terms produces a captivatingly ambivalent picture. Biblical exploration is rooted in a different sphere of discourse than modern political philosophy, as the biblical nation is explicitly defined in ethnic terms. While the concept of a "nation" exists in the Bible, and is apparently a conceptual innovation in Ancient Near Eastern thought,[50] and even if Daniel Gordis is correct in asserting that "the concept of nationhood – of a distinct group identity based on common language, culture, land, and blood ties – was not a modern European innovation, as some scholars proclaim it to be, but rather an integral part of the Jewish tradition from its very beginnings,"[51] nationhood in the Bible is still considered an extension of family. This is evident from the presentation of humanity as the product of three distinct families – Shem, Ham, and Japheth: "These are the groupings of Noah's descendants, according to their origins, by their nations; and from these the nations branched out over the earth after the Flood" (Gen. 6:32). Additionally, this seems to be reflected in the story of the Tower of Babel.[52] In fact, the very appellation "the Children of Israel" illustrates that familial origin is what essentially defines a nation, and as Daniel Block emphasizes, the Bible considers all nations – and not just Israel – extensions of family clans (such as

50. Wolfram von Soden, *The Ancient Orient: An Introduction to the Study of the Ancient Near East* (Grand Rapids, MI, 1994), 13–14.
51. Daniel Gordis, "The Tower of Babel and the Birth of Nationhood," *Azure* 40 (2010): 19–36.
52. See, for example, Theodore Hiebert, "The Tower of Babel and the Origin of the World's Cultures," *JBL* 126 (2007): 29–58.

Edom, Ammon, and Moab), even if it is not at all clear whether these nations also perceived themselves in these terms.[53] Effectively, this perspective characterizes the Jewish people until this very day. As Blaise Pascal famously marveled:

> Advantages of the Jewish people – In this search the Jewish people at once attract my attention by the number of wonderful and singular facts which appear about them. I first see that they are a people wholly composed of brethren, and whereas all others are formed by the assemblage of an infinity of families, this, though so wonderfully fruitful, has all sprung from one man alone, and, being thus all one flesh, and members one of another, they constitute a powerful state of one family. This is unique.[54]

Perception of the nation as an extension of a family (not only in an ideal sense, as reflected in Aristotle, but when members of a nation are considered part of the same "clan") has broad implications in the context of mutual responsibility. This is prominent in biblical laws that require compassion for another member of the community because he is "your brother" (particularly evident in the laws of Lev. 25, Deut. 15, and Deut. 22–25). The law extends the concept of family responsibility to apply between every member of the nation.[55] In this respect, biblical nationalism is an extreme manifestation of the notion of a "natural nation," wherein membership is the automatic result of being born to a certain family. This is consistent with the biblical perception of Israel as a "nation of culture" – as a nation that is distinguished from other nations not merely by its political context, but through its covenant with God, by being "God's nation." Moreover, this is also true, in at least some books of the Bible, in relation to other nations;

---

53. Daniel I. Block, "Nations/Nationality," *NIDOTTE* 4: 968.
54. Blaise Pascal, *Pensées*, trans. W. F. Trotter (New York, 1910), sec. 8, 620.
55. For the notion of the nation as family as a basis for the moral guidelines of the Bible, see W. A. L. Elmslie ("Ethics," in *Record and Revelation*, ed. H. Wheeler Robinson [Oxford, 1938], 275–302), who even included the common covenant of the entire community as part of the moral guidelines.

the culture of Egypt or Amalek can also be traced over the course of the text,[56] among others.[57]

Nonetheless, this must be stated with caution, as the "culture" that defines Israel is not derived from its nature, but from its ancestral history. Abraham was chosen as the father of a nation because of his morality (Gen. 18:19), while Amalek is characterized as God's enemy because it attacked the weak, nascent nation that had only just left Egypt. That is, a biblical nation's culture is determined by its moral decisions. This issue is related to the ambivalence that accompanies the definition of the Israelite nation, which is already reflected in the Abraham cycle on a semantic level.

The distinction between a nation as an extended family and a nation in a political sense is also reflected in the language of the biblical narrative. There are two common biblical expressions for the word nation: "*am*" and "*goy*." The word "*goy*" is usually translated as "nation," while the word "*am*" may be translated as "nation" or "people"; sometimes *am* is used, it seems, to differentiate it from the word *goy* if both are used in the same context (as in Isaiah 2, for example). Speiser claims that these terms actually have different meanings: the term *am* refers to an extended family that has evolved into a nation,[58] while the word *goy* represents a nation

56. Concerning Amalek, see, for example, Jakob H. Grönbäk, "Juda und Amalek – Uberlieferungsgeschichtliche Erwägungen zu Exodus 17, 8–16," *Studia Theologica* 18 (1964): 26–45. Concerning Egypt, see, for example, Asher Weiser, "Egypt in the Bible," *Mahanaim* 105 (1961): 16–24.
57. It is debatable, however, whether this defines the nation according to its culture, or on a literary-symbolic level. Egypt, for example, represents human pride in several prophecies, but Egypt may merely be a *symbol* of pride; this was not necessarily the cultural factor that unified the Egyptian nation into a single political entity.
58. Sometimes the word simply means "family" (as in Gen. 32:8; 48:19; Lev. 21:1–4; Job 18:19). The expression "gathered unto his people" seems to be parallel to the phrase "gathered unto his forefathers" (Bern Alfrink, "L'expression נאסף אל עמיו," *OTS* 5 [1948]: 118–131). The meaning of the word is not limited to the Bible, but appears in other Semite languages. At the end of a broad survey of different languages, Lipiński writes: "In summary, we can say that the West Semitic word *'amm* refers to agnates, both individually and collectively.... The biblical usage of *'am* appropriates this double meaning without any difficulty" (Edward Lipiński, "עַם," *TDOT* 11:169–170).

in the political sense.[59] The choice of a particular word often affects the connotations of a particular phrase: the term *am* is often accompanied by a possessive suffix ("My people," "your people," etc.), while such suffixes are rarely added to the word *goy*. This shows that "*am* is something subjective and personal, *goy* objective and impersonal. Note, '*Ure'eh ki emkha hagoy hazeh*' – 'Consider, too, that this nation is Your people' (Ex. 33:13). The same utterance with the two nouns interchanged would be unthinkable in a biblical context, though not in translation."[60]

Speiser's argument is somewhat overstated; Jacob Licht and Edward Lipiński are more correct in their assertion that sometimes the two words are interchangeable, used in parallelisms, and the word *am* is also sometimes used in a political sense.[61] Aelred Cody's conclusions are also a preferable version of Speiser's, as he claims with more nuance that the words do have different connotations, but in a literary sense,[62] insofar as terminological basis of the word *am* is semantically related to family, so this association arises even when the word is used in the more general sense of "nation." These connotations serve an important function in the construction of the narrative sphere of discourse, and we will see this come into play in the story of Abraham.

Should Abraham be considered the head of a family, or the head of a nation? There is no contradiction between the two roles in biblical thought; on the contrary, Abraham would not be able to establish a nation without first establishing a clan, a tribe. At the same time, the story looks out to the future, anticipating a distant time when Abraham's seed will be as numerous as the stars. In these passages, are Abraham's descendants represented as a "nation" in the political sense, or as a family

---

59. For a philological debate of these two terms, see also Leonhard Rost, "Die Bezeichnungen fur Land und Volk im Alten Testament," in *Das kleine Credo und andere Studien zum Alten Testament* (Heidelberg, 1965), 76–101; Block, "Nations/Nationality," 966.
60. Ephraim A. Speiser, "'People' and 'Nation' of Israel," *JBL* 79 (1960): 158. Abraham Malamat claims that the term "*goy*" also has military connotations, especially in Joshua 5:6 and II Kings 6:18 (Malamat, "On the Study of the Israelite Pre-History of the People of Israel," in *The Controversy over the Historicity of the Bible*, ed. L. Levine and A. Mazar [Jerusalem: Yad Itzhak Ben Zvi, 2001], 112–123), but others reject this claim.
61. Jacob Licht, "*Am*," *Entziklopedya Mikra'it*, 6:235–239; Lipiński, "עם," 174. See also Ronald E. Clements, "גוי," *TDOT* 2:426–427.
62. Aelred Cody, "When Is the Chosen People Called a *Goy*?" *VT* 14 (1964): 1–6.

extended to extremes? Within a broader biblical perspective – to the extent that it can be determined – Israel are presented as both *am* and *goy*, in that its people share common ancestors, but they can also be defined politically, as Speiser shows.[63] A more cautious picture, however, emerges from the Abraham cycle – the term *goy* and its political connotations is used in relation to Abraham's "chosen seed" in only two places. First, in God's first revelation to Abraham: "I will make of you a great *nation*, and I will bless you; I will make your name great, and you shall be a blessing" (Gen. 12:2); and second, in the narrative's explanation as to why God involves Abraham in Sodom's fate, since "Abraham is to become a great and populous *nation* and all the nations of the earth are to bless themselves by him" (18:18).

In both contexts, the reader's vision is directed to the distant future. God's promise to Abraham at the beginning of his journey is not merely a promise for the future, but a blueprint of his entire path: Abraham will eventually establish a great nation, through which "all families of the earth will be blessed." The narrative's intervention in Genesis 18:18, which justifies Abraham's involvement with Sodom's fate, hints to Abraham's broader role and to the purpose of his election, and here, too, the narrative gazes into the future: "Abraham is to become…"

Aside from these two instances, the word *goy* is not used again in relation to Abraham's chosen seed, although it is consistently used in relation to other nations. This is particularly salient during the episode of the commandment of circumcision. Abraham is to be the father of many "nations," "*goyim*," but this particular word and its political connotations are not actually used to describe the chosen seed who will perpetuate the covenant with God:

> As for Me, this is My covenant with you: You shall be the father of a multitude of nations (*goyim*). And you shall no longer be called Abram, but your name shall be Abraham, for I make you the father of a multitude of nations (*goyim*). I will make you exceedingly fertile, and make nations (*goyim*) of you; and kings shall come forth from you. I will maintain My covenant between

63. Speiser, "'People' and 'Nation' of Israel," 162–163.

> Me and you, and your offspring to come, as an everlasting covenant throughout the ages, to be God to you and to your offspring to come. (Gen. 17:4–7)

A multitude of nations will descend from Abraham, but the covenant shall be retained through "your offspring to come," who are not described with the word *goyim*. This is even more striking later on in the narrative, when Ishmael, who is rejected from the chosen line, is described as the founder of a nation with the word *goy* – "As for Ishmael, I have heeded you. I hereby bless him. I will make him fertile and exceedingly numerous. He shall be the father of twelve chieftains, and I will make of him a great nation (*goy*)" (Gen. 17:20) – in contrast to Isaac, whose descendants will perpetuate the covenant: "But My covenant I will maintain with Isaac, whom Sarah shall bear to you at this season next year" (17:21). This phenomenon repeats itself in the story of Ishmael's expulsion from Abraham's household. Both Ishmael's mother and father hear that he is to be the father of a *goy*: "As for the son of the slave-woman, I will make a nation (*goy*) of him, too, for he is your seed" (21:13); "Come, lift up the boy and hold him by the hand, for I will make a great nation (*goy*) of him" (21:18). This phrase is not used in conjunction with Isaac even once; rather, the term "*zera*" meaning "offspring," or "seed," repeatedly occurs. For example, "your offspring (*zarakha*) to come" (17:10), and Isaac's children as well are referred to as "his offspring (*zaro*) to come" (17:19). The definition of Isaac's children does not extend from the family sphere into the national sphere.

This does not seem coincidental. In other stories too, the term *goy*, with all its political associations, applies to other nations, but not to Abraham's seed. During the Covenant Between the Pieces, for example, God declares, "I will execute judgment on the nation (*goy*) they will serve" (Gen. 15:14), while Abraham's seed at the time of their exodus from Egypt, who will already have become a nation, are still referred to as "your offspring (*zarakha*)" (15:13). Abimelech of Gerar also refers to his own people as a "*goy*" (20:4),[64] while Abraham repeatedly hears

64. Speiser, among others, claims that the inclusion of the word *goy* here is a corruption (Speiser, "'People' and 'Nation' of Israel," 159).

blessings showered upon the heads of his "*zera*," "offspring," but not upon the "*goy*" he is to establish.

This distinction is not merely linguistic; a careful reading of these narratives reveals that the text relates to the future nation of Israel not as a nation but as "Abraham's family." This is salient, for example, in the aforementioned narrative of the Covenant Between the Pieces. On one hand, there is a clear national dimension to this revelation. The covenant ends with a description of the borders of the land (including the eastern side of the Jordan), anticipating the nation that will inhabit this territory, coming to fruition in David and Solomon's time. This conclusion would serve well as the ending of a narrative of national-political character, but this is not the case. The chapter opens with Abraham's complaint that he has no "heir" (Gen. 15:2–3); God promises him that he will be granted a son of his own, and that his descendants will one day be too numerous to count. The discussion of an "heir" connotes an intimate family atmosphere, and in this spirit the reader is also introduced to the subsequent discussion of inheritance of the land (I will explore this juxtaposition in depth in the relevant chapter, below). Indeed, the term "*yerusha*," "inheritance," with its striking familial connotations, is repeated in the chapter, mentioned in context of inheritance of the land. God promises "to assign this land to you as a possession (*lerishtah*)," whereupon Abram asks, "How shall I know that I am to possess it (*irashenah*)?" (15:7–8).[65] Therefore, the aforementioned linguistic distinction is consistent with the general atmosphere of this chapter. The nation who will enslave Israel is referred to as a "nation," while Abraham's seed are his "offspring," the "fourth generation" of the head of the clan who will one day return to the land to inherit it.

The theme of Israel as a family also colors the scene concerning circumcision, which is also inherently related to the family sphere. Abraham will father "nations" and "kings" but the covenant will be perpetuated through "your offspring (*zarakha*) to come" (Gen. 17:7), who will one day settle in the land "of your sojourning" (17:7–8).

65. Note that the biblical law of inheritance (Num. 27:8–10) is given in the context of dividing the land into portions, so that "the Israelite law of inheritance originates in the division of land through tribal-familial organization." Samuel E. Loewenstamm, "*Yerusha*," *Entziklopedya Mikra'it* 3:789.

We can now return to the two anomalous places where Abraham's chosen seed is referred to as a *goy* and read them in a new light. Cody demonstrates that Israel is described as a *goy* when the narrative seeks to present them as one nation among many:

> *Goy* is used of the Chosen People because Israel is being considered a *goy* among *goyim,* either because it is being looked upon as an individual within the class, or because the pagans in contexts of national consciousness do not distinguish Israel from other *goyim,* or because God, in upbraiding the infidelity of the Chosen People, reduces it from the preferable status of His *'am* to that of a mere *goy* like all the rest.[66]

In order to emphasize the international significance of these two sources, the appellation *goy* is used. Both sources focus on the relevance of Abraham's seed for the surrounding nations: "I will make you a great nation (*goy*) .... All the families of the earth (*mishpeḥot haadama*) shall bless themselves by you" (Gen. 12:2–3); "All the nations of the land (*goyei haaretz*) are to bless themselves by him" (18:18).[67] Victor Hamilton adds that Abraham's influence on the surrounding nations is actually fulfilled in the plot in Genesis 18, in the context of his concern for Sodom.[68] This reading is supported by Ed Noort's exploration of Abraham's universalistic significance. While arguing that "the linchpin (12:1–3) of the primeval history and the patriarchal narratives breathes universalism," and in the Abraham-Lot cycle, "the question of 18:25 concerns all mankind

66. Cody, "*Goy,*" 2.
67. Regarding this connection, see, for example, Victor P. Hamilton, *The Book of Genesis, Chapters 18–50* (NICOT: Grand Rapids, MI, 1995), 18. Ludwig Schmidt and Claus Westermann surmise that the difference at the end of the linguistic expression between "families of the earth" and "nations of the land" reflects two different sources (Schmidt, *"De Deo": Studien zur Literakritik und Theologie des Buches Jona, des Gesprächs zwischen Abraham und Jahwe in Gen 18, 22ff und von Hiob 1* [Berlin and New York, 1976], 136; Claus Westermann, *Genesis 12–36: A Continental Commentary,* trans. J. J. Scullion [Minneapolis, 1995], 288); however, the familiar phrase incorporating the rarer word "*goyim*" in relation to Abraham's offspring shows that there *is,* in fact, a connection between these two verses.
68. Hamilton, *The Book of Genesis, Chapters 18–50,* 18.

and the mediator is Abraham,"[69] Noort demonstrates that the rest of the narrative is concerned with Abraham's own family and descendants. Aside from these two passages, "the supposed universalism of Gen. 12 is nowhere present" – not even in references to Abraham in later biblical works – and most of the Abraham cycle itself is concerned solely with Abraham's own family: with Lot, Ishmael, and chiefly, of course, the fate of his son and heir, Isaac.[70]

If so, the definition of Abraham's seed as a nation in the Abraham cycle is clearly ambiguous. The promise that a nation is to arise animates God's covenant with Abraham, but there is also noticeable restraint exercised to prevent national connotations from coloring the story. Cody argues that the biblical reservations toward the term *goy* stem from the negative connotations of this word, as it is not used to present Israel as the chosen people, but rather lowers Israel to the level of other political nations (and indeed, this has led to the word "*goy*" becoming a post-exilic term for a non-Jew).[71] The Bible, however, is capable of implementing this word in a positive sense, as in the case of Genesis 12:2 and 18:18. It seems to me that even when Abraham's seed becomes a nation in the active political sphere – a "great nation" ("*goy gadol*") that all nations shall be blessed through – there is clear narrative intent to present this political entity in the context of its family ties; that is, as the product of its "forefathers." The Israelite nation is depicted as the natural, unified progeny of a single family, a "natural nation."[72] This presentation of nationalism commissions more mutual commitment from its members (as expressed, for example, in the story of Lot's rescue from Sodom), which in turn contributes to the members' emotional sense of belonging to their own nation.

This brings us to the unique approach of biblical familial nationalism. Critics of natural-ethnic nationalism have claimed that

69. Ed Noort, "Abraham and the Nations," in *Abraham, the Nations, and the Hagarites: Jewish, Christian, and Islamic Perspectives on Kinship with Abraham,* ed. M. Goodman et al. (Leiden, 2010), 18, 17.

70. Ibid., 13.

71. Cody, "*Goy,*" 1–6.

72. Needless to say, the theory of social contract is not the basis of this kind of nationalism.

this "natural" form of nationalism is liable to degenerate into fascism and negation of the Other – and history has proven them right. The premise of this criticism is clear: reinforcing the national sense of unity through emphasis on natural, unalterable factors constructs an insurmountable wall between members of the community – who were born into these circumstances – and outsiders.

The Abraham cycle, however, despite its emphasis on family as the basis of the nation, presents a completely different approach. Abraham's family is chiefly characterized by its moral quality, and this morality is what serves as the chosen nation's definitive cornerstone: "For I have singled him out, that he may instruct his children and his posterity to keep the way of the Lord by doing what is just and right" (Gen. 18:19). This declaration is followed – and illustrated – by Abraham's efforts to prevent Sodom's destruction. As mentioned, the prevalent position – represented above by Kedourie – attributes common ideals as a collective basis to the liberal definition of a nation, while the tribal-ethnic definition of a nation does not set moral objectives. The biblical ethnic nationalism shatters this dichotomy, however – at least in relation to Israel. As I have already mentioned, it is not entirely clear whether the Bible holds that every nation has a definitive culture it must fulfill,[73] but Abraham's offspring is elected for moral reasons, as the text hints and implies in various ways, and the family-nation Abraham will establish is to be rooted in moral values. In other words, although the nation in question evolves naturally, out of a single family, this "natural" nation is not solely characterized thereby; rather, the narrative employs moral discourse about the nation's foundation upon divine values of righteousness and justice. The nation's morality is an integral part of its character and purpose.[74]

---

73. Some of the philosophers mentioned above relied upon language differentiating between the nations as a gauge for difference in culture (Herder and Fichte). Even if they did not state this explicitly, this can be read in the story of the nations' dispersal (Gen. 10) and the Tower of Babel (Gen. 11). In these narratives, the narrative emphasizes the dispersion of the nations together with the development of their individual languages. According to this reading, the linguistic differentiation between nations hints that each nation has a culture it must fulfill.
74. A similar model appears in Hegel's work "Grundlinien der Philosophie des Rechts," even if it is only similar structurally. When he seeks to explore the "ethical life," he begins by presenting the family as every person's first social framework, and from

Communal Will and Divine Will

This biblical configuration of a nation is described as the result of God's voluntary election of Abraham. According to the social contract theory, the "nation of culture" is based on the "community's will." The Bible exchanges this collective will for the divine will. Therefore, despite the "naturally" evolving depiction of the nation, it is not bound by a deterministic approach which creates the impression of a nation without moral value or purpose. The free will upon which the nation is based facilitates moral discourse; at the same time, however, because a single man is chosen as the father of the nation, the nation is still considered natural. As I mentioned earlier, even though the nation is considered a naturally evolving entity, the culture of this nation is not imposed upon its members merely because they were born into it. The covenant with God is a moral and religious obligation more than a definition of national character.

This approach has several important implications for the Abraham cycle:

- *Rescue mission, not military campaign.* Von Treitschke emphasized the importance of military aggression as an expression of national virility and unity.[75] In his eyes, exercise of national power is an integral part of a nation's definition, and even a supreme value. (Even without adopting his aggressive opinion, it should be noted that in the ancient world, a king established his

---

this framework, a person progresses to "civil society," and eventually encounters "the state," which, in his opinion, is the fulfillment of the ethical ideal. He emphasizes that the ideal collective union (i.e., "the state") should not only be considered as if it were solely intended to safeguard the individual's property and individual freedom (which already occurs in "civil society"), but should comprise the content and purpose of every individual in it, and only through the state can a person find ethical fulfillment (Georg Wilhelm Freidrich Hegel, "Grundlinien der Philosophie des Rechts," in *Werke in zwanzig Bänden*, ed. E. Moldenhauer and K. M. Michel [Frankfurt am Main: Suhrkamp Verlag, 1970], vol. 3, especially no. 258). When Hegel refers to the "general will" as something palpable, which surpasses individual will (even if the individual is not aware of it, Hegel believes, he must submit to it), he already paves the way to the next step of God's will being an expression of general will.

75. Batscha and Yassour, *The Great Modern Political Theories*, 365

might and won over his subjects through his success in war and the extent of his military conquests.) Abraham is also presented as a military figure who leads a campaign (Gen. 14). This chapter is so incongruous with the traditional perception of Abraham's character that many have questioned whether this is an original part of the Abraham cycle. I will discuss this at length below, in the relevant chapter, where I will argue that Abraham's victory awards him not only religious recognition but political renown. However, the battle in question is not the result of a military campaign, but a rescue mission – Abraham seeks to rescue his nephew Lot, who has been taken captive. This motive allows the narrative to hold the rope at both ends – Abraham rises to political fame through the accepted route of a victor returning from the battlefield, but he does not become characterized as a power-hungry conqueror. This is because his underlying motive for attack is moral – saving his nephew, that is, family commitment.[76]

- *Particularism and universalism.* Modern political thought perceives nationalistic separatism as contradictory to universal liberalism. The reasoning is clear, as defining what is "national" inherently defines the Other, who is thereby excluded from the privileges granted to members of the nation.[77] In the wider con-

76. It may well be that for the sake of emphasizing this, Abraham's war is described as reaching until north of Damascus (Gen. 14:15), that is, north of the border of Canaan, which emphasizes that the present war is a rescue mission, and the time of conquering the land is not yet at hand. As we will see, this war granted Abraham rights to the eastern side of the Jordan. I will discuss this at length in my analysis of Genesis 14 and 15.
77. Nonetheless, the beginnings of modern political philosophy already saw thinkers who combined a strong nationalistic approach and liberal-universalistic thought. For example, the French historian Jules Michelet took a liberal stance that developed, on one hand, the importance of the specific nation, but also saw the nation as an agent of universal freedom. In his opinion, history is the story of humanity's struggle for freedom, against nature and fate, and France is the nation that represents this spirit of freedom, which will influence all of humanity in the future. Michelet justified violence and denial of freedom over the course of the French Revolution (such as withholding the right to vote from most of the nation through the monarchical

text of particularism versus universalism, many have correctly stated that the Bible is suspended in unresolved tension; some works are inclined toward one worldview, while others favor the opposite approach. The Abraham cycle also oscillates between these two extremes, which are, nowadays, largely presented as conflicting.

The beginning of the Abraham cycle already establishes that Abraham's election is not a particularistic-chauvinistic election but a choice with universalistic implications: "All the families of the earth shall bless themselves by you" (Gen. 12:3). This idea is confirmed on the eve of Sodom's destruction: "The nations of the earth are to bless themselves by him" (18:18). And it is further reiterated during God's final revelation to Abraham: "All the nations of the earth shall bless themselves by your descendants" (22:18). These universalistic statements frame Abraham's election. They do not state that in the future, all nations will become part of the Hebrew nation, but that they will become "blessed" through it. The narrative thus presents a universalistic view. The post-diluvian world is comprised of many nations, and the story of the Tower of Babel presents this phenomenon as the result of God's will, similar to Herder's approach mentioned previously. It is well known that out of the major monotheistic religions, Judaism is the only one that has never attempted to impose its beliefs and culture upon those outside of the Israelite community. This attitude is already rooted in the Abraham cycle, which anticipates peaceful coexistence with

---

constitution of 1791) for the sake of the Revolution's success, because he believed that the minority sometimes reflects the nation's innermost desires. Due to these approaches, some consider Michelet's works a combination of political and cultural, mystical and historical, chauvinistic and universalistic nationalism. See especially Hans Kohn, *Nationalism: Its Meaning and History* (Malabar, FL, 1982), 97–102; Malach, "The Bases for the Legitimacy of a Jewish Nation-state in a Postmodern Era," 30–31. Alongside the French Michelet, Malach also counts the Italian Giuseppe Mazzini and the Polish national poet Adam Wickiewicz (who, oddly enough, never set foot in Poland). He argues that these thinkers also emphasize, in one way or another, that nationalism is not at odds with universalism, but rather is a preliminary stage of advancing universal concepts.

other nations. At the same time, however, the establishment of the Hebrew nation is an unmistakable process of separation and segregation. Abraham openly fears his son's intermarriage with the daughters of Canaan, similar to God's command for him to leave his hometown and wander to another place. This issue is complex and will crop up repeatedly throughout the different stories. Here, I wish only to draw attention to the fact that in the Abraham cycle, incidents which hint to nationalistic particularism are balanced out by stories that elevate universal benefit as the ultimate objective of Abraham's election. In this context, too, the narrative seems to be holding the rope at both ends, wherein the "natural nation" to evolve from Abraham's seed is also committed to the fulfillment of values of universal justice.

- *Nation and territory*. The "national purpose" of Abraham's election also complicates the issue of the nation's relationship with its land. The promise of inheriting the land is obviously a central, fundamental aspect of the Abraham cycle, and there is virtually no revelation without explicit mention of this promise.[78] At the same time, however, the narrative does not present the land as the nation's birthplace but rather as the land of their destiny. Intriguingly, Israelite culture does not tell itself stories of how its forefathers were born in the land, or of how the land was desolate until its ancestors came to settle it. On the contrary, there is repeated emphasis on Abraham's journey to the land, how the Canaanites already dwelled there (Gen. 12:6 and 13:7), and that his descendants will not immediately inherit the land because "the iniquity of the Amorites is not yet complete" (15:16).[79] This complexity is especially striking in the story of Abram and

---

78. The only revelation which does not explicitly mention the land (Gen. 15:1–6) is balanced out by this promise mentioned in the very next verses (15:7–21), which begin a new revelation, as I will show in my analysis of the two halves of Genesis 15.
79. Moshe Weinfeld claims that besides the Bible, there are no other stories of the origins of the major cultures in the Ancient Near East. The first founding story which shows structural similarity to the Abraham cycle is the story of Aeneas, founder of Ancient Rome (Moshe Weinfeld, *From Joshua to Josiah: Turning Points in the History of Israel from the Conquest of the Land Until the Fall of Judah* [Jerusalem, 1992], 13–26).

Sarai's descent to Egypt (Gen. 12), which interrupts the sequence of his journey to the chosen land, and I will discuss this in depth below. Like the covenant at Sinai, which takes place outside of the borders of Israel, Abraham's election also occurs outside of the territory which his offspring are to inherit, rendering the chosen land a destination rather than a point of origin; it is Israel's destiny, not its birthplace.[80]

- *"The gods of my father."* In his classic 1929 work, *Der Gott der Väter,* Albrecht Alt claims that the ancestral gods did not have a name of their own; rather, they were named for the person who established their ritual worship; thus, he includes the references to "the God of Abraham," "the Fear of Isaac," and "the Mighty One of Jacob." Only later, supposedly, were these gods identified with the Israelite God. Therefore, Alt argues that these ancestral gods were not cosmic deities, or even territorial-national deities, but gods identified with central historical figures, to the extent that they were referred to by the name of these figures (this form of religion, according to Alt, was common in nomadic tribes). This theory was accepted as widely as it was criticized.[81] For our purposes, the crucial aspect of this theory lies in his surprising claim that this phenomenon – the god's naming according to his central worshipper – is only documented in the patriarchal narrative cycles. Claus Westermann, however, is correct in asserting that this testifies to the familial-personal nature of the patriarchal cycles more than to a unique theological practice: "It is only from this context that the titles acquire their meaning."[82] In other words, the obvious familial nature of the patriarchal cycles does not only have bearing on the nation's

80. Similarly, Machinist, "Outsiders and Insiders: The Biblical View of Emergent Israel and Its Contexts," 49.
81. See, for example, Jacob Hoftijzer, *Die Verheißungen an die drei Erzväter* (Leiden, 1956), 84–97; Frank Moore Cross, *Canaanite Myth and Hebrew Epic* (Cambridge, 1973), 3–75; Thomas Edward McComiskey, "The Religion of the Patriarchs: An Analysis of The God of the Fathers by Albrecht Alt," in *The Law and the Prophets,* ed. J. H. Skilton (Nutley, NJ, 1974), 195–206; Kenneth A. Mathews, *Genesis,* vol. 2, 56–60.
82. Westermann, *Genesis 12–36: A Continental Commentary,* 108

definition, but on the construction of its religious infrastructure. God appears to the forefathers privately, addressing them as the heads of the clan, rather than as chief representatives of the nation which is to arise from them.

Nationalism and Morality

Beyond the aforementioned implications, the most important principle that can be derived from the notion of Israel as a natural-yet-ideological nation is related to the field of morality. Once again, the denouncement of marked nationalism is practically a premise of modern political philosophy; the trauma of Nazism certainly serves as a red light against any radical displays of nationalism, but not only Nazi Germany has committed atrocities in its name. The list is long and grows longer with time. At the same time, nationalism has also achieved great things, as Lea Brilmayer neatly states in her opening address to the New York University School of Law:

> One of the puzzling things about nationalism is that it sometimes seems to be a force for good, and sometimes a force for very great evil. At this particular time, we are more likely to think in terms of the evil nationalism brings about; this association is the legacy of the war in the former Yugoslavia, the killings in Rwanda, the ongoing fighting in Chechnya, and many other examples that all too easily come to mind. Nationalism now tends to be associated with barbarism: with genocide, ethnic cleansing, rape and wanton murder. But nationalism can also be a force for great good. When Armenians living in America contribute from their own limited resources to help Armenian earthquake victims, when Eritreans sacrifice their lives to liberate their country from a colonial power, or when Rigoberta Menchu commits herself to a life of personal hardship and danger to advance the human rights of Central American native peoples, it is hard to deny that national sentiment can play a noble role in world events.[83]

83. Lea Brilmayer, "The Moral Significance of Nationalism," *Notre Dame Law Review* 71 (1995): 7.

The solidarity between members of the nations that Brilmayer mentions has been witnessed among Jews throughout history. This phenomenon has baffled cultural researchers, and still remains somewhat of a mystery. There are too many examples to mention, but one notable case is the reaction to the Damascus Affair; Jews the world over endangered their positions and sacrificed their time and resources for the Jews of Syria during that blood libel of February 1840. The Jews of Damascus suffered terribly at the hands of the government.[84] Different scholars point to the Damascus Affair as a climactic point of national solidarity: Jews from across the globe enlisted to help their brothers in a distant land.[85] The Jews who went to extremes to help the victims in Damascus – despite the heavy personal prices they were forced to pay – had never met their Syrian "brothers," nor is it even likely that had they met, they would have been able to communicate through the language barrier. Yet their belonging to the same nation served as sufficient motivation to leave their home for weeks on end in a desperate attempt to prevent injustice to their own people in Syria, while no such efforts were made by the victims' own Arab neighbors.

Of course, this story, and the countless incidents similar to it, do not have the power to negate the grievous atrocities committed in the name of nationalism; this is not my intention. Brilmayer, however, is correct in noting that national solidarity moves citizens to sacrifice themselves for the sake of their people.

I wish to take this observation one step further and assert that nationalism in itself is neither positive nor negative; rather, it is employed to justify positive or negative actions, depending on that nation's culture and regime. For the sake of this discussion, I wish to adopt Brilmayer's working hypothesis:

---

84. George Pieritz, a Protestant missionary, described how the detained Jews were dipped in freezing water, how their heads were squeezed until their eyes popped out, how they were dragged by their ears and set alight. The government even seized and tortured sixty Jewish children between the ages of three and ten in order to pressure their parents into "confessing" about the death of Father Thomas and his Muslim attendant.

85. Jonathan Frankel, *The Damascus Affair: 'Ritual Murder,' Politics, and the Jews in 1840* (Cambridge, 1997).

> The hypothesis I want to investigate here is that nationalism, itself, is morally transparent, and that this fact accounts for its ability to coexist equally well with good and evil. The argument is that the overwhelmingly relevant normative feature of today's nationalism is the justice (or lack of justice) of the claim nationalists advance on behalf of their nation. The single most important normative feature – indeed, perhaps, the only important normative feature – is the right of the nation to the thing that nationalists assert on its behalf, and this right is not itself a consequence of nationalism but a consequence of other underlying moral claims. What matters from a moral point of view is whether the claims of one's nation and co-nationals are worthy, and whether they are pursued by morally acceptable means. Resistance to colonialism, human rights abuses, and dictatorship is just, at least so long as morally defensible means are used, and ethnic cleansing, rape, and genocide are morally wrong; this is not so because of any reasons involving nationalism, but because of other moral features of the situation. Nationalism means simply that one identifies with the claims of one's nations and one's co-nationals, and takes them as one's own. Nationalists act as agents of their nation, and when agents act what matters is the rights of the principal (that is, the nation) rather than the agents' motivations (that is, their nationalism).[86]

This position, even if not universally accepted, is important for the understanding of the legacy that the Abraham cycle leaves for the Israelite nation. Not only do the Abraham narratives not pose a contradiction between nationalism and morality, but on the contrary, Abraham's election is presented as being contingent upon moral values of justice and righteousness. Moshe Weinfeld correctly notes that the description of Abraham's election in Genesis 18:19 implies that the upholding of "justice and righteousness" pertains to Abraham's entire household – that

86. Brilmayer, "The Moral Significance of Nationalism," 7–8.

is, to the entire nation – and not only to the leader himself.[87] As I will posit throughout my analysis of the Abraham cycle, the central question of Abraham's election is explored through pairs of narratives; one of each pair addresses the issue of his continuity from a nationalistic perspective, while the other presents a moral perspective.[88] This is true of the double Ishmael narratives (Gen. 16 and 21), of the story of Lot (Gen. 19 includes two narratives of Lot's escape from the falling city), and of the double tidings of Isaac's birth (Gen. 17 and 18). In each pair, one narrative presents the birth of a nation bound to a covenant with God, while the parallel story depicts the birth of a nation as the result of divine reaction to certain moral actions of the characters. For example, Isaac's birth is justified twice: once in order to perpetuate the covenant with God (Gen. 17), and once as Abraham and Sarah's reward for their hospitality (Gen. 18). This dichotomy, which reoccurs at every narrative junction, ardently clarifies the relationship between nationalism and morality – between Abraham's election for national purposes as well as for moral purposes. Asserting the moral obligations of the nation's founder as a unifying justification of a nation's existence can be considered a revolution in ancient political thought. William Irwin may well be correct in his argument that this revolution was already the result of a more fundamental theological revolution, that of the unique moral values of the God of Israel.[89] In any case, the Abraham cycle introduces a natural (ethnic) nation whose moral purpose and obligations are a fundamental condition for its existence – a natural nation that evolves from a single family yet is inherently established upon free choice.

Moral Nationalism and Post-Modern Nationalism

In Israel, a lively public debate recently raged with regard to the institution of a "Jewish nationality law," which seeks to ratify the State of Israel

87. Moshe Weinfeld, *Justice and Righteousness in Ancient Israel Against the Background of Social Reforms in the Ancient Near East* (Jerusalem, 1985), 125–126.
88. Compare to Thomas L. Brodie, *Genesis as Dialogue: A Literary, Historical, and Theological Commentary* (New York, 2001), 89–94.
89. William A. Irwin, "The Hebrews," in *The Intellectual Adventure of Ancient Man: An Essay of Speculative Thought in the Ancient Near East*, ed. H. Frankfort et al. (Chicago, 1946), 326–359.

as a Jewish-democratic state. One of the main opponents of this law is Prof. Mordechai Kremnitzer, in whose eyes, the "Jewish nationality" of the State of Israel is obvious and inherent, so that there is no need to anchor it through a legal definition:

> The State of Israel is the national state of the Jewish people. It always has been, and will always be. Whether one considers our legal system superficially or in depth, there is only one conclusion: our State is of a Jewish and democratic nature. This is evident from mention of the expression "Jewish and democratic" in our constitution, but not only from that; it is evident from our Declaration of Independence, from the Law of Return, from our festivals and days of remembrance...it is evident from the special status of the Hebrew language.[90]

The nature of this debate reflects a national reawakening of the attempt to define itself in light of contemporary philosophical discourse. This reawakening, of course, is not unique to the State of Israel. According to economist Guy Sorman, a national reawakening in East Asia is quashing liberal European assumptions pertaining to the decline of nationalism and the unlikelihood of war between democracies. In his opinion, Western attention is focused on the economic boom in East Asia, overlooking the fact that the region is sizzling with nationalistic debates that challenge the region's stability as well as the notion that the time of nationalism is long past.[91]

In 2014, Scotland rejected an independence referendum by majority opinion that would have separated them from the United Kingdom. While this decision reflects other factors being privileged over nationalism, the very fact that this issue has come to a head at this point in time – with similar issues bubbling to the surface in other parts of the world – shows that nationalistic sentiment is still stirring across the globe.

90. Mordechai Kremnitzer, "The Jewish State Bill: A Danger for Zionist Enterprise," *Makor Rishon*, May 9, 2014.
91. Guy Sorman, "Where Nationalism Still Matters: Asia's Simmering Political Tensions Defy Conventional Wisdom," *City Journal*, August 20, 2012.

These political factions indicate that questions of nationalism are still relevant, and rather than attempt to quash these issues out of fear from shadows of the past, there is growing need to devote time and effort to formulate a discourse regarding nationalism through the employment of moral terms and obligations. The story of Abraham exemplifies the fusion of nationalistic and moral values; the ancient text has much to contribute to an age-old debate in new guise.

The Line of Terah (Gen. 11:26–32)

Every hero's journey begins with a call to action.[1] In just a few lines, the reader will experience that first moment of revelation, when God appears to Abram and proclaims, "Go forth from your land and from the place of your birth and from your father's house to a land that I will show you" (Gen. 12:1). This is the moment that plants the seed for Abram to become the father of monotheism; it is his "Call to Adventure."

Just before that momentous divine revelation, the text introduces six innocuous verses, ostensibly simply to provide genealogical context to the hero that will emerge in the following chapter. Our hero Abram is introduced at the end of a description of the genealogy of Shem, which culminates with the birth of Terah's three sons: "Terah begot Abram, Nahor, and Haran" (Gen. 11:27). The reader is told of the death of one of the sons, Haran, and Terah's genealogy is followed by a description of his journey to Canaan: "Terah took his son Abram, his grandson Lot, the son of Haran, and his daughter-in-law Sarai, the

1. Although an examination of the Abraham cycle through the lens of Joseph Campbell's "Hero's Journey" paradigm is not the focus of this work, I will point out some of the major milestones that appear in the Abraham cycle that coincide with Campbell's hero cycle.

wife of his son Abram, and set out with them from Ur of the Chaldeans for the land of Canaan; but when they arrived in Haran, they settled there" (11:31).

These six lines depicting the lineage of Terah and his journey to Canaan are in fact the true opening scene of the Abram narrative. We are told of the birth of the brothers Abram, Nahor, and Haran, of Haran's subsequent death and the effect it had on the family dynamic, and of the patriarch Terah's apparent decision to move the family to Canaan. These events are the prequel to the Abram narrative, and beneath the surface they tell a fascinating story of how the man who became the father of the Jewish people left his "land ... birthplace ... and the home of [his] father."

Who Is Our Hero?

Noah marks the tenth generation of Adam's genealogy; Terah marks the tenth in Noah's. It's not clear who the heroes of this story are yet, as we are introduced to a number of Terah's family members in the next few verses. The parallels between Adam's and Noah's lineage nonetheless produce a literary effect: their similarity generates anticipation that a leader might emerge in the next generation.[2] The allusion to the previous biblical "beginnings" implies that the reader is on the brink of a new era.[3] Just as Noah's story began with the enumeration of his lineage, the next chapter in the biblical narrative opens in similar fashion, indicating that a new hero is about to be introduced. The very next verse, however, relates a family tragedy: the death of Terah's son.[4] Abram and Nahor, the remaining brothers, seem to continue

2. See further in Gerhard F. Hasel, "The Meaning of the Chronogenealogies of Genesis 5 and 11," *Origins* 7 (1980): 53–70.
3. Note that according to the "three-son model" Terah (and not Abram) parallels Adam and Noah.
4. The claim that Haran died "in confrontation with Terah" (C. Wynand Retief, "When Interpretation Traditions Speak Too Loud for Ethical Dilemmas to Be Heard: On the Untimely Death of Haran [Genesis 11:28]," *Old Testament Essays* 23 [2010]: 788–803) is, in my opinion, somewhat exaggerated. When the text states that Haran died "*al penei Teraḥ aviv*" (Gen. 11:28), literally translated as "in the presence of," this "presence" is chronological, i.e., in his lifetime.

on comparable paths, each taking a wife – "the name of Abram's wife being Sarai and that of Nahor's wife Milcah, the daughter of Haran, the father of Milcah and the father of Iscah. Now Sarai was barren, she had no child" (Gen. 11:29).

A dramatic family dynamic emerges from the unpacking of the wives' introduction. Milcah and Iscah were the daughters of Haran, together with their brother Lot. We know that upon his brother's death, Abram adopted his nephew, Lot. Here we learn that the recently orphaned Milcah was adopted (by way of marriage) by her uncle, Nahor. And what of the third orphaned child of Haran, Iscah? It would appear that Abram took her under his wing as well. This would appear to be the basis of the midrash that claims that Iscah is Sarai, although this claim is difficult to justify with the plain reading of the text, since Abraham's wife is introduced as Sarai, without the additional detail that Sarai is Iscah.

Abram, the second son, married a woman with no significant lineage – Sarai is presented with no genealogical context. Furthermore, the story makes it clear by mentioning Sarai's infertility that it is unlikely that her union with Abram will yield any further offspring.

This introduction seems to suggest that Nahor will become the story's protagonist: Terah's eldest, Haran, died young; Sarai, wife of Terah's second son, is barren; therefore Nahor, whose wife is deeply connected with the family past, and is presumably fertile, will continue Terah's line. The sudden change of focus afterward to Abram is designed to enhance the sense of divine selection unfolding throughout his story.

The Family Journey

Terah, apparently out of nowhere, picks up his family and moves from Ur of the Chaldeans to Canaan. "Terah took his son Abram, his grandson Lot, the son of Haran, and his daughter-in-law Sarai, the wife of his son Abram, and set out with them from Ur of the Chaldeans for the land of Canaan; but when they arrived in Haran, they settled there" (Gen. 11:31). The text emphasizes Terah's relationships with Abram, his wife, and his nephew Lot, while blatantly omitting Nahor's family. Terah's extended family is tribal in its bonds; the sons have adopted the orphaned children of their brother. When Nahor and his family reappear later in the narrative,[5] it indicates that they too were part of the family's unified journey to another land. Given all this, the reader should find it odd that Nahor is omitted from this part of the narrative.

Furthermore, no reason is provided for Terah's journey to Canaan. Josephus writes that Terah's grief over the death of Haran drove him away from Ur.[6] Others mention Sarai's barrenness,[7] financial reasons, local conflicts,[8] or religious reasons, for his departure.[9] Whatever the cause may be, this apparently intentional lacuna indicates that the reason for Terah's departure plays no role in the story; in fact, its absence might serve as a clue to the story's true purpose and role in the origin story of Abram.

These two glaring omissions – the reason for Terah's journey and the question of Nahor's fate – are linked with the narrative design. Why is Terah's journey – a journey he never sees through; a journey that ends in Haran; a journey that never reaches its final destination – included in the narrative cycle starring his son?

In the next chapter (Gen. 12), God appears to Abram and tells him to go to Canaan. This is perplexing, as it seems that Terah was already on the way to Canaan, with Abram in tow. If this is the case, why did God feel the need to tell Abram to journey somewhere he was already going? Even more perplexing is that this initial revelation of God to

---

5. When Abraham's servant seeks a wife for Isaac (Gen. 24), and when Jacob moves into the house of Laban (Gen. 29–32).
6. Josephus, *Antiquities*, I:152 (Louis H. Feldman, *Flavius Josephus: Translation and Commentary. Volume 3: Judean Antiquities 1–4* [Leiden: Brill, 2000], 55, and see 55n476). See also Yair Zakovitch, "The Exodus from Ur of the Chaldeans: A Chapter in Literary Archaeology," in *Ki Baruch Hu: Ancient Near Eastern, Biblical and Judaic Studies in Honor of Baruch A. Levine*, ed. R. Chazan, W. W. Hallo, and L. H. Schiffman (Winona Lake, IN, 1999), 429–439.
7. Yehuda Kiel, *Daat Mikra*: *Genesis* (Jerusalem, 1997), vol. 1, 205.
8. Edouard P. Dhorme, "Abraham dans le Cadre de l'Histoire," *RB* 37 (1928): 379.
9. I have difficulty with Rabbi Mordechai Breuer's suggestion (*Pirkei Bereshit*, ed. Y. Ofer [Alon Shevut, 1999], vol. 1, 224–225) and Patricia Berlyn's ("The Journey of Terah: To Ur-Kasdim or Urkesh?" *JBQ* 33 [2005]: 73–80) that Terah went to the land of Canaan because it is the land in which God resides, and that Terah felt this deeply in his soul. There is no indication to this effect in the written text. However, according to Abraham ibn Ezra's interpretation, perhaps Breuer's suggestion could be accepted for a different reason, as discussed below.

Abram in chapter 12 is considered the beginning of Abram's journey – "Go forth from your land, from your birthplace, from the house of your father, to a land that I will show you." God's words to Abram, "Go forth from your land," become the lyrical embodiment of his journey for generations to come. God asks Abram to leave everything he knows – his homeland, his birthplace, and the house of his father. This divine edict to leave his home establishes Abram's character as the self-sacrificing, adventurous hero who leaves everything behind to become the father of monotheism, and the messenger of the one true God. It is his first heroic act, an act of blind faith that echoes throughout his entire story. And yet, upon closer inspection, it appears that the text suggests that Abram's leaving his homeland after the divine revelation was nothing more than coincidence. His father, Terah, has already decided to move the family to Canaan. God's revelation to Abram occurred only once the family were already on their way. Practically speaking, Abram had already left his land and his birthplace at the bidding of his father. When God approached Abram in Haran, he had already taken the difficult step to leave the land of his birth. He was, in fact, already halfway through the very journey God commanded him to complete.

The language of "Go forth from *your land* and from *the place of your birth* and from your father's house to a land that I will show you" indicates a level of self-sacrifice and adventurousness that does not align with the apparent chronology of the revelation. It is no great ask for God to command Abram to leave everything he has ever known in Haran – his true home and birthplace was Ur. In fact, God later tells Abram that He "brought you out from Ur of the Chaldeans" (Gen. 15:7), not from Haran. According to the chronological flow of the narrative, it would seem that God came to Abram in the midst of a journey that he undertook at his father Terah's behest. Since Terah's journey to Canaan has no compelling purpose or motivation, the sequence of events here seems coincidental at best.

Of course, we know that Abram's journey is anything but coincidental. This is the starting point of a physical and spiritual journey the entire essence of which is guided by the hand of God. In order to properly understand the narrative, we must discuss the journeys of Terah and Abram on two separate planes: development of the plot, and the literary purpose of the narrative. Terah initiates a journey that is unrelated to God's command; how does this correlate with the command to Abram to journey to that very same destination? Additionally, there must be literary significance to the consecutive *presentation* of the two episodes. Seeking literary significance goes beyond the historical question ("What happened?") and instead relates to the narrative design ("How is the story presented to the reader, and why?").

The Chronological Story

The text relates that Terah begot sons at the age of seventy, and died at 205 (Gen. 11:31). Abram leaves for Canaan on God's command at the age of seventy-five, when Terah is 145 (70+75). The fact that Terah's death (11:32) is recorded *before* God's command to Abram (12:1) creates the false impression that Terah died before Abram left for Canaan, while chronologically Abram arrived in Canaan during his father's lifetime. However, biblical protagonists frequently exit the narrative stage long before their chronological lives are over. For example, though it seems Noah dies long before the Abraham narrative begins, a simple calculation can determine that Noah dies when Abraham is fifty-eight years old. Similarly, Isaac is still alive when his grandson Joseph is sold.[10] Genesis is not a history book, but a sweeping series of portraits tracing a character from birth to death before the next character is introduced. The narrative follows Terah's life: the birth and marriage of his sons (11:27–30), the journey to Canaan that ends in Haran (11:31), and his death in Haran (11:32). The spotlight only falls on Abram once Terah has stepped down, despite the fact that some of Abram's episodes (such as God's revelation and his journey to Canaan) occur during Terah's lifetime.

This narrative style re-illuminates the correlation between Terah's journey and God's revelation to Abram. As the events are clearly not

10. Isaac is sixty years old when Jacob is born, and Jacob is ninety-one when Joseph is born (and so, when Jacob comes before Pharaoh, he is 130 years old and Joseph is thirty-nine). That is to say, when Joseph was born, Isaac was 151 years old, and when Joseph was sold to Egypt at the age of seventeen, Isaac was 168 years old. Isaac died approximately ten years before Jacob discovered that Joseph was alive and governing Egypt, around the time when Joseph was taken from the pit to interpret Pharaoh's dreams.

recorded in chronological order, it is reasonable to assume that Terah's decision to immigrate to Canaan is connected with God's command to Abram to journey to the very same place. The story presented to the reader has Terah leaving for Canaan before his son Abram is visited by God. In fact, chronologically, after Abram is commanded to go to Canaan, his father Terah decides to join him on his journey.

In other words, according to the story's narrative sequence, Terah departs for Canaan before the reader is aware that God had spoken to Abram and commanded him to go, while according to the chronological order of events, after Abram was commanded to go to Canaan, his father Terah decided to join him on his journey.[11]

The chronological sequence of the plot could therefore be described like this: After God spoke to Abram and commanded him to go to the "land that I will show you," Abram then shared this information with his father, Terah. A religious man himself, Terah decided to join his son on his journey. It would be reasonable to assume this version of events based on what we know of the characters involved. Abram had already established himself as a highly moral and spiritual leader. Terah, a pagan, would not have been surprised to discover that his son had been chosen by "a god" to be his benefactor. If that was the case, thought Terah, why shouldn't he and the rest of his family also benefit from Abram's divine sponsorship? Terah therefore decides to join Abram on the journey that this "new" god chose for him to fulfill.

The Literary Story

This version of the story is not presented to the reader in a chronological fashion. We must remember that the biblical text is far more biographical than historical – it seeks to tell the stories of personalities, not necessarily of chronological plot development. The narrative sequence of events not only deviates from the actual timeline, certain verses seem intent on misleading the reader into thinking that Abram received the divine message in Haran, after Terah's journey had begun: "Abram was seventy-five years old *when he left Haran*. Abram took his wife Sarai

11. A similar suggestion is offered by Ibn Ezra and Radak, in their commentaries on the verse.

and his brother's son Lot, and all the wealth that they had amassed, and the people *they had acquired in Haran*; and they set out to go forth to the land of Canaan" (Gen. 12:4–5). The premise of these verses is that Abram set out from Haran, not Ur of the Chaldeans! It is true that Abram departed from Haran after his family had already settled there, but his true journey began in Ur of the Chaldeans, where God first revealed Himself to him. The narrative structure of this story, and the jumbling of the chronological plot points, must intend to tell the story of who Abram was, emphasizing the traits the text deems important to emphasize, and glossing over traits or actions that may disrupt the flow of the moral message.

The text relates to Terah's and Abram's journeys as completely separate – Terah left Ur of the Chaldeans apparently of his own accord, while Abram was commanded by God. The focus of the text on Terah as an independent protagonist contributes to the analogical design of the two journeys: father and son embark on one journey, which is described to the reader as two separate journeys, enabling the reader to compare the individual experiences of father and son. Terah set out for Canaan, but only got as far as Haran. The story omits the reason for Terah's journey, and the reader has no reason to believe the reason behind it is anything but his own free will. In contrast, Abram embarks on his journey "as the Lord had commanded him" (Gen. 12:4). Even if both characters did leave together, there is a literary purpose in presenting the story through two different journeys: one without cause or purpose, which does not culminate in the desired destination, and the other ordained by God, culminating in the desired destination of Canaan.

This presentation of the story also emphasizes the relationship between Abram and the land of Canaan. Abram and Terah's arrivals, although occurring at the same time and place, are also presented as separate. Both Abraham and Terah passed through Haran on their way to Canaan. Terah arrived and settled in Haran – although it was not his original destination, he decided to remain in the city, and so his journey ended there. Abram, however, only "arrived" in Haran. The reason for which he set out on the journey was not yet fulfilled – it was only once he reached Mamre that Abram fulfilled his purpose of "Go forth from your land" and settled in the land of Canaan. Terah's journey precedes

Abram's so that the reader can contrast Terah's choice to remain in Haran with the choice of his son to follow God's command.[12]

Despite the differences, the story is designed to convey the feeling that Abram's journey is a continuation of Terah's; this is the reason that Abram is described as departing from Haran (12:4–5), the very place Terah had ended his journey.[13]

The Complexity of Heroism and Family

Abram's journey is therefore presented ambivalently. While Abram obeyed God's command and left his native land to go toward the unknown, he chose to take Lot and his possessions along with him, elements that seem to be continuous to his father's journey. It would seem that Abram bringing his nephew with him was in conflict with God's directive to leave his family behind. This may be the case, and may also be why the text decided to separate the journey of Terah from that of Abram – to indicate that although they may have traveled together, the impetus and purpose of their journeys were far from being the same. The first chapters of Abram's story, therefore, paint a complex picture of Abram, who faithfully follows God's command and journeys to Canaan; Abram, who physically abandons the house of his father, but maintains an emotional bond by following in his path.

---

12. Compare with Yitzhak Peleg, "Was the Ancestress of Israel in Danger?" *ZAW* 118 (2006): 197–208. According to Peleg, the narrative omits the reasons for Terah's departure from Ur of the Chaldeans because Terah is a secondary character, and only information that is needed to further the plot is provided with regard to secondary characters. I believe the narrative's silence here is critical, as the literary purpose of Terah's character in the narrative is to go without a particular reason, and of his own volition. In this way, Terah is contrasted with Abram.
13. Perhaps the emphasis on the move "from Haran" intends to demonstrate the difference between Terah and Abram; whereas it is Terah's own decision to stay in Haran, Abram is obligated by divine decree to leave Haran and continue to Canaan. Perhaps this is also the reason that Abram's age (Gen. 12:4) and the people accompanying him (12:5) are mentioned in the context of the departure from Haran.

Abram's Journey to Canaan (Gen. 12:1–9)

Abram has received the call, and made the courageous decision to heed it, leaving behind his family and homeland. Now, setting forth on the path prescribed by God, Abram is eager to fulfill his destiny. However, it seems that Abram is still hindered by certain elements of his past that he has not yet entirely renounced. These first steps of Abram's path in Genesis 12 begin with an expedition across the land God promised him, from Shechem, to Bethel, and finally to Hebron. Each landmark on this tour adds another layer to Abram's development, preparing him to begin his destiny as the father of the Jewish people. Obstacles appear in Abram's way to strengthen his resolve; the descent to Egypt, followed by the separation from Lot, shear layers of reluctance from Abram's initial hesitation. The conclusion of this maiden voyage into the land of Canaan sees Abram returning from Egypt to complete the trip he began, and to fully actualize God's commandment to "go forth" to the land he was promised.

The Undisputed Hero

In Exodus, the backstory of Moses' childhood adventures paints a rich picture of the context that shaped Moses as a character. He was the child who grew up in the house of the Pharaoh who became the savior chosen by God to lead the Jews out of slavery. However, here in Genesis, Abram appears on the scene with no such backstory, no indication of why God may have chosen him to be the founding father of the Jewish people. Early midrashic literature sought to fill this void, and integrated foundations of Abram's devotion and escape from the edict of a king, similar to Moses.[1] As we previously discussed, Abram was first introduced to us as one of three sons of Terah. As Abram's role emerges, it seems clear that Abram was introduced in the context of Terah's family in order to highlight the fact that he left them behind when commanded by God. Abraham's lack of an "origin story" here serves to underscore the centrality of choice in his story. Abram made the definitive choice to heed God's call in Ur of the Chaldeans, and throughout the narrative cycle Abram will continue to implement his free will to obey God's commands as His faithful servant. Moreover, the narrative seeks to establish Abram as the undisputable chosen father of the Jewish people. The story gives us no details about the man Abram when he was approached by God – we know nothing of his character, his morality, or his motivations. If the text sought to connect God's choice of Abram with his virtue, his behavior, or his accomplishments, the reader might be able to contest the value of that choice. If Abram's behavior seemed to change, if he made a decision that seemed incorrect – that could invite an argument that perhaps he is "no longer fit" to be God's chosen leader. By omitting any contextual background information, the narrative indicates to the reader that God's choice in Abram was unconditional, and therefore unquestionable.[2]

The First Heroic Cycle

The story of Abram instigates the beginning of the story of the Jewish people. Abram is the first biblical character to undergo the complete hero cycle, and this archetypal role serves as a model for the journeys

1. See the book of Jubilees, chs. 11–12; Genesis Rabba 38. See also Louis Ginzberg, *Legends of the Jews*, trans. H. Szold (Philadelphia, 1961), vol. 1, 203–206; Yair Zakovitch and Avigdor Shinan, *That's Not What the Good Book Says* (Tel Aviv, 2004), 129–137.
2. See more on this topic: Hayyim J. Angel, "The Chosen People: An Ethical Challenge," *Conversations* 8 (2010): 52–60.

of faith undertaken by his children, and for generations to come. Abram's first journey is characterized by the word "*lekh*," "go"; it is a returning motif in his story. Both Abram's initial revelation in Ur of the Chaldeans and his final revelation in which he was commanded to sacrifice his son were formulated using this verb (Gen. 12:1 and 22:2), and on other occasions Abram is also commanded to "walk" ("*hithalekh*" – 13:17 and 17:1). The imagery of walking or going forth exemplifies the shaping of an active and dynamic character. Walking or traveling are symbolic of spiritual vitality and the capacity to begin anew. Abram is expected to leave one land and make room for another, both geographically and emotionally.[3] The repetition of this concept in his initial revelation also emphasizes this point – it was not the "to where" but the "from what" that was a central point here. The initial command omits the destination,[4] and instead focuses on what is being left behind.[5] The purpose of this first step in Abram's narrative is simply to begin the journey.

Abram's obedience here, a key character trait he possesses, is even more powerful against the backdrop of how much he really is leaving behind. "The Lord said to Abram, 'Go forth from your land and from the place of your birth and from your father's house to the land that I will show you.'" The command opens with "your land," and then

3. Compare to Jean-Michel Poirier, "'De Campement en campement. Abram alla au Négev' (Gen 12,9): Le thème de la marche dans le cycle d'Abraham," in *Bible et Terre Sainte: Mélanges Marcel Beaudry*, ed. E. Aguilar Chiu (New York, 2008), 31–45.
4. Compare with the parallel command in the binding of Isaac: "Go forth to the land of Moriah," and with Genesis Rabba 39:9: "R. Levi said: Two times it is stated, 'Go forth,' and we do not know which is more favorable, the first or the second. But since the second says, 'to the land of Moriah,' we now know the second is more favorable than the first." Cf. Hamilton, who notes the stylistic parallel between the two commandments (Hamilton, *The Book of Genesis, Chapters 18–50*, 370–371; 376). See also discussion below about the commandment in the context of the binding of Isaac.
5. Takamitsu Muraoka ("On the So-Called Dativus Ethicus in Hebrew," *JTS* 29 [1978]: 495–498) suggested that the linguistic function of the preposition *lekha* (lit. "for you") in the phrase *lekh lekha* is to focus on the character who takes action, and differentiate the character from their surroundings. This distinction creates an independent identity through differentiation. Rashi's commentary reflects a similar reading: "Go forth – for your own benefit."

escalates to a term with a heavier association of personal connection – "the place of your birth." An even more difficult demand is the separation from "your father's house." The gradual escalation reflects the growing demand of Abram's complete and total disengagement, and indicates the challenge of God's command. This feeling is intensified by the double meaning of the word *moladetekha*, which sometimes is used to refer to a place of birth (e.g., Gen. 31:13) and other times implies family (e.g., Gen. 48:6; 18:9, 11).[6] Identity and self-perception are fundamentally linked with one's family and homeland. Abram's disengagement from both will turn him into an isolated individual with no familial ties. This is an essential step in anticipation of building a new and different life. The two aspects emphasized in the demand to disengage are addressed in God's promises of land and family. The command to "go forth" is not only geographical in nature, but emotional and cultural as well.[7]

Later (Gen. 15:7), God will intimate that Abram was "reborn" when he left Ur of the Chaldeans. From that moment on, God's patronage becomes the replacement for the bond and connection Abram would have received from his family.

In context, the blessing that accompanies the demand seems to be conditional: "Go forth.... And I will make you a great nation, and I will bless you; I will make your name great, and you shall be a blessing. I will bless those who bless you, and curse him who curses you; and all the families of the earth shall be blessed by you."

Thus, if Abram obeys God's command to disengage from his land and family, and go to the land that God will show him, he will receive these blessings. The fact that Abram takes it upon himself to undergo this difficult journey is an indication of his devotion to this new life.

---

6. Brown-Driver-Briggs, *A Hebrew and English Lexicon of the Old Testament* (Oxford, 1906), 409; Menahem Zevi Kaddari, *A Dictionary of Biblical Hebrew* (Ramat Gan, 2006), 588.
7. Nahum Sarna notes that the creation of a monotheistic religion in the area at that time was utterly inconceivable for several reasons, but particularly due to the religious culture. Mesopotamia at the time was saturated in polytheism. Every geographical location and every structure were steeped in symbols of idolatry (Sarna, *Genesis* [JPS Torah Commentary: Philadelphia, New York, and Jerusalem, 1989], 101).

A Blessing for the Ages

God's first promise to Abram is that he will become "a great nation." This promise is reparation for the demand of Abram to disengage from the house of his father. The purpose of severing his connections with the past is to create a future that will spring forth from Abram's own roots. The surprising use of the word "*goy,*" "nation," broadens the scope of this blessing to a national level, well beyond Abram's nuclear family.[8] The phrase "a great nation" will crop up again in the narrative cycle, in relation to both Abram (Gen. 18:18) and Ishmael (17:20, 21:18), and beyond the story cycle, in the Jacob narrative (46:3).[9] Each appearance of the phrase is a reminder of God's initial revelation to Abram. When Moses is told, "Now...that I may destroy them and make of you a *great nation*" (Ex. 32:10), this is an indication that God wishes to turn Moses into "Abram," the father of the new nation.[10]

The second line of the blessing, "I will bless you," is more ambiguous; it is unclear how this blessing will be realized. The Midrash interprets this blessing as a promise of material wealth. The term "blessing" has two essential meanings in the book of Genesis: family and prosperity.[11] Since God has already promised that Abram's progeny will be "a great nation," it is reasonable to assume that this blessing adds the aspect of material wealth. As God has already promised Abram that he will become a great nation, the second blessing probably refers to wealth. The concept of riches as a blessing is established later in the text; throughout the story cycle wealth is regarded as both a blessing (Gen. 13:2) and a point of contention (13:5–13).

---

8. E. A. Speiser, *Genesis* (AB: Garden City, NY, 1964), 162–163.
9. On the similarity between Abram and Jacob's revelations (Gen. 41:1–5), see Westermann, *Genesis 12–36: A Continental Commentary,* 147. Assuming the Jacob narrative refers to the Abraham narrative (in contrast with Weisman, *From Jacob to Israel*), the link should be perceived as a comfort to Jacob, who is required to leave his home and go to Egypt. But God promises him that He will accompany him on his journey, just as He had accompanied his grandfather.
10. The Septuagint was aware of this possibility (Karla R. Suomala, *Moses and God in Dialogue: Exodus 32–34 in Postbiblical Literature* [New York, 2004], 47).
11. See with regard to Isaac, Gen. 27:12 and 29.

God continues, "I will make your name great," meaning that Abram's name will be known to all. Indeed, Abram is the father of monotheism, the first forefather of the world's three major religions. It could be that this wording is an intentional contrast to the previous story of Babel. The builders of the tower express the desire to make a name for themselves: "Come let us build us a city and a tower whose top will reach heaven, to make a name for ourselves, lest we shall be scattered over the face of the whole earth" (Gen. 11:4). The story of the Tower of Babel prefaces the Abraham story. This is necessarily so, as the concept of creating a unique and chosen nation can only be discussed after the scattering of the nations, which had enabled cultural diversity and the ability to privilege one nation over another. However, the statement to Abram is poignant in its contrast to the previous story. One cannot make a name for oneself, as the builders of the tower had believed. God is the only one who can "make a great name" for the one who walks in His path.[12]

In a literal sense, too, Abram's name is ultimately made "greater" – from Abram to Abraham.[13] The literal extension of his name is accompanied

12. See Victor P. Hamilton, *The Book of Genesis, Chapters 1–17* (NICOT: Grand Rapids, MI, 1990), 372; Mark A. Awabdy, "Babel, Suspense, and the Introduction to the Terah-Abram Narrative," *JSOT* 35 (2010): 3–29; Jon D. Levenson, *Inheriting Abraham: The Legacy of the Patriarch in Judaism, Christianity and Islam* (Princeton and Oxford, 2012), 19. Allan K. Jenkins ("A Great Name: Genesis 12:2 and the Editing of the Pentateuch," *JSOT* 10 [1978]: 41–57) posits that this phrase ("to make a great name") in the Tower of Babel story and in Abram's blessing is a motif that strings together all the stories of the patriarchs, and the book of Genesis in general; there is an apparent effort in these verses to create a "literary bridge" between the initiation stories in Genesis and the stories of the patriarchs. Thomas W. Mann ("'All the Families of the Earth': The Theological Unity of Genesis," *Interpretation* 45 [1991]: 341–353) presents Abram's election as a solution for the problems of Genesis 1–11, emphasizing that through Abraham, blessing is channeled to the world instead of curse. Similarly, see Noort, "Abraham and the Nations," 21–22, 29–30. Jenkins ("A Great Name: Genesis 12:2 and the Editing of the Pentateuch") links the naming motif with the selection of the chosen offspring, which could save humanity from its primal sins, as demonstrated in the verses about Noah: "And he named him Noah, saying, this will provide us relief from our work and from the toil of our hands, out of the very soil that the Lord had placed under a curse" (Gen. 5:29). See also M. Daniel Carroll R., "Blessing of the Nations: Towards a Biblical Theology of Mission from Genesis," *Bulletin for Biblical Research* 10 (2000): 21.
13. Previously suggested by Ḥizkuni on Gen. 12:2. See also Genesis Rabba 29:11; Sarna, *Genesis* (JPS Torah Commentary), 124; Mathews, *Genesis*, 114.

by an expansion of the blessing from "a great nation" to "a multitude of nations."[14]

The key word that stands out in this short excerpt is "*berakha,*" "blessing," which is repeated five times. If we follow the root word throughout the blessings, we see the foreshadowing of Abram's character development. Initially, Abram is blessed by God ("I will bless you"), but ultimately his blessing will be spread to others around him; at first to those who are close to him or identify with his cause ("I will bless those who bless you") and eventually to all of humanity ("And all the families of the earth shall be blessed by you").[15] The power of bestowing blessing is transferred from God blessing Abram to Abram himself becoming the source of blessing for others.

The transition from Abram's blessing to the blessing that affects all nations is expressed with a peculiar phrase: "And you shall be a blessing." How can a person become "a blessing"? The most accurate reading is the one suggested by Rashi: "The blessings are entrusted into your hand. Until now, they were in My hand; I blessed Adam and Noah. From now on, you may bless whomever you wish."[16] This phrase creates a delicate balance between the first half of the blessing, which designates him as the father of the chosen nation, and the second half, which delineates his moral obligation to bring blessing to his environment. He is not only blessed himself; he will channel blessing to all nations of the earth. Abram's transformation is not limited to his personal appointment as the leader of the Jewish people; in this role he is to become a source of blessing and moral model for all of humanity.

The Journey Begins

Immediately after receiving the blessing, Abram sets out on his journey to Canaan. God's directions – simply, "Go forth…to a land that I will

---

14. This reading touches on the question of plot development throughout the story cycle. It is possible that the blessing of a multitude of nations is the result of Ishmael's birth (as described in Gen. 16). Had Hagar not been given to Abram, only one nation would have been destined to come from him. At this point in the plot there is no indication of a multitude of nations.
15. See Westermann, *Genesis 12–36: A Continental Commentary*, 146.
16. Rashi on Gen. 12:2.

show you" – are vague at best, and so the route that Abram decides to take through the land takes on special significance. At what point has Abram fulfilled God's command? Upon crossing the border? Arriving at the biggest city? Building a home?

One of the differences mentioned above between Terah's journey and the journey of Abram was expressed in the culmination of the journey: Terah's destination was Canaan, but his journey ended in Haran (Gen. 11:31), while Abram's journey ended in the desired destination (12:5). However, while the verse states that Terah "settled" in Haran, Abram is said to have arrived in Canaan, but no "settling" is mentioned. Abram's journey through Canaan takes him from Shechem to Bethel to Hebron, and it is only there that he finally settles down. This path is anything but arbitrary – in each location, Abram undergoes a change that brings him closer to his destiny. It is only once he settles in Hebron that Abram has finally completed his first quest, and the route to Hebron necessitated the stops along the way.

The roadmap of Abram's journey unfolds as follows:

1. God commands Abram: Go forth.
2. Implementation, stage I: Abram journeys to Shechem and builds an altar.
3. Implementation, stage II: Abram journeys to Bethel and builds an altar.
    - Interjection: Abram goes to Egypt due to the famine, and then returns to Bethel.
    - Interjection II: Abram separates from Lot, and experiences another revelation.
4. Implementation, stage III (final): Abram journeys to Hebron, settles there, and builds an altar.

The first stage of the journey begins with a double description of Abram's actions: "Abram went forth as the Lord had commanded him, and Lot went with him; Abram was seventy-five years old when he left Haran" (Gen. 12:4). The following verse repeats the description of Abram's departure from Haran: "Abram took his wife Sarai and his brother's son Lot, and all the wealth they had amassed, and the persons they had acquired in Haran, and they set out to go forth to the land of Canaan, and they arrived in the land of Canaan" (12:5). The verse does take the journey one step further, since the party's arrival in Canaan is mentioned. But why is the fact that they had departed from Haran, which had already appeared in the previous verse, repeated here?[17] This repetition may give the text an opportunity to emphasize Abram's relationship with Lot. His wife Sarai, the wealth, and the acquired people, are all not mentioned initially; only Lot seems to accompany Abram: "And Lot went with him."

The correlation between the two verses indicates a tension in the delicate relationship between Abram and Lot. In verse 5, Lot is named as one of the many elements included in Abram's journey. Lot is Abram's ward, his adopted nephew; he is thus displayed as one who has no free will. In contrast, the general formulation of verse 4 indicates that Lot is an independent being, who joins Abram on his journey by choice. Here, Lot cannot be portrayed as Abram's subordinate; he is separated from the list since he is an independent character with free will. There is no need to mention Sarai, not because she is less important, but because she is perceived as an organic part of Abram's family; the reader expects her to accompany her husband. In contrast, the mention of Lot in the general description of Abram's journey separates him from the rest of the group. Lot accompanied Abram, despite the fact that he was not an integral part of Abram's journey.

This tension relates to a broader issue that will be clarified as Abram makes his way through that first trip to Canaan: Should Abram have taken Lot with him, despite God's demand to disengage from his father's house? Is Lot's accompaniment of Abram an indication that

17. The verb *halakh* (translated here as "went forth"/"set out") is used in both verses. Use of this verb in the context of the implementation of God's command mirrors the formulation of the command itself: *Lekh lekha* ("Go forth"). However, as we have already mentioned, the verb becomes a key phrase throughout the entire unit. Some translations substituted *halakh* with the verb "departed." For example, the King James Bible translates verse 4: "So Abram departed, as the Lord had spoken unto him...and *they went forth* to go into the land of Canaan." The New International Version substituted the verb in both places: "So Abram left, as the Lord had told him...and they set out for the land of Canaan, and they arrived there." While the text flows better according to these translations, the reader misses out on the delicate wordplay around the integration of this verb, as will be demonstrated below.

Abram did not fully withstand the trial of separating from his past, and that the separation from his father's house was too difficult a trial to endure?[18]

On some level, the same dilemma arises with regard to the assets that Abram took along. The description of "the wealth that they had amassed" deviates from the comparison with Terah's journey (Gen. 11:29–30). We could chalk this up to consistent biblical style;[19] however, not all descriptions of a journey follow this formula. Property was not mentioned in the context of Terah's journey, because whatever he took with him was insignificant to his journey. In contrast, Esau's possessions are mentioned on his journey to Edom, since the wealth of possessions was the reason for his departure: "For their possessions were too many for them to dwell together, and the land where they sojourned could not support them because of their livestock" (36:7).

In what way does mentioning Abram's property contribute to the purpose of the narrative? Perhaps the developing motif of property in the initial stories of the story (Gen. 12–15) should be read as a reaction to the fact that Abram takes his wealth when he departs from Ur of the Chaldeans. Taking possessions might be another example of Abram's reluctance to wholeheartedly obey God's command; is there indeed an expectation that Abram will neglect his possessions and start over financially as well? This quandary will be addressed in the ongoing saga involving Abram's possessions throughout the narrative cycle.

Journey, Interrupted

If we view the actual geographical trip through Canaan as a central part of fulfilling the "Go forth..." command, then we must also attribute great

18. See Cotter, *Genesis*, 91. Andrew G. Vaughn ("'And Lot Went with Him': Abraham's Disobedience in Genesis 12:1–4a," in *David and Zion: Biblical Studies in Honor of J. J. M. Roberts*, ed. B. F. Batto and K. L. Roberts [Winona Lake, IN, 2004], 117–123) writes similarly, that Abram did not adopt Lot formally. Therefore, Lot falls into the category of "the house of Abram's father," and should not have come with Abram to Canaan. He asserts that the lack of a more complete obedience creates a sense of development in Abram's personality, until his final trial of obeying God's command in the binding of Isaac.
19. Cassuto, *A Commentary on the Book of Genesis: From Noah to Abraham*, 277–278. Cf. Gen. 36:30.

significance to the two interjecting episodes that interrupt Abram's expedition through Canaan: the descent to Egypt and the subsequent separation from Lot. Each milestone on this journey is an essential building block culminating in the final act of settling in Hebron and building an altar there.

Abram's travels through the land can be separated into three sections, each culminating in the construction of an altar:

1. Ur of the Chaldeans/Haran to Shechem: "And he built there an altar" (Gen. 12:7)
2. Shechem to Bethel: "And he built there an altar" (12:8)
3. Bethel to Hebron: "And he built there an altar" (13:18)

There are three central stations in Abram's journey through the land: Shechem, Bethel, and Hebron. Abram follows a clear geographical path through the "spine of the land" (see Josh. 20:7).

What is it about these three locations that Abram saw fit to stop in each and build an altar? Rashi, based on the Midrash, saw each of these stops as representing a unique purpose on Abram's journey. This idea relies on the assumption that Abram visited each location in order to pray for a child. Rashi associates Shechem with Abram's grandson Jacob, who would go to battle in the city. Regarding the stop between Bethel and Ai, he writes that Abram heard a prophecy that his grandchildren would succumb to Achan's sin in that place, and for that reason Abram saw fit to stop there and pray. Regarding Hebron, Rashi is silent – indicating that he saw Hebron as the final destination, and so there was no need to explain why he stopped there.

Abram's path – and pit stops – can be viewed from a more logical, geographical perspective, upon an examination of the map of Canaan at the time. Two valleys emerge from the central mountain: the west coast valley in the west, and the Jordan valley in the east. Each stop has a purpose in the journey (and so he builds an altar), but the journey is only complete once he gets to Hebron, where he settles.

The cities mentioned in Abram's journey were settled in the patriarchal era.[20] We are not told about encounters between Abram and the

20. Regarding Shechem, see Lawrence Toombs, "Shechem," *ABD* 5:1174–1186; Shmuel Achituv, "Shechem," *Entziklopedya Mikra'it* 7:662–670. Regarding Bethel and Ai, see

locals, but we do know that Abram sets up camp in settled areas and builds altars, creating a religious-cultural alternative in those major cities. Perhaps this idea is alluded to in the narrative's comment on Abram's first stop, in Shechem: "Abram passed through the land as far as the site of Shechem, at the terebinth of Moreh; *the Canaanites were then in the land*" (12:6). Canaan is not just some territory that Abram intends to settle; it is a holy place, which one can gain the right to settle through one's relationship with God, by building altars.[21]

The two following episodes, discussed at length, should be seen as interruptions to this journey. Indeed, after Abram left Bethel to go to Egypt, he returned to Bethel to complete the trip he had started. This does not make sense geographically, unless we see these two interjecting episodes as interrupting the journey from Shechem to Bethel to Hebron.

It is interesting to note as well that Abram received an additional blessing from God only once he reached Hebron: "Raise now your eyes and look out from where you are, northward, southward, eastward, and westward. For all the land that you see, to you I will give it, and to your descendants forever.... Arise, walk about the land through its length and breadth. For to you I will give it" (Gen. 13:14–17). It is exceedingly odd that God would direct Abram to "arise, walk about the land..." at this point – Abram was quite clearly in the midst of doing just that. It seems that this extended blessing, the promising of the land to the descendants of Abram forever, could only be bestowed once Abram had fully completed God's original request to leave his previous land, both physically and emotionally. In order to understand this better, we must delve into the two interrupting episodes of Abram's descent to Egypt and separation from his nephew.

Harold Brodsky, "Bethel," *ABD* 1:710–712; Umberto Cassuto, "Bethel," *Entziklopedya Mikra'it* 2:61–67; Callaway, "Ai," *ABD* 1:125–130.

21. Yehoshua Gitay, "Geography and Theology in the Biblical Narrative: The Question of Genesis 2–12," in *Prophets and Paradigms: Essays in Honor of Gene M. Tucker*, ed. S. B. Reid (JSOTSup 229: Sheffield, 1996), 209.

Famine and the Loss of Sarai (Gen. 12:10–20)

Abram's Bizarre Behavior

The first of two episodes that interrupt Abram's initial journey into Canaan is Abram's seemingly sudden and perplexing descent to Egypt in the wake of a famine. In light of God's recent promises to Abram, his decision to now leave the Promised Land (before he has even had a chance to settle there) seems odd. Even more bewildering is Abram's proposed plan to present Sarai to the Egyptians as his sister, effectively offering his own wife as a prospective bride to strangers. Abram, righteous and wise, who, a few pages prior, was so ready to go forth on a divinely decreed journey of faith into a strange land, now seems to abandon that journey just as it began, abandoning his own wife along the way.

This is a prime example when careful attention to the literary style of the narrative will make all the difference in understanding the true meaning of the story. Do we truly believe that Abram would abandon his hero's journey so quickly? Is the hero of our story this man who seems to discard his own wife by the wayside in a callous act of self-preservation? Surely not! As we delve into the text, we will see a series of carefully crafted structural parallels in the narrative, revealing the tragic irony that is the true story behind the words.

The first question, of course, is why did Abram leave Canaan in the first place? Yes, there was a famine, but he was in the midst of a heroic journey ordered by God; surely the man who was willing to abandon everything he knew to follow God to a new land could muster enough faith in his God to weather a food shortage. Many commentators point to textual indications that Abram mishandled the crisis. Nahmanides stands out in his harsh review of Abram's actions.[1] Nahmanides initially discusses the literary analogy between the narrative regarding Abram in Egypt and the slavery and redemption from Egypt in the book of Exodus. He explains that this is a realization of the principle "The events of the patriarchs are signs for their descendants," or, in his own formulation, "Nothing was lacking in all the events that happened to the patriarch that would not occur to the children." However, he then adds an additional layer to his interpretation, offering a harsh criticism of Abram's actions: "Our father Abraham unintentionally committed a great sin."[2] Nahmanides focuses on two issues in his criticism. First, there is no justification to leave Canaan in a time of famine, since "in famine God will redeem him from death."[3] According to Nahmanides, only a few verses earlier, while Abram was in Shechem, God had promised him that his offspring would inherit the land; Abram should have trusted God and awaited His assistance.

Nahmanides' second criticism relates to Abram's abandonment of Sarai. Here, too, Nahmanides writes that Abram "should have trusted that God would save him and his wife and all his belongings."[4] Nahmanides concludes that the slavery in Egypt is a punishment of Abram's offspring for the deeds of their forefather: "In the place of justice, there is wickedness and sin."[5]

---

1. Nahmanides on Gen. 12:10.
2. Nahmanides' ambivalence is certainly present in this formulation, regarding Abram's "great sin," which was committed "unintentionally."
3. Paraphrasing Job 5:20: "In famine He will redeem you from death; in war, from the sword."
4. I have presented the two criticisms in the order of appearance in the narrative. Nahmanides intentionally reverses the order, and opens with the sin involving Sarai, which is a greater sin in his opinion. See Avraham Shama, "Processes of Formulation and Changes in Ramban's Critical Attitude Towards Abram's Descent to Egypt (Genesis 12)," *Megadim* 50 (2009): 209–210.
5. Cf. Eccl. 3:16.

The formulation of Abram's request of Sarai only adds fuel to the fire: "As he was about to enter Egypt, he said to his wife Sarai: I know what a beautiful woman you are. If the Egyptians see you, and think, 'She is his wife,' they will kill me and let you live. Please, say that you are my sister, that it may go well with me because of you (*lemaan yitav li baavurekh*), and that I may remain alive thanks to you" (Gen. 12:11–13). Abram's words, "That it may go well for me because of you," reappear later in the story, in the context of the wealth Abram had accumulated in Egypt: "And *because of her, it went well with Abram* (*hetev baavura*). He acquired sheep, oxen, asses, male and female slaves, she-asses, and camels" (12:16). The reappearance of the phrase in this context leads the reader to assume that Abram's intentions were to accumulate wealth through his sacrifice of Sarai, as Rashi emphasizes: "That it may go well for me – i.e., they will give me gifts." If this is the case, Abram's plan is disgraceful. Using Sarai to save his life is surprising and perhaps immoral, but sacrificing his wife to gain riches is appalling.

The Tragic Irony in the Literary Structure

If read this way, there is no doubt that the criticism of Abram is justified. Were this reading correct, I would certainly position myself among Abram's critics. But I do not believe that the story itself is intended as a criticism of Abram.[6] A closer look at the structure of the text reveals a literary design that uncovers the true story as well as the narration's assessment of Abram's actions. The story begins with Abram's "descent" to Egypt due to a "heavy" (*kaved*) famine: "There was a famine in the land, and Abram went down to Egypt to sojourn there, for the famine was heavy in the land" (Gen. 12:10), and ends with Abram's "ascent" to Canaan, "heavy" (*kaved*) in riches: "From Egypt, Abram went up into the Negev, with his wife and all that he

6. According to David J. A. Clines, Abram's initial concerns are invalidated later in the story (Clines, *What Does Eve Do to Help?: And Other Readerly Questions to the Old Testament* [JSOTSup 94: Sheffield, 1990], 68). However, I am not convinced that his interpretation is correct.

possessed, together with Lot. Now Abram was very heavy in cattle, silver, and gold" (13:1–2).

The literary structure of the story is based first and foremost on the geographical movement: Abram "goes down" to Egypt, and eventually "goes up" to Canaan. This is not the story of a man who was compensated for bad behavior, rather of a man who descended into difficulty and then ascended into a form of redemption. To connect these two geographical movements, the text integrated the adjective *kaved* into both sentences, even though that word describes contradictory situations. The former use of the word describes the severe distress caused by the famine, while the latter describes the abundance of Abram's riches.[7] It is difficult to imagine that a story with such harsh criticism of Abram would support a process beginning in such distress and ending with such reward. In fact, the story concludes with Abram having accumulated great wealth, thus fulfilling one of God's initial promises, and reconnecting us to the story arc of Abram's journey into Canaan. The conclusion of the story negates criticism of Abram, and instead portrays him as having accumulated great wealth. It is noteworthy that the reader is not informed at any point that the famine has ended, and the emphasis of the story shifts from the distress of the land to Abram's blessing.[8] This shift of focus to the fact that Abram merits the fulfillment of one of God's promises is important background for the alternative reading we shall now offer.

In his commentary on the Torah, Don Isaac Abrabanel asks what Abram and Sarai's plan was when he decided to go down to Egypt, and what his intentions were when he introduced Sarai as his sister. According to the prevalent position, mentioned above, they had intended for Sarai to be taken by the Egyptians, and Abram would receive gifts in exchange.[9] However, this reading ignores the linear progression of

7. See, among others, Fokkeilen Van Dijk-Hemmes, "Sarai's Exile: A Gender-Motivated Reading of Genesis 12.10–13.2," in *A Feminist Companion to Genesis*, ed. A. Brenner (Sheffield, 1993), 226.
8. Hermann Gunkel, *Genesis – Translated and Interpreted*, trans. M. E. Biddle (Macon, GA, 1997), 172.
9. Van Seters (*Abraham in History and Tradition*, 169) writes that there is full correlation between Abram's plan and the implementation.

the narrative: Abram asks Sarai to introduce herself as his sister, not to separate from him.[10] A more plausible scenario would be that Abram hoped one of the Egyptians would ask "Sarai's brother" for her hand in marriage. A negotiation would ensue, and Abram would ask for an unreasonable bride-price. He could authenticate the process by loosening his demands from time to time, and then pull back. If Abram and Sarai ever felt they were in danger, they could always run away and return to Canaan.[11]

In other words, Abram knew that his wife was beautiful and would be desirable to the Egyptians. He concocted a plan that would act as a stalling tactic should anyone try to acquire her. He never imagined the scenario that actually ensued.

Abram's anxiety about being separated from Sarai ("If the Egyptians see you" in verse 12) is validated ("When Abram entered Egypt, the Egyptians *saw* how very beautiful the woman was" in verse 14). However, the situation quickly escalates to a point where Abram's plan tragically begins to backfire:

"Pharaoh's courtiers saw her (*vayiru ota sarei Paro*)
and praised her to Pharaoh (*vayehalelu ota el Paro*)
and the woman was taken into Pharaoh's palace (*vatukaḥ ha'isha beit Paro*)."

The repetition of the word "Pharaoh" (in the Hebrew hammering at the end of each clause) evokes the sense of disbelief and sudden apprehension in the text: Pharaoh has his eye on Sarai! Within the context of Abram's plan, what price could he possibly name that is too high for Pharaoh? Abram's plan thus fails; he would have been able to "haggle" with the common Egyptians, but he is helpless before the king.

10. That is, unless we accept Rost's suggestion, that the phrase "You are my sister" is a formal divorce formulation. His interpretation relies upon sources regarding Muslim divorce laws. Rost believes that Abram temporarily divorced Sarai, and God's afflictions upon Pharaoh were not punishment for adultery, but an indication that Sarai belongs with Abram (Rost, "Die Bezeichnungen fur Land und Volk im Alten Testament").
11. See Sforno in his commentary on the narrative; Samuel David Luzzatto, *The Book of Genesis*, trans. Daniel A. Klein (Northvale, NJ, 1998), 129; Cassuto, *A Commentary on the Book of Genesis: From Noah to Abraham*, 350.

The verb *re'eh,* "to see," repeating itself here, connects and contrasts Abram's plan with the disastrous reality:

Plan (Gen. 12:12–14)	**Occurrence (Gen. 12:14–15)**
If the *Egyptians see* you...	The Egyptians *saw*...
	Pharaoh courtiers *saw* her

Abram was concerned that the Egyptians would "see" Sarai, and prepared a plan accordingly. But he never expected his wife to be "seen" by Pharaoh's courtiers, or for Pharaoh himself to express interest.

In light of this, let's return to the wording of Abram's original plan, which was the source of the criticism lodged against him by the commentators. Abram wants to present Sarai as his sister "that it may go well with me because of you." Indeed, when Sarai is taken and Abram showered with gifts, the text plays on the situation, "And because of her, it went well with Abram." Did Abram plan to become rich by sacrificing his wife to Pharaoh? Certainly not. The context of the word "*hetev,*" "well," reveals the underlying and heartbreaking irony in what ensued as a result of Abram's plan.

In Abram's plan, he speaks of things going "well for me because of you and that I may remain alive thanks to you." This phrase is shocking; the term *yitav li* generally refers to financial benefit, but if this is the case, it seems as though Abram counts his financial gain ahead of his own life! Rabbi David Kimchi (Radak), among others, comments that Abram is not referring here to two separate benefits, financial and physical. Rather, he writes, the first part of the sentence introduces the second. "That things may go well for me" introduces Abram's wish, that he will retain the gift of his own life. Umberto Cassuto adopts the same reading, understanding that when Abram wishes that things "will go well" for him, the only benefit he desires is his life. If Abram was referencing financial gain, that certainly would have come secondary to saving his life, and the order of the words would have been reversed, looking like this: "That I may remain alive because of you and that things will go well for me." Later, the text repeats the same words in a different context, in order to underscore the horrible irony of the situation. "And because of her, *it went well with Abram*; he acquired sheep, oxen, asses, male and female slaves, she-asses, and camels" (Gen. 12:16). All Abram wanted was for he and Sarai to escape with their lives. Now things have gone "well" for him – he has amassed an incredible amount of wealth, but this treasure is like dust in his mouth, for he has lost his wife![12] The repetition of the word "well" in both instances creates a literary contrast that reveals the true nature of the story.

A Return to the Heroic Cycle

Let us return now to the broader picture – how does this episode contribute to the overarching narrative of Abram's journey to Canaan? Firstly, God's intervention on Abram's behalf to afflict Pharaoh and return Sarai demonstrates the fulfillment of one component of the blessings: "I will bless those who bless you, and curse him that curses you." Even those who wish to harm Abram inadvertently are severely punished.[13] Westermann suggests that omitting the details creates an emphasis on the dialogue between Pharaoh and Abram.[14] I agree with Westermann's assertion that the narrative's silence is telling; however, the emphasis is not on Pharaoh's discussion with Abram, but rather on God's intervention. Instead of discussing the reason for Pharaoh's suffering, the narrative focuses on God's protection of Abram's wife.

12. Cassuto, *A Commentary on the Book of Genesis: From Noah to Abraham*, 350; Nisan Ararat, *Emet VeḤesed BaMikra* (Jerusalem, 1993), 54. Yair Zakovitch (*"I Will Express Riddles of Old": Riddles and Dream-Riddles in Biblical Narrative* [Tel Aviv, 2005], 128) writes: "Abram's inappropriate behavior, his willingness to abandon his wife, to lie and say that Sarai is his sister; all these brought upon him a shameful reward. Abram sold his wife to save himself." Hamilton notes that the other patriarchs gain their fortune as an explicit result of God's blessing, while Abram does not (Hamilton, *The Book of Genesis, Chapters 1–17*, 383); I believe the link is ironic, but instead of a criticism, it deepens the tragic dimension of the story. See further in Jonathan Grossman, *Ambiguity in the Biblical Narrative and Its Contribution to the Literary Formation* (PhD diss., Bar Ilan University, 2006), 45–47.
13. Cf. Gerhard von Rad, *Genesis*, trans. J. H. Marks (London, 1963), 164.
14. Westermann, *Genesis 12–36: A Continental Commentary*, 162. He believes the two dialogues (the dialogue between Abram and Sarai and the dialogue between Abram and Pharaoh) are emphasized, and frame the story on both ends.

Furthermore, this story illuminates the fact that Sarai is meant to accompany Abram on his journey. This might sound obvious, but Abram was commanded to disengage from the house of his father, put his past behind him, and begin anew. Within the context of this command, God had promised Abram that he will become a great nation (Gen. 12:2), and from the outset the text notes that Sarai is barren. Might God not have expected Abram to leave Sarai behind, with the rest of his father's family? This episode, which interrupts Abram's wanderings in Canaan, drives home the explicit statement that Sarai belongs alongside Abram. Sarai was taken from Abram by force, but God returned her. Sarai is an integral part of Abram's future in Canaan.

Not only does Abram reclaim his wife; he also gains an immense fortune. The descent to Egypt concludes with the statement: "Now Abram was very rich in cattle, silver, and gold" (Gen. 13:2). One purpose of this information is to prepare the reader for the conflict of the following literary unit – Abram's separation from Lot due to their amassed wealth. Moreover, this verse serves to emphasize the fact that Abram returned to Canaan not only with his wife, but with cattle, gold, and silver. God's initial blessing seemed to promise wealth; now, that blessing is beginning to be fulfilled. The immense riches Abram acquired in Egypt render irrelevant any possessions brought from his birthplace. The famine in Canaan proved to be a blessing in disguise; through his descent to Egypt and the dangers he and Sarai must face, Abram is granted a new beginning. Perhaps before Abram is able to receive the blessings that await him in Bethel (13:14–17), he must disengage completely from his previous life. Abram's possessions are now presented as having been accumulated after his arrival in Canaan. The famine and the episode in Egypt ultimately become a means for the fulfillment of God's blessings.

In his personal heroic cycle, this story enables utter detachment from Abram's previous life in a maneuver that simultaneously affirms Sarai's status as Abram's chosen life partner and nullifies the possessions he brought with him from his birthplace.

On a national level, the "first couple's" descent into Egypt foreshadows the keystone event in the history of their descendants – the descent to and subsequent Exodus from Egypt years later.

As we noted above, this parallel was emphasized by Nahmanides, and many commentators in his wake have concluded similarly.[15] There are a host of parallels that can be found in a close comparison between the texts:[16]

Abram and Sarai in Egypt (Gen. 12)	**Israel in Egypt (Gen. 43–Ex. 12)**
"Abram went down to Egypt	"They made their way down to Egypt" (Gen. 43:15)
to sojourn there	"We have come... to sojourn in this land...
for the famine was heavy in the land" (v. 19)	for the famine is heavy in the land of Canaan" (Gen. 47:4)
"they will kill me and let you live" (v. 12)	"look at the birth stool: if it is a boy, kill him; if it is a girl, let her live" (Ex. 1:16)

15. See Cassuto, *A Commentary on the Book of Genesis: From Noah to Abraham*, 349–352; Richard Pratt, "Pictures, Windows, and Mirrors in Old Testament Exegesis," *WTJ* 45 (1983): 156–167; Wenham, *Genesis 16–50*, 291–292; Becking, "Abram in Exile: Remarks on Genesis 12, 10–20," in *Die Erzväter in der Biblischen Tradition: Festschrift für Matthias Köckert*, ed. A. C. Hagedorn and H. Pfeiffer (BZAW 400: Berlin and New York, 2009), 42–43; Thomas Römer, "The Exodus in the Book of Genesis," *SEÅ* 75 (2010): 1–20. Van Dijk-Hemmes ("Sarai's Exile: A Gender-Motivated Reading of Genesis 12.10–13.2," 228) used the comparison to the edict to kill the male babies as proof that Abram was correct to fear that the Egyptians would kill him and sustain his wife. See also John Roning, "The Naming of Isaac: The Role of the Wife/Sister Episodes in the Redaction of Genesis," *WTJ* 53 (1991): 19. Rudolf Kilian (*Die Vorpriesterlichen Abrahams-Überlieferungen, Literarkritisch und Traditionsgeschichtlich Untersucht* [BBB 24: Bonn, 1966], 212–213) believes the connection is incidental. Westermann (*Genesis 12–36: A Continental Commentary*, 166) mentions the link between the plagues in Genesis and Exodus, but also believes the parallel is incidental. I believe that in light of the multitude of links, they cannot be brushed aside as incidental.
16. See Rachel Reich, *The Woman Whom Thou Gavest to Be with Me* (Tel Aviv, 2005), 36. I have omitted some links made by Reich that I found unconvincing. Becking mentions two linguistic connections: the roots N-G-A (relating to plague) and SH-L-Ḥ (relating to being sent), and tries to use these links to determine the historical timeframe of redaction in these stories. He believes the story of Abram in Egypt and the Exodus have a common theme: offering encouragement to the nation in times of distress, and particularly in times of exile, when the disappointment of unfulfilled promises is identifiable (Becking, "Abram in Exile: Remarks on Genesis 12, 10–20," 42–44).

"When Abram entered Egypt"	"These are the names of the sons of Israel who entered Egypt" (Ex. 1:1)
"the Lord afflicted Pharaoh and his household with mighty plagues" (v. 17)	"And the Lord said to Moses, 'I will bring but one more plague upon Pharaoh and upon Egypt'" (Ex. 11:1)
"Pharaoh sent for Abram" (v. 18)	"Then Pharaoh summoned Moses and Aaron" (Ex. 8:4)
"take her and be-gone!" (v. 19)	"Take also your flocks and your herds, as you said, and be-gone!" (Ex. 12:32)
"and they sent him off with his wife and all that he possessed" (v. 20)	"The Egyptians urged the people on, impatient to have them leave the country" (Ex. 12:33)
"Now Abram was very rich in cattle, silver, and gold" (13:12)	"Each woman shall borrow from her neighbor…objects of silver and gold… "(Ex. 3:22; 11:2)
	"Moreover, a mixed multitude went up with them, and very much livestock, both flocks and herds" (12:37)
"And he proceeded by stages from the Negev as far as Bethel" (13:3)	"From the wilderness of Sin the whole Israelite community proceeded by stages as the Lord would command" (Ex. 17:1)

The connection between the narratives is striking from a linguistic perspective, but even more so from the perspective of plot. Both describe a descent to Egypt due to famine. Both describe life-threatening danger for the males of the family. They both have as a result divine intervention and physical punishment for the Egyptians. Finally, both end with Israel's triumphant emergence and great wealth. The parallel between the two stories may point to the connection between the fertility of man and land: Abram's temporary disengagement from Sarai mirrors the disengagement of the nation from their land.[17]

17. Reich, *The Woman Whom Thou Gavest to Be with Me*, 35–39.

The captivity in, and redemption from, Egypt are perceived as a necessary introduction to the inheritance of the Promised Land, as described in the Covenant Between the Pieces in Genesis 15. Perhaps Abram's detour to Egypt is an introduction to *his* inheritance of the land. Disengagement from the land nullifies the sense of possession and political control. Canaan is unique, in that the land does not belong to its inhabitants, but rather to God, who is Lord of the land and who will ensure that the land is inherited only by deserving parties. In biblical philosophy, a famine is an indication that the local population has lost its right to continue inhabiting the land (see, for example, Deut. 11:17). Abram, and later Jacob's family, need to leave the land for some time, in order to be granted the privilege of returning and inheriting it. In the spirit of T. S. Eliot:

> And what you own is what you do not own
> And where you are is where you are not.[18]

The unique nationalistic philosophy that underpins Abraham's narrative cycle establishes the new nation upon the foundations of "righteousness and justice," which enables the possibility of a religious life without dependence upon national borders. Abraham only receives the promise of inheritance of the vast land after his descent and exodus from Egypt, because the privilege of inheritance can only be granted after his disconnection from and reconnection with the land. Neither inheritance of the land nor the birth of offspring is granted freely; both are inextricably contingent upon the moral nature of the nation Abram will establish. His separation from the barren land and his barren wife are a necessary precondition for God's promise of fruitfulness, and both will be restored to him with God-given fertility. In order to receive the blessing at Bethel, however, Abram must undergo another separation; this time, from his nephew Lot.

---

18. T. S. Eliot, "East Coker," III, *Four Quartets*.

The Separation from Lot (Gen. 13)

The distressing descent to Egypt behind them, Abram and his family return to Canaan, galvanized and prepared to continue their journey. After the intense experience in Egypt, the innocent reader might overlook the next, seemingly innocuous, trial Abram must undergo on his journey: the separation from his nephew, Lot. This parting of the ways, many commentators feel, had been a long time coming. Even God makes it clear that He was "waiting" for Lot's absence to finally bestow upon Abram the full blessing of the land.

Lot is an enigmatic character throughout the Abram narrative cycles. Commentators expressed ambivalence about Lot's true nature, and he is often perceived as a negative influence. Lot's disposition aside, his role during Abram's descent to Egypt and subsequent return to Canaan remains somewhat of a mystery. The story seems straightforward, however; Abram's sudden shift from reluctance to dissociate from Lot to essentially cutting off ties is abrupt, as is Lot's sudden interest in settling down in Sodom. At the end of the ordeal, the text reveals that it was the separation from Lot that finally rendered Abram ready to receive God's complete blessing in Bethel.

Always the Outsider?

From the onset, the question of Lot's incorporation into Abram's family is apparent. God's directive to leave "your family, your homeland, the house of your father," surely includes Lot, who was considered part of Terah's family. Mention of Lot sporadically occurs throughout the story, until the text somewhat baldly outs him as a misfit when God finally bestows the complete blessing upon Abram only "... after Lot parted from him" (Gen. 13:14). In the description of the initial journey from Haran (12:5), Lot is mentioned immediately after Sarai ("Abram took his wife Sarai and his brother's son Lot"), whereas in our verse Abram's property separates Abram and Sarai from Lot, perhaps an indication that it is property that will ultimately separate the family. Genesis 13:1 depicts Abram and Lot as two separate clans that join together on a journey to Canaan, rather than a unified family.[1] The previous story had described Abram's journey to Egypt, and concluded with the return of Abram and his family to Bethel, to "the site of the altar that he had built there at first" (13:4).[2] Based on the conclusion of that narrative, this story seems to begin in verse 5: "Lot, who went with Abram, also had flocks and herds and tents." Abram's significant wealth is essential to understanding the quarreling of the herdsmen. Some commentators therefore believe this verse begins the story of Abram and Lot's separation.[3] But the earliest

1. Nechama Leibowitz, *Studies in Genesis* (Jerusalem: World Zionist Organization, 1966), 88–89; Sharon Pace Jeansonne, "The Characterization of Lot in Genesis," *Biblical Theology Bulletin* 18 (1988): 124; Zvi Shimon, *Contrast in Biblical Narrative: The Literary Device and the Drama of Choice* (PhD diss., Bar Ilan University, 2009), 265.
2. Cf. Umberto Cassuto, *The "Quaestio" of the Book of Genesis,* trans. M. E. Hartom (Jerusalem, 1990), 248. Cassuto views Lot's mention in Gen. 13:1 as an introduction to the following episode (ibid., 248). However, v. 5 begins with the word "*vegam*" ("also"), which is unusual in an independent unit (Elchanan Samet, *Studies in the Weekly Parasha: Second Series* [Maaleh Adumim, 2004], vol. 1, 46; Hezi Cohen, "Abraham's Separation from Lot [Genesis 13]" *Megadim* 52 [2011]: 9n3). This difficulty will integrate into the analysis of the link between the journey to Egypt and the separation from Lot.
3. For example, Westermann, *Genesis 12–36: A Continental Commentary,* 173–175; Mathews, *Genesis,* 133. According to Mathews, the parallel of "*kaved*" in the beginning of Abram's journey to Egypt (12:10) and the story of Abram's separation from Lot (13:2) serve to link the two episodes (ibid., 132). Many scholars (among them John

possibility for beginning this story is 13:1, since Lot is specifically mentioned in the context of Abram's return to Canaan: "From Egypt, Abram went up into the Negev, with his wife and all that he possessed, *together with Lot*" (13:1). Lot is incorporated into the story of Abram's return to Canaan, despite the fact that he is not mentioned among those who traveled to Egypt. The indefinite parameters of the separation story indicate that the journey to Egypt is connected with the fact that Abram later parts with his nephew. One might say there is a continuous storyline in which Abram and his family journey to Egypt, accumulate wealth, and consequently separate from Lot.[4]

The fact that Abram, throughout this journey, shows such hesitation to separate from Lot is another perplexing question. As we mentioned previously, it seems clear God's command to Abram to leave "the house of [his] father" includes leaving his nephew behind as well. For reasons the text omits, Abram still allows Lot to accompany him on his journey, despite the apparent noncompliance this entails. Now, upon returning from Egypt, separation from Lot becomes a necessity, apparently for logistical reasons.

Abram's method of handling the quarrel between the herdsman provides the text with another opportunity to exemplify Abram's righteousness and compassion, even as it may come in conflict with God's word. "Abram said to Lot, 'Let there be no strife between you and me, between my herdsmen and yours, for we are brothers'" (Gen. 13:8). According to Abram, the argument between the herdsmen represents an argument between Abram and Lot. Abram does not deflect responsibility by blaming the herdsmen; he takes full responsibility for the actions of his employees, despite the fact that the text presents the argument

Skinner, *A Critical and Exegetical Commentary on Genesis*, 2nd ed. [ICC: Edinburgh, 1930], 251) believe Gen. 13:1, which describes Abram's return from Egypt, concludes the previous story, and therefore have a difficult time understanding Lot's mention in the verse, since he had no role (and in fact was not even mentioned) in the Egypt episode. Many assert that Lot's name was a later insertion (among others, Gunkel, von Rad, and Eissfeldt). I believe the vague boundaries of the story relate directly to its message, and should not be viewed as careless editing.

4. For a different formulation based on a similar reading, compare with Otto Procksch, *Die Genesis* (KAT: Leipzig, 1913), ad loc.

as one among the herdsmen. Presumably, Abram's herdsmen know that Abram is superior to Lot. He is Lot's elder and respected uncle, who follows a direct command from God, while Lot is merely the younger nephew who accompanied Abram on his journey. Despite the fact that Abram is the head of the family, his choice to deal with Lot as an equal, "for we are brothers," portrays him as a modest and reasonable leader who values peace within his family unit above his own honor. Again, the Abraham narrative provides us with an intimate view into how our hero ticks. Abraham was chosen by God, yes, but his compassionate intuition, his grace and kindness, render him entirely worthy of his role as the future leader of the Israelite nation, regardless of God's choice.

The Parting of the Ways

Lot is mentioned specifically in the tale of Abram's return to Canaan: "From Egypt, Abram went up into the Negev, with his wife and all that he possessed, *together with Lot*" (Gen. 13:1). Lot is incorporated into the story of Abram's return to Canaan, despite the fact that he is not mentioned among those who traveled to Egypt. The fact that Lot is the only character mentioned by name aside from Abram foreshadows Lot's central role in the following scene. Something happened in Egypt that facilitated the sudden separation.

As we will see numerous times throughout the bible, Egypt is often depicted as a tremendously fertile land, in this case in contrast to the famine-ridden Canaan. We know from historical accounts that Egypt at the time was an advanced, prosperous civilization. Abram's return to Canaan was not motivated by the end of the famine, but rather, his unpleasant experiences in Egypt and the understanding that he must continue the journey commanded to him by God. While in Egypt, Lot's eyes were opened to what a prosperous life might look like for him. His uncle's fixation on his spiritual journey must have felt progressively foreign to Lot. Upon his return to Canaan, Lot was already considering adhering to a more "Egyptian" lifestyle.

Nechama Leibowitz points out how the text elegantly brings us back to the list of returnees in Genesis 13:1 with the order of those traveling to Haran. In the description of the initial journey from Haran (12:5), Lot is mentioned immediately after Sarai ("Abram took his wife Sarai and his brother's son Lot"), whereas in our verse Abram's property separates

Abram and Sarai from Lot, perhaps an indication that it is property that will ultimately separate the family. As mentioned previously, Genesis 13:1 depicts Abram and Lot as two separate clans that join together on a journey to Canaan, rather than a unified family. Perhaps at some point in the journey there was a moment when Lot and Abram could envision joining their two clans seamlessly to achieve Abram's divine mission. However, upon returning from their stint in Egypt, it becomes clear to both uncle and nephew that this will never be the case. Abram still regards Lot with affection, but understands that they needed to separate, which is what leads to the conversation following the shepherds' quarrel.

In fact, it would appear that Abram's separation from Lot begins with the joint journey to Canaan.[5] As mentioned above, there is a continuous storyline in which Abram and his family journey to Egypt, accumulate wealth, and consequently separate from Lot.

Lot expresses his choice to relinquish his portion in God's promise to Abram in the geographical choice to leave the land of Canaan.[6] Abram offers Lot "north or south" (lit. "right or left") of the land, while Lot chooses to travel east of the Jordan River, outside the borders of the Promised Land.[7]

> Lot looked about him, and saw how well watered was all the plain of Jordan, all of it – this was before the Lord had destroyed Sodom and Gomorrah – all the way to Zoar, like the garden of the Lord, like the land of Egypt. (Gen. 13:10)

5. Cf. among others, Speiser, *Genesis*, 9; Kiel, *Daat Mikra: Genesis*, 345; Yael Tzohar, *The Exposition in the Biblical Narrative* (PhD diss., Bar Ilan University, 2005), 94–95; Cohen, "Abraham's Separation from Lot," 9.
6. R. Christopher Heard (*Dynamics of Diselection: Ambiguity in Genesis 12–36 and Ethnic Boundaries in Post-Exilic Judah*, SBLSS 39 [Atlanta, 2001]: 33–34) claims that Lot had no choice but to accept Abram's command. I identify with Zvi Shimon's reading that the narrative describes Lot's choice as one based on financial and ethical considerations (Shimon, *Contrast in Biblical Narrative: The Literary Device and the Drama of Choice*, 270).
7. Walter Vogels, "Lot in His Honor Restored: A Structural Analysis of Gen 13:2–18," *Eglise et Théologie* 10 (1979): 5–12; Larry Randall Helyer, "The Separation of Abram and Lot: Its Significance in the Patriarchal Narratives," *JSOT* 26 (1983): 77–88; George W. Coats, "Lot: A Foil in the Abraham Saga," in *Understanding the Word*, ed. J. T. Butler et al. (JSOTSup 37: Sheffield, 1985), 117.

Lot looks out over the land, and with the image of luxurious Egyptian lifestyle seared in his mind's eye, chooses the most fertile land he can see. The text refers to the destruction of Sodom here intentionally – the reader who is familiar with the dry and barren characteristics of Sodom will wonder how Lot views a lush and fertile land. The journey to Egypt opened Lot's eyes to a lifestyle to which he was previously unaccustomed, in which farmers and shepherds need not rely on rain to sustain them. Lot lifts his eyes and recognizes the area bordering Canaan that is most similar to Egypt, and sets forth to settle there.[8]

The text here is explicit in contrasting Lot's choice to separate with Abram's. Lot chooses Sodom before its destruction, in contrast to God's promise to Abram: "For I give all the land that you see to you and your offspring *forever*." Lot chooses a seemingly fertile and valuable land, but the value of the land is measured in temporary terms, as opposed to Abram's choice to continue wandering in difficult conditions without sufficient pasture, while relying on God's promise that his inheritance of the land will be everlasting. This contrast is communicated to the reader, unbeknownst to Lot, since he is unaware of God's plans for Sodom. Furthermore, an additional evaluation contrasts not just Lot's lifestyle but his values with those of Abram and the reader. The Jordan plain is described as "the garden of the Lord," but also "like the land of Egypt." The two comparisons seem contradictory, until the text elucidates: "Now the inhabitants of Sodom were wicked and sinners against the Lord" (Gen. 13:13). The

8. Meir Lubetski ("Lot's Choice: Paradise or Purgatory," *Jewish Studies at the Turn of the Century* 1 [1999]: 164–172) points out the expression "*kula mashkeh*" (NJPS: "well watered"; lit. "is all drink") is meant to create an association with Egyptian wine. Egyptian hieroglyphics describe heavenly gardens bursting with wine. According to Lubetski, Lot saw the agricultural potential of Sodom, and was contemplating trading his sheep for a career in wine-making. If he is correct, perhaps the final story about Lot, in which he is found drunk with his daughters in a cave in Gen. 19, is an ironic closure to Lot's decision to settle in Sodom. The question relates to the exact geographical location of Sodom, which is disputed among scholars. For a wealth of biblical, historical, and archaeological information on this subject, see James Penrose Harland, "The Destruction of the Cites of the Plain," *BA* 6 (1943): 41–52, and Harland, "The Location of the Cities of the Plain," *BA* 5 (1942): 17–32.

land is indeed fertile, but its inhabitants are evil; Sodom, like Egypt, is a place of questionable values; perhaps the type of place where beautiful women are taken against their will to satisfy the sexual desire of the inhabitants.

The story of the separation places Lot and Abram on two ends of a spectrum with regard to the source of financial security. Lot chooses to settle in a place as similar to Egypt as possible, whereas Abram chooses to continue wandering, while observing God's command to "walk about the land, through its length and its breadth" (Gen. 13:17). Lot chooses apparent abundance, while Abram chooses to put his faith in God.

The Wanderer Settles

Our story continues to emphasize the necessity for Abram to shed Lot in order to receive the complete blessing of the land from God. The journey from Haran is Abram's first heroic journey, setting the tone for him as a protagonist in his own narrative and the future father of a nation. The text accentuates the differences between Lot and Abram in order to position Abram as the unequivocal hero, the righteous man of faith whose moral compass is nearly unwavering.

Abram's Separation from Lot (Gen. 13:8–13)	**God's Revelation to Abram (13:14–18)**
Is not *all the land* before you? Lot looked about him, and saw how well watered was *all* the plain of Jordan, *all* of it	Raise your eyes and see and look out from where you are, to the north and to the south, to the east and to the west.... For I give all the land that you see to you and your offspring...
Before the Lord had destroyed Sodom and Gomorrah	...forever.
So Lot chose for himself *all* the plain of the Jordan, and Lot journeyed eastward	And Abram moved his tent and came to dwell at the terebinths of Mamre, which are in Hebron
Now the people of Sodom were wicked and sinners against the Lord.	And he built an altar there to the Lord.

The text contrasts Lot's choice with God's demand of Abram: Lot raised his eyes and saw *one* specific place ("all the plain of Jordan"), while Abram was asked to look out upon the *entire land* ("north and south, east and west").[9] Whereas Abram had offered Lot "*all the land*," Lot's vision is limited to the plain of Jordan. The word "all" is ironically sprinkled throughout the description of Lot's choice: "Lot looked about him, and saw how well watered was *all* the plain of Jordan, *all* of it"; "So Lot chose for himself *all* the plain of the Jordan." However, the word "all" is omitted in the description of the outcome of Lot's decision: "Lot settled in the cities of the plain" (Gen. 13:12). While Lot *felt* he was choosing a vast area, he abandoned the possibilities of inheriting the "all" that was offered to Abram when he chose to separate from his uncle.

Driving the point home, Genesis 13:14 opens, "And the Lord said to Abram after Lot parted from him." There is no doubt, the blessing that follows could only be given at this moment, now that Abram has completed the dual trials of his experience of losing Sarai in Egypt and dissociating from Lot.

Both in his journey to Egypt and in his separation from Lot, Abram is required to separate from a close family member who has journeyed with him from Haran: he is temporarily separated from his wife Sarai, and permanently separates from Lot (whom he regards as a brother, despite the fact that he is a nephew).[10]

Within the broader concentric structure of the story cycle these two stories are parts of the same literary whole, and they are obviously analogous.

	The Journey to Egypt	**Abram's Separation from Lot**
Introduction	"For the famine was severe in the land"	"Now Abram was very rich in cattle, silver, and gold"
Challenge	Infertile land (famine)	Abundance of property leads to difficulty finding sufficient pasture

9. Compare with Skinner, *A Critical and Exegetical Commentary on Genesis*, 253.
10. Regarding the various biblical connotations of the word "brother," see Michael Fishbane, "The Treaty Background of Amos 1:11 and Related Matters," *JBL* 89 (1970): 313–318.

	Abram is (temporarily) separated from his wife	*Abram is separated from his nephew*
Suggestion	"Please say that you are my sister"	"For we are brothers…please, separate from me"
Conclusion	"The Egyptians saw how very beautiful the woman was"	Lot looked about him, and saw how well watered was all the plain of Jordan, all of it…like the land of Egypt"

Both stories serve as stepping stones on Abram's journey from Haran to Canaan. Abram's distress in both episodes is intensified when considering Sarai and Lot's central role in the fulfillment of God's promises to Abram. Abram departs for Egypt due to the infertility of the land, but in the course of his journey he is separated from his wife, who is also infertile; thus, Abram's separation from his life partner lessens his chances of realizing his destiny as the father of many nations. Since Abram had abandoned the land, and now stands to lose his wife, he thinks he is losing everything – the promise of both land and seed given at his departure from Haran. Similarly, Abram and Lot discover that the land cannot contain both flocks; however, this dilemma leads to a greater challenge to Abram, that of parting with his brother's son, who was perhaps viewed by Abram as a substitute for the son Sarai had not given him.

There are significant differences between the stories, as well. Both open with Abram's suggestion. However, the purpose of Abram's request of Sarai is to *keep* her, whereas the purpose of his suggestion to Lot is to separate them. Both stories culminate with a show of divine perspective on current events: God intervenes on behalf of Sarai and reunites her with Abram, while the divine revelation after the second episode shows God's approval of the separation from Lot.

Both stories seek to clarify a common theme, the question of who is worthy of joining Abram on his journey to Canaan. When God demands that Abram abandon the house of his father, the role of various members of his father's family, namely, Sarai and Lot, becomes unclear. Abram's (failed) attempts to protect Sarai prove that he views her as a worthy partner, and he wants her by his side. More importantly, God's intervention to save Sarai and return her to Abram proves that it is also the will of God to have Sarai join Abram. This idea will be stated explicitly to Abram in Genesis 17, but despite her barrenness, Sarai is clearly given God's approval at this early stage. Alternatively, Abram *chooses* to separate from Lot, and God affirms Abram's decision in His revelation.

Abram took his orphaned nephew under his wing, but as a result of their dispute, and apparent ideological differences, decided to part ways. In doing so, Abram finally fulfills God's initial command to separate from his father's home. If so, we can assert that the episodes leading up to God's revelation to Abram in Bethel, and the explicit blessing of offspring and inheritance of the land, explore Abram's relationship with several entities that call his right to the blessing into question: his relationship with the land, with his wife, and with his nephew Lot. Abram retains and reaffirms his connection with the two entities God is interested in – the land and his wife – but he takes leave from his nephew, who will not walk along the path that leads to a covenant with God.

Lot's Rescue (Gen. 14)

As we begin to familiarize ourselves with our hero in these early episodes, the question of Abram's deservedness arises again and again. True, God chose him, and as readers we accept that divine choice. However, from a literary perspective, we are inclined to examine Abram's character more objectively. Is he truly worthy of the role God has bestowed? Even if the answer is an unequivocal and resounding yes, the reader – and the generations of readers that will follow in Abram's footsteps – yearn for the lessons taught by watching our hero's leadership and morality in action.

The upcoming narratives, particularly the narratives including Lot, set up a contrast for Abram to be judged against – as a moral leader, as a spiritual figure, and in this case, as a diplomatic and military figure. As we familiarize ourselves with our protagonist, we must have an opportunity to perceive him in various situations, to be convinced as readers that he is worthy of God's choice.

Let us begin with what we know of the character, Abram. He is a virtuous man, who welcomes guests with extraordinary kindness and generosity, and exemplifies in all his actions a strong moral backbone. Without a doubt, he is a spiritual man who merits to develop a unique relationship with God. Even in Haran, when we first encounter him, Abram has created a persona for himself as somewhat of a spiritual guru – locals approach him with their woes and look to him as a spiritual guide.

Suddenly, in this chapter, the narrative presents the reader with an episode in which Abraham is portrayed as a master military general. He girds his armor, braces his weapon, and leads an army of three thousand soldiers on a military mission to rescue his nephew. On the way, he mounts a full-scale attack against a powerful military alliance – and wins. Abram the Hebrew is portrayed as a war hero and diplomat who negotiates with ancient kings. If, throughout the story cycle, Abram is consistently depicted as a man of spirit, a prophet, a moralist who promotes justice, an excellent host, and above all as one who merits an everlasting covenant with God, then this portrait is seemingly incompatible with the diplomatic strategist who divides his troops and leads them in a dangerous nighttime rescue operation.

Of course, in the greater narrative, the reader understands the importance of Lot's salvation. We may even perceive how this act of self-sacrifice fits in with the ethical ethos of our protagonist. However, it is nonetheless startling to suddenly view Abram in the role of military leader. Technically speaking, when in his journey did he ever learn to fight? When has there ever been a need to? The question of the source of this aspect of Abram's character, and what its literary significance is in the greater scheme of the story, is perplexing.

Other stylistic differences in this chapter include the absence of active participation by God and His angels, and the absence of Abram's divine blessings, which play a major role in all other Abram narratives. The stylistic characteristics of this episode are foreign to the rest of the Abraham cycle. The narrative includes new motifs that add to the complexity of Abram's character, and the foreign style of the unit is prominent.

Even more puzzling is the question of the details the text *does* choose to share with the reader in its account of the battle. Before Abram and Lot even enter the story, the narrative opens with a long and seemingly convoluted introduction, detailing various aspects of the military figures and actions involved in the battle. Ostensibly, the only real details the reader requires are that the Mesopotamian alliance engaged in warfare in order to thwart a rebellion, and in the process, Abram's nephew was taken prisoner along with his Sodomite cohort. This background is sufficient for a story that centers on the narrative of Abraham in relation to Lot. However, the text provides far more detail of the battles, and deviates sharply from the writing style we are accustomed to.

The portrayal of Abram as a military commander, the absence of explicit divine intervention, and the details of the war of the four kings are all vital to the narrative's significance and messages.

The narrative is divided into three central units:[1]

1. The four kings east of the Jordan go to war (Gen. 14:1–7).
2. Lot is taken captive and rescued by Abram (14:8–16).
3. Abram meets with the king of Sodom and Melchizedek (14:17–24).

The Conquest of the Transjordan

The narrative begins, "It was in the days of King Amraphel of Shinar, King Arioch of Ellasar, King Chedorlaomer of Elam, and King Tidal of Goiim." This opening line itself is out of place – the phrase "*vayehi bimei*" which translates to "in the days of…" is a familiar biblical phrase: "It was in the days of Ahasuerus" (Est. 1:1); "It was in the days of Jehoiakim" (Jer. 1:3). The preface introduces a key figure in the story that will follow – we would assume that the king in whose days the narrative takes place will play a central role, not only in the plot, but in the overarching motif of the story's purpose. Here, *vayehi bimei* introduces a list of Mesopotamian kings whose role in the grander scale of the Abraham narrative is negligible at best.

1. The common position views Lot's captivity as part of the first unit; therefore scholars tend to begin the second unit in Gen. 14:12 or 13. Additionally, most scholars do not view Abram's meeting with the king of Sodom as the conclusion of the second unit – saving Lot from captivity – since the meeting with Melchizedek is a separate unit, which is not an organic part of the story (see Westermann, *Genesis 12–36: A Continental Commentary*, 190–192). The alternative structure suggested above is based on a different interpretation of Abram's meeting with the kings at the end of the story, as we will explain below. For an extensive discussion regarding the possibility of various layers in the chapter see Van Seters, *Abraham in History and Tradition*, 296–308.

In biblical commentary, two different readings have been suggested for verses 1–7. Medieval commentators generally view these verses as introductory exposition reporting the same battle described afterward in the text (verse 8 and on). According to this reading, there was just one battle between the four and five kings, described twice in the narrative. The report begins with an overview of the battle: the identity of the kings and location ("all these joined forces at the Valley of Siddim, now the Dead Sea"), and the reason behind the war (a rebellion against the oppressive four kings). Later, when the narrative discusses the events relating to Lot, the description of the battle is repeated in more detail.[2]

More modern analyses of this narrative claim that the two descriptions relate to two different battles, and that the narrative is written in chronological sequence. The first battle gives context to the second. The four kings were victorious in the Battle of Siddim, and subjugated the nations of the five kings for twelve years. On the thirteenth year, the five kings rebelled. On the fourteenth year the four kings, led by Chedorlaomer, led their troops into battle to suppress the rebellion. After the battle, they pillaged Sodom and took Lot hostage.[3] According to this reading, the exposition is not an introduction relating to the details ahead. Rather, the initial verses describe another battle, which offers background regarding the domination of the four kings in the area, and the rebellion that was repressed in the fourteenth year.

Both interpretations are legitimate, and the plot is unaffected by the difference between these battles. It is unclear, however, as to why the battle is described at such great length. At first glance, the excessive review of the events of the initial battle and the thirteen years that followed do not seem to contribute to the battle or to Lot's captivity. The image of a captured Sodom is ironic in light of the previous story, which provided Lot's motivation to choose to live in Sodom. The previous story described Sodom as a fertile and blessed land, while the

2. See, for example, Cassuto, *The "Quaestio" of the Book of Genesis*, 309; Mathews, *Genesis*, 142–145.
3. See, for example, Westermann, *Genesis 12–36: A Continental Commentary*, 187; Wenham, *Genesis 1–15*, 304–305. Wenham writes that the two battles won by Chedorlaomer and his allies portray Abram as victorious over a king who has already won two battles; see ibid., 313.

very next chapter reveals that Sodom is under the rule of another powerful nation, and the fertility of the land feeds four foreign rulers, who demand an unreasonable levy. Sodom was probably already subject to the four kings when Lot moved there, which intensifies the irony: Lot looked at the land itself, not at the human conduct upon the land. The land was blessed with abundance, but the inhabitants "were wicked and sinners against the Lord" (Gen. 13:3), and the fertility of the land was enslaved to the eastern superpower.[4] This context provides a meaningful literary background to the irony that guides Lot's actions (and dictates Abram's reactions). However, the necessity for the length and detail of this account still remains unclear.

At first glance, the verses in the unit seem out of order. This is how they are ordered in the text:

> 1: "Now, when King Amraphel of Shinar, King Arioch of Ellasar, King Chedorlaomer of Elam, and King Tidal of Goiim"
> 2: "made war on King Bera of Sodom, King Birsha of Gomorrah, King Shinab of Admah, King Shemeber of Zeboiim, and the king of Bela, which is Zoar."
> 3: "All these joined forces at the valley of Siddim, now the Dead Sea."
> 4: "Twelve years they served Chedorlaomer, and in the thirteenth year they rebelled."
> 5–7: "In the fourteenth year Chedorlaomer and the kings who were with him came, and defeated the Rephaim at Ashteroth-karnaim, the Zuzim at Ham, and the Emim in Shaveh-kiriathaim, and the Horites in their hill country of Seir, as far as El-paran, which is by the wilderness. On their way back they came to En-mishpat, which is Kadesh, and subdued all the territory of the Amalekites, and also the Amorites, who dwelt in Hazazon-tamar."

The mention of the five kings in verse 2 is awkward, since verse 3 is a continuation of verse 1. The expression "all these" (verse 3) relates to

4. In the patriarchal era, Egypt was the dominant ruler of Canaanite cities. The rule of Chedorlaomer and his allies in Sodom was unusual, and created a political border that separated Sodom from the rest of Canaan.

the four kings in verse 1, meaning that these are the distant nations who come together at the Valley of Sidim. The list of the five kings should open verse 4, which describes the reason for the attack.[5] This is supported by the syntax, since the ambiguous pronoun in verse 4 ("they" served, "they" rebelled) seems to relate to the previously mentioned five, but after the five are mentioned, the narrative reports the meeting of the four in Siddim, and only then returns to the rebellion described by the pronoun. At first glance there is confusion as to who was subjugated and who rebelled. Apparently, the purpose of the confusion is to position the four and five, names and countries, against each other.[6] For some reason, confusion is privileged over clarity for the sake of placing the kings side by side, resulting in verse 2's placement after verse 1.

Perhaps this curious arrangement relates to an additional question, with regard to the change in the order of the names of the four kings upon their second appearance in verses 8–9:

Verses 1–2	**Verses 8–9**
Now, when King Amraphel of Shinar, King Arioch of Ellasar, King Chedorlaomer of Elam, and King Tidal of Goiim	Then the king of Sodom, the king of Gomorrah, the king of Admah, the king of Zeboiim, and the king of Bela which is Zoar, went forth and engaged them in battle in the Valley of Siddim
made war on King Bera of Sodom, King Birsha of Gomorrah, King Shinab of Admah, King Shemeber of Zeboiim, and the king of Bela, which is Zoar.	King Chedorlaomer of Elam, King Tidal of Goiim, King Amraphel of Shinar, and King Arioch of Ellasar; four kings against the five.

In the second list, the order of the kings is reversed, and the five kings are mentioned before the four. This difference is easily explained by

5. Westermann, *Genesis 12–36: A Continental Commentary*, 193.
6. Westermann, ibid.

the context of the plot. Another surprising difference is the internal order of the list of four kings. In the initial list Amraphel was at the head of the list, whereas the second list opens with Chedorlaomer. The positioning of Chedorlaomer at the head of the list is not surprising in itself, since he seems to be the leader of the four-king superpower: verse 4 states that the five kings were subject to him, and verse 5 has him leading the three other kings in a war of conquest. Therefore, the surprising component is Amraphel's appearance at the head of the first list.

The question, of course, is based on the assumption that biblical lists correspond to the content they express, and that they represent a certain hierarchy. Therefore, when the text lists a person's belongings, their slaves and maidservants will be mentioned before their possessions (for example, Gen. 36:6); Judah will be the first of the tribes mentioned in the order of encampment (Num. 2:3); the burnt offering will open the list of sacrifices (Lev. 1:3, 6:2), and so forth. The second list, which opens with Chedorlaomer, reflects the military and political hierarchy. But perhaps the model of the first list reflects another theme. The names in the first list appear according to alphabetical order in Hebrew: Amraphel, Arioch, Chedorlaomer, and Tidal.[7] This order sets a technical tone of a military chronicle that exists outside the narrative, as if to say, this is not a "story," it is a "dictionary," a technical list of participants taken from a military record.[8] Perhaps this is why the names of the five kings are omitted

7. Avraham Kahana, *Bible Series with Scientific Commentary* (Zhitomir, 1903), 45. For a discussion of when the order of the alphabet was established, see Elie Assis, "The Alphabetic Acrostic in the Book of Lamentations," *CBQ* 69 (2007): 710n1. As alphabetical order is common to western Semitic languages (beginning with Phoenician, and continued in Hebrew and Aramaic), it is reasonable to assume that from the beginning of written language in Israel, the alphabetical order of the consonants was the same as it is today (except for the order of the letters *ayin* and *peh*, which may have changed). In fact, alphabetical order was retained and reflected in the Greek alphabet as well (Joseph Naveh, *Early History of the Alephbet* [Jerusalem, 1997], 174–175), which proves the stability of the accepted alphabetical order.
8. Van Seters (*Abraham in History and Tradition*, 300) believes the first part of the story is taken from an ancient source. However, most scholars agree that the alliance

in the second list. The second list is part of the story, and in the story the four kings are defeated; the omission of their names foreshadows this. This indication of future occurrences has no place in the initial dry and technical description of the war. The technical list blends in with the style of the first unit in the narrative, which is foreign to the Abraham cycle.

The most surprising element in the unit is the detailed description of the places conquered by the four kings. The locations themselves are irrelevant to the story, since Abram only chased the kings once they had left the area and traveled north. Nonetheless, the course of war is described at length. Genesis 14:5–7 mentions four nations (Rephaim, Zuzim, Emim, Horites) who settle four areas (Ashteroth-karnaim, Ham, Shaveh-kiriathaim, and Seir), which were all conquered by the four kings in the fourteenth year. Later, two additional nations/locations were also conquered: the territory of the Amalekites, and the Amorites, who dwelled in Hazazon-tamar. This description plays no part in the present narrative, but the significance of the unit does relate to later Israelite history. Cassuto (followed by others)[9] notes that the names and nations mentioned in our narrative are repeated in Moses' description of the nation's journey to Canaan in Deuteronomy. In Deuteronomy, the directions are reversed: the four kings traveled north to south, while the children of Israel traveled south to north. The context of the journey in Deuteronomy is the prohibition to conquer certain areas from Ammon and Moab, the descendants of Esau and Lot, who received their portions of land from God. While in Genesis 14 the four kings are the conquerors, in Deuteronomy 2 they are Abraham's family (Lot and Esau):

against the eastern kings is incongruent with the patriarchal era (see, for example, Kitchen, "Genesis 12–50 in the Near Eastern World," 71–74).

9. Cassuto, *The "Quaestio" of the Book of Genesis*, 312–313. See also Michael C. Astour, "Political and Cosmic Symbolism in Genesis 14 and in its Babylonian Sources," in *Biblical Motifs: Origins and Transformations*, ed. A. Altmann (Cambridge, MA, 1966), 66–74; and see Zekharyah Kallai, "The Wandering-Traditions from Kadesh-Barnea to Canaan: A Study in Biblical Historiography," *JJS* 33 (1982): 175–184; Mathews, *Genesis*, 143–144.

The Journey of the Four Kings (Gen. 14:5–7)	The Journey of Israel (Deut. 1–3)
...and defeated the Rephaim at Ashteroth-karnaim	It too counted as Rephaim country. It was formerly inhabited by Rephaim, whom the Ammonites call Zamzummim; a people great and numerous and as tall as the Anakites (2:20–21)
the Zuzim at Ham	
and the Emim in Shaveh-kiriathaim	It was formerly inhabited by the Emim, a people great and numerous, and as tall as the Anakites; they are counted as Rephaim, but the Moabites call them Emim (2:11)
and the Horites in their hill country of Seir, as far as El-paran, which is by the wilderness	Similarly, Seir was formerly inhabited by the Horites; but the descendants of Esau dispossessed them, wiping them out and settling in their place (2:12)
On their way back they came to En-mishpat, which is Kadesh, and subdued all the territory of the Amalekites	Thus, after you had remained at Kadesh all that long time, we marched back into the wilderness (1:46)

The mention of Rephaim, Zuzim, Emim, and Horites seems unnecessary both in Genesis, where the list fails to contribute any significant information to the narrative, and in Deuteronomy, where Moses describes the ancient history of the nations who used to inhabit those locations before they were conquered by Ammon and Moab. According to Cassuto, Moses and future generations who conquered these lands generations later were merely pursuing land that was rightfully theirs from the days of Abram.[10]

Cassuto sees the link between the journey of the kings and that of the Israelites as an indication of the nation's merit as they traveled through the Transjordan. Since Abram was victorious over the four

10. Cassuto, *The "Quaestio" of the Book of Genesis*, 312–313; Yoel Bin-Nun, *Chapters of the Fathers: Studies in Narratives of the Patriarchs in the Book of Genesis*, ed. H. Navon (Alon Shevut, 2003), 54–64.

kings (even if symbolically – by returning the Sodomite captives and their belongings), from a broader historical perspective he merited those areas they had captured in the battle of Genesis 14.[11] Following in Cassuto's footsteps, Rabbi Yoel Bin-Nun describes a complex biblical perception of the relationship between the nation of Israel and the Promised Land. According to their view, the inheritance of the land is multilayered: Canaan was promised to Abram at the start of his journey, when he was chosen by God; however, the Transjordan was added to Abram's initial inheritance after his heroic deeds in the War of the Kings. The addition is formalized in the following chapter, during the Covenant Between the Pieces. This is the reason the Transjordan conquests by the four kings are described in such detail. It is no military chronicle with outdated background information; rather, the text provides details that justify Abram's rights to areas in the Transjordan. Cassuto asserts, however, that the link between Genesis 14 and Deuteronomy 1–3 signifies the national right to the Transjordan. This is unlikely, particularly since the context in Deuteronomy is the prohibition on conquering those very same areas from the descendants of Esau.[12] Therefore, the link should be redefined as Abram's right to the Transjordan – which is indeed inherited by his family. The Transjordan is not inherited by the sons of Jacob, but by other rejected members of Abram's family: the offspring of Lot and Esau.[13] Here, too, the familial-nationalistic approach of Genesis comes into play. As the descendants of Lot and Esau are considered part of

11. Similarly, Immanuel Benzinger, "Zur Quellenscheidung in Gen. 14," in *Vom Alten Testament: Festschrift fur K. Marti*, ed. K. Budde (BZAW 41: Giessen, 1925), 21–27. Compare with Astour, "Political and Cosmic Symbolism in Genesis 14 and in Its Babylonian Sources," 74, in contrast with Van Seters (*Abraham in History and Tradition*, 306), who argues that Abram is not portrayed here as obtaining land for himself or his offspring.
12. The narrative connection makes it difficult to accept Mathews' claim that the meaning of the connection between the stories is, "If father Abraham could defeat the invincible Kedorlaomer, the Israelites could take courage facing enemies in their own day" (Mathews, *Genesis*, 144). The context in Deuteronomy is that Israel is *prohibited* from fighting their enemies in Seir, Moab, and Ammon.
13. There is therefore no reason to view Gen. 14:5–7 as a vague geographical description or a later addition (Westermann, *Genesis 12–36: A Continental Commentary*, 193, believes the ancient names of these nations originate in Deuteronomy).

Abraham's family, they are also granted inheritance in Abraham's merit, despite having been rejected from his covenant, and despite the perpetual conflict between Israel and these nations over the course of history. The nature of the initial list of kings, arranged alphabetically, reflects this broader historical perspective. Based on the internal relationship between the four nations, Chedorlaomer should be at the top of the list; however, the significance of the conquests supersedes the boundaries of this narrative and necessitates an order that indicates a broader historical perspective than the temporary political hierarchy of the time.

Lot's Rescue

Genesis 14:8 reviews the battling parties, and concludes, "Four kings against the five." Rashi comments on this mathematical equation: "Four kings against the five – and yet the fewer were victorious. This statement is expressly made to tell you how powerful they were, and yet Abram did not refrain from pursuing them." The reader, who knows that these four kings were northeastern world powers who have subjugated the entire ancient world, would not be surprised that four such kings are victorious over five kings of medium-sized cities surrounding the Dead Sea. The suppression of the uprising was only done in the context of conquering the entire Transjordan. Cassuto, for example, refers to the four kings as "four wretched kings" throughout his commentary. The forces are far from equal, and there is no logical reason to assume the outcome would be different. Therefore, if the mathematical conclusion is meant to address the reader's expectations, it should be read as an ironic comment, mocking the behavior of the king of Sodom: the five kings act as though they have some sort of advantage over the eastern empires. The five kings are the ones who go out to war in the Valley of Siddim; from their perspective, the forces battling are "four against five," when the results of the battle are obvious from the outset.

However, the literary purpose of the mathematical conclusion is to set a tone to the centrality of this world war: nine kings worldwide congregate in the battlefield, from Shinar, Ellasar, Elam, Goiim, Sodom, Gomorrah, Admah, Zeboiim, and Zoar.[14] A tenth king will be mentioned

14. Cf. von Rad, *Genesis*, 177.

at the conclusion of the story – Melchizedek king of Salem, who greets Abram warmly when he returns from the battlefield.

This design is significant to the purpose of the story: for the first time in his narrative cycle, Abram is portrayed as an important figure in the international political realm. The story also reveals that Abram has allies – Mamre, Eshkol, and Aner – as well as a battalion of 318 men.[15] Abram's entry into the military-political arena will be emphasized in his defeat of the four kings: "At night, he and his servants deployed against them and defeated them; and he pursued them as far as Hobah, which is north of Damascus" (Gen. 14:15). Abram's battalion could not have defeated hundreds of thousands of soldiers, and then chased them down; instead, they probably attacked one camp of war prisoners late one night, and released them and their possessions (similar to the military operation managed by Gideon in Judges 7:16–22). However, the phrases "defeated" and "pursued" convey complete military victory. The portrayal of the battle turns Abram into a true and equal statesman: he "defeated" the four kings just as the four kings had "defeated" their adversaries in verses 5 and 7.[16] According to Cassuto, this portrayal of Abram as a military commander merits Abram more land, as we will see later in the Covenant Between the Pieces.

The mockery of the king of Sodom is enhanced by an additional wordplay in the conclusion of the war. The connotation of the word "fell" in the context of the battle (Gen. 14:10) might be "died in battle" (such as Ex. 32:28). The reader's first impression is that the king of Sodom

---

15. Walther Zimmerli writes ("Abraham und Melchisedek," in *Das nahe und dasferne Wort*, ed. F. Maass [BZAW 105: Berlin, 1967], 255–264) that the story reveals that Abram's household consists of approximately one thousand people. Westermann (*Genesis 12–36: A Continental Commentary*, 201) believes this to be impossible, and suggests that the size of Abram's camp is only related to be analogous to the Judges narratives (especially Gideon).
16. Cf. Wenham, *Genesis 1–15*, 314. Westermann (*Genesis 12–36: A Continental Commentary*, 201–202) "accuses" verse 17 of creating the incorrect impression that Abram defeated empires using only foot soldiers. He believes this is nothing but "sloppy editing" and "a false impression." However, we will demonstrate below that this relates to the purpose of the story, which seeks to portray Abram as relevant in the political field.

died at the outset of the battle; only later does it become clear that he was, in fact, in hiding.

The text generates a stark comparison between the fleeing kings of Sodom and Gomorrah and Abram and his troops, who pursue the eastern kings in an attempt to rescue the prisoners. While the kings of Sodom and Gomorrah hide to save themselves, Abram and his allies take action for the good of others. Abram becomes a legitimate candidate for lordship in the land of Canaan; moreover, he valiantly chooses to maintain his status as Lot's patron, even when the latter has chosen to settle in Sodom. The king of Sodom does not take an interest in the captives taken from his city, while Abram, who resides "at the terebinths of Mamre the Amorite" (Gen. 14:13), risks his own life to return the prisoners to safety.

Wealth and possessions are emphasized as a motif in the narrative. The text focuses on these elements when describing the results of the initial battle:

> [The invaders] took all the wealth of Sodom and Gomorrah and all their provisions, and went their way. They also took Lot, the son of Abram's brother, and his possessions, and departed; for he had settled in Sodom. (Gen. 14:11–12)

The four kings "take" two things: "All the wealth of Sodom and Gomorrah and all their provisions," and "Lot... and his possessions." Only later does the reader discover that additional prisoners were taken – "the women and the rest of the people" (Gen. 14:16). The initial omission of this fact, and the excessive focus on the possessions in place of the people, led some commentators to suggest an alternative version; instead of "all their provisions," they suggested "all their prisoners."[17] The fact that the narrative would ignore the prisoners is indeed surprising, and intends to greatly emphasize the possessions motif. From the perspective of the

17. Joseph Halevy, *Recherches Bibliques* (Paris 1895), 331. Westermann writes that there is an incoherence between the military-political narrative, which only notes taking assets, and the family narrative, which mentions captives, particularly Lot (Westermann, *Genesis 12–36: A Continental Commentary*, 198–99).

four kings, the battle centered on the possessions of Sodom; their victory is measured in terms of the wealth they had acquired. This motif will be emphasized in Abram's victory as well, but the people will be mentioned also:

Capture of the Wealth by the Kings (Gen. 14:11–12)	Return of the Wealth by Abram (Gen. 14:16)
[The invaders] took all the wealth of Sodom and Gomorrah and all their provisions, and went their way.	He brought back all the possessions
They also took Lot and his possessions, the son of Abram's brother, and departed; for he had settled in Sodom.	And his brother Lot and his possessions he also brought back,
	and the women and the rest of the people

Abram's retrieval of the possessions mirrors the taking of the possessions: the verb "brought back" appears twice in the former, while "took" appears twice in the latter.[18] When the possessions are returned, they are not attributed to Sodom and Gomorrah, as they are when they are taken. This abbreviation is reasonable, as it will later emerge that Abram has no interest in the possessions. One other difference between the compared scenes is the initial distance placed between Lot's name and his description as "the son of Abram's brother"; Lot's name and relation to Abram are separated by Lot's possessions: "They also *took Lot and his possessions*, the son of Abram's brother." This awkward phrase serves to further emphasize possessions as a major motif in this episode; implying that Lot cannot be separated from his possessions, not even when he is taken captive, not even by a statement revealing his family connections and describing him as Abram's nephew.[19] The formulation is "corrected" after Abram's rescue mission: "And *his brother Lot* and *his possessions* he also brought back." The third and most significant distinction between the two episodes is the mention of the "women and the rest

18. Wenham, *Genesis 1–15*, 315.

19. This is reminiscent of Gen. 12:5. See the discussion of this verse in previous chapters.

of the people," who were apparently also taken captive. Their captivity is only revealed to the reader after Abram rescues them. The fact that the women and the others are an addition is emphasized by the chiastic form of the other components in the verse:

A: *He brought back*
  B: All the *possessions*
    C: And also his brother Lot
  B': And his *possessions*
A': *He brought back*

The reader's impression is that the list of returned components is complete, and includes Lot and possessions.[20] This impression is reinforced by the fact that it mirrors the original list of elements that were taken, and the reader has no additional expectations. It is then related that there were other captives who were returned to Sodom by Abram. The design emphasizes the centrality of possessions, which are given even more attention than the people of Sodom.[21] In a later narrative, Lot will once again be forced to choose between joining his uncle or remaining in Sodom. In that episode, the choice to escape with Abram is one of life or death – and although he does leave Sodom, Lot ultimately opts not to join his life together with Abram. The values and luxuries of Sodomite culture are compelling, and despite the repeated hazard to his life, Lot perpetually chooses to remain. Abram, for his part, continues to attempt to save him.

Abram Takes Action

Up to this point, Abram is not mentioned in the story at all as an active character; it is only when the rumor of recent events reaches Abram's

20. In an attempt to make the translated text flow, the translator sometimes "loses" the wordplay. The Septuagint omits the word *heshev* ("brought back") which appears after Lot's name, and before the women and the rest of the people.
21. Based on verses that depict the women as part of the spoils of war (Deut. 21:10–14, II Kings 5:2), Wenham suggested that the women here are depicted as an element of the spoils (Wenham, *Genesis 1–15*, 315). However, his interpretation fails to relate to the absence of the women from the outset.

ears that the reader is reminded of the context of the story, which is in the middle of the Abraham cycle.

The narrative describes the rumor Abram hears, and then inserts a comment about his allies: "A fugitive brought the news to Abram the Hebrew, who was dwelling at the terebinths of Mamre the Amorite, brother of Eshkol and brother of Aner, these being Abram's allies (*baalei habrit*)" (Gen. 14:13). The reader learns that Abram is not alone; he is surrounded by allies who can assist him in his war. However, since Aner and Mamre do not take part in the actual battle, the mention of these allies seems irrelevant. The names are mentioned again only at the end of the story, when Abram insists that they receive a portion of the spoils (14:24). This, of course is even more surprising. Why are Abram's friends significant enough to warrant mention at the end of the story, when they made no apparent contribution to the war?

Perhaps the verse should be read as preface to the following verse: "When Abram heard that his brother had been taken captive, he mustered his retainers, born into his household, numbering three hundred and eighteen, and went in pursuit as far as Dan" (Gen. 14:14). The distance between Abram's "brother," who dwells in Sodom, and the strangers who surround Abram and become his allies, is emphasized. "Allies" is described using the same word as "covenant" – *brit*, which is one of many links between this narrative and the Covenant Between the Pieces in the following chapter.[22] The covenant with God was previously described as a replacement for family ties; here the allies are replacements for the biological "brother." Abram is not as lonely as one would think, since he forms alliances with the inhabitants of the land. The fact that Abram has allies highlights his devotion to his nephew; when Abram hears that his nephew has been captured, there is no deliberation or hesitation. He takes immediate action: "When Abram heard that his brother had been taken captive, he mustered his retainers." Lot is not described as Abram's "brother's son," but rather as Abram's "brother," both here and in verses

22. Regarding the term *baal brit*, "ally," see Götz Schmitt, "El Berit-Mitra," *ZAW* 76 (1964): 325–327; Ernst Kutsch, "Gesetz und Gnade: Probleme des alttestamentlichen Bundesbegriffs," *ZAW* 79 (1967): 18–35.

14 and 16. While Lot willingly distances himself from his uncle, Abram comes to his nephew's rescue without a second thought.

Abraham's Encounter with the Two Kings

Abram returns from the battle having proved himself an astute and capable military leader. Despite the obvious sting operation perpetrated by his foes, Abram emerged from battle a figure with considerable military prowess. When Abram returns from the battle, he meets with the king of Sodom (Gen. 14:17, 21–24) and Melchizedek, king of Salem (14:18–20). Textually, there is a sudden leap here from the king of Sodom to Melchizedek. Following an introduction in verse 17 that amply prepares the reader for the meeting with the king of Sodom ("The king of Sodom came out to meet him when he returned from defeating Chedorlaomer"), suddenly the reader is told in verse 18 of Abram's meeting with Melchizedek, who is mentioned for the first time ("And King Melchizedek of Salem brought out bread and wine; and he was a priest of God Most High"). Abrabanel aptly asked here, "How did [he] enter into the story of the kings?" echoing the reader's confusion at the king of Jerusalem's sudden appearance in the story. Melchizedek's appearance here is not only unrelated to the story, it disrupts the flow of the narrative. The reader is about to witness the conversation between Abram and the king of Sodom – ostensibly the diplomacy that will end the conflict – and without warning the scene switches to a seemingly unrelated dialogue with a seemingly unrelated character. Just as perplexingly, after the meeting with Melchizedek, the story returns to the dialogue between Abram and the king of Sodom (14:22–24). It seems as though these are two separate stories, serving two separate (rather unclear) purposes.

The stories of Abram's encounters with the two kings both contradict and complement each other. The joint subject – the king of a major city in Canaan greeting Abram upon his return from battle – creates an essential analogy between the two scenes. This analogy is enhanced by the linguistic and textual similarities:[23]

23. See Robert H. Smith, "Abram and Melchizedek (Genesis 14, 18–20)," *ZAW* 77 (1965): 130; Zimmerli, "Abraham und Melchisedek." Both believe that the meeting of Abram

King of Sodom (Gen. 14:17, 21–24)	Melchizedek (14:18–20)
The king of Sodom came out (*vayetze*) to meet him.	and King Melchizedek of Salem brought out (*hotzi*) bread and wine; he was a priest of God Most High.
Abram said to the king of Sodom, "I swear to the Lord, God Most High, Creator of heaven and earth"	blessed be Abram of God Most High, Creator of heaven and earth; and blessed be God Most High, who has delivered your foes into your hand
Give me the persons, and take the possessions for yourself	And he gave him a tenth of everything

Both kings go out to greet Abram. In the Hebrew syntax, Melchizedek's name and title appear before the verb, whereas the verb "came out" precedes the name and title of the king of Sodom. This style often indicates contrast: while the king of Sodom "came out," "*vayetze*," toward Abram, Melchizedek "brought out," "*hotzi*," bread and wine. The unique name Abram uses for God, "God Most High, Creator of heaven and earth," is learned from his meeting with Melchizedek. The significance of the name he gives to God indicates the impact the meeting with Melchizedek had on him.

Some commentators have suggested a chiastic structure for the unit:[24]

A: King of Sodom (v. 17): "When he returned from defeating Chedorlaomer and the kings with him, the king of Sodom came out to meet him in the Valley of Shaveh, which is the Valley of the King."

---

and Melchizedek is a later addition to the original narrative, which had only discussed the king of Sodom. However, neither referred to the dialogue conducted between the two units. In an attempt to establish the uniformity of the text, Wenham emphasized some of the links between various parts of the story (Wenham, *Genesis 1–15*, 305). See also David Elgavish, "The Encounter of Abram and Melchizedek King of Salem: A Covenant Establishing Ceremony," in *Studies in the Book of Genesis; Literature, Redaction and History*, ed. A. Wénin (Leuven, 2001), 506–507.

24. Allen P. Ross, *Creation and Blessing: A Guide to the Study and Exposition of Genesis* (Grand Rapids, MI, 1988), 295. An alternative chiastic structure is suggested by Wenham, *Genesis 1–15*, 315. I am skeptical about the stability of this structure.

B: Melchizedek offers Abram (v. 18): "And King Melchizedek of Salem brought out bread and wine; he was a priest of God Most High."

C: Melchizedek blesses Abram (v. 19): "He blessed him, saying, 'Blessed be Abram of God Most High, Creator of heaven and earth.'"

C': Melchizedek blesses God (v. 20): "And blessed be God Most High, who has delivered your foes into your hand.'"

B': Melchizedek receives from Abram (v. 20): "And [Abram] gave him a tenth of everything."

A': King of Sodom (vv. 21–24): "Then the king of Sodom said to Abram: 'Give me the persons, and take the possessions for yourself.' And Abram said to the king of Sodom, '…as for the share of the men who went with me – Aner, Eshkol, and Mamre – let them take their share.'"

If the structure is convincing, the meeting with Melchizedek and the king of Sodom should certainly be viewed as part of the same organic unit. But even so, why is the meeting with the king of Sodom interrupted by a report about Melchizedek? Verses 21–24 should logically resume at verse 17. Perhaps the two meetings were depicted this way in order to allow for a simultaneous and comparative reading between them. The comparison is enhanced by the similar language used to describe both meetings. The essence of the comparison is Abram's relationship with each of the kings.

Abram clearly regards each king differently. The meeting with Melchizedek emanates pleasant friendship, and an exchange of goods as part of a respectful normative and religious relationship. Melchizedek inexplicably offers Abram "bread and wine." This gift might be a symbol of agreement,[25] although a more likely explanation would be a feast honoring kings.[26] Abram offers Melchizedek "a tenth of everything." The syntax of

25. This was pointed out by Bruce Vawter, *On Genesis: A New Reading* (Garden City, NY, 1977), and later by Elgavish, "The Encounter of Abram and Melchizedek King of Salem," 499–500. The word "blessing" connotes the covenant in this context.

26. See, among others, Wenham, *Genesis 1–15*, 316. But see Rashi: "This is done for those weary from battle," and similarly Sforno. Skinner also views the meal as one offered to

this verse is vague, and since Melchizedek is the explicit noun related to previous actions in the verse, and there is no indication that the subject has changed, at first glance it would seem that Melchizedek is the one who offers Abram a tenth of everything. However, based on the context, it is clearly Abram, the one who has returned with the spoils, who offers Melchizedek a tenth of everything, which is, of course, appropriate since Melchizedek is a priest.[27] The tension between the syntax and the content of the verse forced most translators to make a choice as to how to present this exchange, with the majority identifying Abram as the giver of the tithe.[28]

Even if the reader can easily figure out that it was Abram who gave the tithe, the vague writing style creates a literary awareness that plays an important role in the design of this scene. The reader is made to feel that even if in reality it was Abram who offered the tithe, the literary reality would *justify* a reversal of roles. The advantage of this dual reading is the reciprocal relationship between Abram and Melchizedek,

---

soldiers returning from the battlefield (Skinner, *A Critical and Exegetical Commentary on Genesis*, 268). Hamilton comments that Melchizedek's concern for the soldiers attests to his humane personality (Hamilton, *The Book of Genesis, Chapters 1–17*, 407–408).

27. Some commentators view this scene as etiological with the ritualistic purpose of establishing the receiver of tithes as a priest (e.g., Westermann, *Genesis 12–36: A Continental Commentary*, 203). For additional etiological-ritualistic approaches, see John A. Emerton, "The Riddle of Genesis xiv," *VT* 21 (1971): 414–426.

28. Simcha Kogut, *Syntax and Exegesis: Studies in Biblical Syntax as Reflected in Traditional Jewish Exegesis* (Jerusalem, 2002), 101. See also Michal Peter, "Wer sprach den Segen nach Genesis xiv 19 über Abraham aus?" *VT* 29 (1979): 114–120. Modern translations agree that Abram is the subject of the sentence (e.g., Skinner, Hertz, Cohen, Wenham, Rosenberg, Sherman, Speiser, and Kaplan). Some included Abram's name in their translation: "Abram gave him a tithe of all the booty" (Speiser, *Genesis*, 100; Aryeh Kaplan, *The Living Torah* [New York and Jerusalem, 1981], 65; Robert Davidson, *Genesis 12–50* [CBC: Cambridge, 1979], 32). Hamilton (*The Book of Genesis, Chapters 1–17*, 413n12) sees the tithe as similar to the division of spoils between the fighters and the people who remain in the camp in the war against Midian (Num. 31). However, the narrative does not portray Abram and Melchizedek as a united front against the kings, as in the war against Midian. Elgavish compared the tithe to the division of spoils at the conclusion of the war against Midian, of which a donation was made by the Israelites to the Tabernacle (Num. 31:28–30). He believed the tithe given by Abram to Melchizedek was symbolic of a political alliance, similar to the alliance made between Abram and Abimelech in ch. 21 (Elgavish, "The Encounter of Abram and Melchizedek King of Salem," 502).

as if to say, it really doesn't matter who gave to whom; the two characters are inseparable and equal.[29] Perhaps the two met in the Valley of Shaveh ("equal") for this reason.[30]

The meeting with the king of Sodom leaves the reader with an entirely different impression. In verse 17, the king of Sodom goes out to greet Abram, which creates anticipation for a friendly welcome or a call for peace. Instead, the conversation with the king of Sodom revolves around the question of possessions. The king of Sodom offers Abram the possessions he had recovered from the four kings; but here – in contrast with the episode with Melchizedek – Abram absolutely refuses to accept the offer: "But Abram said to the king of Sodom: I swear to the Lord, God Most High, Creator of heaven and earth; I will not take so much as a thread or a sandal strap of what is yours; you shall not say, 'It is I who made Abram rich'" (Gen. 14:22–23). Various elements in Abram's statement emphasize his hostility toward the king of Sodom:

- Whatever the reason for Abram's refusal, he could have chosen to express himself in another way. Abram's oath expresses firmness and determination. Abram leaves no room for negation or reevaluation.[31] Moreover, an oath in the name of God adds a religious element to his refusal; it is Abram's loyalty to God that prevents him from accepting gifts from Sodom.

29. Hamilton (*The Book of Genesis, Chapters 1–17*, 410) compares the double positions that they both seem to serve: priest and king. In his opinion, Abram functions as a priest in the story as well (he builds altars and performs circumcisions) and is compared to a king (as in the verse "You are a mighty prince among us" of Gen. 23:6).
30. For this meaning of "Shaveh," see BDB, 1001.
31. Similar to Samuel's command to Saul on the eve of the war against Amalek: "Now go and smite Amalek, and utterly destroy all that they have, and spare them not; but slay both man and woman, infant and suckling, ox and sheep, camel and donkey" (I Sam. 15:3). The expression "infant and suckling," like the expression "camel and donkey," signifies "not only an infant, but even a suckling," "not only a camel, but even a donkey," in contrast to "both man and woman," or "ox and sheep," which function as a standard polar merismos (a description of boundaries, which in fact include everything in between. However, see also Adele Berlin, *The Dynamics of Biblical Parallelism* [Grand Rapids, MI, 2008], 7). On the classic merismos, see Louis Alonso Schökel, *A Manual of Hebrew Poetics* (Subsidia Biblica 11: Roma, 2000), 83–84.

- While Abram absolutely refuses to forge a friendship with the king of Sodom, he consistently alludes to his friendly relationship with Melchizedek. Abram repeats the name for God that he had learned from Melchizedek. In other words, Melchizedek taught Abram a divine name, which Abram uses to disengage from the king of Sodom. The word *he'esharti* ("It is I who made Abram rich," v. 23) is reminiscent of the word *maaser* ("a tenth"), which Abram offers Melchizedek (Gen. 14:20).[32] This too is an accentuation of the difference between the king Abram awards with a tithe, and the king with whom Abram rejects any type of association. This reinforces Abram's rejection of the king of Sodom. The reader cannot assume that the reason Abram rejects the king of Sodom so vehemently is his desire to distance himself from the kings of Canaan. Abram's relationship with Melchizedek would make this interpretation unacceptable.
- Abram explains that he does not accept the offer of the king of Sodom so that the latter will not be able to say, "It is I who made Abram rich." This information is offered without further explanation. Is this a personal statement against the king of Sodom? A theological statement? Why is Abram suddenly reluctant to become rich by another king, when in Egypt he had no qualms about doing so? The significance of Abram's refusal needs to be examined within the greater significance of the story as a whole, through the perspective of the recurring motif of possessions.

The distinction between the two kings who met with Abram in the Valley of Shaveh is expressed in the associations with the kings' names. The king of Sodom is called Bera, which, as Rashi points out, connotes evil (from the word *ra*): "Evil toward God and evil toward mankind."[33] The

---

32. Joseph Dore, "La rencontre Abraham-Melchisedech et le probleme de I'unite litteraire du Genese 14," in *De la Torah au Messie*, ed. M. Carrez, J. Dore, and P. Grelot (Paris, 1981), 75–95; Wenham, *Genesis 1–15*, 318.
33. Rashi on Gen. 14:2. Scholars have discussed both the literary and etymological significance of the names of the five kings. See, for example, William F. Albright, "Abram the Hebrew: A New Archaeological Interpretation," *BASOR* 163 (1961): 49; Sarna, *Understanding Genesis*, 111–112; Wenham, *Genesis 1–15*, 309; Hamilton, *The Book*

people of Sodom were described similarly in the previous story: "Now the inhabitants of Sodom were wicked (*ra'im*) and sinners against the Lord" (Gen. 13:13). The king's name therefore represents (or reflects) the nature of his community. Melchizedek's name is more difficult to decipher. The component *zedek* could be part of his full name, or the name Melchizedek could be comprised of two components that describe the nature of the king – *Melkhi* ("my king") *tzedek* ("justice"), whereas his private name is omitted from the text altogether. If *zedek* is part of his personal name, this connotes a positive evaluation of the king. Speiser's interpretation is more technical. To him, Melchizedek means "the just king," as a legitimization of Melchizedek's monarchy (like Sargon the Ashurite).[34] Either way, the concept *tzedek* carries strong, positive connotations. The story that follows will use the same term to describe the relationship between Abram and God: "And because he put his trust in the Lord, He reckoned it to his *just merit* (*tzedaka*)" (15:6). The narrative will use the same term to justify the selection of Abram in the discussion on the destruction of Sodom: "For I have singled him out that he may instruct his children and his posterity to keep the way of the Lord by doing what is *just* (*tzedaka*) and right" (Gen. 18:19). Whether *tzedek* denotes a personal quality, a city, or a name, the associations that accompany the word are unequivocally positive.[35]

What, then, is the literary purpose of the contrast between the two kings? It seems unlikely that Abram had been employed to fight Melchizedek's wars.[36] Rather, presenting the alliance between Abram

---

of Genesis, Chapters 1–17, 401). Elgavish ("The Encounter of Abram and Melchizedek King of Salem," 496) notes the negative connotation, and claims that the names should only be viewed as a literary tool. He suggests that this is the reason the names are not repeated when the names of the four kings are mentioned for the second time (vv. 8–9).

34. Speiser, *Genesis*, 104.

35. Albright asserts that the meaning of the word *Shalem* in the verse is peace, and the combination *melekh shalem*, usually translated as "King of Salem," denotes "man of peace" or "ally" (Albright, "Abram the Hebrew: A New Archaeological Interpretation," 52). According to Albright, this is not just an association but the primary literary significance of the name.

36. Together with Augustine Pagolu, *The Religion of the Patriarchs* (Sheffield, 1998), 188, unlike Loren R. Fisher, "Abraham and His Priest-King," *JBL* 81 (1962): 269.

and Melchizedek contributes to characterization on two levels. Many commentators believe that Melchizedek is a symbol of Jerusalem, based on the etymological identification of "Salem" with "Jerusalem." This interpretation can be found as early as Onkelos' translation of verse 18.[37] It is further reinforced by the identity of Melchizedek as a priest, and by the tithe given to him by Abram.[38]

According to this interpretation, the purpose of the contrast between Melchizedek and the king of Sodom in the story reflects the contrast between Sodom and Jerusalem. This conflict accompanies the reader throughout the Bible, and is expressed explicitly in Isaiah 1 and Ezekiel 23. The story alludes to God's choice of Jerusalem and what the city represents: *tzedaka,* justice. This choice is in itself a rejection of Sodom and the values it represents, as seen in Genesis 19.

However, the evidence that links Melchizedek with Jerusalem is not unequivocal. Moreover, the biblical Salem often connotes the Shechem area, not Jerusalem (see Gen. 33:18).[39] The true literary purpose of Melchizedek's offer is the contrast his character offers to the king of Sodom.[40] The reader might have thought that Abram's participation in the war and the retrieval of Sodom's captives and riches could have been the foundation for a relationship between Abram and the

37. Cf. I Sam. 18:18. This is the impression from the Amarna letters, which refer to Jerusalem as "Uru-salim" ("Uru" probably means "city"). See Westermann, *Genesis 12–36: A Continental Commentary,* 204; Hamilton, *The Book of Genesis, Chapters 1–17,* 409–410.
38. Klaus Baltzer, "Jerusalem in den Erzväter-Geschichten der Genesis? Traditionsgeschichtliche Erwägungen zu Gen 14 und 22," in *Die Hebräische Bibel und Ihre Zweifache Nachgeschichte: Festschrift fur Rolf Rendtorff zum 65. Geburtstag,* ed. E. Blum, C. Macholz, and E. W. Stegemann (Neukirchen-Vluyn, 1990), 3–12; Yairah Amit, "The Place of Jerusalem in the Pentateuch," *Studies in the Bible and Exegesis* 5 (2000): 41–57. Elgavish ("The Encounter of Abram and Melchizedek King of Salem") claims that the root TZ-D-K is frequently incorporated into names of characters associated with Jerusalem, and adds that this identification is apparent in the Genesis Apocryphon found by the Dead Sea.
39. Some ancient translations viewed the word *Shalem* (Salem) as the name of a place (Septuagint; Peshitta; Vulgate). This interpretation is accepted by many modern scholars. Cameron Mackay ("Salem," *PEQ* 80–81 [1948/9]: 127) identifies Salem with a city near Shechem. Elgavish ("The Encounter of Abram and Melchizedek King of Salem," 498) claims that the word Salem indicates both Shechem and Jerusalem.
40. See Leibowitz, *Studies in Genesis,* 93–96.

king of Sodom. The final episode of the story refutes this possibility. Abram's clear disengagement from the king of Sodom illuminates the fact that Lot's rescue was a personal endeavor. Melchizedek, who had nothing to gain from the war, greeted Abram with bread and wine, and Abram offered him his allegiance, while the king of Sodom, who had prisoners and riches returned to his city by Abram, did not go out to greet him with a celebration, and Abram refused to forge any kind of relationship with him.[41]

Abram's disengagement from Sodom is also reflected by the choice of meeting place, "the Valley of Shaveh, which is the Valley of the King" (Gen. 14:17); in other words, not in Sodom. Abram does not return the prisoners to their city. The king of Sodom goes out to him and receives his people in the valley. The geographical locations are symbolic of Abram's values: Abram will not set foot in Sodom. His antipathy toward the people of Sodom relates to their description in the previous chapter: "Now the inhabitants of Sodom were wicked and sinners against the Lord" (Gen. 13:13). This implies that Abram does not reject alliances with Canaanite kings on principle, as illustrated by the fact that Abram does forge an alliance with Melchizedek, a just king with acceptable morals.[42]

Abram's refusal to connect with the king of Sodom might also be expressed by an analogical reading of the narrative alongside the story of Gideon (Judges 6–8). Various commentators note the many links between the stories,[43] some even arguing that the analogy suggests

41. Shamai Gelander ("Defus Sifruti VeHistorya," in *Haim M. I. Gevaryahu: Memorial Volume*, ed. J. Adler [Jerusalem, 1990], 48–56) suggests that the purpose of the scene is to show that although Abram received the honor of kings (when honored by Melchizedek), he was not blinded by this honor when facing the king of Sodom, and was willing to forgo significant riches.

42. Wenham (*Genesis 1–15*, 321–322) writes that Abram's attitude toward the king of Sodom (particularly his impertinent request) foreshadows the future of Sodom, in accordance with, "I shall curse those who curse you" (Gen. 12:3).

43. Among others, Emerton, "The Riddle of Genesis xiv"; Gilad Sasson and Jonathan Grossman, "On Implicit Biblical Analogies in Midrashim of the Sages," *Megadim* 46 (2007): 23–25; R. Yaakov Medan, *The Word Is Very Near – Bereshit* (Tel Aviv 2014), 80–84. John E. Harvey (*Retelling the Torah: The Deuternonmistic Historian's Use of Tetrateuchal Narratives* [JSOTSup 403: London, 2004], 38) shows that the analogy

that Abram's distance from the king of Sodom should be viewed as a rejection of monarchy, as Gideon rejected the kingship he was offered when he defeated the enemies of Israel.[44] This reading might clarify the meeting place in the "Valley of the King," as the Midrash comments in its colorful language: "How do we know that [Abraham] was made king? As it is written, 'To the Valley of Shaveh, which is the Valley of the King.' What is the meaning of 'Valley of Shaveh'? That they all agreed (*shehishvu*) and chopped down cedars and made a chair and enthroned him as their king."[45] This suggestion might be extreme, and there is certainly no explicit offer of kingship; however, the atmosphere of the story certainly supports the concept. In this narrative, Abram becomes an influential political figure and is regarded as such by the inhabitants of the land.[46]

Another interesting element in the conclusion of the story is the absence of Lot. After everything Abram went through to rescue his nephew, one would expect Lot to return to the household of his uncle. Instead, no emotional reunion is mentioned, and the reader only discovers inadvertently in a later story that Lot had in fact returned to Sodom. Instead of mentioning Lot, Abram ensures the just reward of his "replacements," Aner, Eshkol, and Mamre (Gen. 14:24). The final verse of the narrative mentions Abram's current allies; instead

---

between Abram and Gideon goes beyond just Gen. 14 and includes elements of the entire Abraham cycle. See also Nathaniel Helfgot, *Mikra and Meaning: Studies in Bible and Its Interpretation* (Jerusalem, 2012), 55–64.

44. Westermann (*Genesis 12–36: A Continental Commentary*, 202) asserts that Abram's rejection of the offer to become king is similar to Gideon's rejection of the kingship. However, McConville ("Abraham and Melhizedek: Horizons in Genesis 14," in *He Swore an Oath: Biblical Themes from Genesis 12–50*, ed. R. S. Hess, G. J. Wenham, and P. E. Satterthwaite [Carlisle, UK, 1994], 100–101) rejects this conclusion and suggests another context: Gideon is portrayed as a charismatic warrior acting on behalf of his nation and land, while Abram saves his nephew from captivity.
45. Numbers Rabba 15:14 (and parallels).
46. Perhaps this relates to *Ivri,* Hebrew, the unique term used in the narrative to describe Abram. For a broader discussion of various uses of the term, see Nico Adriaan van Uchelen, *Abraham De Hebreeër: Een literair en historisch-kritische studie naar aanleiding van Genesis 14:13* (Assen, 1964). He discusses genealogical aspects (pp. 5–26), geographical aspects (pp. 27–47), the integration of the term in our chapter (pp. 48–70), and the sociological significance of the term (pp. 71–105).

of the anticipated reunion with Lot, Abram's new friends emphasize his absence.

In light of these observations, we can return to the broader meaning of the story. As noted above, one of the dominant and consistent characteristics in the story is the absence of divine intervention. The literary void is filled with stories about Abram, who transforms into a military commander and a politician who associates with Canaanite kings and battles the kings of the east. Until this point Abram merited God's blessings; in this chapter he receives the blessings of Melchizedek.[47] Abram becomes part of the political map of ancient Canaan. He is no longer only a private person who has gained God's protection; he is an important public figure.

The details embedded in the story give the feeling of a historical chronicle. This idea is expressed through the style of the narrative in details such as the alphabetical list of kings and the conquered territories, the number of Abram's troops, and the details of the midnight rescue operation. The difference between the reality of the rescue operation (a nighttime action against one prisoner camp) and the terms in which it is described (as if Abram defeated the entire army and successfully chased them) wishes to portray Abram as a military commander who leads his troops to war. The purpose of this portrayal is to convey that Abram's inheritance of the land is not only a result of God's blessings, but is also due to his own application of wisdom and might in his involvement in local and world politics. On the moral plane, his merit is also expressed by his attitude toward the two kings: he rejects the company of those who are "wicked and sinners against the Lord," and accepts the companionship of those who recognize the Creator of heaven and earth.

This idea also sheds light on the emphasis of the possessions motif. The story ends with Abram's refusal to accept riches, which might have been linked to Abram's refusal to be associated with the values of an evil place, had the previous chapter not revealed that Abram was willing to receive riches from Egypt. We previously noted

47. Wenham (*Genesis 1–15*, 317) views the blessing as a fulfillment of God's promise to Abram: "I will bless those who bless you" (Gen. 12:3).

that the riches Abram received in Egypt were regarded as a fulfillment of God's blessings to Abram. Why can't the Sodomite riches be perceived in the same way?[48]

In the context of Abram's oath, he names God "Creator of heaven and earth." This borrowed title is also an explanation for Abram's refusal to receive possessions from the king of Sodom. Since Abram's mission is to acknowledge God and His possession of heaven and earth, accepting wealth from the king of Sodom, who would take credit for enriching Abram, would contradict his life's work.[49] Abram's statement conveys that becoming rich by the king of Sodom is an alternative to becoming rich by the hands of God. The difference between Egypt and Sodom is the way in which the riches were acquired: in Egypt, God intervened on Abram's behalf, and the "conflict" resulted in Abram becoming rich. Since God does not intervene in Abram's war against the kings, and the battle is won on a natural human plane, receiving riches as a result would not be perceived as connected to God's blessing, and instead might be attributed to the King of Sodom.[50]

Now we can examine the meaning of the narrative and its contribution to the story cycle. The unique design of the story indicates a unique purpose. In this narrative, Abram merits inheriting the land not because he was chosen to be blessed by God, but due to his conduct as an ambassador and an army general, forced to take action against

48. Regarding the legitimacy of Abram taking spoils from the battle he had won, researchers of the era agree that according to prevalent laws of war, the spoils belonged to Abram. See Yochanan Muffs, "Abraham the Noble Warrior: Patriarchal Politics and Laws of War in Ancient Israel," *JJS* 33 (1982): 86n1; Elgavish, "The Encounter of Abram and Melchizedek King of Salem," 502. (Regarding the custom of taking spoils in the Bible itself, see Roland de Vaux, *Ancient Israel: Its Life and Institutions*, trans. J. McHugh [London, 1965], 254–57).

49. This reading is reinforced by Nahmanides' position that "*koneh*," usually translated as "creator," does not actually denote "creator," but rather "owner of." According to this interpretation, Abram's emphasis is not on God as the creator, but rather as the owner of all land and property (see Leibowitz, *Studies in Genesis*, 95–96).

50. Moreover, Sodom is included in the borders of Canaan – the Promised Land. Thus, receiving assets from Sodom is covert approval of Abram's association with the city, as opposed to accumulating wealth in Egypt, which is not included in the promises to Abram.

kings and lead troops in battle. The story focuses on the description of the battle between the kings, thereby emphasizing Abram's entry into a true military arena, and how significant he has become in the political realm. The story lacks God's direct involvement, and the blessings of land and offspring. In this narrative, Abram proves that he is worthy of inheriting the land by natural actions and involvement in the political and military sphere. Abram's political breakthrough is achieved through a story of moral conquest – for the sake of rescuing his nephew, not in order to display his power and might. It should therefore not be surprising that in the next chapter – which is linked with this one – God will make a covenant with Abram, and promise him that he will inherit the Promised Land.

Looking to the Stars (Gen. 15)

Battle-torn, Abram returns in Genesis 15 to continue his spiritual journey. Our hero is changed, perhaps not in his essence – he is still the righteous, peace-loving man we have always known – but certainly in how others perceive him. The meek, trusting servant who followed blindly as God led him out of Haran returns to his camp as a powerful military general and shrewd diplomat. The rescue mission of Lot introduced Abram as a powerful military figure in the region and set a precedent of deference among regional leaders. Even in this valiant initiative, our hero acts out of compassion and a sense of duty. Upon his return to camp, Abram is visited by God in an unprecedented vision. The commanding imagery of the skyscape and the almost romantic ritualism of the covenant solidify God's endorsement of his chosen hero and Abram's reciprocal unwavering faith in his adopted Father.

The Return of the War Hero

Abram has now established himself as a major military player in the region. Abram's lingering emotional connection to his nephew is a recurring issue in the narrative, and here too it is unclear as to whether Abram should have ventured out on this mission to save his estranged kin. Certainly, it is worth mentioning that this battle is the only military initiative in the Bible connected with Abram, and its motivation and purpose is wholly consistent with Abram's character. He may have displayed his military acumen, but the driving factor behind Abram's actions in the previous chapter was compassion. We saw a new side to him, but at his core, Abram is still the virtuous, kind, and compassionate servant of God.

That being said, the detour to rescue Lot was neither divinely directed nor divinely assisted. Perhaps both Abram and God are acutely aware of this, for upon reconvening with God, Abram is immediately reassured: "Fear not." In light of the content of the upcoming blessings, one may assume that Abram's fear relates to the question of whether he will ever produce an heir. However, the text opening line, "After these things…," plainly correlates the adjoining accounts. This introduction gives clear context to Abram's fear; Abram could not have known how the great powers would react to his military action and the release of the prisoners.[1]

God takes it even further when He adds, "Your reward shall be very great." God's encouragement here should be viewed as a transitional passage, which relates to the previous narrative but prepares the ground for the tidings of Abram's heir, which is introduced in the following passage.[2] Not only does God approve of Abram's altruistic initiative to rescue his nephew, He assures our hero that he is still on a trajectory to become the father of a great nation by his own genetic line.

---

1. Among others, Wenham, *Genesis 1–15*, 327.
2. Gary A. Rendsburg ("Notes on Genesis XV," *VT* 42 [1992]: 266–268) suggests that the verb *magen*, shield, in "I am your shield," should be read with a double meaning, denoting both protection and contribution (as in the previous narrative, Gen. 14:20, as well as in Prov 4:9). This is a literary device known as "Janus parallelism" – protection is a reasonable reading based on the beginning of the sentence ("Fear not"), and contribution is reasonable based on the end of the sentence ("Your reward shall be very great"). If the entire chapter is one unit, Kiel might be correct in asserting that God's reassurance of Abram relates to the Covenant Between the Pieces as well, due to the difficult message of enslavement included therein (Kiel, *Daat Mikra: Genesis*, 397).

One Story or Two?

Genesis 15 can be read as either one or two literary units. In the first part of the chapter (vv. 1–6), Abram is promised a son, while in the second part (vv. 7–22), Abram participates in the Covenant Between the Pieces – the covenant of the land. Many commentators believe the two accounts are unrelated. Ḥizkuni, who reads the promise of a son and the promise of the inheritance of the land as two separate units, even claims that the promise of the inheritance of the land occurred prior to the promise of the son.[3] Others argue that the two motifs, the promise of a son and the inheritance of the Promised Land combine to create a unified, thematically consistent whole.[4]

The approach that views the two promises as separate – both in content and chronological context – is compelling. Three textual elements lend themselves toward the view that the two promises should be viewed as occurring in two separate events:

- The opening and closing statements in each promise seem to indicate that the two literary parts are separate. The first promise ends in verse 6 with the concluding declaration, "And because he put his trust in the Lord, He reckoned it to his merit." This certainly reads like a conclusion to the revelation. The following verse, the opening of the second promise, begins by introducing God to Abram: "He said to him, 'I am God who brought you out of Ur of the Chaldeans…'" Surely if this was a continuous dialogue, God would not be compelled to introduce Himself in the middle. It appears that the two promises were delivered at different times.
- There are apparent gaps in time throughout Genesis 15. First, Abram is shown the stars (Gen. 15:5), indicating that the

3. An extension of this claim is mentioned by R. Yaakov Medan. In his view, the covenant was made while Abraham was still in Haran (*The Word Is Very Near – Bereshit* [Tel Aviv, 2014], 94–96).
4. Moshe Anbar, "Abrahamic Convenant – Genesis 15," *Shnaton* 3 (1979): 35; 51; John Ha, *Genesis 15: A Theological Compendium of Pentateuchal History* (BZAW 181: Berlin and New York, 1989), 39. And see further in Ha, ibid., 33–38, for a survey of studies that view the chapter as one unit.

conversation takes place at night. As the text transitions to the Covenant Between the Pieces, the scene describes, "The sun was about to set" (v. 12), and later, "When the sun set and it was very dark" (v. 17). The story cannot be continuous if it begins at night (when the stars are out) and continues at sundown; there is no indication that an entire day has passed between the first and second definition of time.[5] The only explanation is that the two episodes actually take place on entirely different evenings.

- The content of the two promises is presented separately. In the first promise, Abram is promised an heir; in the second, he is promised the land. Although in the future these two tidings are often linked,[6] in this context, each message is portrayed independently of the other, which reinforces the contention that the promises are separate.[7]

Despite these compelling literary indications that the promise of the offspring and the Covenant Between the Pieces represent two separate conversations, there are a number of other parameters that point to a unified story here, or at the very least a strong link between the two

5. This is the evidence offered by the majority of scholars who separate the story into two units; however, the story can still be read as continuous regardless: Abram was told about the multitudes of offspring he is going to father one night, and the following day he received another prophecy regarding the covenant of the land; he proceeded to prepare for the covenant that entire day, and at sunset the flaming torch passed between the pieces, and only then Abram heard the contents of the covenant (see Kiel, *Daat Mikra: Genesis,* 425). In light of this difficulty, Scott B. Noegel suggests that God had taken Abram outside to count the stars during the day, and the statement "If you are able to count them" is rhetorical. He believes that this is symbolic of Abram's test, since he is expected to have faith "blindly." This indeed, should be "reckoned to his merit" (Noegel, "A Crux and a Taunt: Night-Time Then Sunset in Genesis 15," in *The World of Genesis: Persons, Places, Perspectives,* ed. P. R. Davies and D. J. A. Clines, 128–135 [JSOTSup 257: Sheffield, 1998]).
6. See Gen. 13:16.
7. According to von Rad (*Genesis,* 177), the portrayal of Abram's character can be listed among the narrative materials that separate the two units. In the first unit Abram believes God's promise (v. 6), while the second unit opens with Abram doubting God's promise (v. 8). However, von Rad fails to note Abram's doubts in the first unit.

episodes. In order to better understand the link between the two promises, let us examine each one in turn, and then explore their connection.

Look to the Stars

In order to view the promises as a unified text, we must first understand that verses 1–6 are not a verbatim conversation. The words, "Abram said," are repeated several times throughout the story. Ḥizkuni interprets this repetition as portraying the intermittent nature of Abram's prayers – he would pray for a son, then cease for a time, then begin again.[8] More recently, Yitzhak Lev-Ran understands the repetition as an escalating expression of Abram's internal state: At first, Abram only expressed his desire internally – according to Lev-Ran, this expression was harsher, more demanding. It was only later, in the second repetition of "Abram says," that he was able to put his supplication into words.[9] I prefer to read the repetition somewhat differently. Abram's distress at not producing an heir was ongoing; it was an incessant plea. Imagine Abram and Sarai, month after month, year after year, discovering that her barrenness persists. Abram's concern about lack of offspring was a desperate prayer that he voiced at every moment he could find. The repetition, "Abram said," paints a literary picture of a man waiting for years for a response that does not come.[10] Abram prays and prays, and for years God does not respond. There is no answer, no hope, until the night when God finally asks Abram to leave his tent and gaze up at the stars.

Verses 2 and 3 describe Abram's perpetual state of unanswered prayer. That state is not confined to a specific time or place, and so these verses must be read as a description of an ongoing situation, not as the introduction of the conversation. The actual revelation of the two promises begins in verse 4, when God suddenly answers Abram's

---

8. Ḥizkuni on Gen. 15:3.
9. Lev-Ran, *Narrative Modes for Presenting Complexity of Inner Life of Biblical Characters* (PhD. diss., Bar Ilan University, 2009), 51–53.
10. Meir Shiloach, "And He Said … and He Said," in *Sefer Korngreen,* ed. A. Weiser and B. Z. Luria (Tel Aviv, 1964), 251–252. For a critique of Shiloach's analysis see Samuel A. Meier, *Speaking of Speaking: Marking Direct Discourse in the Hebrew Bible* (VTSup 46: Leiden, NY, and Köln: E. J. Brill, 1992), 68–91.

desperate cry. "Behold,[11] the word of the Lord came to him in reply." The word "behold" evokes a feeling of surprise. After all this time, years of Abram's supplication for a son going unanswered, suddenly, on this night, God responds.[12]

If we read the conversation this way, verse 6 is not only a closing statement, but a description of Abram's mental state at the moment when God finally acknowledges his plea. For years he prayed for a son and received no response. Suddenly, God appears to him to relay the promise of the land. But for Abram, any promise from God is meaningless if he has no heir. So, God finally reassures Abram – you will have a son, you do not need to distress over that doubt any more. It will happen. In verse 6 we can almost hear Abram's emotional release that this concern about the unknown has been addressed. Abram releases a grateful sigh of relief, he "put his trust in the Lord" that He would fulfill this promise, and now he is emotionally open to hearing the remainder of the revelation, the promise of the land which was the purpose of this conversation to begin with.

God reassures Abram by taking him outside and having him look at the stars. The act of moving from one realm to the next could be interpreted as either physical or symbolic. The Midrash cites three opinions, the common denominator between them that they represent a change of perspective.[13] Whether God literally pulled Abraham outside of the earthly realm, or if He simply indicated that the stars told a story beyond their astrology, Abraham's exit from the tent is deeply symbolic. The symbolism is not abstract (as in the case of comparing the multitude of offspring to the dust of the earth in Gen. 13:16), but tangible, as Abram is expected to take physical action by *going* outside and *looking* at the stars. Abram undergoes a process in this symbolic act. Going outside the tent represents escaping conventional boundaries. The stars are the unreachable reality beyond concrete everyday life. God's initial response to Abram's doubts is to demand that he expand the boundaries of his belief: Abram must dare to look beyond his reality

11. NJPS omits the word "*Hinei*," "Behold."
12. See I Kings 19:9.
13. Genesis Rabba 44:12.

and aim high, to the stars. Abram's faith is not to be taken for granted. His current reality does not support the fulfillment of God's blessings, and in order to believe, Abram needs to look at the stars.[14]

The Hero's Promised Land

Structurally, the covenant text is directly related to the previous star promise, through a number of repeating words.

The second part of the chapter begins with God's promise to Abram that he will inherit the land: "Then He said to him, I am the Lord who brought you out from Ur of the Chaldeans to give this land to you as an inheritance" (Gen. 15:7). Three verbs mentioned in God's words link the promise to the previous verses and the promise of offspring:

Promise of Offspring	Promise of Land
That one shall not be your heir; none but your very own issue (*asher yetzei mime'ekha*) shall be your heir (Gen. 15:4)	I am the Lord who brought you out (*asher hotzitikha*) from Ur of the Chaldeans
He took him outside (*vayotzei oto haḥutza*)	
What can You give me (*ma titen li*) (v. 2)	to give this land to you (*latet lakh*)
You have granted me no offspring (*li lo natata zera*) (v. 3)	
My steward will be my heir (*yoresh oti*) (v. 3)	as an inheritance (*lerishta*)
That one shall not be your inheritor (*yirashekha*); none but your very own issue shall be your inheritor (*yirashekha*) (v. 4)	

14. Wenham suggested that Abram's faith is mentioned here "because the word of promise had come to him in a crisis situation following the battle of ch. 14" (Wenham, *Genesis 1–15*, 329). I will demonstrate below that the test of Abram's faith becomes the central axis of the entire chapter, beyond the specific scope of Abram's reaction to the battle. See also Matthias Köckert, "'Glaube' und 'Gerechtigkeit' in Gen 15,6," *Zeitschrift für Theologie und Kirche* 109 (2012): 415–444.

In addition to the semantic link between the two promises, the repetition of the verb *yatza* ("go out") portrays the unique relationship between God and Abram. In the promise of the stars, the verb is used to describe the heir, *asher yetzei mime'ekha* (lit. "the one who will *come out* of you"), while in the second promise, God takes Abram "out" of Ur. The comparison is meant to portray God as Abram's adoptive father. Abram was instructed to abandon the house of his own father; the depiction of God as one who "took Abram out," in juxtaposition with the previous promise of an heir, illustrates that leaving Ur was Abram's rebirth to his new father. This scene, in particular, hints at Abram's adoption by God, as some commentators have noted. Abram's complaint that his servant Eliezer will inherit him refers to the ancient social practices: if a man dies without children, his servant is considered his adopted son and heir.[15] While Abram is lamenting that his only son is his "adopted" servant, God hints to him that he, himself, has been "adopted" by God.

God begins His tidings of the land with Abram's departure from his homeland: "I am the Lord who brought you out from Ur of the Chaldeans to assign this land to you as an inheritance." Abram's response is odd. He rejects the promise and demands proof and reassurance that his inheritance of the land will indeed come to pass. Abram's request for concrete commitment, "How shall I know that I am to possess it?" has been interpreted in various ways,[16] but the simple meaning is that Abram is seeking a sign that this destiny will come true.[17] In this context there is no mention of Abram's offspring, and God seems to be implying that Abram's inheritance of the land is imminent. Abram understands that God's promise is not a gift (if it were, Abram would have no choice but to accept it graciously). The Promised Land is portrayed as a replacement

15. As reflected in the Nuzi tablets. See, for example, Parrot, *Abraham and His Times*, 103.
16. See Yehuda Elitzur, "Berit Bein HaBetarim," *Hagut BaMikra* 4 (1984): 34–45. This form of the word, *bama* ("how"), appears only two other times in the Pentateuch. The first is Ex. 22:26's "*bameh yishkav,*" "In what else shall he sleep?" and in Ex. 33:16's "*uvameh yivada…,*" "For how shall it be known that Your people have gained Your favor?"
17. Franz Delitzsch states (*Neuer Commentar über die Genesis* [Leipzig, 1887], 276), "The question is not an expression of doubt, but rather a request." Westermann compares Abram's request to that of Abram's servant, who asks for a sign from God (Westermann, *Genesis 12–36: A Continental Commentary*, 225).

for Abram's place of birth. The inheritance of the land is not a reward or a simple gift, but a destiny. The purpose of Abram's journey is the inheritance of the new land to which he is led. Later, we will discover that the impression that Abram will inherit the land is intentionally misleading; the deceptive language will later play a role in introducing one of the essential messages of the narrative.[18]

The Renewal of Vows

The act of the Covenant Between the Pieces is perplexing from start to finish. At first glance, we may view it as another sacrifice, as the forefathers were wont to perform throughout the Bible, and as Abram himself performed at each step along the way in his heroic journey. The Midrash links the sacrificial animals in the covenant to those found in other sacrificial offerings throughout the biblical text: three goats, one to represent the Pilgrimage sacrifice, one to represent the sacrifice of the new month, and one to represent the individual's sacrifice, and so forth.[19]

However, the major components of a traditional sacrifice are missing from this ceremony – there is no altar, nothing in the passage is sacrificed, and Abram does not use the blood ritualistically. The fire of revelation does not eat the animals, but rather passes between them.[20] Additionally, the text does not describe Abram's action as SH-Ḥ-T, slaughter, as in the case of all biblical sacrifices, but rather as B-T-R, cutting, in Genesis 15:10.

Two other seemingly minor details come together to weave a very different tapestry of this covenant, which begins to emerge as

18. I do not identify with Westermann's assertion that the omission of Abram's offspring is related to Abram's portrayal as a representative of the entire nation (Westermann, *Genesis 12–36: A Continental Commentary*, 224). Abram does act on behalf of the future nation in the context of the Covenant Between the Pieces. However, the omission of his offspring from the formulation of the promise is conspicuous, and therefore plays a literary role in the reading process.
19. Genesis Rabba 44:14.
20. Kiel (*Daat Mikra*, 424) attempts to overcome this difficulty: "If you should wonder what happened to the 'pieces'…some commentators assume that these were burned in God's fire, as we have seen in the inauguration of the altar (Lev. 9:24) and Solomon's Temple (II Chr. 7:1)." The problem with this reading is that it adds elements that are in no way indicated in the text.

a bonding ceremony that is unique in all biblical narrative. First, the gory placement of bloodied pieces of cut animals is described using a surprising phrase. The Hebrew is worded in an almost romantic way, literally reading, "He laid the half of each man (*ish*) toward (*likrat*) its companion (*re'ehu*)," usually meaning, the pieces of each animal were placed across from each other.

The word *likrat*, which denotes "toward/against," implies two opposing biblical connotations: one of friendship and longing ("Joseph ordered his chariot and went toward [*likrat*] Goshen to meet his father Israel" – Gen. 46:29), and the other relating to violence and war ("Sihon gathered all his people and went out toward [*likrat*] Israel ... and engaged Israel in battle" – Num. 21:23). There is no doubt that the connotation of the verse in Genesis is positive, as the sentence ends, "toward *its companion.*"

The literary associations of these chosen words connote closeness and fondness, the feeling of Joseph going toward his father, or Moses meeting with his brother Aaron (Ex. 4:27), or the nation going toward God in Sinai (Ex. 19:17). The choice of words paints a poetic picture of intimacy and intense destiny; this symbolic emotive description does not seem to match the physical reality of what is taking place.

Another noteworthy detail is the "birds of prey" that come upon the carcasses. The birds do not seem to contribute to the development of the plot in any way. It appears that the attack of the birds on the carcasses is purely symbolic. Some commentators perceive the birds of prey as a warning of the punishment that would befall one who might violate the covenant.[21] However, the overarching context of the covenant may suggest an alternate symbolism, as I will describe below.

It is clear that the Covenant Between the Pieces is no standard biblical sacrifice – in fact, it is not a sacrifice at all, but a ceremonial commitment. Commitments in the ancient world included two components: speech and action. The symbolic action varies (such as lifting a hand, placing a hand on the other's thigh, and so on), and is accompanied by words of commitment,

21. E.g., Moshe Weinfeld, "The Covenant of Grant in the Old Testament and in the Ancient Near East," *JAOS* 90 (1970): 198n132; Anbar, "Abrahamic Convenant – Genesis 15," 44. Compare with Jer. 34:19–10.

often with an oath to maintain one's commitment.[22] The Covenant Between the Pieces includes both components: the passage of a smoking oven and flaming torch between the pieces is the symbolic act upon which the covenant is created,[23] and God's words to Abram declare His commitment to Abram's offspring regarding their inheritance of the land.

The Poetic Circle

The verses describing the covenant (Gen. 15:12–16) are designed in a chiastic structure:

A: *As the sun was about to set*, a deep sleep fell upon Abram, and a great dark dread descended upon him.

> **B**: And He said to Abram, "Know well that your offspring shall be strangers in a land not theirs and they shall be enslaved and oppressed for four hundred years. But I will execute judgment on the nation they shall serve, and in the end they shall go free with great wealth.
>
> > **C**: As for you, you shall go to your fathers in peace; you shall be buried at a ripe old age.
>
> **B'**: And they shall return here in the fourth generation, for the iniquity of the Amorites is not yet complete."

A': *When the sun set* and it was very dark, there appeared a smoking oven, and a flaming torch that passed between those pieces.

The setting sun (A and A') frames the chiasm of the covenant. Before the sun sets, a great dark dread falls upon Abram. After the sun has set, a smoking oven and a flaming torch appear and pass between the pieces. The descent of nightfall sets the scene for the revelation of exile. Darkness

22. Elia S. Hartom, "Covenant," *Entziklopedya Mikra'it* 2:350.

23. The etymology of the word "*brit*" is vague (Gordon J. McConville, "ברית," *NIDOTTE* 1:747). Noth suggests, based on texts found in Mari, that the word is derived from the Akkadian word *birit* ("between"), connoting the mutual commitment between two parties (Martin Noth, "Old Testament Covenant-Making in the Light of a Text from Mari," in *The Laws in the Pentateuch and Other Essays* [Edinburgh, 1966], 108–117). If this is correct, the Covenant Between the Pieces visually represents the etymological meaning of the word.

and nighttime are recurrent representation of exile (see especially Jacob's exile to Haran – Gen. 28:11 and 32:32). Therefore, after "the sun set and it was very dark," the timing and backdrop are ripe for Abram to hear about the future exile of his descendants.[24]

The structure gives Abram and God equal roles in order to emphasize the covenant aspect, but Abram is still passive, reminding the reader that although this may be a mutual commitment, in truth it is a divinely initiated commitment, and Abram and God are not truly equal partners.

Element B' continues the story sequence of element B: the enslavement of Abram's offspring in a foreign land, and their exodus with great wealth (B), followed by the return of Abram's offspring to Canaan (B'). The two pieces are structurally linked by the repetition of the number four – "four hundred years" and "fourth generation," and by God's attitude toward the offending nations – judgment of the enslaving nation (B) and of the Amorite when their sin is complete (B').[25] The numeric repetition reinforces the symbolic nature of the covenant. Repeated number four represents the end of enslavement, and the number three repeats itself in the preparation of the ritual, in reference to the heifer, the she-goat, and the ram (Gen. 15:9). The three animals represent the three enslaved generations, cut in half and separated. The young bird and turtledove stand apart; they are not cut, and their number remains undefined. The turtledove and young bird represent the generation that will leave the enslaving country and return to the land. Birds often symbolize freedom in the biblical narrative (for example, Noah's dove in Gen. 8:13, and the leper's bird in Lev. 14:7).[26] Three generations

---

24. See, e.g., Ralph L. Smith's comment on Zech. 1:8: "The night often symbolizes a time of suffering and distress, while the dawn can refer to the time of God's deliverance (Ps. 30:5, 46:5). In the first vision, Zechariah appears as a watchman through the long night of distress and is informed of the first signs of God's return to His people and land" (Smith, *Micah-Malachi* [WBC: Dallas, Texas, 1998], 189).
25. The "fourth generation" might be viewed as the general biblical principle of postponing punishment for four generations (Ex. 20:5 and 34:7; Num. 14:18; I Kings 10:30). According to this reading, "four generations" might have a dual meaning: a completion of exile on the part of the nation, and a completion of the sin on the part of the Amorite (cf. Mathews, *Genesis*, 175).
26. While the bird symbolizes freedom, the dove symbolizes a return home, to one's origins. See Is. 60:8, where doves symbolize the return of the nation to Israel. See also Cassuto,

represented by the cut animals signify God's unfulfilled commitment to Abram, while the dove and bird represent the fourth generation, which will return to Canaan and realize God's promise to Abram.[27]

This leaves element C interrupting the logical sequence of the description of the exile, and emerging as a central axis. God suddenly stops describing the future of Abram's offspring, and turns to focus on his personal future: "You shall go to your fathers in peace; you shall be buried at a ripe old age" (Gen. 15:15). Earlier, Abram had asked for assurance that he would indeed inherit the land; God's earlier promise had portrayed the inheritance of the land to be imminent. In this statement (C), the message of Abram's peaceful aging and death is the answer to Abram's inquiry: the inheritance of the land will not occur in his lifetime,[28] or in the lifetime of his children. The formulation of Abram's question, "How shall I know that I am to possess it?" assumes that Abram will inherit the land himself; God clarifies here that the inheritance of the land is a long-term goal, and will only come to pass after the return of the fourth generation, long after Abram is gone.

With this new perspective in mind, we can now summarize the purpose of the ritual and the covenant. The animals are not sacrificial. Instead, they are symbolic of the commitment of Abram and God to each other. The two parts of the cut animal are personified ("He laid the half of each toward its companion"), indicating the symbolic significance of the act: the two parts of the animal symbolize the two beings that are united in covenant. These are the companions who go "toward" each other. God passes between the parts to symbolize the unification of the severed parts, and to close the gap between them.[29]

A Commentary on the Book of Genesis: From Noah to Abraham, 74–75; Jonathan Grossman, *Creation: The Story of Beginnings* (Jerusalem: Maggid Books, 2019).

27. Cf. Kiel, *Daat Mikra: Genesis*, 425.
28. The statements, "You shall go to your fathers in peace. You shall be buried at a ripe old age," are linked with, "You will send my white head down to Sheol in grief" (Gen. 42:38, 44:29, 31). See Speiser, *Genesis*, 113.
29. I partially agree with Gordon J. Wenham ("The Symbolism of the Animal Rite in Genesis 15," *JSOT* 22 [1982]: 134–137), and Mathews (*Genesis*, 172–173), who view the cut animals as a representation of the suffering of Abram's offspring in Egypt. Mathews notes that the animals do not serve a sacrificial purpose; instead they

The birds of prey that threaten to devour the animals symbolize those who would harm the nation by enslaving them for four hundred years, and threaten to separate them from Lord and land. The enslaving nation attacks both the offspring of Abram and God, by threatening the covenant between them. Abram banishes the birds, thereby protecting his offspring and defending the covenant.[30]

One Story or Two?

Should the two parts of this chapter be viewed as one or two stories? We explored the reasons to separate the narratives above, but there remain several compelling literary parameters to indicate this might be two parts of one whole story.

- The link between the two narratives is apparent in the opening verse to the second message: "Then *He said to him,* I am the Lord who brought you out from Ur of the Chaldeans" (Gen. 15:7). The style indicates a new story; however, it also indicates literary continuity, since the name of our protagonist, Abram, is absent, the text simply referring to "him." Clearly, the reader is supposed to know to whom the verse is referring based on the previous paragraph.[31]
- The similar structure of the two stories suggests a deep link between them:[32]

---

represent the parties in the covenant. I believe God is also symbolized in the animals. The birds of prey were deciphered by Mathews as above.

30. The birds of prey may have been interpreted differently in the Septuagint, which reads "*vayeshev itam Avram,*" "Abram sat with them," instead of "*vayashev otam Avram,*" "Abram returned them." According to this interpretation, Abram does not oppose the birds of prey.
31. Van Seters, *Abraham in History and Tradition,* 257.
32. Similarly, Van Seters, ibid., 260–261 (following Lohfink); Sarna, *Understanding Genesis,* 120–121; Alexander, "A Literary Analysis of the Abraham Narrative in Genesis," 161–164; George W. Coats, *Genesis* (FOTL: Grand Rapids, MI, 1983), 123–24; Wenham, *Genesis 1–15,* 325; Westermann, *Genesis 12–36: A Continental Commentary,* 216; Ha, *Genesis 15: A Theological Compendium of Pentateuchal History,* 39–62; Horst Seebass, *Genesis II. Vätergeschichte I (11, 27–22, 24)* (Neukirchen-Vluyn, 1997), 66; Konrad Schmid, *Erzväter und Exodus: Untersuchungen zur doppelten Begründung der*

Promise of Offspring	The Promised Land
(1) God's promise to Abram	(7) God's promise to Abram
(2–3) Abram's misgivings	(8) Abram's misgivings
(4–5) God's response: the promise of offspring. A reinforcement of the promise with a symbolic act (viewing the stars)	(9) God's response: the promise of land. A reinforcement of the promise with a covenant, which includes a symbolic act (passing between the pieces of animals)
(6) Narrative's conclusion: Abram put his trust in the Lord	(18–21) Narrative's conclusion: God made a covenant with Abram

This similarity cannot be viewed as incidental. Throughout the Abraham cycle, Abram rarely expressing misgivings toward God's promise. Yet here, two consecutive promises elicit a similar response from Abram, followed by a symbolic act. The similarity in plot development also indicates a deep connection between the two tidings.

- There is semantic unity. Key words, or words that share a semantic field, often create uniformity within a literary unit.[33] In both parts of the chapter, Abram uses the unusual name "Lord God" in reference to God (verses 2 and 8). This double appellation only appears twice more in the Pentateuch, both times in Deuteronomy (3:24, 9:26). The appearance of such a rare expression in both units creates a deep semantic correlation between the two parts of the narrative. Moreover, the rare name fills the same semantic function; in both places it is integrated with Abram's doubts regarding the promise he had received: "Lord God, what can You give me, seeing that I shall die childless" (Gen. 15:2); "Lord God, how shall I know that I am to possess

Ursprünge Israels innerhalb der Geschichtsbücher des Alten Testaments (Neukirchen-Vluyn, 1999), 175–176; Thomas C. Römer, "Recherches actuelles sur le cycle d'Abraham," in *Studies in the Book of Genesis: Literature, Redaction and History*, ed. A. Wénin (Leuven, 2001), 200; Mathews, *Genesis*, 161–165. See also Cotter, *Genesis*, 98; Ruth Fidler, "Genesis XV: Sequence and Unity," *VT* 57 (2007): 162–180.

33. See Polak, *Biblical Narrative Aspects of Art and Design*, 90–106.

it" (v. 8).[34] As I already noted at the beginning of the discussion, additional words that link the two parts include, among others, the recurring root Y-R-SH ("inherit"), which appears three times in verses 3–4 and twice in verses 7–8, and the root Y-TZ-A ("go out"), which appears twice in verses 4–5 and once in verse 7. The root Z-R-A ("seed" or "offspring") also recurs in both messages; in the first part as the essence of the tiding, and in the second part, "To your offspring I assign this land" (v. 18).[35]

- In addition to the literary links between the two parts of chapter 15, the entire chapter seems to be related to chapter 14.[36] The chapter's opening, "After these things," already creates a sense of continuity between this story and the preceding passage, but, as mentioned, various commentators have noted a variety of linguistic connections between the two chapters that bind them together. As these connections are evident throughout chapter 15, it seems that the chapter is a single story in dialogue with chapter 14.[37]

Those who view the chapter as one story need to reconcile the need for the ending in verse 6 ("And He reckoned it to his merit") and the new opening in verse 7 ("And He said to him"), as well as the discrepancy between time definitions. Conversely, the position that views the two

34. For various interpretive responses to Abraham's character design in these verses, see: Hayyim Angel, "Learning Faith from the Text, or Text from Faith: The Challenges of Teaching (and Learning) the Avraham Narrative and Commentary," in *Wisdom From All My Teachers*, ed. Jeffrey Saks and Susan Handelman (Jerusalem and New York 2003), 196–201.
35. Rolf Rendtorff, *Das Uberlieferungsgeschichtliche Problem des Pentateuch* (BZAW 147: Berlin and New York, 1977), 75, 79.
36. Regarding these links, see Sarna, *Understanding Genesis*, 121–122; Alexander, "A Literary Analysis of the Abraham Narrative in Genesis," 43–44; André Caquot, "L'alliance avec Abram (Genèse 15)," *Semitica* 12 (1962): 66 (who views ch. 15 as an interpretation of ch. 14); Schmid, *Erzväter und Exodus*, 176–177; Römer, "Recherches actuelles sur le cycle d'Abraham," 205–206; Yehuda Elitzur, "Key Words as Indicators of Hidden Meaning in Biblical Passages and the Question of *MiMoḥorat HaShabbat*," *Megadim* 38 (2003): 34–35.
37. Wenham, *Genesis 1–15*, 325.

parts as two separate units is faced with the issues we raised previously. Each position relies on the proofs it provides.[38]

The lack of ability to reach a satisfactory conclusion as to whether the narrative is one literary unit or two stems not from lack of evidence, but rather from contradictory evidence. The ambivalent delineation of units stems from the intentional design of the chapter, which should be simultaneously viewed as two separate units and as one cohesive story. The complex demarcation may be viewed in three spheres (which do not negate one another):

- God's revelations throughout the story cycle include two components: the assurance of offspring and the promise of land. Genesis 15 presents the reader with an overview of both promises: Abram will have multitudes of offspring, like the stars in the sky, and eventually they will inherit the land.[39] The two tidings are joined together in chapter 15, thereby blurring the boundaries of the chapter. As a result, the reader is exposed to one unit that includes two promises – offspring and land.
- The prayer of the Levites in Nehemiah 9 is the first source that relates to Genesis 15 as one unit. This context might indicate the value of combining the two revelations.[40] The Levites say: "You are the Lord God, who chose Abram, who brought him out of Ur of the Chaldeans and changed his name to Abraham. Finding his heart true to You, You made a covenant with him to give the land of the Canaanite, the Hittite, the Amorite, the Perizzite, the

38. The two interpretations lead to different modes of discussion on the chapter. Viewing the stories as one unit raises the discrepancy between Abram's faith in God ("He put his trust in the Lord") and his later questioning, "How shall I know" (Wenham, *Genesis 1–15*, 331; Wenham suggests that Abram's statement is not a question, but a request for a sign [similar to Nahmanides' interpretation]). In contrast, if the two stories are separate units, Abram's faith and questioning are unrelated and do not contradict one another (Paul R. Williamson, *Abraham, Israel and the Nations: The Patriarchal Promise and Its Covenantal Development in Genesis* [JSOTSup 315: Sheffield, 2001], 98).
39. Similarly, Anbar writes ("Abrahamic Convenant – Genesis 15," 35), "The purpose of adjoining them... was to unite three promises into one festive context: the promise of a son, the promise of multitudes of offspring, and the promise of the land."
40. Cf. ibid., 40–41.

Jebusite, and the Girgashite – to give it to his descendants. And You kept Your word, for You are righteous" (Neh. 9:7–8). The expressions embedded in this prayer are based on Genesis 15:[41]

Genesis 15	**Nehemiah 9**
I am the Lord who *brought you out from Ur of the Chaldeans* (Gen. 15:7)	*You are the Lord* God, who chose Abram, who *brought him out of Ur of the Chaldeans* (Neh. 9:7)
And because *he put his trust in the Lord…* (15:6)	*Finding his heart true to You* (Neh. 9:8)
On that day the Lord made a covenant with Abram, saying, "To your offspring I assign this land" (15:8)	You made a covenant with him to give the land of the Canaanite… (Neh. 9:8)
He reckoned it to his merit (*tzedaka*) (15:6)	And You kept Your word, for You are righteous (*tzaddik*) (Neh. 9:8)

The prayer is designed in a way that defines the correlation between the two parts of the chapter: "Finding his heart true to You, You made a covenant with him." In other words, in the first part of the chapter Abram withstands the test of faith in God's yet-unfulfilled promises, and as a reward for his faith, God makes a covenant with him regarding the land, which will be inherited by his offspring. Gunkel writes similarly: "The fact that this extremely impressive sign of divine grace is only given now, when Abraham's faith has been proven, may be well understood as a religious profundity. The sign that strengthens faith is not given to the unbeliever or the doubter, but to the believer."[42] Based on this depiction, the two parts of the chapter should be viewed as

41. See Mark J. Boda, *Praying the Tradition: The Origin and Use of Tradition in Nehemiah 9* (Berlin, 1999), 101–111 (and discussion there of various positions). Joseph Blenkinsopp (*Ezra-Nehemiah* [OTL: Philadelphia, 1988], 303–304) correctly notes that the prayer in Nehemiah is based both on the Covenant of Circumcision and the Covenant Between the Pieces, and that this fact should be considered in the context of the discussion regarding the time of authorship of Abraham's covenants.
42. Gunkel, *Genesis – Translated and Interpreted*, 179–180. Compare with Köckert, "'Glaube' und 'Gerechtigkeit' in Gen 15,6."

a test of Abram's faith and reward for his devotion. Gunkel views the two units as separate, but since they correlate with each other in this way, they were written as one continuous story.

- Besides these aspects, it seems that the two sections of the chapter are linked through the unique message emphasized in these revelations. Unlike the atmosphere that accompanies God's blessings to Abraham throughout the narrative cycle, the two revelations of chapter 15 express the hardships Abram faces; the emotional and conceptual ordeals of his situation. These revelations implicitly demand Abram's patience and endurance because these blessings will only be fulfilled in the distant future. In the first promise, the blessing of an heir, this emerges from Abram's double prayer. As discussed, the design of Abram's complaint and God's reaction show that Abram regularly appeals to God, expressing his fears and doubts. This design explores the depth of his anguish and misery; the emotional and spiritual trials of his everyday life. Despite all this, it is still stated that "he put his trust in the Lord." This is the fundamental theme of this chapter: not the promise and blessing itself, but Abram's unwavering faith in God despite his harsh reality. This is also the essence of the covenant of this chapter – not the promise of the land, but the postponement of the promise's fulfillment for four hundred years. In this context as well, Abram and his seed must show extraordinary patience before they will be granted dominion over the land; the covenant demands their undying faith and perseverance.

Perhaps this is the reason for the two promises' juxtaposition. Each section relates a different story, but they pose a common challenge: belief in both promises, despite the deferment of their fulfillment. The tidings of seed (in the chapter's first half) and the tidings of the land (in the second) both demand Abram's far-seeing, undying faith. In this sense, Sarai's barren state (and perhaps Rebecca's and Rachel's as well) reflects the land's yearning for its children's return. The womb is a metaphor for the earth, as reflected, for example, in Isaiah's prophecy (Is. 54:1–3):

> Shout, O barren one, You who bore no child! Shout aloud for joy, you who did not travail! For the children of the wife forlorn shall outnumber those of the espoused – said the Lord. Enlarge the site of your tent, extend the size of your dwelling, do not stint! Lengthen the ropes, and drive the pegs firm. For you shall spread out to the right and the left. Your offspring shall dispossess nations, and shall people the desolate towns.

The chapter of the Covenant Between the Pieces discloses, for the first time, the dark world of exile; the travails of separation and severance; the yearning of the believer. Abram's faith that the promise will be fulfilled – even if it tarries – becomes a paragon for the undying faith demanded of his descendants.

Hagar's Flight (Gen. 16)

Ishmael is well known as the brother-rival of Isaac, and the story of his birth is rife with domestic discord. The story of Ishmael's birth embodies the complex family dynamic in Abram and Sarai's home. Although Ishmael did not inherit his father's legacy, the story of his birth is described in extraordinary detail, delving into the inner worlds of each of the characters involved. The theme of freedom and slavery weaves its way through the text, in Abram and Sarai's child-rearing decisions, in Hagar's responses to Sarai, her response later on to the angel that approaches her, in the story of how Ishmael is born, and the prophecy of how he will live out his life.

Hagar's escape from Sarai's home is not a story of jealous women, or a tale of the complexity of having multiple wives, but an origin story that sets the tone for Ishmael's entire life. The "wild ass of a man" was born into slavery, but through his mother's sacrifice becomes free, and a formidable rival to his half-brother. Hagar and Ishmael's story is not only significant to their characters' plotlines. This episode demonstrates the compassion of the God of Abraham, a trait which Abram will be expected to exemplify as he grows into his leadership role. The dynamic between Abram, Sarai, and Hagar is a central catalyst to the progression of the story. In this complex situation, God's messengers step in and provide Abram and Sarai with an important model for behavior that sets the tone for the generations.

In Genesis 15, Abram was promised a son and an heir by God. This is the natural continuation of Abram's heroic journey, and gives the reader a sense that he is advancing in fulfilling his destiny as the father of a nation. As this story unfolds in Genesis 16, however, God's promise fades to the background, and the focus turns to the human initiative as it plays out in the dynamic between Abram, Sarai, and Hagar. The development of the story is deeply correlated with the way the text relates to each of these characters. Since this is a clear continuation of the story of Sarai and Abram's genetic line, we would expect the text to discount the plight of the maidservant, and rationalize Sarai's poor behavior toward her. Surprisingly, there are points which arise from the narrative that indicate the text's apparent harsh judgment of Sarai's actions, and as the story progresses, it becomes clear that its main protagonist is, in fact, Hagar. As the story unfolds, the roles of the characters shift, as they interact with each other and undergo changes within themselves. One moment, Sarai is dominant, the next it is Hagar who is playing the lead. Abram, for his part, seems to remain passive for much of the plot, until the very end, when he bestows a name upon his newborn son – an act which brings the entire narrative full circle.

Domination and Envy

The relationship between Sarai and her maidservant, Hagar, is fraught. Hagar begins her service in the house of Abram as a simple handmaid, a common fixture in ancient domestic life. It is likely that Hagar was one of the handmaids gifted to Abram in Egypt following Sarai's kidnapping by Pharaoh. She soon finds herself an unwitting tool in the formation of her masters' legacy, and – perhaps accidentally, perhaps not – driving a stake in the relationship between Abram and Sarai.

Sarai's distress at being barren drives her to a creative solution – the use of Hagar as a surrogate. This suggestion is first posited in verse 1: "Sarai, Abram's wife, had borne him no children. She had an Egyptian maidservant whose name was Hagar" (Gen. 16:1). Hagar's nationality here may seem like an irrelevant detail. Why should the reader care that Hagar is Egyptian? The mention of Egypt here is poignant. As we saw earlier in the story of Lot, Egypt is symbol of fertility and bounty, an allusion that will recur throughout the book of Genesis. Later in this story, we see that Hagar runs in the direction of Egypt to seek refuge when she escapes Abram's house. In chapters 12 and 16, Egypt also arises as a fertile alternative, when Abram is faced with the infertility of the land, and in chapter 16, as Sarai comes to terms with her own infertility. Here, too, Sarai is forced to consider an Egyptian solution for her barrenness.

The dynamic between the three characters in this episode is complex. Each character approaches the situation from their own perspective, which can feel both reasonable and irrational at the same time, depending on how the reader looks at it. The text utilizes a clever literary technique to convey this complexity, helping the reader to both empathize with and stand in judgment of each of the players. The story begins with two subtly different perspectives – the first-person point of view of Sarai, and the third-person point of view of the narrative text.

Let's examine how the situation is described from the two points of view:

Narrative text (1)	**Sarai's suggestion (2)**
Sarai, Abram's wife, had borne him no children	Look, the Lord has kept me from bearing
She had an Egyptian maidservant whose name was Hagar	Consort with my maid; perhaps I shall have a son through her

Sarai is distressed at a situation that she emphasizes is *her* struggle, not Abram's: "The Lord has kept *me* from bearing. Consort with *my* maid; perhaps *I* shall have a son through her" (Gen. 16:2). In contrast, the narrative perspective returns Abram to the picture, emphasizing the direct effect of Sarai's infertility on Abram – "had borne *him* no children." The two descriptions describe two points of view regarding the same situation.

This is also emphasized in Sarai's conclusion: "Perhaps *I* shall have a son through her," instead of "we" or "you." In addition, Hagar is described in the narration by name and nationality – "an Egyptian maidservant whose name was Hagar." Sarai does not relate to Hagar by name, but rather by position, "my maidservant."

Sarai should not be judged harshly at this point of the narrative; the term "maidservant" is appropriate in the context of Sarai's discussion with her husband, since it is the nature of their relationship that enables Sarai to have Abram's child through Hagar. However, the omission of Hagar's name portrays Sarai's transaction as a technical-legal act, devoid of personal implications. Hagar is not an independent personality, she is nothing more than Sarai's maidservant; Sarai is portrayed as the one affected by the transaction, not Hagar.

Sarai's opening lament, "The Lord has kept me from bearing," paints a sympathetic picture of her character. Sarai is in distress, pained by the reality of her circumstance. That being said, Sarai does not simply accept her destiny, and instead allocates blame elsewhere – she involves Abram, assuming that the fault for the couple's barrenness lies with both of them, and not only with her.

The story unfolds in two parallel parts:

Sarai's suggestion	Look, the Lord has kept me from bearing. Consort with my maid; perhaps I shall have a son through her	And Sarai said to Abram, "The wrong done me is your fault! I myself put my maid in your bosom; now that she sees that she is pregnant, I am lowered in her esteem. The Lord decide between you and me."
Abram's reaction	And Abram heeded Sarai's request	Abram said to Sarai, "Your maid is in your hands. Deal with her as you think right."
Sarai's actions	So Sarai, Abram's wife, took her maid, Hagar the Egyptian ... and gave her to her husband Abram for a wife	Then Sarai treated her harshly

The result: Hagar's reaction	He cohabited with Hagar and she conceived; and when she saw that she had conceived, her mistress was lowered in her esteem	she ran away from her

While Sarai's solution to her infertility began as a cold transaction, as the story progresses we begin to see Sarai's distress at the unintended consequences. Initially Sarai offers Hagar to Abram so that the maidservant would carry a child in her name. The resulting reality is not only is Sarai dissociated from Hagar's pregnancy, but she finds herself lowered in the esteem of her maidservant.

In both instances, Sarai mentions God. She attributes her barrenness to God's hand ("The Lord has kept me from bearing"), and she later calls upon God to mediate between herself and her husband ("The Lord decide between you and me"). Sarai's mention of God highlights His lack of involvement in the scene, even when He is called upon by Sarai to intervene.

The narrative develops in a natural way, through human initiative and reaction. Sarai's dialogue reveals the emotional overload of all characters involved in this brief story. Instead of focusing on the problem of Hagar's scornfulness, she repeats the entire story from her point of view: "The wrong done me is your fault! I myself put my maid in your bosom; now that she sees that she is pregnant, I am lowered in her esteem."

The phrase, "put my maid in your bosom," has surprisingly romantic connotations, considering that Hagar was meant to be no more than a fertile womb in the service of Sarai.

However, if we read the initial interaction carefully, it reveals a similar tone from both points of view:

Narrative text (Gen. 16:3–4)	**Sarai's perspective (Gen. 16:5)**
And gave her to her husband Abram for a wife and when she saw that she had conceived, her mistress was lowered in her esteem	I myself put my maid in your bosom! Now that she sees that she is pregnant, I am lowered in her esteem

In light of this comparison, Sarai has good reason to attribute romantic connotations to the relationship between Abram and Hagar. Sarai's comment, "I myself put my maid in your bosom," parallels "[Sarai] gave her to her husband Abram for a wife." "Wife" is a status that deviates from Sarai's original plan. Based on documents of the era, even if a maidservant were to gain a higher status by providing the master with a son (and, by the way, it was prohibited to banish her and her son), she still would not be given the status of a proper wife. Sarai's intention had been to give Hagar to Abram for the sole purpose of bearing a child, as a surrogate mother.

However, if we follow the two titles used to describe Hagar throughout the scene, we see the difference between Sarai and Abram's view of Hagar's role (and the delicate process Abram undergoes in the narrative). Sarai initially refers to Hagar as a maidservant; once Hagar becomes pregnant, she is suddenly deemed "wife." Despite the title and pregnancy, Hagar later returns to her original status as Sarai's maidservant, both from her own perspective ("Her mistress was lowered in her esteem") and in Sarai's view ("I myself put my maid in your bosom"). After Sarai's criticism of Abram, he also changes his view of Hagar, who returns to her original status as Sarai's servant ("Your maid is in your hands"). The shift in language from "maidservant" to "wife" and back again does not refer to Hagar's legal status – legally, she remains a "maidservant" throughout; despite being chosen for surrogacy, she is not considered to be Abram's legal spouse.

This shift in language seems to be in reference to Abram's treatment of Hagar during her pregnancy, a point which hurt Sarai and emboldened Hagar. When Sarai tells Abram she had placed her maid "in his bosom," she is in fact relating to Hagar's achievement of the unexpected status as Abram's wife. When Abram heard that Hagar was expecting, he would have begun to care for her well-being. While Sarai watched this special treatment, she might have been berating herself for having brought the situation upon herself. The emotional effects of watching a second wife suddenly walk into one's home are not necessarily logical. The barren Sarai sees her husband consorting with another woman, and she cannot stand such a reality. Whether Abram interprets the situation in the same way or not, Sarai's anger leaves an impression on him; he releases Hagar and returns her to Sarai.

Sarai's actions are a result of Abram's reaction, which sets the characters up for the next part of the story. The dynamic between Abram and the two women in the first part of the story is the catalyst for the next scene, when Hagar discovered she is pregnant, "her mistress was lowered in her esteem," and following Sarai's harsh treatment, she "ran away from her." Hagar's actions in the conclusion of the first two scenes prepares the reader for the shift in focus to Hagar in the next scene, which features Hagar as the protagonist.

A noteworthy detail emerges from the scenes discussed above. Abram's passivity in the story cannot be incidental. His inactivity sets this story apart from all others in the Abraham cycle. Even the parallel story of Hagar's dismissal (Gen. 21), which begins with Sarai's initiative to banish "this maid and her son," invites the reader to share Abram's emotions (21:12); ultimately, Abram is the one who acts, following God's revelation (21:14). The gap left by Abram's passivity in the story of Hagar's flight is filled by a new protagonist, Sarai. Sarai initiates the process; Sarai implements her idea; Sarai acts harshly toward her maid, thereby advancing the next stage of the plot. The depth of Sarai's dominance is particularly apparent in the way the text describes Sarai's transference of her maidservant to Abram. The text uses the root L-K-Ḥ ("take"), the common verb describing marriage; however, instead of simply stating "Abram took Hagar," a long and winding verse makes Sarai the subject of the sentence: "So Sarai, Abram's wife, took her maid, Hagar the Egyptian... and gave her to her husband Abram for a wife" (16:3). The lengthy description highlights both Sarai's authority and Abram's inactivity. Abram's thoughts and feelings are concealed, and he seems to be acting only on behalf of his wife's wishes and instruction.

Abram's silence is one of several indicators that the story deviates from God's plan. The Bible is not averse to the prevalent custom of using a maidservant as means of acquiring a child for a childless couple. Therefore, there is no explicit criticism of human initiative with regard to the process of building a family. But it is true that the question of Abram's heir deviates from the regular context of a childless couple. God's promises and the development of the Abraham cycle both indicate that the birth of Abram's son is destined at a specific time. This hits upon one of the central crucial points of the story: the question of whether Sarai's actions were divinely planned – or at least sanctioned – and what were the ramifications of her decisions.

Escape from Torture

The word, *vate'aneha,* used to describe Sarai's harsh treatment of Hagar, may be interpreted in several ways, but there is no doubt that the association of harsh treatment or torture with Sarai may be difficult for the reader to swallow. Radak interprets the verb literally, insinuating actual physical torture on Sarai's part. His analysis is a harsh judgment of Sarai's character, and leaves no room to interpret the "torture" as metaphorical, nor her actions as justified. In fact, Radak's severe assessment of Sarai directly informs his analysis of the story's purpose – to counsel distance from Sarai's unacceptable and cruel behavior.[1]

In contrast, a look at the Code of Hammurabi suggests the possibility of an entirely different explanation of Sarai's "torture." Sarai's actions were not, in fact, torture at all, but the implementation of a common practice. Sarai's behavior may not have been physical, based on section 146 in the Hammurabi Code:

> If a man take a wife and she give this man a maidservant as wife and she bear him children, and then this maịd [will] assume equality with the wife: because she has borne him children, her master shall not sell her for money, but he may keep her as a slave, reckoning her among the maidservants.[2]

The case in our narrative is similar to the case in the law: Hagar the maidservant was given to Abram, husband of the barren mistress, for the purpose of producing a child, and the maidservant assumed "equality

1. Radak on Gen. 15:6.
2. Some translated *imannûši* as a transitive verb: the mistress will appoint her maid to be among the other mothers. I prefer Richardson's translation (*Hammurabi's Laws: Text, Translation and Glossary* [Sheffield, 2000], 87), which reads the verb as passive.

with the wife."[3] In light of this similarity, some interpret the meaning of the verb *vate'aneha* based on the law, "reckoning her among the maidservants."[4]

The details of Sarai's harsh treatment are left to the reader's imagination. While the idea that Sarai physically tortured Hagar seems extreme, the explanation that she was simply conforming to common practice does not quite justify the narration's use of the word "torture." There is certainly an element of judgment of Sarai's character in the language, although we can assume, based on the emotionally fraught context of the story (and, later, the angel's directive to return to her mistress despite the harsh treatment), that Hagar's struggle with her mistress was largely emotional, not physical.

That being said, Hagar responds to Sarai's "harsh treatment" by escaping to the desert. This extreme reaction indicates something worse than standard maidservant working conditions. A pregnant woman, a maidservant at that, is unlikely to run away to the desert alone and without protection unless she has good reason to do so. While Sarai's precise actions are not disclosed, the choice of the verb *vate'aneha*, which has negative connotations throughout the Bible, certainly indicates inflicting suffering. The use of this word certainly underlines the severity of Sarai's treatment of Hagar. To put the negative connotation of *vate'aneha* in context, earlier, in the Covenant Between the Pieces, the same verb was used to describe the harsh treatment and oppression of Abram's offspring,[5] particularly in Egypt.[6] Sarai, who "oppresses" her Egyptian maid, reminds the reader of the Egyptians, the future oppressors of

3. For additional links to Ancient Near Eastern texts, see Speiser, *Genesis*, 120–21; John van Seters, "The Problem of Childlessness in Near Eastern Law and the Patriarchs of Israel," *JBL* 87 (1968): 401–408; Albert Kirk Grayson and John van Seters, "The Childless Wife in Assyrian and the Stories of Genesis," *Orientalia* 44 (1975): 486–485; Hamilton, *The Book of Genesis, Chapters 1–17*, 444–446. For a comparison of this case to a custom reflected in the Nuzi documents, see Parrot, *Abraham and His Times*, 103–104.
4. E.g., Avraham Ahuvia, "An Angel of the Lord Found Her by a Spring of Water in the Wilderness," *Beit Mikra* 39 (1994): 72.
5. "And they shall be enslaved and oppressed (*ve'inu*) four hundred years" (Gen. 15:13).
6. "So they set taskmasters over them to oppress them (*anoto*) with forced labor... but the more they were oppressed (*ye'anu*), the more they increased" (Ex. 1:11–12).

Abram's offspring. The comparison is, of course, unflattering to Sarai; however, the desired consequence is effective – the reader is moved to sympathize with Hagar's pain and misery.

The Meeting at the Spring (Gen. 16:7–14)

Hagar, pregnant and alone, flees to the desert. Ostensibly, Hagar is attempting to head back to her native Egypt. Given the distressing nature of her departure and her physical condition, we can imagine her emotional state. As she makes her way, alone, through the barren wilderness with no planned route, her mind racing with fear and doubt at her actions, Hagar's relief at the discovery of an oasis must have been immense. Hagar's venture into the desert begins with the discovery of the spring and ends with its naming. The spring is far more than a welcome sight at which a desperate runaway may quench her thirst; it lends meaning to the overall story.

In this scene, the geographical backdrop sets the tone for the conversation between Hagar and the angel. The desert symbolizes aridity and barrenness, while the spring or well represents abundance and blessing, especially the blessing of fertility. It is no coincidence that biblical couples meet at wells; the realistic element of young girls drawing water from the well is enhanced by the symbolism of wells as a sign of fertility.[7]

The spring is introduced in two parallel descriptions:

> By a spring of water in the wilderness,
> the spring on the road to Shur.

The spring Hagar happens upon is in the wilderness, far from any settlement, "on the road to Shur."[8] The symbolic dichotomy between fertility and barrenness is woven deeply throughout this scene, both in the imagery of Hagar's physical location, and in the content of the blessing she receives from the angel.

---

7. Alter, *The Art of Biblical Narrative,* 104. See also my discussion on ch. 24.
8. Regarding the identification of Shur, see Jan Jozef Simons, *The Geographical and Topographical Texts of the Old Testament* (Leiden, 1959), 217; Denis Baly and A. Douglas Tushingham, *Atlas of the Biblical World* (New York, 1971), 104.

Hagar is blessed with fertility ("the spring"), but the fruit of her labor will find his place outside a place of settlement ("the wilderness"). This mixed blessing once again reflects the contrast of the blessing in the scene's setting – naming a source of water in the desert transforms a place in the wilderness into one with human significance. Places in the desert are rarely named, since they are not frequented by people. Here, a source of water in the wilderness is given a name, giving it meaning. The angel's blessing foresees Hagar's son making his home in the wilderness and naming places in it, giving them significance, just as Hagar's spring is made significant by its naming.

When the angel appears to Hagar, he addresses her as "Sarai's maidservant," which sets the tone of the dialogue as critical of Hagar's escape. "Hagar, maidservant of Sarai, where have you come from?" Hagar does not argue with this delegitimization. In fact, she fully acknowledges her position: "I am running away from my *mistress* Sarai." Hagar's recognition of her status redirects the criticism against her; even while fleeing from Sarai, she knows her place and obligation.

The angel asks Hagar two questions: "Where have you come from?" and "Where are you going?" Hagar only responds to the first question: "I am running away from my mistress Sarai." The text revealed earlier that Hagar is "on the road to Shur," meaning it is likely that Hagar is heading back to her family in Egypt. Hagar omits her destination in her response to the angel – she is far more intent on running away than she is on arriving at her destination. The angel asks, "Where have you *come* from," and Hagar changes the angel's terminology by answering, "I am *running* away." In Hagar's state of mind, the details of where she came from or where she is going are dwarfed by the overwhelming feeling that she simply had to escape where she was. Even being approached and questioned by a divine being was not enough to jolt Hagar out of her desperate state – the only thing on her mind was escape.

The meeting between the angel and Hagar climaxes in the angel's blessing. Amazingly, the blessing is structured in the same standard format of the blessings given to the forefathers in the book of Genesis, even though the recipient of this blessing is nothing more than an Egyptian maidservant!

The angel's message can be divided into three parts, as the three captions indicate:

- *And the angel of the Lord said to her,* "Go back to your mistress, and submit to her harsh treatment."
- *And the angel of the Lord said to her,* "I will greatly increase your offspring, and they shall be too many to count."
- *And the angel of the Lord said to her,* "Behold, you are with child and shall bear a son. You shall call him Ishmael, for the Lord has paid heed to your suffering. He shall be a wild ass of a man; his hand against everyone, and everyone's hand against him. He shall dwell alongside of all his kinsmen."

The text repeats the heading, "And the angel of the Lord said to her," intimating that the angel was "awaiting a response or action," in the words of Meir Shiloach.[9] Hagar has just escaped her abusive mistress, and a stranger in the wilderness approaches her, urging her to return to that harsh situation.[10] Hagar, in her desperate state, is silent, indicating that she is, at best, disinclined to comply with the angel's directive. As a result, the angel is put in a position of having to convince Hagar to return to her masters.[11]

---

9. Shiloach, "And He Said…and He Said," 251.
10. It is difficult to determine at precisely what point Hagar understands that she is being addressed by an angel. A similar ambiguity is present in Abram's meeting with the angels in ch. 18. Gunkel believed Hagar only realized she was conversing with an angel in vv. 9–12, when the angel blessed her (Gunkel, *Genesis – Translated and Interpreted*, 186).
11. Cf. Ahuvia, "An Angel of the Lord Found Her by a Spring of Water in the Wilderness," 73. In his opinion, Hagar is tired and thirsty, and the angel speaks the thoughts she would have had regardless. He writes that the difficulties of traveling through the desert defeated her, and she reluctantly returned to Sarai's house. His reading is unlikely, since the angel meets Hagar "by a spring of water." In contrast with ch. 21, where Hagar needed her eyes opened in order to find water, in ch. 16 she reached the spring before meeting the angel. Noort writes that Hagar is portrayed as knowledgeable in the paths of the desert. He notes that Shur is several days of travel from Hebron, and the pregnant Hagar made it as far as Shur. In his opinion, there is therefore a similarity between the portrayal of Hagar and the qualities she is told her son will possess – "a wild ass of a man" (Ed Noort, "Created in the Image

However, Hagar is adamant. The promise of innumerable offspring fails to convince the frightened and tortured maid to return to the source of her grief. The angel is compelled to try again, adding yet another blessing, promising Hagar the well-being and success of her unborn child. It is only after this promise that Hagar finally complies with the angel's instruction.

The angel's message escalates in three stages, first attempting and failing to engage with Hagar, until the message is finally received:

1. The angel initially tells Hagar: "Go back to your mistress, and submit to her harsh treatment."[12] This formulation might create the impression that the angel identifies with Sarai and justifies her harsh treatment of Hagar.[13] However, this is a misreading of the verse. The angel does not condone Sarai's actions; rather his statement should be read, "Go back to your mistress *despite* her harsh treatment."
2. In the second phase, the angel attempts to convince Hagar to return to her mistress despite her obvious reluctance to do so. Hagar is promised: "I will greatly increase your offspring, and they shall be too many to count" (Gen. 15:10). Remarkably, the angel's language here is reminiscent of the future blessing bestowed upon Abram at the conclusion of the Binding of Isaac.[14] This parallel is momentous, as it seems to place Hagar on the same level of divine benefit as the forefathers of the Jewish nation. Hagar, who had been chosen to bear the child who would become the heir to Abram's legacy, now finds herself

---

of the Son: Ishmael and Hagar," in *Abraham, the Nations, and the Hagarites: Jewish, Christian, and Islamic Perspectives on Kinship with Abraham*, ed. M. Goodman, G. H. van Kooten, and J. van Ruiten [Leiden, 2010], 39).

12. The angel's words translate literally into "under *her* hand," repeating the expression Abram uses when he permits Sarai to do as she pleases with Hagar.
13. As claims, for example, Elchanan Samet, *Studies in the Weekly Parasha: First Series* (Maaleh Adumim, 2002), 36.
14. "I will bestow My blessing upon you and make your descendants as numerous as the stars of heaven and the sands on the seashore; and your descendants shall seize the gates of their foes" (Gen. 22:17).

homeless and desperate, wandering the desert. The angel assures her that not only is her suffering legitimate, but that to make up for it, God will bestow upon her the same blessing He gave to the descendants of the family who so mistreated her. Hagar's suffering is not insignificant, and her progeny will benefit from her sacrifice.

3. But Hagar remains unconvinced, and unwilling to return to the house of her mistress. Finally, in the third phase, the angel offers Hagar a concrete blessing that relates to her present reality: "Behold, you are with child and shall bear a son..." (Gen. 15:12–13). The angel shares with Hagar the name that will be given to her unborn child. This is another remarkable parallel between God's approach to Hagar and to the families of her masters, the forebears of the nation of Israel. In the next chapter, Abram's second son, Isaac, will also be named by God, in a similarly articulated verse: "God said, 'Nevertheless, Sarah your wife shall bear you a son, and you shall name him Isaac'" (17:19). The fates of Abram's son and Hagar's are compared; God offers patronage to Hagar's son, just as He intends to sponsor Isaac. The angel assures Hagar that she, the mother of the child, will bestow a name upon her son, and not Sarai. In this moment, it finally becomes clear to Hagar that the angel is telling her that she will be free of the burden of her mistress, and that the son she will bear will be her own.

The reasoning behind this change is no less significant: "For the Lord has paid heed to your suffering." This phrase is again reminiscent of the enslavement in Egypt: "I have seen the plight of My people in Egypt, and I have heard their outcry because of their taskmasters; yes, I am mindful of their suffering" (Ex. 3:7). Clearly God identifies with the Hebrew slaves and not with their Egyptian oppressors, just as God seeing Hagar the Egyptian's suffering is a clear indication that He deplores her oppression.

A Mother's Sacrifice for the "Wild Ass" of a Man

Alone in the wilderness, approached by a divine being, Hagar is determined not to heed the angel's blessing. It is not until the angel utters these words that the maidservant's attention is suddenly caught: "He shall be a wild ass of a man; his hand against everyone, and everyone's hand against him; he shall dwell alongside of all his kinsmen." The significance of the metaphor "wild ass" (*pere adam*) is debated among commentators. However, I believe the emphasis here is on the word "wild." Wild, as opposed to domesticated, or in other words, Hagar's son will be a free man, and will not inherit his mother's status as a slave.

In this context, it becomes clear why the angel's third statement is the catalyst that convinces Hagar to comply with the angel's command. Hagar has only just escaped. What horrible fate awaits her and her child should she now return? Surely their enslavement will be longer and harsher now in the wake of her rebellion. The angel reassures the terrified mother-to-be that her unborn child's fate is, in fact, freedom.

The significance of Ishmael's freedom and independence is also essential for understanding the angel's statement, literally, "His hand is in all and the hands of all are in him," which seems to allude to financial success. The significance of the metaphor "wild ass" was debated among commentators. In the book of Job in particular, the wild ass is a paradigm of freedom: "Who sets the wild ass free?... Whose home I have made the wilderness, the salt land his dwelling place? He scoffs at the tumult of the city, does not hear the shouts of the driver; he roams the hills for pasture..." (Job 39:5–7).[15] The reason the wild ass does not hear the shouts of the driver is that the wild ass is never caught, and lives forever free in the wilderness. Gerhard von Rad believes the verse in Job 39 depicts the wild ass in a negative light from a biblical perspective, although not from Hagar's viewpoint: "He will be a real Bedouin, a 'wild ass of a man,' i.e., free and wild, eagerly spending his life in a war of all against all – a worthy son of his rebellious and proud mother!"[16] I believe the symbolic freedom is better explained in the context of the narrative in Genesis 16. Hagar has only recently escaped her oppressive

15. Gunkel, *Genesis – Translated and Interpreted*, 188; von Rad, *Genesis*, 189 (similarly, Kahana, *Bible Series with Scientific Commentary*, 26). The wildness of the ass is also expressed through the breaking of conventions, as reflected, for example, in Job 11:12: "A hollow man will understand, when a wild ass is born a man." This verse indicates that a wild ass is uncivilized, and has to be educated in order to become civilized.
16. Von Rad, *Genesis*, 189.

mistress; what will become of her if she should return to the house of her master and mistress? What will become of the status of her child, now the son of a rebellious maidservant? The angel offers the encouragement Hagar needs to hear: her son will be free as a wild ass.[17] He will live in the desert where none will discipline him, as Ibn Ezra writes: "The most free among people ... none shall rule him outside of his own family."[18]

With the mention of the "hand," the story of Hagar comes full circle. Abram said to Sarai: "Your maidservant is in your *hands*" (Gen. 15:6); the angel ordered Hagar to return to her mistress and submit to the harsh treatment "under her hand" (v. 9). Now the angel informs Hagar that her son will have his own "hand" which will be in high demand. The final part of the blessing, "He shall dwell alongside of all his kinsmen," indicates that Ishmael will inherit his own portion of land, equally among his brothers. Hagar undergoes a metamorphosis from a docile surrogate serving the greater vision of her mistress's family to the mother of a son who will one day be that mistress's son's equal, a free man. The hand that once oppressed her now becomes a symbol of her freedom.

The language and structure of the angel's speech to Hagar is deeply linked with the story of the Covenant Between the Pieces from the previous chapter. In chapter 15, Abram was promised a multitude of offspring (Gen. 15:5); he was told that his offspring will be enslaved and mistreated in a foreign land (15:13); and finally, he is promised that his

---

17. In fact, the verses in Job may well be alluding to Ishmael, who is defined as a "wild ass" in our story, and whose tribes roam the desert. In the parallel narrative in ch. 21, Ishmael is "cast" out to the desert, just like the verse in Job 39:5: "Who sets the wild ass free?" Moreover, in that verse in Job, the wild ass is described as "scoffing," "*yisḥak*," at the "tumult of the city," just as Ishmael "scoffs," "*metzaḥek*," at Isaac prior to his expulsion (Gen. 21:9).
18. Ibn Ezra on Gen. 16:12. See also Noort, "Created in the Image of the Son: Ishmael and Hagar," 35. Stanley Gevirtz and Hamilton understand the word "*adam*," meaning "man," as a derivative of "*adama*," "earth," connoting wilderness. They translate *pere adam* as "wild in the wilderness." See Gevirtz, "Of Patriarchs and Puns: Joseph at the Fountain, Jacob at the Ford," *HUCA* 46 (1975): 43n35; Hamilton, *The Book of Genesis, Chapters 1–17*, 449n3. The word *pere*, meaning "wild," sounds similar to the word *poreh*, meaning "fertile." In this case the image is linked with the blessing Hagar received from the angel. Cf. Amnon Shapira, "He Shall Be a Wild Ass of a Man," *Beit Mikra* 41 (1996): 119–122.

children will be freed, accumulate great riches, and inherit their land. All the elements predicted in Hagar's future seem to be taken from God's covenant with Abram. The text in our story also reminds us of Hagar's Egyptian roots, perhaps to strengthen the link between these two narratives. Abram discovered that his offspring will be tortured in a foreign land – Egypt. In the very next chapter the roles are reversed and Sarai is the one to torture Egyptian Hagar.

The link between these stories goes much deeper than literary comparison, and seems to hint at the text's appraisal of the dynamic between the characters. From the beginning of the story, the reader is perplexed by how to judge Hagar and Sarai. Is Sarai cruel, or is Hagar insubordinate? The dynamic is complex, and perhaps even changes as the plot develops. The narrative link between the Covenant Between the Pieces and Hagar's blessing solidifies our sympathetic perspective of Hagar, and leads to a surprising and poignant ending to her story.

Naming Names (Gen. 16:13–14)

Hagar is shocked by the entire experience of being approached by a divine being amid her ungraceful escape. Her responses to the angel throughout their conversation oscillate between disbelief and outright obstinacy. At the end of his speech, the angel tells Hagar that she will give birth to a son named Ishmael, in recognition of the fact that God heard her plight. Instead of declaring the given name of her unborn son, Hagar responds by giving the angel a name: "And she called the Lord who spoke to her, 'You are El-Roi,' by which she meant, 'Have I not gone on seeing after He saw me!'" (Gen. 15:13). The name El-Roi ("the God who sees me") is redolent of the name Ishmael ("God has heard").[19]

Hagar's act of naming the angel is surprising to say the least. Naming God and His messengers is a rare phenomenon in biblical literature. Usually the name is bestowed by the authoritative figure (often God) unto the lesser character, not the opposite. Apparently, Hagar reacts impulsively, uttering the name of the angel instead of her son.

19. Being heard and seen by God are frequently linked, as in the Exodus narrative: "I have seen the plight of My people in Egypt, and I have heard their outcry because of their taskmasters; yes, I am mindful of their suffering" (Ex. 3:7).

Intrinsically embedded in the story of Ishmael's birth is the suffering Hagar experienced leading up to it.

The text attempts to explain Hagar's reaction: "Have I not gone on seeing after He saw me!" (Gen. 15:13). Hagar's outburst is out of amazement at the fact that she was exposed to an interaction with a Godly being and left unscathed.[20] Remember, this entire story takes place in the whirlwind of Hagar's escape from suffering – an escape which she expected to end, at best, in a fugitive state, having run away pregnant with what was ostensibly her mistress's baby. Still reeling from her anguish and subsequent escape, she finds herself in the wilderness, which, according to prevalent Ancient Near East beliefs, is considered to be a godless place. A disgraced slave alone in the desert would hardly expect a divine being to reveal itself to her, much less bring the exact tidings that will change her life for the better. Hagar names the place of this apparent miracle Beer-lahai-roi ("Well of the Living One Who Sees Me") – another tribute to her amazement at such divine attention. The fact that this name is then accepted is another testament to the importance of the message of Hagar's story, which we will touch upon at the end of this chapter.

The text's transition from the angel to the spring could be interpreted as a formal approval of Hagar's name for the angel, although it could just as easily be viewed the opposite way. The text focuses on the naming of the spring to distract from Hagar's outburst in naming the angel, which may have crossed a line in her interaction with a divine being. Perhaps the text is telling us that even though the name Hagar bestowed on the angel is accurate, she is not in a position to be naming a divine being. Instead, she is allowed to bestow a similar name upon the spring – an act that would be considered within accepted human boundaries.

---

20. Many scholars adopted Wellhausen's interpretation: "Have I seen God and am I kept in life after my seeing?" The advantage of this suggestion is Hagar's reasoning. Just as Manoah fears for his life after meeting face to face with an angel (Judges 13:22), Hagar expresses her wonder at having seen an angel and surviving. The disadvantage is the intense changes the verse must undergo in order to justify this reading, none of which are supported by ancient translations or variants.

The naming of the spring in verses 13–14 brings the story to a poetic end:

> And she *called* the Lord who *spoke* to her, "You are *El-Roi*"
> By which she *said*,
> "Have I not gone on *seeing* after He *saw* me (*roi*)!"
> Therefore the well was *called* Beer-lahai-*roi*
> It is between Kadesh and Bered.

The first three lines begin with speech ("she called," "she said"), and all end with the word "*roi*," relating to vision. As she continues her declaration, Hagar repeats the words "see" and "spoke" when referring to the angel: "The Lord who *spoke* to her," and "after He *saw* me."

Hagar's emphasis on sight is poignant. The verb "to see" and related words ("eyes") are woven throughout the start of the narrative: Abram heeded (*vayishma*) his wife (Gen. 16:2); Hagar saw (*vatere*) she was with child, which made her *view* her mistress in a different light (*be'eneha*) (v. 4); Sarai described from her perspective that Hagar saw (*vatere*) she was pregnant and *viewed* (*be'eneha*) her differently as a result (v. 5). The two verses use the verb "saw" alongside Hagar's "eyes," while Abram's reaction (v. 6) contrasts Sarai's eyes with Hagar's, *hatov be'enayikh,* literally, "what is good in your eyes." The description of Sarai's harsh treatment toward Hagar with the word *vate'aneha* is a play on the sound of the word *ayin* ("eye").

Here, at the end of Hagar's story, the angel's message to Hagar revealed that God had "heard" her plight, and suddenly she sees and is seen entirely differently. The emphasis and subsequent closure surrounding the "see" and "hear" wordplay punctuate the theme of Hagar's journey from the unseen maidservant, to obstinate surrogate, to desperate mother heard by God.

The final note in this poetic conclusion is in Ishmael's name, which means "God heard." Hagar concludes the narrative with the motif of "seeing," noting her awe at having "seen" (or being seen by) God's messenger, which she expresses by naming the angel accordingly. Hagar's entire story in this chapter relates to being seen – she begins as an insignificant housemaid, barely registering on her masters' radar. Once she is given to Abram as a surrogate wife, his attention to her causes her to be seen (or to see herself) too blatantly, and she is banished. As she escapes into the desert, Hagar is distressed that her son will be born into a life of enslaved invisibility, and when the angel finally bestows his blessing, Hagar is in awe that God finally saw her plight, and acted in accordance.

The essence of Hagar's story centers around God's compassion toward her, and the result of that compassion. The final passage of the story brings this theme together by bestowing names on three dimensions: man (Ishmael), God (represented by the angel), and the physical world (the spring). The spring, Beer-lahai-roi is so named because it is the location where Hagar's suffering was finally noticed – she was "seen." Hagar names the angel in a moment of joyful shock when she realized that God had not only seen her, but would alleviate her suffering. Finally, in the resolution to the story, the language shifts from being "seen" to being "heard." Ishmael's name is far more than another iteration of the theme of being noticed by God. In His compassion, God bestows upon Hagar the final, and greatest gift – her own son, a free man, named after the divine answer to his mother's cry. A narrative that began with human initiative, and not by divine decree, changes the face of reality for man, for nature, and for the divine.

God Sees the Suffering of the Oppressed

We can now return to the purpose of the story within the context of the Abram narrative. The evaluation of the characters is widely debated among the commentators. The text clearly identifies with Sarai's plight and pain, and criticizes Hagar's treatment of her mistress. The angel orders Hagar to return home, which downplays Sarai's actions. Although the text doesn't seem to support direct criticism of Sarai's actions, the unusual empathy toward Hagar is nevertheless unequivocal. The fact that a mere maidservant merits a revelation, the content of the blessings, the statement that God has heard her distress, the links to the enslavement of the nation in Egypt and their redemption, and the naming of the angel and spring – all of these indicate that God is on Hagar's side.[21]

21. For more details on this interpretation, see Jonathan Grossman, "Hagar's Characterization in Genesis and the Explanation of Ishmael's Blessing," *Beit Mikra* 63 (2018): 249–286.

According to this narrative, Ishmael was never intended to be Abram's heir. Sarai's plan to offer her maidservant as a surrogate was an act of desperation. God never intended the surrogate to bear the child that would carry on Abram's legacy. Hagar and Ishmael explicitly merit the blessing as a compensation for Hagar's suffering at the hands of her mistress, due to the angel's demand that Hagar return to the place of her suffering. Hagar will suffer under the hands of her oppressor, thereby buying her son freedom, riches, and land, just as Abram's offspring will suffer under their oppressors but will ultimately escape with riches and inherit the land of Canaan. Hagar's blessing is portrayed as a moral compensation for the injustice she endured, unrelated to Abram. Sarai demands, "The Lord decide between you and me." Ironically, her demand is met. God assesses the situation with Sarai and Hagar, and decides to hear Hagar's cries of distress.

There are commentators who believe the Abraham cycle is arranged in a concentric structure around Hagar's flight.[22] According to this position, the story portrays God as a moral god, sympathetic even to the suffering of a lowly maidservant who escaped to the desert. Even Hagar is surprised by the uncommon and unexpected empathy. Even if pointing to the story as the central axis of the Abraham cycle is an exaggeration, the narrative includes certain elements that do not reappear in the story cycle or in biblical literature. One particularly noteworthy element is the intimate relationship between Hagar and the angel, which is expressed in the mutual exchange of names ("Ishmael" – "El-Roi"). In Genesis 16, Hagar is paralleled with Abram in her independent standing before God, and the inheritance of blessings on her own merit. This episode's message is particularly salient in light of one of the narrative cycle's main objectives: to depict the nation of Israel's establishment upon moral grounds. Here, too, in this context, the narrative does not shy away from exploring the moral aspects of national history.

---

22. Such as Cotter, *Genesis*, 84–85; Mathews, *Genesis*, 89–91. Even according to Yehuda T. Radday, who suggested a chiastic structure for the story cycle, the stories of Hagar's flight and the circumcision are the two central stories in the cycle (Radday, "Chiasmus in Hebrew Biblical Narrative," in *Chiasmus in Antiquity*, ed. J. Welch [Hildesheim, 1981], 104–105). See at length in the introduction, regarding the literary structure of the story cycle.

The dynamic between Sarai and Hagar plays out in a delicate tension between the formal norms of their time which may have informed each woman's behavior, and the moral implications of their actions within the biblical narrative. A midrash (Genesis Rabba 5:10) illustrates the delicate contrast between the two characters in a discussion regarding whether God deigned it fitting to speak to both women, or only to the righteous Sarai. True, the midrash says, God only spoke to Sarai, but Hagar attained an elevated form of revelation – the divine appeared before her physically. Although Sarai regained her place of honor as the righteous matriarch, her maidservant, through suffering, achieved divine revelation. In the end, although both women returned to their roles, each was deemed worthy of God's love and attention.

Birth of Ishmael (Gen. 16:15–16)

The story concludes with the birth and naming of Ishmael:

> Hagar bore a son to Abram,
> and Abram gave the son that Hagar bore him the name Ishmael.
> Abram was eighty-six years old when Hagar bore Ishmael to Abram.

All three concluding statements mention Hagar and Abram, emphasizing that Abram's son was borne by Hagar. Sarai's absence in the conclusion is deafening. Hagar has a baby, and Abram gives his son a name. But Sarai is altogether absent. This oversight is surprising, since the purpose of Abram taking in Hagar was to produce a child for Sarai. The heroine who initiated the plot disappears at its conclusion.

Sarai's disappearance and Abram's renewed involvement validate the change in Ishmael's status, and contain implicit criticism of Sarai. Hagar and Ishmael merit an independent blessing, and Ishmael exceeds the purpose Sarai had intended for him. Instead of being Sarai's son, Ishmael becomes the son of his biological mother. When the angel tells Hagar that she will be the one to name her son (Gen. 15:11), he essentially confirms Sarai's loss of control over her maidservant. Several generations later, Leah and Rachel name the children of their maidservants (Gen. 30) as an indication of their "ownership" of the maids and their children. Ishmael becomes Hagar's child when she is given the opportunity to name him, and his status is elevated further when Abram ultimately gives him his name instead of Hagar. Ishmael thus becomes Abram's official firstborn son and heir.

The opposing viewpoints of the two heroines provide the story with two opposing characteristics: Sarai's story is tragic, almost ironic. She wished to give Abram a son, but by bringing her maidservant into her house for this very purpose, she creates an alternative heir to her own son. By mistreating Hagar, Sarai brings about God's blessings for Hagar. Hagar's story is one of salvation and redemption. God is portrayed as one who hears the cries of the oppressed and the lowest rungs of society's hierarchy; a maidservant will be compensated by God for her suffering at the hands of her mistress.

And where does Abram stand? He tells Sarai, "Your maidservant is in your hands," negating his relationship with Hagar. But at the end of the story, he names his son Ishmael, as the angel had told Hagar she would name her son. In the present narrative Abram's role is paired with God. As long as God remains uninvolved, Abram, too, is passive, while after the angel says that God has seen Hagar, Abram actively names his son. At the end of this story, Abram once again emerges as the hero who walks with God; he internalizes God's message of compassion and models it toward the mistreated maidservant. The story of Hagar's escape, even with all its intricacies and drama, ends by showcasing Abram as the moral backbone of his future nation.

The Covenant of Circumcision (Gen. 17)

Abram's hero cycle takes place on two parallel planes – the national and the personal. Abram is the divinely chosen leader of the future Jewish nation, and serves as the original model of the nation's value system. On the other hand, Abram is also an individual, whose inherent personal creed and development as a person are the qualities which render him worthy as the chosen leader in the eyes of the reader and his future people.

At the center of Abram's journey is the Covenant of Circumcision, in our chapter. This covenant is the center of the relationship between God and Abraham. More importantly, it is the center of Abram's chosen-ness, both as an individual and as a leader. As such, the covenant serves as the central point of Abram's entire heroic cycle. These promises are etched in the collective memory as the inception point of the unique relationship between God and the Jewish nation for generations to come.

This episode is written in a beautifully delicate and powerful style, nodding to the deeper literary meaning of the centrality of the covenant to the story. The covenant sends a significant message, on both the individual and national plane. We must know and trust Abram both as the divinely chosen leader of the nation, and also as the righteous role model whose chosenness is clearly deserved. The narrative adeptly weaves the centrality of these two points into the concentric nature of the chapter, resulting in a powerful message not only in the content of the promises, but in their literary structure as well.

Personal Covenant

Abram is the archetypal origin hero of the Jewish nation. As such, the two main covenants he binds with God serve as prototypes of all the biblical covenants that come afterward.[1] Despite the similar terminology, the two covenants could not be more different. In the Covenant Between the Pieces, Abram is portrayed as a passive character who practically commits to nothing. His passivity is highlighted by the fact that he "falls asleep" while God passes between the cut pieces. Additionally, the only information Abram is given that would directly affect his life related to his death at an old age. In other words, Abram would not witness the fulfillment of his covenant with God. While he believes God's plan and commitment to his offspring, the covenant has no direct impact on his life, and its delivery in chapter 15 is unidirectional. Some define the covenant as a "political-national-historical treaty,"[2] in contrast with the Covenant of Circumcision, which was wholly personal.

The Covenant of Circumcision is personal and reciprocal. It features a mutual commitment between Abram and God. The chapter is devoted to God's dialogue with Abram – out of twenty-seven verses in the chapter, eighteen are spoken by God.[3] Abram's name is changed to Abraham, indicating a changed status before God, and he is called to take action and circumcise himself, his son, and the men of his household. The covenant is implemented immediately – "on that very day" (Gen. 17:23), and not four hundred years later, as in the Covenant Between

1. Thomas Edward McComiskey, *The Covenants of Promise: A Theology of the Old Testament Covenants* (Grand Rapids, MI, 1985), 139–177. Concerning the relationship between the two covenants, see Thomas Desmond Alexander, *From Paradise to the Promise Land: An Introduction to the Main Themes of the Pentateuch* (Grand Rapids, MI, 1998), 52–54; Yitzchak Etshalom, *Between the Lines of the Bible: Genesis: Recapturing the Full Meaning of the Biblical Text* (Jerusalem and New York, 2015), 106–118.
2. Bin-Nun, *Chapters of the Fathers*, 44–48.
3. Yitzhak Moshe Emanueli, *Genesis – Commentary and Insights* (Tel Aviv, 1978), 254.

the Pieces.[4] The Covenant of Circumcision is not a "national covenant," but rather a "personal/familial covenant."[5]

The text highlights the intimate, personal nature of the circumcision through the use of the verb *halakh* ("go/walk"). In fact, God asks Abram to walk "before" Him, a phrase which evokes an image of Abram walking almost literally beside the Divine, indicating an intimacy between them. This word has escorted Abram throughout his journey, from the very moment God first turned to him and commanded, "*Lekh lekha*," "Go forth." Since that moment, Abram walked (*halakh*) through the land, interacted with the inhabitants (Gen. 12:6; 13:7), and negotiated with the leaders (14:17–24). The Covenant Between the Pieces formalized God's commitment to Abram with regard to the land (15:18–21). In the Covenant of Circumcision, Abram is expected to engage once again in the act of going forth, and walking before God. Abram's relationship with God becomes more intimate after the Covenant of Circumcision; the inclusion of the verb *halakh* brings this part of the story full circle, indicating that our protagonist has ascended another level on the journey that began with the opening "*Lekh lekha*" in chapter 12.

Concentric Structure

In this chapter, the text utilizes the use of the concentric structure beautifully, weaving together a narrative whose twists and turns continually

4. Alexander's formulation is misleading: "As in 15:1–6, the promise of a son prepares the reader for future developments in the cycle" (Alexander, "A Literary Analysis of the Abraham Narrative in Genesis," 48). While the two messages prepare the reader for the rest of the cycle, Gen. 15 is designed as a promise for the distant future, while the promise of a son in the Covenant of Circumcision is given a specific time in the near future (17:21).
5. For another definition of the correlation between the two covenants, see Thomas Alexander, "Abraham Re-Assessed Theologically," in *He Swore an Oath: Biblical Themes from Genesis 12–50*, ed. R. S. Hess, G.J. Wenham, and P. E. Satterthwaite (Carlisle, UK, 1994), 7–28; Williamson, *Abraham, Israel and the Nations*. Alexander and Williamson emphasize the condition element: while the Covenant Between the Pieces is unconditional, the Covenant of Circumcision is conditional. They also emphasize the replacement of the promises of land and offspring with a more universal approach in the Covenant of Circumcision, which continues the blessings of ch. 12. See also Speiser, *Genesis*, 126, who believes the two chapters express different approaches to the term "covenant."

wind their way back to the central message.[6] The chapter includes two parallel halves (Gen. 17:1–14, 15–27), concentrated around the central axis: the circumcision. Since chapter 17 is the general central axis of the entire Abraham cycle, the commandment of circumcision (and Abram's and Sarai's name changes, which enclose it on both sides) become the focal point of the entire story cycle. The concentric structure repeats itself several times over: chapter 17 is the central axis of the entire Abraham narrative, and the circumcision and name changes are the focal point of this chapter. With the name change in the center, this is the "official" transformation of Abram and Sarai to the mother and father of the Jewish nation.

Let us begin by looking at the outer concentric structure:

A: Introduction (Abram is ninety-nine) (Gen. 17:1)
Abram was ninety-nine years old.

> **B: Beginning of revelation (v. 1)**
> The Lord appeared to Abram.
>
> > **C: Covenant and the promise of fertility (vv. 1–2)**
> > "I am El Shaddai. Walk in My ways and be blameless.
> > I will establish My covenant between Me and you, and I will make you exceedingly numerous."
> >
> > > **D: Abram's reaction (Abram throws himself on his face) (v. 3)**
> > > Abram threw himself on his face.
> > >
> > > > **E: Name change for Abram; the promise of kings (vv. 3–8)**
> > > > And God spoke to him further, "As for Me, this is My covenant with you: You shall be the father of a multitude of nations. And you shall no longer be called

6. Sean E. McEvenue (*The Narrative Style of the Priestly Writer* [AnBib 50: Rome, 1971], 157–58) named the structure a "palistrophe." Cf. Grayson and Van Seters, "The Childless Wife in Assyrian and the Stories of Genesis," 179–193; Alexander, "A Literary Analysis of the Abraham Narrative in Genesis," 170–17; Radday, "Chiasmus in Hebrew Biblical Narrative," 105; Wenham, *Genesis 16–50*, 17. In addition to the structure, McEvenue suggests a classic parallel of the two parts of the chapter (*The Narrative Style of the Priestly Writer*, 158–159). He also notes the continuity throughout the chapter: "The chapter always moves from intention to fact, and from vague to specific" (McEvenue, ibid., 156).

Abram, but your name shall be Abraham, for I make you the father of a multitude of nations. I will make you exceedingly fertile, and make nations of you; and kings shall come forth from you…

F: The covenant sign (vv. 9–14)

You and your offspring to come throughout the ages shall keep My covenant. Such shall be the covenant between Me and you and your offspring to follow which you shall keep: every male among you shall be circumcised…

E': Name change for Sarai; the promise of kings (vv. 15–16)

As for your wife Sarai, you shall not call her Sarai, but her name shall be Sarah. I will bless her; indeed, I will give you a son by her. I will bless her so that she shall give rise to nations; rulers of peoples shall issue from her."

D': Abraham's reaction (Abraham throws himself on his face) (vv. 17–18)

Abraham threw himself on his face and laughed, as he said to himself, "Can a child be born to a man a hundred years old?"

C': Covenant and the promise of fertility (vv. 19–21)

"Nevertheless, Sarah your wife shall bear you a son, and you shall name him Isaac and I will maintain My covenant with him as an everlasting covenant for his offspring to come. As for Ishmael, I have heeded you. I hereby bless him. I will make him fertile and exceedingly numerous. He shall be the father of twelve chieftains, *and I will make of him a great nation.*"

B': End of revelation (v. 22)

And when He was done speaking with him, God was gone from Abraham.

A': Conclusion (Abraham is circumcised at ninety-nine) (vv. 23–27)

Abraham was ninety-nine years old when he circumcised the flesh of his foreskin.

A-A' – Abraham's Age

The emphasis on Abram's age underscores the timing of the Covenant of Circumcision. "Abraham was ninety-nine years old." Since Abram is nearly one hundred years old at the time of the Covenant of Circumcision, one might have expected a more dramatic, symbolic round number to indicate Abram's age. A round number would have contributed to the sense of a new beginning in the life of the protagonist, complete with a new covenant and a new name. But "almost one hundred" is exactly what this detail is meant to convey. In addition to the admiration of Abram's continued devotion to God despite his old age, the text wishes to indicate that the main event is yet to come. The covenant is complete only when God's promise to Abram is fulfilled.[7] The covenant precedes the birth of Isaac, so that Isaac could be born *into* the covenant; this event only takes place when Abram turns one hundred.

B-B' – "Seeing" God

The repetition of the root word R-A-H ("to see" – here, "appeared") again emphasizes the personal nature of this covenant between Abram and God. Analysis of other divine revelations will reveal a distinct differentiation between those which include a visual component and those which do not. This covenant could be compared with Abram's previous revelation in Shechem, which was also a visual revelation: "The Lord appeared to Abram and said, 'I will assign this land to your offspring.' And he built an altar there to the Lord who had appeared to him" (Gen. 12:7).[8] In Abraham's journey, a revelation from God that incorporates a vision indicates an emphasis on the personal aspect of the revelation. In the Covenant of Circumcision, the text adds an unusual description: "And God went up (*vayaal*) from Abraham," a phrase which does not repeat itself elsewhere. The verb *vayaal* seems a more appropriate description of an angel (e.g., Judges 13:20, and cf. Gen. 18:33, 35:13).[9] The personification

7. Cf. Westermann, *Genesis 12–36: A Continental Commentary*, 257.
8. Cf. Hamilton, *The Book of Genesis, Chapters 1–17*, 460; Kiel, *Daat Mikra: Genesis*, 444.
9. Although Gen. 35:13 states, "And God went up from him at the spot where He had spoken to him," and indeed Jacob's name is changed as well, "*Elohim*" here refers to the angel, not to God Himself. See Jonathan Grossman, "'What You Vow, Fulfill': The Meaning of Jacob's Struggle with the Angel," *Megadim* 26 (1996): 19–20.

of God, who descends to the land and returns to His place at the conclusion of the revelation, might be related to the mutual design of the covenant, as if to say, in order to make a covenant with man, God must materialize Himself, abandoning the divine realm for some time.

C-C' – Blessing of Fertility

The blessing of this covenant is fertility, the end to the long suffering of a couple grappling with their barrenness. Here, God is referred to for the first time as "El Shaddai." Some suggest the name Shaddai derives from "*sadeh,*" "field."[10] Others link the term with "*shadayim,*" "breasts," as a symbol of breastfeeding and abundance.[11] Some connect Shaddai with the Akkadian *šadû,* mountain[12] (with some even claiming that the Hebrew word for mountain, "*har,*" comes from the same etymological root as the word *shad*).[13] In any case, all appearances of the combination "El Shaddai" in Genesis are linked with the blessing of fertility,[14] supporting the position that connects *Shaddai* with fertility.[15] On a deeper level, this revelation of God's new name and the new name given to Abram coincide with the great blessing of fertility bestowed on Abram in this

10. Manfred Weippert, "Erwägungen zur Etymologie des Gottesnames 'El Ŝaddaj," *ZDMG* 111 (1961): 42–62. Similarly, some linked the name El Shaddai with the Amorite god "Baal Sadeh" ("Lord of the Field"). See Jean Ouellette, "More on 'Êl Šadday and Bêl Šadê," *JBL* 88 (1969): 470–471; Lloyd R. Bailey, "Israelite 'Ēl Šadday and Amorite Bêl Šadê," *JBL* 87 (1968): 434–438.
11. Dhorme, "Abraham dans le Cadre de l'Histoire"; Maurice A. Canney ("Contribution and Comments: Shaddai," *The Expository Times* 34 [1923]: 329–333) believed the name represented a feminine matriarchal entity before it was attributed to God.
12. *Šadû* A, CAD, Ṣ, 49–58.
13. William F. Albright, "The Names Shaddai and Abram," *JBL* 54 (1935): 180–187.
14. The only deviation is Gen. 43:14: "May El Shaddai dispose the man to mercy toward you…" However, while the context of the verse is the unity of the family, from Jacob's perspective the subject of concern is the survival of his sons.
15. I am not convinced by Joseph Fleishman's assertion that this is the preferred name for God in the patriarchal narrative (Fleishman, "Name Change and Circumcision in Genesis 17," *Beit Mikra* 46 [2001]: 310). *YHWH* and *Elohim* are integrated in patriarchal texts no less than El Shaddai; moreover, the phenomenon should not be evaluated with statistical tools. The name is more common in fertility and family contexts, since it is connected with the blessing of fertility.

covenant.[16] Before, in the Covenant Between the Pieces, Abraham was also promised a son – the son that would continue his line and inherit his leadership role. Here, Abraham and Sarah are promised an end to their infertility – a son to bring them the personal joy of parenthood, regardless of his destiny.

A Moral Archetype for the Ages

At the outset of the covenant, the expectations are set between the two parties:

> Abram's commitment: "Walk in My ways and be blameless."
> *I will establish My covenant between Me and you*
> God's commitment: "I will make you exceedingly numerous."

This short statement summarizes the conditions of the covenant. Abram has to walk in God's ways, while God commits to making Abram "exceedingly numerous." "My covenant" connects the two commitments. This is the essence of the covenant, while the following verses contain extensions and consequences. God's commitment is clear, and centers on fertility. However, the expectation from Abram is vague: "Walk in My ways and be blameless." Clearly walking in God's ways indicates, in general terms, "fearing God" and "committing to His will."[17] The phrase "walking before God" is generally interpreted as "at the service of God," but in the context of the Abraham narrative cycle the demand is dramatized by the use of the verb H-L-KH ("go/walk"), which has accompanied our hero intensively throughout his journey, as we discussed above.

In addition to the demand to walk in God's ways, Abram is told to "be blameless." While some read the phrase as a result of the

---

16. Westermann believed the unique name El Shaddai indicates the unique revelation to the forefathers, which is different from revelations to the nation, and not only different in content (Westermann, *Genesis 12–36: A Continental Commentary*, 258).
17. Gunkel, *Genesis – Translated and Interpreted*, 263; von Rad, *Genesis*, 193; Speiser, *Genesis*, 124. According to Abraham's servant, he was told: "The Lord, whose ways I have followed, will send His angel with you and make your errand successful" (Gen. 24:40). Cf. Hezekiah's prayer: "Please O Lord, remember how I have walked before You sincerely and wholeheartedly" (II Kings 20:3, Is. 38:3).

previous demand (i.e, "You will be blameless as a result of walking in God's ways"),[18] or a completion of the previous statement (i.e., "Walk in God's ways, completely, blamelessly"),[19] the phrase might express an independent demand.[20] While the imperative to "walk in God's ways" is religious in nature, blamelessness has an ethical-moral standing. Many verses interpret "blameless" as "honest and fair": "He who lives without blame, who does what is right, and in his heart acknowledges the truth" (Ps. 15:1–2).[21] This interpretation is emphasized in Psalms 101, which combines *halakh* with *tamim*, "blameless:"[22]

> I will study *the way of the blameless*; when shall I attain it? *I will walk without blame* within my house. I will not set before my eyes anything base. I hate crooked dealing. I will have none of it. Perverse thoughts will be far from me. I will know nothing of evil.... My eyes are on the trusty men of the land, to have them at my side. He who *walks the way of the blameless* shall be in my service. He who deals deceitfully shall not live in my house; he who speaks untruth shall not stand before my eyes.

18. "Thus you will be perfect" (Gunkel, *Genesis – Translated and Interpreted*, 263).
19. This position might be based on Weinfeld's claim that the phrases discussed here have an Akkadian parallel: "Walk in My ways" parallels *ina mahriya ittalak*, and "be blameless" parallels *ittallaku šalmiš* (Moshe Weinfeld, *Deuteronomy and the Deuteronomic School* [Oxford 1972], 76–77). Since the parallel for "be blameless" includes walking, perhaps "be blameless" defines "walk in My ways," creating a hendiadys.
20. Westermann, *Genesis 12–36: A Continental Commentary*, 259.
21. According to Craigie, the meaning of living without blame is interpreted in light of the correlation between v. 2 and v. 3: "Three positive conditions are followed by three negative conditions, then two positive followed by two negative – total ten" (Peter C. Craigie, *Psalms 1–50* [WBC: Dallas, Texas, 1998], 150). He parallels "walking blamelessly/no falsity."
22. According to Briggs, the introduction to the psalm was a late addition, and originally the psalm began, "I will live without blame" (Charles Augustus Briggs and Emily Grace Briggs, *A Critical and Exegetical Commentary on the Book of Psalms* [ICC: Edinburgh, 1907], 313–314). This position emphasizes the link of the psalm to the Covenant of Circumcision even more. However, his position is based on pure speculation.

The psalmist's blameless conduct is expressed through moral sensitivity and a rejection of evil; he wishes to be enveloped in a society of those who walk in the way of the blameless – who do not deal deceitfully or speak untruths.[23]

The demand to be socially ethical is integrated into the covenant of those who walk with God. The verse is based on the concept that Abram is expected to walk in God's ways not only religiously, but socially and ethically, by being benevolent and just. Abram must be beyond reproach not only in the eyes of his people, but in the eyes of the global community. His righteousness in the eyes of the nation is paramount to creating the Jewish nation who will be "a light unto the nations." Abraham's unyielding moral compass is the epitome of human morality – his righteousness sets the tone for the nation he will sire.

D-D' – Abram Throws Himself on His Face

While Abram throws himself on his face in reaction to both of God's messages, there seems to be a real difference between the two episodes. The first time Abram falls (Gen. 17:3), he does so as an expression of awe and respect. The revelation began with God's appearance before Abram (17:1). Hiding one's face is the appropriate reaction (see Ex. 3:1; 33:20–34:8; Lev. 9:24–25; I Kings 18:39; 18:1 and 28), and falling on one's face indicates self-deprecation before God. In contrast, the second time Abram throws himself, he does so in laughter: "Abraham threw himself on his face and laughed" (Gen. 17:17). These two actions seem to directly contradict each other; I believe this conflict is an intentional literary device. Abraham laughs skeptically, yet throwing himself down diminishes the effect of his skepticism.[24] The laughter directly affects the name of the child, which makes the element of laughter essential to this tiding (and to the tidings of chapter 18, as demonstrated there). Abram's laughter expresses wonder and

23. Mitchell Dahood translated "*holekh tamim*" as "the man of blameless conduct" (Dahood, *Psalms* [AB: Garden City, NY, 1970], 1). Regarding v. 7 as an antithesis of v. 6, see Briggs and Briggs, *Psalms 1–50*, 315.

24. Cf. Gunkel, *Genesis – Translated and Interpreted*, 266.

surprise at the impossible breach of the natural order: a woman of ninety bearing a child. The element of surprise is known to be an essential comedic element, which leads to laughter. God commemorates Abram's laughter, which expresses the miraculous conditions of his son's birth, through Isaac's name.[25]

E-E' – The Name Change

The name change is the turning point for Abram and Sarai in their literary journey. In fact, the names themselves are not the essence, but the fact of transition. The name change symbolizes the completion of the covenant with God, the completion of the journey that began with *Lekh lekha* – "Go forth."

After Abram-Abraham's reaction to God's message, God's commitment is explained further: "I will make you exceedingly fertile (*hifreti otkha meod meod*)" (Gen. 17:6). The blessing is an expansion of the generic "be fruitful and multiply" (Gen. 1:28 and 9:1), and the same roots (*pru urvu*) are used in Abraham's blessing ("*arbeh*" in 17:2, and "*hifreti*" in 17:6), but expanded beyond the scope of the original blessing (*meod meod*).[26] A comparison of Abraham's blessing (E) with Sarah's (E') shows that the parallel is complete, with one major distinction:

25. This seems to be the reason there is no criticism of Abram's laughter, in contrast with the parallel in ch. 18, where Sarah is criticized for laughing in a similar context. The lack of criticism is established by the fact that God commemorates Abram's laughter in the son's name, which shows that God does not perceive his reaction in a negative light – or it would not be commemorated in his name. When tidings of a child are delivered to Sarai in ch. 18, no name is mentioned. See discussion below on the correlation between the two chapters, and why Sarah's laughter is criticized. For different interpretive responses to God's different attitude to the laughter of the two characters, see Hayyim Angel, "Learning Faith from the Text, or Text from Faith: The Challenges of Teaching (and Learning) the Avraham Narrative and Commentary," in *Wisdom from All My Teachers*, ed. Jeffrey Saks and Susan Handelman (Jerusalem and New York 2003), 204–206.
26. A similar literary phenomenon occurs in the description of the fertility of Jacob's offspring in Egypt (Ex. 1:7), which leans on the basic blessing "Be fruitful and multiply," but also expands the original blessing. See Jonathan Grossman, "Deliberate Misuse of Idioms in the Biblical Narrative," *Tarbitz* 77 (2008): 39–40.

Abram – Abraham (Gen. 17:3–6)	Sarai – Sarah (Gen 17:15–16)
And God spoke to him further	And God said to Abraham
As for Me, this is My covenant with you: You shall be the father of a multitude of nations	
And you shall no longer be called Abram, but your name shall be Abraham, for I make you the father of a multitude of nations	As for your wife Sarai, you shall not call her Sarai, but her name shall be Sarah
I will make you exceedingly fertile	I will bless her; indeed, I will give you a son by her
and make nations of you	I will bless her so that she shall give rise to nations
and kings shall come forth from you	rulers of peoples shall issue from her
I will maintain My covenant between Me and you, and your offspring to come, as an everlasting covenant throughout the ages, to be God to you and to your offspring to come. I assign the land you sojourn in to you and your offspring to come, all the land of Canaan, as an everlasting holding. I will be their God.	

The two basic components of name change and the blessing of fertility are repeated in both blessings. The change to each of the names is identical: an addition of the letter *heh,* and both blessings of fertility include components of "nations" and "rulers/kings." The one change seems to be the covenant: whereas Abram's name change is enveloped in the covenant, which is mentioned at the beginning and end of the blessing, the covenant is omitted altogether from Sarai's blessing.

This inconsistency is related to the ambivalent position of women with regard to circumcision. Sarai was not mentioned in the Covenant Between the Pieces, or in any of the revelations prior to chapter 17. This is the first time Sarai seems to be regarded as Abram's partner in his covenant with God; she, too, merits a name change and a personal blessing.[27] On the other hand, the terms of the covenant relate to Abram and are not even mentioned in Sarai's blessing, and the covenant sign is performed in Abram's body and not Sarai's.

There are a number of opinions among the commentators as to the meaning of the name changes. The Midrash viewed the addition of the letter *heh* as an indication of an aspect of God's name (*YHWH*) being inserted into Abram's name.[28] Some commentaries have noted that the addition of the letter *heh* actually enables the intentional play on the words "*av hamon goyim,*" "father of a multitude of nations," which is directly linked with the name change.[29] A more felicitous option views the name change as an expression of fertility; the increase of the blessing of fertility is expressed through the expansion of the names. The diverse uses of the letter *heh,* which can serve as either a vowel or a semi-consonant, enable this addition to act as both an expansion of the noun and an addition of a consonant, altogether enhancing the possibilities of the name.[30]

---

27. In contrast with previous revelations, now Abram has a son, Ishmael, who will be mentioned in Abram's reaction to God's promise. Perhaps this is the reason for the emphasis on Sarai's partnership in the covenant and Abram's blessings, as opposed to previous revelations.
28. *Midrash Aggada,* vol. 2, 79, in Menachem Mendel Kasher, *Torah Shelema,* vol. 2, 696. See also Zohar, *Lekh Lekha,* 96a; Kiel, *Daat Mikra,* 451. Heinemann (*The Methods of the Aggadah,* 106) discusses Philo's position that the meaning of the name is changed as well.
29. See Rashi, Ibn Ezra, and Samuel David Luzzatto on Gen. 17:5. Similarly, see for example Parrot, *Abraham and His Times,* 83n51; Mathews, *Genesis,* 202.
30. As various scholars have shown, there is no significant etymological difference between Abram and Abraham, and they seem to be different dialects of the same name (Hans Bauer, "Die hebräischen Eigennamen als sprachliche Erkenntnisquelle," *ZAW* 48 [1930]: 73–80, 75). Montgomery added that the same is true of the names Sarah-Sarai (James A. Montgomery, "The *hemzah-h* in the Semitic," *JBL* 46 [1927]: 144).

The multitude of possible explanations is itself, perhaps, proof that the new names themselves are not the focus. Rather, the fact of the transition itself is what is paramount. When Pharaoh changed Joseph's name to Zaphenath-paneah, he indicated that Joseph was "reborn" into Pharaoh's patronage; Joseph became a member of Pharaoh's household, and merited a new name that expressed his new position.[31] The change from Abram to Abraham should be viewed in a similar light. The name indicates a new beginning, a new chapter; but since God is the one who gives Abraham his new name, the name also indicates Abraham's dependence on God, who takes Abraham in under His patronage. The new name expresses his new position. Abraham commits to walking in God's ways, while God spreads His wings over Abraham and adopts him like a son.[32]

The change in Abraham's name could also be viewed as the final stage in completely disconnecting from the house of his idolatrous father, Terah. All members of Terah's household were given idolatrous names (Nahor, Haran, Milcah, Sarai), and Abram's name was no different (cf. Josh. 24:2).[33] Abram was expected to disengage from the house of his father and seek out not only a new land, but also a new theology. The name change "is another stage... continuing his disengagement from his land, the place of his birth, and his father's house."[34] Abram left behind his Mesopotamian past – culminating in the change of his name – and arrived in Canaan, God's realm, where he will start anew under the

31. See Hamilton, *The Book of Genesis, Chapters 1–17*, 507; Jonathan Grossman, *Joseph: A Tale of Dreams* (Rishon LeZion, 2021), 217–235. See also Dvir, *Biblical Proper Names and Their Mission*, 28–29: "The name is a sign of subordination and subjugation; of ownership." Pharaoh Nekho changes the name of Eliakim, son of Josiah, to Jehoiakim in II Kings 23:34. The meaning of the name remains the same; the change signifies Jehoiakim becoming a ruler on behalf of the Egyptian Pharaoh. Similarly, the king of Babylon changed Mattaniah's name to Zedekiah in II Kings 24:17, to express the commitment of the Judean kingdom to Babylonia.

32. Symbolically, the addition of a letter from God's name indicates a unique internal connection created by the covenant, which is expressed by God changing Abram's name.

33. Dhorme, "Abraham dans le Cadre de l'Histoire"; Fleishman, "Name Change and Circumcision in Genesis 17." Cf. Wenham, *Genesis 16–50*, 252.

34. Fleishman, "Name Change and Circumcision in Genesis 17," 313.

auspices of his God. As this marks a "new beginning" for Abraham, this revelation also refers to the "nations," a reference that does not appear often in the Abraham narrative. God's first revelation to Abraham (Gen. 12:2–3) reveals that Abraham will be the father of a "nation," and here too, when his new name symbolizes a new beginning, nationalistic terminology features.

F – The Covenant Sign

The center of the covenant is the circumcision, and the circumcision itself is a chiastic structure. It is as if to say, this is it, this is the moment, the focal point, the moment that will live on as a legacy for generations. The entire text is pointing to it. The circumcision is a sign, to walk with God, and to remain "blameless" – the circumcision is as much a reminder to be a good person as it is to be a good Jew.

At the center of the covenant structure is the commandment of circumcision itself:

A: As for you, you and your offspring to come throughout the ages shall *keep My covenant.*

B: Such shall be the covenant between Me and you and your offspring to follow which you shall keep: *every male among you shall be circumcised.*

C: You shall circumcise the *flesh* of your foreskin, and that shall be the *sign of the covenant* between Me and you.

D: And throughout the generations, every male among you shall be circumcised at the age of eight days. As for the homeborn slave and the one bought from an outsider who is not of your offspring,

D': they must be circumcised, homeborn, and purchased alike.

C': Thus shall My covenant be marked in your *flesh* as an *everlasting covenant.*

B': And if any *male* who is *uncircumcised* fails to *circumcise* the flesh of his foreskin, that person shall be cut off from his kin.

A': He has broken *My covenant.*

Within the concentric structure of the entire episode, the commandment of circumcision as well appears here in a chiastic, central design. If the covenant of circumcision is the central point of the story, the epicenter of this divine promise is twofold: (1) the act itself, (2) as sign of the covenant. The binary focal points of the covenant are interrelated and significant. Initially (C) the removal of foreskin is defined as the *covenant sign,* while later (C') circumcision is called the actual covenant: "Thus shall *My covenant* be marked in your flesh." Verse 10 expresses a similar idea: "Such shall be *the covenant*... every male among you shall be circumcised."

The definition of circumcision as a sign indicates that the act is a reminder of the covenant, not the essence of the covenant. If circumcision is a sign, it is meant to remind Abraham of his commitment to walk in the ways of God and be blameless. We find a similar model with Noah after the flood: the content of the commitment is the avoidance of a flood, and the rainbow is a sign – a reminder of the commitment (Gen. 9:13).[35] According to the formulation that depicts circumcision as the actual covenant, the obligation to circumcise parallels God's promise of fertility. Many commentators viewed the removal of the foreskin as Abram's commitment in the covenant, and as the content of the covenant. But, verse 11 provides us with clarity: "You shall circumcise the flesh of your foreskin, and that shall be the sign of the covenant between Me and you." The removal of the foreskin is a sign of commitment to the content of the covenant. The verses that seem to indicate otherwise should be viewed as a metonymy: since circumcision is the "covenant sign" and a reminder of the covenant, the covenant is represented by the flesh itself. The covenant is not theoretical or abstract; rather, the

35. Compare with McComiskey, *The Covenants of Promise,* 139–177. Fox writes that the sign of circumcision is a reminder of the covenant directed at God, which parallels the rainbow (Michael V. Fox, "Sign of the Covenant: Circumcision in the Light of the Priestly 'ot' Etiologies," *RB* 81 (1974): 595–596). As he emphasizes, this has much significance, because unlike the common ancient world beliefs, circumcision is not considered a form of magical protection in itself, but rather only functions as a sign of the covenant. Regardless, Hamilton (*The Book of Genesis, Chapters 1–17,* 470–472) debated the moot question regarding toward whom the symbol is directed.

essence of the covenant is in the flesh, which symbolizes man's yielding to its obligations.

The significance of removing the foreskin is puzzling, to say the least. If the circumcision functions as the sign of this essential covenant, one would expect the sign to be in plain sight. After all, the phylacteries, which are also called a sign, are worn on the head, like a crown. Here, however, the sign of the Covenant of Circumcision is in a hidden place. Even more puzzling is another matter. Although Sarah's name is also changed in the story, the sign is exclusively in the male body. Could not another sign that is in plain view, and that involves women as well, have been selected? Bekhor Shor suggests that the sign needs to be hidden "so that the gentiles should not say about Israel that they are blemished."[36] According to his interpretation, hiding the covenant is the chief factor in God's choice of the sign. However, the assumption that circumcision was not known because of the location of the sign is unrealistic. Additionally, an essential part of the concept of a sign is the statement that accompanies the sign. Even if the sign causes physical damage, the statement should be public; a defect that declares devotion to the God of the forefathers.

Since the content of the covenant is specifically linked with the blessing of fertility, the covenant sign is made in the reproductive organ. In the past, removal of the foreskin was considered a coming-of-age or initiation rite. However, several factors attest to the fact that in the Bible, circumcision is not perceived as an initiation rite. For one, all members of Abraham's household, regardless of age, were required to undergo circumcision. Additionally, the usual age for performing circumcision is eight days old. Furthermore, in the Bible, the ceremony was never performed by priests nor any figures of authority.[37] The sign indicates the essence of the covenant. God committed to bless Abram's fertility, while Abram committed to walk blamelessly in the ways of God. The mutual commitment – the acceptance of El Shaddai as the God of Abraham

36. Rabbi Joseph Bekhor Shor on Gen. 17:11. He also views maintaining the laws relating to menstruation as the female alternative to circumcision.

37. Eric Isaac, "Circumcision as Covenant Rite," *Anthropos* 59 (1965): 450. And see the conclusion of this chapter, below.

and his descendants, meriting the blessing of fertility – is expressed by a mark on the reproductive organ of those loyal to El Shaddai.

The structure raises several key points that clarify the narrative. First, the structural link between Abraham and Sarah, which relates to the birth of Isaac. Second, the focus on the command for future generations to circumcise all male children. Third, the frame that emphasizes that Abram is "not yet one hundred." All these indicate that the story has not reached its conclusion.

How Does Ishmael Play into the Covenant?

Meanwhile, where does Ishmael fit into this covenant? Following the story of his birth, we know that Abraham considers Ishmael a legitimate son, and an inheritor of some sort. However, Isaac has clearly been chosen as the beneficiary of the line of power as it relates to the Jewish nation.

Here again, the literary structure of the text clarifies Ishmael's position, which undergoes a veiled transformation throughout the chapter. Isaac is unequivocally the central son in the covenant from God's perspective; however, Abraham's request, "O that Ishmael might live by Your favor" (Gen. 17:18), creates an overt conflict between the two sons, which demands an explicit divine resolution. Verses 19–21, where God relates to Ishmael, are also concentric:[38]

A: "Nevertheless, Sarah your wife shall bear you a son."

> **B:** "And you shall name him Isaac; and I will maintain My covenant with him as an everlasting covenant for his offspring to come."
>
> > **C:** "As for Ishmael, I have heeded you. I hereby bless him. I will make him fertile and exceedingly numerous. He shall be the father of twelve chieftains, and I will make of him a great nation."
>
> **B':** "But My covenant I will maintain with Isaac,"

A': "whom Sarah shall bear to you at this season next year."

---

38. McEvenue, *The Narrative Style of the Priestly Writer*, 175; Alexander, "A Literary Analysis of the Abraham Narrative in Genesis," 172; Wenham, *Genesis 16–50*, 26.

God clarifies the distinction between Isaac, the chosen son, and Ishmael, the son of the maidservant. However, God admits, "As for Ishmael, I have heeded you…" He seems to divide the blessings of fertility between the two sons. As we saw in the previous chapter, Ishmael's status was changed at least in part by virtue of his mother's suffering and God's acceptance of her prayers. Here, we see that this is only part of the story – Ishmael is also blessed by virtue of his connection with Abraham.

The verses emphasize the preference of Isaac over Ishmael, and the parallel tracks their lives and fortunes take, despite their shared father: God tells Abram twice that the everlasting covenant will be realized through Isaac, not Ishmael. Nonetheless, Ishmael's inclusion specifically in the center of the text cannot be ignored, and the blessing he merits has to be clarified.[39] The wording of the blessing is similar to the blessings directed at Abram in previous chapters; however, the parallel between Ishmael's blessing and the one given to Abram earlier in the chapter is apparent. God says in reference to Ishmael: "I will make him *fertile* and *exceedingly numerous,*" mirroring Abram's blessing in verse 2: "I will make you *exceedingly numerous,*" and verse 6: "I will make you *exceedingly fertile.*" Similarly, God says in reference to Ishmael: "He shall be the father of *twelve chieftains,* and I will *make of him a great nation,*" mirroring Abram's blessing in verse 6: "I will *make nations of you*; and *kings* shall come forth from you." Ishmael disengages from the covenant that will be maintained by Isaac; nevertheless, he stands to inherit Abram's blessing of fertility.

This division is apparent from the general chiasm in the chapter, which parallels the verses regarding Isaac and Ishmael's blessings with God's initial message. The similar wording links the two episodes and indicates a division between the sons:

---

39. John Goldingay, "The Place of Ishmael," in *The World of Genesis; Persons, Places, Perspectives,* ed. P. R. Davies and D. J. A. Clines (Sheffield, 1998), 147.

Component C (Gen. 17:1–2)	Component C' (Gen. 17:19–21)
I will establish My covenant between Me and you	I will maintain My covenant with him as an everlasting covenant for his offspring to come.… But My covenant I will maintain with Isaac
and I will make you exceedingly numerous	As for Ishmael, I have heeded you. I hereby bless him. I will make him fertile and exceedingly numerous. He shall be the father of twelve chieftains, and I will make of him a great nation.

While component C introduced the covenant and the blessing of fertility, the parallel C' clarifies that the covenant will be maintained through Isaac, while the blessing of fertility is given to Ishmael. This conclusion might seem implausible; Sarah is also blessed with fertility, a blessing that clearly will be fulfilled through her only son. However, the structure and development of the text indicate that Abraham's outburst led to the inclusion of Ishmael in the dialogue, warranting him a blessing that was originally part of the covenant. The conclusion is therefore that Isaac's fertility will stem from his inclusion in the covenant, while Ishmael's fertility is unconditional on a religious or mutual covenant.

Ishmael's unique status is also expressed in relation to his blessing in the previous chapter, particularly in reference to the implied meaning of his name in each of the chapters. In chapter 16, Ishmael's name signified God having heard Hagar's distress. Hagar's blessing of fertility is portrayed as her compensation for suffering at the hands of her mistress. These accusations are diminished in chapter 17, and Ishmael's name takes on new meaning: "As for Ishmael, I have heeded you (*shematikha*)" (Gen. 17:20). According to this declaration, the name and blessing of Abraham's son are not a compensation for Hagar's suffering, but rather for Abraham's request, "May it be that Ishmael live by Your favor" (v. 18). In chapter 17, Ishmael's status is not a criticism of Sarai, but rather a merit to Abram, whose offspring – even the one who is not part of the covenant – is blessed. In chapter 17, Ishmael inherits the blessing of fertility not because of his mother, but because of his father.

The feeling that Ishmael was not originally supposed to be included in the narrative is apparent from the concluding verses (A'). These verses (Gen. 17:23–27) are also designed concentrically:

A: "Then *Abraham* took *his son Ishmael,* and *all his homeborn slaves and all those he had bought,* every male in Abraham's household, and he *circumcised* the flesh of their foreskins"

B: "*on that very day,* as God had spoken to him."

C: "Abraham was ninety-nine years old when he circumcised the flesh of his foreskin."

C': "And his son Ishmael was thirteen years old when he was circumcised in the flesh of his foreskin."

B': "*On that very day*"

A': "*Abraham* and *his son Ishmael* were *circumcised,* and *all his household, his homeborn slaves and those that had been bought from outsiders,* were *circumcised* with him."

The center of the structure focuses, surprisingly, on Abraham and his son – Ishmael. The narrative begins by stating Abram's age, and ends by repeating his age, this time alongside the age of his son. These details specify Ishmael's status, which is improved throughout the story. Following Abraham's request on behalf of his son, Ishmael merits a portion of Abraham's blessing.

Circumcision for the Generations

We cannot conclude this chapter without noting the biblical innovation regarding circumcision, which was prevalent in the ancient world. Although many cultures have documentation on circumcision,[40] as

40. Cf. Jer. 9:24–25 (Sarna, *Genesis* [JPS Torah Commentary], 132). See the review by Fox, "Sign of the Covenant"; Jack M. Sasson, "Circumcision in the Ancient Near East," *JBL* 85 (1966): 473–476; Westermann, *Genesis 12–36: A Continental Commentary,* 165; Sarna, *Genesis* (JPS), 131–133; Hamilton, *The Book of Genesis, Chapters 1–17,* 469; Robert G. Hall, "Circumcision,'" *ABD* 1:1025–1031; Fleishman, "Name Change and Circumcision in Genesis 17," 314; Nick Wyatt, "Circumcision and Circumstance: Male Genital Mutilation in Ancient Israel and Ugarit," *JSOT* 33 (2009): 405–431.

noted in a variety of biblical sources,[41] commentators debate the source of the custom and the purpose of circumcision in other nations.[42] Since circumcision affects the reproductive organ, the custom seems to relate to fertility. This idea is reinforced by the ancient custom to circumcise men before marriage in particular.[43] There are two major differences between biblical circumcision and the prevalent custom in the Ancient Near East. First, the context of the law portrays circumcision as part of a covenant, and the removal of the foreskin is a "sign" of the covenant between Abraham (and his offspring) and God.[44] Second, biblical circumcision is performed on infants at the age of eight days, and not as a rite of passage prior to marriage.[45]

These two details shed a unique light on circumcision, and on the purpose of the narrative in Genesis 17. The covenant sign is performed in the reproductive organ, because the essence of the covenant relates to the blessing of fertility.[46] But the covenant is not as significant to the infant as it is to his parents. The performance of circumcision on a helpless baby makes the sign into a testimony of the covenant between the *parents* and

---

41. See, for example, the Dinah narrative in Gen. 34, Moses and Zipporah in the encampment in Ex. 4, and Jer. 9:24–25. Sarna suggests that the Passover law that excludes the uncircumcised from the sacrifice attests to the widespread "pre-Sinai" circulation of the law of circumcision (Sarna, *Genesis* [JPS], 132). Also, according to the biblical narrative, the law was given to Abraham, and there is no reason his children should not know and follow the law. John Goldingay claims correctly that the integration of circumcision in the Dinah narrative creates an ironic effect. See Goldingay, "The Significance of Circumcision," *JSOT* 88 (2000): 9–10.
42. Hall, "Circumcision," 1025. See Fleishman's summary of the debate ("Name Change and Circumcision in Genesis 17," 314).
43. Hamilton, *The Book of Genesis, Chapters 1–17*, 46. Sasson ("Circumcision in the Ancient Near East," 474) raises the possibility that this is a rite of passage.
44. Sarna, *Genesis* (JPS), 132; Fox, "Sign of the Covenant"; Hall, "Circumcision," 1027.
45. See, among others, Wyatt, "Circumcision and Circumstance."
46. See especially Isaac, "Circumcision as Covenant Rite." Fleishman views sexual purity as the essence of the covenant and the distinction of the offspring of Abraham from the prevalent sexual morality in Egypt and Canaan (Fleishman, "Name Change and Circumcision in Genesis 17"). He demonstrates that the inheritance of the land is dependent on maintaining high moral sexual standards, and that this concept manifests in the book of Genesis as well.

their god.[47] A circumcision at the age of thirteen (i.e., Ishmael's) could mean a rite of passage; however, circumcision at eight days is part of the birth rituals.[48] When parents circumcise their son, they recognize that God has fulfilled His commitment to the fertility of Abraham's offspring. Simultaneously, by circumcising their son, the parents enter their son into the family covenant with God. Since the sign of the covenant is in the reproductive organ, the next generation to be born to the circumcised baby will be born into the sanctity of the covenant, because his parents had walked in the ways of El Shaddai. Each circumcision represents a multi-generational acceptance of the covenant: the parents who make the covenant, the baby who will be an instrument for the covenant sign, and the next generation to be born of the covenant sign.

In light of all this, Abraham's age is an appropriate frame for the Covenant of Circumcision. As we noted earlier, the timing of the covenant when Abraham was "almost one hundred" was an indication that the real and essential starting point would only occur when Abraham was one hundred: "But My covenant I will maintain with Isaac, whom Sarah shall bear to you at this season next year" (Gen. 17:21). Abraham circumcises himself one year before the birth of Isaac, to ensure that the process of Isaac's conception and birth is included in the covenant.

This is the central essence of the Covenant of Circumcision, not only for Abraham, but for all the generations that follow. The covenant requires three participants: the parents, already bound by the covenant, who introduce the child into it; the child who enters the covenant; and

---

47. The fact that the parents are the focus of the covenant and not the circumcised baby is emphasized in Ishmael's circumcision. Abraham is obligated to circumcise Ishmael; nonetheless, Ishmael is not included in the Covenant of Circumcision, as God says: "But My covenant I will maintain with Isaac." The demand for circumcision at eight days might relate to a broader biblical concept relating to "the eighth day," particularly in relation to the purification process, which lasts seven days and requires a sacrifice on the eighth day. Wyatt ("Circumcision and Circumstance," 416) views circumcision as a type of sacrifice, shedding new light on the "eighth day" concept in Ex. 22:9 and Lev. 22:27. Others view the removal of the foreskin as a protection from the constant threat to those who would violate the covenant. See Isaac, "Circumcision as Covenant Rite."

48. Wyatt, "Circumcision and Circumstance," 411–412. See also Isaac, "Circumcision as Covenant Rite," 450.

the third generation, as symbolized by the reproductive organ of the child undergoing circumcision. Abraham needed to enter first himself into the Covenant of Circumcision, in order to lead his son, and his progeny, into the ternary, eternal, bond.

Comparison with the Rainbow Covenant

As we mentioned above, the broader purpose of the Covenant of Circumcision becomes apparent in light of the contrast with the Rainbow Covenant. The language and style of the two covenants are similar:[49]

Abraham's Covenant (Gen. 17)	**Noah's Covenant (Gen. 9)**
I make you the father of a multitude of nations; I will make you exceedingly fertile	Be fertile, then, and increase; abound on the earth and increase on it.
I will maintain My covenant between Me and you, and your offspring to come…	I now establish My covenant with you and your offspring to come, and with every living thing that is with you – birds, cattle, and every wild beast as well – all that have come out of the ark, every living thing on earth. I will maintain My covenant with you.
…as an everlasting covenant throughout the ages	For all ages to come.
You shall circumcise the flesh of your foreskin, and that shall be the sign of the covenant between Me and you	I have set My bow in the clouds, and it shall serve as a sign of the covenant between Me and the earth.
as an everlasting pact.	I will see it and remember the everlasting covenant.

49. See, among others, Isaac, "Circumcision as Covenant Rite," 451; McEvenue, *The Narrative Style of the Priestly Writer*, 170–171; McComiskey, *The Covenants of Promise*, 139–177; Cassuto, *The "Quaestio" of the Book of Genesis*, 18–52, 41–43.

Additionally, God's demand, "Walk in My ways and be blameless," is reminiscent of the characterization of Noah: "Noah was a righteous man; he was blameless in his age – Noah walked with God" (Gen. 6:9). The narrative attests that Abraham did "as God had spoken to him" (17:23) just as Noah did "as God had commanded him" (7:16).[50]

Despite the obvious link between all covenant narratives, these two seem to have a special affinity.[51] The Covenant of Circumcision is portrayed as though it promotes the Rainbow Covenant to another level. There are four advances from the Rainbow Covenant to the Covenant of Circumcision:

1. **The partnership**: After the flood, God made a covenant with "all flesh," including animals. This fact is emphasized four times in the text,[52] starting from the very first declaration regarding the creation of a covenant: "I now establish My covenant with you and your offspring to come. And *with every living creature* that is with you... every beast of the earth." (Gen. 9:9–10). And similarly, the covenant sign – the rainbow – is "a sign that I set for the covenant between Me and you and *every living creature* with you, for all ages to come" (9:12). Further, God states, "I will remember My covenant, which is between Me and you and *every living*

50. The link between the Covenant of the Rainbow and the Covenant of Circumcision is expressed in Ezekiel's chariot vision: "From what appeared as his loins up, I saw a gleam as of amber – what looked like fire encased in a frame; and from what appeared as his loins down I saw what looked like fire. There was a radiance all about him. Like the appearance of the bow that shines in the clouds on a day of rain, such was the appearance of the surrounding radiance. That was the appearance of the semblance of the presence of the Lord" (Ezek. 1:27–28). Ezekiel describes a fire and radiance "from his loins down," and compares the radiance to a rainbow.
51. Regarding the linguistic formulations that distinguish the covenant narrative, see George E. Mendenhall, "Covenant Forms in Israelite Tradition," *BA* 17 (1954): 50–76; Moshe Weinfeld, "ברית," *TDOT* 2:253–279; Dennis J. McCarthy *Treaty and Covenant: A Study in Form in the Ancient Oriental Documents and in the Old Testament* (Analecta Biblica 21: Rome, 1978).
52. McEvenue demonstrated that in God's address to Noah in 9:8–10, those affected by the covenant gradually expand, and ultimately include all animals (McEvenue, *The Narrative Style of the Priestly Writer*, 73).

creature of all flesh... an everlasting covenant between God and *every living creature* of all flesh that is upon the earth." (9:15–16). Finally, the conclusion of the narrative states: "That shall be a sign of the covenant that I have established between Me and *all flesh that is on earth*" (9:17). In contrast, the Covenant of Circumcision includes only Abraham and his offspring. Abraham is promised that he will be "father of a multitude of nations" (17:4). The formulation of the covenant constantly repeats the exclusivity of those included in the covenant. Unlike the detailed list in the Rainbow Covenant, the Covenant of Circumcision has only the intimate description "between Me and you and your offspring to come." Anyone outside Abraham's family is not included in the covenant.[53]

2. **Location:** The purpose of each of the covenants leads to the implementation of each covenant in a different location. The word "earth" appears seven times in the text of the Rainbow Covenant. Since the purpose of covenant is the maintenance of the world, the covenant is valid everywhere. In contrast, the Covenant of Circumcision is only maintained within the narrow borders of Canaan: "I assign the land you sojourn in to you and your offspring to come, all the land of Canaan as an everlasting holding, and I will be their God" (Gen. 17:8). Abraham and his offspring will inherit the land of Canaan, where God will be acknowledged as the Lord of Abraham's offspring.[54]

---

53. As noted previously, Westermann believed that the Covenant of Circumcision reflects a universalistic approach, similar to Gen. 12:3, since in both instances the blessing is said to affect many nations. While Abram is blessed that he will be father to many nations, the nations to merit God's blessing in the Covenant of Circumcision are those descended from Abraham; this is not a universal approach, but rather a blessing to Abraham's extended family. In contrast, the blessing in Gen. 12:3 relates to nations that are independent of Abraham.
54. Some, such as Lohfink, understand the biblical description of Canaan as "Land of the Fathers" as lacking any particular religious indications. However, this possibility is not apparent in Ex. 6, particularly compared with Ex. 3–4. Rashi writes (confirmed by reliable manuscripts cited by Avraham Grossman in *Rashi* [Jerusalem: Zalman Shazar Center, 2006], 174): "There: 'I will be their God,' but one who dwells outside

3. **Scope**: While the scope of the covenant is reduced, human commitment in the Covenant of Circumcision is expanded. The Rainbow Covenant is predominantly God's commitment, but there seems to be an expectation of human contribution: man is expected to reproduce, while God commits not to destroy the world with another flood. This demand was stated twice in the covenant, as a literary frame for the unit before the covenant: "Be fertile and increase, and fill the earth" (Gen. 9:1), and "Be fertile, then, and increase, abound on the earth and increase on it" (9:7). The demand is to devote oneself to a natural survival instinct. The demands are mutual in that both parties have committed to maintain the existence of the world. In contrast, God's demand of the party to circumcision is religious: "Walk in My ways and be blameless" (17:1).
4. **Who bears the sign:** Finally, the party responsible for maintaining the sign varies in each of the covenants. While God commits to "set My bow in the clouds" (Gen. 9:12–14), Abraham is the one who must maintain the sign of the Covenant of Circumcision: "You shall circumcise the flesh of your foreskin, and that shall be the sign of the covenant between Me and you" (17:9–11).

These four differences stem from the fact that God's covenant with Noah is a natural covenant, which relates to the very existence of the world. In this covenant, there is a human commitment is to be fruitful and multiply, that commitment relates to all living beings at all times, and its nature is unrelated to religion. In contrast, the Covenant of Circumcision relates to a specific group, which committed to walking in the ways of God; the covenant is therefore religious in nature. A religious declaration by those committed to the covenant is necessary, and so the maintenance of the covenant sign is incumbent upon man. Upon the birth of his son, God's faithful subject will declare his commitment to God, and acknowledge the source of his fertility. Such a statement could not be expected in the Rainbow Covenant, which comprises all living beings, and the earth itself.

---

the land, it is as though I am not their God" (Rashi on Gen. 17:8). The author there discusses Rashi's unique approach toward the Land of Israel.

The Covenant of Circumcision is the central axis upon which the Abraham narrative unfolds. It is the moment in which Abraham changes – literally, his name changes – from chosen individual to leader of a chosen nation. From now on, every story in Abraham's journey will reflect this dichotomy – Abram, the man, will continue to learn and grow as a servant of God; Abraham, the leader, will undergo great hardship and emerge victorious as he lays the groundwork for the nascent nation he will lead.

Angels Eat and Sarah Laughs (Gen. 18:1–16)

For some time now in Abraham's journey, he has been the obvious protagonist of God's master plan. Just as obvious is the reality that God must facilitate the birth of a son and heir to continue Abraham's legacy. And yet, the message that Sarah and Abraham will bear a son is told not once, but twice, in incredible detail. The first occurrence was God's revelation to Abraham during the Covenant of Circumcision, and the second took place when divine messengers visited the couple's tent. What is this literary device, how does it serve the narrative, and most importantly, what does it teach us about the birth of Isaac, and, correspondingly, the Jewish nation?

Beginning or Continuation?

The beginning of the story in chapter 18 is, by all accounts, the beginning of a new chapter. The text has been divided this way by essentially anyone who ever bothered to divide it in the first place – it is verse 1 of chapter 18, the first sentence of a Masoretic chapter division (*seder* 15), and the beginning of a new weekly reading portion ("*Vayera*"). It is odd, then, that the opening line of a decidedly new narrative would begin by referring to the protagonist not by name, but by an ambiguous pronoun. "The Lord appeared to *him* by the terebinths of Mamre; he was sitting at the entrance of the tent as the day grew hot" (Gen.

18:1). If this is the opening line of a new story, how do we know who the text is talking about? The Lord appeared to *him*…" To whom? The text continues in this way in the verses that follow. "*He* was sitting" (who was?), "*he* saw" (who did?), "as soon as *he* saw them, *he* ran" (who?), "*he* bowed to the ground, and *he* said" (who?). Who is performing all these actions? *Who*?

Obviously, the text is referring to Abraham. However, the narrative connection to the Covenant of Circumcision that occurred in the previous chapter is not completely clear. One possibility is that having stated previously that Abraham was dwelling in tents by the terebinths of Mamre (Gen. 13:18), the text directly continues that narrative here with the opening verse, "The Lord appeared to him by the terebinths of Mamre."[1] However, the talmudic Sages generally viewed this narrative as a continuation of the immediately preceding Covenant of Circumcision, some contending that the angels came to visit the elderly Abraham as he was recovering from his circumcision.[2] Even so, the structure reminds the reader of a previous disclosure of a future heir – in chapter 16, when God told Abram that he would sire a son through Hagar.

The thematic links between chapters 16 and 18 are clear: each tale involves the tidings of a son and heir, delivered by angels to each of Abraham's wives. The two narratives are also theologically related, which will be further discussed in the context of chapter 21. The story of Ishmael's birth ends with Abram: "Hagar bore a son to Abram, and Abram gave the son that Hagar bore him the name Ishmael; Abram was eighty-six years old when Hagar bore Ishmael to Abram" (Gen. 16:15–16). The presumptuous opening pronoun in chapter 18 might rely upon this previous verse and describe "him" sitting in the terebinths of Mamre. The angels who met Hagar return from that encounter and proceed to Abraham's tent. The desert revelation by the spring, delivering tidings of a son who will leave home and roam the wild,

1. Talia Rudin-O'Brasky, *The Patriarch in Hebron and Sodom (Genesis 18–19)* (Jerusalem, 1982), 48–49.
2. Bava Metzia 86b. See survey by Rudin-O'Brasky, *The Patriarch in Hebron and Sodom*, 34–35.

now comes inside Abraham's tent, bringing the promise of an heir to Abraham's home.

The link to Ishmael's birth aside, the apparent continuation of the story contrasted with the clear unanimous division of the literary units is perplexing. This apparent disparity highlights the question that lies at the heart of the chapter: Why is another revelation regarding the birth of Isaac necessary, immediately after Abraham was told in the Covenant of Circumcision that Sarah will give him a son?

Laughter

One of the most puzzling details of this story is Abraham and Sarah's laughter. The angels inform Abraham that Sarah will have a baby "next year" (Gen. 18:14), just as God had told Abraham that his son will be born "at this season next year" (17:21). Abraham laughed in disbelief when he heard God's tidings, since "can a child be born to a man a hundred years old, or can Sarah bear a child at ninety?" (17:17). Sarah reacted similarly, and for the same reason, when she heard the prediction: "Now that I am withered, am I to have enjoyment – with my husband so old?" (18:12).

The repetition of laughter stories, as well as their given explanations for laughing, are strange. It is apparent why Abraham laughed. After years of infertility, after the saga of siring a child through a surrogate, Abraham is told by God that he will bear a son through his wife Sarah. Abraham, so utterly shocked and overjoyed, bursts out laughing at the thought – a laughter that no doubt turned to tears of incredulous joy. However, some time later, angels arrive at Abraham and Sarah's tent and turn to Sarah, telling her that she will bear her husband an heir. Sarah's outburst of laughter and disbelief mirrors Abraham's incredulity in the previous scene. Are we really meant to believe that this is the first time Sarah heard this news? Again, after decades of struggles, of barrenness, of unfulfilled prayers and dashed hopes, Abraham finds out his wife Sarah will have a child. He bursts out laughing and … goes back to whatever task was at hand? He doesn't drop everything to run home to tell his wife the good news? Was the angels' message at the doorstep truly the first time Sarah received this information?

Certainly, some commentators insist that Abraham did indeed withhold the revelation from Sarah after the circumcision, or perhaps that Sarah did not believe it was true until she heard it from the angel's mouth.[3] Nahmanides suggests that Abraham did not disclose to Sarah the divine message about a son, possibly because Abraham believed, as the prophet Amos declares (Amos 3:7), that God will only act once He relays His secrets to His prophets. Alternatively, Nahmanides writes, Abraham may have been so busy fulfilling the commandment to circumcise himself and his entire household that he forgot to mention the prophecy to his wife.

Regardless, in highlighting Sarah's laughter, the focus of the narrative shifts from Abraham to Sarah and may offer an explanation as to the repetition of the story.[4] From a literary analysis perspective, it is clear that the Covenant of Circumcision is the story of Abraham discovering that he will sire an heir through Sarah. The arrival of the angels to bear the same tidings at the couple's tent is entirely Sarah's story. The apparent repetition of these tidings will become clearer as we analyze the text itself.

The Unknowing Protagonist, the Knowing Reader

The first significant literary device we notice in this narrative is a split in perspective as the story unfolds. There is an ongoing disparity between information that the text relays to the reader and the information relayed to the main character, Abraham. The very first verse describes God appeing to Abraham, yet does not record any direct conversation. The simplest way to read this, as suggested by Rabbi Samuel ben Meir (Rashbam), is to see the first verse as a title description to the entire story; it introduces the topic by explaining how the revelation that will follow came to pass. However, I believe the narrative here is a bit more complex, in that the text intentionally creates a feeling of watching the story unfold from two perspectives.

---

3. Hamilton, *The Book of Genesis, Chapters 18–50*, 13. See also Derek Kidner, *Genesis* (TOTC: London, 1967), 132.
4. A similar approach was suggested by McEvenue, who believes ch. 17 is familiar with the narrative of ch. 18. However, according to McEvenue the two narratives relate to each other, while Zakovitch believes the narratives complete each other (McEvenue, *The Narrative Style of the Priestly Writer*, 153–154).

While the reader is aware that the men who arrive at Abraham's tent are in fact part of a divine revelation, to Abraham they appear to be three guests in need of rest and shelter. Using this device, the text creates a feeling of mystery and suspense in the storytelling – the reader watches in eager anticipation as Abraham scurries about, preparing his home for houseguests that he does not realize are divine beings. Abraham simply believes he is acting with kindness, as he normally would. Meanwhile, the reader breathlessly waits to see how the event pans out, knowing that Abraham's behavior in this situation could very well affect the nature of divine beings' message. If Abraham is kind, the message may be encouraging. But what if he turns them away? If Abraham fails this trial testing the extent of his kindness and grace, he may be deemed unworthy of the angels' blessed tidings. Of course, Abraham has no idea he is being tested; only the knowing reader experiences this scene in all its suspenseful uncertainty.

In this covert test of Abraham's hospitality, his every move matters. The text goes into great detail outlining Abraham's behavior and state of mind throughout the scene. At each juncture, the text reveals Abraham as a genuine host, intensely concerned for his guests' every comfort, and engaging every aspect of his substantial household to ensure the guests feel welcome and contented.

The moment Abraham caught his first glimpse of the strangers in Genesis 18:2 is described in two sentences, both of which begin with the word "*vayar,*" "he saw":

- "He lifted his eyes and *he saw,* and behold! There were three men standing near him."
- "*He saw,* and ran from the entrance of the tent to greet them and bowed to the ground."

First, Abraham notices the guests unexpectedly from afar. We know they were unexpected because of the use of the word "*hineh,*" "behold," in the first verse. The text continues on to repeat the verb *vayar* upon seeing the strangers, and then Abraham runs to greet them. This repetition is significant – Abraham first notices the strangers approaching, and "sees" that they should be welcomed. Three strangers at a considerable distance arouse in Abraham the feeling of responsibility for their comfort and well-being.

The renowned "entrance of the tent," which later becomes the sigil of Abraham's family, plays a central role. It appears twice in the first few verses and reemerges later in the story as well, in the episode with Lot in Sodom. The entryway in which Abraham sat (Gen. 18:1), and later runs out from (18:2), symbolizes the transition and boundaries between inside and out.[5] Throughout this story, the entryway is a defining motif. Abraham brings outsiders into his home, and as a result, he is about to discover that the boundaries of his home will expand by means of a son. By inviting guests into his home, Abraham quite literally opens the door to divine blessing.

The constant back-and-forth of plural and singular throughout the language of the story gives the reader the exhilarating feeling of perpetually bouncing back and forth between Abraham's perspective and the omniscient narrator. The singular reinforces the divine revelation: God, the main speaker, is present in Abraham's tent, while the plural reflects Abraham's perception: three passers-by in need of assistance. The writing style is confusing,[6] and begins as early as Abraham's discussion with his guests:

> He said, "My Lords, if I find favor in your (singular) eyes, do not go on past your (singular) servant. Let a little water be brought; bathe your (plural) feet and recline yourselves (plural) under the tree. And let me fetch a morsel of bread that you (plural) may refresh yourselves (plural); then you (plural) shall pass, for this is why you (plural) have passed by your (plural) servant." They (plural) replied, "Do as you have said."[7]

---

5. See also Ex. 33:7–11, Num. 12:5, Deut. 22:21, Judges 19:26–27. See also Rüdiger Bartelmus, "פתח," *TDOT* 7:173–191.
6. See Rudin-O'Brasky, *The Patriarch in Hebron and Sodom*, 31–32, who notes that the confusion is continued in Gen. 19:18–19. However, the reason is easier to determine there than in ch. 18.
7. Instead of, "You have passed by (*avartem*) your servant," the Septuagint reads, "You have turned aside (*sartem*) your servant." Some prefer this version (Charles James Ball, *The Book of Genesis: Critical Edition of the Hebrew Text* [Leipzig: J. C. Hinrichs, 1896], 68). I believe the constant use of the verb *avar*, to pass ("My Lords, if it please you, do not go on *past* your servant ... then you shall *pass*, for this is why you have passed by your servant") is intentional, and emphasizes Abraham's perception of the

This shifting continues throughout the narrative: the three men wash their feet, lean under the tree, eat, and ask Abraham about the whereabouts of his wife. The tidings are delivered in the singular: "Then he said, 'I will return to you next year, and your wife Sarah shall have a son!'" (Gen. 18:10).

Preparing the Meal

The chaotic writing style, jumping from one perspective to the other and back again, also heightens the feeling of Abraham's somewhat frenetic running around as he prepares to serve his guests. He hurries to Sarah and gives specific instructions, and he chooses the calf himself and gives it to the servant. Sarah is issued three commands (no words are recorded, by the way, between Abraham and the servant): "(1) Be quick, (2) [take][8] three seahs of choice flour! (3) Knead and make cakes!" These clipped commands add to the feeling of chaos, in addition to switching back and forth between addressing the guests in the plural and singular forms. This frenzied scene only underscores Abraham's devotion to hospitality. Abraham is clearly energetic and seeks to be involved in every detail of the preparation of the feast. Imagine Abraham, animated and eager, running into the kitchen to check on the status of the meal Sarah was preparing for their guests: Is it ready? Knead the bread! How wonderful it is that these people have come! With the same enthusiasm, he then runs to the herd,[9] finds a "tender and choice" calf, and hands it to the servant himself.

The Midrash offers an interpretation that even though the guests arrived in a group, that group contained one main leader, with two

---

situation, and the fortuitousness of his unexpected guests (cf. Rudin-O'Brasky, *The Patriarch in Hebron and Sodom*, 54). Garsiel demonstrates that "*ivrim*," "Hebrews," is always used in connection to the verb "to pass" (Garsiel, *Biblical Names: A Literary Study of Midrashic Derivations and Puns*, 40). Perhaps here, too, the use of the verb is alluding to Abraham, who is called an "*ivri*."

8. In his haste, Abraham apparently "forgot" to say the word "take"!
9. Anthony Abela notes a break in the chain of Genesis 18:7a, which features an inverted word order (object, verb, subject), and he claims that it expresses how Abraham ran out to his herd, which was kept at a distance from his living quarters. Thus, the phrase is best translated as, "Even to the herds did Abraham go in all haste" (Abela, "Difficulties for Exegesis and Translation: The Inversion of Genesis 18:7a," *Bible Translator* 60 [2009]: 1–4).

secondary associates.[10] This might explain Abraham's alternating use of the plural and singular in addressing them, as he may have at times been speaking to the group as a whole, and other times addressing only the leader (identified by the midrash as the Divine). If we continue this train of thought and perceive the leader of the guests as God Himself, much of the confusion in the text seems to dissipate. This approach, which identifies God as the main "guest," relies heavily on the title description of the story – "And God appeared to him" – as well as on the instance later in the story in which one of the messengers is referred to as God (Gen. 18:13). Later, when Abraham argues with God over the fate of Sodom, the text seems to indicate that parts of Abraham's conversation with the messengers is in fact a conversation with God – indicated by the fact that while Abraham is arguing with one messenger, characterized as God, the two others make their way to Sodom (v. 22). Rashbam suggests that in a group of any three messenger angels, one carries the weight of the Divine name, and may therefore be seen as His representative, if not God Himself.

Even if we accept this approach, there is literary value to the intense fluctuation from singular to plural, confusing language apparently generating two perspectives in the same narrative. The perspective of the reader, who sees that it is (the singular) God who has visited Abraham's tent, tells a different story than Abraham sees, as the (plural) guests make their way to his home. Abraham's "mistake," of course, is no coincidence. For some reason, God prefers to mislead Abraham, at least initially, and the messengers take part in this theater by agreeing to rest and eat as Abraham prompts.

While the meal is being prepared, Abraham offers his guests rest ("Recline under the tree"); in practice, "he waited on them under the tree as they ate." While the story began with the visitors "standing" over Abraham, now he "stood" over them, to serve them. The opening scene of Abraham's hospitality (and clandestine test of his kindness) begins to come full circle. Abraham's diligence and generosity are expressed through the difference between his initial modest offer and the feast he serves the messengers, which included cakes (instead of bread), a

10. Genesis Rabba 48:10.

tender calf, curds, and milk. Each dish's preparation is described with the word "*vayikaḥ,*" "and he took," in parallel to his initial offer to "take" water and some bread. The reader watches on as Abraham passes and surpasses the test of his virtue and kindness. As the hospitality scene comes to an end, there can now be no doubt in the reader's mind that the messengers' divine revelation will be a joyous and beneficial tiding.

Let us return to the message itself. After the hospitality scene, we are still left with the question of why the messengers have arrived in the first place. They already delivered the message of Isaac's birth to Abraham in chapter 17, and presumably, Abraham shared this information with his spouse. In order to understand the purpose of the apparent repetition, let us compare the two deliveries of the message – the first directed at Abraham, and the second at Sarah.

- **The Message's Recipient:** Both messages pertain to the couple, but one is addressed to Abraham, and the other focuses upon Sarah. In the Covenant of Circumcision, God appears to Abraham: "I will bless her; indeed, *I will give you* a son by her" (Gen. 18:16). Sarah will be blessed but she will birth *Abraham's* son. This is consistent throughout the chapter: "God said, 'Nevertheless, Sarah your wife *shall bear you* a son'" (17:19), and, "But My covenant I will maintain with Isaac, whom Sarah shall bear *to you* at this season next year" (17:21). In contrast, the visitors' message is directed toward Sarah. Although they do not address Sarah directly (probably due to etiquette), they ask about her whereabouts before they begin to speak (18:9). This emphasizes that she is their recipient, as the message itself repeatedly clarifies: "Then he said, 'I will return to you next year, and *your wife Sarah* shall have a son'" (18:10), and again afterward,[11] "I will return to you at the time next year, and *Sarah shall have* a son" (18:14).

---

11. Based on the comparison of the two chapters, von Rad incorrectly states that Sarah was the protagonist of Gen. 17 (von Rad, *Genesis*, 197). Although Sarah is paralleled with Abraham in chapter 17, and is portrayed as his partner, the emphasis of the chapter is on Abraham, as opposed to chapter 18. Regarding Sarah as the main

- **Who Laughed?:** As with the previous distinction, the recipient of each message is the one to react with laughter. Abraham laughs after receiving tidings of Isaac's birth during the Covenant of Circumcision in Genesis 17, and Sarah reacts the same way in Genesis 18.[12]
- **Content:** The messages also differ significantly in content. In both narratives, the elderly couple is told that they will bear a son, but the function and purpose the child will serve is dramatically different in each of the stories. In this scene in Abraham and Sarah's tent, the angels emphasize the birth itself; not a word is mentioned about the child's unique destiny or historical significance. The purpose of the child is to bring joy to his elderly parents, who have waited for so long to hold a child in their arms. In contrast, the Covenant of Circumcision defines Isaac's role as the guardian of the covenant.[13] Abraham's future son is entrusted with a national-historical mission: "You shall name him Isaac, and I will maintain My covenant with him as an everlasting covenant for his offspring to come.... My covenant I will maintain with Isaac, whom Sarah shall bear to you at this season next year" (Gen. 17:19–21).
- **The Child's Name:** In the Covenant of Circumcision, Abraham's son is named, while the divine visitors do not discuss the name of the child. Sarah's laughter and the ensuing dialogue allude to Isaac's name, but it is not mentioned explicitly. The absence of the name is particularly surprising, when we consider that birth tidings often include this component (see the tidings

---

character with regard to the tidings of the birth of Isaac, see Westermann (*Genesis 12–36: A Continental Commentary*, 279), who believes that in the nuclear story the message was delivered directly to Sarah.

12. God's reaction to the laughter in the two narratives should also be compared. Sarah's laughter is questioned, while Abraham's laughter is not, although I believe Abraham's laughter in the Covenant of Circumcision is not taken lightly. However, as already mentioned, the fact that Isaac's name commemorates this laughter shows that Abraham's reaction is not openly criticized.
13. Cf. McEvenue (*The Narrative Style of the Priestly Writer*, 154), who believes ch. 17 relies on ch. 18.

to Hagar in Gen. 16:11, and see as well I Kings 13:2, Is. 7:14–16, I Chr. 22:9–10).[14]

- **Divine Names:** In the Covenant of Circumcision, with the exception of the introduction as *El Shaddai*, God is referred to as *Elohim*, while Genesis 18 uses *YHWH* throughout the narrative.
- **The Nature of the Revelation:** The Covenant of Circumcision is a prophetic revelation: *Elohim* reveals Himself to Abraham, who in turn "falls on his face." In the angel narrative, God meets with Abraham in his tent and appears to him in some sense in an anthropomorphic form. Instead of a formidable prophetic revelation, the setting is intimate and personal.

If we look at these six details side-by-side in each story, a clear dichotomy arises that sheds light both on the nature of repetition of the message, as well as the dichotomous nature of Abraham's overall narrative.

Throughout Abraham's heroic journey, two plot threads emerge over and over again, at times separate, at others intertwined. The first is the "covenant thread": the national-historical story behind the establishment of the nation. The second is the "personal thread," the story of Abraham and Sarah's private life. While both threads have theological significance, the covenant thread is naturally ideological-theological, clarifying God's plan to establish a nation, while the personal thread describes the couple's everyday lives and challenges. The couple's infertility has great bearing on each thread. A son and heir is necessary to maintain the covenant, establish a nation, and realize God's promises to Abraham. On an entirely separate plane, Abraham and Sarah's natural desire for a child is independent of the historical ideology that they are expected to promote. Like any other couple, Sarah and Abraham yearn to raise a child of their own.

---

14. Noted by Alexander ("A Literary Analysis of the Abraham Narrative in Genesis," 202–203). The problem led Van Seters to read the birth and naming of Isaac as a direct continuation of the angels' tidings in ch. 18 (Van Seters, *Abraham in History and Tradition*, 203 and 209–221).

The two juxtaposed and consecutive tidings demonstrate two aspects of the message of Isaac's birth. The son promised to Abraham in the Covenant of Circumcision will be the successor of his covenant with God: "But My covenant I will maintain with Isaac" (Gen. 17:21). The child's name is bestowed in the first message because his destiny awaits him even before his conception.

In contrast, the divine messengers bring tidings to Abraham and Sarah's home irrespective of the child's destiny. The child is not named; rather, the promise focuses upon the fulfillment of Abraham and Sarah's personal longing for a child. *They* are the focus of the blessing; they deserve a child because they are good and decent people, champions of the values of benevolence and justice, regardless of the covenant between them and God.

This distinction clarifies other literary components that characterize the two messages as separate episodes. Both Abraham and Sarah live their lives on both planes: both are significant with regard to the covenant, and both have their own hopes, dreams, and ambitions. When the covenant is emphasized, however, Abraham is the protagonist, and the story revolves around him. Abraham is the focus of these national-historical narratives because he was the one selected to establish God's nation, while Sarah joined the journey as his wife. Therefore, in the Covenant of Circumcision, *Abraham* is given a son; the son is a continuation of Abraham's choices and values. However, Sarah is the focus of the personal episode. She is the mother burdened with the weight of infertility, the wife who so longed for a child to raise that she offered her own maidservant as a surrogate.

The interchangeable names for God throughout the story may also function as a literary tool. Cassuto,[15] among others, discusses whether the use of the name *Elohim* in Genesis 17 contributes to the nature and purpose of the narrative, and whether the use of *YHWH* contributes to the purpose of Genesis 18. *Elohim* is essentially a general name that expresses divine power, while *YHWH* is used as God's private name, which differentiates Him from hundreds of gods that were worshipped in the ancient world. Throughout the Abraham cycle, the

15. Cassuto, *The "Quaestio" of the Book of Genesis*, 18–52.

name *YHWH* is used in narratives with an intimate setting; in other words, stories of a personal encounter with God. *YHWH* is the appropriate name for Sarah's story, where God responds personally to His creations, whereas the name *Elohim* sets the appropriate tone for the obligations and commitments of making a covenant with God in the Covenant of Circumcision.

This difference is also reflected in the reason for the birth of a child in each episode. In Genesis 17, Abraham is given a son to maintain his covenant with God. Isaac is not born as a result of Abraham's virtue, but as part of God's historical design.[16] The personal story of Genesis 18, on the other hand, is deeply rooted not in divine but human actions. In this episode, God is not portrayed as an initiator, but as one who reacts to human initiatives. What, then, is the reason for giving Abraham and Sarah a son in this chapter?

The answer, of course, lies in the great hospitality with which Abraham and Sarah received the strangers. The purpose of the divine messengers' visit seems to be the discussion with Abraham regarding the destruction of Sodom (Gen. 18:17), not to deliver tidings of a birth that was already revealed to Abraham in the Covenant of Circumcision. However, when the visitors arrived at Abraham's tent, they were received with such gracious human initiative that Abraham was rewarded with additional blessing.[17] This blessing, indeed, almost seems to be offered

16. Compare with Frank H. Polak: "Humility in view of divine sovereignty is also the point of the tale about the revelation of divine identity to Abram and the circumcision command (Genesis 17). This narrative is characterized by the use of three different names.... The use of the personal name fits the idea of divine-human communication. However, when Abraham reacts to the divine call, the narrative prefers the appellation: 'Abram threw himself on his face; and God spoke to him further' (17:3). Thus the narrative presents Abraham's point of view as a devoted servant who loyally accepts the commands of his overlord" (Polak, "Divine Names, Sociolinguistics and the Pragmatics of Pentateuchal Narrative," in *Words, Ideas, Worlds: Biblical Essays in Honour of Yairah Amit*, ed. A. Brenner and F. Polak [Sheffield, 2012], 171–172).

17. Regardless of whether this is a normal procedure that reflects the life of wanderers (Shapira, "He Shall be a Wild Ass of a Man," 54) or a historical deviation, Abraham's character is portrayed nobly. Even if he acts in accordance with the customs of the time, he is praiseworthy.

as a host-gift.[18] In Genesis 18, Abraham and Sarah are granted a son as a reward for their good deeds, not as part of a divine plan to maintain the covenant with Abraham's offspring.

In fact, the angels allude to this when they ask for Sarah: "They said to him, 'Where is your wife Sarah?' And he replied, 'There, in the tent'" (Gen. 18:9), hinting that she is being granted a blessing "in the tent" because of her activity "in the tent." The tent is certainly an appropriate location for the news of expansion of the family. In this chapter, Abraham and Sarah are rewarded according to the principle of "measure for measure." They hospitably nurtured their guests, and are rewarded with a child to nurture.[19] They opened their home to others, expanding their household from without, and are rewarded with a household expanding from within.[20]

There is a striking similarity between Sarah's story in Genesis 18 and the episode of Elisha and the Shunammite woman in II Kings 4.[21] There, the Shunammite woman takes great pains to make Elisha

18. See Rudin-O'Brasky, *The Patriarch in Hebron and Sodom*, 63–64, and Jonathan Grossman, "Two 'Doubled' Narratives in Genesis: Hagar's Departure (16; 21) and the Announcement of Isaac's Birth (17–18)," *Megadim* 29 (1998): 9–30.

19. Walther Eichrodt, *Theology of the Old Testament*, trans. J. A. Baker (OTL: Philadelphia, 1961), 144.

20. This reading was previously suggested by Ronald E. Clements (*In Spirit and in Truth: Insight from Biblical Prayers* [Atlanta, 1985], 24–25). Rudin-O'Brasky (*The Patriarch in Hebron and Sodom*, 74) also noted the link between the hospitality motif and the message of fertility. However, she believes the link is missing in our narrative, since Abraham was previously promised a son as part of his destiny, so the son cannot be portrayed as a reward for Abraham's hospitality. Even if the link between hospitality and the promise of fertility is not overt, it is certainly implied in the text, and reinforced by the reappearance of the two threads in additional duplicate stories in the cycle.

21. Regarding the parallels between Gen. 18 and Elisha's interaction with the Shunammite woman, see Leila Leah Bronner, *The Stories of Elijah and Elisha as Polemics Against Baal Worship* (Leiden, 1968), 86–99; Rudin-O'Brasky, *The Patriarch in Hebron and Sodom*, 66–72; Kiel, *Daat Mikra: Genesis*, 498 (who differentiates between an angel and a prophet); Mordechai Sabato, "The Story of the Shunammite Woman," *Megadim* 15 (1992): 45–52; Uriel Simon, *Reading Prophetic Narratives* (The Biblical Encyclopedia Library and Bialik Institute: Jerusalem, 1997), 279–316; Yairah Amit, "Elisha and the Great Woman of Shunem: A Prophet Tested," *Zmanim* 77 (2001): 4–11.

comfortable in her home, like Abraham and Sarah did with the messengers. Like the messengers in Genesis, Elisha promises that the Shunammite woman and her elderly husband would be granted a son (II Kings 4:13), "At this season this time [next year], you will be embracing a son," which directly alludes to Genesis 18. In the Elisha narrative, the Shunammite woman is granted a son as a reward for her hospitality, just as Sarah and Abraham are granted a son for welcoming strangers into their home. Just as Sarah laughed in disbelief at the prospect of bearing a child, the woman responds, "Please my lord, man of God, do not delude your maidservant" (II Kings 4:16). Many have noted that the analogy between the two narratives implies a criticism of Elisha, in having overstepped his authority by promising a child to the barren woman.[22] Regardless, the narrative clearly links the concept of fertility as a reward for hospitality to strangers, and in this respect, the Elisha story relies on the model presented in the Abraham story.

The two narratives foretelling the birth of Isaac (Gen. 17 and 18) indicate that he is to be born twice: once in the name of *Elohim*, as the heir of Abraham, and the maintainer of God's covenant, and once in the name of *YHWH*, as Sarah's pride and joy. The story in Genesis 21 tells parallel accounts of Isaac's "double" birth – born once as the heir to a great nation, and again to his overjoyed parents.

> *YHWH* took note of *Sarah* as He had promised,
> and *YHWH* did for *Sarah* as He had spoken.
> Sarah conceived and bore a son *to Abraham* in his old age
> at the set time of which *Elohim* had spoken.

---

22. See Sabato, "The Story of the Shunammite Woman," 48; Simon, *Reading Prophetic Narratives*, 301; Yairah Amit, *Reading Biblical Narratives*, 7; Yosef Marcus, "The Role of the Prophet in Israel – The Figure of the Shunammite Woman as a Case Study," *Megadim* 51 (2010): 33. Skinner claims that although the phrase in II Kings 4:16 and 17 of *ka'et ḥaya*, "this time [next year]," is incompatible with the narrative in Kings, the author is influenced by Gen. 18 (Skinner, *A Critical and Exegetical Commentary on Genesis*, 301). Wesley J. Bergen demonstrates that the use of this phrase with regard to Elisha shows an implicit criticism, indicating that unlike the angels, Elisha is out of place predicting a birth (Bergen, *Elisha and the End of Prophetism* [JSOTSup 286: Sheffield, 1999], 98–99).

> *Abraham* gave his newborn son, whom *Sarah* had borne him, the name of Isaac.
> And when his son Isaac was eight days old, *Abraham circumcised him*, as Elohim had commanded him…
> *Sarah said, "Elohim has brought me laughter."*

It is particularly the name *YHWH* that is used in Genesis 21:1 in conjunction with "taking note" and fulfilling His promise to Sarah. A number of commentators interpret "took note," "*pakad*," to mean "visited," in correlation with the words of the divine guest: "I will revisit you next year" (Gen. 18:10).[23] They view Genesis 21 as a direct extension of Abraham's hospitality, and a direct fulfillment of the tidings delivered on that occasion. The focus on Sarah in this verse correlates with the message intended for Sarah, in the name of *YHWH*. The next verse conveys the second perspective of Isaac's birth. God is called *Elohim*, since this second aspect is a fulfillment of *His* promise to Abraham in the Covenant of Circumcision. These verses focus on Abraham, and occur "at the set time" that *Elohim* had stated on that occasion. Isaac's naming and circumcision, and finally, Abraham's age, all correspond to the Covenant of Circumcision, while Isaac is said to bring the joy and comfort to Sarah that she had not dared to wish for.

Isaac is a different son to each of his parents. He is the son of Abraham and Sarah, and also the son of Sarah and Abraham. He is the joy of an old and childless couple, and he is the heir to the forefather of a new nation, the keeper of Abraham's covenant with God. Similarly, God plays two roles. In the Covenant of Circumcision, He establishes a nation, while in the hospitality narrative He displays divine morality, and rewards kindness to human beings with the expansion of the home and the comfort of a son.

The episode ends with Sarah's laughter at the news of her child's impending birth and a surprising exchange between Sarah and God. The angel informs Abraham: "I will return to you next year, and your wife Sarah shall have a son!" (Gen. 18:10), which elicits disbelief: "Sarah laughed to herself, saying, 'Now that I am withered, am I to have enjoyment – with

23. Hamilton, *The Book of Genesis, Chapters 18–50*, 12.

my husband so old?'" (v. 12). The text interrupts the sequence of the message and response to add the two following details: "Sarah was listening at the entrance of the tent, which was behind him" (v. 10), and, "Now Abraham and Sarah were old, advanced in years; Sarah had stopped having the way of women" (v. 11).

The first detail explains how Sarah was able to hear the divine messenger's words to Abraham even though she was in the tent: the divine messenger could not see Sarah since the tent was behind him, but Sarah, who stood at the entrance to the tent, was able to overhear the conversation. The second intriguing detail seems to legitimize Sarah's reaction. The text reminds the reader that Sarah and Abraham were exceedingly old; in addition, Sarah was no longer menstruating, so it was physically impossible for her to bear a child. Sarah's laughter relates directly to this detail, since she says, "Now that I am withered, am I to have enjoyment" (paralleling "Sarah had stopped having the way of women") and "my husband so old" (paralleling "Abraham and Sarah were old").

This complexity creates a delicate and balanced critique of Sarah's reaction: while Sarah's laughter is inappropriate, it is also understandable. The text "interrupts" yet again when Sarah denies her laughter: "Sarah lied, saying, 'I did not laugh,' *for she was frightened*" (Gen. 18:15). This interruption also minimizes the disapproval of Sarah, who only lies because she is nervous (and perhaps only laughs nervously as well, and not for lack of faith).[24]

There is a jarring contrast between the depiction of Sarah's actions and the unequivocal and harsh reprimand she receives. The dramatic ending – "You did laugh!" – continues to resonate after the story is over. Sarah does not know the speaker is a divine messenger, and so, there is no reason to portray her hesitation as a lack of belief in God. Sarah probably interprets the conversation as a polite blessing by strangers who are utterly unaware of her situation. Her laughter expresses her pessimism in light of repeated disappointment. Her lack of belief in herself and her future are the setting for God's intervention. The words "Is anything too wondrous for the Lord?" teach Sarah that she must not give up hope, even in the face of nature and logic. The test of Sarah's

24. Procksch, *Die Genesis*, 120.

faith, as in Søren Kierkegaard's perception of faith, was an expectation to continue believing during the very darkest of hours, even when the possibility of childbearing seems impossible.

Perhaps this is the result of the gap between what Sarah says to herself, "Now that I am withered, am I to have enjoyment – with my husband so old?" (Gen. 18:12), and how God repeats her words. Sarah mentions her own age as well as Abraham's, while God omits her description of Abraham: "Why did Sarah laugh, saying, 'Shall I in truth bear a child, old as I am?'" (18:13). While traditional exegesis derives from this verse that one is permitted to lie in order to keep the peace,[25] perhaps the change serves to focus Sarah's laughter on herself, rather than upon her husband. Sarah's challenge was to believe that she, and not only others, could be the receptacle of God's blessing.

The element of laughter, which is central in both narratives, carries significant weight in the scene, which concludes with the word "laugh." Perhaps the angels' insistence that Sarah laughed indicates that Sarah's laughter has additional significance (and that her son's name is implied in this action).[26] Why is this laughter so significant?[27]

Sarah's disbelief contributes to the unique and miraculous atmosphere surrounding the birth of her son, which culminates in the statement, "Is anything too wondrous for the Lord?"[28] Had the characters in

---

25. Genesis Rabba 48:18, Yevamot 65b. More accurately, God did not lie; He only spoke a partial truth.

26. Westermann, *Genesis 12–36: A Continental Commentary*, 282; Hamilton, *The Book of Genesis, Chapters 18–50*, 14. See also Zakovitch, *"I Will Express Riddles of Old": Riddles and Dream-Riddles in Biblical Narrative*, 134, who discusses Isaac's name, which represents both delighted laughter and laughter of disbelief.

27. Megan E. Warner proposes that Isaac is taken from Sarah at the binding of Isaac as a punishment for her laughter (Warner, "Keeping the Way of YHWH: Righteousness and Justice in Genesis 18–19," in *Universalism and Particularism at Sodom and Gomorrah*, ed. Z. Garber and R. Libowitz [Atlanta, 2012], 113–128). According to this reading, it is clear why this laughter is so important prior to Abraham's debate about the fate of Sodom (which, Warner argues, conceals a debate about the future of his own son).

28. Compare with Jean Louis Ska, "Gn 18,1–15 alla prova dell'esegesi classica e dell'esegesi narrative," *Asprenas* 40 (1993): 5–22. The root P-L-E, "wondrous," is used in other biblical texts, connoting supernatural divine intervention (e.g., Ex. 3:20). See Paul Kruger, "פלא," *NIDOTTE* 3:616.

the story taken the tidings at face value, the reader might have believed their age was not a factor, perhaps due to their era and their lifespans. The laughter – and the process of denial and reaffirmation – indicates that something truly wondrous, which defies the laws of nature, is about to happen. The couple had given up on their ability to conceive – the very idea of conception becoming utterly preposterous – and God now offers them a surreal blessing. This clarifies that the impending birth is not natural, but miraculous – so miraculous that both characters are moved to laughter. Laughter helps Abraham and Sarah internalize the illogical reality born of God's intervention. Their openness will allow the impossible into their home.[29]

Now we can better understand the ambivalence between the text's sympathy for Sarah's laughter, and God's criticism of her reaction. Sarah is in contrast to Michal, daughter of Saul, who mocks David as he dances before God's ark. Michal's mocking laughter was punished with childlessness, while Sarah's laughter leads to the conception of a child. The episode ends with the statement, "You did laugh," because laughter is what opens Sarah's heart and womb.[30] Laughter, by its very nature, is rooted in surprise. Only one who can be surprised, can laugh; Sarah's astonishment, expressed by her laughter, is what opened the door for her to give birth.

---

29. This approach was expressed in a poem by Alexander Pushkin, in *Eugene Onegin*, trans. Babette Deutsch (Baltimore, 1964):

    ... Indeed, thrice blessed / Is he who can believe a fiction, / Who, lulling reason, comes to rest
    In the soft luxury of feeling. / Like a poor sot to shelter reeling /
    Or (since it's ugly to be drunk) / An incest in a flower sunk;
    But wretched is the man who never / Can be surprised, who is not stirred
    By a translated move or word, / Who cannot feel: he is too clever,
    Whose heart experience has chilled, / Whose raptures are forever stilled.

30. Recent studies have shown a physiological connection between laughter and conception. See Shevach Friedler, "The Effect of Medical Clowning on Pregnancy Rates after In Vitro Fertilization and Embryo Transfer," *Fertil and Steril* 95 (2011): 2127–2130.

The Debate over Sodom's Destruction (Gen. 18:16–33)

The two juxtaposed stories in chapter 18 are, arguably, the most iconic episodes in Abraham's journey, at least insofar as Abraham as a heroic character is concerned. For generations, children throughout the world have sat, wide-eyed and in awe, as they learn the dual lessons of hospitality and the value of a life from Abraham's actions in Genesis 18. If nothing else, these two stories are Abraham's legacy to his children; they are the stories from which we paint the image of Abraham the man, from the first moment we meet him at the apron strings of our mothers. Abraham, the father of a people, is a man of endless kindness, who welcomed everyone to his tent, who could not stand to see even one human life unduly destroyed.

Analysis of the narrative does not disappoint – the text seems to view the debate over Sodom as a direct continuation of the story of Abraham and Sarah's hospitality, linking these two stories inextricably. The question of where one story ends and the other begins (or if, in fact, this is one episode or two) has been widely debated.

There is a certain shift in the narrative. Genesis 18:16, in one verse, closes one unit and opens the next: "The men set out from there and looked down toward Sodom, Abraham walking with them to see them off." This shift acts as an organic segue from one scene to the next, and not, as some commentators posit, as an introduction to the Sodom narrative[1] or a conclusion of the previous story.[2]

The verse certainly disbands the characters from the previous scene. However, the phraseology can only be interpreted as a natural continuation of one cohesive story with, "And the men set out *from there*." "There" can only be understood in relation to the previous scene. The description of Abraham, who accompanies them to "see them off," is simply a direct continuation of his role as a host. However, the verse also has the angels looking toward Sodom, clearly introducing a new chapter. Thus, the angels go to Sodom for the purpose of evaluating the city, to determine whether it should be destroyed. One of the "visitors," in fact, stays behind to discuss that very matter with Abraham.

Despite the link between Abraham's visit and the Sodom narrative, there is reason to view the latter as an independent episode that should be read separately from the angels' visit. The story forms an *inclusio*, opening in Genesis 18:16: "The men set out from there and they looked down toward Sodom (*vayashkifu al penei Sedom*), Abraham walking with them to see them off," and ending in Genesis 19:27–28: "And Abraham… looked down toward Sodom (*vayashkef al penei Sedom*) and Gomorrah and all the land of the Plain, and he saw the smoke of the land rising like the smoke of a kiln."[3]

1. E.g., Skinner, *A Critical and Exegetical Commentary on Genesis*, 303; Speiser, *Genesis*, 132; Coats, *Genesis*, 139 (he emphasizes the profound connection between the two units); Wenham, *Genesis 16–50*, 40 (he provides one general title for chs. 18–19: "The Overthrow of Sodom and Gomorrah," which he views as one story); Hamilton, *The Book of Genesis, Chapters 18–50*, 14.
2. Von Rad, *Genesis*, 203. Von Rad is aware that Gen. 18:16 prepares the ground for the following unit, but chooses to view the verse as the conclusion of the hosting narrative: "Any reader feels v. 16 is, to some extent, a conclusion." This was also surmised by Yitzhak Avishur, as is evident from the title of his article, "The Angels' Visit with Abraham (Gen. 18:1–16) and Its Parallels in Ugaritic Literature," *Beit Mikra* 32 (1986): 168–177.
3. For example, Wenham, *Genesis 16–50*, 41, 49; Mathews, *Genesis*, 221. The unique significance of Gen. 19:29, which provides an outsider's look on the narrative, will be discussed in due course.

The structure of Abraham's debate with God over the fate of Sodom also shares a number of links with Lot's later discussion with the angels, indicating that verse 16 is the beginning of the story of Sodom, and not the continuation of the angels' visit. Abraham attempts to save the city and is unsuccessful (Gen. 18:22), while Lot makes a great impression on the angels and succeeds in saving Zoar (Gen. 19:23–26).

On the other hand, the link between the arrival of the angels in Sodom (Gen. 19:4–11) and Lot leaving the city sheds light on the reason Lot is saved, and connects directly back to the story of Abraham's hospitality. Lot invites strangers into his home and protects them. They reward him by taking him out of his home when it is destroyed, and protecting him when his life is endangered. The design of the text supports the reading that views Lot's rescue in light of his good deeds. As we will discuss below, this precisely echoes the reasoning behind the angels' bestowal of good tidings on Abraham and Sarah.

The link between the story of the divine visitors to Abraham's tent and his debate with God over Sodom seems to be intentionally muddled. It is clear that the text wishes to begin a new scene in verse 16; however, the numerous literary links between the two stories indicate that we cannot ignore the lessons learned in the beginning of chapter 18 when analyzing Abraham's actions in the second half of the chapter. Abraham's altruistic actions toward the angels sets the stage for God's decision to involve him in the judgment of Sodom.

Who Were the Angels?

Let us return momentarily to the scene of Abraham and Sarah's hospitality. As we have mentioned previously, the text utilizes a literary device in this story to "hide" information from its protagonist, while bringing the reader in on the full picture. Abraham and Sarah act genuinely and innocently when they receive the three strangers so generously to their tent, and have no idea that the visitors are in fact divine messengers.

The characters' lack of knowledge does more than display for the reader the extent of the couple's generosity. Upon analysis of the text, we see that Abraham's behavior, despite his lack of knowledge of the divine beings, actually changes the messengers' behavior.

God and His delegation come to Abraham for the particular purpose of discussing the destruction of Sodom. However, when the delegation arrives, Abraham's warm hospitality is so extraordinary that it warrants a reaction. The divine visitors are so overwhelmed by the couple's hospitality and kindness, they feel they must bestow a blessing before delving into the true reason for their visit. The discussion of Sodom was therefore delayed until after Abraham and Sarah's hospitality was rewarded with the tidings of a son.

The fact that Sarah laughed at the angels' tiding of a son underscores this idea that the couple had no idea that their guests were divine beings. Certainly, Sarah would not have laughed had she recognized the angel. However, coming from a stranger, the blessing, "May you bear a son," would naturally elicit an abashed chuckle from the gracious hostess who knows that such a blessing is not likely to come to fruition.

It all comes together, several verses later, to answer the question on all of our minds in the next story: What on earth gives Abraham the right to argue with God's ruling regarding Sodom? The answer may be twofold. Firstly, Abraham didn't know it was God he was dealing with in the tent, and that's exactly what gives him the right. The fact that Abraham didn't know demonstrates his pure altruism and generosity, qualities that give God pause and allow Him to consider Abraham's arguments.

The text gives us further justification for Abraham's actions by way of offering a window into God's "thoughts," as it were (Gen. 18:17–19):

> Now the Lord had said: Shall I hide from Abraham what I am doing? Abraham is to become a great and populous nation, and all the nations of the earth are to bless themselves by him; for I have singled him out, that he may instruct his children and his posterity to keep the way of the Lord by doing what is benevolent and just, in order that the Lord may bring about for Abraham what He has promised him.

These unusual verses provide a glimpse into the reasoning behind God's choice of Abraham. Although at first glance, the verses may seem disruptive to the story, they are in fact perfectly placed. They explain why God shared His plan to destroy Sodom with Abraham.

There is added value in the placement of the verses at this point – between the tidings of the son and the argument about the destruction of Sodom. God's vague statement, "Shall I hide from Abraham what *I am doing*" (not "what I *will do*," or "what I am doing *with Sodom*") enables the reader to understand His meaning more broadly.[4] God is referring here not only to hiding His plans for Sodom, but also retroactively – His hiding the divine identity of the three visitors to Abraham and Sarah's tent.

This interpretation of the text sheds light on the previously discussed question of why the blessing of the son was repeated (once in the Covenant of Circumcision and then again at the tent), and as we mentioned above, why Sarah laughed again. As we said, the visitors came with an entirely different intention – to discuss the fate of Sodom with Abraham. After being treated so well by their hosts, they bestowed a second tiding on Abraham and Sarah out of a spontaneous feeling of gratitude. From Abraham and Sarah's perspective, the visitors were simply human strangers, and Sarah's laughter at their tidings nothing more than a polite reaction to a well-meaning (and seemingly impossible) wish. If so, the reason the angels' visit was not disclosed from the outset was in order to emphasize Abraham's "interference" with God's plan. Abraham's hospitality was entirely voluntary, and to his credit, his actions should not be viewed as premeditated. Abraham took people into his home of his own free will, for entirely unselfish reasons; the angels felt indebted and responded by offering Abraham and Sarah the blessing of a son. It was only in verses 17–19, after the visitors "recovered" from the meal and the couple's hospitality, that they could get down to the business for which they were sent.

It is clear why the two stories – of Abraham's hospitality, and of the argument about Sodom – are presented separately. Just as clear is the link between the two narratives, since the purpose of the messengers' divine visit was to discuss Sodom's fate. This link is far more than a technicality in the story; the connection between Abraham's hospitality and the message that he will produce a son, and the story of the messengers' journey to Lot's home, runs deep. Rashbam emphasizes

4. Hamilton, *The Book of Genesis, Chapters 18–50*, 17. See also the discussion in Jerome T. Walsh, *Style and Structure in Biblical Hebrew Narrative* (Collegeville, MN, 2001), 134.

this connection in his claim that the argument over Sodom took place with the same "lead messenger" who visited Abraham's tent.[5] Proof of this lies in the final verses of the argument over Sodom: "And God left when He finished speaking to Abraham, and Abraham returned to his place" (Gen. 18:33), followed immediately by, "And the *two* messengers came to Sodom that evening" (19:1). It would appear from this sequence that the reference to God who engaged in discussion with Abraham was the first of the messengers who arrived at his tent, leaving the remaining two to make their way to Sodom alone. It would seem, then, that the purpose of the messengers' visit was, indeed, to decide and deliver the fate of Sodom, and was immaterial to the narrative of Abraham and Sarah's hospitality, or to the news they received regarding their legacy.

Prayer for Sodom Is About Justice, Not Kindness

Coming on the coattails of the archetypal scene of Abraham's hospitality, it is no surprise that our elementary school teachers ingrained the scene that follows into our hearts as a further display of Abraham's compassionate nature. However, in truth, Abraham's argument for the salvation of Sodom was a legal one, not a moral one.

"Abraham came forward and said, 'Will You sweep away the innocent along with the guilty?... Far be it from You to do such a thing, to bring death upon the innocent as well as the guilty, so that innocent and guilty fare alike. Far be it from You! Shall not the Judge of all the earth deal justly?'" (Gen. 18:23–25).[6] God's position, according to Abraham, is that the whole city should be destroyed, the innocent along with the guilty. God does not correct Abraham on this point, and the conclusion of the dialogue confirms that if ten righteous people are not found in the city, the entire city will be destroyed, including the handful of righteous people who might exist.

5. See also Mordechai Breuer, *Pirkei Bereshit*, ed. Y. Ofer (Alon Shevut, 1999), vol. 2, 390–395.
6. In contrast with Nathan MacDonald, "Listening to Abraham – Listening to Yhwh: Divine Justice and Mercy in Genesis 18:16–33," *CBQ* 66 (2004): 25–43, who believes that Abraham's prayer is based on the two components of divine justice and mercy.

According to Abraham's position, the people of the city should be spared because of merit of the righteous people: "What if there should be fifty innocent within the city; will You then wipe out the place and not forgive it for the sake of the innocent fifty who are in it?" (Gen. 18:24). Both positions are surprising within the context of justice, since we would expect the middle ground, of punishing the guilty and sparing the innocent. This option is not raised at any stage of the legal dialogue, although Abraham certainly knows that God is capable of and will most definitely save the innocent despite destroying the city. This is, in fact, how the story plays out: Lot is spared, while his guilty neighbors meet their demise.

Abraham is not praying for God's compassion – this is a given. He argues for the legal precedent God sets by destroying the entire city. Abraham, the leader of a nation set to become the model of ethics throughout the known world, demands that God convey the statutes of justice by which He will pass judgment.

Two key words repeat themselves throughout the dialogue to emphasize the legal aspect of Abraham's argument – "place" and "city." From the outset, Abraham does not argue for the *people*, but for the *place*: "Will You then wipe out the *place* and not forgive it?" (Gen. 18:24). God's response to Abraham's request mirrors His intentions: "If I find within the *city* of Sodom fifty innocent ones, I will forgive the whole *place* for their sake" (v. 26). The next stage of the discussion continues to revolve around the city, with Abraham pleading: "What if the fifty innocent should lack five? Will You destroy *the whole city* for want of the five?" (v. 28). Some might say "city" is a metonymy for "the people in the city." The punishment of the people is described as inadvertent, collateral damage: "Then the men said to Lot, 'Whom else have you here? Sons-in-law, your sons and daughters, or anyone else that you have in the city – *bring them out of the place,* for we are about to destroy *this place*; because their outcry before the Lord has become so great that the Lord has sent us to destroy *it*'" (vv. 12–13). Lot understands perfectly, and conveys the message to his sons-in-law: "Up, get out of this place, for the Lord is about to destroy *the city*" (v. 14). Later, "The angels urged Lot on, saying, 'Up, take your wife and your two remaining daughters, *lest you be swept away because of the iniquity of the city*'.... So the men seized his hand ... and left him *outside the city*" (vv. 15–16). This description is apparent in the destruction itself as well: "He annihilated *those cities and the entire Plain,* and all the inhabitants of the *cities* and the vegetation of the ground" (19:25).

The people seem to only be destroyed because they are "inhabitants of the cities," just as the "vegetation of the ground" was destroyed along with the city. When Abraham went to "look down" upon the result, "he saw the smoke of *the land* rising" (Gen. 19:28), and the conclusion of the destruction is described in the same terms: "Thus it was that, when God *destroyed the cities of the Plain* and *annihilated the cities* where Lot dwelt..." (v. 29). The cities of Lot were destroyed – and he had to extract himself from the city to be saved. Looking back, the city – not the people – appears to be the center of the discussion from the outset, since God went "to see whether they have acted altogether according to her cry that has reached Me." Indeed, the Midrash notes that "it does not state 'their cry,' but rather, 'her cry.'"[7] "Her" can also refer to the city of Sodom as a unit. Additionally, the choice of punishment is the ultimate proof that the city was being judged, rather than the people. Instead of sending a plague or wild animals to hurt the people, God chooses to destroy the infrastructure of the cities itself. The lush, fertile land of Sodom becomes a desolate wasteland.

The text's focus on the "place" and the "city" reflects each party's perception of retribution on the eve of the destruction. "The place" is a symbol of the entire population, as one unit, or one culture. This is a public trial. The biblical text is familiar with the concept of national retribution,[8] though here the retribution is municipal in nature. The

7. Genesis Rabba 49:6. Based on the word "her cry," the midrash goes on to describe several incidents of abused girls in Sodom, whose outcry was the reason God decided to destroy Sodom (see Theodore-Albeck ed., 505). The literal meaning in the text regards the entire city as one unit.
8. For example, God threatens to destroy the people of Israel after the Sin of the Golden Calf, despite the active participation of only three thousand people (Ex. 32:28). Similarly, the nation is punished for the sin of a single person in the case of Achan (Josh. 7:1). And in the narrative about Korah, his actions lead to a plague in the nation (Num. 16:22). For a survey of the concept of biblical retribution, see Weiss, *Scriptures in Their Own Light: Collected Essays*, 512–548.

people of a city share a culture, which is examined and judged by God. Perhaps in the context of personal retribution, God will decide to rescue someone from destruction, but this is not the level on which the discussion between God and Abraham is conducted. Their discussion is about "place" – will the place be destroyed or maintained?[9] The conclusion necessitates an examination of the definition of the public. Abraham believes that the place could be defined by a small group. Ten (but no fewer!) righteous people are sufficient to categorize the city as a righteous city.[10] Some might view this as a leaning toward benevolence in judgment, but this is still a far cry from Abraham asking for the city to be spared.[11] Apparently, human perspective can drive judgment toward compassion, and a rejection of punishment.

---

9. There is no evidence for the claim that Gen. 18 reflects a primitive stage of biblical retribution. For example, David Daube writes, "From a precise legal perspective this is still an earlier phase" ("Rechtsgedanken in den Erzählungen des Pentateuchs," in *Von Ugarit nach Qumran: Beiträge zur alttestamentlichen und altorientalischen Forschung*, ed. O. Eissfeldt [*ZAW* 77: Berlin, 1958], 41). See Wiess' response in *Scriptures in Their Own Light: Collected Essays*, 47–49. Similarly, there is no prophet more outspoken about personal retribution than the prophet Ezekiel (for example, Ezek. 18:4, "The person who sins, only he shall die"), but when he speaks about Jerusalem and the Land of Israel, he says,

   > O mortal, set your face toward Jerusalem and proclaim against her sanctuaries and prophecy *against the Land of Israel*. Say to *the Land of Israel*, thus said the Lord: I am going to deal with you! I will draw my sword from its sheath and *I will wipe out from you both the righteous and the wicked*. In order to wipe out from you both the righteous and the wicked, My sword shall assuredly be unsheathed against all flesh from south to north. And all flesh shall know that I the Lord have drawn My sword from its sheath, not to be sheathed again. (Ezek. 21:7–10)

10. Joseph Blenkinsopp summarized the different positions that address why Abraham did not continue arguing for fewer than ten righteous people ("Abraham and the Righteous of Sodom," *JJS* 33 [1982]: 119–132). He also mentions Schmidt's claim that ten is the minimal number that can be considered a group or public (Schmidt, *"De Deo,"* 151–56). This approach is also reflected in the rabbinic law that a *minyan*, or prayer group, must consist of at least ten members (Walter Brueggemann, "A Shape for Old Testament Theology, 1: Structure Legitimation," *CBQ* 47 [1985]: 410).
11. Benno Jacob makes a similar suggestion, although he believes that Abraham did not ask God to spare the actual sinners. Rather, Abraham thought the sinners should die and the city should be spared in merit of the righteous (Jacob, *The First Book of the Bible: Genesis*, trans. E. I. Jacob and W. Jacob [New York, 1974], 121–22).

Biblical philosophy does not view mercy and justice as conflicting values.[12] This is apparent from the phrase "benevolent and just" (*tzedaka umishpat*), which describes Abraham's household, and is stated as the reason God feels compelled to share His plans for the destruction of Sodom with Abraham (Gen. 18:19). The phrase should be viewed as a hendiadys that expresses a broader brand of social justice, which goes beyond the legal sense.[13] God Himself is described in the same terms: "For I, the Lord, act with kindness, justice and benevolence (*mishpat utzedaka*) in the world, for in these I delight, declares the Lord" (Jer. 9:23), as is the expectation of mankind: "Do what is just and benevolent (*mishpat utzedaka*). Rescue from the defrauder him who is robbed, do not wrong the stranger, the fatherless, and the widow, commit no lawless act, and do not shed the blood of the innocent in this place" (Jer. 22:3). Benevolence, i.e., extralegal mercy and compassion, enhances justice; the combination of these qualities leads one to protect the weak and prevent wrongdoing.[14]

Abraham's mission is reinforced by the Sodom episode. His sensitivity to morality is demonstrated in his attempt to persuade God to be not only just but benevolent, and this delays punishment for as long as possible, so that merit can be found. Abraham is the ultimate defense attorney; he pleads for justice for the lowest common denominator, demanding that God not only show compassion but to proclaim a precedent. How many righteous people must there be in a city to save it from the legal sentence of destruction?

Our childhood image of Abraham remains rooted in kindness and compassion, but also takes on a more complex, and perhaps more powerful, facet. Yes, Abraham was kind, but at his core he was the leader of a nation that sought to bring universal values of justice and ethics to

---

12. Skinner, for example, writes, "In the Old Testament, righteousness and clemency are closely allied: there is more injustice in the death of a few innocent people than in the sparing of a guilty multitude" (Skinner, *A Critical and Exegetical Commentary on Genesis*, 305).
13. David J. Reimer, "צדק," *NIDOTTE* 3:763–764; Weinfeld, *From Joshua to Josiah*; Kaddari, *A Dictionary of Biblical Hebrew*, 679.
14. See also Hos. 2:21, Mic. 6:8, and Zech. 7:9–10.

the world. This is his role, as the leader of a nation that was destined to become a model of moral behavior for generations to come.

"And I Am But Dust and Ashes"

The argument between God (or the angel) and Abraham is one of the most audacious scenes in biblical literature. Whereas religious theology generally emphasizes human emptiness in the presence of God, Abraham is called upon to express his opinion on divine justice, and actively participate in the final verdict. The scope of the discussion goes beyond Sodom to the essential judicial principle of judging a group that includes various types of individuals. The justification for including Abraham in the process is noted in the verses that introduce the argument with a rare report of God's "thoughts" (Gen. 18:19):[15]

> For I have known him,[16]
> so that he may instruct his children and his posterity
> to keep the way of the Lord
> by doing what is benevolent and just,
> so that the Lord may bring about for Abraham what He has promised him.

---

15. Cf. Hamilton, *The Book of Genesis, Chapters 18–50*, 17. Wenham writes that the senior angel is addressing his two companions, who are about to depart for Sodom (Wenham, *Genesis 16–50*, 50). A similar suggestion was previously offered by Nahmanides, who suggests that God had addressed the heavenly angelic host.
16. The Masoretic text has "*ki yedativ*," literally, "For I have known him." NJPS translates this as, "For I have singled him out." The Septuagint, Samaritan, and Vulgate translations offer a more comfortable reading: "For I know *that* he instructs his children..." (Moshe A. Zipor, *The Septuagint Version of the Book of Genesis* [Ramat Gan, 2005], 232). This interpretation is also reflected in our version of Onkelos' translation (although Nahmanides cites another version): "It is known to Me that he instructs his children..." The Masoretic text sees the verb Y-D-A ("know") as a formal verb denoting choice (see Herbert B. Huffmon, "The Treaty Background of Hebrew Yada," *BASOR* 191 [1966]: 34–35), and it carries a more intimate and personal connotation than the parallel verb B-Ḥ-R ("to choose"), which is prevalent in Deuteronomy (Terrence E. Fretheim, "ידע," *NIDOTTE* 2:411; Mathews, *Genesis*, 223). See more on the use of this verb below.

According to the Masoretic text (the Septuagint has a different version), Abraham was chosen for two reasons.[17] The first reason relates to the education of his family in the ways of God; in other words, Abraham's actions. The second reason relates to God's actions for the benefit of Abraham: the fulfillment of the blessings that had been bestowed upon him. Since Abraham intends to instruct his family in the ways of God – justice and righteousness – he is invited to take part in the design of this path, by witnessing the process of God's judgment and contributing his own understanding. Abraham will learn from the *tze'aka* ("cry") emanating from Sodom how better to distribute *tzedaka* ("righteousness").[18] The scene is exceedingly bold in the context of religious philosophy, since Abraham's "partnership" with God is explicit; God and Abraham contemplate the verdict of Sodom together.[19] This dialogue emphasizes the development of Abraham's position in the second half of the story cycle. God appears to Abraham in anthropomorphic form, and Abraham is asked to "advise" God on judicial matters. In recognition of his position,

17. Unlike in modern Hebrew, "*lemaan*" ("so that") in the biblical text does not always denote purpose or intent, but can signifiy a result. Compare for example Ex. 20:12, Deut. 5:25. Here, it seems to indicate a result or requirement of God's choice. Thus, Gunkel (*Genesis – Translated and Interpreted,* 201) and Westermann (*Genesis 12–36: A Continental Commentary,* 289) note that this is the only place in the patriarchal narrative that presents the choice of the forefathers as conditional on their deeds.
18. The wordplay between *tzedaka* (righteousness) and *tze'aka* (cry) is implemented in Isaiah, who relies on our verses in his prophecy, "But behold, injustice for righteousness (*tzedaka*), but behold, a cry (*tze'aka*)" (Is. 5:7). See John N. Oswalt, *The Book of Isaiah, Chapters 1–39* (NICOT: Grand Rapids, MI, 1986), 154n22; Mathews, *Genesis,* 224–225.
19. An extreme expression of this position is a rabbinic view that Gen. 18:22, "Abraham remained standing before the Lord," represents a theological editing correction (*tikkun soferim*), while the original text stated that God stood before Abraham (Genesis Rabba 49:7). See Carmel McCarthy, *The Tiqqune Sopherim and Other Theological Corrections in the Masoretic Text of the Old Testament,* OBO 36 (Freiburg and Göttingen: Universitaetsverlag, 1981), 70–76. See also Skinner, *A Critical and Exegetical Commentary on Genesis,* 304–305. However, there is a literary advantage to the Masoretic version. The link between the description here of Abraham standing before God and the description earlier of standing to serve his guests (Gen. 18:8) is noteworthy. Perhaps this connection indicates a similarity of position – Abraham tends to the well-being of his guests, and later to the fate of an entire city.

Abraham will emphasize the difference between him and God throughout the dialogue (such as, "I am but dust and ashes").

Some have noted a contradiction between the two verses that conclude God's thoughts (Gen 18:20–21):

> Then the Lord said, "The outrage of Sodom and Gomorrah is so great, and their sin so grave!"

> "I will go down to see whether they have acted altogether according to the outcry that has reached Me; if not, I will take note."

God initially comments on the severity of the outcry of Sodom and Gomorrah, and the gravity of their sin,[20] while in the subsequent verse, God expresses His intention to investigate the city in order to determine whether the outcry is justified,[21] and the situation is as bad as it seems.[22] However, the verses offer the necessary context for the arrival of the angels in Sodom. Even after God has noted the severity of the sin, He does not hasten to punish before conducting a thorough investigation. Nahmanides perceives this apparent conflict as a depiction of God's thought process as He assesses the situation.[23] If so, these verses represent a gap in knowledge between Abraham and the reader, since Abraham would assume that the messengers are on their way to Sodom to destroy it, not to evaluate it.

---

20. Abraham's possessions were previously described as *kaved* ("heavy") in the introduction to his separation from Lot (Gen. 13:2). Abraham's wealth does not prevent him from seeking out justice, in contrast to Sodom, which is lush and rich, yet full of sin and the outcries of the oppressed.
21. *Tze'aka* and *ze'aka* are entirely interchangeable, and used for variety. (See I Sam. 4:13–14; Is. 65:14, 19; Jer. 25:34, 36; Jer. 48:3–5; Neh. 5:1, 6.) See August H. Konkel, "זעק," *NIDOTTE* 1:1131, but also see Ronald L. Bergey, *The Book of Esther: Its Place in the Linguistic Milieu of Post-Exilic Biblical Hebrew Prose* (PhD diss., Dropsie College, Philadelphia, 1983), 121, who writes, "It is clear that in exilic and post-exilic times a change occurred in the use of the emphatic sibilant *tz* in comparison to the use of the voiced sibilant *z* in the verb *tzaak-zaak* and noun *tzaaka-zaaka*."
22. See discussion in Schmidt, *"De Deo,"* 131–164.
23. Nahmanides on Gen. 18:20–21.

Rashi (among others) views the verses not as part of God's thought process, but rather as part of God's dialogue with Abraham. This interpretation is possible, since Abraham responds directly to this: "Abraham came forward and said, 'Will You sweep away the innocent along with the guilty?'" (Gen. 18:23). However, the sequence of the verses indicates a break in this proposed dialogue of God's decision to investigate (v. 21), and then the angels journeying to Sodom while Abraham continued to stand before God (v. 22). Only after this does it cite Abraham's response. So, reading the verses as part of God's thought process, and not in dialogue with Abraham, is a more viable possibility. According to this reading, God's exact conversation with Abraham regarding His intent is not revealed in the text, which leads to a difference between the information possessed by Abraham and the reader. In the initial episode, the reader knew the identity of Abraham's guests, but Abraham did not; here Abraham might be under the impression that the angels are already on their way to destroy Sodom, while the reader knows the angels are going to Sodom to investigate, and that the verdict is not yet known. Abraham's initial reaction indicates his lack of information: "Far be it from You to do such a thing, to bring death upon the innocent as well as the guilty!" (Gen. 18:25). This gap might have diminished the extent of Abraham's influence on God's decision.

The legal debate is designed as a negotiation between merchants. Abraham uses colloquial rhetoric to convince God that ten righteous people are sufficient to save the city.[24] We will elaborate on this below.

The discussion is framed by the meeting and departure of the characters (Gen. 18:22–33). This frame highlights the unique reciprocity that is expressed in the discussion itself. There is no doubt that God is the one in control; it is Abraham who stands before God, and He alone will determine the fate of the city. And yet, Abraham and God together reflect upon Sodom and discuss the future and appropriate response to the sin of the city.

24. Regarding the common nature of negotiation in this episode, see Mordecai Roshwald, "A Dialogue between Man and God," *SJT* 42 (1989): 154; Ehud Ben Zvi, "The Dialogue between Abraham and Yahweh in Gen 18.23–32: A Historical-Critical Analysis," *JSOT* 53 (1992): 36; Jack R. Lundbom, "Parataxis, Rhetorical Structure and the Dialogue over Sodom in Genesis 18," in *The World of Genesis: Persons, Places, Perspectives*, ed. P. R. Davies and D. J. A. Clines (JSOTSup 257: Sheffield, 1998), 141.

Three changing elements are included at every stage of the discussion: the text's introduction, Abraham's argument, and God's response. The introductions become shorter and shorter through the dialogue. The first three introductions include two verbs: "Abraham *came forward* and he *said*" (Gen. 18:23), "Abraham *answered*, and he *said*" (v. 27), and "He *spoke* to Him again, and *said*" (v. 29). The last three arguments are briefly prefaced with "and he said" (vv. 30, 31, 32). The transfer from the first model to the second is somewhat gradual. Although the third argument is prefaced with two verbs, Abraham's name is omitted, in contrast with the initial two arguments. The writing style phases out the narrative and enables the characters to converse "directly" ("showing" instead of "telling"), resulting in a lively and animated dialogue.[25]

Following the process of Abraham's arguments is complex. After setting the parameters of the discussion at fifty righteous people, Abraham avoids directly lowering the "price" to forty-five. Instead, he presses, "What if the fifty innocent should lack five? Will You destroy the whole city for want of the five?" (Gen. 18:28). The formulation of the argument presents the absurdity of destroying a city *due to the absence* of five people. God's response indicates that although He accepts Abraham's argument, rhetoric will not help Abraham in this instance: "I will not destroy if I find forty-five there" (v. 28). Abraham continues in kind, focusing on the number (rather than the absence) of righteous people.

Abraham introduces his arguments using two models of humility:

> **Phase II:** "I venture to speak to my Lord, I who am but dust and ashes" (Gen. 18:27)
> **Phase IV:** "Let not my Lord be angry if I go on" (v. 30)
> **Phase V:** "I venture again to speak to my Lord" (v. 31)
> **Phase VI:** "Let not my Lord be angry if I speak but this last time" (v. 32)

The first argument does not include a show of humility, since Abraham has to test the waters by posing his initial question, to see whether there

25. For more on this literary method, see Peter J. Rabinowitz, "Showing vs. Telling," in *The Routledge Encyclopedia of Narrative Theory*, ed. D. Herman et al. (London, 2005), 530–531.

is any flexibility on God's part. Surprisingly, the third argument – "What if forty should be found there" (Gen. 18:29) – is not introduced with Abraham begging his pardon. Following Abraham's responses reveals that he uses two alternate formulations: "I venture to speak," and, "Let not my Lord be angry." The purpose of the alternation seems to be creative variation, but since the discussion is designed as a negotiation, the variation serves a rhetorical purpose as well: Abraham does not want to sound repetitive. He wants each of his arguments to sound independently convincing, not as a mere expansion of his previous request. The alternation makes each phase sound like a new argument, when contrasted with the preceding argument. The identical models also include small variations, such as the omission of "I who am but dust and ashes" from the fifth argument.

As mentioned above, Abraham's rhetorical style and the development of the dialogue are designed like a buyer and a merchant haggling over the price of a product. This enhances Abraham's personal involvement in the subject matter. To Abraham, justice and charity are not abstract ideals; he is personally invested in these principles, and is willing to haggle with God to ensure their implementation.

Small variations can be detected in God's responses, but He refrains from revealing His methods of administering justice in the world. In fact, the divine position is only detectable through the analysis of Abraham's counter-arguments. The only detail revealed directly about God is His willingness to investigate the outcry from the city, and destroy the city if He finds that the outcry is justified. Abraham is the active conversant, while God only reacts. This is apparent from God's choice of words, which mirrors Abraham's arguments. When Abraham asks, "*Will You... not forgive* it *for the sake* of the innocent fifty?" (Gen. 18:28), God responds in kind, "*I will forgive* the whole place *for their sake*" (v. 26). When Abraham asks, "*Will You destroy* the whole city for want of the five?" (v. 28) and God responds again in kind, "I *will not destroy*" (v. 28). Although the response does not correlate at every stage, the initial phases set the tone of the discussion and enhance the feeling that Abraham initiates and God responds.

The theological ramifications of this episode are overwhelming. As von Rad notes:

> The paragraph is concerned with an important theological matter. God does not wish that Abraham learn of the frightful event at Sodom only, as it were, from without. God intends to tell him whom He, God, has called into a relationship of trust (*yedativ*, "I have made him acquainted with me"), so that God's act outside, in history which otherwise is hidden from man, shall be revealed to him. He is to understand what will happen in Sodom![26]

Despite von Rad's justified enthusiasm, he has failed to note the more dramatic implications of the verses, in that nowhere in the narrative does God instruct Abraham about divine justice, so that Abraham will know how to pass along God's message to his children. Moreover, God seems to seek Abraham's opinion on the distribution of justice, and perhaps, at first glance, even changes His mind as a result of Abraham's arguments. In contrast with other biblical texts, Genesis 18 seems to suggest that God could benefit from the human perspective on justice and benevolence. The premise of the narrative is that man can understand divine justice, and is expected to argue when God seems to be acting unjustly, and moreover, his arguments might be accepted! Although the ultimate decision is left to God's discretion, Abraham's opinion is portrayed as influential. He is called upon to assist God in defining the boundaries of justice.[27]

The conclusion of the legal debate is that if ten righteous people are found in Sodom, God will avoid destroying the city for their benefit. God had declared His intention to investigate the city before His debate with Abraham, but when their debate reaches its end, it is unclear

26. Von Rad, *Genesis*, 204–205.

27. Some commentators find Abraham's involvement theologically disturbing, and question whether God really needs "an outside perspective" to perceive the catastrophic effect of destroying the cities. Some view God giving Abraham the opportunity to change His mind as evidence of His mercifulness. MacDonald suggested an entirely different interpretation for the one-sided dialogue. He portrays Abraham as bursting through an open door. Abraham encourages the negotiation, and God agrees with each of Abraham's arguments, indicating that He will follow Abraham's suggestion. MacDonald claims that Abraham could have saved Sodom had he asked, but he underestimated his influence (MacDonald, "Listening to Abraham – Listening to Yhwh," 34–41).

whether Abraham changed a divine decree, or whether this was God's intention from the outset. Abraham had assumed that God's intention was to destroy the city even if there were righteous people in it, but this presumption is never verified in the text. Abraham's participation in designing divine justice is diminished by the vagueness of God's initial position.

The conclusion of the discussion is that the city must be investigated. The following chapter therefore becomes the realization of Genesis 18. The angels do not journey to Sodom for the purpose of destroying the city, but rather to investigate; the result of their inquiry will determine the outcome of the verdict and the future of the city. This assumption deeply affects the interpretation of Genesis 19.[28]

This sheds a new light on the invisible conflict between Abraham and the people of Sodom. Abraham brings guests into his home and cares for their comfort, while the people of Sodom seek to harm outsiders; Abraham instructs his children in the ways of *zedaka* – benevolence, while the dwellers of Sodom cause *ze'aka* – an outcry; God "knows" Abraham, and, after His investigation, He "will know" what goes on in Sodom (Gen. 18:21). As Hamilton noted sarcastically: "Or again, perhaps the narrative wants to draw a contrast between Yahweh who knew Abraham and the Sodomites who wanted to 'know' Lot's guests (19:5). Here benign knowledge and diabolical knowledge are juxtaposed."[29]

---

28. Eliezer Schweid writes, "God, who agrees to the claims of his advocate without contest, already knows that there are not even ten righteous in Sodom, and its doom is sealed.... It stands to reason that the angels were sent to Sodom to carry out the verdict that had already been sealed and to rescue the lone righteous man who had not sinned" (Schweid, *The Philosophy of the Bible as Foundation of Jewish Culture*, trans. L. Levin [Boston, 2009], 125). Schweid's comment ignores God's stated wish to investigate the city; there is no indication from the text that the results of the investigation are known in advance.
29. Hamilton, *The Book of Genesis, Chapters 18–50*, 18–19.

Sodom's Destruction and Lot's Rescue (Gen. 19:1–29)

Lot's name is conspicuously missing from the debate over the fate of Sodom. One might even assume that Lot has left the city, since his uncle does not mention him even once while pleading for the lives of Lot's neighbors. In fact, Lot returns to Abraham's story in Genesis 19 for a fascinating encore, serving as the symbolic figure of the angels' judgment of his city. Lot's fate is one of the focal points of the narrative – what will happen to Lot if Sodom is destroyed? On a parallel plane, as the angels examine the virtues of Sodom against its sins, Lot himself wavers between both sides. In the end, the story of Sodom is told through Lot's actions and his inactions.

Lot's escape from the angels' verdict is not, however, a result of his righteousness. "Thus it was that when God destroyed the cities… God remembered Abraham and removed Lot from the midst of the upheaval" (Gen. 19:29). Lot's rescue is attributed in this verse to the merit of Abraham. The concentric structure of the Abraham cycle parallels the two narratives about Lot's rescue. In Genesis 14, Abraham saves Lot from captivity, and in Genesis 19, Abraham's merit leads once again to Lot's escape from disaster. When the threat was political-military (Gen. 14), Abraham intervened directly on Lot's behalf. When the source of the threat is God (Gen. 19), it is again Abraham's merit that "intervenes" on Lot's behalf. In both cases, Lot owes his life to Abraham.

Nonetheless, this verse requires interpretation. The verse seems to offer an outside perspective on the long and detailed story of the investigation of Sodom. The story frame ("looking down" at the city in Gen. 18:16 and 19:28) excludes the verse entirely. Additionally, the use of the name "*Elohim*" here is foreign and inconsistent. Despite the apparent insight offered by the verse, it reasonable for us to look for another explanation for Lot's rescue within the confines of this story.

The Angels Arrive in Sodom (Gen. 19:1–3)

Up to this point in the story, Abraham's guests are referred to as "people." However, upon their arrival to Sodom, the text reveals their true identity, and calls them "angels." As the story unfolds, the text alternates between calling the messengers "people" and "angels," ostensibly depending on whose perspective the text is speaking from. The angels arrive at Sodom as God's messengers, and at His command, and therefore, they are regarded as "angels" in the introduction to the story. However, since they appear to Lot and the townspeople in human form, they are referred to as "people" throughout the text (with the exception of Gen. 19:15).

We meet Lot as the angels enter the city. "The two angels *arrived* in Sodom in the evening, and Lot was *sitting* in the gate" (Gen. 19:1). Lot's location on the border of the city is symbolic of the ambiguity of his position – is he a true Sodomite, or an outsider? The gate indicates that either could be the case – Lot sits at the gate as an indication of his official position,[1] as opposed to his permanent place of dwelling.[2]

1. See Gen. 23:10, 18; Deut. 21:19; 22:15, 24; Prov. 24:7; and Jer. 20:2. Therefore, the verse, "Her husband is prominent in the gates as he sits among the elders of the land" (Prov. 31:23), indicates a public position held by the husband of the woman of valor. The significance of the gate in the biblical era is apparent from archaeological digs, prominently in the findings of the city of Bethsaida in the Galilee, where large altars and other ritual accessories were discovered at the gate. The view of the gate as a definition of the city might be the reason for the obligation to place a mezuza on one's doorpost. See Richard Hess, "שער," *NIDOTTE* 4:208–211; Ze'ev Herzog, "Fortifications (Levant)," *ABD* 2:844–852.
2. Wenham (*Genesis 16–50*, 54), William James Lyons (*Canon and Exegesis: Canonical Praxis and the Sodom Narrative* [JSOTSup 352: London, 2002], 215–216), and

Or, perhaps Lot wishes to see that guests are coming to town and offer them protection before the townspeople get their hands on them. Rashi, inspired by the Midrash, saw Lot's position as an official appointment: "He was appointed judge over the judges."[3] In this case, Lot's stance at the gate would have been a temporary one, and not indicative of his place of residence. Rabbi Joseph Bekhor Shor saw the description of Lot "sitting" at the gate as indicating an ongoing status. Meaning, in other words, Lot's residence, where he was "sitting," was close to the gate: "He resided there, for he did not reside inside Sodom, but rather close to the gate, as it is written, '…pitching his tents near Sodom' [Gen. 13:12]."[4] Bekhor Shor reads the verb Y-SH-B ("to sit") here as connoting a permanent dwelling, comparing its use to the same verb used to describe Lot's decision to settle in Sodom in the first place in Genesis 13. Perhaps the connection indicates that the current situation stems from Lot's initial decision to settle in Sodom.

Bekhor Shor's interpretation results in a strong parallel between Lot's story and that of Rahab, the woman who received Joshua's spies in Jericho and ultimately aided in their escape. Rahab's house was "at the outer side of the city wall and she lived in the actual wall" (Josh. 2:15) just as "Lot was sitting *at* (lit. "in") *the gate*." In view of this, Lot's residence at the gate is appropriately symbolic. While residents of a city are those who dwell within the walls of the city (see Ex. 20:10, Deut. 5:14),[5] Lot and Rahab dwell on the borders of the city. Thus, they are associated with the city, but are not "insiders." Their position on the borderline requires a decision: Are they in or out? Do they view themselves as part of the city (and fated to be destroyed with its residents), or do they stand apart (providing themselves with the option of escaping the fate of the city)?[6] Lot's position creates contradicting impressions. Is Lot's assimilation in the evil city so complete that he has risen to an official

Mathews (*Genesis*, 4) all question the position that places Lot at the gate as a judge, asking why, according to this interpretation, is he sitting at the gate alone?

3. Rashi on Gen. 19:1.
4. Bekhor Shor on Gen. 19:1.
5. Hess, "שַׁעַר," 209.
6. As previously noted, in the angels' tidings to Sarah, the entrance to the tent had a significant literary role, symbolizing the invitation Abraham extends to his guests,

position of power within his community, or is his position at the gate an indication that he can leave the city at will?[7]

The imagery of the border also underscores the investigatory nature of the angels' visit – they have arrived in the city in order to examine its virtues and vices and to make a ruling. Sodom's fate has not yet been sealed – it hangs in the balance, on the border between exoneration and condemnation.

Lot's immediate reaction to the angels bodes well for his future ruling, and that of his city – he models his uncle Abraham's alacrity and enthusiasm for hospitality. Lot receives the angels with generosity, offering them a warm bed and food to fill their bellies. The angels reject Lot's offer, a refusal that seems to be linked with the fundamental plot. The angels were charged with the task of investigating the deeds of the city, and examining whether it contains any righteous people.[8] If the angels had gone to Lot, they could investigate Lot's family, but not the general culture of the city. This explains the seemingly rude statement of the angels, "We will spend the night in the square" (Gen. 19:2). They were, in fact, providing an explanation of their refusal, in that the purpose of their visit was to investigate the city, and they need to spend the night in the town square, where they can gather information about the social situation in the city.[9] Lot's insistence changes the anticipated course of the plot. The angels would have been "forced" to wait until morning before they were able to conduct their investigation,[10] had the entire city not shown up at Lot's doorstep and demonstrated prevalent social

---

which parallels the expansion of the tent with the blessing of a son. The symbolism of the entrance in the Sodom narrative will be discussed below.

7. Compare to Robert I. Letellier, *Day in Mamre, Night in Sodom: Abraham and Lot in Genesis 18 and 19* (Biblical Interpretation Series 10: Leiden, 1995), 140.
8. Keil and Delitzsch, *Biblical Commentary on the Old Testament*, 232.
9. As opposed to Wenham, *Genesis 16–50*, 54, who viewed their refusal as unexplained for the purpose of enhancing the tension.
10. Paul Tonson views the angels' refusal of Lot's offer as part of a consistent pattern that is repeated in a number of scenes: 1) Offer or demand, 2) Refusal, 3) Repetition of the offer or demand. In this context, the refusal enhances Lot's hospitality, and comments on his nature (Tonson, "Mercy without Covenant: A Literary Analysis of Genesis 19," *JSOT* 95 [2001]: 102–103, 108, 111).

customs; whereupon the angels were able to proceed with their investigation within the confines of Lot's house.

The Townspeople

The people who gather around Lot's house inadvertently ease the angels' mission, since the angels no longer have to go out into the town to inspect the culture of the city. The Sodomites offer themselves for judgment, and unwittingly step into their own trial. The text emphasizes the fact that the entire city congregated around Lot's house by using three different phrases: "The townspeople, the people of Sodom, gathered about the house:

1) From young to old,
2) All the people
3) To the last person."

This emphasis validates this experience as a binding inspection of the city: God and Abraham had agreed that if ten righteous people are found Sodom will be spared. The gathering of the entire city around Lot's house, with the intention of harming his innocent guests, unequivocally negates the possibility of ten righteous people.

The rumor had spread through the city like wildfire – "They had not yet lain down" (Gen. 19:4) – and the entire town suddenly congregates around Lot's house. No explanation is provided as to how or why the news had spread so fast, and this literary gap is left to the reader's imagination. One midrash attributes the rumor to Lot's gossipy wife.[11] Alternatively, Lot had invited his guests in a public place, and was undoubtedly seen as he walked through town with two strangers.[12] Regardless of the reason, however, this omission serves to highlight the eagerness of the townspeople to come and harm strangers who made the grave mistake of visiting Sodom. The

11. Genesis Rabba 51:5.
12. See discussion in Wenham, *Genesis 16–50*, 54, regarding whether Lot was the only judge to invite guests to his home, as opposed to the other elders at the gate, or whether Lot sits at the gate alone.

arrival of guests is big news, since it provides an opportunity for the Sodomites to unleash the evil within.

The people surrounding the house wish to "know" the guests (Gen. 19:5). At this stage, the reader might wonder what it is that the townspeople want. The meaning of this knowledge gets to the heart of what, in essence, was the city of Sodom's sin. At this point in the narrative, that question remains unanswered. The verb Y-D-A ("to know") had appeared twice before within the narrative, both in positive contexts. God describes His view of Abraham in Genesis 18:19: "For I have known him (*yedativ*), that he may instruct his children and his posterity to keep the way of the Lord by doing what is benevolent and just." In Genesis 18:21, the verb is used to describe the alternative to the justification of the outcry emerging from the city: "If not, I will take note (*edaa*)."[13] Based on these previous uses, the innocent reader might assume the townspeople wish to "get to know" Lot's guests.[14] It is their hospitality that stands in judgment, and is this test which they fail to pass under the messengers' watchful eyes. If, indeed, Sodom's sin was lack of hospitality, this would contrast nicely with the story of Abraham and Sarah,

13. The expression is difficult, and there are three approaches to its interpretation: Some (such as the Ḥizkuni) believe the verb connotes fondness and blessing, similar to its usage regarding Abraham ("I have known him"). According to this interpretation, after investigating the city, God will decide whether to punish the city with destruction, or *bless* the city. In contrast, others (see Rabbenu Baḥya ben Asher, and D. Winton Thomas, "Julius Furst and the Hebrew Root," *JTS* 42 [1941]: 65, among others) interpret *edaa* as indicative of punishment. A third and simpler approach reads the verb as a conclusion of the entire sentence, as if to say, "I will go down to see whether they have acted according to the outcry that has reached Me, or not, I shall know." For this approach, see Rashi, Bekhor Shor, John A. Emerton ("A Consideration of Some Alleged Meanings of *yd'* in Hebrew," *JSS* 15 [1970]: 171), Westermann (*Genesis 12–36: A Continental Commentary*, 284), and Robert Alter (*Genesis – Translation and Commentary* [New York, 1996], 81). All of the approaches above do not diminish the significance of the integration of the verb twice in the verses, one in relation to Abraham and again in relation to Sodom.

14. Some scholars actually posit this. See Scott N. Morschauser, "Hospitality, Hostiles and Hostages: On the Legal Background to Genesis 19.1–9," *JSOT* 27 (2003): 461–485. He writes that the townspeople had security concerns regarding these strangers. See Brian Doyle, "'Knock, Knock, Knockin' on Sodom's Door': The Function of פתח/דלת in Genesis 18–19," *JSOT* 28 (2004): 431–448, and the next footnote.

from which the messengers had just arrived, literally and thematically. However, the false impression is immediately corrected by Lot, who knows his town. He understands that the townspeople intend to sexually assault his guests.[15] Lot's reaction seems to corroborate the view that the Sodomites' sin was sexual in nature, and any misdemeanor in hospitality or lack thereof was merely secondary to sealing their fate. The Sodomites, despite their riches, not only behaved poorly by not supporting the needy, but they also sought to harm them. This is their true sin, and the reason they were condemned.

Lot's reaction to this understanding is horrifically shocking. He offers to substitute his two virgin daughters, "who have not known a man" (Gen. 19:8), to the townspeople in lieu of the guests. It is at this moment that we begin to see a Lot that might have shed the teachings of his uncle and adopted a Sodomite system of values. The double usage of the verb Y-D-A throughout the text further emphasizes this striking contrast. Y-D-A expresses the unique intimacy between God and Abraham, a connection based on justice and benevolence, but also the blatant wickedness of Sodom, whose people would use a sacred act to promote evil.

This should also be viewed as the context of the sin of Sodom. Early and modern commentaries have two primary approaches toward their sin. One approach focuses on the sin of preventing hospitality, while the other focuses on the sexual offense of rape or homosexuality.[16] The main contrast between Lot and the Sodomites is expressed in the text as the difference in attitude toward guests; Ezekiel reinforces

---

15. Doyle ("Knock, Knock, Knockin' on Sodom's Door," 437–438) claims that Lot misunderstood the request of the Sodomites. According to him, they wished only to become acquainted with Lot's guests, since, unlike Lot, they recognized the guests as angels, while Lot perceived the request to "know" them as sexual. Doyle concludes that the sin of Sodom was vanity, since the townspeople had assumed that they could meet with angels despite their inferiority. However, it would appear that the angels' retribution against the townspeople and the ultimate destruction of the city indicate that Lot had understood the intent of the townspeople much better than Doyle did.
16. See the survey by James Alfred Loader, "The Sin of Sodom in the Talmud and Midrash," *Old Testament Essays* 3 (1990): 231–245, and Doyle, "Knock, Knock, Knockin' on Sodom's Door," 431–448.

this view in his description of Sodom: "Only this was the sin of your sister Sodom: arrogance! She and her daughters had plenty of bread and untroubled tranquility; yet she did not support the poor and the needy" (Ezek. 16:49–50).

Sodom's financial power did not lead its residents to "support the poor and the needy," despite their God-given ability to do so. Ezekiel ignores the sexual motif, which in Genesis as well is not portrayed as the chief sin of the city. The sexual assault on the guests emphasizes the lack of morality toward the apparently defenseless visitors, who lack the protection of family. Not only do the townspeople refrain from offering guests food and shelter, they also take advantage of their vulnerability and seek to harm them.[17]

Before Lot's response to the demand of the townspeople, he indicates his position with another seemingly innocuous but symbolic action: "Lot went out to them to the entrance, and shut the door behind him" (Gen. 19:6). Closing the door seems, at first glance, to be entirely superfluous, a detail unnecessary to the progression of the narrative. Technically, Lot has to close the door in order to prevent the mob from entering his home.[18] However, the door appears twice more, once when the townspeople threaten to break it down in verse 9, and again when the angels reach outside the door to pull Lot inside in verse 10. The repeated reference to the door serves a symbolic-literary purpose.[19]

---

17. Even if the sexual issue is not the essence of the sin, Mathews might be correct that words with sexual connotations are deliberately scattered throughout the text. He emphasized the verb "*bo*," "to come toward," in vv. 3, 5, 8, 9, and 10, and the verb "*yishkavu*," "they lay down," in v. 4 (Mathews, *Genesis*, 233).
18. Bruce K. Waltke and Cathi J. Fredricks, *Genesis: A Commentary* (Grand Rapids, MI, 2001), 265–281, correctly note that this detail portrays Lot as self-sacrificing, blocking his escape route into the house. Waltke also connects this closing of the door to God closing the door to Noah's ark (Gen. 7:16). Hamilton has noted this similarity as well (Hamilton, *The Book of Genesis, Chapters 18–50*, 37).
19. Doyle sees "door" ("*delet*") and "entrance" ("*petaḥ*") as key words which link Genesis 19 with Genesis 18, where Abraham sits at the entrance to his tent. To him, the door symbolizes a place of revelation, similar to the entrance of the Tent of Meeting (Doyle, "Knock, Knock, Knockin' on Sodom's Door," 442–448). This symbolism is congruent with the position that the townspeople sought to meet with the angels of God.

The door separates the townspeople from the angels; Lot stands at the threshold and has to determine where he belongs. Does he identify with the Sodomites, the people among whom he chose to dwell, or does he belong in his own house, which is separated from the events that take place outside? Lot goes out, and later goes back in; the door opens and closes. The literary reality creates a distinction between the "few righteous people" inside the house, and the wicked on the outside.[20]

Lot's address is confusing. He does all that is in his power to protect his guests; he prevents the angry mob from breaking into his house to harm his people. Lot stands apart from the culture of the city. He takes pity on passers-by and defends them faithfully. Ironically, it is the people of Sodom who point to Lot's righteousness: "But they said, Move away! They said, the fellow dwells here as a stranger, and now he passes judgment! Now we will deal worse with you than with them" (Gen. 19:9).

The repetition of "they said" deepens the barrier between Lot and the townspeople. Initially, they tell him to leave, a demand for separation from them. The second statement reveals their true feelings toward Lot: "The fellow dwells here as a stranger, and now he passes judgment!" Lot is perceived as a stranger in Sodom, who could never belong – because his culture is rooted in justice. The phrase "*vayishpot shafot*" ("he passes judgment") has been interpreted by some as denoting authority, instead of judgment.[21] However, the use of the verb SH-F-T (lit. "to judge") is not accidental. Lot wishes to distribute justice, identifying himself with Abraham, who instructs his household in the ways of "justice and benevolence" (Gen. 18:19).[22] Lot thereby chooses to walk in the way of God, who is also called "Judge of all the earth" by Abraham (Gen. 18:25), instead of the ways of Sodom. While the townspeople clearly meant to mock Lot, they inadvertently saved him from

20. Jonathan Jacobs views the emphasis on the door as an indication of the concept of "measure for measure." He writes, "Lot shuts the door in a heroic act, in order to protect his guests from the Sodomites who wish to harm them. In a positive 'measure for measure,' the angels reward Lot when the people of Sodom turn on him, and close the very same door, protecting their protector" (Jacobs, *Measure for Measure in the Storytelling Bible* [Alon Shevut, 2006], 83).
21. Mathews, *Genesis*, 237.
22. Compare with Alter, *Genesis*, 86.

the fate of Sodom by categorizing him as part of Abraham's house, which is based in justice and benevolence.

However, the offer Lot makes to give up his daughters – assuming he was serious – is shocking, and readers throughout history have found the passage difficult to comprehend.[23] In Lot's zealousness to protect his guests, he is apparently willing to sacrifice his virgin daughters. Lot is charged with the protection of his own flesh and blood, but his daughters will pay the price for his charitable act of protecting the foreigners. The irony of Lot's offer is indicated in Lot's use of the roots *ra* ("evil") and *tov* ("good"): "I beg you, my friends, do not commit such an evil (*al tare'u*). Look, I have two daughters who have not known a man. Let me bring them out to you, and you may do to them as is good in your eyes (*katov be'enekhem*)" (Gen. 19:7–8). Ironically, Lot employs ethical semantics, portraying himself as one who fights against evil, while he is willing to commit the unspeakable act of throwing his own daughters into the hands of a depraved mob.[24] Later, in another context, Lot will express his fear of being caught up in the fate of the city, "lest the evil stick to me and I die" (19:19). Here, one might say some of Sodom's evil seems indeed to have stuck to Lot.

Lot's character is therefore portrayed ambivalently, as a generous and kind host, but also as a villain who is willing to abandon his daughters to a gang of rapists.[25] This ambivalence will accompany Lot throughout the story.

At this point the text stops "showing" (the characters' voices are no longer heard) and begins "telling" (describing the events from

23. Regarding the possibility that Lot's suggestion was insincere, see Lyn M. Bechtel, "A Feminist Reading of Genesis 19:1–11," in *A Feminist Companion to Genesis*, ed. A. Brenner (Sheffield, 1993), 108–128.
24. See Phyllis Trible, *Texts of Terror: Literary-Feminist Readings of Biblical Narratives* (London, 1984), 75; Bechtel, "A Feminist Reading of Genesis 19:1–11," 108–128; Robert D. Sacks, *A Commentary on the Book of Genesis* (Adelaide, 1990), 132. Sacks views Lot's request, "I beg you, my friends, do not commit such an evil," as evidence of Lot's cowardice.
25. The title of Laurence A. Turner's paper ("Lot as Jekyll and Hyde: A Reading of Genesis 18–19," in *The Bible in Three Dimensions: Essays in Celebration of Forty Years of Biblical Studies in the University of Sheffield*, ed. D. J. A. Clines et al. [JSOTSup 87: Sheffield, 1990], 59–98) is a harsh expression of this idea.

a third-person perspective). The distant perspective enables the text to describe both the actions of the townspeople and the angels. The townspeople press Lot to let them in, and threaten to break down the door. The people inside send out a hand and pull Lot inside, and close the door. The door becomes the object of struggle between the two groups. The reader is called upon to differentiate between Lot and the Sodomites. Lot "urges" (*vayiftzar*) the angels to come to his home (Gen. 19:3) and the Sodomites "urge" (*vayiftzeru*) Lot to let his guests out so that they could have their way with them (v. 9). The use of the same verb (P-TZ-R – "urge") indicates the difference between Lot, who wishes to host and protect his guests, and the townspeople, who would take the guests out of the house to harm them.[26]

The text misleads the reader by using the same name – "*anashim*" ("people") – for the two opposing groups. Lot's guests are called *anashim* (vv. 5, 8, 12, and 16), as are the Sodomites (vv. 4, 11). The "people" approach the door and try to break it down, but it is also the "people" (the angels) who send out their hand and bring Lot inside. The protector has become the protected. In most instances, the context allows the reader to determine which group is being referred to, but Genesis 19:10 is confusing: "And the people sent forth their hand (*vayishleḥu haanashim et yadam*)..." Reading the verses consecutively, the *anashim* seems to refer to the Sodomites, who were discussed in the previous verse: "They approached to break down the door..." Since there is no direct indication that the subject has been changed, the verse might imply that the townspeople stretched out their hand to break down the door as they had intended.

Moreover, the expression "to send forth one's hand" is frequently used in the context of doing others harm, as in: "Do not send forth your hand against the boy, or do anything to him" (Gen. 22:12), "So I will send forth My hand and smite Egypt" (Ex. 3:20), "Yet He did not send forth His hand against the leaders of the Israelites" (Ex. 24:11), "David said to his men, 'God forbid I would do such a thing to my lord, the Lord's anointed, to send forth my hand to him'" (I Sam. 24:6), and

26. Yehuda Kiel, *Daat Mikra: Genesis* (Jerusalem, 2000), vol. 2, 31; Mathews, *Genesis*, 234.

many other examples.[27] This association bolsters the reading that views the Sodomites as the ones who extend a hand to break the door and harm Lot's guests. It is only later in our verse, with the phrase "and they brought him into the house," that it is revealed that the hand was in fact extended by the "*anashim*" who are inside the house, and not by the Sodomites on the outside. Apparently, the extension of the hand here is intended to help, not harm.[28]

The temporary ambiguity regarding the identity of the "people" in the verse is not accidental.[29] The writing style has a dramatic effect, giving a sense of the chaos in the scene.[30] The reader's confusion also reflects the ambivalence of Lot, who has to decide who to side with. With which "people" does Lot identify?

The overt conflict is enhanced by the subtle pitting of the two groups against one another. The two groups of "people" confront each other in three focal points:

1. While the Sodomites want to break down the door, the angels close the door (Gen. 19:10). In view of the significant symbolism of the door in the narrative, the conflict over the door can be given symbolic meaning, in that the townspeople wish to nullify the border between good and evil, while the angels attempt to reconstruct those boundaries. The boundaries are unequivocal in

27. Such as Ex. 9:15; I Sam. 22:17; I Sam. 26:11, 23; Est. 2:21; 3:6; 6:2; 8:7; 9:2; Job 1:12.
28. One could suggest that the earlier "*anashim*" indeed refers to the Sodomites, and it is only beginning with the verb *vayaviu* ("and they brought") that the angels are referenced, indicating that they were saving Lot from the harm the other "*anashim*" wished to inflict upon them.
29. On the implementation of this literary technique in the biblical narrative, see Meir Sternberg, "Delicate Balance in the Story of the Rape of Dinah: Biblical Narratives and the Rhetoric of the Narrative Text," *Literature* 4 (1973): 223. And see Grossman, *Ambiguity in the Biblical Narrative*, 10, 49–51.
30. Yossefa Rahman suggests that the confusion between the "people" in the story (angels and Sodomites) is meant to exhaust the reader: "The effect of exhaustion is theatrical; it enables the narrative to affect the reader's mind and emotions, and create an illusion of encountering angels" (Rahman, "The Embarrassment Effect in the Sodom and Gomorrah Narrative [Gen. 18–19]," in *A Light for Jacob*, ed. Y. Hoffman and Frank H. Polak [Jerusalem, 1997], 191).

the conclusion of the episode: "And the people who were at the entrance of the house, young and old, they struck with blinding light, so that they were helpless to find the entrance" (v. 11).[31]

2. Both groups ask Lot to remove the people under his care. The Sodomites demand, "Where are the men who came to you tonight? Bring them out (*hotzi'em*) to us, that we may know them" (Gen. 19:5), while the angels command, "Whom else have you here? Sons-in-law, your sons and daughters, or anyone else that you have in the city – bring them out (*hotze*) of the place!" (v. 12).[32] Neither of the demands are carried out. However, while Lot objects vehemently to the request of the townspeople, he (reluctantly) agrees to cooperate with the angels. Despite Lot's ambivalence, he leans toward justice and righteousness, and attempts to prevent overt evil. Thus, he identifies with the people inside his house.
3. Lot uses similar wording when he addresses both groups:
   - "*I beg you,* my friends, do not commit such a wrong. *Behold,* I have two daughters..." (Gen. 19:8–9).
   - "*I beg you,* my lord! *Behold,* You have been so gracious to your servant..." (vv. 18–19).

Lot goes in and out and then back in again. With each move, the tension grows. Which side will he choose? Despite the complex evaluation of Lot (due to the offer of his daughters), the subtleties of the plot seem to indicate that Lot chooses to identify with the "people" he brought into his home, and to separate himself from the townspeople.

---

31. Stuart Lasine ("Guest and Host in Judges 19: Lot's Hospitality in an Inverted World," *JSOT* 29 [1984]: 40) interprets the scene as comical. The Sodomites seek the entrance, and cannot understand why it can't be found.
32. The root Y-TZ-A ("to go out") is repeated throughout the narrative, appropriately for a narrative about saving a man from the destruction of his city. Lot *goes out* to the townspeople to protect his guests, and suggests that he will *send out* his daughters as a replacement for his guests (Gen. 19:6–8). After the angels tell him that the city will be destroyed, he *goes out* to his sons-in-law, and tells them to *get out* of Sodom (v. 14). This theme will be discussed further with regard to the sun, which also "*comes out*" (v. 23).

The Verdict and Lot's Escape

After the previous scene, it comes as no surprise to the reader when the angels declare their verdict: "Then the people (i.e., the angels) said to Lot, 'Whom else have you here? Sons-in-law, your sons and daughters, or anyone else that you have in the city – bring them out of the place, for we are about to destroy this place; because the outcry (*tzaakatam*) against them before the Lord has become so great that the Lord has sent us to destroy it'" (Gen. 19:12–13). The divine dilemma that opened the narrative – "I will go down to see whether they have acted altogether according to her outcry (*tzaakata*) that has reached Me; if not, I will take note" (18:21) – is finally resolved. The outcry was entirely justified, and the city must be destroyed.[33]

Lot's inherent ambivalence as a character is further reflected in how he relays the news of Sodom's destruction to the members of his household. If we compare the angels' instructions to Lot's repetition, we see that he omits the reason for Sodom's destruction in his explanation to his family:

The angel's instructions to Lot (Gen 19:12–13)	**Lot's advice to his sons-in-law (Gen. 19:14)**
Whom else have you here? *Sons-in-law, your sons and daughters,* or anyone else that you have in the city	So Lot went out and spoke to *his sons-in-law, who had married his daughters,* and said
bring them out of the place	*Up, get out of this place,*
For we are about to *destroy* this place	for the Lord is about to *destroy* the city
because their outcry before the Lord has become so great that the Lord has sent us to destroy it.	

33. Initially, in Gen. 18:21, the "outcry" is attributed to the city, and stated in the singular. However, in Gen. 19:13, the angels tell Lot that "their outcry" has become intolerable, emphasizing the many individuals harmed by the city's culture. Although the angels specify that God had sent them to destroy the city, one can still assume that the verdict is dependent upon the angels' findings. In other words, the angels are instructed to destroy the city in the event that the city is found guilty, and ten righteous people cannot be found.

This omission is incredibly telling. While Lot believes the angels and adheres to their instructions, he does not accept everything they say. Lot hesitates to stand before his sons-in-law and declare that the financial prosperity of their city was accompanied by an immoral culture. The textual criticism of Lot is apparent in the reaction of his sons-in-law: "He seemed to his sons-in-law as one who jests" (Gen. 19:14). Their rescue would have been based on their connection with Lot, since they are married to Lot's daughters.[34] Lot's failure to sound convincing indicates that he does not identify with the cause wholeheartedly.[35] Something in Lot is reluctant to leave town. Although he had decided to listen to the angels (whose powers he witnessed when they blinded the townspeople at his door), his doubt is expressed through his sons-in-law's disbelief.[36] Essentially, this seems to be the chief function of his sons-in-law in the story. Their lack of faith and decision to stay behind reflects Lot's own doubts.

Lot's narrow escape is filled with complications, serving to highlight his emotional attachment to the city: "As dawn broke, the angels urged Lot on.... Still he delayed. So the men seized his hand, and the hands of his wife and his two daughters – in the Lord's mercy on him – and brought him out and left him outside the city" (Gen. 19:15–16). The angels have to urge Lot to escape, but even after they warn him, he continues to delay, and there seems to be no way to get him out of town other than by gentle force, and the angels literally take Lot by the hand

34. The continuation of the narrative shows that Lot had daughters who died in Sodom. The angels tell Lot, "Up, take your wife and your two *remaining* daughters" (Gen. 19:15), indicating that Lot has daughters who are not with him, presumably the married daughters, married to his previously mentioned sons-in-law (see Ibn Ezra's commentary on Gen. 19:14). Paul Tonson writes that the daughters who escaped were engaged, not married, to the sons-in-law who refused Lot's advice that they escape the city. This would create symmetry between the fallen, i.e., Lot's wife and two sons-in-law, and the rescued, i.e., Lot and his two daughters (Tonson, "Mercy without Covenant," 100n7). According to Tonson, each of the people who were saved lost a spouse; this idea provides an interesting background for the following narrative about Lot and his daughters in the cave.
35. As opposed to being a mere expression of contempt toward Lot, as is generally assumed (e.g., Coats, "Lot: A Foil in the Abraham Saga," 123).
36. Regarding the implementation of this literary technique in the biblical narrative, see Yitzhak Lev-Ran, *Narrative Modes for Presenting Complexity of Inner Life of Biblical Characters* (PhD. diss., Bar Ilan University, 2009).

and lead him out. Lot's indecisive behavior accentuates just how deep-seated his ambivalence regarding Sodom is; even as the city is about to be burned to the ground, he cannot bring himself to leave it behind.

Lot and his family need to be torn from the city, even in the face of its impending destruction. The angels, for their part, do their best to instill a sense of urgency in Lot. The chiastic structure of the angel's instructions portray the twofold significance of the escape from Sodom:[37]

A: Flee for your life!
  B: Do not look behind you
  B': And do not stop anywhere in the plain
A': Flee to the hills, lest you be swept away!

The angel's wording, "Flee to the hills, lest you be swept away (*tisafeh*)," is reminiscent of Abraham's discussion with God regarding the destruction of Sodom. Abraham uses the expression "swept away" twice in his initial argument against the destruction: "Will You sweep away (*tispeh*) the innocent along with the guilty?... Will You sweep away (*tispeh*) the place and not forgive it for the sake of the innocent fifty who are in it?" (Gen. 18:23–24).[38] The context implies that the city's punishment might affect Lot despite his innocence. Although he is given the opportunity to run, if he delays, he might be "swept away" in the fate of the city.

And yet, even as he flees, Lot's character betrays him. The angels urge him to escape as far as possible, but Lot – perhaps out of laziness, or a lingering affection for his city – refuses to stray too far. Lot's request from the angels has two parts (Gen. 19:19–20):

1. "You have been so gracious to your servant, and have already shown me so much kindness in order to save my life; but I cannot flee to the hills, lest the evil stick to me and I die."
2. "Look, that town there is near enough to flee to; it is so small (*mitzar*)! Let me flee there – it is so small (*mitzar*) – and let my life be saved."

---

37. Regarding the structure of the verse, see Mathews, *Genesis*, 239–240.
38. Hamilton, *The Book of Genesis, Chapters 18–50*, 43.

Inadvertently, Lot saves the city of Zoar with his request. The expression "*mitzar,*" "small," mentioned twice in verses 19–20 and the root of the name Zoar, is fitting. Lot's intention was small-minded – to save himself, to attempt to remain close. It almost goes unnoticed by Lot that he has succeeded in supplicating a divine being to save a city condemned to death. This, in contrast with Abraham's petition on behalf of a city he has little or no connection with, is just another indicator of Lot's nature. The literary contrast between Lot and Abraham comes full circle: Lot left his uncle and went to Sodom in search of the luxury and fertile land; in the end it was the contrast between the fertility and Sodom's lack of generosity that led to her demise.

The severity of the punishment inflicted on Lot's wife is the final detail that stresses the importance of disconnecting from Sodom both physically and emotionally. The angels' demand, "Do not look behind you," seems strategic – as they flee the scene of destruction, time and focus is of the essence. It would be understandable that Lot and his family would steal one last glance as their home goes up in flames. Lot's wife's punishment, however, shows us just how untenable Lot and his family's position was. Until the end, it is not clear that Lot and his household were prepared to renounce their Sodomite citizenship. Any inkling of residual emotional connection, as Lot's wife demonstrated here, would unequivocally tie their loyalty – and therefore their fate – with the evildoers of the city. Looking back at the city creates an emotional bond of identification and grief over the destruction; the one who looks back identifies with the city, and is therefore destroyed along with it.

In sharp contrast to Lot's wife, Abraham, too, gazes out at the smoldering remains of Sodom, and in his gaze, as well, we must infer his internal emotional state. "Abraham got up early the next morning to the place where he had stood before the Lord, and, looking down (*vayashkef*) toward Sodom and Gomorrah and all the land of the Plain, he saw the steam of the land rising like the smoke of a kiln" (Gen. 19:27–28). The verse seems to summon the storyline full circle to where it arguably began – in the place where Abraham pled with God for the salvation of Sodom. Although Abraham had no part in Sodom's destruction, this conclusion frames the scene clearly as a central point in Abraham's narrative.

Abraham's gaze down on the burning city (*vayashkef*) is echoed years later, as another entity peers down over the precipice of a similar destruction: "At the morning watch, the Lord looked down (*vayashkef*) upon the Egyptian army from a pillar of fire and cloud, and threw the Egyptian army into a panic" (Ex. 14:24). God watches as the evildoers of Egypt are swept away in the parting of the Red Sea. God looks down on the Egyptians in the process of their destruction, while Abraham looks down on Sodom after it is destroyed. God and Abraham agree on the terms of the fate of the city. As a result, God destroys Sodom, and Abraham "looked down" upon the city. The repeated phrase is an expression of Abraham's partnership with God.

In this light, we can discuss the centrality of time in the story and how it hints to cooperation between Abraham and God. The story opens with Abraham sitting at the entrance to his tent "at the heat of the day." The angels come to Sodom "in the evening." The angels urge Lot to leave "as dawn broke." God rains fire on the cities when "the sun came out." Finally, the story concludes with a description of the time in reference to Abraham, who began the cycle: "Abraham got up early the next morning."[39] The chronological sequence of the story weaves Abraham's actions into those of God and His angels.[40]

The first conclusion had described Abraham looking down on Sodom and viewing the aftermath of the destruction. The second conclusion describes God's mindfulness of Abraham, which is the reason He had rescued one of the residents of Sodom. Genesis 19:29 is designed in a chiastic structure:

---

39. Cf. Gunkel, *Genesis – Translated and Interpreted*, 212.
40. The comparison of the steam rising from the city to "smoke of a kiln" is used at Sinai. When God appears in the image of fire on the mountain, "the smoke rose like the smoke of a kiln" (Ex. 19:18). The fire and brimstone of Sodom leave a scorched and smoky land. Note that the focus of the verse continues to refer directly to the land: "He saw the steam *of the land* rising like the smoke of a kiln." Smoke is often mentioned in the context of the destruction of a city (Josh. 8:20–21, Is. 9:17). The use of the word *kitur* ("steam") is an interesting deviation. Mathews notes that in the sacrificial world, smoke relates to incense, and the verb *lehaktir* (from the root K-T-R) is used to describe the act of offering incense (Mathews, *Genesis*, 242n467). Perhaps there is an attempt to link Sodom's fate with sacrifice.

> **A:** Thus it was that when *God* annihilated the cities of the Plain,[41]
>
> **B:** *God* remembered *Abraham,*
>
> **B':** and removed *Lot* from the midst of the upheaval
>
> **A':** when He overturned the cities where *Lot* dwelt.

The link between the two parts of the verse is apparent. The frame of the statement reveals that God destroyed Sodom, while the central content describes His kindness toward Abraham and Lot. But there is also a distinction in the focus of each part. The first half of the verse emphasizes God (who destroys and remembers), while the second half emphasizes Lot (who is sent away from the city). Two different verbs describe the destruction of the city: "*shaḥet,*" "annihilated," and "*hafokh,*" "overturned." The two parts also distinguish between the cities that were destroyed, which are initially referred to as "the cities of the Plain," and later as "the cities where Lot dwelt."[42] These differences correlate with the two focal points of the verse. The term *shaḥet* is extremely harsh, and expresses total obliteration. The second half of the verse, which describes Lot's rescue, uses a "gentler" verb of *hafokh,* which expresses the substitution of one situation for another (see, for example, Ex. 7:15; 7:17 and 20; 14:5; Lev. 13:3–4; Deut. 23:6). A person can be saved from an upheaval (*hafekha*), but not from annihilation (*hashḥata*).[43] The third difference correlates with the purpose of the first two: when the subject of the verse was annihilation, the cities of the plain were a geographical datum, but when the text shifts its attention

41. *Hashḥit* denotes complete and total destruction, while *hafakh* literally means to "turn over" or "reverse," and is used in various biblical contexts connoting an upheaval or destruction. While NJPS translates Gen. 19:29's *beshaḥet* as "destroyed," and *hafokh* as "annihilated," and though it is true that the meaning of the two words is the same in the verse, the first Hebrew term should be translated with harsher connotations than its counterpart.
42. The second part of the verse has an internal chiastic structure of its own:
    A: "... and removed *Lot*
    B: from the midst of the *upheaval* (*hafekha*)
    B': when He *overturned* (*bahafokh*) the cities
    A': where *Lot* dwelt."
43. See Robert B. Chisholm, "הפך," *NIDOTTE* 1:1048–1050; Kaddari, *A Dictionary of Biblical Hebrew,* 224–225.

to Lot, the cities are also described from his perspective: they are his home. The Sodomites view Lot as a temporary resident and provide excellent references for his rescue: they do not see him as one of their own. The term "dwelt" that describes Lot's relationship with the city revisits the question of Lot's merit. Does Lot really stand apart from the residents of Sodom? The word Y-SH-B ("to sit/dwell") was a key word in the narrative describing Abraham's separation from Lot.[44] The text there was implicitly critical of Lot when he chose to "dwell" in Sodom, where the people were "very wicked sinners against the Lord," when he separated from Abraham (Gen. 13:12).

Additionally, the statement, "God remembered Abraham," is reminiscent of another case of destruction: "God remembered Noah" (Gen. 8:1).[45] In the Noah narrative, God remembers the person He saves, whereas in Lot's case, God remembers not Lot, but Abraham.[46] This detail highlights the main message conveyed by the verse: Lot is not saved by his own merit but by the merit of his uncle. Perhaps the fact that Abraham is mentioned (instead of Lot, who parallels Noah in the story) is the reason that the destruction is repeated using the verb *shaḥet,* which parallels the use of the word in the Flood narrative (Gen. 6:17, 9:11–15). This way, the reader, who is reminded of the Flood and Noah's rescue, becomes more surprised when God remembers Abraham instead of Lot.[47]

The verse roars in deafening silence regarding the souls of Sodom, lost in her destruction. What was Abraham feeling when he watched the smoke rising from what was once a great city? Apparently, there were not even ten righteous people in the whole area, and an entire region was lost. What did Abraham assume became of his nephew? No

---

44. Mathews, *Genesis,* 243.

45. NJPS translates *vayizkor* as "was mindful of" in Gen. 19:29, and "remembered" in Gen. 8:1.

46. Wenham, *Genesis 16–50,* 59. He claims that this refers to Abraham's prayer in Gen. 18, which brings about Lot's salvation (ibid., 59–60). In my opinion, Lyons is correct that the phrase refers to "ancestral merit" in a more general sense (Lyons, *Canon and Exegesis: Canonical Praxis and the Sodom Narrative,* 203–206, 249–250).

47. However, it is noteworthy that the verb *shaḥet* was also integrated into the narrative about the angels in Sodom (Gen. 19:13, and see also 13:10).

reunion is reported between Abraham and Lot; in fact, the two characters do not meet again, as far as we know, after Abraham rescues Lot in Genesis 14. The gaping lack of closure in the story of Abraham and Lot could be filled with various feelings (anger? bitterness? reconciliation?). The choice of silence sustains the detachment between the characters. Lot will not be Abraham's heir or successor. Whatever his destiny, his tie to his uncle's story has been severed.

Why Was Lot Saved from Sodom?

As Sodom's ashes burn, and Abraham looks out over the result of divine judgment, a penetrating question rises with the smoke. Why was Lot saved from Sodom? Was he righteous? This is possible, although his obvious hesitation to separate from Sodom even as it burned is troubling – not to mention the fact that he appeared willing to sacrifice his own daughters to a violent mob. Even if Lot *was* a righteous man, he was in the minority. This was the very conclusion of the discourse between Abraham and God – if there were fewer than ten righteous citizens in Sodom, it would be condemned to destruction – it and all of its citizens within.

A return to Genesis 19:29 may reveal the true reason of Lot's redemption. "Thus it was that, when God destroyed the cities...God remembered Abraham and removed Lot from the midst of the upheaval." According to this verse, Lot was saved on Abraham's merit alone, but the verse is not an integral part of the narrative, and is rather inserted as an addendum.[48] Based on the concentric structure of the narrative we mentioned above, verse 29 lies outside the story. The narrative has a solid frame in the parallel scenes at the beginning and end of the story: before the angels depart from Abraham, they "look down" at Sodom (Gen. 18:16), and after the destruction Abraham "looks down" at the destroyed plain (19:27–28). Genesis 19:29 remains outside these boundaries. It further stands apart from the rest of the narrative in the name used to describe God. The name *YHWH* is used consistently throughout

48. August Dillmann, *Genesis, Critically and Exegetically Expounded*, trans. William Baron Stevenson (Edinburgh, 1897), vol. 1, 112, sees this verse as the first of two addendums, the second being the narrative about Lot and his daughters in a cave.

the narrative (from the beginning of Gen. 18), while verse 29 calls God by the name "*Elohim.*"

Throughout the story, Lot must decide on which side of the door he belongs. Does he identify with the culture of Sodom, or did he build a home that is separated from the culture of the city? Lot needs the angels to physically pull him into the house, and then urge him out of the city. That being said, there is no question that his hospitality toward the angels and attempt to rescue his guests portray Lot as charitable and separate from the culture of the city. The analogy between Lot's hospitality and Abraham's, Lot's insistence that the angels come and stay with him, and his self-sacrifice in attempting to protect them, all portray Lot as one who is worthy of being saved by his own merit.[49] Lot's rescue is described in greater detail even than the destruction, which is narrated in only two verses.[50] The rhythm of the narrative and the emphasis on Lot's attempt to save his guests demonstrate that Lot's rescue is as a result of the way he treats his guests.

If so, two reasons for Lot's rescue are described in the text. Throughout the narrative, Lot's hospitality and the protection of his guests are described as the reason for his rescue. There is no need for the correlation to be explicit; Lot's actions speak for themselves. In the concluding verse, however, another viewpoint attributes Lot's rescue to God's remembering of Abraham. Here, Lot is saved because of Abraham's merit.

---

49. Many scholars consider the analogy to Abraham as a credit to Lot, among others, Skinner, *A Critical and Exegetical Commentary on Genesis*, 307; Julian Morgenstern, *The Book of Genesis: A Jewish Interpretation* (New York, 1965), 126; Schmidt, *"De Deo,"* 141; Vawter, *On Genesis: A New Reading*, 235–236; Thomas Desmond Alexander, "Lot's Hospitality: A Clue to his Righteousness," *JBL* 104 (1985): 289–291; Clements, *In Spirit and in Truth: Insight from Biblical Prayers*, 20; Ben Zvi, "The Dialogue between Abraham and Yahweh in Gen 18.23–32," 42; Victor H. Matthews, "Hospitality and Hostility in Genesis 19 and Judges 19," *BTB* 22 (1992): 6; Wenham, *Genesis 16–50*, 55–56; Ilona N. Rashkow, "Daddy-Dearest and the 'Invisible Spirit of Wine,'" in *Genesis: The Feminist Companion to the Bible*, ed. A. Brenner (Sheffield, 1998), 106–107. See also Lyons, *Canon and Exegesis: Canonical Praxis and the Sodom Narrative*, 219–222.
50. Westermann, *Genesis 12–36: A Continental Commentary*, 299.

This duality sheds new light on the ambivalence of Lot's character throughout the narrative. There is clear sympathy with Lot, but there are also indications that Lot is more connected with the culture of Sodom than it seems. The most obvious indication is Lot's willingness to offer his daughters to the mob outside his house. However, his delays in physically leaving the city also express his hesitation toward disengaging from the city, and so does his lack of ability to convince his sons-in-law. From this perspective, Lot's wife plays a key role in the narrative. The text offers no background on the wife; her origins, Sodomite or otherwise, are unknown.[51] But the fact that she is swept away in the destruction of the city indicates that she is ultimately judged as a Sodomite. Lot's wife had failed to sever her emotional and ethical ties with the city. The angels take her out of the city but could not take the city out of her. Lot's sons-in-law might be an expression of Lot's ambiguity, but his wife's fate is certainly a manifestation of his doubts.

The incident of Lot's wife completes the analogy between Lot and Abraham. As previously mentioned, the angels' visit to Lot (Gen. 19) and to Abraham (Gen. 18) are described in similar terms.[52] The comparison relates, among other things, to the protagonists' wives:

51. See, among others, Dillmann, *Genesis, Critically and Exegetically Expounded*, 113–114, who speculates she was not a Sodomite, since Lot is described as master of a household with possessions in Gen. 13, and was therefore likely already married.

52. See Van Seters, *Abraham in History and Tradition*, 215–216, who notes seventeen distinct parallels between the narratives. See Rudolf Kilian, *Die Vorpriesterlichen Abrahams Überlieferungen*, 150–151; Robert C. Culley, *Studies in the Structure of Hebrew Narrative* (Philadelphia, 1976), 54–55; Lyon, *Canon and Exegesis: Canonical Praxis and the Sodom Narrative*, 218; Letellier, *Day in Mamre, Night in Sodom*, 39–41; Rendsburg, *The Redaction of Genesis*, 49. Rendsburg notes the motifs of "entrance" and the similarity of the minor characters in the two narratives. Hamilton, *The Book of Genesis, Chapters 18–50*, 30, adds that there is similar wordplay with the verb *yada* ("know"). The solid link between the two scenes proves that the stories are not completely separate as stated by Kilian ("Zur Uberlieferungsgeschichte Lots," *BZ* 14 [1970]: 23–37) and Martin Noth (*A History of Pentateuchal Traditions*, trans. B. W. Anderson [Englewood Cliffs, NJ, 1972], 151–154).

	Abraham	**Lot**
Meeting the Angels	The Lord appeared to him by the terebinths of Mamre; *he was sitting at the entrance of the tent in the heat of the day.*	The two angels arrived in Sodom *in the evening,* as *Lot was sitting in the gate of Sodom.*
	Looking up, he *saw* three men standing near him. *As soon as he saw them, he ran from the entrance of the tent to greet them and bowed to the ground.*	*When Lot saw them, he rose to greet them and bowed low with his face to the ground.*
	he said, My lords, if it please you, *do not go on past your servant* Let a little water be brought; bathe your feet and *recline under the tree*… and let me fetch a morsel of bread that you may refresh yourselves; *then go on* – seeing that you have come your servant's way.	*he said,* Please, *my lords, turn aside to your servant's house* *to spend the night,* and bathe your feet… *then you may be on your way early.*
	They replied, Do as you have said.	But they said, "No, we will spend the night in the square." But he urged them strongly, so they turned his way and entered his house.
Preparing the Meal	Abraham hastened into the tent to Sarah, and said, Quick, three seahs of choice flour! Knead and make cakes…. Then Abraham ran to the herd, took a calf, tender and choice, and gave it to a servant-boy, who hastened to prepare it. He took curds and milk and the calf that had been prepared and set these before them; and he waited on them under the tree as they ate	He prepared a feast for them and baked unleavened bread, and they ate.

	Abraham	**Lot**
Identity	They said to him, *Where is your wife Sarah*? And he replied, There, in the tent.	And they shouted to Lot and said to him, *Where are the men who came to you tonight*? Bring them out to us, that we may be intimate with them.... Look, I have two daughters who have not known a man. Let me bring them out to you, and you may do to them as you please.
Tidings	Then one said, I will return to you next year, and your wife Sarah shall have a son! Sarah was listening at the entrance of the tent, which was *behind* him	Then the men said to Lot, Whom else have you here? Sons-in-law, your sons and daughters, or anyone else that you have in the city – bring them out of the place. For we are about to destroy this place; because the outcry against them before the Lord has become so great that the Lord has sent us to destroy it.
Doubt	And Sarah laughed to herself, saying, Now that I am withered, am I to have enjoyment – with my husband so old?	But he seemed to his sons-in-law as one who jests.
Fate of the Wife	I will return to you at the time next year, and Sarah shall have a son.	Lot's wife looked back, and she thereupon turned into a pillar of salt.
Conclusion	The men set out from there and looked down toward Sodom, Abraham walking with them to see them off.	Abraham rose early in the morning to the place where he had stood before the Lord, and, looking down toward Sodom and Gomorrah and all the land of the Plain, he saw the steam of the land rising like the smoke of a kiln.

Based on this analogy, some have claimed that Lot's character pales in comparison with Abraham.[53] Of course, some differences can be chalked up to the difference in situation. Abraham's guests had arrived midday, while Lot's visitors had arrived at his door in the middle of the night. It is difficult and unusual to slaughter cattle and cook it after dark, while the unleavened bread Lot offers is an appropriate food for an evening meal because it is quick to prepare. By the same token, Lot offers his guests to spend the night, an offer absent from Abraham's hospitality, likely also due to the time of day. The other differences between Lot and Abraham as hosts are slight, and seem to point to the similarities between the two men as greater than the contrast.

The main distinction is the content of the angels' tidings. While Sarah receives a message of life and fertility, Lot is given an omen of death and destruction. But therein also lies the similarity. Abraham is awarded a son as a reward for his generosity toward strangers, and Lot is offered his own life in recognition of his hospitality. However, while Abraham involved Sarah in his kind hospitality, and Sarah cooperated fully with her husband, out of her devotion to the values they both held true, Lot's wife is entirely absent from the interaction with the guests.[54] This detail stands out because of the comparison above. In light of the fate of Lot's wife, it is reasonable to assume that her lack of participation in Lot's hospitality is deliberate. Sarah, who shares her husband's generosity, merits a blessing of fertility. Lot's wife, who fails to identify with his values, is cursed with salt. Salt is antithetical to fertility, as salted land loses its vitality and can never grow.[55]

---

53. Some, however, read this comparison as implicit criticism of Lot. See Keil and Delitzsch, *Biblical Commentary on the Old Testament*, 233; Coats, *Genesis*, 141, 143; Waltke, *Genesis: A Commentary*, 265–281; Turner, "Lot as Jekyll and Hyde," 94–95; Hemchand Gossai, *Power and Marginality in the Abraham Narrative* (Lanham, MD, 1995), 76–81.
54. Gossai, *Power and Marginality in the Abraham Narrative*, 80–81, contra Lyons, *Canon and Exegesis: Canonical Praxis and the Sodom Narrative*, 218, who writes, "He, or as with Abraham, more likely his female family… hurriedly bakes unleavened bread."
55. See, for example, Judges 9:45. And see Ps. 107:34, Jer. 17:6, and Zeph. 2:9. See Victor P. Hamilton, "מלח," *NIDOTTE* 2:947–949. Compare with John Gray, *Joshua, Judges, and Ruth* (New Century Bible Commentary: London, 1986), 325; Daniel I. Block, *Judges, Ruth* (NAC: Nashville, 1999), 330.

In the context of the narrative, the women cannot be separated from their husbands. Abraham is praised in the text for sharing his values with his household; Abraham and Sarah are partners in their good deeds, and the servants also participate. Abraham is portrayed as a patriarch who "instructs his children and his posterity to keep the way of the Lord," not only by setting a personal example of kindness toward strangers, but by expecting the entire household to participate. In contrast, although Lot's kindness and hospitality is indisputable, it remains a personal quality, rather than a shared value and a household philosophy. Lot's sons-in-law mock his ideas; his wife is part of the Sodomite culture, instead of a daughter of the house of Abraham. The reader will meet Lot's daughters in the following episode, and they will be portrayed in a Sodomite light. Lot's family could be a manifestation of his own psyche – they could represent his repressed pull toward Sodom and all that it represents.

The ambivalent portrayal of Lot serves two purposes. The first relates to the question of Abraham's continuity, and the second relates to Lot's rescue. As long as Abraham has no heir, Lot will be portrayed as an alternative to his son. Throughout the Abraham cycle, Lot is depicted as an elusive part of Abraham's household. After the separation in Genesis 13, Abraham saves Lot in Genesis 14, and the question of inheritance is revisited. The Sodom narrative portrays Lot as a successor to Abraham's values, in that he invites guests to his home, feeds them, and defends them. But his lack of ability to instruct his family in the ways of Abraham negates his ability to be a true heir.[56]

I would like to point out another phenomenon that occurs in the analogy between Abraham's hospitality in Genesis 18 and Lot's in Genesis 19. At its core, the comparison between the two characters is clear. Abraham welcomes his guests in parallel to Lot welcoming guests. The messengers, of course, are parallel to themselves in each story. Abraham's family (Sarah and the youth) correlate to Lot's family (his wife, daughters, and sons-in-law). And of course, Sarah's fertility stands in stark contrast to Lot's wife's transformation into a pillar of salt, as does the "laughter" mentioned in each episode – Sarah's laughter at

56. Cf. Turner, "Lot as Jekyll and Hyde," 59–98.

the revelation that she will bear a son in contrast to the sons-in-laws' jeering laughter at Lot's warnings.

There are, however, several incidences in which the characters shift from their corresponding players. Two such incidences occur with the messengers, in which they act not in parallel with themselves, but rather in contrast to a different character. The messengers' question to Abraham, "Where is Sarah your wife?" correlates to the Sodomites' demand of Lot, "Where are the people that came into your home?" For some reason, in this case the messengers are compared with the people of Sodom. It is possible that this comparison is meant to emphasize the feeling of confusion that Lot experiences in that moment. It is no coincidence that the Sodomites and the messengers are repeatedly referred to with the same term, "people." Lot stands before a momentous decision: Will he join these "people" or those "people"?

The second example of role switches in the comparison between the two stories occurs at the end. Both narratives end with the characters gazing out at Sodom – the messengers heading out toward the city in the first story, and Abraham peering out at Sodom's ashes in the second. The parallel between Abraham and the messengers is also no coincidence; throughout this conflict, Abraham has consistently been portrayed on the side of God. Together they determined how to suitably deal with Sodom with justice and compassion, and Abraham is tasked with relaying these values to his progeny. The literary frame of this story opens with the messengers standing with God and approaching Abraham's tent, and concludes with Abraham standing by God's side, ready and willing to carry on His divine creed.

The double narrative of Lot's rescue becomes a model of two different types of biblical narratives relating to redemption: redemption based on hospitality and kindness, and redemption based on association, what we refer to as merit of the forefathers.

The Merits of Redemption

As a legacy, Lot leaves much to be desired. Indeed, his character is repeatedly raised and rejected as a possible option as an heir to Abraham. However, as discerning readers of the biblical text, we cannot ignore the intentionality of the story's perpetual return to Lot as a driving character. Lot represents the ultimate foil for Abraham – he symbolizes the life Abraham selflessly left behind, and his weak attempts to emulate Abraham's ethical behavior sharply contrast the ease and confidence which with Abraham utilizes his moral compass.

The lengthy description of Lot's rescue in this chapter is the pinnacle of this comparison between uncle and nephew. Lot's rescue reverberates on a literary plane through two additional episodes which appear much later on in the biblical narrative, and in so doing, the story of Lot conveys a powerful and enduring message for the generations to come.

Lot's Escape from Sodom and Israel's Escape from Egypt

Lot's offering of unleavened bread to his guests may have been a consequence of convenience; however, following the Midrash, Rashi comments: "He baked unleavened bread – for it was Passover."[57] This commentary opens up a fascinating window of comparison between Lot's story and Exodus. In fact, the exact phrase, "*umatzot*," "and unleavened bread," appears only in these two narratives (Gen. 19:3 and Ex. 12:8).[58] Both narratives attribute a unique role to the doorway as an indication of those worthy of saving. Festive meals are conducted in both instances on the night before the redemption. Both meals included unleavened bread. And "destructive" angels feature in both stories.

On a linguistic plane, Pharaoh's command in Exodus 12:31, "Up, depart from among my people," bears a striking similarity to Lot's advice to his sons-in-law in Genesis 19:14, "Up, get out of this place." The need for haste, and in this context the use of the uncommon root M-H-M-H ("delay"), is also emphasized on both occasions: "Still he delayed (*vayitmahma*). So the men seized his hand … and brought him out and left him outside the city" (Gen. 19:16), compared to, "And they baked unleavened cakes of dough that they had taken out of Egypt … since they had been driven out of Egypt and could not delay (*lehitmahmeha*)." The "smiting" of the Sodomites – first with blindness and later with death – is of course reminiscent of the plagues on Egypt. It is noteworthy that the analogy between Sodom and Egypt began at an even earlier stage, when Lot

57. Rashi on Gen. 19:3.
58. However, see also Judges 6:19–21, I Sam. 28:24.

chose to disengage from Abram and go to Sodom, because he saw it was "like the land of Egypt" (13:10). The similarity between Lot's escape from Sodom and the exodus from Egypt is therefore not surprising.

Lot and the Rescue of Rahab

The second story with surprisingly deep literary ties to Lot's rescue is that of Rahab's rescue from Jericho in Joshua 2. The two spies sent by Joshua, who come to Jericho and are hosted in Rahab's house, are also called *melakhim,* which can mean messengers but also "angels" (6:25), like the two angels who come to Sodom and are hosted in Lot's house.[59] Just as the Sodomites asked Lot to bring out (*hotzi'em*) his guests, so too the king of Jericho orders Rahab to "bring out (*hotzi'i*) the men who came to you and entered your house" (Josh. 2:3). In both cases the hosts protect their guests and refuse to surrender them on demand, while risking their own lives to protect them. The similar wording supports this analogy: the expression "*terem yishkavu(n),*" "they had not yet lain down," appears only in these two biblical texts (Gen. 19:4 and Josh. 2:8).[60] Additionally, the verbs *yode'a* ("know") and *bo* ("come") are used intensively in both narratives, with interchangeable sexual and non-sexual connotations.[61] The "closing of the gate" in Joshua 2:7 (*vehashaar sagaru*) is phrased similarly to the "closing of the door" in Genesis 19:10 (*hadelet sagaru*). And Rahab's advice to the spies, "Make for *the hills, lest* the pursuers come upon you" (Josh. 2:16), is reminiscent of the angels' advice to Lot: "Flee *to the hills, lest* you be swept away" (Gen. 19:17).[62] Various

---

59. Regarding this analogy, see F. Langlame, "Josué II et les traditions de l'Héxateuque," *RB* 78 (1971): 5–17, 161–183, 321–354 (with seventeen linguistic links between the stories!); Lewis Daniel Hawk, *Every Promise Fulfilled: Contesting Plots in Joshua,* Literary Currents in Biblical Interpretation (Louisville, 1991); Yair Zakovitch, *Through the Looking Glass: Reflection Stories in the Bible* (Tel Aviv, 1995), 83–86; Richard D. Nelson, *Joshua* (OTL: Louisville, 1997), 43–44; Pamela Tamarkin Reis, "Hagar Requited," *JSOT* 87 (2000): 75–109.
60. Zakovitch, *Through the Looking Glass: Reflection Stories in the Bible,* 83–84.
61. Grossman, *Ambiguity in the Biblical Narrative and its Contribution to the Literary Formation,* 129–131.
62. Note the reverse analogy: God's angels are compared with Rahab, instead of Joshua's spies. The reader of the Rahab narrative has to ask, who is protecting whom? This point supports Zakovitch.

interpretations have been offered for this analogy, including the obvious motif of evaluating a city for the purpose of judging its right to continued existence. The spies, who are compared to God's angels, return with an evaluation of Jericho and, when this is then compared with the Sodom narrative, it implies that their judgment, like that of the angels in Sodom, is what justifies God's decision to destroy the city.

The duality of the Lot narrative enables the analogy with each of these additional biblical tales. All three stories describe the liberation of a single house within an entire city that faces destruction or severe punishment.[63] There is, of course, a great difference between the redemption of the nation of Israel from Egypt, which is part of a broad divine plan delivered in Genesis 15, and the rescue of Rahab.

Israelite history goes through a fundamental and dramatic change on the night of the Exodus; their redemption is not described as a reward for good deeds, but rather as a result of the merit of their forefathers, specifically the covenant between God and Abraham: "God remembered His covenant with Abraham and Isaac and Jacob" (Ex. 2:24), and, "I have remembered My covenant" (Ex. 6:5).[64] This concept – redemption as a result of the merit of the forefathers – is so central to the Exodus story that it becomes an archetypal pillar in the identity narrative of the Israelite nation from that moment forward.

However, it would appear that the undeserving Israelite nation in Egypt were not the first to be saved in the merit of their fathers. Genesis 19:29 clearly indicates that Lot's salvation, in the end, is attributed to the merit of Abraham's actions. Lot was rescued by virtue of the merit of his "father."

On the other hand, the link to Rahab underscores the second reason for Lot's rescue: Rahab is saved not because of a divine plan but because of her actions. Rahab endangers her life to protect the spies, and they repay her appropriately by sparing her life when the city is destroyed.

---

63. The Exodus and the capture of Jericho include an explicit date. Regarding the date of the destruction of Sodom, see Genesis Rabba 50:12.

64. The reason for the Exodus from Egypt is more complex. Two different reasons are stated in the two prophetic inaugurations of Moses: the merit of the forefathers and the unjust suffering of the nation. However, addressing the injustice done to the Hebrews is not like Lot creating his own merit.

Lot is rescued due to Abraham's merit, but also, in spite of God's plan, due to his own actions. Lot endangers his life to protect the angels, and they in turn protect him when the city is destroyed.

These two aspects of Lot's merit can be viewed as a continuation of the double tidings of Isaac's birth in Genesis 17 and 18. Both of these stories are told twice, each iteration reflecting a different perspective. As we noted earlier, the birth of Isaac in Genesis 17 relates to the implementation of God's plan, while the tidings in Genesis 18 portray Isaac's birth as a personal reward to Abraham and Sarah for their hospitality. Similarly, Lot was rescued from Sodom as part of the selection of Abraham (expressed in the text by the name *Elohim*), but also due to his own actions (expressed in the text by the name *YHWH*).

Although the text separates the two reasons for Lot's redemption, they seem to be linked. The narrative that relates Lot's actions indicates a criticism of Lot, which enables a consistent reading in the final verses, which say that Lot was rescued by the merit of his uncle (implying, but not on his own merit). But since Lot's hospitality is comparable to Abraham's, the reader is left with the impression that Lot has learned the ways of his uncle. This is not a literary analogy but an actual influence of one character on another. Rashi comments on why the verse describes Lot sitting at the gate in Genesis 19:1: "He learned from the house of Abraham to seek guests."[65] Abraham's merit is apparent in the conduct that he passes on to his nephew. Perhaps Genesis 19:29 indicates that although Lot is saved by Abraham's merit, Lot has to be worthy of saving, and he proves his worth by emulating the ways of Abraham.

65. Rashi on Gen. 19:1. See also Genesis Rabba 50:4.

Lot's Daughters (Gen. 19:30–38)

The story of Lot and his daughters in the cave is certainly disturbing. One cannot help but wonder what purpose it serves, both in the greater Abraham narrative and on its own, in the retelling of its gruesome details. From a literary perspective, it is fascinating. The plot of the story closes several logistical gaps in the overall narrative, giving closure to Lot's journey as a character, as well as winding up the account of Terah's genealogy. However, a purely literary reading of the story reveals a poetic layer to the episode that may give us some insight as to its metaphorical purpose.

The story must be examined on four levels. First, as a story in and of itself, with an examination of the Bible's judgment of its characters – what were their motivations, and more importantly, were they justified? The second level is how the story of the cave culminates the story of Lot's rescue from Sodom. Thirdly, how this episode completes the story of Lot's separation from Abraham. Finally, the story of Lot and his daughters in the cave provides closure to the chronicle of Terah's genealogy which began when we were first introduced to Abraham and his nephew.

A Dual Narrative

The opening verse of the story (Gen. 19:30) sets the dual tone: Lot's departure from Zoar is recounted twice, each time evoking entirely different emotions from the reader.

First half	Second half
Lot went up from Zoar	for he was afraid to dwell in Zoar
and settled in the hill	and he settled in a cave
with his two daughters;	he and his two daughters.

The initial delivery of this detail is neutral: Lot "went up" from Zoar, while the second part of the verse introduces a disturbing reason: Lot "was afraid to dwell in Zoar."[1] Both parts of the verse then describe Lot's new location: the first half of the verse describes Lot settling "in the hill," the second part "in a cave." The final clause in each part describes the characters, emphasizing the fact that Lot's daughters are with their father in the cave on the hill.

Despite the obvious correlation between the two parts of the verse, each part is accompanied by an entirely different atmosphere. The first part delivers the information dryly and neutrally: Lot traveled from Zoar and settled on the hill with his two daughters. The second part essentially repeats the same information, but the details are accompanied by intense emotion. Lot's desire to leave the area of Zoar stems from panicked distress, and Lot does not settle in the comfort and abundance of a mountainside, but hides in a dark cave.[2]

The cave is a symbolic device in this narrative. Cave-dwellers escape the reality outside a cave, but are also susceptible to dangers from within. Other biblical stories involving caves relate to escape and

1. Regarding the timing of Lot's escape from Sodom in relation to the destruction of the other cities, see Lyons, *Canon and Exegesis: Canonical Praxis and the Sodom Narrative*, 250–251.
2. Cf. Ilona Rashkow, "Sexuality in the Hebrew Bible: Freud's Lens," in *Psychology and the Bible: A New Way to Read the Scriptures: From Freud to Kohut*, ed. J. H. Ellens and W. G. Rollins (Westport and London, 2004), 62. Rashkow sees the cave as a symbol of Sheol, of death.

death. Sarah is buried in a cave in the field of Ephron (Gen. 25); the five southern kings escape Joshua's sword and hide in a cave, which becomes their prison and ultimately the place of their death (Josh. 10). Saul falls into the hands of David when he enters a cave (I Sam. 24). Obadiah hides one hundred prophets in a cave to protect them from Jezebel (I Kings 18:3–4). These connotations can create a distressful atmosphere in a seemingly innocent caption such as: "A maskil of David, while he was in the cave: a prayer" (Ps. 142:2). That psalm concludes with the speaker's plea: "Free me from prison, that I may praise Your name" (v. 8), indicating that the cave was a metaphor for the poet's emotional prison.[3] There is no contradiction between Lot dwelling in a cave or a hill; however, the atmosphere that accompanies the description of each of these locations is entirely different.[4]

The third clause of each part of the introduction presents a fascinating, if nuanced, distinction between the two accounts of Lot's retreat from Zoar. Both parts of the verse clarify that Lot did not travel from Zoar alone but with his two daughters. The first part of the verse reads "with his two daughters," while the latter part of the verse reads "he and his two daughters." Whereas the initial formulation created a sense of unity in the family (Lot the father travels with his two daughters), the absence of "with" in the second part of the verse leaves the reader with the impression of two separate groups (Lot, and his daughters).

This binary design is an early indicator to the reader that this story should be perceived on several levels. The narrative could be read both as a continuation of the Sodom narrative and Lot's escape from the city (which represents the second part of the exposition), and as an ultimate realization of the "line of Terah," which had introduced the Abraham cycle, through the birth of Ammon and Moab (the first part of the exposition). In relation to the destruction of Sodom narrative, Lot hides in a cave, and a tension is apparent between him and his daughters.

3. See also the opening verses of Ps. 57.
4. Perhaps the word "*me'ara*," "cave," is a play on the word "*Amora*," translated as "Gomorrah" (Talia Sutskover, "Lot and His Daughters [Gen 19:30–30]: Further Literary and Stylistic Examinations," *JHS* 11 [2011]: 11n25). Lot escaped Sodom and "*Amora*," but ended up in a *me'ara*. Will his fate in the latter be an improvement on the former?

With regard to the Abraham cycle as a whole, Lot leaves Zoar and seeks another home. He settles on the mountains with his daughters and is involved in the creation of two nations, Ammon and Moab.

What Were Lot's Daughters Thinking?

The palpable, uncomfortable question underlying this entire episode has been debated widely throughout the centuries. What on earth were Lot's daughters thinking when they intoxicated their father and lay with him in order to become pregnant?

Two main schools of thought attempt to make sense of this unthinkable act. The book of Jubilees (16:8–9) states:

> And [Lot] and his daughters committed sin upon the earth, such as had not been on the earth since the days of Adam till his time; for the man lay with his daughters. And behold, it was commanded and engraved concerning all his seed, on the heavenly tablets, to remove them and root them out, and to execute judgment upon them like the judgment of Sodom, and to leave no seed of the man on earth on the day of condemnation.

Jubilees makes no attempt to disguise its criticism of Lot, proceeding to compare the future of Lot's descendants with the punishment inflicted on Sodom. Lot may have been temporarily saved from the fate of Sodom, but he did not escape the influence of its culture, and therefore will ultimately share its fate.[5] The daughters, too, have been unduly influenced by the immorality of their hometown, and the act they perform is clearly appalling.

On the other hand, Josephus defends the daughters, saying, "And the virgins, having supposed that all of mankind had been obliterated, had sexual relations with their father, having taken care beforehand to

5. On the dual representation of Lot in Jubilees see Jacques van Ruiten, "Lot versus Abraham: The Interpretation of Genesis 18:1–19:38 in *Jubilees* 16:1–9," in *Sodom's Sin: Genesis 18–19 and Its Interpretations*, ed. E. Noort and E. Tigchelaar (Leiden, 2004), 29–46.

escape notice."[6] In this school of thought, Lot's daughters, who were innocent virgins, perceived themselves in the same situation as Noah's family following the Flood. With the population of the world eliminated, what choice did they have but to carry on the human race? The fact that they knew they would have to intoxicate their father in order to achieve their goal clearly indicates that they, too, recognized how unpalatable this act truly was, but they felt they needed to go through with it anyway.

Various rabbinic sources illustrate the ambiguity surrounding judgment of Lot's daughters. Some sources define the daughters' act as a mitzva: "R. Ḥiyya bar Avin said that R. Yehoshua ben Korḥa said: A person should always come first with regard to a mitzva, for in reward of the one night that the elder daughter [of Lot] preceded the younger, she [the elder daughter] merited four generations of monarchy in Israel" (Nazir 23b–24a).[7] Other sources refer to the act as a sin: "R. Yehuda ben Simon and R. Ḥanin said in the name of R. Yoḥanan: Lot's daughters sinned and yet, became pregnant. In what merit? In the merit of 'Moab' [so named after Abraham,] '*Mi av*,' 'He who is [called] father,' as it is said of Abraham, 'For I have made you the father of many nations'" (Genesis Rabba 51:11).[8] The gap between defining the daughters' act as a sin versus a mitzva is enormous, and the diverse assessment of Lot's daughters continued throughout history and in modern critical analysis.[9] Nahmanides paints a picture of the daughters' approach hovering over a delicate line of shame and earnestness:

> They said, "Let's perform the correct act, for God will have mercy and give us a son and a daughter, and replenish the world from them, because 'He will build a world of compassion' (Ps. 89:3),

6. Josephus, *Antiquities*, 1:205; Feldman, *Flavius Josephus: Translation and Commentary*, 77–78.
7. This statement also appears in Bava Kamma 38b and Horayot 11a. The statement is not disputed in any of the parallel sources.
8. In Genesis Rabba 51:10, R. Huna contrasts Lot's daughters with the Moabite women of Num. 25, and concludes that Lot's daughters are praiseworthy, while R. Shimon contrasts them with Ruth (Ruth 3), and criticizes them.
9. The ambiguity toward Lot's daughters and the nations born of them is duly noted by Noort, "Abraham and the Nations," 13–15.

and it is not in vain that God saved us." They were modest and did not want to ask their father to marry them, as a Noahide is allowed to marry his daughter. Alternatively, the act was viewed as terribly ugly in those generations, and was never done. And so, our rabbis denigrate Lot terribly.

The commentators who deny any criticism of the daughters base their position primarily on three details:

1. The elder daughter introduces her idea by stating: "Our father is old, and there is not a man on earth to consort with us in the way of all the world" (Gen. 19:31). The daughter's actions are not based on lust or promiscuity, but rather on her desire for continuity. She assumes that "there is not a man on earth to consort with us," and that her father is the only option for the survival of the human species. This detail seems reminiscent of the actions taken by Tamar and Ruth to ensure their respective family lines, and these women are viewed positively for doing so.[10]
2. The fact that both daughters become pregnant after spending one night with their father might signal that divine assistance is involved. Lot's daughters are described as virgins (Gen. 19:8), so conceiving on the night of their deflowering defies known statistics. Once again, Lot's daughters are reminiscent of Tamar, who conceives Judah's child after one sexual interaction with him on the roadside.
3. The etiological conclusion of the narrative describes the establishment of the two nations Ammon and Moab. The story ends on a positive note. Even if the reader is averse to the two nations, the establishment of two nations should clearly be deciphered as a reward for the actions of the daughters in the context of the narrative.

10. Many scholars have noted this threefold link. See especially Harold Fisch, "Ruth and the Structure of Covenant History," *VT* 32 (1982): 423–437, and Alter, *Genesis*, 90. Tamar seduced Judah on the highway by pretending to be a prostitute. The Ruth narrative is more complex; although the idea of seduction is suggested by Naomi, Ruth seems to have decided not to utilize this option (see Grossman, *Ambiguity in the Biblical Narrative and its Contribution to the Literary Formation*, 232–238).

At the same time, the narrative certainly includes indications of criticism. The Bible is particularly sensitive to incest. The disregard of this taboo is attributed to the Canaanites, and stated as the reason they lose their claim to the land. While the correlation between incest and the Canaanites is merely alluded to in Genesis (9:18–27),[11] Leviticus names the act of incest after the Canaanites: "You shall not copy the practices of…the land of Canaan to which I am taking you; nor shall you follow their laws" (Lev. 18:3). These customs are the reason the Canaanites were banished (Lev. 18:24–30; 20:23–24). From this perspective, the reader should not take the daughters' actions lightly: the act itself is powerfully negative. The difference between Lot's daughters and the stories of Tamar and Ruth is fundamental: Tamar and Ruth do not copulate with their father, an unspeakable act in biblical philosophy.[12] In addition to the severe sin of incest, the daughters add to their negative evaluation by tricking their father.

Surprisingly, both positions are supported by the text – as we can see, minor details throughout the text point alternately to either deep criticism or lauding approval of the daughters' intentions. This paradoxical nature of the storytelling underscores the ambiguity in the story with which commentators struggled throughout the generations.

There is another possibility of reading the text, adopted by Rashi, Philo, and Rabbenu Baḥya. It challenges the assumption that both daughters are criticized equally in this episode. I wish to explore this direction. The duality of the narrative expresses itself in the subtle literary differences between the two daughters. Perhaps in this understated way the text is suggesting that we judge them separately.

The Elder Daughter and the Younger Daughter

The names of the daughters are not revealed in the narrative. Instead, they are referred to by their age hierarchy, "the older one" and "the younger one."[13] There is literary value to naming the daughters by their family

---

11. See especially Cassuto, *A Commentary on The Book of Genesis: From Noah to Abraham*, 149–158.
12. Fisch, "Ruth and the Structure of Covenant History," 433.
13. This detail led to a debate among scholars regarding the possibility of an ancient Moabite tale at the core of the narrative. Bernhard Stade (*Geschichte des Volkes Israel* [Berlin, 1887–1888], 118) rejected this assumption based on the omission of

status instead of their individual names. The two daughters are not independent characters; their purpose is to shed light on Lot's action (or in this case, inaction). By emphasizing the different status of the two sisters, the reader is invited to evaluate the actions of each sister separately. The elder sister makes her suggestion out of her position of authority. As the elder sister, she initiates action. In fact, the younger sister might have felt obligated to take her advice because of this. The text indicates that the younger sister acts in accordance with the authority of the older sister, and not of her own volition.

The elder sister states the motive for seducing their father: "Our father is old, and there is not a man on earth to consort with us in the way of all the world" (Gen. 19:31). Lot is described as "old," which might mean one of two things: either Lot is too old to remarry and bear more children,[14] or the sisters have to act fast before their father dies.[15] Either reason is appropriate in the context of the scene.

The assessment of the situation by the elder daughter can be interpreted in more than one way. Lot's daughters might indeed be under the impression that the catastrophe they had witnessed was worldwide, like Noah's flood, and that their father is the only surviving male.[16] This should be ample justification for consorting with their father. Even according to a more minimalistic interpretation, which states that there

---

the daughters' names. Gunkel (*Genesis – Translated and Interpreted*, 216) refuted this claim, since the names could have been omitted in the transfer to the biblical text.

14. Westermann, *Genesis 12–36: A Continental Commentary*, 313; Hamilton, *The Book of Genesis, Chapters 18–50*, 51, among others.

15. Gunkel, *Genesis – Translated and Interpreted*, 217. Arnold Ehrlich (*Mikra KiFeshuto* [New York, 1969], vol. 1, 51) uniquely reads it as, "Our father is so old, he is akin to a small child, and we can do as we wish with him." Regarding the daughters' motivation, see Eliezer Schlossberg, "There Is Not a Man on Earth to Consort with Us in the Way of All the World," *Sinai* 111 (1993): 146–161.

16. Rashi, Ibn Ezra, Rashbam, and Bekhor Shor offer like commentary on Gen. 19:31. Gunkel (*Genesis – Translated and Interpreted*, 217) notes the similarity to God's instruction to take male and female species into the ark "to keep seed alive upon all the earth" (Gen. 7:3). He believes the similarity enhances the impression that the daughters believe there is no one left. See also Skinner, *A Critical and Exegetical Commentary on Genesis*, 313; Speiser, *Genesis*, 145; Westermann, *Genesis 12–36: A Continental Commentary*, 313.

is no man to consort with *right now*,[17] or that their father will no longer take care of them and provide them with a husband,[18] her intentions are clearly not promiscuous or ritualistic. The daughter's motive clearly and directly relates to her desire to have children. At the very least, the action should be viewed as desperate.[19] Desperation links this narrative with other biblical seduction narratives. Biblical incest narratives initiated by men (e.g., Amnon and Tamar, or Absalom and David's wives) are frequently an expression of a struggle for control, while incest stories initiated by women (e.g., Lot's daughters, or Judah and Tamar) express a desire for family continuity.[20]

Over the course of two nights, Lot had relations with each of his daughters after drinking wine; both daughters were impregnated as a result, and each gave birth to a boy. The facts are identical, but the events of each night are described using different words. Most commentators agree that there are no significant differences in the content of the narratives. Even so, the literary details reveal fascinating differences in how the text reacts to each sister. Whereas the occurrences of the two nights are indeed identical, the choice of words and reflected meanings vary:

	First Night: Elder Daughter	**Second Night: Younger Daughter**
Initiative	And the older daughter said to the younger, "*Our father* is old… Let us make *our father* drink wine and then we shall lie with him and preserve our family line through *our father*."	The next day the older daughter said to the younger, "Last night I lay with *my father*. Let us get him to drink wine again tonight, and you go in and lie with him so we can preserve our family line through *our father*."

17. Hamilton, *The Book of Genesis, Chapters 18–50*, 51.
18. Wenham, *Genesis 16–50*, 61.
19. E.g., Keil and Delitzsch, *Biblical Commentary on the Old Testament*, 237, write that the daughters thought no one would want to marry them, since they are the sole survivors of God's curse. Speiser (*Genesis*, 145) writes, "All of this adds up to praise rather than blame."
20. Athalya Brenner, "On Incest," in *A Feminist Companion to Exodus to Deuteronomy*, ed. A. Brenner (Sheffield, 1994), 127.

Giving the father wine	So they made their father drink wine that night…	That night also they made their father drink wine
Relations with the father	and the older one came (*vatavo*) and lay with her father (*et aviha*)	and the younger rose (*vatakom*), and lay with him (*imo*)
Lot's lack of awareness	and he did not know when she lay down or when she rose.	and he did not know when she lay down or when she rose.
Thus the two daughters of Lot came to be with child by their father		
Birth of the son	The older one bore a son	And the younger also bore a son
Naming the son	and named him Moab	and she called him Ben-Ammi
Etiological conclusion	he is the father of the Moabites of today	he is the father of the Ammonites of today

The events of both nights are initiated by the elder daughter. This shared fact actually breaks the full comparison between the two nights, since it is the younger daughter who lies with her father on the second night. The younger daughter could have spoken instead of the elder, saying, "Last night *you* lay with our father. Let us get him to drink wine again tonight, and *I* will go in and lie with him so we can preserve our family line through our father." Instead, the reader is presented with an older sister who initiates while the younger sister is hesitant, perhaps even reluctant, to take action. In addition to the initiative of the older daughter on the second night, there are other subtle differences that do not seem arbitrary. On the first night the elder daughter consistently refers to the father in the plural: "*Our father* is old…. Let us make *our father* drink wine…and preserve *our family* line through *our father*." On the second night, the older daughter seems to distinguish between the sexual act and the desired result. She refers to the father in the singular – "*my* father" – when recalling the sexual act of the previous night, and she continues to use the singular "*my* father" when encouraging her sister to give the father wine and lie with him. She only reverts to the plural "*our* father" in reference to the desired outcome of preserving the family line by bearing a child. This style enables the elder sister to repeat her suggestion while sublimating the demand of her younger sister. The older daughter never verbalizes that her sister is required to lie with "her father." This blunt description is reserved for her own actions on the previous night. On the second night, "he" is to be given wine, and the younger daughter will lie with "him." The indirect terms do not change the meaning, but they do offer sublimation.[21]

The slight variations are extremely significant, and subtly imply a difference in how each daughter approached the acts they performed with their father. The older daughter's action is described with the verb "*vatavo*," "and she came," whereas the younger daughter's action is described with the verb "*vatakom*," "and she rose."[22] Within the context of the narrative, the verb *vatakom* prepares the reader for the main act, which appears in the form of another verb later in the same sentence.[23] The choice of *vatavo* is clever, since this verb is often used in the Bible to describe sexual relations. Although it is not used with a sexual meaning

---

21. Geoffrey Leech (*Semantics* [Harmondsworth, 1974], 22–23) notes that word order affects both meaning and perception. Perhaps the changed word order in the sentences describing the daughters giving their father wine also contributes to sublimation of the act. In the description of the first night, the direct object ("their father") is adjacent to the verb, and the sentence is concluded with the time adjunct ("that night"); in the description of the second night the direct object ("their father") is distanced from the verb, and the time adjunct ("that night also") is placed between them. The more loaded sentence, "They gave their father wine to drink," does not appear in the description of the second night. Here, too, the formulation does not change the meaning, but is presented in a more delicate way, diminishing the harsh reality of the daughters getting their father drunk.
22. The Septuagint unifies the two formulations, so instead of "the younger rose and she lay with him," it has, "and the younger *came* and lay with her *father*." By doing this, the Septuagint undoes the difference of verbs, as well as the differences in describing the subject. Some preferred the Septuagint's unified description (Ball, *The Book of Genesis*, 71); however, I believe the subtle differences between such similar texts carry significance.
23. The Septuagint transfers the verb to the older daughter's initiative: "Let us make our father drink wine, and let us lie with him, and let us raise up (*nakim*) seed from our father." Had the Septuagint maintained the description of the younger daughter found in the Masoretic text, the result could have been a clever word play: the daughter rose in order to *raise up* the father's seed. However, the Septuagint uses the verb *vatavo* ("and she came") to describe the actions of the younger daughter as well.

in Genesis 19:32, the complementary meaning of the verb integrates nicely with the general atmosphere of the verse.[24]

The absence of *vatavo* from the description of the younger daughter seems deliberate. The verb is used twice in the words of the older daughter. First with the elder daughter's speech preceding the first night, with direct sexual meaning, "There is not a man on earth to consort with us (*lavo aleinu*) in the way of all the world" (Gen. 19:31). And then it is used on the second night, with the meaning of getting from one place to another: "And you go (*uvo'i*) and lie with him, that we may maintain life through our father" (v. 34). In light of the older daughter's statement, the reader anticipates the use of the verb in the description of the younger daughter's actions, as a direct parallel to her older sister in the first night. Instead, the narrative reads, "And the younger rose," perhaps by using a less provocative verb hinting at the younger daughter's shame or hesitancy in the moment.

The choice of *vatakom* as a replacement for *vatavo* also plays a part in construing the younger sister's actions. The verbs "*kam*" and "*shakhav*" have opposite meanings in various biblical contexts. For example, "If people quarrel and one person hits another with a stone or with their fist and the victim does not die but is confined to bed (*lemishkav*), if he should arise (*yakum*) and walk outside…" (Ex. 21:18); "Like a lion they crouch and lie down (*shakhav*), like a lioness; who dares to rouse them (*yekimenu*)?" (Num. 24:9); "Speak of them when you sit at home and when you walk on the way, when you lie down (*uveshokhbekha*) and when you get up (*uvkumekha*)" (Deut. 6:7); "So she lay (*vatishkav*) at his feet until morning, but arose (*vatakom*) before anyone could be recognized" (Ruth 3:14). The two verbs appear as antonyms in our narrative as well: "And he did not know when she lay down (*veshikhva*) or when she rose (*uvkuma*)" (Gen. 19:33, 35). Thus the ambivalence of the younger daughter is tangible as she *rises* in order to *lie* with her father. She

24. Mathews (*Genesis*, 233) notes that verbs with sexual connotations are purposely incorporated throughout the narrative about the angels in Sodom ("*shakhav*," "*bo*," "*yada*"), even if in the present narrative they are used in a non-sexual sense. The use of *baa* with regard to the elder daughter's actions carries similar significance. See also Sutskover, "Lot and His Daughters," 2–11.

seems to be acting against her better judgment, and against her instincts, in contrast to the elder daughter who *comes* and *lies*.

Additional subtleties correspond with these distinctions. The father is mentioned explicitly in the action of the older daughter ("and the older one came and lay with *her father*"), whereas the father is not mentioned directly by title in the actions of the younger daughter ("and the younger rose and lay with *him*"). Here, too, the discrepancy is deliberate, and is confirmed by its effect on the naming of the sons. The older daughter who lay "*et aviha*," "with *her father*," names her son "*Moav*," "*from father*," whereas the younger daughter who lay "*imo*," "with *him*," names her son "*Ammon*," "*of him*."[25] The elder daughter flaunts the act she performed with her father in the naming of her child, while the younger daughter seems to attempt to veil the source of her son's conception with euphemism.

While the differences above may be vague, the description of the sexual acts themselves is definitive. Various texts indicate that "*shakhav et*" represents a forced sexual act in which the partners are unequal, while "*shakhav im*" represents a mutual sexual act. This is evident in Abimelech's reprimand to Isaac, "What is this you have done to us? One of the men might well have lain with (*shakhav... et*) your wife, and you would have brought guilt upon us" (Gen. 26:10).[26] The word "*et*" emphasizes the magnitude of disaster that could have been brought upon a man who would have wrongfully lain with Rebecca. So, too, with regard to Dinah,

25. Yair Zakovitch, "Explicit and Implicit Name-Derivations," *HAR* 4 (1980): 168–169.

26. Avraham Ahuvia, "The Expressions '*Shakhav Im*' and '*Shakhav Et*' in the Bible," *Beit Mikra* 40 (1995): 276–278; Hilary B. Lipka, *Sexual Transgression in the Hebrew Bible* (Sheffield, 2006), 185–199. Harry Orlinsky claims that Malbim and Ehrlich both comment in this direction. Regarding Malbim, see Malbim's commentary on Lev. 20 (*HaTorah VeHaMitzva*, 109), which states (in contrast to what we propose above) that *shakhav et* indicates that the submissive partner enjoys the sexual act, while *shakhav im* indicates a lack of enjoyment by the submissive partner. Malbim presents a similar analysis in his book, *Ayelet HaShaḥar* 51:529. Regarding Ehrlich, see his commentary on Gen. 39:7 (*Mikra KiFeshuto*, 107). See also Moshe Greenberg, *Ezekiel 21–37* [AB: New York, 1997], 477). For criticism of the division suggested above, see Harry Orlinsky, "The Hebrew Root ŜKB," *JBL* 63 (1944): 30.

"He took her, and he lay with her (*vayishkav ota*), and he violated her" (Gen. 34:2).[27]

In contrast, sexual relations between Jacob and his wives are described using the preposition "*im.*" Rachel tells Leah, "He can lie with you (*yishkav imakh*) tonight in return for your son's mandrakes.... So he lay with her (*vayishkav ima*) that night" (Gen. 30:15–16).[28] The clearest demonstration of this distinction is in the narrative about the rape of Tamar in II Samuel 13. When Amnon's initially attempts to seduce Tamar, he says, "Come and lie with me (*shikhvi imi*), my sister" (II Sam. 13:11). After she refuses, the rape is described as, "And he refused to listen to her, and he held her forcefully and violated her and lay with her (*vayishkav ota*)" (v. 14). This division is not entirely consistent throughout the biblical text (and more inconsistent in biblical law than biblical narrative),[29] but the difference is starkly apparent in the present narrative. The older daughter lies "*et,*" emphasizing the rape of the old drunken father who cannot discern left from right. The younger daughter lies "*im,*" which de-emphasizes the rape. The change does not reflect a new

---

27. This is assuming Dinah was indeed raped, as is generally presumed (see Mary Anna Bader, *Sexual Violation in the Hebrew Bible: A Multi-Methodological Study of Genesis 34 and 2 Samuel 13* [SBL 87: New York, 2006], 9n1). If Dinah and Shechem's relationship was consensual, this verse cannot be used as proof for my position. See Lyn M. Bechtel, "What If Dinah Is Not Raped," *JSOT* 62 (1994): 19–36; Tikva Frymer-Kensky, "Virginity in the Bible," in *Gender and Law in the Hebrew Bible and the Ancient Near East,* ed. Victor H. Matthews, Bernard M. Levinson, and Tikva Frymer-Kensky (Sheffield, 1998), 79–96; Lipka, *Sexual Transgression in the Hebrew Bible,* 184–199; Nick Wyatt, "The Story of Dinah and Shechem," *UF* 22 (1990): 433–458. Mayer Gruber ("A Re-Examination of the Charges Against Shechem Son of Hamor," *Beit Mikra* 157 [1999]: 127) writes, "It is clear that there is not even the slightest hint that Shechem the son of Hamor raped Dinah." For criticism of this approach, see Paul R. Noble, "A 'Balanced' Reading of the Rape of Dinah: Some Exegetical and Methodological Observations," *Biblical Interpretation* 4 (1996): 173–203; Susanne Scholz, *Rape Plots: A Feminist Cultural Study of Genesis 34* (New York, 2000). See also Gen. 34:7, 35:22, and I Sam. 4:22.
28. See the words of Potiphar's wife to Joseph (Gen. 39:7) as well as II Sam. 11:11, 12:24.
29. See in particular: Deut. 22:25, 28. On the unique combination *lishkav etzla* (Gen. 39:10), see Orlinsky, "The Hebrew Root ŜKB," 34–36. This is a deliberate digression from the regular combinations because of a literary tactic (Grossman, "Deliberate Misuse of Idioms in the Biblical Narrative," 38–39).

chain of events; Lot is just as unaware of his daughter's violation on the second night as he is on the first. However, the choice of words changes the atmosphere of the second night and seems to perceive the younger daughter in a more favorable manner.

The Message in the Literary Analysis

The impact of this analysis on our judgment of the sisters is complex. Their initiative is described favorably, and their intention is described as pragmatic, not promiscuous or self-indulgent. Nonetheless, there is room to question whether the daughters felt repelled by their actions, despite their desperation. In this context, the complementary meanings, the specific choice of words, and the delicate contrast between the sisters paint two different pictures of the two nights. While the description of the younger daughter sublimates the vulgarity of the father's rape, the older daughter's actions are described openly and explicitly. There is a distinction between the evaluation of the older and younger daughters.

The Talmud (Bava Kamma 38b) reflects this subtle difference in a fascinating way:

> The Holy One, blessed be He, does not deprive any reward due to any creature, even if only for pleasant diction. For regarding the elder daughter, who named [her son] "Moab," the Holy One, blessed be He, said to Moses, "Do not harass the Moabites or provoke them to war" (Deut. 2:9) – battle against them is forbidden, but imposed forced labor is allowed. But regarding the younger daughter, who named [her son] "Ben-Ammi," the Holy One, blessed be He, said to Moses: "When you come to the Ammonites, do not harass them or provoke them to war" (Deut. 2:19) – meaning, at all; they may not even be subjugated to forced labor.

The premise of this passage is that the younger daughter gave her son a more modest name than that given by the older daughter. The difference in naming the sons is extremely significant to the author of this rabbinic text; he sees the names as the core of a more favorable general attitude toward Ammon. Medieval commentators such as Rashi and Rabbenu Baḥya also evaluated the younger daughter more favorably on the basis of this text. We have demonstrated here that the design of the narrative alludes to such a similarly complex and subtle assessment.

In light of this analysis I would like to return to the correspondence between the older sister's suggestion and the execution of her plan. The accepted premise is that the older daughter intended to have each daughter lie with her father on a different night. Therefore, the execution is compatible with the original plan. However, there is no indication in the elder sister's verbalization of her plan that that was indeed her intention. In fact, the older daughter initially spoke in the plural about the actions of giving the father wine and lying with him: "Let us make *our father* drink wine and then *we shall* lie with him and preserve our family line through *our father*" (Gen. 19:32). However, in the account of the following events the giving of wine is described in the plural – "So *they* made their father drink wine," whereas the older daughter proceeded to act alone: "And *the older one* came and lay with her father" (v. 33). When push came to shove, the initial partnership made way for the brave older daughter's action, while the younger daughter seemed to have lost her nerve to act out the plan the sisters had agreed upon.[30] One might argue that both daughters could not have lain with their father simultaneously, but this argument does not clarify why the younger daughter needs to be convinced of the plan again on the second night. The reader is left with the impression that the plan was not completed on the first night due to the hesitation of the younger daughter.

Why are the daughters presented differently? The younger daughter is commended for her hesitance; the text presents her lying with her father against her better judgment and out of desperation.

In this first moment of their origin stories, the narrative projects a different attitude toward Moab than toward Ammon. This distinction is expressed in the law prohibiting marriage with Ammon and Moab (Deut. 23:4–7):

> No Ammonite or Moabite or any of their descendants may enter the assembly of the Lord, not even in the tenth generation. For they did not come to meet you with bread and water on your way

30. A similar suggestions was made by Sutskover, "Lot and His Daughters," 49.

> when you came out of Egypt, and he hired Balaam son of Beor from Pethor in Aram-Naharaim to pronounce a curse on you. The Lord your God would not listen to Balaam but turned the curse into a blessing for you, because the Lord your God loves you. Do not seek their peace or their prosperity as long as you live.

Ammon and Moab seem to have equal status; they are mentioned in one breath. Additionally, the reason for the directive (*they* did not come to meet you) and the concluding remarks (*their* peace; *their* prosperity), which are stated in the plural, relate equally to both nations. However, the central reason for the directive focuses on Moab (and is therefore delivered in the singular), "And he hired Balaam son of Beor…" This lengthy statement points to specific animosity between Israel and Moab, which is deeper than the animosity with Ammon. There is no clear historical evidence for such a distinction,[31] but ancient Hebrew poetry does reflect such a distinction. As opposed to Moab and Edom, the people of Ammon were not mentioned negatively in the Song of the Sea (Ex. 15) or in Balaam's poem (Num. 24:17). While this point is not the main purpose of the story, however, the nuanced literary motifs woven in the text lend themselves to the reasoning behind the slightly differing evaluation of Moab and Ammon later on in the biblical narrative.

I believe the delicate distinction between the daughters serves an additional literary purpose. One literary view sees this as an innovative concept of preference toward the younger sibling, since the elder daughter is presented as the initiator, while the younger sister is frightened and hesitant.[32] I believe the opposite to be true: the hesitation of the younger daughter is commended in the narrative. The presentation of the younger daughter highlights the fact that what the sisters felt compelled to do should have been avoided altogether, had they had a choice. On the literary plane, the presentation of the younger sibling

31. The two are frequently mentioned as a pair in biblical texts. See Timothy D. Finlay, *The Birth Report Genre in the Hebrew Bible* (Tübingen, 2005), 203. Oded claims that the hostility toward Ammon seems to have evolved later than that toward Moab and Edom (B. Oded, "*Ammon,*" *Entziklopedya Mikra'it* 6:254–271).
32. Sutskover, "Lot and His Daughters," 7.

in a more positive light is part of a known motif of preference for the younger sibling in the book of Genesis.

It is noteworthy that the present narrative was placed between the message of the birth of Isaac (Gen. 17–18) and the realization of that message (Gen. 21). Once again, in this context Lot can be compared to Abraham. Lot has two daughters, and Abraham two sons. Just as Abraham's elder son Ishmael acts inappropriately (Gen. 21:9) and preference is given to the younger (Isaac), Lot's elder daughter takes the initiative and lies with her father, and her younger sister is preferred as a result. Lot's journey continues to parallel that of his uncle, and once again he and his household seem to fall short.

The Evaluation of Lot

Lot himself remains entirely passive throughout the scene, a point which is driven home by an unflattering play on the word "*yada*." Lot's ignorance of the events is described in the same words on both occasions: "He did not know (*yada*) when she lay down or when she rose" (Gen. 19:33, 35). This detail is necessary to point out at the conclusion of the first night, since it explains how the daughters were able to get away with the second night. Reiterating Lot's ignorance on the second night, however, seems entirely unnecessary. In fact, it serves only to elevate anticipation of Lot's response, which is then piercingly absent. Throughout the biblical narrative the verb Y-D-A' ("to know") interchangeably denotes the sexual act and intellectual understanding. The word play surrounding Lot in this scene creates a sense of harsh irony: Lot "did not know" that his daughters "knew" him.[33] While the daughters are active in a way that exceeds their normal role, their father is utterly passive, and so ignorant of his surroundings that he is unaware of what his own body is doing.[34]

---

33. Melissa Jackson, "Lot's Daughters and Tamar as Tricksters and the Patriarchal Narratives as Feminist Theology," *JSOT* 98 (2002): 39.

34. Otto Rank's theory overloads the text with more information than it contains. Perhaps he is correct, and the purpose of portraying Lot as passive is to exempt him of responsibility for violating the taboo of incest. However, he went too far with the claim that the story demonstrates Lot's secret lust for incest (Rank, *The Incest Theme in Literature and Legend: Fundamentals of a Psychology of Literary Creation*, trans. G. C. Richter [Baltimore, 1992], 303). Shira Stav ("Fathers and Daughters: The Incest

Lot's ignorance is enhanced by the notorious analogy with Noah and his sons after the flood (Gen. 9:18–27). The flood had destroyed all of humanity, leaving only Noah and his family, and the perception of Lot's daughters is that they, too, are the sole survivors of the destruction of the world. Noah became drunk inside his tent, and Lot becomes drunk in his cave on the hill. Noah's son viewed his father's nakedness in his drunken state, and Lot became engaged in incestuous relations with his daughters.[35]

The analogy is broken, however, by the father's reaction to his child's action. Noah "woke up from his wine *and knew* what his youngest son had done to him" (Gen. 9:24). Noah's lucidity led him to regain control; he blessed his two sons, and cursed his youngest son. In contrast, Lot "did not know" what his daughters had done.[36] The first appearance of the statement might have portrayed Lot as a victim, but the emphasis of the repetition portrays Lot as someone who has given up. Lot loses not only his wife and daughters, but his own vitality and will to live.

Trap," *Theory and Criticism* 37 [2010]: 87) has written similarly: "The sexual act is characterized by increased, aberrant, and redundant activity (the act occurs twice), as well as lethargy and senselessness, which represent the deep denial that is an integral part of all fatherly desire." Such readings refer to the fact that Lot offers his daughters to the townspeople, demonstrating his subconscious lust toward them (Rashkow, "Daddy-Dearest and the 'Invisible Spirit of Wine,'" 82–107). J. Cheryl Exum ("Desire Distorted and Exhibited: Lot and His Daughters in Psychoanalysis, Painting, and Film," in *"A Wise and Discerning Mind": Essays in Honor of Burke O. Long*, ed. S. M. Olyan and R. C. Culley [Providence, RI, 2000], 94) attributes the secret lust to the author. See also Elke Seifert, "Lot und seine Töchter: Eine Hermeneutik des Verdachts," in *Feministische Hermeneutik und Erstes Testament: Analysen und Interpretationen*, ed. H. Jahnow (Stuttgart, 1994), 48–66. Despite well-known postmodern predilections, commentators should read the text rather than conform the characters to their philosophies.

35. Westermann viewed the analogy as part of the literary motif "fertility after destruction," which relates to the establishment and characterization of nations (Westermann, *Genesis 12–36: A Continental Commentary*, 312; see also Coats, *Genesis*, 147). However, the correlation between the scenes involves concrete literary elements, such as drunkenness and incest with children.

36. Turner, "Lot as Jekyll and Hyde," 98; Hamilton, *The Book of Genesis, Chapters 18–50*, 52; Mathews, *Genesis*, 245.

In light of this, Lot's daughters are correct. Without taking action, Lot's line might end (and according to their perception, the end of Lot's line will be the end of mankind). Lot's lack of knowledge stems from his choice to know no more; he had hidden in his cave and allowed himself to become oblivious to the surrounding reality.

The Epilogue to the Destruction of Sodom

The scene between Lot and his daughters in the cave is the clear culmination of the story of Sodom's destruction. In terms of plot continuity, the scene in which Lot and his family flee Sodom sets the details for the following scene in the cave. "As dawn broke, the angels urged Lot on, saying, 'Up, take your wife and your *two remaining daughters,* lest you be swept away because of the iniquity of the city.' Still he delayed. So the men seized his hand, and the hands of his wife *and his two daughters*... and brought him out and left him outside the city" (Gen. 19:15–17). The detail is likely emphasized in preparation for the story of the daughters in the cave: Lot escapes with his wife and two daughters, and then the wife is lost, leaving Lot and his daughters. The elder daughter's words, too, "There is not a man on earth to consort with us in the way of all the world," can only be explained in relation to the destruction of Sodom. Lot and his daughters come to the hill because "he was afraid to dwell in Zoar" (v. 30), a fear that can only be explained if the reader is aware of the previous story.[37] In fact, Lot's arrival on the hill relates directly to the angel's instructions, "Flee to the hills, lest you be swept away" (v. 17).[38]

The ambiguity of Lot's household at leaving the culture of Sodom is integrated into this scene as well. Lot's daughters give him wine to drink, just as Lot offered his guests wine (Gen. 19:3).[39] In both

37. Among others, Coats, "Lot: A Foil in the Abraham Saga," 125.
38. Coats, ibid., 146.
39. On the motif of food and drink in rape narratives, see Yael Shemesh, "Biblical Stories of Rape: Common Traits and Unique Features," *Studies in Bible and Exegesis 6* (2002): 324–325. Shemesh notes that the motif appears in the Sodom narrative, as well as the concubine of Gibeah story and the rape of Tamar – all the biblical rape narratives aside from Dinah's. The motif has unique significance in the rape of Lot by his daughters, since the motif is essential in advancing the plot.

instances the drinking is offered as literary context for the demand to sexually abuse the drinkers. The sexual motif links the cave scene with the broader narrative through the choice of words. The verbs *shakhav* ("lie") and *yada* ("know") are used regarding both the angels who come to Sodom, and the cave scene. While the neutral meaning of the verb *shakhav* is used in the Sodom narrative (19:4), the sexual connotation is clearly implied in the cave narrative (19:32, 33, 34, and 35). The neutral meaning of the word *yada* is used in the cave scene (19:33, 35) but has a clear sexual connotation in the Sodom narrative (19:5, 7). Whatever the sisters' motives, their behavior certainly echoes that of their former kinsmen.

The final question we are left with is, truly, why is this story included in the Abraham narrative? What purpose does it serve? Whereas Abraham was somewhat involved in the destruction of Sodom narrative, the story of Lot's daughters is utterly unrelated to Abraham.

As we have seen numerous times in Lot's exploits, the texture of the phrasing and key motifs create a veiled connection with the broader Abraham narrative, establishing Lot and his household as a foil to that of Abraham.

The statement by the eldest daughter regarding her father's old age in the context of fertility (Gen. 19:31) links the scene to the angels' visit to Sarah, who laughed at their tidings of fertility because of her husband's old age (18:12).[40] Sarah's barrenness is somewhat reminiscent of Lot's wife, who turns into a pillar of salt – the symbol of infertility. The issue of family continuity in both scenes is based on the old age of the father, but is ultimately resolved.

Rabbinic commentary notes the ironic link of the relationship between Lot and his daughters in the scene in Sodom and that in the cave.[41] The Sodomites wish to force themselves upon Lot's guests, and he offers his daughters for their sexual pleasure instead. Eventually, the very same daughters force themselves upon Lot in the cave. This irony goes beyond mockery of Lot's suggestion and indicates a connection

---

40. Hamilton, *The Book of Genesis, Chapters 18–50*, 51; Mathews, *Genesis*, 246.
41. *Midrash Tanḥuma, Vayera* 12.

between Lot and the townspeople, as he personally engages in the sexual act he had offered them.[42]

As I mentioned above, the text seems to view Lot's innocence or lack thereof as complex, but leans toward a positive evaluation based on the fact that he is ultimately saved by the merit of his own actions. The rescue story is devoid of explicit criticism of Lot in order to enable a reading that portrays him as worthy of being saved. In this epilogue, however, Lot's offer to the vicious mob outside his door is finally criticized.[43] The implicit criticism of Lot who "did not know" is obvious in the harsh irony with which the text utilizes those same words to describe the old man in the cave.

The analogy with the Abraham and Sarah episode continues to raise more criticism against Lot. Each family is faced with the challenge followed by a resolution of the problem of family continuity. Whereas Abraham and Sarah's problem is resolved by God's intervention, it is the daughters' actions that solve the question of Lot's continuity. The divine intervention in Isaac's birth comes as a stark contrast to the incestuous act that leads to the birth of Ammon and Moab. Sarah, who is a full partner to her husband's hospitality, enjoys the reward of a miraculous birth, while Lot's nameless and discourteous wife turns into a pillar of salt.[44] Lot, like Abraham, invited people into his home; like Abraham, he was rewarded for his hospitality. But Abraham, who shared his values with his wife, was able to also share his reward of fertility with his wife, while Lot, who did not instruct his family in the ways of his beliefs and was willing to give up his daughters for rape and possibly worse, was rewarded with fertility through an incestuous act with his daughters.

There are several theories regarding the universal taboo on incestuous relations. According to the biological theory, the aversion to incest reflects the natural need to prevent the unwanted genetic results of intra-family breeding. In 1934, Edward Westermarck proferred that

42. See Cheryl H. Smith, "Challenged by the Text: Interpreting Two Stories of Incest in the Hebrew Bible," in *A Feminist Companion to Reading the Bible: Approaches, Methods and Strategies*, ed. A. Brenner and C. Fontaine (Sheffield, 1997), 114–135.
43. Katherine B. Low, "The Sexual Abuse of Lot's Daughters: Reconceptualizing Kinship for the Sake of Our Daughters," *JFSR* 26 (2010): 40.
44. Polak, *Biblical Narrative Aspects of Art and Design*, 196–197.

the abstention from incest is part of the evolutionary process of natural selection. He believed that only people who possessed an instinctive aversion to incest survived.[45] Anthropologists and psychologists challenged this idea and claimed that the prohibition attests to a natural attraction, which needs to be limited by instating a law.[46]

A widely accepted alternative theory was suggested by Claude Levi-Strauss. He believed the prohibition on incest was not focused on preventing intra-family relations, but rather on forcing the family to marry the daughter outside the hereditary line, in what he called "the alliance theory." Application of this theory through exogamy enables the growth and development of society, and the creation of broad and supportive social networks.[47] In light of this theory, the incestuous narrative involving Lot cruelly mirrors Lot's choice to settle in Sodom.

Both Lot and Abraham exhibit hospitality, which is based on the need to open one's door and utilize one's good fortune for the benefit of a foreigner. The sin of the people of Sodom was their refusal to use their fortune and prosperity to benefit others. Despite the fertility of their land and the wealth of their community, they only sought to harm visitors who come to their city. Incest is thus an expression of the refusal to open the closed gates of family and share the wealth. The fact that Lot's fertility remains inside the family unit is another indication of the negative values on which his Sodom-based family was raised.

Lot's Daughters in the Context of the Abraham Cycle

The story of Lot's legacy also serves to complete the story of Terah's genetic line. The verb Y-SH-B ("to sit/dwell"), which is emphasized in the text, carries dramatic significance with regard to Lot's character throughout the Abraham cycle. The verb initially appears with regard to the separation of Abraham from Lot, because "their possessions were so great, they could not *dwell* together" (Gen. 13:6), and "the Canaanite and

45. Edward Westermarck, *Three Essays on Sex and Marriage* (London, 1934), 147.
46. E.g., James George Frazer, *Totemism and Exogamy: A Treatise on Certain Early Forms of Superstition and Society* (London, 1910), 97–98. Freud also adopted this position.
47. Claude Levi-Strauss, *The Elementary Structures of Kinship*, trans. J. H. Bell, J. R. von Sturmer, and R. Needham (Boston, 1969), 481.

Perizzites were then *dwelling* in the land" (13:7); therefore, each chose to settle in a different location: "Abram *dwelt* in the land of Canaan, while Lot *dwelt* in the cities of the Plain" (13:12). Lot's choice related specifically to the fertile land of Sodom, which was "well watered" (13:10). The war in Genesis 14 affected Lot who, in contrast to Abraham, "*dwelt* in Sodom" (14:12). In the narrative about the destruction of Sodom, Lot is seated (*yoshev*) at the gate of the city (19:1), and the narrative concludes by reminding the reader that Lot had chosen to settle in Sodom: "Thus it was that when God destroyed the cities of the Plain and annihilated the cities *where Lot dwelt*..." (19:29). The epilogue opens with the same root: "Lot went up from Zoar and *dwelt* in the hill country with his two daughters, for he was afraid to dwell in Zoar; and he and his two daughters *dwelt* in a cave" (19:30). Lot's story culminates on the hill, instead of his original choice of the plain. Without mentioning Abraham's name, the text introduces an additional retroactive evaluation of Lot's choice in juxtaposition with Abraham's.[48] Abraham's choice to continue journeying through Canaan with God as his guide gives him greater stability than Lot, who is guided by a desire for stability but seeks it in a godless place.

The story brings to a close the broader circle of Terah's line. The biblical narrative's interest in Lot's story and the establishment of Ammon and Moab is surprising, as is the interest in Ishmael, since they disengage from the house of Abraham.[49] In truth, the biblical text is consistent in its utmost concern for the establishment of family. The book of Genesis is internally structured according to the establishment of families and the tracking of family lines.[50] Since the Abraham cycle began with the line of Terah (Gen. 11:27), the cycle alludes to the establishment of Nahor's line (22:20–24), through Lot (19:36–38) and of course, ultimately, through Abraham. In spite of the mockery and

---

48. The Plain relates also to the location of Sodom. See, among others, Harland, "The Location of the Cities of the Plain," 45. See also Gen. 11:2, which might indicate a general preference of hill-dwelling as opposed to settling in the valley.
49. Von Rad, *Genesis*, 219–220.
50. Keil and Delitzsch, *Biblical Commentary on the Old Testament*, 35–37; Thompson, *The Origin Tradition of Ancient Israel: The Literary Formation of Genesis and Exodus 1–23*, 167–172; David M. Carr, *Reading the Fractures of Genesis: Historical and Literary Approaches* (Louisville, 1996).

criticism of Lot, the birth of Ammon and Moab is a positive development in the establishment of the Haran-Lot branch of the Terah line. In this establishment of the three genetic lines of Terah, Abraham finally completely fulfills the commandment to separate from his father's house. He is no longer Abram, son of Terah; Abraham is the father of his own nation, as his brothers carry on their own ancestral lines.

Abraham and Sarah in Gerar (Gen. 20)

An inattentive reader might find themselves experiencing a bit of *deja vu* at the beginning of the story that follows that of Lot's daughters in the cave. Abraham and Sarah leave Canaan, encounter an enemy ruler, Abraham presents Sarah as his sister, and she is taken to be wed to another man. *Hold on a moment... haven't I read this story already...* ? Yes, just eight chapters prior, Abram and Sarai leave Canaan in the wake of a famine, and Sarai is taken by the Pharaoh after Abram claims she is his sister. This narrative was odd enough the first time around, in Egypt – what purpose could a parallel narrative serve a second time round? More to the point, why are our characters putting themselves once again in this perilous situation?

The meaning of a story is created throughout the reading process – the timber and pace by which certain plot points unfold, which creates the tone, the tension, and significance in the narrative. Some details that might seem trivial at first glance become deeply significant in the context of the full narrative. The information is offered in a deliberate order that affects the reading process and the deciphering of the story. The Gerar narrative is a classic example of this literary style, where information provided at the end of the narrative sheds new light on the entire story.

The text seems to be extremely critical of Abraham in this narrative – a point which would be easier to swallow if not for the context in which the story of Gerar is told in the Abraham journey. Abraham has just pled to save an entire city and rescued his undeserving nephew from certain death. The previous episode with Lot and his daughters seems to have been presented, among other things, as a foil to Abraham's character, emphasizing his unyielding moral compass in contrast to that of Lot. Most obviously, Abraham has actually been through this story before, with the Pharaoh in Egypt. Surely the biblical text does not intend to present this narrative in Gerar to display Abraham's *lack* of character development since the previous event? And yet, the criticism in the superficial reading of the text is undeniable.

Everything about this narrative lends itself to a dual reading. The first reading will be an evidentiary analysis of the story as it is written. The second reading, in the context of the final verse, will reveal a plot twist that will turn our initial analysis on its face. The revelation at the end of the narrative will jolt us back to the beginning to read the whole story in a new light.

Egypt and Gerar

The brevity and omission of explanations in this story imply that this episode of "the endangered ancestress" relies on the narrative in Genesis 12. On one hand, there is no need to explain why Abraham tells his wife to pretend she is his sister, or why the king of Gerar takes Sarah (Gen. 20:2). The information provided in the parallel narrative in Genesis 12 is presumed in Genesis 20. On the other hand, there are several meaningful plot points in our story that are absent from the story in Genesis 12. One major question in the story of Abram and Sarai in Egypt is why Abram feels morally justified in leaving Canaan, after God has explicitly commanded him to traverse the land. That question is absent from the story of Gerar, since it is located within the boundaries of Canaan. This fact could be interpreted both positively and negatively. Abraham should be praised for keeping his family in Canaan. Alternatively, what reason justifies Abraham exposing his family to the dangers of Gerar?

On that note, Genesis 12 leaves open the question of whether Sarai had been violated by Pharaoh or not. "In addition to avoiding stating explicitly whether such actions took place," writes Reuben Aharoni, "the narrative uses ambiguous terms such as, 'The woman was *taken* to the house of Pharaoh,' and 'I *took* her to be my wife.'"[1] Even if God had afflicted Pharaoh before he had had a chance to do anything to Sarai,[2] there is no explicit statement to that effect. In contrast, in Genesis 20, God Himself says, "I knew that you did this with a blameless heart, and so I kept you from sinning against Me. That was why I did not let you touch her" (Gen. 20:6).

Another perplexing issue to be addressed is the question of Abraham's behavior with Abimelech. While Abraham does not attempt to justify his lie to Pharaoh, Abraham does attempt to justify his lie by explaining to the king of Gerar, saying, "And besides, she is in truth my sister, my father's daughter though not my mother's" (Gen. 20:12). Yet, even so, Abraham had misled the king to assume he was not married to Sarah.

The final puzzling difference between these narratives relates to the gifts that Abraham receives from each king, which are presented in a different light in each of the stories. Pharaoh's gifts are offered as part of Abram's deception, as a dowry for Sarai: "And because of her, it went well with Abram; he acquired sheep, oxen, asses, male and female slaves, she-asses, and camels" (Gen. 12:16). In contrast, Abimelech's gifts are offered legitimately. In fact, the gifts were offered after Abraham's secret was revealed (20:14).[3]

On its face, it would seem that the story of Abraham in Gerar portrays Abraham as hesitantly misleading at best, and intentionally duplicitous toward Abimelech and callously unempathetic to Sarah at worst. Abimelech, for his part, seems to play the role of the gracious innocent. He is accused of a terrible act, and in response welcomes Abraham

---

1. Reuben Aharoni, "Three Similar Stories in Genesis," *Beit Mikra* 24 (1979): 219.
2. As Cassuto firmly believes is the case (*A Commentary on the Book of Genesis: From Noah to Abraham*, 356), and as opposed to Peleg, "Was the Ancestress of Israel in Danger?" 197–208.
3. Aharoni ("Three Similar Stories in Genesis," 222) writes that Abraham is portrayed differently as well. While in the Egypt narrative he is a "common wanderer," in the Gerar narrative he is "chosen by God, and a prophet," who can heal Abimelech and his household with his prayer.

and Sarah into his home with generosity and grace. The external structure of the plot certainly raises questions regarding how this narrative contributes to our understanding of Abraham and the journey we have experienced with him as a character thus far.

Some suggest that the purpose of Genesis 20 is to moderate the criticism of Abraham in Genesis 12.[4] However, an analysis of the narrative actually indicates that there is greater criticism of Abraham present in the Gerar story. The second narrative certainly shifts the focal point to the ethical plane,[5] but Abraham is not portrayed in more positive light.

The narrative lends itself to a dual reading, and the final verse reveals a critical detail that was previously concealed from the reader. The new information creates a demand for a second reading of the story.[6] We will therefore attempt to read this episode with emphasis on the narrative's criticism of its characters; once we reach its conclusion, however, we will be forced to retrace our steps and reanalyze the narrative as a whole.

---

4. Gelander writes, "Apparently the link between the three narratives [Gen. 12, 20, and 27] indicates a correction and improvement of [Abraham's and God's] image" (*Studies in the Book of Genesis*, 87–88). See, among others, Van Seters (*Abraham in History and Tradition*, 167–191) and Westermann (*Genesis 12–36: A Continental Commentary*, 159–168, 316–319); Yair Zakovitch and Avigdor Shinan, *Abram and Sarai in Egypt* (Jerusalem, 1983), 141. J. Cheryl Exum ("Who's Afraid of the 'Endangered Ancestress'?" in *The New Literary Criticism and the Hebrew Bible*, ed. D. J. A. Clines and J. C. Exum [JSOTSup 143: Sheffield, 1993], 91–113) believes, with scant evidence, that the three narratives express ambivalence toward the idea of the woman being taken by a stranger, which is viewed as both a threat and a secret desire, and that the fantasy is sublimated from one episode to the next, with the characters eventually overcoming that forbidden desire.
5. Aharoni, "Three Similar Stories in Genesis," 222.
6. Moshe Garsiel (*The First Book of Samuel: A Literary Study of Comparative Structures, Analogies and Parallels* [Ramat Gan, 1983], 85–89) believes there is an implied criticism of Saul from the outset, which only becomes apparent at the end of his monarchy. With regard to this phenomenon in the Abraham and Abimelech narratives, see Tzvi Novick, "'Almost, at Times, the Fool': Abimelekh and Genesis 20," *Prooftexts* 24 (2004): 277–290; Grossman, *Ambiguity in the Biblical Narrative and its Contribution to the Literary Formation*, 251–265.

From Sodom to Gerar

The narrative opens, "Abraham journeyed *from there* to the region of the south and settled between Kadesh and Shur, and he settled in Gerar." The phrase *from there* demands attention – from where? Usually in such biblical descriptions, this phrase is used to link the new journey to the previous location. When Abraham journeys from Shechem to Bethel, the verse reads, "From there he moved on to the hill country east of Bethel… and he built there an altar" (Gen. 12:8). Abraham's journey is portrayed as ongoing, so his journey "from there" intends to relate directly to the previously mentioned location where Abraham previously built an altar. In this case, figuring out the place of departure in Abraham's journey to Gerar is not as simple as looking at the previous verse. The scene preceding the journey was not about Abraham, but about Lot's daughters.[7] The use of the phrase seems to create a sense of continuity where there is none. The last place we saw Abraham was looking out over the destruction of Sodom. The text here appears to indicate that Abraham's journey to Gerar is somehow linked to the episode in Sodom.

The association is not entirely far-fetched; from a literary perspective, there are overlaps between the episodes in Sodom and in Gerar. Both journeys involve punishment of the locals due to sexual corruption, and in both stories someone is saved from punishment due to Abraham's merit (Gen. 19:29; 20:17).[8] Abimelech's plea, "Will you slay a nation, though innocent?" (20:4), eerily echoes Abraham's supplication to God on behalf of Sodom (a literary connection we will explore later in this chapter).[9]

In the context of Abraham's journey, these episodes also coalesce nicely as a literary lead-up to the birth of Isaac. The three stories

---

7. Following the Midrash, Rashi does link the two stories: "Abraham journeyed from there: When he saw that the villages were destroyed and travelers ceased, he journeyed from there. Alternatively, he distanced himself from Lot, who had acquired a bad reputation, because he had been intimate with his daughters" (Rashi on Gen. 20:1).
8. Additional links will be addressed below, and are noted by Hamilton, *The Book of Genesis, Chapters 18–50*, 58–59; Mathews, *Genesis*, 248–249.
9. Diana Lipton, *Revisions of the Night: Politics and Promises in the Patriarchal Dreams of Genesis* (JSOTSup 288: Sheffield, 1999), 52.

preceding the birth of Isaac relate to the sexual corruption in the societies that surround Abraham: the rape of visitors (Sodom), incest (Ammon and Moab), and taking the wife of another (Gerar). Interestingly, the severity of the crime gradually diminishes. The Sodomites had premeditated intent to harm Lot's guests; while Lot's daughters were fully aware of their actions, the motives for their actions were positive (to sustain the family line). And while Abimelech took another man's wife, he did so innocently, without a full awareness of his actions.

In contrast to Canaanite culture, Abraham is destined to be "a blessing to all the nations" by teaching his children "to keep the way of the Lord by doing what is benevolent and just" (Gen. 18:19). While the sexual conduct of the people of the land is immoral, Isaac is born and immediately circumcised as part of Abraham's covenant with God, which obligates him, like his father, to be benevolent and just. Abraham had come "from there," but journeys beyond, distinguishing himself with loftier values and higher morality than the cultures he encounters on his way.

That said, the tone of the narrative is critical of Abraham's behavior toward Sarah and Abimelech in Gerar. If the only link to Sodom relates to the contrast between Abraham and the morally decrepit Sodomites, the episode in Gerar struggles to uphold Abraham's character as the perpetual moral indicator. There is no apparent reasoning behind Abraham's decision to travel to Gerar, which leads us to believe that his deception with Abimelech is voluntary. If this is so, where does this narrative place our hero on his journey to become the moral leader of the Jewish nation?

Abraham as the Anti-Hero

The opening scene between Abraham and Sarah sets a tone immeasurably different from the couple's descent to Egypt. "Abraham said of (*el*) Sarah his wife, 'She is my sister.' So King Abimelech of Gerar took Sarah." While the preposition "*el*" usually denotes "to" or "toward," here it is used as "of" or "regarding."[10] Genesis 12:11 uses this phrase "*vayomer el*," as well, yet it is in communication with his wife. The contrast emphasizes the absence of direct communication between Abraham and Sarah in

10. And indeed, all modern translations translate "of Sarah" instead of "to Sarah."

Genesis 20. In Egypt, Abraham – sensitive to his bride, uneasy about his actions – justifies his actions to Sarah, and seems to have asked for her permission to act as he did (Gen. 12:11–13). In contrast, the succinctness of the Gerar text creates the impression that Abraham's actions are automatic. The verse creates anticipation for direct communication between Abraham and Sarah ("Abraham said to his wife Sarah"), but in reality Abraham speaks *of* her, instead of communicating *with* her. Abraham had asked Sarah whether she would pretend to be his sister *before* they reached Egypt (12:11). In contrast, only once Sarah and Abraham reach Gerar is the plan exposed to the reader. The conversation between Abraham and Sarah may have indeed taken place as well on the way to Gerar. However, the text intentionally omits it in order to set a certain tone for the reader. The impression we get is that, while Abraham felt conflicted about the correct approach in Egypt, upon entering Gerar he presents Sarah as his sister without a second thought.

Abimelech's reaction is similarly succinct, contributing to the technical and straightforward tone of the narrative. Pharaoh had taken Sarah after hearing rumors of her beauty, while the king of Gerar takes her seemingly for no particular reason. Even if the reader is capable of filling in the narrative gap him- or herself, the fact that it is not written explicitly has bearing upon the plot design.

As the character of Abimelech develops over the course of the narrative, the reader also begins to wonder why Abraham had felt the need to deceive the king in the first place. Abimelech, whose virtue apparently makes him worthy of a divine revelation, is horrified at his mistake when the truth about Sarah finally comes out. It would seem that Abraham is unrightfully suspicious of the king's character, assuming that he would steal another man's wife with no misgivings or concern about the moral implications of the act. As we will see below, the method by which Abraham deceives Abimelech is also stingingly wily. He claims Sarah is his "sister," which was true in the sense that they belonged to the same clan, but intentionally misleading in its implication that being "brother and sister" would preclude the possibility of their marriage. Abraham's deception of the king at this point in the narrative seems petty and cruel, particularly since his reasoning for doubting the king's intentions in the first place seems unreasonable.

Abimelech as the Hero

Astonishingly, Abimelech, the foreign king who has played no role in the Abraham narrative until this point, receives a divine revelation. Although the content of the revelation is largely negative, the fact of God's communication directly with the king establishes Abimelech in this story as a protagonist, worthy of divine attention and contrasted with his Egyptian counterpart.[11]

Our positive assessment of Abimelech is reinforced by his response to God's reprimand. The text insists, "Abimelech had not approached her," meaning that, although Abimelech had "taken" Sarah, he had not violated – or "taken" – her in the biblical sense. Abimelech responds to God's rebuke in a sentence that shocks us with its familiarity: "Will You slay people, though innocent?" (Gen. 20:4). The last time we heard these words uttered to God, it was from the lips of our hero, Abraham: "Far be it from You to do such a thing, to bring death upon the innocent as well as the guilty.... Shall not the Judge of all the earth deal justly?" (18:24–25).

The links to Abraham do not end there; both plaintiffs use the term "*tzaddik*," "innocent,"[12] and design their rhetorical question in a similar manner; both turn to God using the name "*Adonai*," "Lord" (Gen. 18:27). The premise of both statements is that God is just and will not punish the innocent.[13] The demands for justice by both Abraham and Abimelech clearly portray the latter in a positive light. As well, the phrasing of Abimelech's declaration of innocence, "My heart was blameless and my hands were clean," is similar to God's demand of Abraham to "walk in My ways and be blameless" (17:1). In fact, the context of God's demand of Abraham was the Covenant of Circumcision, which is based on the reciprocity between fertility and sexual purity.[14]

11. Robert Alter, *The Five Books of Moses* (New York and London, 2004), 98.
12. Regarding the term "*tzaddik*" as a key word of chapters 18–20, see: Yitzchak Etshalom, *Between the Lines of the Bible: Genesis: Recapturing the Full Meaning of the Biblical Text* (Jerusalem and New York, 2015), 119–129.
13. Davidson, *Genesis 12–50*, 81; Robert W. L. Moberly, *Genesis 12–50* (OTG: Sheffield, 1995), 71–72.
14. Similarly, Cotter, *Genesis*, 131–132. The grammatical link is sufficient for the desired effect on the reader's consciousness, especially in light of the broader connection

Abimelech parallels Abraham's position in the Sodom narrative, but also in the Covenant of Circumcision: he is blameless, and expects God to reciprocate impartially. This comparison, seemingly out of nowhere in the context of the greater Abraham narrative, is both enthralling and perplexing.

Abimelech in this scene is a deeply sympathetic character. The justification of his actions is not eloquent or well expressed; the brief successive syllables and repetitive information ("He himself [*halo hu*] said to me, 'She is my sister!' And she also said [*vehi gam hi*], 'He is my brother!'") express the confusion and embarrassment of one who has fallen into a trap. An allusion to this trap might even be found in God's accusation: "You are to die because of the woman that you have taken, for she is the wife of another man (*vehi be'ulat baal*)." The phrase *be'ulat baal*, which denotes "a married woman," is found in only one other biblical reference, Deuteronomy 22:22: "If a man is found lying with the wife of another man (*be'ulat baal*), both of them – the man and the woman with whom he lay – shall die." Both verses sentence the offender to death; however, the law in Deuteronomy specifies that both the man and the woman who engage in such an act must die, while in Genesis the "wife of another man" is the only one of the two who is aware of her status. Beneath the surface of God's severe accusation, the reader must wonder whether Abraham and Sarah should be blamed for Abimelech's actions, rather than the innocent and deceived king.

Despite the initial accusation against Abimelech, God acknowledges his innocence and justifies his actions. Abimelech uses the word "*gam*," "also," twice in his plea of innocence (Gen. 20:4–5), and the phrase appears twice in God's response, to emphasize that God is indeed on Abimelech's side: "I also (*gam*) knew that you did this with a blameless heart, and so I also (*gam*) kept you from sinning against Me" (20:6).

God's reference to Abimelech's "blameless heart" is a direct response to Abimelech's appeal, "My heart was blameless and my hands were clean." God accepts the fact that Abimelech was deceived.[15]

---

between the two characters, which is based on additional components as noted below.

15. Wenham (*Genesis 16–50*, 71) writes that the reader realizes at this stage that Abimelech never touched Sarah due to his illness, based on the comparison with ch. 12. However,

The concentric structure of the dream accentuates God's approval:[16]

A: You are to *die*
  B: because of the woman that you have taken, for she is *the wife of another man.*
    C: Now Abimelech had not approached her.
      D: He said, "O Lord, will You slay people even though *innocent*?
        E: When I did this, my *heart was blameless* and my hands were clean."
          F: And God said to him in the dream,
        E': "I knew that you did this with *a blameless heart,*
      D': and so I kept you from sinning against Me.
    C': That was why I did not let you touch her.
  B': Therefore, restore the *man's wife* – since he is a prophet.
A': He will intercede for you – so you may live. If you fail to restore her, know that you shall *die*, you and all that are yours."

This structure emphasizes the apparent divine corroboration of Abimelech's claims. Even the characterization of Abimelech as "righteous" in his grievance against God earns approval in this retelling, "And I kept you from sinning against Me" (Gen. 20:6).

The phrase "*lo netatikha lingo'a eleha,*" "I did not let you touch her," further emphasizes that Abimelech was distant from sin. The common phrase used to describe contact with another is "*naga be-*" (cf. Gen. 26:11, Ex. 19:12). The expression *lingo'a eleha* conveys a greater distance, closer in meaning to the text's description, "Abimelech had *not approached her.*" The phrase *lingo'a* means "to touch," and it is a clever pun of another word with the same letters "N-G-A," "affliction," creating a grammatical association with the parallel story of Pharaoh, who had suffered afflictions as a result of taking Sarah (Gen. 12:17). While

there is no reason to assume the narratives will have an identical outcome, and the reading consciousness cannot be based upon this assumption.

16. Thomas Desmond Alexander, *Abraham in the Negev: A Source-Critical Investigation of Genesis 20:1–22:19* (Carlisle, UK, 1997), 39.

God afflicted Pharaoh for taking Sarah, He helped Abimelech avoid sin (and thus, affliction) by speaking to him. Despite the overwhelming evidence in favor of Abimelech, this is an indication that Abimelech's innocence should be attributed not to his righteousness but to God's intervention.[17] Additionally, although God repeats Abimelech's remark about his blamelessness, He omits the "cleanliness of his hands."[18] These two details, which will be discussed further below, do not detract from Abimelech's innocence in the sin that is initially attributed to him.

The second part of God's response to Abimelech includes instructions on how to correct the situation, and the demand to return Sarah to Abraham. In this section of the discussion, Abimelech seems to inhabit a role that feels more familiar for a character of his kind in the Abraham narrative. In contrast with the previous conversation with Abimelech, God takes a harsher tone with regard to Abimelech's future actions (Gen. 20:7): "And now (*ve'ata*), restore the man's wife – since he is a prophet, he will intercede for you so you may live. If you fail to restore her, know that you shall die, you and all that are yours."

The word "*ve'ata*," "and now," is a common opening to the conclusion of a speech. In view of all that was previously stated, Abimelech is expected to take action to rectify the situation. Abimelech is given two options. He can either "restore" or "fail to restore," and as a result, he can "live" or "die," respectively.

In light of Abimelech's seemingly sympathetic position in the narrative, and God's assurance of his blamelessness, God's threatening tone seems out of place, as does the possibility that Abimelech will fail to return Abraham's wife. If Sarah was taken innocently and under false pretenses, there is no reason to assume that Abimelech would not rectify the situation. The threat of punishment is expanded beyond Abimelech, and includes his dynasty and household, "you and all that are yours." The severity of the threat indicates divine wrath toward Abimelech. Even according to the "best case" scenario, in which Abimelech returns Sarah, Abimelech's survival can only be ensured with Abraham's intervention once his wife is returned. In other words, Abimelech's life is very much

17. Cf. Wenham, *Genesis 16–50*, 71.
18. See Rashi on Gen. 20:6.

in danger. The reason Abraham can save Abimelech's life by interceding on his behalf is his identification as a "prophet." Clearly, the significance of the king's divine revelation was previously overrated. Otherwise, why would Abimelech need Abraham's intervention if Abimelech himself can communicate with God?[19]

The second part of God's response conveys anger at Abimelech, indicating that God supports Abraham's initial assessment and suspicion of the king. This ambiguity of the text's evaluation of Abimelech is intentional, sowing the seeds for an analysis of the narrative which – like our evaluation of Abimelech's character – could go either way.

Early Next Morning

In keeping with the vague ambiguity of the two protagonists, the text opens the next verse with another familiar expression: Abimelech "rose early the next morning (*vayashkem... baboker*)." This expression is present in all stories surrounding the Gerar narrative (Gen. 19:27, 21:14, 22:3), but all three narratives remark on *Abraham's* early rise in the morning. The Talmud viewed the expression as a connotation of activism and enthusiasm to fulfill a task: "The zealous are early [to perform] their religious duties, for it is said, 'And Abraham rose early the next morning.'"[20] Abimelech's eagerness to fulfill God's command continues the trend of "walking in Abraham's ways." Not only does Abimelech argue morality with God, he also wakes up early to heed the word of God!

Abimelech's urgency does not bring him to Abraham's doorstep immediately. First, he gathers his servants and shares the contents of his dream.[21] Until this moment, the reader was unaware of any involvement

19. Ruth Fidler, "Abimelech's Dream in the Context of the 'Matriarch in Danger' Genre," *Turra* 2 (1991): 28. See also Yael Shemesh, "Lies by Prophets and Other Lies in the Hebrew Bible," *JANES* 29 (2002): 81–95. Perhaps the definition of Abraham as a prophet emphasizes Abraham's greatness in comparison to Abimelech, so though Abimelech has a divine revelation, he is not categorized as a prophet like Abraham.
20. Pesaḥim 4a.
21. The king's address to his servants is linked to his reprimand of Abraham. From a literary perspective Abimelech might have summoned his servants and Abraham simultaneously.

of Abimelech's household in the story, and Abimelech's disclosure of his own folly seems noble; he could have returned Sarah to Abraham discreetly. This implies that like Abraham, Abimelech is intent on teaching his household justice and righteousness. He is not ashamed of his mistake, which he uses to demonstrate the correct path.[22] The reaction of Abimelech's people, "And the men were greatly frightened," indicates shared values and moral discourse. The root Y-R-A, which denotes both fear and sight, is used interchangeably in the parallel narratives of Genesis 12 and 20: Whereas "Pharaoh's courtiers *saw* (*vayir'u*) her and praised her to Pharaoh" (Gen. 12:15), Abimelech's servants "were greatly *frightened* (*vayir'u*)" (20:8). Abimelech only addresses Abraham after he has informed the people of his household, who react to the news with great fear.

Abimelech vs. Abraham

Abimelech accuses Abraham of acting against laws of natural morality, which he views as a great sin. Abimelech testifies that he is honest, in contrast with Abraham who has brought "so great a guilt upon me and my kingdom" (Gen. 20:9), and describes taking another man's wife as "things that ought not to be done."[23] Since Sodom was described in similar terms of great sinfulness and immorality (Gen. 18:20), Abimelech's accusation seems to compare Abraham to the Sodomites, and indicate that he, too, practices sexual immorality!

The repetition in verses 9–10 ("Abimelech said…") seems to indicate Abraham's astonished silence at the king's accusation.[24] Abraham

22. "Who wants to admit publicly that he has been tricked? His willingness to be open and tell the truth contrasts with Abraham and his subterfuge" (Hamilton, *The Book of Genesis, Chapters 18–50*, 67).
23. The expression *ḥataa gedola* ("a great sin") has the connotation of sexual sins in Ancient Near Eastern literature (Jacob J. Rabinowitz, "The 'Great Sin' in Ancient Egyptian Marriage Contracts," *JNES* 18 [1959]: 73; William L. Moran, "The Scandal of the 'Great Sin' at Ugarit," *JNES* 18 [1959]: 280–281; Jacob Milgrom, *Cult and Conscience: The Asham and the Priestly Doctrine of Repentance* [Leiden, 1976], 132–133; Sarna, *Genesis* [JPS], 143). Abimelech seems to be using a common term for a sexual offense.
24. Alter, *The Five Books of Moses*, 99. Based on this suggestion, it should have been included in what Shiloach calls "waiting for a response or reaction" (Shiloach,

is dumbfounded at the severe allegations made against him. His silence may also echo the realization that they contain a grain of truth; had God not intervened, Abraham would have been responsible for a great sin.

Abraham's justification, "I thought surely there is no fear of God in this place, and they will kill me because of my wife" (Gen. 20:11), supplies the reader with ample information to know that Abraham is in the wrong. In addition to the overwhelming evidence that Abimelech is just, honest, and moral, his servants react to his revelation by becoming "greatly frightened (*vayir'u meod*)" (20:8) in direct contrast with Abraham's assertion that "there is no fear of God (*yirat Elohim*)."[25] The design of the narrative compares Abraham's concern with the reaction of the servants. Abimelech rises early and speaks to his servants, and to Abraham. A comparison of the dialogues reinforces the ironic link between Abraham's wrong assessment and the true colors of Gerar:

Abimelech and his Servants (Gen. 20:8)	**Abimelech and Abraham (Gen. 20:9–11)**
Abimelech called for (*vayikra*) his servants	Abimelech called for (*vayikra*) Abraham…
and told them all that had happened (*hadevarim ha'eleh*).	"What, then, was your purpose in doing this thing (*hadavar hazeh*)…"
and the men were greatly frightened.	"I thought surely there is no fear of God in this place, and they will kill me because of my wife!"

"And He Said… and He Said," 251). Shiloach instead attributes this to the group in which the dual caption differentiates between "two claims" (ibid., 253). However, both Benno Jacob (*The First Book of the Bible: Genesis*, 132) and Claus Westermann (*Genesis 12–36: A Continental Commentary*, 325) believe that the first caption relates to a general criticism (to which Abraham was not expected to respond), while the second was a concrete question to which Abraham was expected to offer a response.

25. Similarly, see Emanueli, *Genesis – Commentary and Insights*, 198; Wenham, *Genesis 16–50*, 72; Westermann, *Genesis 12–36: A Continental Commentary*, 324–25. Alter (*Genesis – Translation and Commentary*, 94) writes, "In the event, he is entirely wrong: Abimelech is a decent, even noble, man." Wenham (*Genesis 16–50*, 68) also noted a concentric structure surrounding v. 8, which describes Abimelech's conversation with his servants. This position gives centrality to Abimelech's speech and the servants' reaction, which affects the evaluation of the characters.

Abraham further justifies his deception by explaining that Sarah is indeed his "sister," insofar as she is a member of his family. Some commentators "justify" Abraham's formulation based on marriage documents found in Nuzi. The word "sister" may have been used in the context of a betrothal (the agreement was generally made between a brother of the bride and the future husband).[26] Some believe the terms "wife" and "sister" were identical in Nuzi culture.[27] The word "sister" is often "borrowed" to connote "love" and "wife."[28] This alternative meaning is particularly prevalent throughout the Song of Songs 4:9–12: "You have captured my heart, my sister, my bride.... How sweet is your love, my sister, my bride!... A garden locked is my sister, my bride, a fountain locked, a sealed up spring."[29] According to this idea, Abraham did not lie when he called his wife "sister," even if by using an ambiguous term he created the impression that he was not Sarah's husband. While this suggestion is attractive, the text fails to support this reading.[30] The term "sister" in reference to one's wife is found nowhere in the Abraham cycle outside

26. Ephraim A. Speiser, "The Wife-Sister Motif in the Patriarchal Narratives," in *Biblical and Other Studies*, ed. Alexander H. Altmann (Cambridge, MA: Harvard University Press, 1963), 15–28.

27. Paul Koschaker, "Fratriarchat, Hausgemeinschaft, und Mutterrecht in Keilschriftrechten," *ZA* 41 (1933): 1–89. This hypothesis was rejected by various scholars, such as Thompson, *The Historicity of the Patriarchal Narrative: The Quest for Historical Abraham,* 315–330. For a detailed discussion on this issue see Samuel Greengus, "Sisterhood Adoption at Nuzi and the 'Wife-Sister' in Genesis," *HUCA* 46 (1975): 5–31; Barry L. Eichler, "On Reading Genesis 12:10–20," in *Tehillah le-Moshe: Biblical and Judaic Studies in Honor of Moshe Greenberg*, ed. M. Cogan, B. L. Eichler, and J. H. Tigay (Winona Lake, IN, 1997), 24–26, 32–33; Barry L. Eichler, "'Say That You Are My Sister': Nuzi and Biblical Studies," *Shnaton* 3 (1978): 108–115.

28. E.g., Benno Jacob, *The First Book of the Bible: Genesis*, 89; Sarna, *Genesis* (JPS), 95; Zakovitch, *"I Will Express Riddles of Old": Riddles and Dream-Riddles in Biblical Narrative*, 141.

29. See also Prov. 7:4. Regarding the meaning of sister, see Ludwig Koehler and Walter Baumgartner, *Lexicon in Veteris Testamenti Libros* (Leiden 1953), 31 ("Zur Geliebten"); BDB, 27 ("Beloved, Bride").

30. See Shemesh, "Lies by Prophets and Other Lies in the Hebrew Bible," 81–95; Jonathan Grossman, "The Use of Ambiguity in Biblical Narratives of Misleading and Deceit," *Tarbitz* 73 (2004): 483–515. Thompson writes, "Speiser's 'interpretation' of Gen. 12, 20 and 26 is not based on the Genesis text, but is rather the construction

the three narratives at issue of Genesis 12, 20, and 27. In fact, the term used in this way is not found anywhere else in the entire Pentateuch.[31]

But, more to the point, Abraham's response fails to justify the possibility of the immoral outcome of his lie, which could have led to illicit relations between his wife and Abimelech! Abimelech is not concerned with Abraham's semantics, but rather with the detrimental consequences of Abraham's dishonesty.[32] As Nahmanides writes:

> I did not know the sense of this apology. Even if it were true that she was both his sister and his wife, but when they desired her as a wife, and he told them, "She is my sister," in order to mislead them, he already sinned against them, bringing them to perpetrate a "great sin," and it didn't matter whether it was true or not.[33]

When Abraham provides an additional explanation with the word "*vegam*," "also" (Gen. 20:12) conveys Abraham's embarrassment and confusion; even *he* realizes that the initial explanation was insufficient ("I thought surely there is no fear of God in this place, and they will kill me because of my wife"), and so he offers another reason for his actions, worse than the one before.[34] Abraham had requested of Sarah, "Let this be the kindness that you shall do me," while her kindness toward

---

of a historical hypothesis based on historical record" (Thompson, *The Historicity of the Patriarchal Narrative: The Quest for Historical Abraham*, 235).

31. However, the term "brother" *is* found in reference to males who are not blood relations (Gen. 17:7, 29:4, 31:37). This might support the position that there is a half-truth in Sarah referring to Abraham as "brother."
32. Mathews (*Genesis*, 258) writes harshly, "The impotent excuses the patriarch presents casts him in an even more distasteful light."
33. Nahmanides on Gen. 20:12.
34. Abimelech's reference to Abraham as Sarah's "brother" at the conclusion of the narrative (Gen. 20:16) does not prove that Abraham's claim "was accepted by Abimelech" (Fidler, "Abimelech's Dream in the Context of the 'Matriarch in Danger' Genre," 26–27). Abimelech's formulation is meant to be sarcastic. Sarna (*Genesis* [JPS], 103) argues that the fact that the Isaac narrative in Gen. 26 uses this same "sister" motif proves that it is unrelated to any actual paternal connection. This argument further weakens Abraham's claim in the eyes of the reader, who is familiar with all three texts.

Abraham was damaging to others. Abraham has difficulty defending himself in light of Abimelech's claim, "You have done to me things that ought not to be done!"[35]

The moral appraisal of the characters in the narrative is deepened by the comparison of the two dialogues on which the story is based: one between God and Abimelech in his dream, and the other between Abraham and Abimelech. While Genesis 12 focuses on the events, Genesis 20 concentrates on the evaluation of the various characters through the two dialogues:

	God and Abimelech	**Abimelech and Abraham**
The characters meet	God came to Abimelech in a dream by night and said to him	Abimelech called for Abraham and said to him
Accusation: The sin of taking another man's wife	You are to die because of the woman that you have taken, for she is married to another man	"What have you done to us? What wrong have I done that you should bring so great a guilt upon me and my kingdom? You have done to me things that ought not to be done!" "What, then," Abimelech demanded of Abraham, "was your purpose in doing this thing?"
The narrative justifies the "defendant"	Now Abimelech had not approached her.	

35. The word "*ḥesed,*" "kindness," which Abraham uses to describe Sarah's willingness to pretend she is his sister, also appears in the context of incest between a brother and sister in Lev. 20:17. Calum M. Carmichael (*Law, Legend, and Incest in the Bible: Leviticus 18–20* [Ithaca, 1997], 14–44) believes the order of Leviticus 18 correlates with the stories in Genesis, and that the prohibition on incest between a brother and sister is a response to the sister-wife stories in Genesis. See also Tirzah Meacham, "The Missing Daughter: Leviticus 18 and 20," *ZAW* 109 (1997): 254–259.

	God and Abimelech	Abimelech and Abraham
Defense	He said, "O Lord, will You slay people even though innocent? He himself *said to me,* 'She is my sister!' And *she also said, 'He is my brother.'* When I did this, my heart was blameless and my hands were clean."	"I thought," said Abraham, "surely there is no fear of God in this place, and they will kill me because of my wife. And *also,* she is in truth my sister, my father's daughter though not my mother's; and she became my wife. So when God made me wander from my father's house, I said to her, 'Let this be the kindness that you shall do me: whatever place we come to, *say there of me: He is my brother.*'"
Reconciliation	And God said to him in the dream, "I knew that you did this with a blameless heart.... Therefore, restore the man's wife – since he is a prophet, he will intercede for you – so you may live. If you fail to restore her, know that you shall die, you and all that are yours."	Abimelech took sheep and oxen... and he restored his wife Sarah to him. Abraham then prayed to God, and God healed Abimelech and his wife and his slave girls, so that they bore children.

Both dialogues center on the allegations of immorality and defense by the accused, and in both cases, the two parties eventually reconcile. According to the table above, Abimelech parallels God – God accuses Abimelech of immorality, and Abimelech accuses Abraham of unethical conduct. Before Abimelech responds to God's accusations, the text sides with him ("Now, Abimelech had not approached her"). This literary justification is not paralleled in the case of Abraham. The word "*gam,*" "also," is used in the responses to both accusations, as is the repetition of the deception ("he is my brother"). These links reinforce Abimelech's grievances. Even Abraham admits the deception, using the very same formulations Abimelech had quoted. The third part of each interaction creates an atmosphere of appeasement, and God's demands of Abimelech are met at the conclusion of the second dialogue.

Abimelech thus seems to have the upper hand in the ethical debate with Abraham. This is based not only on the positive characterization of Abimelech, but also God's express approval, Abimelech's eagerness to rectify the situation, the text's portrayal of Abimelech's household as God-fearing, Abraham's mistaken lack of faith in a God-fearing community, and Abraham's unsatisfying explanations regarding potentially disastrous behavior.

Abimelech's position as the justified hero in this exchange seems to be solidified when, instead of becoming angry with Abraham at his deception, the king treats Abraham and his household to a generous feast, heaping gifts upon them with grace and magnanimity. Abimelech's actions are recorded without interruption (Gen. 20:14–16):

> Abimelech took sheep and oxen, and male and female slaves, and gave them to Abraham;
> and he restored his wife Sarah to him.
> And Abimelech said, "Here, my land is before you; settle wherever you please."
> And to Sarah he said, "I herewith give your brother a thousand pieces of silver; this will serve you as vindication before all who are with you, and you are cleared before everyone."

Abraham and Sarah's reunion is not described in the text. The text also fails to disclose whether Abraham accepts Abimelech's generous offers of land and silver, and Sarah's reaction to Abimelech's suggestion is omitted. The text conveys a sense of activity and eagerness on the part of Abimelech, who wants to make things right and compensate those who were hurt in the process. The focus on Abimelech's actions demonstrates how much more he gave than what God had demanded of him, which was simply to return Sarah to her legitimate husband.[36] This might be viewed as a happy conclusion to the story, and the evaluation of Abimelech's character remains altogether positive.

---

36. Cf. Westermann, *Genesis 12–36: A Continental Commentary*, 319.

Abimelech's gifts set him apart from Pharaoh. While Pharaoh offered Abraham goods when he thought he was receiving Sarah in return, Abimelech offered Abraham cattle and silver when he knew he would have to return Sarah. The text creates a correlation between Sarah and the gifts that almost trivializes her as one of the many objects offered to Abraham. The strange order, which places the gifts before Sarah, is reminiscent of the order of the text in the Egypt narrative, where the gifts are offered as a dowry. Here, however, the gifts are offered as part of Sarah's return to her husband.

When Pharoah had discovered that Abraham had made a mockery of him and his kingdom, who were afflicted by Abraham's God, Pharaoh had banished him from his land and wanted nothing to do with him (Gen. 12:20). In stark contrast, in addition to offering Abraham gifts, Abimelech invites him to stay as a permanent resident in his land, despite the deceit he had suffered (20:15). The climax of Abimelech's decency is with regard to Sarah. He announces publicly that Abraham and Sarah are legitimately married, and then proceeds to appease Sarah.

Sarah's appeasement is not a necessary detail to further the plot, and serves the sole purpose of emphasizing Abimelech's kind nature. He humorously relates to Abraham as Sarah's "brother," perhaps also demonstrating his acceptance of the excuse Abraham offers for his lie.[37] Various explanations have been offered with regard to Genesis 20:16: "And to Sarah he said, 'I herewith give your brother a thousand pieces of silver; it will serve you as a covering of the eyes before all who are with you, and you are cleared before everyone.'"[38] Abimelech's declaration

37. Skinner (*A Critical and Exegetical Commentary on Genesis*, 319) suggests that the gifts to Sarah are a cynical act. When a single woman is harmed, she receives gifts, while the husband is compensated for damage done to a married woman. Abimelech compensates Sarah as though she had been a virgin. However, I believe that Abimelech's act is not cynical, but particularly sensitive to Sarah, who personally suffered.

38. The verse is difficult, and various interpretations were offered. Many view the pronoun "*hu*" (translated above as "it"; lit. "he") in the phrase, "it will serve you as a covering of the eyes," as a reference to the money. Westermann (*Genesis 12–36: A Continental Commentary*, 317) and von Rad (*Genesis*, 229) suggest that the money was a "covering of the eyes," as in, a vindication, for all those who desired and "put their eyes on" Sarah. In other words, a protection from criticism. This explanation correlates with their interpretation of the rest of the verse, "and you are cleared

regarding Abraham and Sarah's married status prevents such a mistake from being made by others. Whereas Pharaoh looks after his own interests, Abimelech attempts to prevent future injustice.

In conclusion, the text directs criticisms at Abraham, while Abimelech is portrayed as acting on a higher moral plane. God reveals Himself to Abimelech and speaks with him. He accepts and reinforces Abimelech's innocence, which is also supported by the narration. Abimelech is open with his subjects about his dream and his mistake, and they react appropriately. Despite Abraham's deceit and inadequate explanations, Abimelech offers him gifts and land.

On Abraham's part, the story offers no overt justification for going to Gerar (unlike when they went to Egypt, no famine is mentioned here). The absence of dialogue between Abraham and Sarah depicts the deceit as standard procedure for them ("...whatever place we come to, say there of me: He is my brother"). Abimelech is critical of Abraham, and Abraham fails to offer a satisfactory explanation for his actions. As the story draws to a close, Abimelech is clearly portrayed as the "bigger man," so to speak, and Abraham, with all the moral high ground we have attributed to him in his journey thus far, comes out patently deficient as our hero.

The Plot Twist

Just as Abraham turns to exit the scene, in the penultimate verse, the text drops a bombshell that changes the entire course of the story. Abraham

---

before everyone." Similarly, Rashi writes: "A covering of the eyes – this will cover the eyes of anyone with you, so that they will not denigrate you. For had I returned you empty-handed, they could say, 'After he violated her, he returned her.' Now that I had to spend much money and to appease you, they will know that I returned you against my will, and through a miracle." Dillmann writes that this is Abimelech's confession about what he did to Sarah (*Genesis, Critically and Exegetically Expounded*, vol. 2, 123). Similarly, Wenham (*Genesis 16–50*, 74) suggests that the "cover" is for "Sarah's eyes," as a bribe to make her overlook and forgive what Abimelech had done to her. Chaim Gilad ("Hine Hu Lakh Kesut Einayim," *Beit Mikra* 22 [1977]: 45) explains that the pronoun *hu* refers to an actual cover for her face, worn by married women to alert others of their status. For other suggestions that involve altering the text, see, among others, Ball, *The Book of Genesis*, 72; Gunkel, *Genesis – Translated and Interpreted*, 222; Skinner, *A Critical and Exegetical Commentary on Genesis*, 319–320.

prays to God, "And God healed Abimelech and his wife and his slave girls, so that they bore children…for the Lord had closed fast every womb of the household of Abimelech because of Sarah, the wife of Abraham" (Gen. 20:17–18).[39] This new information is shocking. It changes the reader's entire perception of the exchange between Abraham and Abimelech, and suddenly provides important context to Abimelech's actions, and, consequently, our evaluation of his character.

As it turns out, Abimelech did not act out of the kindness of his heart when he returned Sarah to Abraham. Instead, he was fearing for his life and for the generations of progeny who would never be born. In kidnapping Sarah, Abimelech had brought a terrible plague upon his family. Abimelech's household was in an upheaval before they had learned of Abimelech's dream, due to the unknown and life-threatening plague that tortured their wives. The fear of the servants in Genesis 20:8 might not have been a reaction to Abimelech's revelation at all, but to the realization that the epidemic is divine in nature. The fear, then, was not a spiritual reaction to sexual immorality, but a natural fear for their health and lives.

Suddenly, three phrases in the text are given new meaning. As previously noted, while God repeats Abimelech's remark about his blamelessness, He omits the "cleanliness of his hands." Rashi comments, "It is true that you did not intend at first to sin, but you cannot claim purity of hands, for it was not due to you that you did not touch her. Rather, I prevented you from sinning."[40] Rashi's commentary might seem inappropriate according to the initial reading, since even God justifies Abimelech. However, based on the new information offered at the

39. Commentators debate the meaning of the phrase, "For the Lord had closed fast every womb." Rashi on Gen. 20:17 opines that pregnant women were prevented from giving birth. Radak similarly suggests this possibility, but alternatively suggests, in accordance with one position found in Bava Kamma 92a, that the entire kingdom was also blocked from urination and defecation (see Rabbenu Baḥya here as well). Wenham and others claim that in addition to preventing childbirth, the epidemic created temporary infertility (Wenham, *Genesis 16–50*, 74).

40. Rashi on Gen. 20:6.

conclusion of the narrative, God had also chosen to punish Abimelech for his actions.[41]

The affliction also sheds new light on the use of the verb "*lingo'a,*" "to touch." We previously thought that the text differentiated between God's conduct toward Pharaoh, who was afflicted "with mighty plagues" *(nega'im gedolim),* and Abimelech, who is prevented by God from touching Sarah with, "I did not let you touch her" (*lo netatikha lingo'a eleha*). However, in light of the information offered at the conclusion of the narrative, apparently Abimelech did suffer a plague at God's hands. The previous distinction between Abimelech and Pharaoh is withdrawn in the final verse, which uses the identical formulation with regard to Abimelech as in the case of Pharaoh:

> Genesis 20:18: "For the Lord had closed fast every womb of the household of Abimelech *because of the matter of Sarah, the wife of Abraham.*"
> Genesis 12:17: "But the Lord afflicted Pharaoh and his household with mighty plagues *because of the matter of Sarai, the wife of Abram.*"

Whereas the use of *lingo'a* was previously perceived as a distinction between the two narratives and the two characters, based on the new information the words should be viewed as a link and bond, in the spirit of the following midrash:

> It was taught in the name of R. Eliezer ben Yaakov. We know that Pharaoh was plagued with leprosy and Abimelech with the closing up [of the orifices]. How do we know that what is said here is to be applied there, and vice versa? That is why "because

41. Meir Sternberg (*The Poetics of Biblical Narrative: Ideological Literature and the Drama of Reading* [Bloomington, 1985], 315–316) and Novick ("'Almost, at Times, the Fool': Abimelekh and Genesis 20," 277–290) believe the "second reading" reveals that it was Abimelech's illness that prevented him from approaching Sarah, and that Abimelech was not so "innocent." I believe the second reading does not detract from the first, and should not be viewed as a "correction," but as an additional perspective.

> of the matter of" (*al devar*) occurs in both places, in order that an analogy should be drawn (*gezera shava*).[42]

Lastly, Abimelech's accusation that Abraham brought a "great a guilt upon" Abimelech and his kingdom (Gen. 20:9) should also be read in a new light. Whereas in the initial reading the "guilt" seemed to refer to the sin of taking another man's wife, in light of the new information the integration of "kingdom" seems to indicate that the guilt that Abimelech lays upon Abraham's conscience is not the guilt of immorality but rather of the plague he brought Abimelech's kingdom.[43]

This analysis illuminates the use of the name *YHWH* in the final verse. In the Egypt narrative, God afflicts Pharaoh, and God is called *YHWH* throughout the narrative. In the Gerar narrative, however, God is called *Elohim*, since Abimelech is initially evaluated positively, and *Elohim* is an appropriately universal name that relates to foreigners as well as the chosen people.[44] The universal name enables an intimacy between the king and God, who speaks in a language Abimelech can understand. Abraham's reference to God in the plural in Genesis 20:13 (lit. "when they caused me to wander from my father's house") conveys the feeling that the entire chapter is conducted on Abimelech's semantic playing field. Abimelech understands that Abraham's God protects him, just as Abimelech's own god protects him. At the conclusion of the story, when the reader discovers that God afflicted Abimelech, the text created a distance between God and the foreign king, by calling God by the name reserved for His chosen people.

The essential question we are left with is, of course, why this information was concealed instead of being integrated into the appropriate place in the narrative. One could argue that this is a literary device, intended to heighten tension, and that when the reader discovers the "truth" at the end of the narrative, the initial reading should be entirely

42. Genesis Rabba 41:2.
43. In this view, the phrase *ḥataa gedola* ("a great sin") expresses the result of the sin (in other words, the punishment). See Kaddari, *A Dictionary of Biblical Hebrew*, 290. BDB interprets the word *ḥet* ("sin") as an expression of punishment, but not *ḥataa*.
44. Cf. Albert Šanda, *Moses und der Pentateuch* (Münster: Aschendorffsche Verlagsbuchhandlung, 1924) 24–30; Cassuto, *The "Quaestio" of the Book of Genesis*, 45.

abandoned.[45] This hypothesis, however, completely ignores the powerful effect the initial reading creates. Yes, the new information might illuminate various details in the narrative, but it does not eliminate the reading experience. The surprising detail offered just as the reader believes the story is over does not change the first reading, but rather creates two parallel readings of the narrative, thereby creating a dialectical critique of Abimelech's character.

Throughout the initial reading the reader identifies with Abimelech, who falls into a trap set by Abraham and Sarah. Discovering the affliction – the motive behind the king's action – provides the reader with the opportunity to view Abimelech as a more complex character, who was perhaps not altogether deserving of the entirely positive reviews he was previously offered. This complexity might diminish the empathy toward Abimelech, but should not invalidate the reader's compassion altogether, since Abimelech is wronged, and suffers, and indeed rectifies the situation in accordance with God's instructions.[46]

Both Abraham and Abimelech are the subjects and victims of this twofold narrative. Whereas the initial reading is critical of Abraham's behavior, the second reading is more critical of Abimelech. The ambivalent assessment of Abimelech in the narrative is cleverly embedded in the links to the destruction of Sodom. The links are apparent both in the narrative materials and the fabric of the language.

---

45. Gunkel, *Genesis – Translated and Interpreted*, 219.
46. Von Rad (*Genesis*, 223) addressed the dual reading of the story, while considering the synchronic element: "One could almost say that our story has two faces, an ancient and a modern. Ancient is the emphasis on Abimelech's guilt: the king infringed on another's marriage which was absolutely protected by the divinity.... In contrast to that is the advanced reflection over the subjective ignorance that caused Abimelech to act in good faith. Indeed, the personal blamelessness of the heathen king is delineated by the narrative to the profound humiliation of Abraham." Compare to Ruth Fidler, *"Dreams Speak Falsely?" Dream Theophanies in the Bible: Their Place in Ancient Israelite Faith and Traditions* (Jerusalem, 2005), 109, who focuses on another difference: "On the one hand, this is the implementation of divine will, that preventing Abimelech from approaching Sarah saves the king from sin (instead of punishing him). On the other hand, there is an emphasis on Abraham's prophetic prayer which heals Abimelech and the women of his household." See also Cotter, *Genesis*, 134.

As previously noted, both narratives share a common theme: the sexual corruption of the people of the land. This corruption led to the destruction of Sodom, and almost led to Abimelech's demise. Some have compared Abraham's estrangement from his wife for the sake of his own safety to Lot offering his daughters to the mob outside his house in order to save his guests.[47] Both narratives include a moral argument against God's judgment, resulting in Abraham's prayer for the "defendant." Both narratives discuss the dwelling of a "stranger" among the people of the land (Lot in Genesis 19:9 and Abraham in 20:1). Finally, both narratives portray a sexual offense against guests/foreigners within the boundaries of the land of Canaan.

The texts also share similar phrases that link the two stories:

1. Abraham asks Sarah, "This is the kindness that you shall do me (*ḥasdekh asher taasi imadi*)" (Gen. 20:13), in a similar formulation to Lot's request of the angels, "You have been so gracious to your servant, and have already done me so much kindness (*ḥasdekha asher asita imadi*) in order to save my life" (19:19).
2. God warns Abimelech, "If you fail to restore her, know that you shall die, you and all that are yours (*vekhol asher lakh*)" (20:7), just as the angels had warned Lot, "Sons-in-law, your sons and daughters, and all that are yours (*vekhol asher lakh*) in the city – bring them out of the place" (19:12).[48]
3. Abimelech demands of God, "Will You slay people even though innocent?" (20:4), in correspondence with Abraham's statement, "Far be it from You to do such a thing, to bring death upon the

---

47. Gossai, *Power and Marginality in the Abraham Narrative*, 111–139; Hamilton, *The Book of Genesis, Chapters 18–50*, 58.
48. Mathews (*Genesis*, 255) felt this statement is reminiscent of the description of Abraham's wealth in Gen. 12:20, "They sent him off with his wife and all that was his (*vekhol asher lo*)," and in Gen. 13:1: "From Egypt, Abram went up into the Negeb, with his wife and all that was his (*vekhol asher lo*), together with Lot." However, the phrase "*vekhol asher lo*" is a common formulation. The motivation to link the expressions must be based on other similar phrases throughout both literary units.

innocent as well as the guilty, so that innocent and guilty fare alike.... Shall not the Judge of all the earth deal justly?" (18:25).[49]

4. As mentioned above, the formulation, "He rose early the next morning (*vayashkem... baboker*)," appears in both narratives (20:8 and 19:27).

The shared motifs, the analogous phrases, and the proximity of the texts within the Abraham cycle reinforce reading the Gerar narrative in relation to the destruction of Sodom. Commentators debate whether a literary analogy demands an exact parallel to the character in the corresponding story (a "static analogy"),[50] or whether it can be based on links between varying characters in each of the stories (a "dynamic analogy").[51] Indeed, sometimes the contrast with a variety of characters better serves the purposes of the analogy.[52] In the analogy above, Abimelech in Gerar is compared to Abraham in the Sodom narrative (e.g., challenging God's judgment, and rising early in the morning), and Abraham in Gerar is compared to Lot in Sodom (e.g., the separation from the wives, the "kindness" request). But other components in the text compare Abimelech to Lot (e.g., the threat to everything one has, the need for the intervention of others to save one's life). In this case, the inconsistency serves the purpose of the analogy. Abimelech seems at times to be an ethical alternative to Abraham, but not always. He sometimes requires the strong hand of God Himself to prevent him from immorality. Abimelech might remind the reader of Abraham, but the parallel is incomplete, and before long he is compared to Lot, another morally questionable character.

There are no winners in the moral debate between Abimelech and Abraham. While initially Abimelech seems to have the upper hand, the

49. Lipton, *Revisions of the Night: Politics and Promises in the Patriarchal Dreams of Genesis*, 52.
50. Paul R. Noble, "Esau, Tamar, and Joseph: Criteria for Identifying Inner-Biblical Allusion." *VT* 43 (2002): 219–252.
51. Rendsburg, *The Redaction of Genesis*; Craig Y. S. Ho, "The Stories of the Family Troubles of Judah and David: A Study of Their Literary Links," *VT* 49 (1999): 514–531.
52. Jonathan Grossman, "Dynamic Analogies in the Book of Esther," *VT* 59 (2009): 394–414.

final verse moderates this conclusion. Even after the moderation of the final verse, however, the results are overwhelming. Thus, in the midst of the Abraham cycle, the reader is presented with an alternative moral figure, which successfully challenges Abraham's morality, occurring shortly after God attests, "I have singled him out, that he may instruct his children and his posterity to keep the way of the Lord by doing what is just and right" (Gen. 18:19). Since God's choice is based on Abraham's morality, is Abraham more worthy than Abimelech, who is on a similar moral plane?[53] The order of the narrative designs Abimelech as a moral character. Even if the conclusion of the story demonstrates that Abimelech's actions are not entirely voluntary, the reader is left with an uneasy feeling with regard to Abraham.

The undermining of Abraham's morality is devastating within the context of the Abraham cycle. There are references to the story throughout the rest of the cycle which attempt to deal with these implications and correct this impression. As we noted above, the final verses of the Gerar narrative subvert the negative impression of Abraham. Next, after the unrelated episodes of the birth of Isaac and the eviction of Ishmael (Gen. 21:1–21), Abraham and Abimelech interact once more, in the episode discussed below. Later, the binding of Isaac declares Abraham's "fear of the Lord." And lastly, Isaac's Gerar narrative in Genesis 26 clarifies the preference for Abraham and his offspring. In contrast with Abraham, Isaac goes to Gerar because of a famine, and despite the fact that Rebecca was not taken to the king's palace, Abimelech acts like Pharaoh and banishes Isaac from his land.[54] Here, Abimelech demonstrates that when he is not threatened, he is not eager to please Abraham's family.

This narrative is intentionally creating a sense of doubt surrounding Abraham's morality, offering Abimelech as a possible contender for the role of moral high ground. Following Sodom in the context of the greater Abraham narrative, we may have felt confident that Abraham

53. Bin-Nun, *Chapters of the Fathers*, 109.

54. Van Seters (*Abraham in History and Tradition*, 177–180) notes correctly that the narrative in Gen. 26 contains motifs that are similar to the Egypt narrative (Gen. 12) and the Gerar narrative (Gen. 20). He writes that the final narrative in Gen. 26 responds to both.

was indeed the one true leader, worthy of God's attention. Although the episodes with Lot reinforced Abraham as the divinely chosen protagonist, the text here intimates that Abraham's journey to chosenness is still incomplete. His most challenging test is still to come, in the binding of Isaac, and the text implies here that the result of that trial is anything but guaranteed.

Birth of Isaac and Ishmael's Expulsion (Gen. 21:1–21)

The dual reading of the episode with Abimelech has planted a seed of doubt as to whether Abraham's position as the one ethical leader in his region is deserved. Abimelech had been portrayed in the beginning of the previous scene as a morally sound king, deserving of divine revelation, and even described using many of the terms and expressions we had previously attributed to Abraham alone. Although the end of that episode had revealed Abimelech's true nature, the effect of our doubt in Abraham's unequivocal moral authority lingers. Throughout the next few chapters, the text swings intentionally in the opposite direction, attempting to restore the reader's faith in Abraham – first, in the plot twist at the end of the initial Abimelech episode, and then, when the two leaders meet again in the quarrel over the wells in Genesis 21, and finally, in the story of the binding of Isaac. One by one, each of these stories seeks to rebuild the reader's feeling of trust in Abraham, after having been plunged abruptly into doubt in the episode with Abimelech.

The stories of Isaac's birth and the expulsion of Ishmael come in the middle of the narrative of Abraham and Abimelech. Genesis 17 and 18 had brought tidings of the birth of a son and heir to Sarah and Abraham within the year, and the promised son is finally born in Genesis 21. It is safe to assume that the narratives embedded between promise and implementation – the destruction of Sodom (Gen. 19) and Abraham and Sarah in Gerar (Gen. 20) – occurred over the course of that same year. Since Genesis 21 begins with Sarah's conception, presumably she conceived shortly after leaving Gerar.[1] The chronological proximity is also expressed on the literary plane, through joint narrative materials. The Gerar narrative ends with God opening the wombs of the women of Abimelech's household (20:17–18), while the following narrative describes God fulfilling His promise to Abraham and Sarah and opening Sarah's womb (21:1). Perhaps the previously discussed integration of the name *YHWH* in the last verse of the Gerar narrative also serves the purpose of linking the two narratives, since Sarah's conception is in the name of *YHWH*. Additionally, the phrase "For the Lord had closed fast (*atzor atzar*) every womb" (20:18) is reminiscent of Sarah's infertility, which she had previously described in similar terms, "The Lord has closed me up (*atzarani*) from bearing" (16:2).[2] Moreover, the placement of the next episode in the Abraham-Abimelech relationship (the quarrel and covenant over the well in 21:22–34) after the birth of Isaac and expulsion of Ishmael reinforces the link between the episodes, and might be the purpose of the order of the narratives. In an attempt to create a more comfortable reading, Josephus placed the quarrel at the end of the Gerar narrative, but in so doing lost the literary link between the births.[3]

Some view the link as a contrast. While God prevented birth from the women of Abimelech's household, He offered Sarah the gift of fertility. The midrashic texts reflect this debate. For example, Genesis Rabba 53:1 states:

> "And the Lord remembered Sarah as He had said." This is what the verse states, "I have brought low the high tree, and made high the low tree, dried up the green tree, and made the dry

1. Cf. Clines, *What Does Eve Do to Help?: And Other Readerly Questions to the Old Testament*, 75–76; Hamilton, *The Book of Genesis, Chapters 18–50*, 73n7.
2. Mathews, *Genesis*, 260.
3. Josephus, *Antiquities* 1:212 (Feldman, *Flavius Josephus: Translation and Commentary*, 80).

> tree flourish. I am the Lord; I have spoken, and I have done it" (Ezek. 17:24).... R. Berekhya expounded the verse, "I am the Lord; I have spoken, and I have done it." Where did He speak it? – "At the set time I will return unto thee... and Sarah shall have a son" (Gen. 18:14). "And I have done it" – "And the Lord did unto Sarah as He had spoken." "And all the trees of the field shall know" refers to the people, as you read, "For the tree of the field is man" (Deut. 20:19). "That I the Lord have brought down the high tree" alludes to Abimelech; "Have exalted the low tree" – to Abraham; "Have dried up the green tree" – to Abimelech's wives, as it is written, "For the Lord had fast closed up all the wombs of the house of Abimelech" (Gen. 20:18). "And have made the dry tree to flourish" alludes to Sarah. "I am the Lord; I have spoken." R. Yudan said: Not like those who speak but do not act. R. Berekhya commented, "I am the Lord; I have spoken." Where did He speak it? "At the set time I will return unto thee," etc. "And I have done it." Thus it is written, "And the Lord did unto Sarah as He had spoken."

The phrase at the end of Ezekiel's prophecy, "I am the Lord; I have spoken, and I have done it," appears very similarly in the story of Sarah's conception of Isaac, "And the Lord did unto Sarah as He had spoken" (Gen. 21:1), and perhaps it is this link that serves as the source of the midrashic interpretation. According to this view, the proximity of the stories intends to present a contrast. In the first story, God "brings low the high tree" and "dries up the green tree" by preventing Abimelech's wives from conceiving. In the other story, He "exalted a low tree" and "made the dry tree flourish" when He blessed Sarah's womb with the miracle of life.

In contrast, the following midrash supports a comparison between the two stories (*Midrash Tanḥuma, Vayera* 14):

> The Holy One, blessed be He, said: Abraham prayed to Me on the evil Abimelech's behalf, and I had mercy on him, and remembered Abraham together with him, as it says, "And God healed

> Abimelech and his wife and his women and their children," in the same way that, "And God remembered Sarah."[4]

This midrash draws a comparison between the two narratives, noting God's "remembrance" of both Abimelech's wives and Sarah. In fact, the Talmud derives from the juxtaposition of the stories a principle that "anyone who requests mercy on behalf of someone else, and he has the same need, he will be answered first."[5]

The approach that compares Sarah's conception to Abimelech's women portrays Abimelech as a positive character, while the contradictory view portrays Abimelech in a negative light. As previously noted, this tension regarding Abimelech's evaluation is encouraged by the narrative.

God Remembered Sarah

We have already discussed how the story of the prediction of Isaac's birth, literarily speaking, is told in two parts, one from the personal perspective, and one from the national perspective. Here, too, that dichotomy continues with the narrative focusing first on the parental experience of Sarah, the mother, and then on that of Abraham, the father.

The first verses of Genesis 21 open with the fulfillment of God's promises to the couple. The execution mirrors the double promise to Abraham in the Covenant of Circumcision (Gen. 17) and to Sarah in the tent (ch. 18). In Genesis 21:1, "*YHWH* took note of Sarah as He had promised, and did for Sarah as He had spoken." The name *YHWH* and the focus on Sarah indicate that this verse correlates with the promise of Genesis 18. There, Sarah is the focus of the angels' promise, which is given in the name of *YHWH*.

---

4. See a similar interpretation by Yair Zakovitch, *Introduction to Inner-Biblical Interpretation* (Kadima, 1992), 39, who believes that the last two verses of Genesis 20 are a late midrashic addition designed to generate such a link between the narratives.
5. Bava Kamma 92a.

In Genesis 21:2, Isaac's birth is described once again: "Sarah conceived and bore a son to Abraham ... at the set time of which *Elohim* had spoken." This time, the focus of the verse is on Abraham and "*Elohim*'s" promise to Abraham. Abraham then names his son and circumcises him (Gen. 21:3–4). The story of Isaac's birth culminates in a festive announcement: "Now Abraham was a hundred years old when his son Isaac was born to him" (21:5). These components all correlate with God's promise to Abraham in Genesis 17, where the Covenant of Circumcision is made between *Elohim* and Abraham. There, a child is promised "at a given time" (17:21), the child shall be named Isaac (17:19), and the son will be circumcised (17:9–14).

The word "*pakad*" in the first verse has been interpreted in a number of ways. The generally accepted translation is "God remembered Sarah." The verse has also been translated as "God visited Sarah," which is fitting as a realization of the previous promise, "I will return to you at the time next year, and Sarah shall have a son" (Gen. 18:14). Although an actual physical visit is not described, the text might be deliberately creating the association with the previous visit by the angels, to enhance the sense that God took note of Sarah as a fulfillment of the promise in Genesis 18.

Reactions to the Birth (21:6–8)

Abraham and Sarah's reactions to the birth differ as well, reflecting their emotional states and circumstances when Isaac is born. Both parents react with laughter and joy. Sarah declares that "God has brought me laughter; everyone who hears will laugh with me" (Gen. 21:6). Abraham is described as holding "a great feast" when Isaac is weaned, thus including those around him in his joy.[6] Abraham and Sarah experience the joyous birth of their son differently, and the difference is expressed through the description of each parent's reaction.[7] While the narrative

6. About the idea of a "feast" as a social function, see Alan W. Jenks, "Eating and Drinking in the Old Testament," *ABD* 2: 252–253, and Robert H. O'Connell, "שתה," *NIDOTTE* 4:261.
7. Many scholars view the description of Abraham making a feast in v. 8 as an introduction to the following scene of Ishmael's expulsion, and background for Sarah's assessment of Ishmael being "*metzaḥek*," with a negative connotation of laughter. This connection is highlighted by various modern translations for Gen. 21:9, such as

allows Sarah to speak about her feelings ("showing"), Abraham's happiness is expressed through his actions ("telling"). The reader is therefore given an opportunity to experience Sarah's happiness ("God has brought me laughter"), but also become aware of the complexity of her social situation as a barren woman, despite the happy ending ("Everyone who hears will laugh with me [*yetzaḥak li*[8]])." Her second statement is introduced with a new caption, "*And she said,* 'Who would have said to Abraham that Sarah would suckle children! Yet I have borne a son in his old age.'" This statement expresses her frustration from the long years of her childless marriage, the shared disappointment, and perhaps the guilt over her inability to give her husband a son.[9] In contrast with Sarah's complex emotions, the report of Abraham focuses on his actions. He does not speak, and no emotions are described. Nonetheless, the "great feast" Abraham makes in honor of Isaac's weaning expresses his joy. The phrase "*mishteh gadol,*" "a great feast," appears only one other time in Tanakh (Est. 2:17), and the emphasis on the "greatness" of the feast indicates that the size or nature of the feast was unusual.[10]

---

the New International Version translation, "*But* Sarah saw." While Gen. 21:8 might be viewed as a transition between the birth of Isaac and Ishmael's laughter, the celebration of Isaac's weaning cannot be entirely separated from the joy of his birth. Krzysztof Sonek (*Truth, Beauty, and Goodness in Biblical Narratives: A Hermeneutical Study of Genesis 21:1–21* [BZAW 395: Berlin and New York, 2009], 62, and see 147) proves this point from the literary style. Gen. 21:8 reports Abraham's actions ("telling"), which correlates with the initial verses in the chapter, while Gen. 21:9–10 describes Sarah's emotions, which were previously described in her own words ("showing"). The latter style correlates with the following unit.

8. See, for example, Benno Jacob, *The First Book of the Bible: Genesis,* 136–137, unlike others who translate "*yetzaḥak li*" as "will laugh about me."
9. Sarah declares, "Who would have said (*mi milel*)..." Nahum Sarna ("Genesis 21:33: A Study in the Development of a Biblical Text and Its Rabbinic Transformation," in *From Ancient Israel to Modern Judaism: Intellect in Quest of Understanding: Essays in Honor of Marvin Fox,* ed. J. Neusner, E. S. Frerichs, and N. M. Sarna [BJS 159: Atlanta, 1989], vol. 1, 146) connects this to the unusual Aramaic verb *milal* in a wordplay on *mila* – circumcision.
10. Rashi, based on the Midrash, understands "a great feast" as "a feast involving the great leaders of that generation: Shem, Eber, and Abimelech." This reading is possible in the context of Est. 1:3 as well, where Ahasuerus explicitly invites "the nobles and governors of the provinces in his service." Alternatively, "great" might simply describe the number of people (O'Connell, " 261, "משתה") and amount of effort that was put into the feast.

An additional difference between Abraham and Sarah relates to the timing of their reaction. Sarah is delighted at Isaac's birth – "I have borne a son in his old age," and expresses wonder at the nursing stage – "that Sarah would nurse children!" In contrast, Abraham's reaction to the birth of his son is delayed until after he is weaned: "The child *grew up and was weaned,* and Abraham held a great feast on the day that *Isaac was weaned.*" The reader gets the sense that the celebration of Isaac's birth was an ongoing event that lasted through the years of his infancy. The joy extends from Sarah's wonder to Abraham's feast, becoming a permanent feeling throughout the early years of Isaac's life. In addition to prolonging the description of the happiness related to Isaac's birth, the text distinguishes between "Abraham's son" and "Sarah's son." This correlates with the "purpose" of the son in Genesis 17 and 18. Sarah had wanted nothing more than to hold a baby in her arms and nurse her very own child, and Abraham desired a son to maintain God's covenant and carry on the family line. Isaac's birth is the greatest joy of Sarah's life; his weaning, in fact, is a sad day for her, the separation of a child from his parents as he grows independent. From Abraham's perspective, as long as his son is suckling at his mother's breast, he cannot be educated and trained to be Abraham's successor. Once Isaac is weaned, he is ready to begin his life as the heir of Abraham's household and his covenant with God.

The two narratives of mother and father paint a picture of each parent's experience at the unlikely and blessed event of their son's birth. Sarah is "remembered" or "visited" by God. She is wholly entrenched in the miracle of pregnancy, childbirth, and weaning. Abraham has a son born "to him." He assumes the responsibility of bringing the child into the covenant with God by circumcising him. Following the circumcision, as we will see, Abraham seems to enter the picture fully only once Isaac is weaned and is old enough to begin his education. For Sarah, Isaac's birth is the fulfillment of a lifelong dream of motherhood. For Abraham, it is the foundation of his legacy.

Isaac's name is a reflection of the journey his parents went through to bring him into the world. The laughter is mentioned twice in Sarah's speech: "God has brought me *laughter*; everyone who hears will *laugh* with me." The repetition of this verb links directly back to Sarah's laughter when she was given tidings of a son in Genesis 18:12. However, here, Sarah admits that she was wrong to doubt God's promise. Now Isaac's name no longer commemorates Sarah's doubt, but rather her joy and wonder at the birth of her son. This might be the reason behind the absence of the common naming structure, in which a name is assigned and then explained. Abraham names the child in Genesis 21:3, but the reason for Isaac's name is explained only three verses later (Gen. 21:6).[11] The omission of the explanation indicates that while Abraham is obligated by divine decree to name his son Isaac (17:19), the name is also indicative of Sarah's change of attitude, from a laughter that once indicated doubt, to a laughter of joy.

Ishmael's name is implied in this context as well: "...everyone who *hears* (*hashome'a*) will laugh (*yitzḥak*) with me." The juxtaposition of these two verbs – *hashome'a yitzḥak* – might predict the tension between the two brothers, and indicate that the tension exists from the moment of Isaac's birth. [12]

Isaac's birth is described in similar terms to the birth of Ishmael,[13] with two significant differences:

The birth of Isaac (Gen. 21:2–5)	The birth of Ishmael (16:15–16)
Sarah conceived and bore a son to Abraham in his old age	Hagar bore a son to Abram
at the set time of *which God had spoken*	
Abraham gave his newborn son, whom Sarah had borne him, the name of Isaac	and Abram gave the son that Hagar bore him the name Ishmael
And when his son Isaac was eight days old, Abraham circumcised him, *as God had commanded him*	
Now Abraham was a hundred years old when his son Isaac was born to him	Abram was eighty-six years old when Hagar bore Ishmael to Abram

11. Cf. Mathews, *Genesis*, 257.
12. Cf. Garsiel, *Biblical Names: A Literary Study of Midrashic Derivations and Puns*, 156.
13. Erhard Blum, *Die Komposition der Vätergeschichte* (WMANT 57: Neukirchen-Vluyn, 1984); Ernst Axel Knauf, *Ismael: Untersuchungen zur Geschichte Palästinas und Nordarabiens im 1. Jahrtausend v. Chr* (Wiesbaden, 1985).

Both births include three components: the birth itself, the naming of the child based on previous instructions,[14] and Abraham's age. Isaac's birth, however, includes an additional component, circumcision, and more significantly, Isaac's birth includes two statements attributing Isaac's birth and circumcision to God's promise: "which God had spoken" and "as God had commanded." Isaac's birth and Abraham's actions are described in light of the covenant between Abraham and God. Sarah gave birth to a son as God had promised, and Abraham circumcised his son as God had commanded. This atmosphere is absent from the birth of Ishmael. The birth of Isaac stands out as an essential part of the covenant, unlike the birth of Ishmael. The conclusion of each story is nuanced accordingly. So, while Abraham is eighty-six "when Hagar bore Ishmael to Abram," he is a hundred "when *his* son Isaac was born *to him*."

These differences are essential in setting the tone for the provocation and subsequent actions of the characters as the two boys begin to take their places within the family dynamic.

Sarah Expels Ishmael from the House

As the two half-brothers grow up under the same roof, the tension that was foreshadowed at Isaac's birth (and was likely inevitable given the circumstances of Ishmael's birth) comes to a head. Sarah observes Ishmael "playing" and demands his expulsion. Many interpretations were offered in an attempt to decipher Ishmael's "playing," which is described by the verb "*metzaḥek*" (Gen. 21:9). The verb in its simple form generally denotes the positive action of joyful laughter, while the active-intensive form (*pi'el*) used in relation to Ishmael can carry negative connotations and additional meanings. Since Ishmael's "playing" was the reason for Sarah's insistence that he be banished from the house, clearly the action has an important role in the separation of the boys and

14. Hamilton (*The Book of Genesis, Chapters 18–50*, 73) writes, "'Isaac' is God's choice for the name of this child. 'Ishmael' was Abraham's choice for the name of his firstborn. 'Ishmael' evolves as a name only after the child's birth. 'Isaac' is revealed as the name for the second child before he is even conceived." He concludes accordingly that in the naming process, Isaac, and not Ishmael, seems to be Abraham's successor (ibid., 74). However, the angel had ordered Hagar to name her son Ishmael before he was born (Gen. 16:11), and Abraham did.

in Ishmael's rejection. God had previously revealed to Abraham in the Covenant of Circumcision that Ishmael would not be the one to carry on the covenant (17:21). However, the biblical narrative often justifies a divine decree through the characters' choices and actions. Ishmael's action in this narrative serves to justify God's decision to eliminate him as the heir to Abraham's covenant with God.

Throughout the ages, *metzaḥek* has been interpreted in a number of ways, each painting a different picture of the context of Sarah's decision. If the word shares the meaning of its simpler form, "playing," Sarah's actions are called into question. We can understand how seeing Ishmael growing up side-by-side with Isaac might have been painful for her, considering the tensions present between the two mothers, but this still wouldn't justify such vindictive behavior. Some see the obvious connection between *metzaḥek* and *yitzḥak* (Isaac) as an indication that Ishmael's "playing" was in fact him pretending to be Isaac.[15] This rebellious behavior would certainly justify Sarah's fear of her beloved son's place being usurped by a child she saw as undeserving. Other translations also opt for a more negative connotation, translating *metzaḥek* as "mocking."[16] Further complicating matters, Ishmael is portrayed throughout the narrative alternately as a "boy" and as a "child," leaving some doubt as to his true age. If he was indeed a child, the "playing" could be nothing more than innocuous childish behavior. However, as we will see below, it would appear that Ishmael was in fact a young man, and not a child. If this is the case, "playing" might take on a more insidious connotation.

The possible meanings of the active-intensive form (*pi'el*) of the verb TZ-Ḥ-K in the biblical narrative split into two categories,[17] one

15. J. Cheryl Exum and J. William Whedbee, "Isaac, Samson, and Saul: Reflections on the Comic and Tragic Visions," in *On Humour and the Comic in the Hebrew Bible*, ed. Y. T. Radday and A. Brenner (JSOTSup 92: Sheffield, 1990), 127.

16. Samuel Rolles Driver, *The Book of Genesis*, Westminster Commentaries (London, 1916), 210–211.

17. For a broad discussion of this verb and humorous biblical narratives, see Athalya Brenner, "On the Semantic Field of Humor, Laughter, and the Comic in the Old Testament," in *On Humour and the Comic in the Hebrew Bible*, ed. Y. T. Radday and A. Brenner (JSOTSup 92: Sheffield, 1990), 46–52.

being "to laugh, jest, play, fool around" (as in Gen. 19:14), the other being "sexual activity" (as in Gen. 26:8 or 39:17).[18] The former, as we saw above, could be interpreted with either a positive or negative connotation, depending on the context. However, if the latter interpretation is what Ishmael was doing, Sarah's actions suddenly become understandable. Ishmael, who is not yet married, may be engaging in illicit sexual activity while under the same roof as his infant brother, which would alarm Sarah's motherly instinct. According to the chronological sequence of the Abraham cycle, Ishmael should be sixteen or seventeen at the time of his expulsion. Ishmael was born when Abraham was eighty-six (16:16), and was was circumcised at thirteen (17:25). Isaac was born one year later, when he was fourteen. Ishmael was expelled when Isaac was weaned, presumably two or three years later. Indeed, the latter definition of the verb *metzaḥek* would certainly be developmentally appropriate with regard to Ishmael.

If this is the case, it would seem that Ishmael was influenced by Canaanite sexual norms instead of the principles that govern his father's household. Ishmael is contrasted with Isaac, a son recently born into the already-present reality of a covenant through circumcision, a covenant that represents, among other things, higher sexual standards. As we have noted, all of the narratives since the Covenant of Circumcision relate to sexual ethics: the Sodomites who want to rape their guests (after Lot made them a feast); Lot's offer of his daughters; the incest between Lot and his daughters (after they made him drink wine); Abraham's wife in the house of Gerar; and finally Ishmael, who "fools

18. BDB, 850. The Akkadian verb *tzahu* has a double meaning as well: "to laugh, to smile, to be seductive, to sexually seduce (including acts outside of accepted norms)" (CAD, Ṣ, 64–65). The verb *tzaḥak*, "laughed," is found in Arabic, Syrian, and Ugaritic as well (Brenner, "On the Semantic Field of Humor, Laughter, and the Comic in the Old Testament," 46–47). On the relationship between the Akkadian and Hebrew verbs, see Joseph Fleishman, "The Expulsion of Ishmael," *Beit Mikra* 44 (1999): 154–155, and n41 in reference to additional studies. On the double meaning of the verb *tzaḥak* in Gen. 39:17, see Sternberg, "The Structure of Repetition in Biblical Narratives: Strategies of Informational Redundancy," 142–143; Polak, *Biblical Narrative Aspects of Art and Design*, 76; Grossman, *Ambiguity in the Biblical Narrative and Its Contribution to the Literary Formation*, 102–104.

around" after Abraham's feast, and is thus banished.[19] Aside from the obvious impropriety, Ishmael's behavior could be interpreted by Sarah as an indication that he has chosen to live by values not accepted in the Sarah-Abraham home. As such, she would be justified in demanding his expulsion.

Sarah's demand to banish the "slave's son" is better understood in light of the laws of the time. The Code of Hummurabi and documents found in Nuzi relate at length to the legal status of a maidservant offered by the wife for the purpose of childbearing. Scholars dispute the practical application that the Code of Hammurabi had in society, but nonetheless, they are in agreement that the code reflects active social-legal awareness.[20] Law 146 arranges the status of a maidservant, to prevent the mistress from selling her after she has borne children to the master, stating, "Because she has borne children, her mistress shall not sell her."[21] According to this law, and the similar law found in Nuzi, Sarah's demand is neither fair nor appropriate.[22] However, two other laws in the Hammurabi code clarify Sarah's demand. Law 170 states as follows:

> If his wife bear sons to a man, or his maidservant have borne sons, and the father while still living says to the children whom his maidservant has borne: "My sons," and he count them with the sons of his wife; if then the father die, then the sons of the

19. Reis ("Hagar Requited," 95–96) suggests that the word *metzaḥek* denotes inebriation: Ishmael drank at Abraham's feast (the word for feast, *mishteh*, is derived from the verb *lishtot* – "to drink," specifically drinking wine). The verb *metzaḥek* is also used with regard to Lot's view in the eyes of his sons-in-law (Gen. 19:4), and Lot, too, later shows an affinity with the bottle. Reis believes Ishmael's inebriation explains Ishmael's rapid dehydration the following day.
20. "The reasonable conclusion is that the judges rule according to legal norms and not according to the book. In other words, the legal codes reflect prevalent custom, and prevalent custom is not evidence of following the rulebook" (Jacob Joel Finkelstein, "*Mishpat, HaMishpat BaMizraḥ HaKadmon,*" *Entziklopedya Mikra'it* 5:611).
21. "Hammurabi's Code of Laws," *Exploring Ancient World Cultures,* trans. L. W. King, www.cawc.evansville.edu/index.htm.
22. Parrot, *Abraham and His Times,* 103–104.

> wife and of the maidservant shall divide the paternal property in common. The son of the wife is to partition and choose.

The following law (Law 171) states that if the father failed to call the sons of the maidservant "my sons" throughout his life, the sons of the maidservant cannot share in the goods of their father's house along with the sons of the first wife. They are released, and the first wife has no right to enslave them or their mother, but they have no status in their father's household.

Clearly Sarah disputes Ishmael's status in her statement, which explicitly refers to Ishmael as "the son of that slave," and not "Abraham's son." Perhaps Sarah's emphasis relates directly to the abovementioned law. Sarah links her demand to expel Ishmael to her concern for Isaac's inheritance – "for the son of that slave shall not share in the inheritance with my son Isaac." Although this claim is part of a broader issue that relates to Ishmael "playing,"[23] Sarah chooses to focus on the issue of inheritance. While there may be hefty emotional baggage behind Sarah's decision, she emphasizes the legal argument in her demand. Her case for Ishmael's expulsion carries legal validation in accordance with prevalent inheritance laws.

However, the verbal definition of the child as his father's son affects both the emotional bond and legal attitude toward that child. Therefore, when Abraham's displeasure with the idea is expressed in the following verse, Ishmael is fittingly referred to as "his son." The contours of Abraham's relationship with Ishmael is the source of disagreement between Abraham and Sarah.[24]

---

23. Norbert Lohfink ("ירש," *TDOT* 6:967) writes that Sarah's claim relates to Abraham's heir as the future head of the family, not just a bequeathing of property and possessions.
24. Nechama Leibowitz insists that Abraham views Ishmael as "his son" ("How to Read a Chapter of the Bible," 136). See Ina Willi-Plein, "Power or Inheritance: A Constructive Comparison of Genesis 16 and Genesis 21," in *Genesis, Isaiah and Psalms: A Festschrift to Honour Professor John Emerton for his Eightieth Birthday*, ed. K. J. Dell, G. Davies, and Y. Von Koh (VTSup 135: Leiden, 2010), 40. The situation seems to be more complex, however. While Abraham initially views Ishmael as "his son," when he sends him away in Gen. 21:14, Ishmael is once again referred to as "the boy." This internalization is the main process Abraham undergoes in the story. See Willi-Plein, ibid., 42.

This disagreement between Abraham and Sarah is not new or surprising – Sarah's difficulty with Hagar and Ishmael, coupled with Abraham's feeling of being torn between his two "families," has been a recurring motif throughout their shared story. Once again, Abraham heeds his wife's words. However, his love for and commitment to Hagar and their son do not allow him to expel the two quite as Sarah may have wished. Although Sarah uses the term "*garesh*," "cast out," in practice Abraham's actions are described with the word "*vayeshalḥeha,*" "he sent her away," using the legal term for freeing a slave. Abraham sends away "his son"; in that label he reaffirms his love for the boy, as well as assuring his legal status as a rightful heir.

Regardless, the general atmosphere of the episode is reminiscent of prevalent norms. The expulsion of Ishmael includes two elements that reflect the laws of the time. First, the laws relate to a situation in which the first wife births sons; otherwise, the status of the maid remains undisputed. The narrative opens with the birth of Isaac, which puts Ishmael's status into question. Second, both laws ultimately leave the status of the children to the father's discretion. The father's portrayal of his relationship with each boy determines whether they are legitimate sons, and this fact directly affects their rights as their father's heirs.[25]

Ishmael Is Sent to His Destiny

As we noted above, Abraham views Ishmael as his son (Gen. 21:11). This is apparent as early as the Covenant of Circumcision, when Abraham asks God to take care of Ishmael (17:18). Although God agrees with Sarah in principle,[26] He addresses Abraham's concern for his son: "But God said to Abraham: Do not be distressed over the boy or your

25. On the significance and ramification of the recognition of a child in Mesopotamian law, see Fleishman, "The Expulsion of Ishmael," 13–41. On the recognition of children in biblical literature, see Fleishman, ibid., 42–56. Fleishman believes that in biblical literature, the recognition of an individual as one's child is unrelated to the relationship between the parents. See Fleishman, ibid., 55–56.
26. "One could call vs. 12 f. the 'tense moment' in the structure of the narrative, for the reader has not expected that God would be on Sarah's side, but rather on Abraham's" (Von Rad, *Genesis*, 228).

maidservant; whatever Sarah tells you, do as she says, for it is through Isaac that offspring shall be continued for you. As for the son of the maidservant, I will make a nation of him, too, for he is your seed" (21:12–13). God refers to Ishmael as "the son of the maidservant," in correlation with Sarah's demand, but earlier he is referred to as "the boy" and Hagar as "your maidservant." God agrees with Sarah's demand, but not out of identification with her reason, though Isaac is the sole heir to Abraham's household and faith. But the expulsion will provide Ishmael with the opportunity to establish a nation of his own: "I will make a nation of him."

The term "son" or "child" links one with one's parents, while the term "boy" portrays Ishmael as an independent personality, with an independent potential.[27] Ishmael is not expelled as the son of the slave, but as a boy. While Sarah banishes him from Abraham's house to make room for Isaac, God focuses on Ishmael's own future. Ishmael is "the son of the maidservant," but also a "boy" who is Abraham's "seed."[28] As such, he is sent away to realize his potential and establish a nation.[29]

This new theme is expressed through the verb used in the expulsion of Ishmael. We noted earlier Sarah's demand of "cast out (*garesh*) that maidservant and her son," and while God agrees with this demand, "Whatever Sarah tells you, do as she says," Abraham only "sends her away

27. Cf. Hamilton, *The Book of Genesis, Chapters 18–50*, 81.

28. Grintz (*The Book of Genesis: Its Uniqueness and Antiquity*, 54) inaccurately wrote: "We now understand why the author explained, time and time again, that Ishmael is indeed Abraham's son.... In other words, despite the expulsion, Ishmael is still 'a son'!" However, God defines Ishmael as "the son of the maidservant," not the son of Abraham.

29. God also tells Abraham, "Do not be distressed over...your maidservant," whereas the narrative only expressed Abraham's concern about his son. While Bekhor Shor interprets the addition as God addressing Abraham's innermost fears (not only regarding Ishmael, but about Hagar as well), Reis ("Hagar Requited," 98) believes this to be a criticism of Abraham, who should have been more concerned with his servant. Both interpretations are supported by the fact that as opposed to Sarah, who calls Hagar "*that* maidservant," God calls Hagar "*your* maidservant."

(*vayeshalheha*)."[30] Although the verbs *garesh* and *shalaḥ* are frequently used as a pair (such as Ex. 6:1, 11:1), the connotations of each vary. G-R-SH implies a cruel eviction, while SH-L-Ḥ is a milder word, indicating that Ishmael is being "sent" from this home on to the next stage in his journey. Abraham did as Sarah had said, and as God had commanded him – but instead of casting Hagar out, harshly and cruelly, he simply sent her away.

The verb change touches on one of the essential themes of this narrative. The term G-R-SH ("cast out" or "drive off") is usually used in the context of expulsion *from* a particular place, with no regard for the destination. For example, in Exodus 2:17, the sheepherders came and "drove off" Reuel's daughters. The girls were free to go anywhere they pleased; the herders only wanted them to vacate the well.[31] In contrast, separations that focus on the destination rather than the origin frequently use the tern SH-L-Ḥ ("send away"). For example, in Genesis 8:8, Noah "sent out (*vayeshalaḥ*) the dove to see whether the waters had decreased." Similarly, the angels tell Lot regarding Sodom that "the Lord has sent us (*vayeshalḥenu*) to destroy it" (Gen. 19:13).

This distinction is particularly notable in the expulsion of Adam from the Garden of Eden. There, both verbs appear side by side: "So the Lord God sent him (*vayeshalḥehu*) from the Garden of Eden to till the soil from which he was taken. He drove the man out (*vayegaresh*) and stationed east of the garden the cherubim and the fiery ever-turning sword, to guard the way of the tree of life" (3:23–25). The verbs are carefully placed in correlation with the content, indicating two separate movements – going out *from* a place, and moving *toward* a destination.[32] God *sends* (SH-L-Ḥ) Adam "to till the soil

30. The verb *shalaḥ* is also used to describe Abraham's separation from the sons of his concubines: "But to Abraham's sons by concubines Abraham gave gifts while he was still living, and he sent them away" (Gen. 25:6).
31. Similar examples include Ex. 33:2, Job 30:5.
32. Note the wordplay between "the Lord God sent him" and God's concern in the previous verse, "lest he send his hand (*pen yishlaḥ yado*) and take also from the Tree of Life." According to Cassuto (*A Commentary on the Book of Genesis: From Adam to Noah*, trans. Israel Abrahams [Jerusalem: Magnes Press, 1961], 173), "God

from which he was taken." The emphasis of this verse is on the destination and purpose to which Adam was sent. The following verse, which emphasizes the involuntary separation from the Garden of Eden, reads "He drove the man out (*vayegaresh*)." This verse emphasizes the origin, not the destination.[33]

This distinction touches on one of the essential themes of the expulsion of Ishmael. Sarah's goal is to distance Ishmael from Abraham's home, to prevent him from inheriting with Isaac. Abraham is unhappy about the demand, but God's revelation supports Sarah's position. However, the revelation also revealed new information about the banished son: "As for the son of the maidservant, I will make a nation of him, too, for he is your seed" (Gen. 21:13). Apparently, Abraham's son has a glowing future outside his father's home. Sending Ishmael away no longer has to be viewed as an expulsion, but rather as a branching out of Abraham's family. This is, at least, the intention. However, soon after their departure, Hagar and Ishmael find themselves on the brink of starvation, dying in the wilderness.

Ishmael's Salvation

Hagar's pain and frustration at being expelled from the house of her master and the father of her child is but a prelude to a greater suffering: looking on helplessly as her son perishes in the desert. Hagar, the discarded slave and suffering mother, has been a sympathetic character. As the episode in the wilderness evolves, Hagar's affability wanes. The wilderness is cruel, and as their journey continues, Hagar and Ishmael find themselves in mortal danger. At this point, Hagar seems to cruelly abandon her son in his time of need, and Ishmael emerges from the scene having pivoted to the role of protagonist, now with a compelling origin story to accompany him.

The use of the root SH-L-KH, in opposition to the other words we have found, must be examined in this scene. Hagar "cast off (*vatashlekh*) the boy under one of the bushes" (21:15). The verb

---

did not just 'send him forth,' an act that would not have precluded all possibility of his returning, but 'He drove him out' – completely."

33. See further in Jonathan Grossman, *Creation: The Story of Beginnings*, 106–107.

could easily have been replaced with a more moderate phrase such as, "And she put the child into it and placed it (*vatasem*) among the reeds by the bank of the Nile" (Ex. 2:3). "Casting off" is more often associated with casting away inanimate objects or corpses.[34] Other narratives that describe people being "cast off" intend to express unique violence and a deliberate annulment of humanity. This is the case with Joseph's brothers who "took him and cast him (*vayashlikhu*) into the pit" (Gen. 37:24), and in Jeremiah, "So they took Jeremiah and they cast him (*vayashlikhu*) into the pit" (Jer. 38:6, 9). Additionally, Ishmael is referred to as "the boy" in this scene, rather than "her son." The narrative is designed to create a distance between Hagar and Ishmael. She could only bring herself to "cast him off," dissociating herself from him. Hagar's distance from her son is repeated three times.

Hagar positions herself "*kemitḥavei keshet,*" "a bowshot away," a phrase which appears nowhere else in biblical literature. Hagar's abandonment of her son is a violent act of maternal rejection. The reader might empathize with Hagar's difficulty at watching her son's suffering, but her actions are unthinkable from a mother's perspective. She brings his death closer by leaving him alone, by failing to hold his hand in his final hours. The psychological effect of Hagar's distance echoes loudly in Ishmael's choice of profession later in life, when he becomes an archer (Gen. 21:20).[35] References to bows and arrows are relatively rare in biblical narratives. The mention of this weapon twice in one narrative implies a link between the two appearances. In light of the above, one might say Ishmael experiences his mother's distancing as

34. BDB, 1020–1021.

35. The Septuagint reads, "And he grew and dwelt in the wilderness, and became an archer." The Masoretic text, which reads "*roveh kashat*" is repetitive (sometimes translated as "great archer" or "skillful archer," but more literally translates as "archer bowman"). For this reason, some prefer *keshet* (Zipor, *The Septuagint Version of the Book of Genesis*, 263) or *kashet* (Gunkel, *Genesis – Translated and Interpreted*, 229). According to the latter version, the link between Hagar's distance ("a bowshot away") and Ishmael's profession (*roveh keshet*) is enhanced. It is possible that "*roveh*" should be understood as a an older youth (as in Gen. 25:23).

abandonment. Ishmael spends his life trying to bridge that distance, by shooting at what is out of reach.[36]

In the midst of this pitiful, tragic scene, Hagar bursts into tears. One verse later, God reacts to the cries – of Ishmael: "God heard the cry of the boy" (Gen. 21:17). This is the first we hear of Ishmael's cries. Until this point, the text laid its scene with the tragic mother at the center, coping with the unbearable pain of watching her son suffer. Hagar finally breaks down, and the text prepares the reader for God's reaction to Hagar's emotional outburst, only to surprise the reader with God's reaction to the crying of the boy. While Hagar distanced herself from her son, God heard his cry. The angel's implicit reprimand of Hagar reinforces this assumption: "What troubles you, Hagar? Fear not, for God has heeded *the cry of the boy* where he is." The angel notes ironically that while Hagar abandoned her son, God heard his cries, "where[ever] he is." The angel therefore calls Hagar to action, "Come, lift up the boy and hold him by the hand."[37] The situation requires the support of a mother, despite Hagar's distress.[38] Interestingly, despite the fact that Ishmael's name takes on new meaning – "for God (*Elohim*) has heeded (*shama*) the cry of the boy" – he is not mentioned by name even here.

This episode is the origin story of the character Ishmael that will become a great nation, as his mother was promised all those years ago in the wilderness. In order to claim his destiny, Ishmael undergoes this excruciating initiation. Banished from the house of his father, and then

36. Alternatively, one might say that Ishmael adopted his mother's attitude toward stressful situations, in creating distance. He shoots at far-away things, not needing to look his prey in the eye. His arrow does the job while he stands at a comfortable distance.

37. Trible (*Texts of Terror: Literary-Feminist Readings of Biblical Narratives*, 20) notes the use of the word "*yad*," "hand," which characterized Hagar's flight, rebellion, and suffering (Gen. 16:6, 9, 12). Trible reads the narratives as one unit, and points to a decline in Hagar's emotional state. She views the Sarah-Hagar relationship as the focal point of both narratives, and sees no implied criticism of Hagar, who is caught in a conspiracy to prefer Sarah's offspring to the son of the Egyptian maidservant.

38. I disagree with Benno Jacob's assumption that "although she says that the child will die and that she does not want to see it die, she sits within sight waiting for help" (Jacob, *The First Book of the Bible: Genesis*, 138). I believe the narrative emphasizes the fact that Hagar distances herself, and there is no indication that she seeks help.

cast aside to die by his mother. Although the words do not share a root, the actions of both parents have a similar sound: *vayeshalḥeha* ("he sent her away"), and *vatashlekh* ("she cast [him] off").[39]

In his darkest hour, after both parents had abandoned Ishmael, only God could hear Ishmael's cry. God will be with him in the wilderness, where he will grow and become a great nation. We already know that Ishmael will fulfill his destiny outside the house of Abraham. This destiny is reinforced by the angel's words, "For I will make a great nation of him." "A great nation" is, of course, reminiscent of Abraham's blessings, but the combination of great nation and the verb "*asimenu,*" "I will make him," is used only in one other biblical narrative. In God's revelation to Jacob on the eve of his descent to Egypt, He tells Jacob: "Fear not to go down to Egypt, for I will make you there (*asimekha*) into a great nation" (Gen. 46:3).[40] Like Ishmael, Jacob is forced to leave his home and the land of his fathers. God's encouragement at this crossroads is based on the assumption that Jacob's great destiny can only be realized through a disengagement from his homeland. He will become a great nation – but in Egypt. The angel similarly encourages Hagar. Ishmael will fulfill his destiny far from Abraham's home, and will become a great nation – but only in the wilderness.[41]

The Story of Two Sons

Starting from both the literal and figurative conception of Isaac and Ishmael's story, these narratives demand a comparison. Is this the story of a "rough draft" (Ishmael) that was discarded once the "real deal" (Isaac) came along? Perhaps it is the bedrock on which an eons-long brotherly rivalry is forged? Most likely it is both, and each story, as each father-son relationship contributes to Abraham's journey as a father and a patriarch. This is one narrative with two different focal points, built in a chiastic structure:

39. Hamilton, *The Book of Genesis, Chapters 18–50*, 83.
40. Mathews, *Genesis*, 274.
41. The promise creates yet another link between the Covenant of Circumcision and the flight of Hagar, which was addressed in the analysis of Gen. 16. Here the context of the link is the fulfillment of both promises: God accompanies those who were banished, and will see that they become a great nation in another land.

- **A: God's blessing – the birth of Isaac (Gen. 21:1–5)**
  - **B: Sarah laughs at the birth of her son (vv. 6–7):** Sarah said, "God has brought me *laughter*; everyone who hears will *laugh* with me." And she added, "Who would have said to Abraham that Sarah *would suckle children*! Yet I have borne a son in his old age."
    - **C: Abraham and the weaned Isaac (v. 8):** Abraham held a *great feast* on the day that Isaac was *weaned.*
      - **D: Sarah demands Ishmael's expulsion (vv. 9–11):** *The matter distressed* Abraham greatly, for it concerned a son of his.
      - **D': God supports Sarah's demand (vv. 12–13):** But God said to Abraham, "Do not *be distressed* over the boy or your slave..."
    - **C': Abraham and the expelled Ishmael (v. 14):** Abraham rose the next morning, took some bread and *a skin of water,* and gave them to Hagar. He placed them over her shoulder, together with the child, and *sent her away.*
  - **B': Hagar cries at the dying of her son (vv. 14–16):** And she wandered about in the wilderness of Beersheba. *When the water was gone from the skin,* she cast off the child under one of the bushes, and went and sat down at a distance, a bowshot away; for she thought, "Let me not look on as the child dies." And sitting thus afar, *she burst into tears.*
- **A': God's blessing – the rebirth of Ishmael (vv. 17–21)**

The structure of the narrative emphasizes the contrast between the birth of Isaac and the expulsion of Ishmael. Before Isaac was born, there was no disputing Ishmael's place and standing in his father's house; once Isaac is born, the status of the son of the slave is questioned, and he is sent away. The structure represents the story of the two brothers. The first part is about a brother who entered the house of Abraham, and the second part is about the brother who had to leave the house of Abraham. Sarah's demand (D) belongs to the first half of the narrative, since from Sarah's perspective the purpose of Ishmael's banishment is to eliminate possible competition for Isaac's inheritance and position as Abraham's heir. In contrast, the divine revelation that supports Sarah's demand (D') belongs to the second part, which contains a promise that Ishmael will become a great nation. The divine revelation is the introduction to the Ishmael narrative.[42]

The parallel emphasizes different parental situations with regard to their children; this difference is particularly apparent in the description of the two mothers (B–B'). Sarah, who finally "holds" the son she had endlessly prayed for, laughs joyously, while Hagar "casts off" her son, is forced to distance herself from his fate, and turns away to cry in misery. While Sarah is delighted by the abundance of milk that fills her breasts for her baby, Hagar watches her dying son without an ability to provide him with the water of life. A similar distinction is apparent in the father's description in relation to each of his sons (C–C'). Abraham celebrates the day of Isaac's independence from his mother with a great feast, while Abraham sends Ishmael away with only enough bread and water to sustain him until he reaches his final destination, far from Abraham's home.

The two parallel halves of the narrative contrast the happy parents who bring a new child into their home, and the unhappy parents who are forced to separate from their son. Since Ishmael and Isaac have different mothers, the distinction between them becomes clearer throughout the plot, but the contrast in Abraham's relationship with each of his sons is more complex. The heart of the transformation in the story involves the development of Abraham's character. Initially he is "distressed" over the expulsion of "his son" (Gen. 21:11) and is reluctant to listen to Sarah, until God Himself intervenes and tells him not to be distressed. In God's revelation, Ishmael is referred to as "the boy" (v. 12),[43] and when Abraham finally sends Ishmael away, he is "the child" – not "his child" (v. 14).

42. Garsiel (*Biblical Names: A Literary Study of Midrashic Derivations and Puns*, 156) notes that the names Isaac and Ishmael have opposite meanings in the narrative. Sarah saw Ishmael *metzaḥek* ("laughing" or "playing") and God told Abraham *shema bekola* ("listen to her"). The structure of the story parallels these two statements.

43. See, among others, Hamilton, *The Book of Genesis, Chapters 18–50*, 81.

The two reversed parts of the story focus on the development of two characters: Abraham and Ishmael. Abraham internalizes the fact that Ishmael is not "his son," and will not be the one to "carry on his name." This development is linked with Ishmael's changing status; initially he is to be "driven off" or banished; but in reality he is "sent away." The focus is not on Ishmael leaving the house of his father, but rather on the destiny that awaits him in the desert, where God will accompany him and bless him.

Against this background, I wish to explore the narrative frame (A–A'). As we already mentioned, the two halves of the story mirror each other, pitting Isaac's relationship with his parents against Ishmael and his parents. The two frame components, however, do not oppose each other. God initially blesses Sarah and her son, and eventually blesses Hagar and her son; not only by saving Ishmael from thirst, but by watching him closely as he grows up: "God was with the boy, and he grew up" (Gen. 21:20). This connection shows that Ishmael's rescue is configured as a rebirth. In the fiery heat of the desert, God appears and drags him from death's door by opening his mother's eyes. In a certain sense, Abraham's circumcision of Isaac (A) is parallel to Ishmael's marriage, arranged by Hagar (A'), as both are related to fertility and family continuity. Thus, in parallel to Isaac's naming at the beginning of the chapter, the episode concludes with an implicit explanation for Ishmael's name: "And God heard (*vayishma*) the cry of the boy.... Fear not, for God has heard (*shama*) the cry of the boy" (21:17). Perhaps the reason Ishmael's name is omitted from the text until this point is that he had lost the name given to him by his father when he lost his status, and had to regain an independent name through his rebirth. His name represents the reason for his rescue: God had heard Ishmael's prayers, and helped him when his own parents had abandoned him, in the theme of Psalms 27:10, "Though my father and mother abandoned me, the Lord will take me in." God opened Hagar's eyes so she could sustain her son, just as Sarah nursed her child.[44] Finally, Isaac's growth to maturity ("the child grew up") is mirrored by Ishmael's development, but while Isaac's

44. The Septuagint reads, "God opened her eyes, and she saw a well of *water of life*" (Zipor, *The Septuagint Version of the Book of Genesis*, 261) in correlation with

development is accompanied by his father, who celebrates his weaning with a great feast, Ishmael is accompanied by a surrogate father who accompanies him to maturity: "God was with the boy and he grew up."

Perhaps Ishmael is portrayed as a young boy because the narrative is designed as a birth story. While a simple calculation of the chronological data proves that Ishmael is not a child but a young man, his rebirth necessitates a depiction of one who is placed to be carried by Hagar, and requires the protection of adults. Only at the end of the story does the boy "grow up." Ishmael, who is abandoned under one of the bushes, is like a fetus waiting to burst into reality. This transformation can only occur far from Abraham's house, in the wilderness.[45]

The concluding verses clarify how the Ishmaelite tribes, the archers, settled in the desert, and explain their link to Egypt. God is with the boy and he grows up. He dwells in the wilderness and becomes a bowman. He lives in the wilderness of Paran, and his mother obtains a wife for him from the land of Egypt (Gen. 21:20–21). The verses also conclude the final separation of Ishmael from his father.[46] The involvement of the mother in her son's marriage is unusual, particularly in light of the fact that Ishmael is portrayed as a grown man who has developed a livelihood and has settled in Paran. Instead of Ishmael "taking a wife,"

Gen. 26:19. Some scholars prefer this version (e.g., Ball, *The Book of Genesis*, 73), which emphasizes Ishmael's rebirth: the well symbolizes a new life for the dying boy.

45. Some central motifs of this scene are narrative conventions symbolizing "rebirth," which feature in both biblical and extra-biblical literature. In this context, the motif of the child's separation from his parents as a prerequisite to rebirth is especially noteworthy. See more in Jonathan Grossman and Sara Daniel, "'Like Arrows in the Hand of the Warrior, So Are Youths': Reading Ishmael's Expulsion in Genesis 21 in Light of Hermann Hesse's 'Siddhartha,'" *Hebrew Studies* 57 (2016): 73–91; Jonathan Grossman, "The Expulsion of Ishmael Narrative – Boundaries, Structure and Meaning," in *Doubling and Duplicating in the Book of Genesis: Literary and Stylistic Approaches to the Text*, ed. Elizabeth R. Hayes and Karolien Vermeulen (Winona Lake, IN, 2016), 27–37.

46. Mathews (*Genesis*, 274) writes, "He is the son of a slave woman, married to an Egyptian, lives outside normal social bounds, and is remembered for his hostilities." See also Benno Jacob, *The First Book of the Bible: Genesis*, 193. According to an etiological reading of this narrative, this is not only the geographical location, but the cultural location as well: the reader is exposed to the source of their independence, and the chronicle that led to their savagery.

his mother arranges one for him from her homeland. The description is generally incongruent with the book of Genesis, in which fathers – not the mothers – take a wife for their sons from their place of origin, or send a messenger in their place (Gen. 24; 28:1–5; 29:19; 34:4; 38:6, 8; 41:45).[47] The narrative alludes to why Abraham is not the one to obtain Ishmael's wife. Hagar's continued involvement indicates that Ishmael was not abandoned in the desert, and he continues to be cared for by his mother. Hagar appropriately selects a wife for her son from her place of origin; the conclusion of the story therefore determines that Ishmael is Hagar's son, not Abraham's.[48]

The culmination of the narrative ending with Ishmael in Beersheba would have been appropriate, a place where Hagar had lost her way, and where Ishmael nearly dies and is miraculously reborn. However, had Ishmael settled in Beersheba, he would have been "too close" to Abraham and Isaac. Beersheba is an integral part of Canaan, and at times a holy site for the Israelite nation. The unrealized anticipation that Ishmael should end up in Beersheba emphasizes the distance between him and Abraham. Ultimately, Ishmael's marriage to an Egyptian woman places him on the Egyptian side of the border with his mother, instead of the Canaanite side with Abraham.[49]

Hagar's Return to the Wilderness

Hagar finds herself once again expelled from her masters' home and on the brink of disaster in the wilderness. Hagar as a character has proven

47. Hamilton (*The Book of Genesis, Chapters 18–50*, 85–86) is mistaken in writing that Hagar providing Ishmael with a wife was the prevalent custom. The father was responsible for marrying his children, not the mother.
48. Hamilton (ibid., 86) notes that just as Abraham took a wife for his son from his homeland (Gen. 24), Hagar has Ishmael marrying an Egyptian from her homeland: "An Egyptian with an Egyptian and an Aramean with an Aramean."
49. Ultimately, the reader associates Beersheba with Abraham, and so it turns out that although Ishmael separated from his father and was "born again," he also continues his father's blessing. One can read with similar ambivalence the process that Ruth goes through, who starts anew in Beit Lehem but also maintain the name of her deceased husband. See further in Jonathan Grossman, "Reading Ruth with Winnicott: Boaz and Naomi as 'Transitional Objects,'" in *Gleanings: Interdisciplinary Reflections on Ruth*, ed. Stuart Halpern (New Milford, CT, and Jerusalem: Maggid Books, 2019), 25–38.

infinitely versatile, her story providing a foil for Sarah and Abraham's development as a couple and as parents. Her son becomes the anti-hero rival of Abraham's heir. At the same time, Abraham's compassion is put to the test when he is forced to choose between his progeny, and his development as a father is underscored in how he reacts in each situation. Now, once more, Hagar finds herself in need of divine mercy, and God intervenes, modeling a precedent of compassion that recognizes no bloodline.

The literary and grammatical parallels between Hagar's two jaunts into the wilderness are apparent.[50] The differences between the stories allow us a glimpse into how the characters involved have developed since the first story began. Both stories follow this general outline:

1. Hagar, along with her son (in the womb in Gen. 16 and on her shoulders in Gen. 21), is separated from the house of Abraham.
2. Both separations are linked with Sarah (her actions or demand).
3. Hagar and her fetus/son venture into the wilderness in the south.
4. God's angel appears to Hagar in the vicinity of water and blesses her offspring.
5. Ishmael's name is given significance in each of the episodes. While he is named in Genesis 16 in commemoration of God hearing Hagar's suffering, his name is given a new and independent meaning when God hears his suffering in Genesis 21.

The two narratives are also linked through similar language:

1. Abram "heeded (*vayishma*) Sarai's request" in Genesis 16:2, while in Genesis 21:12, God commands Abraham, "Whatever Sarah tells you do as she says (*shema bekola*)."[51]

---

50. Cf. Thomas B. Dozeman, "The Wilderness and Salvation History in the Hagar Story," *JBL* 117 (1998): 23–43; Willi-Plein, "Power or Inheritance: A Constructive Comparison of Genesis 16 and Genesis 21," 33–44.
51. Needless to say the verb *shema* ("to hear") carries unique significance in the Ishmael narratives. See Garsiel, *Biblical Names: A Literary Study of Midrashic Derivations and Puns*, 121, who writes that *shema* is a key word in Gen. 16.

2. Both narratives feature the motif or keywords of "*shema*" ("to hear") and "*re'eh*" ("to see").[52] In Genesis 16, the pair affects the naming of the child (*yishmael*) and of the place (*el-ro'i*).[53]
3. In both narratives the angel addresses Hagar with a question: "Hagar, slave of Sarai, where have you come from, and where are you going?" (16:8); "What troubles you, Hagar?" (21:17).

Although the stories are similar, there are significant differences between them. The distinguishing elements in each narrative emphasize specific factors that contribute to the individual purpose of each of the narratives; by contrasting the narratives, we may define the unique purpose of each one.

- *The Protagonist:* The protagonist of the story of Hagar's flight (Gen. 16) is Sarai. The narrative opens with Sarai's barrenness and ownership of an Egyptian maidservant (16:1); Sarai initiates the idea of using Hagar as a surrogate mother (16:2), and makes this suggestion to Abram, while focusing on her personal gain, saying, "Perhaps I shall have a son through her." Abram "heeded Sarai's request," once again emphasizing that Sarai is the active and leading character in the story, while Abram is entirely passive: his opinions are not expressed, he fails to investigate the matter; he just listens to his wife. As we noted in our analysis of Genesis 16, Sarai's dominance is expressed through the use of the verb L-K-Ḥ ("to take/to marry") in relation to Hagar: "So Sarai... *took* her maid... and gave her to her husband Abram as concubine" (16:3). While Abram will be the one to have marital relations with Hagar, Sarai is the one who "marries her." The plot is therefore driven by Sarai. She initiates Hagar's

52. Regarding this pair of keywords in the biblical narrative, see Amos Frisch, "SH-M-A and R-E-H as a Pair of Leitwörter," *Proceeding of the Twelfth World Congress of Jewish Studies* Division A (1999): 89–98; Samuel L. Terrien, *The Elusive Presence: Toward a New Biblical Theology* (San Francisco, 1978). Regarding the pair of verbs in relation to the link between the two narratives, see also Trible, *Texts of Terror: Literary-Feminist Readings of Biblical Narratives*, 26.
53. Garsiel, *Biblical Names: A Literary Study of Midrashic Derivations and Puns*, 119.

relationship with Abram, she suffers the implications of that relationship and chooses to react by mistreating Hagar, and she drives Hagar away by reacting as she does. Abraham, for his part, seems to stand idly by. In Genesis 21, too, Sarah seemingly initiates the expulsion (21:10), but this time, Abraham takes a clear stand: "The matter distressed Abraham greatly" (21:11).[54] Abraham undergoes a process of change throughout the narrative. He initially views Ishmael as "his son," but ultimately recognizes that he is merely "the child"; he is initially distressed, but ultimately understands that the expulsion of Ishmael is part of God's plan. Abraham is more active as well. He rises early, prepares food for the journey, helps Hagar pack, and sends her off. The expulsion narrative emphasizes Abraham's actions in light of the change he undergoes.[55]

- *The Content and Recipient of the Blessing (and the Judgment of Hagar):* We already mentioned the literary links between Hagar's flight and the preceding narrative – the Covenant of Circumcision – in our analysis of Genesis 16. Hagar's character is compared to the offspring of Abraham, who are sentenced to suffer under Egyptian rule but promised that they would someday be free.[56] Hagar is therefore compared to Abraham, in that she, too, would merit land and the blessing of fertility.[57] Hagar's blessing is a compensation for her suffering, and a reward for returning to Sarai's home as she was instructed by the angel. In the parallel expulsion narrative, Hagar once again hears a blessing by the angel of God; however, this time the blessing is not

54. Von Rad, *Genesis*, 227.
55. Cf. Yair Zakovitch, "The Exodus from Egypt in Genesis," *Al Haperek* 3 (1987): 32n6.
56. Trible (*Texts of Terror: Literary-Feminist Readings of Biblical Narratives*, 20) also compares Gen. 21 to the Exodus from Egypt, but her interpretation is that the comparison between Israel and Hagar portrays Hagar as disadvantaged and wronged, as opposed to the Israelite nation, who had God at their side throughout the process.
57. This detail is especially prominent if one accepts Philip Drey's position that the placement of Hagar's escape between the two covenants affects the reading of the story (Drey, "The Role of Hagar in Genesis 16," *AUSS* 40 [2002]: 179–195). However, he believes Hagar's escape is a fulfillment of the promise of great nations, since God saved Hagar's son and promised her that he would become a great nation.

> addressed to her directly, but to her son. The angel does not offer Hagar a new blessing. He simply reveals God's promise to Abraham, using the same words, "I will make a (great) nation of him too" (Gen. 21:13). Since Hagar's actions are criticized in the narrative, there is no justification for a new blessing. The reason for the blessing is not Hagar's suffering, or her distress; Ishmael is blessed in this case because he is Abraham's son. In contrast with Genesis 16, the blessing of Ishmael is not compensation or reward; it is part of God's historical plan for Abraham and his descendants.[58]

These are the two central differences between the narratives. There are a number of other differences worth noting:

- The reason for Hagar's flight is her relationship with Sarai. Hagar does not show respect toward her mistress, and as a result Sarai mistreats her, a tension that leads to Hagar's escape. In contrast, the reason for Hagar's expulsion in Genesis 21 is Ishmael's conduct, and the issue of the inheritance of Ishmael and Isaac. In other words, the reason for the expulsion involves the relationships of the next generation.[59]
- In the escape narrative, Hagar is the initiator of the separation from Abram's household. Abram and Sarai are not even aware

58. F. Charles Fensham, "The Son of a Handmaid in Northwest Semitic," *VT* 19 (1969): 318. Trible (*Texts of Terror: Literary-Feminist Readings of Biblical Narratives*, 22) writes that now that Ishmael received a second blessing, this time as Abraham's offspring, the blessing to Hagar become obsolete, and her significance is diminished. There is no justification for reading the second blessing as a replacement of the first; Trible prefers this interpretation, which supports her claim that Hagar is discriminated against. In this context, I disagree with Ehrlich (*Mikra KiFeshuto*, 57–58) who writes, "The first story [the escape of Hagar] indicates what God will do for those who are part of the household of Abraham our forefather – even for a maidservant. The last story [the expulsion] shows that God would change His ways when the attendant is no longer part of Abraham's household." I believe the opposite to be true: the first story portrays Hagar as an independent personality, while in the second she only merits her blessing due to her relationship with Abraham!
59. Van Seters, *Abraham in History and Tradition*, 39; Willi-Plein, "Power or Inheritance: A Constructive Comparison of Genesis 16 and Genesis 21," 199–200.

of her decision to flee, and God is uninvolved until He addresses Hagar's distress in the wilderness. In contrast, in the expulsion narrative, the separation from Abraham's house is initiated by divine decree.

- When Hagar escapes to the wilderness, the angel suggests a name for her unborn child, and her son is indeed named Ishmael by Abram.[60] In contrast, Ishmael's name is not mentioned once in the expulsion narrative. This detail contributes to the independent purpose of each narrative. In the expulsion narrative, Ishmael is blessed by the merit of being Abraham's offspring, while in the escape story, Hagar receives blessings for Ishmael independently of Abram.
- The revelation: When Hagar flees, the angel finds her by a spring and speaks with her. The conversation is direct and personal, as though two people were speaking with each other. This quasi-human element is emphasized in the fact that the angel "found her" (Gen. 16:7).[61] In the expulsion story the angel did not "find Hagar," and he does not converse with her. Rather, he "called to Hagar from heaven" to deliver his divine message.[62]
- An additional distinction, which led to the narrative's separation into various sources, is the use of different names for God in each of the narratives: the name *YHWH* is used throughout the escape narrative, while the name *Elohim* is prevalent in the expulsion narrative.

60. When Hagar escaped in Gen. 16, both Ishmael and the well are given names, as opposed to Gen. 21, where only Ishmael was named (Garsiel, *Biblical Names: A Literary Study of Midrashic Derivations and Puns,* 119). See also Skinner, *A Critical and Exegetical Commentary on Genesis,* 324; Thomas Desmond Alexander, "The Hagar Traditions in Genesis 16 and 21," in *Studies in the Pentateuch,* ed. J. A. Emerton, VTSup 41 (Leiden: Brill, 1990), 133. Gunkel (*Genesis – Translated and Interpreted,* 229) believes the expulsion story originally included a naming of the well, which was omitted due to the alternative name in the following chapter.
61. The root M-TZ-A, which denotes "to find," is used in the context of direct contact (e.g., Gen. 37:15–16). Ehrlich (*Mikra KiFeshuto,* 57) notes that the phrase implies a chance meeting.
62. As opposed to Gunkel (*Genesis – Translated and Interpreted,* 228), who viewed the conversation as divine, similar to the Burning Bush.

The different objectives in each of the stories can be understood in light of these differences. Hagar's flight is a personal-ethical narrative, involving a quarrel between a maidservant and her mistress, causing the maidservant to flee. She is ultimately encouraged to return to her former position by an angel of God, who promises her compensation for her suffering. The plot is driven by the choices made by the characters in the narrative: Sarai offers Hagar to Abram, Hagar does not show respect to her mistress, and then Sarai is unkind to her maidservant. God becomes involved in the narrative only after Hagar escaped, in response to her distress and unfair treatment. The dialogues in the narrative are all personal and intimate: Sarai complains to Abram and he responds, the angel speaks to Hagar and encourages her, and the angel even suggests a name for her unborn child. The name *YHWH* is appropriately used for God, who becomes involved at a personal level and is even concerned with the distress of a suffering maidservant.

In contrast with the escape narrative, the expulsion narrative is an extension of the historical-national axis of the Abraham cycle. This is a story about the implementation of God's plan. Even if Sarah initiates the expulsion, she is not the force behind the plot, which is ultimately only implemented because of God's revelation to Abraham. This is not a personal or private quarrel between two characters. Instead, the argument relates to the essential issues of Abraham's inheritance and Abraham's heir. Sarah's motive is not personal. She acts out of concern for the legal status of her son. God's intervention in the argument between Sarah and Abraham is crucial, since the main purpose of the story is to distance Ishmael from Abraham and his chosen offspring. Statements regarding the establishment of the nation (such as, "For it is through Isaac that offspring shall be continued for you," in Gen. 21:12) are entirely absent from the escape narrative. Ishmael's "rebirth" and blessing are part of the fundamental theme of Abraham's choice: even Abraham's rejected sons are blessed, and they, too, fulfill the blessing to Abraham that he will be "the father of a multitude of nations," despite the fact that they do not inherit his covenant with God.

The personal tone that accompanied Hagar's flight is absent from the expulsion narrative. While Ishmael's name is given in the initial narrative, in the expulsion story he is not referred to by name, but rather by his position ("son," "boy"); he is a nameless child. The angel in the expulsion narrative appears to Hagar "from heaven," as opposed to the personal treatment she had received previously. The name *Elohim* reflects the universal administration of history by God. This is the appropriate name for a narrative that points history in the direction of the divine plan.

This essential distinction is expressed in the formulation of the blessing Hagar receives.[63] When she flees from Sarai, the angel blesses her with a multiplicity of offspring: "I will greatly increase your offspring" (Gen. 16:10). However, when she is expelled from Abraham's home, the angel blesses Hagar with the promise that "a great nation" will come from Ishmael. As mentioned in the introduction, the word nation, "*goy*," has national connotations, and features appropriately in the context of Ishmael's expulsion. This, too, is the expression of the distinction between a narrative about choice and rejection, which includes a general national message (Gen. 21) and a personal-ethical narrative, whose purpose is to support and encourage a woman in distress (Gen. 16).

The main difference between the two narratives relates to Hagar and Ishmael's status. In the private story of a maidservant who escaped from her mistress out of misery, God addresses Hagar and compensates her for her suffering. In contrast, Ishmael's expulsion is part of God's original plan, which is mapped out before Abraham knows he will father Isaac (Gen. 17:19–21).

The protagonist of each of the narratives is changed accordingly. Abraham was chosen to father a new nation. Therefore, the narrative describing the choice of Isaac and the rejection of Ishmael focuses on Abraham. The reader is exposed to his dismay, and to his ultimate decision (after God's encouragement) to disinherit the son of the maidservant. Abraham is also the one to actively send away Hagar and her son. Sarah represents the personal yearning of a simple couple for a child, and the household that reflects Abraham's education and personality, independent of the broader national and divine context. Therefore, she plays a defining role in Hagar's flight, which is a story of personal and internal affairs in Abraham's household and family.

63. See further in Grossman, "Hagar's Characterization in Genesis and the Explanation of Ishmael's Blessing."

Ishmael's position differs from that of the other rejected members of Abraham's family (Lot and Esau). In Genesis 16, he receives an independent blessing that is unrelated to his relationship with Abraham. Perhaps this is also the explanation for Ishmael's place of dwelling in the desert of Paran, south of Canaan, in contrast with Lot and Esau who inherited areas east of the Jordan River.

In earlier expulsions in Genesis, those who were rejected from before God went to the east. Adam went east of the Garden of Eden (Gen. 3:24),[64] and after Cain murders his brother, he also "left the presence of the Lord and settled in the land of Nod, *east* of Eden" (4:16).[65] Lot chooses the Transjordan, and travels east (13:9–13) to what became the land of his descendants, Ammon and Moab. Esau travels to Seir, south of the Transjordan and east of Canaan. And the sons of Abraham's concubines are sent away "eastward, to the land of the East" (25:6). As mentioned in the discussion of Genesis 14, Cassuto has demonstrated the link between their settling east of Canaan, and Moses' warning to the Israelite nation that they may not conquer those areas, which were given as an inheritance by God (Deut. 2:4–20),[66] while Ishmael's absence is notable in the verses discussing portions of land surrounding Canaan that were given by God as an inheritance to Abraham's offspring. The absence is linked with another anomaly: Ishmael is Abraham's only rejected offspring who fails to settle in the east, and chooses instead to settle in the desert of Paran (Gen. 21:20–21).

The story of Ishmael's expulsion seems to function as an etiological explanation for this anomaly.[67] Hagar's flight, Ishmael's expulsion, and the double revelation in the wilderness explain why the Ishmaelites

64. See Cassuto, *A Commentary on The Book of Genesis: From Adam to Noah*, 174.

65. See Claus Westermann, *Genesis 1–11: A Continental Commentary*, trans. J. J. Scullion (Minneapolis, 1994), 314 ("It is not a piece of geographical information but a reference to life 'outside,' in a state of alienation from God").

66. Cassuto, *A Commentary on The Book of Genesis: From Noah to Abraham*, 367.

67. Noort writes that "the author looks at nomadic life in complete amazement and astonishment. Nomads and nomadic life are strange and dangerous to him. They are a threat. Nevertheless, these people are brothers and neighbours; and although they are distant brothers, they are still family" (Noort, "Abraham and the Nations," 17). Nomads were a regularly encountered Other in everyday life, and this episode seeks to explain why and how they came to thrive in the desert.

settled in the harsh environment of the desert. There, Hagar was ordered to return to Sarah and suffer her harsh treatment. There, her eyes were opened to the well that hid in the dunes of the burning sand. These episodes suggest that the Ishmaelites learned to thrive in the wilderness because *there* they were blessed by God. *There* God "was with the boy and he grew up" (Gen. 21:20). The flight narrative emphasizes the location of the angel's revelation to Hagar. The exact location is named in its conclusion: "Therefore the well was called Beer-lahai-roi; it is between Kadesh and Bered" (16:14). This emphasis anticipates that this location will become their home, that the wild nature of the "wild ass of a man," ancestor of the Ishmaelites who are able to thrive in the wilderness, is the result of divine compensation for Hagar and her son. God promises Abraham that Ishmael, too, will be the father of a great nation; as part of Abraham's offspring, he will inherit an independent portion of land in the south – the site of his mother's double revelations, where she learned to "see" where water hides in the wilderness, and where Ishmael was raised by God and bloomed in the harsh desert environment.

The Treaty with Abimelech (Gen. 21:22–34)

As was mentioned earlier, the birth of Isaac and expulsion of Ishmael interrupted the seemingly far less compelling story of Abraham's relationship with the gentile king Abimelech. To avid readers of the Abraham journey, the lengths to which the text goes to detail these stories, as well as the dual tone of both narratives, seem odd. It is unclear what role Abimelech plays in Abraham's heroic journey to merit such attention, and the continued ambiguity of the text surrounding which man has the moral high ground is difficult to swallow for supporters of the Abraham character.

The next episode in the Abraham-Abimelech relationship is postponed until after the birth of Isaac and expulsion of Ishmael (Gen. 21:1–21), despite the fact that this episode is a direct continuation of the "sister-wife" episode in Genesis 20. Continuity is apparent from Abimelech's request that Abraham "will return the kindness that I have done for you, to me and to the land in which you have sojourned" (21:23), and from literary links between the texts.[1] The significance of this delay should presumably be found in the link

1. Coats (*Genesis*, 155) writes that a literary frame surrounds both units. It opens with "He settled in Gerar" (Gen. 20:1) and concludes with "And Abraham resided in the land of the Philistines a long time" (21:34).

between the current unit (the treaty of Abraham and Abimelech) and the previous or following units (the birth of Isaac and expulsion of Ishmael or the binding of Isaac). The treaty narrative begins with a time reference to the previous episode: "At that time…" (21:22).[2] However, textual links also exist between the treaty narrative and the binding of Isaac,[3] and the episode might appear here so that the binding narrative can be read on the background of the treaty narrative.[4] Another possibility is that postponing the treaty episode enabled the juxtaposition of the closed wombs of Abimelech's household and Sarah's birth. Additionally, the significance of the treaty between Abraham and Abimelech is validated with the birth of Isaac; had the treaty taken place before his birth, the responsibilities of the treaty might only have obligated Abraham and Ishmael. Forging the treaty after Isaac's birth means that Isaac is included in the pact, and clarifies the significance of the treaty.[5] Another obvious link exists between the treaty narrative and the expulsion of Ishmael: wells. Abraham banishes his son, who as a result almost dies of dehydration, but is saved when his mother is made aware of a well in the wilderness, while in the treaty narrative Abraham fought over wells with the people of Gerar. In both narratives, the well is necessary for the very existence of the relevant party – "obtaining a source of life in the wilderness."[6] The dispute between Abraham and Abimelech is a matter of life and death. Additionally, Hagar is

2. Coats, *Genesis*, 155.
3. See Bin-Nun, *Chapters of the Fathers*, 107.
4. One purpose of the treaty narrative is etymological, regarding the name Beersheba (Coats, *Genesis*, 155–57). According to this reading there is another link between the narratives: the sanctified location is named Beersheba in commemoration of Abraham's pact with Abimelech, while in the binding of Isaac narrative the sanctified place is named Adonai-yireh, in commemoration of his relationship with God. Note that the binding narrative concludes with a double mention of Abraham's return to Beersheba (Gen. 22:19): "Abraham then returned to his servants, and they departed together for Beersheba; and Abraham stayed in Beersheba."
5. Emanueli (*Genesis – Commentary and Insights*, 293) suggested that the pact between Abraham and Abimelech took place at the great feast Abraham held in Gen. 21:8, "Therefore there was no need to announce their arrival."
6. Alter, *The Art of Biblical Narrative*, 182.

lost in the wilderness of Beersheba, and the name Beersheba is given meaning in the treaty narrative.[7] Another connection between the episodes, which touches upon the scene's narrative objective, is a phrase that appears in both of them: "God was with the boy" (21:20) and "God is with you in everything that you do" (21:22). As Thomas Brody writes, the connection shows that "despite the separation of Abraham and Ishmael, God is with both."[8] In our story, however, the latter declaration is made by Abimelech, a gentile king, and the significance of this will be clarified below.

In the grand scheme of things, Abimelech should be nothing more than a background character, whose only purpose is to shed light on some virtuous aspect of our protagonist. Perhaps this is indeed his function; however, the literary importance of the Abimelech episodes establishes a vivid setting from which the more climactic episodes in the Abraham journey commence. This detailed, often convoluted, backstory sets the tone for a far more dramatic reveal in the Abraham journey, just around the corner.

The Moral High Ground

The ambiguous tone of the narrative from the first Abimelech-Abraham interaction continues here as well. The text seems to be telling two separate stories simultaneously – one of two leaders engaging in a friendly treaty, and the other, of two men locked in a dispute that requires diplomatic acumen to achieve a ceasefire. In the first (Gen. 21:22–24, 27, 31), Abraham agrees to Abimelech's offer to make a friendly pact, and the place is named Beersheba in commemoration of the pact ("*sheba*" from the root SH-B-A – "to take an oath"). The second narrative (21:25–26, 28–30, 33) is about a treaty that resolves a long-term conflict over wells, and validates Abraham's claim to Beersheba. Abraham plants a sanctified tree in commemoration of

7. See Hamilton, *The Book of Genesis, Chapters 18–50*, 87. Hamilton added other less convincing elements, such as Abraham providing Hagar with bread and water compared with Abraham giving cattle to Abimelech.
8. Brodie, *Genesis as Dialogue: A Literary, Historical, and Theological Commentary*, 262.

the validation.[9] According to this position, the narratives should be read in the following order:[10]

The Friendly Treaty	The Ceasefire
(22) At that time Abimelech and Phicol, chief of his troops, said to Abraham, "God is with you in everything that you do. (23) Therefore swear to me here by God that you will not deal falsely with me or with my kith and kin, but will deal with me and with the land in which you have sojourned as loyally as I have dealt with you." (24) And Abraham said, "I swear it." (27) Abraham took sheep and oxen and gave them to Abimelech, and the two of them made a pact. (31) Hence that place was called Beersheba, for there the two of them swore an oath. (32) When they had concluded the pact at Beersheba, Abimelech and Phicol, chief of his troops, departed and returned to the land of the Philistines. (34) And Abraham resided in the land of the Philistines a long time.	(25) Then Abraham reproached Abimelech for the well of water which the servants of Abimelech had seized. (26) But Abimelech said, "I do not know who did this; you did not tell me, nor have I heard of it until today." (28) Abraham then set the seven ewes of the flock by themselves, (29) and Abimelech said to Abraham, "What mean these seven ewes which you have set apart?" (30) He replied, "You are to accept these seven ewes from me as proof that I dug this well." (33) Abraham planted a tamarisk at Beersheba, and invoked there the name of the Lord, the Everlasting God.

9. See von Rad, *Genesis*, 230–232. Some scholars viewed this as a combination of two sources (Gunkel, *Genesis – Translated and Interpreted*; Skinner, *A Critical and Exegetical Commentary on Genesis*; Procksch, *Die Genesis*. The division above is based on their analysis). Others viewed the section as one primary source with added narrative sections (e.g., Dillmann, Speiser, and Coats). However, an alternative position values the current design of the narrative, regardless of the original sources (Wenham, *Genesis 16–50*, 91).
10. Gunkel (*Genesis – Translated and Interpreted*, 230–231) discusses the issue at length. The division of verses above is based on Skinner, *A Critical and Exegetical Commentary on Genesis*, 325, although he fails to note the double pacts in 27 and 32. For alternate suggestions, see Gunkel, ibid.; Westermann, *Genesis 12–36: A Continental Commentary*, 346.

Both narratives include similar elements. There is a dialogue between Abraham and Abimelech, Abraham presents Abimelech with cattle, there is testimony of commitment (an oath and "proof"), and finally, significance is given in both narratives to the name Beersheba, the first narrative relating the name "sheba" to the oath, and in the second, "sheba" commemorating the seven (*sheva*) ewes that are proof of Abraham's ownership of the well.

The division into two separate narratives is convincing: whereas the narrative begins in an atmosphere of friendship and appeasement, the second scene brings forward hostility between the parties. Some commentators did not view the two stories as separate or contradictory, but saw the disagreement over ownership of the well as a difference between friends and allies, whose treaty was stable enough to withstand the crisis without resulting in real conflict.[11] This reading is difficult to accept, since the design of the characters in each of the episodes is indeed contradictory: a different character is responsible for the commitment in each of the narratives, and a different character compels the other to act. From the political perspective, Abraham is the stronger presence in both narratives, which explains why Abimelech is interested in a pact. From an ethical perspective, however, Abimelech seems to be more powerful; he asks Abraham for a treaty because Abraham is indebted to him, and Abraham seems to have no choice but to take an oath. In contrast, in the second scene, Abraham accuses Abimelech of immoral conduct.

It is true that the narrative should not be viewed as two separate stories, but rather as a complex account that intentionally presents opposing facts. Sarna provides evidence toward the unity of the narrative based on the prevalence and centrality of the number seven throughout the narrative. In addition to Abraham offering Abimelech seven ewes, and the name of the place that commemorates this number, the names "Abraham" and "Abimelech" each appear seven times throughout the

11. Coats (*Genesis*, 156) attempts to prove the unity of the narrative from the mention of cattle in both narratives. However, the cattle is not a viable link since it serves a different purpose in each of the narratives. Speiser (*Genesis*, 160) also claims there is no room to divide the narrative, but failed to explain why. Nahmanides on Gen. 21:23 preceded Coats with a similar explanation.

narrative.[12] Sarna therefore views the narrative as a harmonious unit, despite the intentional incongruities that enhance the purpose of the narrative, as demonstrated below.

Abimelech's request is based on two elements: God's blessing to Abraham, and Abraham's moral obligation to Abimelech after the king had treated him so generously in the sister-wife episode, despite Abraham's unfounded accusation against him. Abimelech's recognition that "God is with you in everything that you do" plays an important role in the purpose of this scene. Abimelech reflects Abraham's political acceptance by the people of the land. The acknowledgment by a foreign king of Abraham's covenant with God is a new stage in the establishment of Abraham's rights to the land. But the second element founds the pact on the unique relationship between Abraham and Abimelech. As Abimelech says, "Return the kindness that I have done for you." This moral claim refers to the kindness with which Abimelech had treated Abraham, which he now expects Abraham to repay. Instead of banishing Abraham in anger for the wife-sister scandal (as Pharaoh did), Abimelech offers him riches and permanent residency in Gerar. The term "*ḥesed,*" "kindness," was the phrase Abraham used when he had asked Sarah to pretend she was his sister (Gen. 20:13). Abimelech repays this dubious "kindness" with true kindness. There is no acceptable response to the moral demand other than "I swear it" (21:24).[13]

---

12. Sarna, *Genesis* (JPS), 145.
13. The relationship between "*ani*" and "*anokhi,*" both meaning "I," has received much scholarly attention. It is generally agreed that the word "*anokhi*" emphasizes the speaker more, while "*ani*" is usually used in certain phrases. For more on this issue, see Friedrich Giesebrecht, "Zum Hexateuchkritik: Der Sprachgebrauch des Hexateuchischen Elohisten," *ZAW* 1 (1881): 177–276; Samuel Rolles Driver, "On Some Alleged Linguistic Affinities of the Elohist," *The Journal of Philology* 11 (1882): 201–236; Cassuto, *The "Quaestio" of the Book of Genesis*, 101–104; *HALOT* 1:72; BDB, 59. Yechiel Bin-Nun (*Eretz HaMoriya: Pirkei Mikra VeLashon*, ed. Yoel Bin-Nun [Alon Shevut, 1996], 115–116) writes that the form *anokhi* is integrated in contexts where the speaker has difficulty expressing himself, or is ambivalent about his own actions. If his assumption is correct, Abraham's *anokhi* is appropriate in this context, since he cannot act entirely according to his own free will; Abimelech's kindness obligates him.

Had the narrative then proceeded to Abraham's oath, the conclusion and message of the narrative would have been as follows: Although God is with Abraham in everything that he does, Abimelech has the moral upper hand, and Abraham's commitment toward Abimelech is the only reason he agrees to the treaty. To negate this conclusion, Genesis 21:25–26 causes the reader to rethink the relationship between Abraham and Abimelech. Before Abraham actually takes the oath, the dispute over the wells emerges. Here, the relationship is reversed. Apparently, Abimelech's servants steal Abraham's wells, but Abraham decides to keep silent until Abimelech expresses interest in a treaty, and reminds Abraham of his old debt. Abimelech cannot come up with satisfactory reasons or shed his responsibility for the actions of his servants. Nonetheless, Abraham "took sheep and oxen and gave them to Abimelech" (Gen. 21:27). In our conclusion of our analysis of Genesis 20, we referred to the links between the well narrative and the Gerar narrative. There, we noted the role reversal in each of the scenes: the wrongdoer in the first scene (Abraham) becomes the accuser in the second scene, while the accuser in the Gerar narrative (Abimelech) becomes the wrongdoer in the well narrative.[14] Abimelech's accusation in the first episode ("What have you done to us?" in 20:10) becomes his defense in the second ("I do not know who did this," in 21:26). Abimelech reprimands Abraham, "Why did you see fit *(ma ra'ita)* to do this thing?" and later defends himself, "I do not know (*lo yadati*) who has done this thing." [15]

The integration of the conflict into the narrative is essential to prevent the impression that Abraham commits to a treaty because of

14. See Grossman "The Use of Ambiguity in Biblical Narratives of Misleading and Deceit," 487–490. Wenham (*Genesis 16–50*, 90) suggested the following structure: "The tale itself consists of one scene (vs. 22–33) made up of three speeches by Abimelek, Abraham's responses, and some short concluding comments." However, in the well scene Abraham is the speaker and Abimelech responds, which is significant in understanding the interchangeable roles in the scene.

15. The verbs "to see" and "to know" are almost synonymous in the biblical narrative (Isaac Leo Seeligman, *Studies in Biblical Literature*, ed. A. Hurvitz, S. Japhet, and E. Tov [Jerusalem, 1992], 153; Yair Zakovitch, *"Man Sees Only What Is Visible But the Lord Sees into the Heart": Disguise and Retribution in Biblical Narrative* [Jerusalem, 1998], 17).

Abimelech's moral superiority following the sister-wife narrative. This conclusion is reassessed and sublimated. The interchangeable roles demonstrate that Abimelech, too, stammers when faced with an ethical grievance, while Abraham knows how to offer generous gifts to one who brought him harm.

After the grievance is resolved, Abraham and Abimelech come to an agreement. While Abraham's commitment was previously described as his willingness to take an oath, the final agreement takes a different tone, "And the two of them made a pact" (Gen. 21:27). The verse implies a mutual commitment rather than a one-sided oath.[16] This discrepancy is even more apparent in the etymological conclusion of the narrative: "Hence that place was called Beersheba, for there *the two of them* swore an oath" (21:31). Perhaps the emphasis of this equal standing is the reason for the repetition of Abraham and Abimelech's names an identical number of times in the text. Abimelech no longer has the moral upper hand; the treaty is made between equals.

A True Ally

The narrative could easily have ended here, when another surprising element is mentioned: the seven ewes that Abraham had separated from the others (Gen. 21:28). The text is vague regarding whether the ewes are part of Abraham's original gift to Abimelech or a separate parting gift. The text indicates that the ewes should be viewed as one detail of the general gift Abraham offered Abimelech: a definite article precedes the mention of the cattle, "*the* seven ewes," indicating that these were previously mentioned.[17] Additionally, the text omits a repetition of the verb "Abraham took" before Abraham sets the ewes aside, implying that they were present.[18]

16. Therefore, the assertion that verse 27 is a direct continuation of verse 24 (e.g., Westermann, *Genesis 12–36: A Continental Commentary*, 348) contradicts the primary purpose of the narrative. Verse 27 indicates the change that Abraham's commitment underwent since his suggestion in verse 24.
17. Even Westermann, who believes verse 27 is not attributed to the same source as verse 28, admits that verse 28 refers to verse 27 (*Genesis 12–36: A Continental Commentary*, 349).
18. Wenham (*Genesis 16–50*, 93) claims that the definite article before the cattle refers to the author's future comment; Abraham's clarification in the next verse that

This writing style is clarified in light of the previously mentioned link between the dispute over the well and the sister-wife episode. There, too, Abimelech had offered Abraham cattle (and more), and there, too, Abimelech's gifts were to be "evidence" of sorts, where the thousand pieces of silver were to serve as proof that Sarah and Abraham are married, just as the seven ewes were to serve as proof of Abraham's ownership of the well. The gifts serve a dual purpose. They are proof of Abraham's generosity despite the injustice of Abimelech's actions, but also proof of Abraham's ownership of the well, paralleling the purpose of the silver in the Gerar narrative. The giving of cattle is repeated twice to emphasize the dual role of the gift.

Abraham's generosity is highlighted when we consider the prevalent Hittite law regarding concealment of an ownership mark on a lost sheep:[19]

> If anyone finds a ram and removes the brand, [if] its owner traces it out, he shall give seven sheep; he shall give [specifically] two ewes, three rams, [and] two lambs and he shall pledge his estate as security.[20]

If this law reflects the accepted norms of the time, the one expected to give "seven ewes" is the offender who took possession of stolen property.[21] Here, Abraham offers seven ewes to the offender who had stolen

---

Abimelech should take "the cattle" proves that he is not referring to cattle that were already taken by Abimelech. However, the following verse could also be read as a detail of the previous generalization: Abimelech specifically takes the cattle at this point.

19. This law does not relate to common theft (which according to section 59 of Hittite law obligates the thief to pay the sum of fifteen sheep), only to indirect theft – finding a ram and removing the owner's identification sign.
20. Section 62, based on translation by ANET, 192. The conclusion of the law is unclear. See Harry A. Hoffner, *The Laws of the Hittites: A Critical Edition* (Leiden, 1997), 168–169; Meir Malul, *Law Collections and Other Legal Compilations from the Ancient Near East* (Haifa, 2000), 229n9. This is a common signature in Hittite laws, which might signify: "It is the right of the harmed party or the people of his household to demand compensation from the household of the offender" (Singer, *The Hittites and Their Civilization*, 130).
21. Similar to Prov. 6:30–31: "A thief is not held in contempt for stealing to appease his hunger; yet if caught he must pay sevenfold; he must give up all he owns." The

his wells. Abraham thus reciprocates Abimelech's kindness, and the two characters carry equal weight on the reader's moral scale.

The newfound reciprocity between the two characters also clarifies the concluding verses (Gen. 21:31–34). As mentioned above, the text emphasizes that the location was named Beersheba "for there *the two of them* swore an oath." The narrative opened with Abimelech's demand that Abraham will swear an oath, and Abraham agreed (vv. 23–24). The process described above led to the desired conclusion of a reciprocal oath between equals. This conclusion could only be reached by integrating the dispute over the well into the treaty process. The "pact" is mentioned twice, in verses 27 and 32, both in the plural to emphasize the reciprocity between the two parties. The concluding verses note that both Abimelech and Abraham returned to the land of the Philistines, and that Abraham remained there "a long time." Abimelech originally requested a treaty of friendship on the basis of his kind offer of land; Abraham's ultimate acceptance of Abimelech's offer indicates the close bond between them.

Abraham Begins to See God's Promises Coming True

The journey that Abraham began when he "went forth" from his land for the first time in Ur of the Chaldeans has been arduous and punctuated by diversions. He was forced to leave the land due to famine, nearly killed by the Egyptian king who wanted to take his wife, battled a war, saved his nephew and watched the destruction of a city, experienced domestic strife, sired two sons and banished the eldest. God had promised Abraham that he would become the leader of a new nation. Yet at every turn, he seems to move one step forward, two steps back. Despite all this, Abraham's faith has not wavered. God, for His part, has fulfilled at least one promise – Sarah gave birth to Abraham's heir. And yet, it would not be surprising if Abraham was beginning to feel as if the remainder of God's vision for him was still far in the future. His personal familial destiny is slowly becoming a reality, but how can he grow into the leader of a nation when he still has not fully settled in his new home?

Septuagint has David respond to Nathan regarding the sin of stealing the sheep from the poor (II Sam. 12:6): "He must pay sevenfold."

The episodes between Abimelech and Abraham mark a notable turn in the fulfillment of God's promise. Abimelech's acceptance of Abraham's rights to the land creates a border at Beersheba between Abraham and the king of Gerar. Abraham, finally, begins to see the fruits of his journey panning out. He has signed a treaty with the local king and established a set boundary to his land. Abraham's settlement in the land begins to take on a feeling of permanence. As a result, Abraham plants a tamarisk and "invokes the name of the Lord" (Gen. 21:33). God's promise to him is coming true. The text emphasizes Abraham's feeling of settling down by contrasting it with the return of Abimelech and the chief of his troops to the land of the Philistines (v. 32). This detail is unnecessary, as the text did not previously mention that Abimelech and Phicol had come to Abraham; there is no need to mention their return home. Perhaps the purpose of this information is to emphasize the distinction between Abimelech and Phicol, who return to the land of the Philistines, and Abraham, who "planted a tamarisk at Beersheba." They leave, and Abraham remains.

The Tamarisk Tree

The planting of the tree carries clear symbolic significance, reflecting Abraham's feeling of settling down at last in the promised land. The tamarisk is mentioned in two other biblical narratives. The first is, "When Saul heard that David and the men with him had been located, Saul was then in Gibeah, sitting under the tamarisk tree on the height, spear in hand, with all his courtiers in attendance upon him" (I Sam. 22:6). And the second, "Then they took the bones and buried them under the tamarisk tree in Jabesh, and they fasted for seven days" (I Sam. 31:13). We can infer from the story about Saul that the tamarisk was a giant tree, which could provide plenty of shade to the king's weary cohort. Such a tall tree, planted in the hot wilderness of Beersheba, would certainly serve to provide respite to all those who happened upon in it in their travels. Abraham's planting of the tamarisk tree is not only a symbol of Abraham's family taking up roots in the land; the tree is a symbol of all that Abraham and his household represent. Abraham has reclaimed his stolen wells and in doing so protects his family. He then plants a tree on his land to ensure the benefit of all those who may pass by. This has been and will always be the motif of Abraham's actions, in any situation. He establishes both his physical and moral presence in the land in one symbolic action.

The planting of trees for the benefit of passers-by is not a new concept. Indian emperor Ashoka the Great, who ruled in the years 273–232 BCE, carved inscriptions of Buddhist wisdom on pillars and rocks throughout his empire, for the purpose of educating the people in Buddhist ways. One inscription described the deeds of the king:

> Along roads I have had banyan trees[22] planted so that they can give shade to animals and men, and I have had mango groves planted at intervals of eight krosas, I have had wells dug, rest-houses built, and in various places, I have had watering-places made for the use of animals and men. But these are but minor achievements. Such things to make the people happy have been done by former kings.[23]

Despite the many centuries separating Ashoka from Abraham, the needs of travelers for water wells and the shade of trees did not change much. In addition to claiming the wells that he had created, Abraham plants shade trees to enable his own herdsmen – and perhaps other passers-by as well – to have respite from the hot sun.

However, the planting of the tree specifically in the context of the pact with Abimelech remains unclear. Some note that Abraham's journey through Canaan consistently relates to trees.[24] Abraham's first stop was at the terebinth of Moreh (Gen. 12:6). Later, Abraham built an altar near the terebinths of Mamre (14:13), where he was visited by the angels (18:1). Abraham invited the angels to "recline under the tree" (18:4), and later served them "under the tree" (18:8).[25] But this

22. The translator added in a footnote: "This is the ficus of Ngalnesis – a tree with a broad and extensive top."
23. Edicts of Ashoka, Rock Edict Nb7.
24. Among others, Wenham, *Genesis 16–50*, 94; Hamilton, *The Book of Genesis, Chapters 18–50*, 93; Mathews, *Genesis*, 282.
25. Sarna ("Genesis 21:33: A Study in the Development of a Biblical Text and Its Rabbinic Transformation," 71) notes that the word "tree" is designated by the definite article (*ha'etz*), in reference to a specific and well-known oak in the terebinths of Mamre.

is the first time Abraham plants a new tree. The tree is symbolic of a new future; instead of Abraham's previous reliance on existing trees, Abraham creates and contributes something of his own. Additionally, the type of tree stands out,[26] since this is the first mention of a tamarisk in the Abraham cycle.[27] Sarna compares the planting of the tree to the building of an altar in other narratives, and adds that the tree was the foundation of the later temple of Beersheba.[28] Sarna's position is well based in the text, since when Abraham builds an altar he invokes the name of God (12:8; 13:4; Isaac in 26:25), and here Abraham invokes the name of God as well when he plants the tree. The broad concentric structure of the Abraham cycle (as described in the introduction) also presents invocation of God's name alongside the tamarisk in parallel to the invocation of God's name alongside the building of the altars in 12–13. However, the link between the altars and the tree also highlights the fact that Abraham did not build an altar in Beersheba, and that the tree was a replacement of the usual altar rather than an addition to it.

The main significance of the event, as noted earlier, was the fact that Abimelech wished to make a treaty with Abraham, expressing the acceptance of Abraham's position by the nations of the land. As Bekhor Shor states, "Kings make treaties with him in recognition of his greatness."[29] Creating a pact indicates the realization that Abraham is not a nomad who will eventually abandon the area. Abimelech asks that Abraham take an oath in the name of God, that he will not lie to him and to the three generations that follow (Gen. 21:23). The perspective of time signifies that Abimelech is aware of Abraham's permanency on the land. Planting a new tree appropriately signifies Abraham's confidence that he

26. Hamilton (*The Book of Genesis, Chapters 18–50*, 93n28) notes the possibility of a deliberate link between tamarisk and the Akkadian word *ašlu* ("rope") and in the biblical context (as well as texts found in Nuzi) it is also denoted as "region" or "estate." The Septuagint and Vulgate translate accordingly.

27. Assuming this is the correct reading. Gunkel (*Genesis – Translated and Interpreted*, 233) raises the possibility that the original text read *Asherah*, and the word was changed to prevent idolatrous connotations. Whether the tamarisk is a correction or not, there is significance to the deviation from Abraham's oak.

28. Sarna, "Genesis 21:33: A Study in the Development of a Biblical Text and Its Rabbinic Transformation," 69–75.

29. Bekhor Shor on Gen. 21:33.

will enjoy the fruits (or shade) of the tree in years to come. Subsequently, Abraham invokes the name "*El Olam*" – "Everlasting God."[30]

This divine appellation is also associated with the specific kind of tree Abraham planted – a tamarisk. Many commented that one of the tamarisk's distinguishing characteristics is its long life span,[31] and its perennial quality symbolizes eternity and perpetual renewal.[32] In a certain sense, planting a tamarisk also suggests permanent residence in the land, even more than the erection of an altar. Unlike André Parrot's formulation that "Isaac built an altar at Beersheba (Gen. 26:25), at the place where Abraham had *only* planted a tamarisk tree,"[33] this planting should not be considered inferior or preliminary to the building of an altar. In context of the promise of the land, the tree stands for eternal blessing.

Once Abraham's position is recognized by the kings of the land, Abraham looks to the everlasting quality of God, the giver of his land, who serves as a permanent assurance that Abraham's offspring will inherit the land: "In other words, after so many delays, the promises of land and descendants at last seem on their way to fulfillment."[34]

Abraham seems to have completed the journey he began so long ago, when God first appeared to him in Ur of the Chaldeans. He has faced trials and tribulations and emerged from them as a virtuous,

30. Gen. 21:33. This phrase also denotes "a long time" in Ugaritic as well. See Anthony Tomasino, "עולם," *NIDOTTE* 3:345–351. Von Rad (*Genesis*, 232) objects to the common translation for *"el olam"* as "eternal," or the German *"ewig,"* since the biblical term denotes "forever," but not in the sense of "beyond time." Therefore, von Rad translates it as, *"Des Gottes der Urzeit an* – the God of Primeval Times" (*Das erste Buch Mose: Genesis* [Göttingen: Vandenhoeck und Ruprecht, 1958], 201–202).
31. Harold G. Stigers claims that because of this quality, its planting in the narrative symbolizes the perpetual need to recall God's kindness with humanity (Stigers, *A Commentary on Genesis* [Grand Rapids, MI, 1976], 187).
32. Davidson, *Genesis 12–50*, 90; Yehuda Kiel, *Daat Mikra: Genesis*, vol. 2, 209. (He holds that the tamarisk symbolizes the ongoing covenant between Abraham and Abimelech.) See also Shlomo Weissbluth, "'Abraham Planted a Tamarisk at Beersheba, and Invoked There the Name of the LORD, the Everlasting God' (Gen. 21:33)," *Beit Mikra* 36 (1990): 11–19.
33. Parrot, *Abraham and His Times*, 111n4 (italics mine).
34. Wenham, *Genesis 16–50*, 94.

faithful servant of God. He and Sarah were rewarded for their kindness and patience with the miraculous birth of their son. He has arrived in the promised land, established diplomatic treaties with the local government, and he has an heir to accept his teachings. Abraham's journey seems complete. His faith is absolute, his reward has been given. It would be terrible if, after all this, Abraham found himself facing the most agonizing trial of all.

Binding of Isaac (Gen. 22:1–19)

The binding of Isaac is the formative story of Abraham as a character. This is the moment that separates Abraham from any other literary heroic figure. The test of the binding is a trial by fire, pushing both our protagonist and us as readers to the furthest edge. Abraham emerges from the test of the binding with a renewed divine promise. The legacy of that promise will protect his progeny for generations, and the enormity of his trust in God will be lauded universally as the ultimate moment of faith.

The binding narrative has captivated commentators for centuries. The simplicity of its prevailing message is poignant. The deeper literary planes of the text offer a far more complex and universal message, while leaving some burning questions painfully unanswered.

Abraham and Isaac depart on the journey to Mount Moriah together. Who will return from that journey, and in what state, remains unclear. What occurs on that mountain will be etched into the hearts of father and son, and will forever change not only their lives but the lives of their descendants after them.

Introduction I: Did Abraham Pass the Test?

The binding of Isaac has been discussed broadly from a variety of perspectives throughout the generations, as Edward Greenstein notes, "No narrative in the Hebrew Bible has evoked so many readings, and so many passionate ones, as the 'masterpiece' known to Christians as the sacrifice of Isaac and to Jews as the binding of Isaac or *Akedah*."[1] One particularly significant introductory question to this narrative is whether or not Abraham passed the test to his faith. This issue was debated on both the moral-philosophical plane and the historical-literary plane. Immanuel Kant is a prominent representative of the position that undermines the common conception of Abraham faithfully withstanding God's test. Kant's ethical philosophy is based on the values of freedom and personal autonomy. Kant writes in the *Conflict of the Faculties*:

> For if God should really speak to man, man could still never know that it was God speaking. It is quite impossible for man to apprehend the infinite by his senses, distinguish it from sensible beings, and recognize it as such. But in some cases man can be sure that the voice he hears is not God's; for if the voice commands him to do something contrary to the moral law, then no matter how majestic the apparition may be, and no matter how it may seem to surpass the whole of nature, he must consider it an illusion.[2]

He relates this matter specifically to the binding of Isaac:

---

1. Edward L. Greenstein, "Reading Pragmatically: The Binding of Isaac," in *Words, Ideas, Worlds: Biblical Essays in Honour of Yairah Amit*, ed. A. Brenner and F. Polak (Sheffield, 2012), 102.
2. Immanuel Kant, *The Conflict of the Faculties (Der Streit der Fakultaten)*, trans. Mary J. Gregor (New York: Abaris Books, 1979), 115. Kant repeats this principle several times throughout his work. He writes in *Religion Within the Limits of Reason Alone* (1960, 171): "After all, the revelation has reached the inquisitor only through men and has been interpreted by men, and even did it appear to have come to him from God Himself (like the command delivered to Abraham to slaughter his own son like a sheep) it is at least possible that in this instance a mistake has prevailed."

> We can use, as an example, the myth of the sacrifice that Abraham was going to make by butchering and burning his only son at God's command (the poor child, without knowing it, even brought the wood for the fire). Abraham should have replied to this supposedly divine voice, "That I ought not to kill my good son is quite certain. But that you, this apparition, are God – of that I am not certain, and never can be, not even if this voice rings down to me from heaven."[3]

Assuming that revelation will by nature always be debatable, Kant concludes that morality takes precedence over revelation; therefore, Abraham should have rejected, or at least argued with, the voice that ordered him to sacrifice his son with the claim that it is not the voice of God. Kant's position is based on two assumptions: the morality of God and the questionability of His revelation to man.[4] The fact that Abraham was willing to sacrifice his son – a norm that is considered an "abhorrent act that the Lord detests" (Deut. 12:31) according to biblical standards – demonstrates an immature relationship with God, and a moral and spiritual failure.

The second approach, which relates to the narrative sequence, is based on an analysis of the text. Omri Boehm's extreme position is a meaningful introduction of the broader discussion below. Boehm believes the binding narrative is the result of intervention by a late redactor. To him, the original narrative included no revelation – not initially (Gen. 22:11–12), and not "a second time" (vv. 15–18). His position is based mainly on the interchangeable names for God in the narrative. The two

3. Kant, *The Conflict of the Faculties*, 115. On the rational theory, which, according to Kant, should prevail over biblical theology in the binding narrative, see Jon D. Levenson, "Abusing Abraham: Traditions, Religious Histories, and Modern Misinterpretations," *Judaism* 47 (1998): 260–262.
4. Maimonides believed one can prove the certainty of revelation from the binding narrative, claiming that Abraham would not have gone to sacrifice his son had he not been certain that God had indeed spoken with him (*Guide for the Perplexed*, III:26). Rabbinic literature alludes to the dilemma with a story of the devil, who attempts to plant uncertainty in Abraham's mind regarding the revelation. See *Midrash Tanḥuma, Vayera*, 22.

revelations utilize the name *YHWH,* while most of the narrative makes use of the name *Elohim*:

> In the original account Abraham actually disobeyed the divine command to slay his son, sacrificing the ram "instead of his son" (v. 13) on his own responsibility. This interpretation thus brings together the textual and narrative understandings of the text, explaining the reason for the later redaction of this story: anxious to conceal Abraham's disobedience, a later redactor interpolated the figure of the angel, thereby shifting responsibility for interrupting the test from Abraham to the angel.[5]

According to Boehm, Abraham's failure (in the "original account") was his inability to slaughter his son, and finding a last-minute replacement in the form of a ram. This approach describes a reverse failure from the position presented above. While Kant believes Abraham had failed by adhering to the command, Boehm claims that Abraham failed by backing out.

Despite the essential differences between the two approaches, they both make the same methodical error of excessive interference by the reader. A reader can only decipher the existing text. While Hans-Georg Gadamar and others correctly assert that the reader's perception of the narrative is influenced by culture and personality, an honest reading of the text takes it at face value, instead of bending it to the reader's worldview. Kant undermined the meaning of the text, while Boehm subverted its existence; these challenges enabled them to reach the conclusion that Abraham failed the test of the binding. The design of the narrative indicates that Abraham passed the test ("For now I know that you fear God" – Gen. 22:12), and is commended by God for his actions. Therefore, there is no justification for the omission of the initial revelation (vv. 11–12) from the narrative sequence. Abraham is portrayed as

5. Omri Boehm, *The Binding of Isaac: A Religious Model of Disobedience* (New York, 2007), 23. See also Boehm, "The Binding of Isaac: An Inner-Biblical Polemic on the Question of 'Disobeying' a Manifestly Illegal Order," *VT* 52 (2002): 1–12.

one who has proven his fear of God through great difficulty, and has merited God's blessing as a result.

Nonetheless, the position that views Abraham's actions as a moral failure is understandable. The binding narrative stands out in the Abraham cycle. Until this point, Abraham was portrayed as a highly moral character, who is particularly concerned with the good of others (such as saving Lot in Gen. 14, generous hospitality in Gen. 18, and so on). The text in fact indicates that Abraham was selected because of those qualities: "For I have singled him out, that he may instruct his children and his posterity to keep the way of the Lord by doing what is charitable and just" (Gen. 18:19). The ethical worldview that was developed and encouraged by the book of Genesis up to now is suddenly shattered. The previously mentioned verses about Canaanite customs are particularly jarring in this context (Deut. 12:30–32):

> When the Lord your God has cut down before you the nations that you are about to enter and dispossess, and you have dispossessed them and settled in their land, beware of being lured into their ways after they have been wiped out before you! Do not inquire about their gods, saying, "How did those nations worship their gods? I too will follow those practices." You shall not act thus toward the Lord your God, for they perform for their gods every abhorrent act that the Lord detests; they even offer up their sons and daughters in fire to their gods.

The custom of sacrificing children is idolatrous, and detested by God. These verses clarify Kant's claim that Abraham should have refused God's command, since the God of Abraham would never ask him to sacrifice his son. Perhaps the test to Abraham's faith was the internalization that despite the human desire represented by idol-worshippers to sacrifice that which is most precious to one's god, the God of Abraham is not worshipped in a way that contradicts natural morality.

However, this understanding does not justify Kant's reading. Since Abraham is portrayed in the narrative as withstanding the test, Kant's question should address the text itself. Why is Abraham, in the final narrative of the story cycle, to act in a way that defies the very premise of his selection, as well as the underlying assumptions of biblical ethics? Conversely, Boehm's reading adds a true challenge to the analysis of the text. What accounts for the sudden change and possibility of a replacement for Isaac? Does the possibility not indicate that Abraham could have offered a replacement from the outset?

Introduction II: The Narrative Structure

The binding of Isaac should be read both as a story in and of itself, and in the context of its literary surroundings. The narrative begins, "And it was after these things," a familiar phrase in the biblical text, which, Rabbi Samuel ben Meir (Rashbam) aptly specifies, should be interpreted as "in light of these things," directly connecting the new narrative with the previous one.[6] In this case, however, it is unclear what "these things" are. As we mentioned before, there is a strong argument for the progression of the plot from the episodes between Abraham and Abimelech, which seems to see Abraham settling down into the role God promised him, to the sudden call from God to test His servant's faith one last time. Of course, conceptually, the binding of Isaac follows quite naturally from the story that is often referred to as the "Binding of Ishmael." After Ishmael's expulsion, there is no longer any doubt as to which son will become the heir to Abraham's legacy – and as such, the context of God's test becomes all the more horrific and significant.

This story is the final chapter of Abraham's journey. The following denouement of Sarah's death and the search for Isaac's bride outline the future of the nation Abraham birthed. However, as far as our hero, Abraham, is concerned, the binding of Isaac represents his final trial, the climax of his journey, and, if he succeeds, will end in his return home. This is the last time God appears to Abraham. The text illustrates the closing of this heroic cycle by repeating the poignant words with which it commenced: "*Lekh lekha*," "Go forth." This phrase appears only in these two biblical narratives.[7]

6. Rashbam on Gen. 22:1.
7. Noted by Martin Buber (*Darko shel Mikra* [Jerusalem, 1997], 293–294) in his discussion on key words.

The similarities between the opening and closing episodes of Abraham's heroic journey are numerous. Both begin with a repetitive, listed command (Gen. 12:1: "Go forth from your land, and from the place of your birth, and from your father's house" and 22:2: "Take your son, your favored one, whom you love, Isaac"), and the repetition serves as a rhetorical design of an inward spiral. This gradual design is apparent throughout the Abraham cycle, but particularly in the first and final narratives.[8] Additionally, the characterization of the destination is similarly vague in both narratives (12:1: "...to the land that I will show you" and 22:2: "...on one of the heights that I will point out to you"). The implementation also begins similarly (12:4: "Abram went forth as the Lord had commanded him" and 22:3: "He set out for the place of which God had told him"). Lot joined Abraham on his journey to Canaan, and now his son Isaac accompanies him on his journey to Moriah. These two units are parallel within the concentric structure of the entire narrative sequence.

Comparing Abraham's first test and his last clarifies the purpose of the narrative on three levels. First, the two narratives might be viewed as a literary frame (*inclusio*) for Abraham's heroic cycle. The first and last tests of Abraham's faith present the reader with the foundation for the selection of Abraham, and his suitability for his designated role: Abraham obeys God even in the most difficult commands. The second level relies upon the first: the final test might be viewed as continuous to the initial command, since the common theme is Abraham's disengagement from his surroundings. In the first test, Abraham is asked to disengage from his past, while in the final test, he is asked to abandon his future.[9]

The third level, based upon the first two, is the distinction between the two tests. Despite the similarities mentioned above, there is a major discrepancy between the two commands. While God requires Abraham

---

8. Cf. Yairah Amit, "Progression as a Rhetorical Device in Biblical Literature," *JSOT* 28 (2003): 3–32.
9. Herschel Shanks, "Illuminations: Abraham Cut off from His Past and Future by the Awkward Divine Command 'Go You!'" *Bible Review* 3 (1987): 8. Similarly, Benno Jacob, *The First Book of the Bible: Genesis*, 143; Terrence E. Fretheim, "The Book of Genesis: Introduction, Commentary, and Reflections," in *The New Interpreter's Bible*, ed. L. E. Keck et al. (Nashville, 1994), 495.

to leave his past behind him, He accompanies the demand with a promise of offspring and multiple blessings (Gen. 12:2).[10] The journey toward the unknown promises to be beneficial to Abraham. Despite the difficulty of leaving one's past behind, Abraham did so in anticipation of a better future. In this respect, the disengagement from Abraham's family is not comparable with the command to leave his home behind and sacrifice his only son on a deserted hilltop. In addition to the obvious emotional effects, Abraham is expected to sacrifice all that he has worked for. The death of Isaac is not only the death of a beloved son, but also the death of Abraham's hopes and God's promises. The contrast demonstrates the great difficulty of the final test, since this new command undermines the achievements of all the other tests. In this light, the link becomes almost ironic.

We must pay special attention to a mutual component in the two narratives. As noted above, the exact destination remains unknown to Abraham when he embarks on his journey "to the land that I will show you" and "on one of the heights that I will point out to you." This detail has no direct bearing on the development of either of the plots. In Genesis 12, Abraham simply arrives in Canaan, while in the binding narrative Abraham "looked up and saw the place from afar" (Gen. 22:4). The initial concealment of the exact destination creates an anticipation that the plot will revolve around this issue, perhaps through an explanation of how Abraham knew he had arrived, or the significance of the discovery of the location. The absence of this theme emphasizes the true purpose of the initial concealment: God will lead the way. Abraham might know where to go, but the place is selected by God.[11] The naming

10. Indeed, Trible stresses that the lack of blessing mentioned in the command to sacrifice his son highlights the difficulty of this trial in relation to God's first command to Abram to go to Canaan, where the blessings were already incorporated in the command (Phyllis Trible, "Genesis 22: The Sacrifice of Sarah," in *"Not in Heaven": Coherence and Complexity in Biblical Narrative*, ed. J. P. Rosenblatt and J. C. Sitterson, Jr [Bloomington, 1991], 172).
11. This undermines Mordechai Cogan's suggestion that the absence of the binding narrative from Solomon's Temple stems from the emphasis that "the location of the Temple was selected by God, not by man. The possibility of a historical site is negated, since it would detract from the Deuteronomistic concept of divine selection" (Cogan, "'The City that I Chose' – The Deuteronomistic View of Jerusalem,"

of the mountain in Moriah signifies this concept: *Adonai-yireh* – "The Lord will show" (meaning, He will select the location). The wording links the selected location to the selected sacrifice, as Abraham explains ominously to Isaac: "God will see to the sheep for His burnt offering" (v. 8). God releases just enough information to start Abraham embarking on his task, but in the end, the final reveal is in God's hands.

The Test

The opening verse immediately reveals to the reader that the following episode is a "test." "And it was after these things, God tested Abraham" (Gen. 22:1). An avid reader of biblical texts should be surprised by this spoiler at the very beginning of the story. The text, as we have come to see, is far more likely to withhold this information from the reader in order to create a sense of anticipation – the reader waits in suspense to see what will be the outcome of God's command. In this case, the text seems to take pity on the reader's sensitive soul. The act that God commands Abraham to perform is so unthinkable, so abhorrent, that the text cannot allow the reader to believe that it is in fact God's intention, even for a moment. This explanation, however, does not exactly coincide with the text itself – even though we are told this is a test, there is no assurance that this means that Isaac's life will not be taken. Perhaps that sacrifice itself is the test. The reader's horror remains; until the very end, we are still unsure what the outcome will be. Instead, defining the event as a test emphasizes another point altogether: God has no need for human sacrifice.[12] Even if God had asked Abraham to go through

---

Tarbitz 55 [1986]: 307). This is indeed a central idea; however, it is already reflected during the binding. See Isaac Kalimi, "The Land of Moriah, Mount Moriah and the Site of Solomon's Temple in Biblical Historiography," *Shnaton* 11 (1997): 185.

12. Cf. Jan P. Fokkelman, *Reading Biblical Narrative: An Introductory Guide*, trans. I. Smit (Louisville, 1999), 124. Another thesis was proposed by Aharon Koller. In his opinion in the first part of the narrative God is presented as one who is interested in human sacrifices, while in the second half of the narrative it becomes clear that a father is not allowed to sacrifice his son (Aaron Koller, *Unbinding Isaac: The Significance of the Akedah for Modern Jewish Thought* (Philadelphia and Lincoln, 2020]). In what follows, I will also rely on the division of the story into two, but in my opinion even in the first part God is not really presented as someone who wants human sacrifices but wants to try Abraham.

with sacrificing Isaac, it would only have been a test of Abraham's faith, not a divine need for human sacrifice.[13]

Here I Am

God beckons Abraham, and Abraham immediately responds, "*Hineni*." Abraham's response expresses utter obedience. The Hebrew term "*hineni*" is difficult to translate. Some translate it as, "Here I am,"[14] and others make do with the generic "Yes."[15] The response "*Hineni*" expresses so much more than its literal directive. The word denotes acquiescence to any command, and indicates absolute compliance and obedience.[16] The exact meaning of the word is particularly significant in the story of the binding, since it is one of the key words in the text, repeated three times across the narrative.[17] "*Hineni*" encapsulates an entire world of emotion and context. Like lovers who need only to utter the words "I love you" to convey the infinite depth of their sentiment, "*Hineni*" in the binding

13. Others view the caption from a psychological perspective: "The fear and trepidation for the fate of Isaac, who is to be sacrificed by his father, might impact the reader's mental equilibrium" (Shmaryahu Talmon, *Darkhei HaSippur BaMikra*, ed. G. Gil. [Jerusalem, 1965], 31). See also Jacob Licht, *Testing in the Hebrew Scriptures and in Post-Biblical Judaism* (Jerusalem, 1973), 21; Sarna, *Genesis* (JPS), 393; Yair Zakovitch, "Foreshadowing in Biblical Narrative," *Beer Sheva* 2 (1985): 86; Tzohar, *The Exposition in the Biblical Narrative*, 50–59.
14. This is the common translation. See, among others, NJPS, NAS, NAU, NIB, NIV, NRSV.
15. See James L. Crenshaw, *A Whirlpool of Torment: Israelite Traditions of God as an Oppressive Presence*, Overtures to Biblical Theology 12 (Philadelphia, 1984): 19; Stanley D. Walters, "Wood, Sand and Stars: Structure and Theology in Genesis 22:1–19," *Toronto Journal of Theology* 3 (1987): 301; Hamilton, *The Book of Genesis, Chapters 18–50*, 97.
16. BDB, 244. Another option, which is farther from the literal meaning, but closer to the definition of the phrase, is "Ready!" (Speiser, *Genesis*, 162; see the translation of the New American Bible).
17. Uriel Simon, "Notes on the Binding of Isaac," *Hagut BaMikra* 1 (1973): 163–170; Emanueli, *Genesis – Commentary and Insights*, 305–306; Yosef Tsamudi, *A Second Look at the Bible* (Tel Aviv, 1997), 163–165; Licht, *Testing in the Hebrew Scriptures and in Post-Biblical Judaism*, 116–117; Polak, *Biblical Narrative Aspects of Art and Design*, 230–32; Jonathan Jacobs, "Willing Obedience with Doubts: Abraham at the Binding of Isaac," *VT* 60 (2010): 557–558.

narrative conveys the same ineffable depth of emotion between the players in this dramatic scene.

God expresses His command to Abraham deliberately and gradually. "Take your son, your favored one, whom you love, Isaac." The undertone of this design clarifies that God knows exactly what He is asking of Abraham.[18] Lest one think that perhaps God, who sees the world on the broadest scale, in His infinite wisdom, might not understand the very human pain He is possibly causing Abraham in asking him to sacrifice his son, God explicitly names the stakes. God is fully aware of the meaning of the human relationship between Abraham and his cherished son. Take your son – *for whom you waited so long*; your favored one – *yes, the progeny of your wife, Sarah*; whom you love – *the child who has become your everything*; Isaac – *the boy born to you in miraculous joy*. God Himself emphasizes Isaac's uniqueness and Abraham's love. Nonetheless, God demands that Abraham make this ultimate sacrifice.

The Mountain

Isaac's sacrifice cannot take place in Beersheba or by the terebinths of Mamre; Abraham is required to travel to the land of Moriah and sacrifice his son there. This demand is linked with the sanctification of the "one place," which is emphasized throughout Deuteronomy. The journey to Moriah itself adds another layer to the test, in that the voyage forces Abraham to accept his decision anew every step of the way. But where is the mountain located?

II Chronicles 3:1 identifies the Temple Mount as the mountain of Moriah: "Then Solomon began to build the House of the Lord in Jerusalem on Mount Moriah." This reading is ratified by Abraham's naming of the mountain: "And Abraham named that site Adonai-yireh, whence the present saying, 'On the mount of the Lord there is vision'" (Gen. 22:14). The simplest interpretation would link a place in which

18. Skinner, *A Critical and Exegetical Commentary on Genesis*, 328. See also Sean E. McEvenue, "The Elohist at Work," *ZAW* 96 (1984): 323; Hamilton, *The Book of Genesis, Chapters 18–50*, 102; Polak, *Biblical Narrative Aspects of Art and Design*, 284; Amit, "Progression as a Rhetorical Device in Biblical Literature," 6–8.

God is "seen" and where people are "seen before Him" to Jerusalem.[19] The "land of Moriah" in Genesis is therefore commonly believed to be Jerusalem.[20]

Some commentators, however, object to this identification, noting, among other things, that there would be no need for Abraham to lug firewood to the Judean Hills. This school of thought points to Mount Sinai as the sanctified location of the sacrifice. Commentators debate the Jerusalem-Sinai question. Already in the Talmud, they debated the significance of the name "Moriah" as indicating its location.[21] One opinion states that Moriah indicates the place where "*horaa*," "teaching," emanated for the people of Israel, identified as the location of the Sanhedrin, in Jerusalem, which made rulings of law. The other opinion identifies the mountain as a place where "*mora*," "fear," emanated for the world. Rashi, in his commentary on the Talmud, first suggests that this may also be a reference to the impressive Jerusalem, a display of Israel's greatness to the world. His second suggestion, more relevant to us, is the possibility that this refers to Mount Sinai at the revelation of the Torah, which put fear in the hearts of all those who heard about it (as he cites Ps. 76:9, "The earth feared, and was silent").

There are compelling arguments for both locations. The identification of Moriah with Mount Sinai would reinforce the link between the binding narrative and two other narratives that took place in that location. First, the revelation at Sinai, which includes grammatical and thematic links to the binding narrative, and second, Elijah's escape to Mount Horeb.[22]

---

19. See in particular Umberto Cassuto, *Biblical and Canaanite Literatures: Studies on the Bible and Ancient Orient* (Jerusalem, 1979), 93–95; S. E. Loewenstamm, "Moriah, the Land of Moriah," *Entziklopedya Mikra'it* 5:458–460.
20. See also *Jubilees* 18:13; Josephus, *Antiquities* I:224 (Feldman, *Flavius Josephus: Translation and Commentary*, 86 and n692. Josephus understands the command as not only to go to the land of Moriah, but to "Mount Morion").
21. Taanit 16a.
22. Regarding the link between the revelation at Sinai and the binding of Isaac, see Jonathan Grossman, "The Binding of Isaac and the Sinai Covenant," in *The Sacrifice of Isaac in Israeli Eyes: Memorial Volume to Yitzhak Hirschberg*, ed. I. Rosenson and B. Lau (Tel Aviv, 2003), 355–364. Regarding the link between the binding narrative and Elijah's journey to Mount Horeb, see Devorah Spiro-Applebaum, "Between Isaac's

In addition to the significance of the identification in relation to the nature of Jerusalem and the sanctification process of the Temple Mount, determining the location of the sacrifice directly affects our perception of the purpose of this narrative as a whole. The new name of the location, Adonai-yireh, is appropriate for both Mount Sinai and Temple Mount. However, if the land of Moriah is the Sinai desert, the binding narrative should be read as an introduction to the revelation at Sinai. In this case, the element of "sight" is the crux of the narrative, and it is this element that is expanded to become a public revelation on Sinai. The firestone and knife (*esh umaakhelet*) of the binding become the consuming fire (*esh okhelet*) at the mountaintop in the Sinai revelation (cf. Gen. 22:7 and Ex. 24:17). Conversely, if the binding narrative took place in Jerusalem, the narrative is an introduction to Solomon's Temple and the inauguration of sacrificial custom on Temple Mount. The focus of this reading would be the sacrifice of the ram as a replacement of Isaac, and a sanctification of the altar in Jerusalem by Abraham, through the binding of Isaac.

Despite the importance of this question, the answer remains ambivalent. The significance of the absence of the binding narrative in Kings and the absence of a direct reference in Chronicles is impossible to decipher. The silence might serve a literary purpose, just as Abraham gathering the wood contributes to the design of his character and mood. Nonetheless, the prominence of the expression "the place" leads to the inclination to perceive Jerusalem as the site of the binding, as we will see below. The loneliness that accompanies the narrative does not characterize the geographical location of the narrative but the emotional space of the characters within.

Preparation

Abraham's mouth and heart remain mysteriously sealed throughout the narrative. He neither argues nor expresses emotion, and the text fails

---

Ascent (to the Altar) and Elijah's Ascent (to Heaven)," *Megadim* 45 (2007): 9–19. Yairah Amit ("The Place of Jerusalem in the Pentateuch," 51–52) writes, "Perhaps Abraham, like Elijah, who also departed from Beersheba, travelled in the direction of Horeb, which is referred to as 'the mountain of *Elohim*' and once as 'the mountain of *YHWH*.'"

to divulge his feelings (as opposed to his distress about Ishmael in Gen. 21:12). Instead, the narrative focuses on his intensive activity through a plethora of verbs: arose, saddled, took, split, set out. Replacing speech and emotions with concrete actions preserves the unattainability of Abraham's emotional state. In a state of horror and shock, it is perhaps the most human reaction in the world to busy oneself with the external preparations. Abraham cannot stop for a moment, cannot utter a word, for if he opens his mouth, the primal cry of his terrible suffering may burst forth and never cease.

Privileging silence over the attempt to formulate Abraham's unfathomable sorrow in words recalls Michel de Montaigne's essay "Of Sorrow." He writes about an artist who attempted to express the grief of those who watched Iphigenia's sacrifice, and having depicted them with "the utmost power of his art, when he came to that of her father, he drew him with a veil over his face, meaning thereby that no kind of countenance was capable of expressing such a degree of sorrow."[23] Focusing on Abraham's intensive activity serves as such a veil, hinting that such emotion cannot be expressed in mere words.

Nonetheless, a careful analysis of the verse might provide a glimpse into Abraham's emotional state. His absolute compliance might not indicate unequivocal identification with God's command. Within the context of compliance one might find hesitation and an attempt to postpone the act. Despite the difficulty of God's command, Abraham is still, after all, the devoted and faithful servant he has always been. Rashi stresses Abraham's haste to implement God's command early in the morning:

> "Arose early": He hastened to [perform] the commandment.
> "He saddled": He himself, and he did not command one of his servants, because love causes a disregard for the standard [of dignified conduct].
> "On the third day": Why did He delay from showing it to him immediately? So that people should not say that He confused

23. Michel De Montaigne, *The Complete Works, Comprising His Essays, Letters, and Journey Through Germany and Italy*, ed. William Hazlitt (Philadelphia, 1850), 30.

> him and confounded him suddenly and deranged his mind; that if he had had time to think it over, he would not have done it.[24]

The approach is generally accepted in modern commentary as well. Abraham's early rising demonstrates his haste. His personal preparation for the journey instead of commanding his servants shows his industry. His preparation of the wood in his house instead of delaying until he reaches Moriah indicates his urgency.[25] All of these details paint a picture of a person who does not hesitate to do as he is told.[26]

Nonetheless, others have claimed that the verse describing Abraham embarking on his journey portrays hesitation and an attempt to delay the binding. Some noted the literary procrastination which emerges from the comparison of Abraham's implementation with God's command:[27]

Command (Gen. 21:2)	**Implementation (21:3)**
	So Abraham woke early next morning, and saddled his ass
Take *your son*, your favored one, *Isaac*, whom you love,	and *took* with him two of his servants and *his son Isaac.*
	He split the wood for the burnt offering,
and *go forth* to the land of Moriah.	and he arose, and he *went forth* to the place of which God had told him.

24. Rashi on Gen. 22:3–4.
25. E.g., Hamilton, *The Book of Genesis, Chapters 18–50*, 107.
26. Harold Fisch (*The Holy Scriptures* [Jerusalem, 1977], 175–176) suggests that Abraham purposely rose early to ensure that Sarah was not present when he embarked on his journey.
27. Jacobs, "Willing Obedience with Doubts: Abraham at the Binding of Isaac." Also compare Shalom Carmy's criticism of Trible's analysis of the *Akeda* narrative: Shalom Carmy, "A Room with a View, but a Room of Our Own," *Tradition* 28 (1994): 50–54.

While Abraham rises early in the morning, the saddling of the ass does not move the plot forward and seems like an unnecessary description – as though Abraham is adding tasks to his list in order to delay the implementation of God's command. While God commands Abraham to "take" Isaac, Abraham "takes" two servants, and only then, almost as an afterthought, does he take his son Isaac as well. God's emphasis on Isaac's singularity is contrasted by Abraham taking two servants in addition to his son.[28] Abraham is not prohibited from taking an entourage along on the journey, but saddling the ass and taking the servants are actions that stray from the formulation of the commandment. Splitting wood at this point – despite the long journey to the mountains, where presumably trees can be found – is Abraham's way of delaying the inevitable.[29] Perhaps Abraham had hoped that his willingness to prepare for the journey would suffice, and God would call off the binding. "Abraham broadcasts his message to the heavens: See, I am serious; I've taken everyone and I've even hewn wood for the sacrifice. Is this not sufficient proof of my willingness to obey God?"[30]

Each of these approaches focuses on a different emotional plane, and each can find support in the text. Abraham's activity indicates that he ultimately succumbs to the will of his master, while the hesitations are indicative of his emotional state. The delays and added actions indicate Abraham's difficulty in fulfilling God's command, though there is no doubt in his mind that what the Lord has commanded he must obey.

Another distinction emerges from the comparison. While the command focuses on the place ("*Go forth* to the *land of Moriah,* and offer him *there* as a burnt offering on *one of the heights* that *I will point out to you*"), it is Abraham's actions that are emphasized, and the location

28. Alternatively, Trible claims that Isaac is actually placed in the spotlight in this verse because he is surrounded by six verbs, three on either side: "And he rose early – saddled – took – *his son Isaac* – split – arose – set out" (Trible, "Genesis 22: The Sacrifice of Sarah," 173–174).
29. On splitting the wood as a delaying tactic, see Jon D. Levenson, *The Death and Resurrection of the Beloved Son* (New Haven, CT, 1993), 135.
30. Jacobs, "Willing Obedience with Doubts: Abraham at the Binding of Isaac," 554n17. See also Boehm, *The Binding of Isaac: A Religious Model of Disobedience*, 41–48.

briefly hinted at ("He *went forth* to the place of which God had told him"). From the divine perspective, the location is crucial, while in Abraham's emotional state the horrific action he is required to perform blocks out all other details; the place is insignificant compared with the enormity of what Abraham is expected to do. Once Isaac is out of danger, the place will become significant to Abraham as well, and Abraham will be the one to name the mountain in commemoration of the event.

Abraham Speaks

Abraham's silence throughout this story has been deafening. We can only infer the emotional turmoil Abraham experiences as he makes his way to the mountain accompanied by Isaac and the two servants. We can infer, as well, the deep well of faith from which Abraham pulls in order to obey God's commandment. However, both Abraham's anguish and loyalty remain tacit as we watch the father and his son on their final journey.

On the third day, Abraham finally breaks his silence. "On the third day Abraham looked up and saw the place from afar." We do not know how Abraham recognized his destination. According to midrashic texts, Abraham saw "a cloud tied at the top of the mountain."[31] This idea might be based in the analogy mentioned above between the binding narrative and the covenant at Sinai (Ex. 24), and the rabbis transferred the explicit cloud from Sinai to Abraham's Moriah.[32]

Since the first, simple utterance of acceptance, "Here I am," Abraham has been silent. Now, as he approaches his final destination and begins the final climb up the mountain to sacrifice his son, Abraham speaks out. We might expect our protagonist to proclaim his everlasting love to his son or to gird his resolve in a reiteration of his faith in preparation for the final, most difficult step. In his first words in days, Abraham turns, not to his son nor to God, but to his servants, issuing a lengthy and wholly ordinary list of instructions – "You stay here, Isaac and I will be back in a bit."

31. Genesis Rabba 56:1.
32. Sasson and Grossman, "On Implicit Biblical Analogies in Midrashim of the Sages," 26–30.

The literary purpose of the servants is vague from the outset and yet here Abraham's longest speech is made to them. Later, as we will see, the binding narrative returns to the servants: "Abraham then returned to his youths, and they departed together for Beersheba" (Gen. 22:19). On the other hand, after Isaac is saved, he is never mentioned again in the narrative.

The literary purpose of the servants seems to be their absence from the central act.[33] The initial focus on the servants emphasizes Abraham and Isaac's separation from them, and enhances the intimacy of the second leg of their journey. The servants represent the mundane, while Abraham and Isaac proceed to do something extraordinary. Abraham distinguishes between the servants ("*You* stay here with the ass") and himself and Isaac ("*The boy and I* will go up there"). The linguistic fabric highlights the distinction between the two groups:

The Servants	**Abraham and Isaac**
Then Abraham said to his youths (*ne'arav*),	The boy (*naar*) and I
You stay here	*will go up there*
with the ass	we will worship and we will return to you."

The "youths" (*ne'arim*) are contrasted with the "boy" (*naar*).[34] One party "stays," while the other goes "up there." The clever use of wordplay emphasizes the distance between those who remain and those who continue on their journey. While the former remain "here," "*po*," the latter proceed "up there," "*ko*."[35] The servants are designed as a contrast to Abraham and his son, who depart from the mundane reality represented by servants and asses. Abraham turns to the servants and says,

33. The emphasis on a minor character in a narrative sometimes serves to highlight the absence of that character later on. On this literary technique, see Jonathan Grossman, "The Vanishing Character in Biblical Narrative: The Role of Hathach in Esther 4," *VT* 62 (2012): 561–571.
34. Cf. Hamilton, *The Book of Genesis, Chapters 18–50*, 108.
35. Mathews, *Genesis*, 292.

"You stay here with the ass." Something extraordinary is about to occur, an intense and unforgettable act, and we must face it alone.[36]

At the end of the story, Abraham returns to the mundane reality represented by his servants. The binding is an isolated incident, disconnected from logical psychological context. The event cannot be explained by any external parameter; any outside view cannot fully comprehend the occurrence. As Abraham and Isaac make their final steps toward the binding, all tethers to reality must be left behind.

Up the Mountain

After leaving the servants and the ass behind, father and son embark on the second part of their journey. The second leg of the journey, like the first, is filled with verbs describing Abraham's actions: "Abraham *took* the *wood* for the burnt offering and *put it on* his son Isaac. He himself *took* the *firestone* and the *knife*; and the two *walked on* together" (Gen. 22:6). Here, too, the items that Abraham takes with him are listed in detail.

The new start separates the journey into two parts. The first stage included servants and an ass, while the second is the intimate journey of father and son. Some read Abraham's placement of the wood "on his son Isaac" as an intentional irony, since Isaac will later be put on those same pieces of wood in Genesis 22:9. More significantly, placing the wood on Isaac separates "Abraham items" and "Isaac items." The repetition of the verb "he took" distinguishes Isaac and the wood from Abraham with his knife and firestone. Isaac carries the wood on which he will later be sacrificed; they will be burned together. Abraham carries the knife and firestone; these are his responsibility as the bringer of the sacrifice. At the same time, the wood is not as nightmarish a substance in this context as the knife and firestone, which are killing instruments. Abraham distances his son from the more frightening elements, protecting him in whatever way he could.[37]

36. Emanueli, *Genesis – Commentary and Insights*, 303. Benno Jacob (*The First Book of the Bible: Genesis*, 495) compares this to the reinstitution of the Sinai covenant after the sin of the Golden Calf. There, too, the "people" and "cattle" were forbidden to approach the mountain (Ex. 33:3). He also compares the event to the High Priest entering the Holy of Holies in Lev. 16:17.

37. Compare to von Rad, *Genesis*, 240; Trible, "Genesis 22: The Sacrifice of Sarah," 175.

The firestone, the wood, and the knife contribute to the sequence and advance the plot. When Abraham set out on his journey, he took "his ass and took with him two of his youths and his son Isaac" (Gen. 22:3). Now that Abraham has disengaged from the servants and the ass, the narrative focuses on smaller items that are not symbolic of the journey but of the impending sacrifice.

The absence of the donkey and servants enables a constructive dialogue that portrays the father-son relationship in an intimate and loving light. Abraham is consistently referred to as Isaac's "father," while Abraham addresses Isaac with an endearing "my son" every time he speaks. The familial terms highlight the difficulty and tragedy of Abraham's test. This is especially apparent in the first line of the dialogue: "Then Isaac said to his father Abraham, 'Father!' And he answered, 'Yes, my son'" (Gen. 22:7). This stage, which lacks any content of substance, is rare in the biblical narrative, and has no impact on the remainder of the dialogue. The sole purpose of the opening sentence is the emphasis on the father-son relationship. But Abraham's response is noteworthy due to his repetitive use of the phrase "*Hineni*" – "Here I am."[38] As noted earlier, the phrase expresses absolute compliance; an early agreement to any possible demand. Abraham expresses this compliance toward God, but also toward his son.[39] The tension in the narrative reaches its climax: Abraham is not a coldhearted father who is indifferent to the fate of his son; Abraham's dual loyalty will force him to choose between his God and his son. The Danish philosopher Søren Kierkegaard developed the idea of Abraham's complete loyalty to his son in his book, *Fear and Trembling*. He believed that the paradox of faith is expressed by Abraham's love for Isaac, which is only intensified in the binding narrative.[40]

---

38. See Devora Steinmetz, *From Father to Son: Kinship, Conflict, and Continuity in Genesis* (Louisville, 1991), 51–53; Wenham, *Genesis 16–50*, 101; Buber, *Darko shel Mikra*. The prominence of the word in the narrative led JoAnne Tucker and Susan Freeman (*Torah in Motion: Creating Dance Midrash* [Denver, 1990], 27–28) to create a "binding dance" based on the rhythm of the phrase "*hineni*."
39. Note the ironic wordplay between Abraham's response to his son "*hineni*," and the son's question: "Here is the fire (*hineh ha'esh*) and wood, but where is the lamb for the burnt offering?" (Gen. 22:7).
40. Kierkegaard, *Fear and Trembling*. See also Boehm, *The Binding of Isaac: A Religious Model of Disobedience*, 101–109.

Isaac's question reminds the reader once again of the threatening knife, this time by its omission. Isaac mentions the wood and the firestone when he asks what it is they are sacrificing (Gen. 22:7), but he fails to mention the knife. The reader knows that Abraham and Isaac are traveling with a knife, so perhaps Isaac's omission, in addition to the question itself, indicate that he is beginning to suspect the identity of the sacrifice. Isaac's knowledge is crucial to the analysis of the emotional state of the characters in the narrative, but Abraham's response only adds to the ambiguity.

In the initial dialogue, Abraham chose to omit the true destination and purpose of his journey (Gen. 22:5). In response to his son's question, Abraham refrains from lying and says: "God will see[41] to the sheep for His burnt offering, my son" (v. 8). Abraham's response led to two interpretations of his position. Medieval commentators view Abraham's response as having a double meaning, which hints at the bitter truth. Rabbi David Kimhi (Radak) writes:

> He offered him a response that could be understood in two ways. According to one, "my son" addresses the questioner, as in "Here I am, my son." In other words, "My son, God will see to the sheep for His burnt offering," He knows the sheep, and He will provide it for us. Alternatively, "God will see to the sheep for His burnt offering," and who is that sheep? It is "my son"! Isaac understood that he would be that sheep. Therefore it is written, "And the two of them walked on together."[42]

Isaac might have understood from Abraham's response that he is the sacrifice; the missing sheep, Abraham's evasive answer.... In a time and place where sacrificing children was not entirely uncommon, this might have been sufficient for Isaac to figure it out. However, Radak's claim that Abraham grammatically hinted at the fact is unsatisfactory. Abraham's

41. Regarding the verb R-A-H, "to see," denoting "to select," see Greenstein, "Reading Pragmatically: The Binding of Isaac," 120n32. Greenstein notes that the verb "to see" includes both meanings in Akkadian literature as well.

42. Radak on Gen. 22:8. Rashi and Bekhor Shor suggest similar interpretations.

use of the affectionate term "my son" overlaps with the multiplicity of familial terms throughout the dialogue,[43] so there is nothing unique about this particular reply.

Others claim that Abraham's response demonstrates his confidence that ultimately a sheep will be sacrificed, and not his son. Frank Polak writes, "This response can resolve the distinction between God's demand and the love of the son. These things do not only attest to total acceptance of God's command, but also to utter confidence in the fact that 'God will see to the sheep for His burnt offering.'"[44] However, this suggestion ignores the order of the details in the narrative and the building tension toward a solution that the reader is unaware of at this point. When rereading the story, one might insert new meaning into Abraham's words, in light of the ram that is ultimately sacrificed.[45] At this stage, however, neither the reader nor Abraham have any way of knowing that Isaac will not be sacrificed on the altar.[46]

This idea is highly significant in the design of the character of Abraham. When Abraham sets out to sacrifice his son, he is utterly convinced that his son will be sacrificed. The narrative demonstrates Abraham's great fear of God and complete devotion to His will. Conversely, Abraham faces the impossible question by Isaac; he wants to protect him from the bitter truth, but cannot bring himself to lie

---

43. See Sarna, *Genesis* (JPS), 152; Wenham, *Genesis 16–50*, 108–109.
44. Polak, *Biblical Narrative Aspects of Art and Design*, 285. For an expansion of this approach and its representatives, see Greenstein, "Reading Pragmatically: The Binding of Isaac," 121.
45. Don Isaac Abrabanel comments on Gen. 22: "The text signifies that anything that was spoken [by Abraham] in passing, even as a deferral for the purpose of keeping the peace, came true, like the words of a man of God who cannot speak falsely." While Polak believes Abraham was expressing his wish, according to Abrabanel, Abraham was not aware of the significance of his statement. Cf. Hamilton, *The Book of Genesis, Chapters 18–50*, 113 (in the context of his commentary on the ram). On Abrabanel's general theory regarding ambiguous phrases, see Jonathan Grossman, "Abrabanel's Stance towards the Existence of Ambiguous Expressions in the Bible," *Beit Mikra* 52 (2007): 126–138.
46. Kierkegaard views this as Abraham's greatest quality; particularly the magnitude of his faith. Abraham accepts God's command, but still believes "it is through Isaac that offspring shall be continued for you."

to his son at this time. Abraham's solution is an evasive and ambiguous answer. His simultaneous inability to face his son with the truth and his inability to lie reinforce the difficulty of his situation and the immensity of his test.

The question of Isaac's knowledge is one of the great unanswered mysteries of the narrative: Did Abraham have to struggle with Isaac and bind him against his will? Did Isaac understand and cooperate? Before and after the dialogue between Abraham and Isaac, the text has the same description, "And the two of them walked on together" (Gen. 22:6, 8). If Isaac understood or even suspected that he was the sacrifice, the identical phrase would be read entirely differently. If Isaac continued walking to his own sacrifice, it would indeed be together with his father, with the same intent.

Abraham Picks Up the Knife

Prior to the two conversations, between Abraham and the servants and then between Abraham and Isaac, the text opened by letting us know that the final step of the journey was about to begin: "He went forth to the place of which God had told him" (Gen. 22:3). Following the dialogues, the text returns to the plot sequence and relates, "They arrived at the place of which God had told him" (v. 9). After Abraham and Isaac's dialogue, Abraham no longer is described as walking in the singular but rather in the plural; Abraham and Isaac walk side-by-side.

The rhythm of the narrative changes significantly in the following scene. After three days of walking and nothing to report, suddenly the reader is provided once again with a plethora of verbs associated with Abraham's actions (Gen. 22:9): "They arrived," "Abraham built," "he laid out," "he bound his son," "he laid him on the altar," "Abraham picked up the knife to slay his son." The sudden activity is particularly apparent in the additional verb integrated into the text when Abraham takes the knife (v. 10): "And Abraham sent forth (*vayishlaḥ*) his hand, and he took (*vayikaḥ*) the knife to slay his son." There is a sudden deceleration in the pace of the narrative as the moment of truth – of test – approaches. The scene seems to play out in those final moments in slow motion – the hand raises, the knife is clutched, the moment is upon us. All the while, Abraham and Isaac remain silent. What more can be said?

As the moment of sacrifice advances, the text flashes back on the previous episodes in which Abraham has built an altar. The phrase "Abraham built *an* altar *there*" is the standard description for the construction of altars in the Abraham cycle (Gen. 12:7, 8:13, 8:18), and has been used to indicate that the altar was built in a specific location.[47] Here, in Genesis 22:9, the word "altar" is preceded by the definite article in its initial appearance, "*the* altar," indicating that not only the location is significant, but that the entire purpose of the sacrifice itself is unusual. Abraham tentatively lays out the wood on the altar, and in doing so not only delays the inevitable – he is disrupting the usual process of a sacrificial offering. The sacrificial world values the act of preparing the wood for sacrifice (e.g., Lev. 1:7). However, the fire is commonly lit before the sacrifice is placed (Lev. 1:7–8; 6:5). In this case, Abraham binds his son and places him on the wood that is on the altar, without lighting a fire. Furthermore, sacrifices are commonly slaughtered prior to placing them on the altar – Abraham binds Isaac to the altar while he is still alive. Ordinary sacrifices are slaughtered and then burned upon the altar unbound.[48]

Some commentators have suggested that different customs prevailed between the sacrifice of children and animals.[49] However, God specifically defined Isaac's sacrifice as a "burnt offering," linking the command with the world of animal sacrifice. Some view the distinction as proof that Abraham never had intended to sacrifice Isaac (and that Abraham decided of his own volition to sacrifice the ram as a replacement). Therefore, instead of lighting a fire on the wood, Abraham bound his son upon the altar but left him alive.[50] However, the narrative process,

---

47. In contrast with Noah's altar, which was built in an insignificant location: "Then Noah built an altar to the Lord" (Gen. 8:20). See also Gen. 26:25 (Isaac in Beersheba) and 35:7 (Jacob in Bethel).
48. Jacob (*The First Book of the Bible: Genesis*, 498) claims that the binding of animals in Leviticus is obvious, and therefore not written explicitly. However, even if the animal is bound for slaughtering, it is not placed bound on the altar. Wenham wants to prove from Abraham's need to bind Isaac that Abraham knew Isaac might resist. His lack of resistance proves his devotion to God as well (Wenham, *Genesis 16–50*, 109).
49. Levenson, *The Death and Resurrection of the Beloved Son*, 135.
50. Boehm, *The Binding of Isaac: A Religious Model of Disobedience*, 47.

and especially the statement "Abraham raised his hand and took the knife *to slay his son,*" leave no room to doubt Abraham's intentions.

We must examine the order of sacrifice from a literary perspective rather than one related to realia. Had there been fire on the altar, the angel would have had to appear to Abraham and stop him before he had placed Isaac on it. Of course, if Abraham had slaughtered his son before placing him on the altar, the angel would have had to intervene earlier as well. The current order of events enables the angel to appear when Isaac is bound and already upon the altar. The wood beneath him prevents the suspicion that Abraham was not willing to go through with his plan to the bitter end. Everything was prepared, and from a dramatic perspective the reader's nerves have been stretched to their limit. The narrative pushes the dramatic moment until the very end; the altar is prepared, the boy is bound, and only then does the angel appear and prevent Abraham from slaughtering his son. After Abraham "sent forth his hand" (Gen. 22:10), the angel can intervene and call out to him, "Do not send forth your hand!" (v. 12).

Passing the Test

The abrupt conclusion to Abraham's test of faith brings the entire narrative full circle. The text emphasizes the parallel by repeating the call of Abraham's name ("He said to him, 'Abraham'" and, "Abraham! Abraham!") and his response ("Here I am") on both occasions. The command to sacrifice Isaac includes the terms, "Your son, your favored one, Isaac," and when the test is terminated the angel commends Abraham, "You have not withheld your son, your favored one."

Despite the similarities that create this parallel, there are three minor distinctions in the formulation of each revelation. In the first revelation, God appears to Abraham, while in the second, the message is delivered by "an angel of the Lord…from heaven."[51] Additionally, in the first revelation, Abraham's name is called once ("He said to him, 'Abraham'"), while in the second, Abraham's name is called twice ("Abraham! Abraham!"). These two distinctions stem directly from the context of each scene. Both indicate that Abraham is coming closer to

51. On the change from *Elohim* to *YHWH,* see below.

God – the repetition of Abraham's name is clearly a sign of intimacy as well as urgency, and the appearance of an angel in the book of Genesis often indicates greater intimacy. This was apparent in the two tidings of a son brought to Abraham and Sarah by angels (Gen. 17–18). The more intimate, personal message was delivered by angels (Gen. 18) while the national message, which is unrelated personally to Abraham and Sarah as a couple, was delivered by God Himself (Gen. 17). Here, too, the content of the initial message necessitates a distance that does not take the collapse of Abraham's personal life into consideration, and so, the message is delivered by *Elohim,* the God of the universe. Conversely, the emotive and dramatic halt to the sacrifice, coupled with a message of reconciliation, is delivered by an angel. Addressing Abraham by calling out his name twice conveys a similar placating message, as in the case of Jacob on the eve of his departure from the land (46:2), Moses at the burning bush (Ex. 3:4),[52] and Samuel in his inaugural revelations (I Sam. 3:4). The revelation in each of the scenes above is delivered in a pacified and encouraging atmosphere. Calling Abraham's name twice and the appearance of an angel are both an appropriate introduction to rescuing Abraham's son.[53]

The third and final difference between the initial command and the angel's arbitration relates to the references to Isaac. God commands Abraham to sacrifice Isaac using the terms "your son, your favored one, *whom you love,* Isaac." When the test is stopped, the angel commends Abraham, "You have not withheld your son, your favored one." The angel omits Abraham's love for his child; Abraham expressed his absolute willingness to sacrifice that which is dearest to him to God, requiring him to overcome his love for Isaac in order to do so. Love cannot be mentioned while Abraham still holds the slaughtering knife in his hand.

52. On the comparison between the binding of Isaac and the revelation at the burning bush, see Norman Habel, "The Form and Significance of the Call Narrative," *ZAW* 77 (1965): 301–302.

53. Some scholars write that calling a name twice is an element used when God or an angel attempt to stop the protagonist from acting (Gunkel, *Genesis – Translated and Interpreted,* 235; Benno Jacob, *The First Book of the Bible: Genesis,* 144; Hamilton, *The Book of Genesis, Chapters 18–50,* 111–112). This interpretation fits the binding narrative and the burning bush (Ex. 3:5), but not in Samuel's inaugural revelation.

The scene ends with Abraham naming "the place." The term "the place" accompanies the entire narrative and becomes one of the focal points of the story, starting with God's command to go to an unidentified location in the land of Moriah (Gen. 22:2), through Abraham's journey with his servants to "the place of which God had told him" (v. 3) until finally Abraham "saw the place from afar" (v. 4). When Abraham leaves his servants behind and walks alone with his son, finally "they arrived at the place of which God had told him; Abraham built the altar there" (v. 9). Finally, the "place" is revealed, and ultimately named as one of the central motifs of the story (v. 14). The group Abraham travels with is reduced until the text can focus on father and son. In correlation, the vague and general destination is narrowed down from one of the hilltops in "the land of Moriah" to a place that is visible, but "from afar," until finally Abraham and Isaac arrive at the place, and Abraham sanctifies the location by building an altar. Finally, "the place" is given a name in commemoration of the event. The purpose of this gradual focus is, of course, to serve as background for the sanctification of the mountain. It is noteworthy that Abraham does not name the place when he builds the altar, or even after experiencing the relief of the rescue of his son. Instead, the naming is delayed until after the sacrifice of the ram.

The Encore

The dramatic scene comes to a climax with Abraham's hand wielding the knife over his son, the angel's impassioned cry to stop, and finally the incredible relief of realization that the entire episode was a test. As the characters decompress, a ram serendipitously appears to provide a "replacement" for Isaac as the sacrifice. The scene ends with a beautifully wrapped finale – God has received His sacrifice, the characters may now return to their lives, and the literary cycle has come full circle. The etymological note ("Abraham named that site Adonai-yireh") is a common ending to a biblical narrative, and one we have encountered previously in Genesis 16:14, 19:37–38, and 21:31.

This ending to the narrative would be more than satisfactory. However, following the sacrifice of the ram and the naming of the location, the story moves forward in an addendum. Suddenly, the angel returns to bestow a blessing upon Abraham. The text itself corroborates the feeling of a postscript to the original story: "And the angel appeared to Abraham a second time." Why is the angel's promise only mentioned in the second, surprising revelation, after the ram is sacrificed, rather than during the first revelation? Why wouldn't the blessing be included in the "main" narrative? Moreover, what is the significance of this additional blessing vis-à-vis the promises, blessings, and covenants that God has bestowed upon Abraham during the entire narrative cycle of his journey?

The focal point of this promise that concludes the narrative is Abraham's offspring. The blessing (Gen. 22:17) has three components. First is the multiplicity of Abraham's offspring: "I will bestow My blessing upon you and make your descendants as numerous as the stars of heaven and the sands on the seashore." Second is their success at conquest: "And your descendants shall seize the gates of their foes," and third is their political success: "All the nations of the earth shall bless themselves by your descendants." The relevance of the blessing is obvious. Once Abraham shows his willingness to abandon his only child out of loyalty to God, the multiplicity and success of his offspring by God is a fitting and encouraging message.

The blessing seems to be designed in a concentric structure:[54]

A: Because you have done this
  B: and have not withheld your son, your favored one,
    C: I will bestow My blessing upon you
  B': and make your descendants as numerous as the stars of heaven and the sands on the seashore; and your descendants shall seize the gates of their foes. All the nations of the earth shall bless themselves by your descendants,
A': because you have obeyed My command.

The structure signifies the internal process, where the frame of the blessing (Abraham's actions) justifies its content (God's blessing).

---

54. For an alternative chiastic structure, see Yitzhak Avishur, "The Narratives of the Binding of Isaac and Abraham's Exodus from Haran – Structure, Style and Language," in *Studies in the Archaeology and History of Ancient Israel*, ed. M. Heltzer, A. Segal, and D Kaufman (Haifa, 1993), 96.

The blessing is explicitly designed as a reward for Abraham's actions, in contrast with all other blessings in the Abraham cycle.

Throughout Abraham's journey, the reader has struggled with the dichotomy of his chosenness by God. On one hand, God's choice of Abraham is a divine revelation, unconditional and unencumbered by cause and effect – God chose Abraham because Abraham is who He chose. On the other hand, the narrative has continually placed Abraham in situations that highlight his character and his moral fiber – proving to the reader that Abraham, on his own, is more than worthy to inherit the role that God has chosen for him.

When we first meet Abraham at the beginning of his story in Genesis 12, God's blessings are a destiny and an unconditional promise. The concluding narrative of the cycle after the binding of Isaac portrays the blessings as a reward for Abraham, who proved that he deserves to be blessed.

We can see this difference in the changing order of the narrative. Genesis 12 is written in the following order:

1. **Command**: "*Go forth* from your land and from the place of your birth and from your father's house to the land that I will show you."
2. **Blessing**: "I will bless those who bless you, and curse him that curses you; And all the families of the earth shall bless themselves by you."
3. **Implementation**: "Abram took his wife Sarai ... and they set out for the land of Canaan."
4. **Building an altar**: After reaching Canaan and another revelation in the terebinths of Mamre, Abraham "built an altar there to the Lord who had appeared to him."

All four components are present in the binding narrative, but the order is changed:

1. **Command**: "*Go forth* to the land of Moriah."
2. **Implementation**: "So early next morning, Abraham saddled his ass and took with him two of his servants and his son Isaac ... and he set out for the place of which God had told him."

3. **Building an altar:** "Abraham built the altar there.... And Abraham named that site Adonai-yireh."[55]
4. **Blessing:** "I will bestow My blessing upon you and make your descendants as numerous as the stars of heaven and the sands on the seashore; and your descendants shall seize the gates of their foes. All the nations of the earth shall bless themselves by your descendants."[56]

The context of the blessing in Genesis 12 demonstrates that the blessing should be viewed as conditional. If Abraham agrees to God's demand to journey to Canaan, he will merit multiple blessings. The integration of the blessing in the command makes the blessing itself a source of encouragement to Abraham to begin his journey. The blessings are offered to him, and all he has to do is "go forth" and take them. In contrast, the binding narrative delays the promises to the end. Abraham cannot be promised a multitude of offspring on his way to sacrifice his only child; such a promise would undermine the nature of the test. Nonetheless, the nature of the promise changes as a result. Here, the promise is no longer an encouragement to act, but a reward for having acted.

In light of all this, the content of the blessing is all the more surprising. One would have expected Abraham to be rewarded for his extreme fidelity with a new blessing, but the content of the blessing is identical to previous blessings Abraham had been given in various stages of his journey through Canaan.[57] The blessing might be viewed as a reinforcement or culmination of all previous blessings.[58] But the context of the blessing ("Because you have done this and have not

55. The nature of the altar in each of the narratives is entirely different. Nonetheless, Avishur ("The Narratives of the Binding of Isaac and Abraham's Exodus from Haran – Structure, Style and Language," 100–101) compares the construction of the two altars, and the contrast emphasizes the delay of the promise in the narrative.
56. "We should consider the fact that once more in Abraham's story, between these two incidents, God said of Abraham, 'All the nations of the earth are to bless themselves by him' (18:18)" (Buber, *Darko shel Mikra*, 294).
57. In reference to the metaphor of stars and sand, see Gen. 13:16; 15:5; 17:2. Regarding overcoming enemies, see Gen. 15:7–21. In reference to the blessing of the people of the land, see Gen. 12:3.
58. Emanueli, *Genesis – Commentary and Insights*, 308.

withheld your son ... because you have obeyed My command") indicates that Abraham's actions merit something new.

Three possible solutions are offered to this dilemma. Bin-Nun claims that while the content of the blessings is not new, since the selection of Abraham was questioned in Gerar, there is a need to reaffirm the original blessings:

> When Abraham agreed to make a pact and take an oath with Abimelech, and their agreement is officially sanctioned, a question might be raised regarding the selection of Abraham, regarding his designation, and particularly regarding the promise of the land. Perhaps Abimelech is also deserving? Why should Abraham be given more blessings than Abimelech? The binding of Isaac responds to these misgivings.... [T]he purpose of the test is to renew Abraham's selection after his descent to Gerar and the land of the Philistines ... to reinstate his mission, to renew his destiny, to restore the selection and blessing.[59]

Alternatively, some commentators reject the basic assumption that the blessing is the same as the previous ones, and they attempt to find something new about the promise that follows the binding of Isaac. Gordon Wenham explains that the phrase "*barekh avarekhekha*," "in a blessing I will bless you," indicates a special blessing. He also finds the innovation in the multiplicity of offspring promised to Abraham. While the image of the stars was used previously, the metaphor of sand is new. Wenham also finds innovation in the promise of land. To him, the statement "Your descendants shall seize the gates of their foes" is concrete, as opposed to previous theoretical promises of land without a promise of military victory.[60]

The difficulty with Wenham's reading is that richer literary metaphors do not indicate an innovative message. Although the sand metaphor was not previously used, the metaphors of sand or stars represent the same thing: a multiplicity of offspring. The festive occasion might

59. Bin-Nun, *Chapters of the Fathers*, 108–11.

60. Wenham, *Genesis 16–50*, 111–12.

call for new metaphors and poetic language,[61] but does it not also call for additional reward?

A third option adopts the assumption that the content of the blessing contains no innovation. The innovation of the blessing in the binding narrative is not in its content, but in its legal validity. I think that Radak (on Gen. 22:16) was right to emphasize the novelty of this revelation as an "oath." The blessing's novelty lies in its caption: "By Myself I swear" (Gen. 22:16). This is the only time that Abraham is vowed something by God. In fact, this is God's only oath toward one of the forefathers. When God speaks to Isaac, he reinforces "fulfilling the oath that I swore to your father Abraham" (26:3–5). Unlike previous blessings, a promise is binding. God promises in His own name – He is bound to His word. The purpose of the blessings bestowed upon Abraham at the start of his journey was to set goals. If the following generations cease from walking in God's ways as Abraham had instructed them, God is not bound to those blessings, since Abraham's offspring no longer realize the destiny that merits those blessings. A covenant obligates both parties, even if one is a lord and the other a vassal; the violation of the covenant by one party exempts the other from all obligations. Conversely, an oath is unconditional. Abraham's willingness to sacrifice his son bought him an everlasting oath. The nature of the blessing therefore correlates with its place in the story cycle. In the opening narrative, Abraham was encouraged to pursue a blessed destiny, while in the culminating narrative, he is given blessings he earned by his own deeds. The final words God utters to Abraham in the cycle are "You have obeyed My command."

Although the promise could simply be attributed to the enormity of the test, it might also be a manifestation of "measure for measure." God's unconditional commitment is a reaction to Abraham's unconditional loyalty. When the episode is read in its wider context, it emerges that Abraham had the legal right (which, in this context, also reflects the moral right) to refuse God's command to sacrifice his son. God had told Abraham in the Covenant of Circumcision that the covenant would be implemented through Isaac: "Sarah your wife shall bear you

61. Robert W. L. Moberly, "The Earliest Commentary on the Akedah," *VT* 38 (1988): 318.

a son, and you shall name him Isaac; and I will maintain My covenant with him as an everlasting covenant for his offspring to come.... But My covenant I will maintain with Isaac, whom Sarah shall bear to you at this season next year" (Gen. 17:19–20). The general promise of offspring was anchored in a concrete promise that Isaac would be born in one year, and that Isaac would be the one to maintain God's covenant. Assuming that God would have allowed Abraham to slaughter Isaac, His command would have been a violation of His covenant with Abraham. Abraham therefore had every legal and moral right to refuse. Nonetheless, Abraham's unequivocal loyalty led him to follow God's command. By doing so, he expressed unconditional devotion to God, independent of the actions of the "other party." Abraham's devotion overpowered the content of previous covenants and mutual agreements. Every step of the three-day journey to Moriah was an expression of utmost faith in God, despite His violation of the covenant from Abraham's perspective. God's response is a promise. The blessings are now anchored and independent of Abraham's loyalty. Even if Abraham's offspring should sin and become unfaithful to the covenant, they will maintain the merit of the binding of Isaac, and their relationship with God will prevail.

In light of the link between the test and the result, the blessing is an appropriate conclusion for the narrative, and cannot be viewed as a later addition. While one would have expected the promise to follow Isaac's rescue, instead, the angel only delivers the message of the promise in a second revelation, after the sacrifice of the ram and the naming of the mountain.

The purpose of a "false conclusion" is often to surprise the reader with an additional element or stage that seems unnecessary to the progression of the plot.[62] The design of the binding narrative in this way contributes to the portrayal of Abraham's character, since Abraham acts without intending to be rewarded. While the blessings in Genesis 12 accompanied the demand to "go forth," here the blessings are "appended" to the main message of the text, instead of distracting from Abraham's true and unadulterated intention. The blessing is not

62. See further in Jonathan Grossman, *Text and Subtext: On Exploring Biblical Narrative Design* (Tel Aviv, 2015), 210–218.

the main purpose of the narrative, but the realization of Abraham's faith and loyalty. Abraham did not act in order to be blessed. As a result of his absolute faith, Abraham's children will benefit from absolute loyalty from God – regardless of their actions, they will always be protected by their forefather's sacrifice.

The Binding as a Precedent for Worship of God

The opportune appearance of the ram is a clear literary tool, although its purpose is less straightforward. The narrative portrays the ram as a substitute for Isaac. The parallel between God's command and Abraham's actions indicates that the offering is indeed "in place of his son."[63] Despite the wider parallel, however, there is an essential distinction in the nature of each of the sacrifices. The angel's revelation prevents Abraham from slaughtering his son (Gen. 22:12), but does not include a command to sacrifice another animal in his stead. The ram is offered voluntarily, whereas the son was to be offered by divine command. The process of replacing Isaac is described as Abraham's initiative, the initial mandatory offering replaced with a voluntary offering.

In order to understand the ram's significance in the narrative, we must analyze the story's structure, beginning with the question of where the story "splits" – what moment can we point to as the narrative's climax? Some view the short dialogue between Abraham and Isaac on the final leg of their journey to the mountain (Gen. 22:7–8) as the climax of the narrative. This dialogue is bordered at both ends with the statement, "And they walked on together" (vv. 6 and 8), which emphasizes the dialogue that occurs between the two statements. Some note that the dialogue is the heart of a concentric structure throughout the

63. The word "*aḥar*" (lit. "after") in Gen. 22:13 complicates the verse: "When Abraham looked up, his eye fell upon a ram *after*, caught in the thicket by its horns." Numerous attempts have been made to decipher the odd expression, including the adoption of the alternative version recorded in several Masoretic manuscripts (and some translations), substituting "*aḥar*," meaning "after," with "*eḥad*," "one," meaning one ram. See a list of manuscripts in Skinner, *A Critical and Exegetical Commentary on Genesis*, 330. This version reinforces the link between Isaac who is called "*yeḥidekha*," "your only one," and the "one" ram.

narrative (apart from the second revelation of the angel), and view the dialogue as "the dramatic climax of the narrative."[64]

However, from a literary viewpoint, the transition from verse 10 to verse 11 should be viewed as the climax: "And Abraham took the knife to slay his son. Then an angel of the Lord called to him from heaven." This is the "solution stage" – the angel stopped Abraham from slaughtering his son. The change in the plot is marked by the change in God's names. From verse 11 onward, God is referred to as *YHWH*,[65] in contrast with the first part of the narrative, where God is called *Elohim*.[66] The division of a unified narrative into two parts, each represented by another name, is unusual in biblical literature. This obvious division of the narrative does not occur in the dialogue between Abraham and Isaac (vv. 7–8) but in the angel's revelation (v. 11), which is also marked by the change in God's name.

The significance of this division is the parallel it creates between the two halves of the narrative, which centralizes the sacrifice of the ram as a parallel to Abraham's preparations to sacrifice Isaac. The initial caption in which God turns to Abraham ("He said to him, 'Abraham,' and he answered, 'Here I am'" [Gen. 22:1]) is paralleled by the angel's demand of Abraham ("Then an angel of the Lord called to him from heaven: 'Abraham! Abraham!'" [v. 11]). God's initial demand, "Take your

64. Avishur, "The Narratives of the Binding of Isaac and Abraham's Exodus from Haran – Structure, Style and Language," 93; Jacques B. Doukhan, "The Center of the Aqedah: A Study of the Literary Structure of Genesis 22:1–19," *AUSS* 31 (1993): 17–28. Avishur views Gen. 22:13 (!) as the conclusion of the narrative. Both consider the dialogue between Abraham and Isaac as the central axis of the concentric structure.

65. The integration of the name *YHWH* in v. 11 is problematic for those who attribute the narrative to E; some therefore viewed the integration of *YHWH* as an addition by the final redactor (Skinner, *A Critical and Exegetical Commentary on Genesis*, 330).

66. The phrase "For now I know that you fear God (*Elohim*)" in the second part strays from the division. However, "Fear of God" should be viewed as an idiom. See, for example, Deut. 25:18, Job 1:8, Eccl. 7:18. Regarding the characterization of Job as *yere Elohim*, it should be remarked that this may be one element within a broader analogy, as convincingly suggested by Judy Klitsner, *Subversive Sequels in the Bible: How Biblical Stories Mine and Undermine Each Other* (Jerusalem, 2011), xx–xxiv; Nathaniel Helfgot, *Mikra and Meaning: Studies in Bible and Its Interpretation* (Jerusalem, 2012), 65–71.

son, your favored one, whom you love, Isaac" (v. 2), is paralleled by the angel's demand, "Do not send forth your hand against the boy, or do anything to him." The first part of the narrative describes Abraham lifting his eyes and viewing "the place" from afar (v. 4), which is paralleled by Abraham lifting his eyes to see a ram caught in the thicket (v. 13).[67] Finally, God's command to "offer him there as a burnt offering" (v. 2) is paralleled by Abraham's initiative: "Abraham went and took the ram and offered it up as a burnt offering *in place of his son*" (v. 13). The verbs *lakaḥ* ("took"), and *halakh* ("went"), which reference Abraham's actions in the first part of narrative, when he takes his son and goes to offer him as a sacrifice to God, reappear in the second part when Abraham "takes" the ram and "goes" to sacrifice it instead of his son.

First half	Second half
He said to him, "Abraham," and he answered, "Here I am" (v. 1)	Then an angel of the Lord called to him from heaven: "Abraham! Abraham!" (v. 11)
"Take your son, your favored one, whom you love, Isaac" (v. 2)	"Do not send forth your hand against the boy, or do anything to him." (v. 12)
Abraham saw "the place" from afar (v. 4)	Abraham lifted his eyes and saw a ram caught in the thicket. (v. 13)
"Offer him there as a burnt offering" (v. 2)	Abraham went and took the ram and offered it up as a burnt offering *in place of his son.* (v. 13)

The text clearly portrays the ram as a replacement for Isaac, despite the fact that God requested no such compensatory act from Abraham. The sacrifice of the ram points to the greater purpose of the binding narrative. Many commentators emphasize the test element as the main purpose of the narrative, and indeed, for readers it is difficult to imagine that the dramatic point of Abraham's sacrifice might not be the main purpose of the story. Of course, the test is the central point of the narrative, as

67. For another arrangement of the verses and the claim that v. 13 parallels vv. 7–8, see Mary Douglas, *Thinking in Circles: An Essay on Ring Composition* (New Haven, CT, and London, 2007), 23.

it relates to the development of Abraham and the legacy he creates for his offspring. However, only the first part of the narrative emphasizes the test, while the second focuses on the significance of sacrificing animals – and this is the crucial point – thereby eliminating the need to sacrifice children. The first part of the narrative certainly expresses the unyielding obedience expected of Abraham. The polemic against child sacrifice does not emerge in the first part of the narrative. On the contrary, the position of the first part seems to be that if God should demand such a thing, a true believer would have to acquiesce. The second part of the narrative, however, reveals that there is no real need for child sacrifice, and a replacement is sufficient.

The binding narrative is an introduction to the perception of sacrifice in Israel, including the appropriate mood and the purpose of the sacrifice. Once God exempts Isaac, He does not request an alternative animal sacrifice. Sacrificing the ram is Abraham's decision, and he was the one who made the ram into a replacement for his son. By Abraham's choice, the narrative does not end with Isaac's rescue.

It makes sense, then, that the mountain is only named after the sacrifice of the ram. Abraham sanctifies the altar and the location, both to become models for future sacrifices by Abraham's offspring. The narrative establishes an important precedent in the ethos of the Jewish nation: that sacrificing an animal to God demonstrates unequivocal loyalty to God, as though one were willing to sacrifice that which is dearest.[68] In the religious climate in which Abraham lives, human sacrifice was common. Indeed, the God of Israel, according to this analysis, has every right to request human sacrifice. However, He does not need it. Later, the Bible will state explicitly that human sacrifice is an "abhorrent act that the Lord detests" (Deut. 12:31). The God of the Israelites is satisfied with His worshippers' intent – they must be willing to sacrifice their children, but, as exemplified in Abraham's test, God will never ask this of them. The animal sacrifice is sufficient to denote the servants' absolute faith.

As we have mentioned previously, changing names and titles in the biblical narrative carries literary significance, and in this narrative,

---

68. On the sacrifice of animals as a substitution for human sacrifice, see references in Gunkel, *Genesis – Translated and Interpreted*, 236.

the name of God changes as the narrative progresses. *Elohim* as a general name represents the strength and might of God, while *YHWH* is the exclusive name of the Lord of Israel. In the first part of the narrative, God portrays Himself as one of the ancient gods, hungrily demanding human sacrifice. However, when the God of Abraham reveals His true intention and lack of desire for human sacrifice, His private name emerges: "Then an angel of *YHWH* called to him from heaven.... Do not send forth your hand against the boy, or do anything to him!" At the start of the narrative God claimed what is rightfully His, while the culmination of the narrative reveals that God has no interest in human sacrifice, but only the loyalty of his servants instead.[69]

The Return Home

The terrible event behind them, Abraham and his son ostensibly return together from Mount Moriah, perhaps shaken, perhaps strengthened by a renewed bond forged in the fire of trauma and survival. The journey to the binding teemed with extraneous detail, the suspense of each step palpable in the text. Now, as Abraham heads down the mountain, the reader's mind swarms with unanswered questions: What is Isaac thinking right now? Having seen with his own eyes Abraham's willingness to sacrifice his own flesh and blood, does Isaac still walk "together" with his father, in-sync in mutual conviction and faith? Do they speak at all?

These questions remain unbearably unanswered. Isaac is conspicuously absent from the end of this story, an omission so palpable it led one midrashic tradition to conclude that Isaac was indeed slaughtered.[70] According to the midrash, he died, went up to heaven, and remained there for three years, and only returned to earth when Rebecca arrived with Abraham's servant. Ibn Ezra (on Gen. 22:19) was familiar with the tradition, which he rejected: "Isaac was not mentioned because he was his [Abraham's] property. Anyone who says he slaughtered him and

69. "The purpose is to convey that in theory one should be willing even to sacrifice a son to the high divine presence of the universe, while in practice the God of Israel, Hashem, does not demand such sacrifices. On the contrary, He neither accepts them nor permits them" (Cassuto, *The "Quaestio" of the Book of Genesis*, 46).
70. *Midrash HaGadol* on Genesis. See also Ḥizkuni on Gen. 22:19.

left him and then he returned to life – contradicts the text." Ibn Ezra views the absence of Isaac as no different from an omission in any other text. The reader is meant to understand that Isaac had accompanied his father on the journey back home. However, his need to object to the position that Isaac was slaughtered and returned to life indicates that the tradition was not unpopular.[71] There is no question that Ibn Ezra is correct; the assumption that Isaac was slaughtered indeed negates the text.[72] But while the early tradition negates the text itself, it was almost certainly based on the atmosphere of the concluding verse. Although Isaac returned to Beersheba with Abraham and the servants, the ending generates the dramatic impression that Abraham had returned alone, without his son.[73] The ram that was sacrificed in Isaac's stead represents the sacrifice of Isaac himself.

This realistic representation links Isaac to the mountain, which in some sense he can never leave. The narrative successfully and powerfully represents two opposing ideas: Abraham's absolute loyalty to God, to the point of sacrificing his own son, and God's objection to the sacrifice of children. Abraham's ram sacrifice sufficed to express his unequivocal loyalty; from the perspective of Abraham's withstanding of God's test, it is as though Isaac was indeed sacrificed, and left up on the mountain.

The Oath

The narrative of the binding concludes with a delicately woven but meaningful nod to the legacy of the binding for generations to come. Our protagonist, Abraham, "returns" to Beersheba. Returning to one's home is a classic story ending, but since the narrative had failed to mention that Abraham had departed from Beersheba, his "return" seems out of place. Not only does Abraham return, the text continues, "And Abraham

71. Medieval Jewish commentators were sensitive to readings of the text that might reinforce Christian beliefs. Ibn Ezra's rejection might be based on this concern.

72. Kierkegaard suggests alternative endings for the narrative. According to one, Isaac stopped believing in God. According to another, after the binding Abraham could never find happiness again.

73. Trible expressed this similarly, but she focused on Abraham's emotional detachment from his son (Trible, "Genesis 22: The Sacrifice of Sarah," 181).

stayed in Beersheba" (Gen. 22:19). The city of Beersheba becomes the final chord of the entire binding narrative.

Previously, Abraham had named Beersheba in commemoration of the oath between him and Abimelech (Gen. 21:31). The binding story concludes by repeating the soulful note of the word "oath." That utterance reverberates in the Abraham journey; the city named for one oath now welcomes our hero back into her gates under the protection of the divine oath. Abraham's chosenness and the divine promise is an oath that will endure for generations.

Sons of Nahor (Gen. 22:20–24)

Winding Down Abraham's Journey

The binding narrative is unquestionably the closing event of Abraham's literary heroic cycle. Isaac returns from the binding as the unequivocal living heir, and from that point on the story shifts to establish and ensure that legacy. As Abraham's cycle draws to a close, the text provides closure to the genealogical list that began Abraham's journey, detailing the sons of Nahor, his brother. Genealogical lists are generally presented for the reader's benefit, but the text makes a point of indicating that this list of Nahor's sons was delivered directly to Abraham: "Some time later, Abraham was told, 'Milcah too has borne children to your brother Nahor'" (Gen. 22:20). One could read the list in light of the birth of Isaac. Just as Abraham had a son, his brother Nahor also had sons.[1]

However, the juxtaposition of Nahor and Abraham's sons is steeped in tragic irony. Abraham and Sarah waited many years for their son, who finally came in their old age. After Isaac was born, Abraham almost lost him. Nahor, on the other hand, has twelve sons.

1. Westermann, *Genesis 12–36: A Continental Commentary*, 366–67. Westermann claims that based on this detail the list was originally adjacent to Gen. 21:1–8 (the birth of Isaac). The units can be linked despite the episode of Isaac's binding and "rebirth," which interrupts the sequence.

While Abraham took Sarah's maidservant to overcome Sarah's fertility problem, and ultimately had to send that son away, his brother Nahor took a concubine so that he could have twelve sons instead of eight (at this point in the narrative, the reader has not yet been introduced to Keturah, who bears six more sons to Abraham). The clean transition between the two episodes, and the opening remark, "And it was after these things," highlights this irony. Perhaps this is the reason for the emphasis that the list is not only intended for the reader but for Abraham as well. One might imagine Abraham returning to his tent after the binding ordeal, and hearing the news of his brother's impressive family. We will delve into what that encounter may have looked like later on in this chapter.

Sons of Terah

The purpose of this genealogical tree can be viewed in three different contexts. On a literary-structural plane, this list completes the "line of Terah" (Gen. 11:27) which opened the Abraham narrative cycle. The cycle follows three branches of Terah's descendants: Haran – through Lot – culminating in Terah's great-grandsons Ammon and Moab; Nahor, who has twelve sons; and particularly the Abraham branch, the narrative protagonist, who had a son at one hundred years of age, and nearly sacrificed him to God. The list of Nahor's sons indicates that the line of Terah culminates in Ur of the Chaldeans.[2] Since according to the common reading Milcah, Nahor's wife, is the daughter of Haran, who dies in his father's lifetime (11:29), the marriage of Isaac (son of Abraham) to Rebecca (granddaughter of Nahor and Haran's daughter Milcah) reunites all three family branches. Mentioning Nahor's sons here contributes to the conclusion of the Abraham cycle: Abraham's last revelation sealed his story, and all that is left is to report about the remaining brother. This frame is supported by the artistic structure of the entire unit, and defines the narratives that follow as an appendix to the story cycle.

---

2. "[R]eminding us that the tradition we are reading is really the *Toledoth* of Terah, of which the story of Abraham is but a part" (Thompson, *The Origin Tradition of Ancient Israel: The Literary Formation of Genesis and Exodus 1–23*, 99).

Rebecca

In the context of character and plot development, the purpose of the list is obvious: to introduce Rebecca as Isaac's bride-to-be, the perpetuator of the Abrahamic line. Rashi writes:

> When he returned from Mount Moriah, Abraham thought, "Had my son been slaughtered, he would have died without children. I should have married him to a woman of the daughters of Aner, Eshkol, or Mamre." So the Holy One, blessed be He, announced to him that Rebecca, his mate, had been born. That is why it says, "And it was after these things" – after his thoughts following the binding.[3]

The suggestion that Rebecca – and therefore the future genetic line of Abraham – is the main point of the list is strongly supported by the text. While the focus of the episode is the sons of Nahor, when the narrative reaches Bethuel, there is a diversion from the list for the purpose of mentioning Nahor's granddaughter Rebecca. Nahor's grandson Aram is also mentioned in the list (Gen. 22:21), not as a separate stage but as part of the description of the life of his father.[4] In addition to skipping a generation by mentioning Rebecca, the appearance of women in biblical genealogical lists is rare. Family lines focus on sons, since they are the successors of the dynasty. As daughters traditionally joined their husband's family, there is no reason to mention them in a genealogical list.[5] Therefore, the mention of Rebecca is unusual and surprising, and

---

3. Rashi on Gen. 22:20.
4. However, the mention of Aram – even if merely as an extension of his father – is related to the centrality of Aram in the broader biblical consciousness. In addition to the long-lasting political dispute with Aram, Abraham's family that remained in Mesopotamia is referred to as Aram, and the place of origin is called "Paddan Aram." Regarding Aram's relationship with Nahor (as opposed to the sons of Shem in Gen. 10:22), see Yehoshua Guttman, "Aram," *Entziklopedya Mikra'it* 1:573–577.
5. The name Maacah at the end of the list of the concubine's children might be the name of a girl or a boy. The fact that the name is mentioned in the list would indicate that Maacah is a son, but the biblical name is more commonly feminine (II Sam. 3:3; I Kings 15:2; I Chr. 2:48; 7:15–16; 9:35). Some early commentators (e.g., Sforno) and some modern scholars (e.g., Sternberg, *The Poetics of Biblical Narrative: Ideological*

probably anticipates Isaac's future right after his rescue. Mention of Rebecca will be followed by news of the death of Sarah.

However, the mention of Rebecca is an insufficient explanation for the entire list. Certainly the sons of Nahor's concubine Reumah, for example, do not contribute to this purpose. The list should therefore be viewed in light of the important role played by the family of Nahor throughout the remainder of Genesis narratives (sending Abraham's servant to Nahor's family; Jacob's escape to Haran) and as a foreshadowing whose contribution will only become clear in future narratives.

This might be the reason the list is not reported to the reader, but rather described as news heard by Abraham. Abraham has to have information about the birth of the sons of Nahor, so that he knows to send his servant there to find a wife for his son.[6]

The Life That Would Have Been

The third layer of analysis of the genealogical list is theological in nature. The list of Nahor's children should not be read outside its literary context. In fact, a special effort is made to link the episode with Abraham's life. According to the two contexts mentioned above, Nahor's sons parallel Abraham's family – from the joint father to the reunification of the next generation. But the parallel can also be viewed as a contrast. The abovementioned irony of mentioning Nahor alongside Abraham

Literature and the Drama of Reading, 133) therefore note that Maacah was a daughter, not a son. However, the name Maacah was originally linked with a geographical region (II Sam. 10:6), and in other places probably indicates a masculine name (I Kings 2:39; I Chr. 11:43; see Kaddari, *A Dictionary of Biblical Hebrew*, 642). Therefore, Maacah is more likely to be a son than a daughter.

6. See Nahum Sarna, "The Anticipatory Use of Information as a Literary Feature of the Genesis Narratives," in *The Creation of Sacred Literature: Composition and Redaction of the Biblical Text*, ed. R. E. Friedman (Berkeley, 1982), 76–84. The claim above does not contradict Wenham's position that the statement, "Bethuel birthed Rebecca," should be attributed to the narrative, and should not be viewed as part of the rumor that reached Abraham. Based on this assumption, Wenham claims that there is no reason to say Abraham knew about Rebecca before sending his servant, and that Abraham sent his servant based on the information that his brother Nahor had established a family (Wenham, *Genesis 16–50*, 120).

in reference to fertility and establishing a family is in itself part of the purpose of the list.

The journey of the Abraham cycle began with Abraham's departure from his family with a promise that by leaving his past behind him he goes toward a better future, and will become a great nation. Contrasting Nahor with Abraham undermines this perception. Apparently Nahor, who stayed behind in Ur of the Chaldeans, and did not even join his father on the first leg of the trip that ended in Haran, was blessed with fertility and many sons, while Abraham, who went to Canaan as he was commanded, was blessed with one son, after great difficulty.

With this message, Abraham is faced with the future he did not choose, the path he did not take. Had he stayed in Ur of the Chaldeans, like his brother Nahor, perhaps he, too, would have been surrounded by children and grandchildren. Instead, Abraham and Sarah struggled for years for their only son, and he was almost lost to them forever.

As Abraham's personal story draws to a close, both he and the reader are reminded of the promise that began his journey. God's promise opened with the words, "Go forth..." These words launched our hero on a long and arduous journey. Yes, there is divine reward at the finish. However, even though Abraham's part in it may be coming to a close, the journey is far from over. This is the story of the birth of a nation, and Abraham is but the opening act. God's promises to Abraham are thus portrayed as intended for future generations, not to be enjoyed by Abraham himself. The inheritance of the land was delayed to the distant future (Gen. 15:13–16), and the blessing of fertility will also not be fulfilled in the days of Abraham. The juxtaposition with Nahor seems to indicate that had Abraham remained in Haran, he might have had his brother's luck. Nonetheless, Abraham chose to follow God's command, and his blessings will be fulfilled in the time of his children, and the nations they will establish.

Sarah's Burial (Gen. 23)

At this point, Abraham's narrative cycle has essentially come to an end. His journey as our hero is over, although the next stories of Isaac, and then Jacob, have not yet commenced. The stories that bridge these two narratives serve to pass the torch, from the "founding generation" to the new generation. In the next few episodes, Abraham and Sarah pass away, making way for Isaac and Rebecca to take center stage. Abraham does not witness any other divine revelation in the purchase of the cave of Machpelah nor in the search for Isaac's wife, making the blessing he received at the end of the binding his final divine blessing. While the transition from Abraham to Isaac is clear after the binding, who will replace Sarah as foremother remains to be seen, which may explain why that particular story is recounted in such detail.

Sarah's death is a significant turning point in Abraham's journey. After the binding of Isaac, Abraham's heroic cycle begins to wane, shifting the focus from our protagonist's development to the establishment of his continuing legacy. The loss of Sarah may be shattering for Abraham personally, but his path forward is clear – in the burial of his life-long partner, Abraham enacts the first step in establishing his progeny's settlement and legacy in their own land. The purchase of the cave of Machpelah is far more than a procurement of convenience or necessity – it is the first cornerstone in ensuring the next generation's everlasting birthright. The biblical text of this narrative seems verbose and convoluted, dragging the reader through a perplexing exchange between Abraham and the Hittites, raising questions about Abraham's motivations and the purpose of the narrative as a whole. In the end, the lengthy dialogue will stand for generations as the moment of foundation for the Abraham line's origin in the land of Canaan.

What Is the Focus of the Story?

Is the story of Genesis 23 the story of Sarah's burial, or is it the story of the purchase of the cave of Machpelah? Ostensibly, the narrative could have a dual focus – Abraham has to bury his recently deceased wife, and therefore needs to purchase an appropriate burial cave. Although logically the purchase of the cave should serve the main purpose of burying Sarah, the length and detail of the retelling of Abraham's purchase indicates that the purchase of the cave is itself the purpose of the narrative, and not the burial. Although the burial of Sarah may be the impetus, the negotiation and final purchase of the cave is the central focus point of this story. We see this most clearly when we compare the deaths of the other foremothers with that of Sarah. The death of the foremothers is only mentioned when serving another purpose in the narrative. The deaths of Rebecca and Leah are not mentioned at all, and Rachel's death is only revealed as the context for the birth of Benjamin and the reason for her burial outside the cave of Machpelah. Similarly, Sarah's death and burial are discussed as context for the purchase of the cave of Machpelah, which is the main purpose of the narrative. This is evident from the lengthy description of the negotiation and purchase of the cave, and from the repetitive conclusion (Gen. 23:17–20):

> (I) So passed Ephron's land in Machpelah, near Mamre – the field with its cave and all the trees anywhere within the confines of that field – to Abraham as his possession, in the presence of the Hittites, of all who entered the gate of his town.
>
> (II) And then Abraham buried his wife Sarah in the cave of the field of Machpelah, facing Mamre – now Hebron – in the land of Canaan.

(III) Thus passed the field with its cave from the Hittites to Abraham, as a burial site.

After concluding the purchase of the field (I) and the burial of Sarah (II), the concluding verse of the entire chapter reiterates the purchase of the field (III), indicating that the purchase was indeed the main purpose of the narrative.[1]

If this is the case, we might wonder if the arduous dialogue between Abraham and the Hittites is intended to distract the reader from the importance of the purchase. The text's description of Abraham's negotiations is lengthy and convoluted – why does the reader need to "sit through" the entire conversation? Later, when Jacob purchases a field in Genesis 33:19, the biblical text notes succinctly: "The parcel of land where he pitched his tent he purchased from the children of Hamor, Shechem's father, for a hundred kesitahs" (Gen. 33:19). The basic details – buyer, seller, and price – are sufficient to describe the purchase of the plot, while the negotiation over the Machpelah cave is described in excruciating detail. It would seem that the centrality of the dialogue and negotiations supersede the purchase of the field and cave, and should be viewed as the main purpose of the narrative.

After a series of narratives centering on saving members of the next generation from death – Lot in Sodom, Ishmael in the wilderness, Isaac on Mount Moriah – this story focuses on the death of the founding generation. Sarah dies "in Kiryat Arba – now Hebron" (Gen. 23:2). The significance of the place of Sarah's death would become apparent when Abraham purchased the plot and field. Here, it is introduced using both the contemporary and ancient names of the city. This nomenclature sets a tone that will continue throughout the story of a legal and binding transaction. There is no reason to remind the reader of the ancient name of Hebron unless the purpose is to ensure that there is no doubt as to the exact location and geographical parameters of the place under discussion. In the same way that a legal document dating back to the 1800s indicating transfer of ownership might specify a piece of land "in the State of Virginia, formerly of the 13 British Colonies...," the narrative

1. Hamilton, *The Book of Genesis, Chapters 18–50*, 136.

specifies the city of Hebron, known formerly as Kiryat Arba. The reference to all known names of the city is the first indication of a legal-formal setting for the episode that follows. Since the act of purchasing the land carries broad and deeply significant legal ramifications, the official atmosphere necessitates an accurate identification of the place, as well as a clarification that the place in question is "in the land of Canaan.

Although the literary purpose of this narrative centers around Abraham's acquisition of the cave of Machpelah and its national ramifications, the text also offers the reader a peek into the personal experience of the widower's grief: "and Abraham came to mourn for Sarah and to bewail her" (Gen. 23:2). Abraham's mourning is a rare glimpse into the relationship between Abraham and Sarah; Abraham feels genuine grief over the loss of his wife, who had traveled with him in partnership from the outset of his journey.

Negotiation

The dialogue between Abraham and the Hitties begins with what seems like a simple request for a favor, and at some point transforms into a binding legal discussion with long-lasting ramifications. The main driver of the labyrinthine tone of this conversation seems to be Abraham, who opens with one request and switches gears seemingly quite suddenly in the middle of the discussion. The fact that the text includes the full report of the negotiation between Abraham and the Hittites seems superfluous as well. Commentators explain this in a number of ways. Some suggest that the legal problem Abraham had to overcome – and the reason for the negotiation – is the Hittite prohibition to sell land to strangers. Since Hittite law prevents a foreigner from acquiring proprietary rights to land, Abraham had to convince the Hittites to stray from the standard procedure so that he could bury his wife.[2] The custom is

---

2. Ezra Zion Melamed, "Purchase of the Cave of Machpelah," *Tarbitz* 14 (1942): 11–18. As we discussed in our introduction, Lehmann also sees Hittite law as the necessary background for understanding our chapter, but in a different way. He believes that the extended dialogue between Abraham and the Hittites is related to their desire not to own part of a property, since they would have financial obligations toward the king by owning even a part of the land (Lehmann, "Abraham's Purchase of Machpelah and Hittite Law," 15–18).

reflected in the biblical concept of the return of lands to their owners: "But the land must not be sold beyond reclaim, for the land is Mine; you are but stranger residents with Me" (Lev. 25:23). Since the Israelites are defined as "stranger residents" on God's land, they are forbidden from selling the land permanently, and can only work the land as "leaseholders." According to this suggestion, Abraham outwitted the system by acquiring the cave as "a gift."

Others reject the idea that the Hittite law is the background for the narrative.[3] Other than Abraham's reference to himself as a "resident alien," there is no real discussion of the Hittite prohibition to sell land. In fact, the moment Ephron and Abraham come to a financial agreement, Ephron seems to have no qualms about selling both cave and field. The possibility that Abraham had to overcome the challenge of the Hittite custom does not justify the lengthy dialogue, as the specific legal problem is not emphasized in the text. Moreover, this explanation fails to explain the drawn-out dialogue about the sale, as it would have sufficed to declare that the entire town was aware of the matter.

The inclusion of the dialogue is an important decision on the part of the biblical text to reinforce the overall purpose of Abraham and the Hittite's negotiation. Upon analysis of the conversation, we see that the dialogue between Abraham and the Hittites includes ambiguous speech, statements of etiquette, and deliberate misleading on both sides. While the Hittites portray themselves as extremely generous, their sincerity is questionable.[4] Abraham, too, is responsible for a major deceit in the negotiation. Ironically, the key verb throughout the unit is "*shema*," "to hear," also supported by "*oznei benei ḥet*," "the hearing of the Hittites" (lit. "the ears of the Hittites").[5] The repetition of the

---

3. Gene M. Tucker, "The Legal Background of Genesis 23," *JBL* 85 (1966): 77–84; Raymond Westbrook, "Purchase of the Cave of Machpelah (Gen. 23)," *Israel Law Review* 6 (1971): 29–38.
4. See Meir Sternberg, "Double Cave, Double Talk: The Indirections of Biblical Dialogue," in *Not in Heaven*, ed. J. P. Rosenblatt and J. C. Sitterson (Philadelphia and Bloomington, 1991), 28–57.
5. Polak shows that the opening of speeches with the verb root "to hear" is a common biblical phenomenon also prevalent in Ugaritic literature; only in the latter, the root functions as the opening of the instructions of an authority (such as a god or

verb emphasizes what is lacking in the narrative. The two sides failed to really "hear" one another, because each related to the conversation from a different perception of the reality, and repeated their ideas without listening to the other.

The negotiation between Abraham and the Hittites undergoes several stages, and in that process morphs from one kind of conversation to another altogether. Naturally, each speaker represents a new stage in the dialogue on a structural plane. However, the dialogue between Abraham and the Hittites is also accompanied by other indications of the various stages. Each of the three stages of the dialogue opens with Abraham rising to bow down to the Hittites: "Then Abraham rose from beside his dead, and spoke to the Hittites" (Gen. 23:3); "Abraham bowed low to the people of the land, the Hittites" (v. 7); and "Abraham bowed low before the people of the land" (v. 12).[6] Additionally, each of the three stages includes a statement that alludes to burying the dead: "That I may remove my dead for burial" (v. 4); "If it is your wish that I remove my dead for burial" (v. 8); and, "That I may bury my dead there" (v. 13). Finally, each stage of the dialogue concludes with a Hittite reference to Abraham's need to bury his dead: "Bury your dead in the choicest of our burial places" (v. 6); "Bury your dead" (v. 11); and "Go and bury your dead" (v. 15).[7] This repetition reflects the paradox we mentioned earlier between the two layers of the narrative. Abraham's need to bury

---

king), and this language also features in the Bible (Frank Polak, "Epic Formulae in Biblical Narrative and the Origins of Ancient Hebrew Prose," *Te'uda* 7 [1991]: 27–28). This claim increases the irony in this story: each of the parties presents themselves as most genial, but uses a formula that suggests authority and command.

6. The narrative concludes: "Thus the field with its cave was established away (*vayakom*) from the Hittites to Abraham, as a burial site" (23:20). Perhaps the integration of the verb *vayakom* ("to rise") is a wordplay with the initial description "Abraham *rose* from beside his dead."
7. Reversal of the order in the final stage, "*ve'et metekha kevor*," lit. "your dead bury," instead of "bury your dead," is the stylistic signature of the conclusion of a biblical narrative. The repetition itself sometimes "invites" variety and a change of the structure of a sentence (Shamir Yona, "Stylistic and Syntactic Variants in Repeated Texts in the Bible," in *Yitzhak Avishur Festschrift*, ed. Michael Heltzer and Meir Malul [Tel Aviv: Archaeological Center Publications, 2004], 225–232).

his deceased wife is the repeated motivation for the purchase of the cave – but it is the purchase itself that is the true focal point of the story.

Stage I: The Gift

Abraham begins with self-definition: "I am a resident alien among you." The definition is crucial, since the fact that as a foreign resident Abraham owns no land is the reason for his distress. As a shepherd Abraham was able to wander without a real need for ownership of land, but now that he has a wife to bury, the absence of owned land has become a real problem that requires the assistance of the Hittites.

Abraham asks of the Hittites: "*Give me* a burial site among you,[8] that I may remove my dead for burial." The phrase "*tenu*" ("give") has been interpreted in a number of ways. Some commentators suggest an indication of transfer of property (whether as a gift[9] or in exchange for money).[10] Another meaning of the word, found in other biblical contexts, is permission, responsibility, or opportunity, without the transfer of ownership – Abraham is asking for permission to bury his wife among the tombs of the Hittite families.[11] The verb *tenu* is used in both contexts throughout biblical text. The verses that refer specifically to changing hands do not always denote the transfer of ownership. In I Samuel 17:10, Goliath challenges the Israelites to war and says: "I herewith defy the

8. NJPS translates "*tenu li*" as "sell me." As I will clarify below, this prevents the reader from sensing the process that unfolds over the course of their exchange.
9. The gift option is raised by Nahmanides on Gen. 23:6. A similar interpretation was offered by Melamed, "Purchase of the Cave of Machpelah," 11–18.
10. Westbrook, "Purchase of the Cave of Machpelah (Gen. 23)," 29–38. Abraham Sivan ("The Negotiations over the Cave of Machpelah," in *The Book of Sivan – A Collection of Studies in Memory of Shalom Sivan*, ed. Abraham Even-Shoshan et al. [Jerusalem: Kiryat Sepher, 1979], 207–215) offers a similar interpretation. See also Melamed ("Purchase of the Cave of Machpelah," 11): "Firstly it is noteworthy that throughout the episode the verbs *makhar* ('to buy') and *kanah* ('to sell') are absent, and replaced by the verb *natan* ('to give') which generally denotes giving for free, as a gift." Amit writes that the phrase is ambiguous, meaning either payment with money, or a gift (Amit, *Reading Biblical Narratives: Literary Criticism and the Hebrew Bible*, 52). However, it can also hint to the granting of permission without the transferal of ownership, as mentioned above.
11. E.g., Gen. 20:6; 39:4; Num. 20:21; Num. 21:23. See BDB, 681.

ranks of Israel. Give me (*tenu li*) a man and let us fight it out!" Clearly Goliath had no intention of possessing ownership over the man sent by the Israelites.[12]

The most convenient reading of the verb *tenu* in Abraham's request is therefore a request to bury Sarah in a plot on Hittite land. Abraham does not indicate transfer of ownership; the gravesite would remain the property of the Hittite family.[13] Abraham encourages the Hittites to believe this was his intention by adding the word "*imakhem*," "among you," indicating that he seeks a family that will allow him to bury Sarah in their own family plot, among their own deceased. Abraham's initial introduction as a foreigner creates the atmosphere of one in need, asking a favor of those in a position to offer help.

Meir Sternberg claims that the term *aḥuzat kever* ("burial site/estate") proves that Abraham's intention was ownership, and that it is the Hittites who use ambiguous phrases throughout the discussion.[14] If this were true, then Abraham should have clarified that he had wanted "a burial cave – for an estate." Instead, Abraham's phraseology can easily be interpreted as a desire for a cave that is the estate of one of the Hittite families.[15] The phrase "*tenu li... imakhem*" ("give me... among you") is quite ambiguous, a fact that is expressed in the interchangeable modern translations for this verse. Most translations offered the literal translation "*give* me a burial plot *with you*,"[16] while others translate based on

---

12. In the Abraham narrative, see Gen. 15:10; 18:7; 21:14; 24:32.
13. This reading might be supported by Hieronymus' translation of Abraham's request: "*Advena sum et peregrinus apud ius, data mihi ius sepulcri vobiscum*" – "I am a foreigner and a wanderer among you, give me the right of burial in your midst." See Abraham J. Brawer, "The Negotiations for Purchasing a Tomb in Hebron," *Beit Mikra* 4 (1966): 92–94.
14. Sternberg, "Double Cave, Double Talk: The Indirections of Biblical Dialogue," 31.
15. As explained below, the ambiguity here is intentional. Eventually the Hittites – and the reader – will discover that Abraham had intended to purchase the plot and transfer ownership. The use of the confusing phrase is intentional: while Abraham's true intention is hinted, the Hittites understand his intentions differently.
16. RSV, NKJV, KJV and others. Wenham (*Genesis 16–50*, 122) translated similarly, but emphasized Abraham's intention of transfer of ownership: "Abraham is asking for ownership of a piece of land" (Wenham, ibid., 127).

the broader context, "*sell* me a burial site *among you.*"[17] This translation, which took into account the broader situation in the narrative, resolved the ambiguity that enabled an interpretation of Abraham's request as a favor. However, the narrative indicates that Abraham encouraged the mistaken interpretation of his words.

Intention aside, the response of the Hittites proves that they understood Abraham's request as a favor, not a desire for transfer of ownership (Gen. 23:6):

> Hear us, my lord: you are the elect of God among us.
> In the choicest of our burial places bury your dead;
> None of us will withhold his burial place from you for burying your dead.

The Hittites view Abraham's request as one that honors them, since he is considered "the elect of God" among them. In fact, the families might have fought among themselves to have Abraham bury Sarah in their plot. A joint burial would create an intimate connection with Abraham, whose reputation evidently precedes him, and who is also known to be exceedingly wealthy.[18] The response indicates that the Hittites interpret Abraham's request as an appeal to open one of their family burial plots for him, turning the grave into a joint grave, while the ownership of the grave is maintained by the Hittite family. This understanding is emphasized in two elements of their response:

---

17. NJPS and Sarna, *Genesis* (JPS), 157–158. A similar translation is found in NIV; NAB; NIB.
18. Emanueli (*Genesis – Commentary and Insights*, 316–317) notes that the Hittites' response indicates that Abraham intentionally avoided mentioning his desire to purchase the plot. Emanueli believes that this was because the "trends of the time do not allow prosaic words such as 'buying' or 'selling.' This terminology would be appropriate among traders in the marketplace, not among respectable company." Kiel also explains that Abraham employed intentional ambiguity, but gives a different interpretation, similar to Amit's aforementioned explanation: "Since Abraham was aware of the legal status of a foreign resident, he avoided using the word 'purchase' or 'sell,' and preferred the verb 'to give' (*natan*), which denotes a gift, but can also indicate sale or possession" (Kiel, *Daat Mikra: Genesis*, 140).

- "The choicest of *our* burial places.... None of us will withhold *his* burial place from you." This formulation indicates that ownership will be maintained by the Hittite family, while Abraham is welcome to select any grave he sees fit.
- "None of us will withhold his burial place from you *for burying your dead.*" The Hittites explicitly note the purpose of the transaction: they will enable Abraham to bury his wife. No transfer of ownership is implied in any way.

The two-part response ends with an epiphora ("bury your dead"), which acknowledges Abraham's sense of urgency: the Hittites can see that Abraham requires an immediate solution, which they are quick to offer.[19] This completes the first stage of the dialogue, which could by all accounts be deemed a success. The Hittites agree to Abraham's request to bury his wife in one of their graves, and seem delighted with the opportunity to make such a connection with this highly esteemed individual. The issue, it appears, is resolved, to the benefit of both sides.

Stage II: An Offer of Payment

The second stage opens with Abraham bowing before the Hittites in recognition of the kindness they had offered him.[20] In this context a new appellation is given to the Hittites: "Abraham bowed low to *the people of the land,* the Hittites." (Gen. 23:7) The phrase "people of the land" has different meanings in various biblical contexts, and sometimes refers to a specific group within the general population.[21] In the context of our

19. Cf. Sternberg, "Double Cave, Double Talk: The Indirections of Biblical Dialogue," 30. Regarding this function of the epiphora, see Polak, *Biblical Narrative Aspects of Art and Design,* 35–36; Grossman, *Text and Subtext: On Exploring Biblical Narrative Design,* 105–115.
20. The narrative offers a look at accepted norms of trade in the ancient world, and anthropologists utilize the narrative to assess customs such as the grandiloquent flattery, which might be part of the etiquette (such as, "You are the elect of God among us"), or Abraham's low bow. See Nathan MacDonald, "Driving a Hard Bargain? Genesis 23 and Models of Economic Exchange," in *Anthropology and Biblical Studies: The Way Forward,* ed. M. I. Aguilar and L. J. Lawrence (Leiden, 2004), 81–90.
21. E.g., Ernest W. Nicholson, "The Meaning of the Expression *am hā'āres* in the Old Testament," *JSS* 10 (1965): 59–66; De Vaux, *Ancient Israel: Its Life and Institutions,*

narrative, the phrase might refer to the elders of the community or the rulers who have the power to pass the possession of land from a tribe member to a foreigner in need.[22] However, based on the context, the phrase might simply and literally mean local landowners – people who possess the land and have the power to sell.[23] According to this possibility, the term is an early indication that Abraham is about to ask for something that strays from his original request for a burial plot, and that his request will require the consent of local landowners.

Abraham continues to refer to his original request, based on the agreement of the Hittites: "If it is your wish that I remove my dead for burial, you must agree to intercede for me with Ephron son of Zohar" (Gen. 23:8). Abraham repeats the crux of his request to bury his dead, and seemingly verifies the need for special permission to enter the grave of one of the Hittite families. Abraham's following statement supports this understanding: "Let him give me (*vayiten li*)[24] the cave of Machpelah that he owns, which is at the edge of his land" (v. 9). Abraham once again uses the verb *vayiten* ("let him give"). Previously Abraham requested the burial cave as a favor, without transfer of ownership. It would seem that from the moment that Abraham pointed to the cave, which was not a designated burial place, the Hittites realized they did not entirely understand Abraham's request. But in the next sentence Abraham suddenly changes his tone: "Let him give it to me, *at the full price*, for a burial site in your midst." This statement is a sharp turning point in the dialogue. Here Abraham clarifies, for the first time, exactly what he wants: not permission to bury his dead in a Hittite burial cave, but ownership over the cave "at the full price." Abraham repeats his

---

70–72; *HALOT* 2:838–839; John Tracy Thames, "A New Discussion of the Meaning of the Phrase *'am hā'āreṣ* in the Hebrew Bible," *JBL* 130 (2011): 109–125.

22. Wenham (*Genesis 16–50*, 127) raises this as a possibility, but ultimately leans toward the second possibility.
23. Abraham J. Brawer ("Am HaAretz KiFeshuto BaMikra," *Beit Mikra* 15 [1970]) makes this sweeping claim regarding all biblical references to "the people of the land." Regarding our verse, this claim was made by De Vaux (*Ancient Israel: Its Life and Institutions*, 70–71) and Hamilton (*The Book of Genesis, Chapters 18–50*, 130).
24. The Masoretic text reads "*vayiten*," "let him give," while NJPS translates based on context: "Let him *sell* me the cave." However, as explained below, the development of the discussion uses the ambiguous word *natan* to misrepresent Abraham's intention.

initial request, but rewords the request to make his intention to purchase the cave clear. Instead of asking: "*Give me* a burial site *among you*, that I may remove my dead for burial" (v. 4), Abraham reiterates: "Let him *sell it to me*, at the full price, for a burial site *in your midst*." Only now it becomes apparent to the Hittites – and the reader – that Abraham's intention was to purchase the cave and acquire full rights to the land; he had no intention of burying his wife in a Hittite cave, but in his own cave, which happens to be located in their midst.

In light of this new development, Ephron's public reaction requires careful examination: "Ephron the Hittite answered Abraham *in the hearing of the Hittites, all who entered the gate of his town*, saying: No, my lord, hear me: I give you the field and I give you the cave that is in it; I give it to you in the presence of my people. Bury your dead" (Gen. 23:12).[25] Ephron begins with a refusal of Abraham's request ("No, my lord"),[26] and makes a seemingly generous counter-offer. Instead of Abraham purchasing the cave, Ephron offers him the cave free of charge, as a gift. Yitzhak Moshe Emanueli writes: "Ephron refuses: 'No, my lord.' His refusal is not aimed at Abraham's proposal, but at the idea of the sale. To sell – under no circumstances! To give away for free – absolutely!"[27] Gunkel adds a positive evaluation, explaining that Ephron did not reject Abraham's request, but rather, accepted it with the additional magnanimous omission of the point of payment."[28]

---

25. Various interpretations have been offered for the phrase "all who entered the gate of his town." Some view the phrase as idiomatic, denoting the elders or leaders of the community, who possess the power to approve or reject public action (Ephraim A. Speiser, "'Coming' and 'Going' at the City Gate," *BASOR* 144 [1956]: 20–23), while others claim that the phrase indicates ordinary citizens who have the right to vote on public matters (Gunkel, *Genesis – Translated and Interpreted*, 271). Another position understands the expression literally: all of those who came to the town gate, whether they are permanent citizens or foreign visitors (Hamilton, *The Book of Genesis, Chapters 18–50*, 134).
26. According to the Masoretic text, Ephron answers "*lo*," "no" (see Ziony Zevit, "Expressing Denial in Biblical Hebrew and Mishnaic Hebrew, and in Amos," *VT* 29 [1979]: 506, among others). However, Gunkel reads "*lu*" as in, "if only, my lord" in correlation with v. 13 (Gunkel, *Genesis – Translated and Interpreted*, 271).
27. Emanueli, *Genesis – Commentary and Insights*, 318.
28. Gunkel, *Genesis – Translated and Interpreted*, 271.

Gunkel portrays Ephron as generous in the extreme, insofar as while Abraham had asked to purchase the cave, Ephron was willing to give it away free of charge. Ephron emphasizes that Abraham can have free access to the field any time he wishes to visit the burial cave. However, it is obvious that Ephron had no intention of offering Abraham a large field free of charge,[29] so his offer of access refutes the view of Ephron's offer as excessively generous. Ephron's offer reflects the negotiation etiquette of the time: while Ephron offers Abraham the field for free, it is clear that Abraham's response must be a refusal of the offer. This negotiation custom still prevails in Damascus and Egypt,[30] and Abraham J. Brawer offers a firsthand account of the custom:

> In my morning in Hebron, winter of 1914…the negotiation between the seller of locally made primitive glass artifacts and myself was done in Ephron style: "Take it for free, sir, it would be my honor to offer you this gift." I refused to accept it for free, and certainly paid more than the customary price. I asked the man who accompanied me – a local Jew – what the seller would have done had I taken the item for free? "Had you taken it for free," he responded, "then you would have created a bond of friendship with him, and you can't refuse a friend if he says to you, 'What a nice watch!' According to local custom, you would then have been obligated to give the watch to your 'friend.'"[31]

Ephron repeats the combination of the verb *natan* ("to give") and *lekha* ("to you") three times:

> I give to you the field
> I give to you the cave that is in it
> I give it to you in the presence of my people

29. Wenham, *Genesis 16–50*, 128.
30. Delitzsch, *Neuer Commentar über die Genesis*, 335–336.
31. Brawer, "The Negotiations for Purchasing a Tomb in Hebron," 94.

The first combination relates to the field. The second relates to the cave. And the third might relate to the combination of the field and the cave. Many commentators view this as Ephron's attempt to profit from the sale of the entire field, instead of merely the cave. However, offering Abraham a cave within a field owned by Ephron might create difficulties in following generations. A burial cave generally serves an entire family, and any time a descendant would want to visit the burial cave, permission would have to be granted by the Ephron family. Therefore, at this stage, Ephron's offer seems logical, not devious. His deviousness will only become apparent in the next stage of negotiation.[32] Given the rationale behind Ephron's negotiation tactics, it is apparent why Abraham insists on paying for the cave in full. Sarah's death may have started a timer on the urgency of the purchase of a burial site, but the grave of the Israelite nation's foremother could never sit on the land of strangers. Today, thousands of years later, the devout still visit the cave of Machpelah in Hebron in tribute to the ancients who were buried there. Even in his grief, Abraham knew that this plot of land needed to remain, unequivocally and without cessation, the legal property of his children for generations to come.

Stage III: At Any Cost

By this point, all the cards are on the table. Abraham repeats his desire to purchase the field with money, and Ephron reluctantly agrees. The change from Abraham's perspective is, of course, the field, which was not part of his initial request. Even if Ephron intends to extort money from Abraham (and as stated above this might not be the case), Abraham is disinclined to argue with him, and readily agrees to purchase the field in addition to the cave. Ephron's asking price might be indicative of his character: Abraham needs a burial cave and is therefore limited in his ability to negotiate, and Ephron takes full advantage of Abraham's distress. There is not enough evidence for us to determine whether four

32. However, it is not specified that the cave is inside the field, so the comment above is left to the reader's evaluation of Ephron. Since later on Ephron is portrayed as devious, the integration of the field at this stage might be an early sign of his slyness.

hundred shekels of silver is a realistic or excessive price,[33] but compared with other biblical accounts, the price seems high. Joseph was sold as a slave for twenty shekels of silver (Gen. 37:28). A field that is planted with "a homer of barley seed" (approximately four hundred liters) is estimated at fifty shekels of silver (Lev. 27:16). A virgin's dowry (Deut. 22:29) and the value of the most expensive category of person (Lev. 27:3) is fifty shekels of silver. Based on these records, Ephron elevated the price, and took advantage of Abraham's personal situation for personal gain. The high asking price supports the position that Ephron seemingly displays charity and generosity, while in practice he has no intention of offering a bargain to a man in need of burial for his wife.[34] Nonetheless, Abraham is responsible for the primary deception in the dialogue. Abraham's desire is not financial gain – in fact Abraham fails to bargain over price at all, and willingly pays Ephron's asking price without argument. The text is designed to encourage a misunderstanding of his request. The contribution of the deliberate portrayal of Abraham misleading Ephron requires attention.

Abraham's ambiguity contributes to the contractual rhetoric of his speech. Abraham portrays the Hittites as friends and good neighbors, who would not refuse him a favor during hard times. Initially he creates empathy by defining himself as an "alien resident," which portrays the Hittites as the lords of the land, and Abraham as inferior to them. Abraham immediately proceeds to compliment them: the man they view as "the elect of God among us" wishes to forge a long-lasting relationship with them, through common burial. A joint grave creates a close connection between the Hittites and Abraham's family, who will customarily bury everyone in the family plot. A partnership centered around burial is everlasting, since there is nothing more permanent than death. Having received such a compliment, the hearts of the Hittites opened to Abraham's plight. Eventually it will become apparent that Abraham really sought something else, but the lasting first impression melts the ice and creates fertile ground for a successful agreement.

33. Wenham, *Genesis 16–50*, 129. See II Sam. 24:24; Jer. 32:9; I Kings 16:24.

34. See, among others, Sternberg, "Double Cave, Double Talk: The Indirections of Biblical Dialogue," 28–57.

Regarding Abraham's apparent deceit, the text raises one possible understanding of his intentions, but then rejects that possibility with another explanation – an effective literary tool in a narrative whose purpose is not transparent. Simply ignoring a possible explanation would not leave a strong impression on the reader; raising and then rejecting a viable possibility turns the rejection into a statement that becomes part of the hidden message of the narrative.[35]

The text initially portrays Abraham as seeking a partnership with the Hittites – this desire is rejected not only by the text but by Abraham himself. Abraham explains that he had not intended to ask the Hittites for a favor, but rather to purchase the grave "at the full price." The purchase of the burial ground negates the concept of a partnership with the Hittites, and of joint burial. Instead, Abraham wants full rights to the cave, which will serve himself and his offspring – to the exclusion of the Hittites.

Abraham's initial duplicity, at least from a literary perspective, turns out to be a methodology to ensure the incontrovertibility of the cave's legal and binding transfer from the Hittites to the Abrahamic line. Abraham stresses the "possession" of the land, a term which carries broad significance in Genesis, being the term God uses when He promises the land to Abraham (Gen. 17:5; 48:4).[36] The purchase of the Machpelah cave is the beginning of Abraham's realization of his possession of Canaan, alongside – not along with – the Hittites. The purchase is not the act of creating a partnership, but rather part of the process of

---

35. As noted above in the discussion on the binding of Isaac. There are many examples of this literary technique. Sternberg (*The Poetics of Biblical Narrative: Ideological Literature and the Drama of Reading*, 200–201) offers one example involving another Hittite. In II Sam. 11:13, the narrative describes Uriah the Hittite in Jerusalem: "But in the evening, [Uriah] went out to sleep in his resting place." The initial impression is that David, in trying to get Uriah to go home, succeeded in his scheme, and Uriah went to his regular resting place, in his home. In fact, David's regular resting place is described in the same terms in v. 2. However, the remainder of the verse reveals that Uriah in fact slept "with his lord's officers"; this surprising statement, which negates the resting at home, is then reinforced by the explicit statement: "He did not go down to his home."
36. Wenham, *Genesis 16–50*, 127. See also Gillis Gerleman, "Nutzrecht und Wohnrecht: Zur Bedeutung von אחזה und נחלה," *ZAW* 89 (1977): 313–325.

separation and distinction from the people of the land, a theme that is continued in the following narrative when Abraham sends his servant to find a wife for Isaac.

The Stories' Endings

The dual narrative of Sarah's death and the purchase of the cave of Machpelah comes to a dual conclusion, nicely rounding out the literary structure we observed from the outset. The final "*shama*" ("to hear") appears in the final verse: "And Abraham heard Ephron."[37] Despite the statement of the text about Abraham listening to Ephron, the Hittites are the ones who accept Abraham's terms; ultimately the cave and field became Abraham's property. Verse 16 offers another detail regarding the sale that was previously omitted: "Abraham heard Ephron. Abraham paid out to Ephron the money that he had named in the hearing of the Hittites, four hundred shekels of silver at the going merchants' rate." Even when Ephron demanded a high price for the field, he never mentioned the "going merchant's rate." The term refers to currency that can be used anywhere and is accepted by any merchant. Perhaps the detail is only noteworthy at the payment stage and not in the discussion of terms, but perhaps the surprise indicates that for all of Ephron's high-minded talk he accepted the payment of premium currency for his land.

The two narratives wrap up in two parallel conclusions: the outcome of the legal transaction, and the laying to rest of Sarah. The first is, aptly, reminiscent of a legal contract. The text provides a detailed account of the transaction, which seems almost like a quote from a proprietary contract: "...the field, with its cave, and all the trees anywhere within the confines of that field" (Gen. 23:17).[38] The mention of witnesses supports the impression of a legal contract, "in the presence of the Hittites..." (v. 18).[39] Linguistically, this passage completes the

37. NJPS translates this as, "Abraham accepted Ephron's terms."

38. Skinner, *A Critical and Exegetical Commentary on Genesis*, 338; Gunkel, *Genesis – Translated and Interpreted*, 272; von Rad, *Genesis*, 244; and many others.

39. On the use of similar formulations in Ancient Near East contracts (with regard to v. 16), see Speiser, *Genesis*, 171.

narrative with a return to verbiage used in the beginning of the story. The repetition is evident both in content and in the fabric of the language:

Gen. 23:17–18	**23:20**
So passed Ephron's land in Machpelah, near Mamre	Thus passed
the field with its cave and all the trees anywhere within the confines of that field – passed	the field with its cave
to Abraham as his possession, in the presence of the Hittites, of all who entered the gate of his town.	from the Hittites to Abraham, as a burial site.

Following the closure of the cave's purchase, the text circles back to the narrative frame – the death of Sarah is brought back to the reader's consciousness: "And then Abraham buried his wife Sarah in the cave of the field of Machpelah, facing Mamre – now Hebron – in the land of Canaan" (Gen. 23:19). The statement seems like the perfect conclusion to the event that opened the narrative and triggered the story. Sarah died, and Abraham had to find a place to bury her. Finally, Abraham purchased a field with a burial cave, and buried Sarah. The closure also generates a linguistic *inclusio*: Sarah died "in Kiryat Arba – now Hebron – in the land of Canaan (v. 2); Sarah was buried "in the cave of the field of Machpelah, facing Mamre – now Hebron – in the land of Canaan" (v. 19).

The initial conclusion describes the purchase of the field and cave from Ephron "in the presence of the Hittites, of all who entered the gate of his town." Ephron is named as the seller of the land, and the Hittites serve as witnesses, who approve the transfer of ownership over the field from Ephron to Abraham. The second conclusion names the Hittites as the sellers, and Ephron is not mentioned at all: Abraham purchases the field "from the Hittites." The reader knows from the detailed negotiation that Ephron is the actual seller. However, within the literary context there is an emphasis on the Hittites as an ethnic group rather than on Ephron the owner. The second conclusion indicates that the purchase of Machpelah relates to national affairs, and that the significance of the purchase is that Abraham acquired land from the Hittites. This distinction is also apparent in the definition of the purchase. In the initial conclusion the land is given to Abraham as "a possession," while the function of the land in the second conclusion is "a burial site." The second conclusion de-emphasizes the actual purchase, and focuses instead on the purpose – Sarah's burial. Since Sarah's burial is described after the first conclusion, one might view the two conclusions as two stages. Initially, Abraham purchased the land, and once it was taken into his possession, he decided to bury his wife there, ordaining the land as a burial ground. Nonetheless, the fact that Abraham purchased the land is repeated in verse 20, in a new context.

The two conclusions indicate that the story should be read in two different contexts. The dialogue demonstrates that Abraham purchased the field legally and honestly, for a handsome sum. The reference to the contract in the initial conclusion ensures that the purchase cannot be contested in future generations. The second conclusion indicates a broader context. Abraham did not purchase the field from Ephron, but from the Hittites. The purpose of the purchase was not for profit but for a burial, which represents permanent and everlasting possession. While the initial conclusion highlights the first purchase of land in Canaan by Abraham, the final conclusion reveals the historical significance of the purchase, which returns to the initial report of Sarah's death and the need to bury her.

Abraham will not inherit the Promised Land in his lifetime (Gen. 15:13–16), though he does plant the seeds of inheritance before he departs. Abraham receives official rights to the Beersheba wells before the binding, and after the binding, Abraham purchases land. Although neither could be viewed as the inheritance of Canaan promised to Abraham, both episodes should be appreciated for their historical symbolism: the Philistines and the Hittites both acknowledge Abraham's rights to the land; Abraham plants a new tree in his land and buries his wife in a burial ground that unequivocally belongs to him.[40]

---

40. Cf. von Rad, *Genesis*, 244–245; Speiser, *Genesis*, 171–172; McEvenue, *The Narrative Style of the Priestly Writer*, 142; Brevard S. Childs, *Old Testament Theology in a Canonical Context* (Philadelphia, 1986), 219. However, see also the critique on the theological reading by Westermann, *Genesis 12–36: A Continental Commentary*, 376, and Coats,

The negotiation over Ephron's field therefore functions in a broader context. Ephron might have attempted to take advantage of the opportunity to increase his earnings, but symbolically, in addition to purchasing a burial ground for his current needs, Abraham also purchased a field that could be planted for the future. He, too, will be buried in the cave, but his offspring will enjoy the fruits of the field and see the fulfillment of God's promise that Abraham's family will inherit the land.

Genesis, 164–165. According to Coats, "It is simply a report of acquisition of burial property," while Westermann believes the narrative is intended to encourage the exiled who could not bury their dead in their homeland.

Finding a Wife for Isaac (Gen. 24)

Although Abraham's continuing legacy is secured with Isaac, the bridge to the next generation cannot be complete until Rebecca comes onto the stage. Without her, the Abrahamic line cannot continue. Following the binding narrative on Mount Moriah, Abraham returns home with the express mission to secure the next generation in his line. Isaac, however, seems to disappear. The topic of Abraham's successor was a key theme throughout his narrative – his mother, father, half-brother, and step-mother suffered greatly in order to solidify Isaac's role as the inheritor. However, once father – and son, presumably – have passed the final test of faith in the binding story, Isaac remains blatantly absent from the task of arranging his own marriage and ensuring the continuity of his genetic line.

Abraham needs a successor who will carry on the values he established, who will be willing to make the difficult decisions required of a leader. For all his virtue, Isaac's journey led him in a completely different direction. He is still the inheritor, still the successor, but the experience on the mountain has left him a changed man – the brush with death seems to have left Isaac wedged perpetually between heaven and earth, experiencing life on a spiritual, metaphysical plane. For the Abrahamic line to succeed, Isaac will need a partner who emulates

Abraham's character traits of action and pragmatism. Isaac is about to transition into the role of protagonist in his own story, and he needs a strong wife by his side.

Rebecca is the heroine our new hero needs. She represents the first generation after Abraham, the first born into the birthright, and therefore the first that has not experienced firsthand the arduous journey Abraham overcame to found his dynasty. The trials Rebecca must overcome in the coming story test not only her virtue and kindness, but her courage – like her future father-in-law, Rebecca heeds the hero's call and leaves her home and family behind to forge her destiny in a foreign land.

The Messenger's Mission

The search for Isaac's wife is the longest story in the Abraham cycle, and perhaps in the Pentateuch. Hamilton noted: "It is interesting that the longest chapter in Genesis is given over to discussion of marriage and not, say, to the creation of the world or the covenant with Abraham."[1] The length of the narrative stems from the fact that the story is recited twice: once by the text and again by the servant, who retells his experience to Rebecca's family. The repetition phenomenon is a well-used literary technique in the biblical narrative, and the review of a detail or even several details is not uncommon. In this chapter, however, the entire story of the servant's adventure is repeated, for no apparent reason.

The story's structure is simple:

> **A: Canaan**: The servant receives instructions to bring back a wife for Isaac (Gen. 24: 1–9).
>
> > **B: Haran**: The servant's experiences by the well (vv. 10–28).
> >
> > **B': The house of Bethuel**: The servant reviews his experiences (vv. 29–61).
>
> **A': Canaan**: The servant returns with a wife for Isaac (vv. 62–67).

The text could easily have summarized the servant's review in a brief statement, as in the conclusion of the narrative: "The servant told Isaac all the things that he had done" (Gen. 24:66). However, it is exactly

1. Hamilton, *The Book of Genesis, Chapters 18–50*, 138.

that succinct closing line that sheds light on the necessity for the story's loquaciousness. The servant leaves his master, Abraham, on a quest. He returns from the quest, again to his master – Isaac. The lengthy narrative, the repetition, and the experiences of the servant on his sojourn in Canaan constitute a dramatic shift in the Abraham story – in fact, in the Abrahamic dynasty as a whole. He departs a servant of Abraham, and returns a servant of Isaac.

Abraham's Motive and Instructions to the Servant

The reader should not be surprised that a wife has to be sought for Isaac. The ongoing analogy between the two sons of Abraham necessitates a review of Ishmael's marriage. The tidings of Ishmael's birth are delivered by an angel (Gen. 16:11), he is saved from death by means of a revelation (21:17), and his mother takes a wife for him from her homeland, Egypt (21:21). The major events of Isaac's life follow a similar path. He is conceived after the revelation of an angel (18:9), his life is saved by means of another revelation (22:11–12), and the next anticipated event should be his father finding him a wife from his homeland, Haran.[2] The opening line of the narrative ("Abraham was now old, advanced in years") also sets a scene of a man caring for the needs of his sons before he dies.[3] The story prepares the reader for the upcoming passage of generations. Sarah dies in the previous narrative, and now Abraham arranges his son's marriage, to ensure continuity and succession. The generational change is also indicated in the depiction of the servant as "old": "Abraham said to his servant, the elder of his household, who had charge of all that he owned" (24:2). The era of Abraham is nearly over; he is old, and his servants are old. Isaac's marriage to the right bride is crucial so that he can take over Abraham's estate and become his successor.

The servant is clearly introduced as a proxy for Abraham on the impending journey. The servant is described with parallel terms to Abraham:

---

2. Sternberg, *The Poetics of Biblical Narrative: Ideological Literature and the Drama of Reading*, 132.
3. Some translations even relate that Abraham was "well stricken in age" (JPS 1917; ASV 1901), but this is melodramatic.

Genesis 24:2	**Genesis 24:1**
Abraham said to his Servant, the elder (*zekan*) of his household	Abraham Was now old (*zaken*), advanced in years
who had charge of all (*bekhol*) that he owned	and the Lord had blessed Abraham in all things (*bakol*)

God blessed Abraham "in all things," but the one in charge of "all" that Abraham was blessed with was Abraham's servant. The servant acts with Abraham's authorization; he is as Abraham's own right hand. There are two approaches among the commentators to the servant's placement of his hand on Abraham's thigh. Ibn Ezra writes that the placing of the servant's hand under the thigh of the master symbolizes a certain passing of agency from the master to the servant, a commitment of loyalty from the servant, and the placing of faith and authority to act on the master's behalf. He notes that this practice was common even in his time in India. Neither Ibn Ezra nor Rashbam (who writes similarly) saw a direct connection between the placement of the hand and the oath that was made. Rashi, on the other hand, takes a completely opposite approach: "The oath-taker must hold in his hand an item related to a commandment, such as a Torah scroll, or phylacteries; circumcision was his [Abraham's] first commandment, and so held a dear place in his heart." Rashi's commentary assumes two details. One, that the phrase "thigh" was in fact a euphemism for the circumcised member. Second, that just as Israelite law requires an oath-taker to hold a religious object, the same requirement falls on the servant of an Israelite. If this is the case, Abraham asks his servant, "Put your hand under my thigh," as a reinforcement of the oath he is about to take. This symbolic act is reenacted by Jacob on his deathbed: "And when the time approached for Israel to die, he summoned his son Joseph and said to him, 'Do me this favor, place your hand under my thigh as a pledge of your steadfast loyalty: please do not bury me in Egypt'.... And he said, 'Swear to me.' And he swore to him. Then Israel bowed at the head of the bed" (Gen. 47:29–31).[4]

The expression "*yotzei yerekh,*" "fruit of loins," does seem to indicate that the thigh (*yerekh*) is symbolic of the reproductive organ. The

4. See further in Jonathan Grossman, *Joseph: A Tale of Dreams* (Rishon LeZion 2021), 490–491.

symbolism to the covenant, to fertility, and to familial continuity are clear. Abraham's senior servant, who is trusted with everything that Abraham has, is perceived as part of his family; having him take the oath over the reproductive organ turns the oath into a commitment to family.[5] Jacob too, issues this oath in the context of generational continuity – Jacob makes Joseph promise that he will bury Jacob in the family plot of the Machpelah cave. Abraham transforms his servant into his proxy, his right hand and the messenger tasked with the crucial mission to ensure the continuation of his genetic line by marrying off his son.

The question arises from the text as to whether Abraham intended for his servant to choose a bride for Isaac from amongst his own family. Abraham's request, "You will not take a wife for my son from the daughters of the Canaanites among whom I dwell, but will go to my land and the place of my birth,[6] and get a wife for my son Isaac" (Gen. 24:3–4), can be understood in two different ways, depending on the interpretation of the term "the place of my birth." As previously noted in the discussion of God's initial command to Abraham, the biblical term *moledet* ("birth-land") denotes both "the place of one's birth" (e.g., Gen. 31:13) and "family" (e.g., Gen. 48:6; Lev. 18:9 and 11). Perhaps Abraham simply wanted his servant to find Isaac a bride from the area of Haran. The other possibility is that Abraham instructed his servant to return to Haran because he was looking for a bride from within his own family – indeed, he emphasizes that the servant return to "the house of my father." The servant supports this reading of Abraham's instructions in his report to Rebecca's family: "Now my lord made me swear, saying, 'You shall not get a wife for my son from the daughters of the Canaanites in whose land I dwell; but you shall go to my father's house, to my kindred, and get a wife for my son'" (24:38). But the details of his report seem to deliberately change Abraham's request; the servant

5. See Klaus Koch, "*Pahad jishaq*: eine Gottesbezeichnung?" in *Werden und Wirken des Allen Testaments: Festschrift für Claus Westermann*, ed. R. Albertz et al. (Göttingen, 1980), 113–114.
6. NJPS translates this as "the land of my birth," omitting the dual reference. See discussion below.

drops "my land" and "my birthplace," but adds "my father's house," and "my kindred," which Abraham had not specified. The fact that the servant changes the wording might indicate that the simple reading of Abraham's reference to "the place of my birth" refers to the land without reference to the family. Abraham's original intention was not to send his servant specifically to his family but to his homeland.

This is not to say that Abraham represents a philosophy that objects to marrying outside of the tribe; rather, his decision reflects a desire to create a distance between him and the Canaanites.[7] Presumably, Abraham is concerned about becoming overly involved with the people of the land. Abraham's covenant with God separates him from those people, and his loyalty to this principle is shown in the previous chapter, when he purchased the cave of Machpelah. The servant's account to the family strays from Abraham's initial intentions. We will analyze this discrepancy later in the narrative. For now, Abraham's request is clear – find Isaac a bride from the land of his birth.

The initial instructions to the servant seem relatively straightforward; if we consider that Abraham is getting on in years, the decision to send a servant to Canaan in his stead seems reasonable. When the servant questions Abraham's instructions, Abraham unwittingly reveals an additional layer that may be driving his decision. The servant asks, "What if the woman does not consent to follow me to this land, shall I then take your son back to the land from which you came?" (Gen. 24:5). This is a rational question, since Abraham had stated that he is not willing to have his son marry a Canaanite woman. If Abraham's main goal is to perpetuate the family lineage, then he should not mind Isaac leaving the country for that purpose.

Abraham, however, responds ardently:

7. Some read "*moladeti*" as "the place in which I was born," but in reference to Abraham's family. Radak writes on Gen. 24:4: "To the place of my birth – the city in which I was born, which is Ur of the Chaldeans; in other words, that is where his family will be found, and he hinted to him about Rebecca, because he was told that she was born." Gersonides suggests: "[T]his is the reason Abraham selected a daughter of his own country, and specifically of his own family. He ordered his servant to take a wife for Isaac from there, and if he could not find one from his family, he should take one from his land."

> The Lord, the God of heaven, who took me from my father's house and from my native land, who promised me on oath, saying, "I will assign this land to your offspring" – He will send His angel before you, and you will get a wife for my son from there. And if the woman does not consent to follow you, you shall then be clear of this oath to me.

Abraham's reaction, awash with emotion, seems to cry out, *On no account must you take my son back there!* Abraham seems to dread the possibility of his son returning to the place he left, though he also conveys his confidence that God will assist the servant. God "took" Abraham from his "native land," and will help his servant "take" a wife for his son "from there." The parallel wording to Abraham's first divine revelation here is haunting. Abraham, at the end of his life, seeks to ensure the continuation of his lineage. However, the genetic line is only part of the story. Abraham was taken by God from his homeland, followed Him blindly on a complicated journey – both physically and spiritually. That process changed Abraham, it formed him into the patriarch he is today. Peering over the precipice at the advent of a new generation, he may fear that they will not retain the lessons his journey has imprinted upon him. Abraham designs the concept of the woman following the servant to Canaan as the mirror image of his own journey "from there." Rebecca is portrayed from the outset as Abraham's literary counterpart: both leave their native land and the house of their father to go to the same unknown land. Rebecca is not only a prospective wife and foremother, she is the symbol of hope for continuing Abraham's legacy.

The scene concludes with the servant's oath to follow his master's instructions, which is reinforced by placing his hand "under the thigh of his master." The "hand" plays an important symbolic role throughout the narrative. The following verse states: "Then the servant took ten of his master's camels and set out, taking *in his hand* all the bounty of his master" (Gen. 24:10). Rebecca's hand will feature later in the story: "She quickly lowered her jar *upon her hand* and let him drink" (v. 18), causing the servant to take "a gold nose-ring weighing a half-shekel, and two gold bands for her *hands,* ten shekels in weight" (v. 22; see also v. 30). The "hand" element emphasizes the mutual generosity throughout the narrative: the servant gives what is in his hand, while Rebecca gives what is in hers. The hand in the oath, placed by the servant under Abraham's thigh, takes on another role: the hand of the servant is part of Abraham, enabling the hand to take Abraham's fortune. The actions of the servant are in Abraham's name and for his benefit. The hand links the events throughout the narrative – Rebecca's generosity and the servant's loyalty – which strive to realize Abraham's request. Each stage of the story leaves the mission in someone else's "hands."

The promise mentioned in Abraham's instructions (Gen. 24:3) and the conclusion of the first scene (v. 9) is particularly noteworthy. The promise motif is reminiscent of the two previous narratives: the oath between Abraham and Abimelech (21:31), and God's promise to Abraham at the conclusion of the binding narrative (22:16). Here the servant promises his master that he will follow his instructions. The previous promises related to the distant horizon of future generations. The oath between Abraham and Abimelech and their offspring was marked by the planting of a tree by Abraham, and invoking the name of an everlasting God, which indicates His ability to realize His promises for future generations (21:33). Needless to say, God's final revelation to Abraham, which is delivered at the conclusion of the binding narrative, looks to future generations. Here, too, on a smaller scale, the narrative relates to future generations: Isaac's marriage to the right woman is crucial to the education of future generations in the ways of God, and essential to the maintenance of God's covenant. Abraham links the two oaths. When he asks his servant to promise, he reminds him: "The Lord, the God of heaven, who took me from my father's house and from my native land, *who promised me on oath*, saying, 'I will assign this land to your offspring' – He will send His angel before you, and you will get a wife for my son from there" (v. 7). The repetition of the promise links the servant's mission with the process of Abraham's selection and his blessings. The literary role of the promises in the final Abraham narratives is to digress from the concrete here and now, and link the events with the more profound theme, "The Making of a Nation."

The Servant's "Divination Game"

The servant sets out, as directed by Abraham, to Aram-naharaim, equipped with "ten of his master's camels" (Gen. 24:10), and "all the bounty of his master" – a load that amounts to a small fortune in ancient times. In the servant's prayer, we begin to see the first foretaste of the dramatic change that the characters are to undergo by the end of this ordeal. In his prayer by the well, the servant emphasizes his position and acknowledges that the success of his mission would be God's kindness toward his master, Abraham. However, the servant is not the only one with this title: Isaac is also referred to as "God's servant" in the servant's prayer (v. 14). While a social-legal servant cannot be compared to a spiritual servant of God, the wordplay is not incidental. Abraham could easily have been referred to as God's servant, but Abraham remains the servant's master throughout the dialogue. The changing references to the characters play an important role in the narrative, and the reference to Isaac in the same name as the servant is deliberate. The positions of Abraham, the master, the servant, and Isaac, the master's son and servant to God, will take a dramatic turn at the conclusion of the narrative. To add to the confusion, the servant refers to Isaac using the same term as he uses in reference to himself: the reader might wonder to which of the "servants" God "decreed" the appropriate maiden, and there is need for clarification that the "servant" is, in fact, Isaac.

In an innocent statement that is characteristic of the early stages of a narrative, the text describes the servant going "to Aram-naharaim, to the city of Nahor" (Gen. 24:10). This parenthetical mention of Nahor plants the early seeds of the plot in the reader's mind, although the servant remains in the dark. He has to reach Abraham's place of birth, whether or not his family still resides there, and there is no indication that he is aware that he has reached the boundaries of Nahor's city. In fact, the servant does not even ask the townspeople about Nahor and his family, as Jacob does when he arrives in the city (29:5–6). The family is not the servant's main concern, and not the purpose of his mission.

The servant camps outside of the city, by the well, at "the time when women come out to draw water" (Gen. 24:11). To avid readers of biblical text, the time and location of the servant's campsite is delightfully fitting. In the context of the book of Genesis, we know that there is no more fitting location to arrange a match than by a well. The symbology of the oasis in the desert is clearly tied to fertility, and we know that couples throughout Genesis will meet their betrothed while drawing water from a well. However, the story of Rebecca – though it is the first chronologically – diverges from the "normal" well narrative. In the narratives of Jacob (Gen. 28) and Moses (Ex. 2) at their respective wells, the stranger arrives at the well and proves to be a savior of the shepherdesses who required assistance drawing water. The detail is not insignificant. A man protecting his future wife is the perfect pattern for a good match in the ancient world. A man's sensitivity toward a woman shows that he is a good match for her, and proves his moral worth.

In the Rebecca narrative, however, the roles are reversed: "The maiden to whom I say, 'Please, lower your jar that I may drink,' and who replies, 'Drink, and I will also water your camels' – let her be the one whom You have decreed for Your servant Isaac." The servant portrays himself as the one in need of assistance. He requires the help of the maiden to draw water for him and his camels.

Robert Alter paints a beautiful picture of this role reversal, claiming that the nature of the encounters next to the wells foreshadows the nature of the couples who meet there. Jacob, who overcomes the obstacle of the rock covering the well in his meeting with Rachel, demonstrates that

> Jacob will obtain the woman he wants only through great labor, against resistance, and even God's will, in the relevant biblical idiom, "shut up her womb" for years until she finally bears Joseph. For Rebecca and Isaac, however, Isaac remains a largely passive character in their marriage. It is Rebecca that will drive the plot of their lives – indeed, she is the craftiest and most forceful of the matriarchs. It is no surprise then, that she would take on a dominant role in her betrothal scene.[8]

---

8. Alter, *The Art of Biblical Narrative*, 53–54. Similarly, Hamilton, *The Book of Genesis, Chapters 18–50*, 148; Lieve M. Teugels, "'A Strong Woman, Who Can Find?' A Study of Characterization in Genesis 24, with Some Perspectives on the General Presentation of Isaac and Rebecca in the Genesis Narrative," *JSOT* 63 (1994): 88–104. See

The scene at the well is not only an introduction to the Jacob narrative, in which Rebecca plays an important role, but is also part of the concluding narratives of the Abraham cycle. In other words, even in this stage of the story there seems to be a need for the description of Rebecca's activity in relation to the servant – Isaac's representative in the match.

Instead, the narrative continues the theme that Abraham originated. The text portrays Rebecca as a mirror image of Abraham. Rebecca is the one being tested in this match, not Isaac (as Jacob and Moses are in their marriage stories). The challenge of the narrative is Rebecca's. Will she, like Abraham, choose to leave her land and abandon the house of her father to go to a foreign land and mother a budding nation? Rebecca's actions will determine whether she is worthy of joining the house of Abraham; her kind actions are emphasized, to demonstrate that they are comparable to those of the servant's master. The servant focuses his prayer on his master, not on the intended groom: "God of *my lord Abraham,*[9] grant me good fortune this day, and deal graciously with *my lord Abraham* .... Thereby shall I know that You have dealt graciously with *my lord*" (Gen. 24:12–14). Although Isaac is mentioned ("Let her be the one whom You have decreed for Your servant Isaac"), God's kindness in finding him the right match will be with Abraham.[10] Beyond the technical fact that Abraham was the one to send his servant on this mission, the bride they seek has to be appropriate for the house of Abraham. Rebecca needs to be far more than a good match; she must be capable of carrying the weight of Abraham's legacy.

Rebecca's success in passing the servant's test may seem like a simple outcome, perhaps even a predictable literary device in a story that is rife with archetypal, even fairy-tale-like motifs. However, this is no Cinderella story – the method by which the servant tests his potential future mistress, as well as the text's interpretation of the outcome, tells a deeper story.

---

also George Savran's opinion below that these breakings of conventions stem from the fact that the servant is not looking for a wife for himself (Savran, "The Character as Narrator in Biblical Narrative," *Prooftexts* 5 [1985]: 4).

9. NJPS, like other modern translations, translated the word *adonai* in reference to Abraham as "my master" throughout the story.
10. Hamilton, *The Book of Genesis, Chapters 18–50*, 145.

In order to understand the outcome of the test, we must first familiarize ourselves with the art of divination, which was ubiquitous in ancient times. In a world where life and death ebbed and flowed at the whims of a pantheon of gods, believers searched for any way they could find to attempt to interpret the gods' intentions and their effects on humanity. Ancients would practice haruspicy, inspecting the size, shape, and color of animal livers, for example, to foretell the future based on their findings. Another technique, consisting of pouring oil into water and examining the bubbles and rings, relied on minute differences in the exact size of the bubble or the shape of the lines.[11] There was no logical link between the action and the prediction, apart from the imagined connection fashioned in the minds of the diviners. From a modern perspective, this arbitrary methodology for predicting the future may seem primitive. However, the art of divination was considered definitive. The essence of divination was in the details – the slightest change in shape, color, or grammar could drastically alter an outcome.

Returning to our story, we see that the servant seems to engage in a manner of divination in order to aid in his search. He uses the verb "*hakreh*," "grant me success," and an indication of time ("this day"). The phrase "Let her be the one whom You have decreed for Your servant Isaac" is especially redolent of divination – but the content of his test relates to the qualities of the maiden. Many commentators perceive this to be a test of character rather than an attempt at prediction.[12] The integration of the word *ḥesed* at the beginning and end of the servant's prayer ("Deal *graciously* with my lord" and "You have dealt *graciously* with my lord") creates a consciousness of the requirement for kindness of anyone who would wish to join the household of Abraham. This is the challenge set before any candidate for the wife of Isaac. Although the formulation might sound like divination, the servant seeks to examine the characteristics of the maiden; he is well aware

11. E.g., Isaac Mendelsohn, "Divination," *IDB*, vol. 1, 856–858.
12. Cf. Abrabanel's commentary on Gen. 24; Wenham, *Genesis 16–50*, 153; Leibowitz, *Studies in Genesis*, 157–161.

of the central quality expected of Isaac's wife.[13] Nonetheless, there is a reason the servant formulates his prayer in a way that correlates with the world of divination. The tension between prediction based on magic and an examination of the maiden's qualities is exactly the point at which Rebecca fails the servant's test – and in turn succeeds at a far greater trial.

This paints a picture of the value system of the Jewish people. Rebecca did not pass the test of the guessing game – she passed a far more valuable test in the eyes of the biblical ethos.

Rebecca at the Well

The scene is set – the servant waits patiently by the well, the criteria for discerning a deserving bride for his master's son clear in his mind. Rebecca, the striking young woman, steps onto the scene and immediately catches the servant's eye. At this point, the text confides in the reader: "Rebecca, who was born to Bethuel, the son of Milcah the wife of Abraham's brother Nahor, came out with her jar on her shoulder" (Gen. 24:15). The reference to Abraham, Rebecca's grandfather's brother, and to the mother, Milcah daughter of Haran, leaves no room for doubt. The reader is meant to know that the servant has met with a candidate from Abraham's own family, as per the instructions of his master, while the servant is entirely unaware that the maiden's father is a descendant of two of Abraham's brothers. This is a literary device that serves to shift the reader's focus from the question of the maiden's identity – which is known in advance – to the actions of the oblivious characters.[14] In this case, the reader is given the opportunity to examine the process of exposure of the maiden's character and true identity. As mentioned, Rebecca is the one who must prove herself, and the reader can sit back, mesmerized by her actions, understanding how her kindness will ultimately drive the plot.

---

13. Sternberg, *The Poetics of Biblical Narrative: Ideological Literature and the Drama of Reading*, 137.
14. See Polak, *Biblical Narrative Aspects of Art and Design*, 174–75. Gérard Genette (*Narrative Discourse: An Essay in Method* [Ithaca, 1980]) writes similarly regarding prolapses. See also Talmon, *Darkhei HaSippur BaMikra*, 27–31.

The impeccable timing of Rebecca's arrival points to some level of divine intervention: "He had scarcely finished speaking, when Rebecca ... came out with her jar on her shoulder" (Gen. 24:15). Divine intervention is embedded in this narrative. God ensures that all the pieces of the puzzle are perfectly aligned – the well, the servant, the prayer, the girl. However, the maiden still has to prove herself worthy by exposing her attributes. The test is outside the divine realm, and Abraham's servant, along with the reader, looks to the maiden and her free will to determine whether she is the answer to his search. Rebecca has the choice to deny the request of the servant. Divine decree or not, God can only bring the characters together in an opportune moment – it is up to Rebecca to realize her own potential by acting with kindness out of free will.[15] The preparation mission creates an anticipation of meeting with an angel, following Abraham's statement: "The God of heaven, who took me from my father's house and from my native land.... He will send His angel before you" (Gen. 24:7). In light of the prevalence of angels (specifically by a well) in other stories in the cycle, it is reasonable to expect an angel to appear in order to assist the encounter. However, the lack of appearance of an angel sends an important literary message: the characters determine their own future by their moral actions. The servant will have to logically determine whether Rebecca is the right woman for his master's son.

Upon laying eyes upon Rebecca, the servant's interest is piqued. His explicit request fresh in his mind, he observes the maiden's actions in anticipation – will she perform the exact sequence of actions he determined as the test? In order for his divination to work, Rebecca must perform the actions precisely as he articulated – there can be no digression. So, did Rebecca pass the test?

---

15. This correlation between divine decree and human choice is characteristic of the book of Ruth, and perhaps indicated in Esther as well. See Ronald M. Hals, *The Theology of the Book of Ruth* (Philadelphia, 1969); Jonathan Grossman, *Esther: The Outer Narrative and the Hidden Reading*, Siphrut: Literature and Theology of the Hebrew Scriptures 6 (Winona Lake, IN, 2011), 119.

Servant's Prayer (Gen. 24:13–14)	Rebecca's Action (15–20)
Here I stand by the spring as the daughters of the townsmen come out to draw water	Rebecca ... came out with her jar on her shoulder. The maiden was very beautiful, a virgin whom no man had known. She went down to the spring, filled her jar, and came up
let the maiden to whom I say, "Please, lower your jar that I may drink,"	The servant ran toward her and said, "Please, let me sip a little water from your jar."
and who replies, "Drink –	"Drink, my lord," she said, and she quickly lowered her jar upon her hand and let him drink.
'and I will also water your camels'	When she had let him drink his fill, she said, "I will also draw for your camels, until they finish drinking." Quickly emptying her jar into the trough, she ran back to the well to draw, and she drew for all his camels.

The dilemma is clear. Rebecca seems to have proven herself worthy of Abraham's household. Not only did she agree to let the stranger drink from her jar, she also offered to water all of his camels, without even being asked. The rules of divination, however, demand a high degree of accuracy. Since the signs are magical, even a minor change is highly significant. For example, in the inspection of animal livers there is a difference between the message conveyed by "a head crushed like a needle," a "caught nose," a "face facing left," and two parts of the liver intertwined "like string." Initially, Rebecca seems to fulfill the prediction accurately. The servant had anticipated that she would ask him to drink, and she says, "Drink, my lord" (though some claim that even at this point, Rebecca's polite addition of "my lord" strays from the formulation). After this promising beginning, the reader expects Rebecca to continue in correlation with the servant's prediction, and offer to water his camels. Instead, Rebecca "quickly lowered her jar upon her hand

and let him drink." Only after Rebecca has confirmed that the servant drank his fill, does she offer, "I will also draw for your camels, until they finish drinking."

In truth, the servant put Rebecca at a disadvantage by deviating himself from his own test. He had stated that he would turn to a maiden who would come to him, but when he saw Rebecca he "ran toward her" (Gen. 24:17). The reason the servant decided to run to Rebecca is explicit: "The maiden was very beautiful."[16] Running negates the ability to allow the magic to work, since divination is based on the assumption that there is a predetermined decision, and divination uncovers messages sent by the gods. Therefore, any human intervention or action might lead to the wrong conclusion. However, even if the servant's intervention had been acceptable in the reality of divination, Rebecca's reaction creates a greater dilemma. It would seem that Rebecca, for all her kindness and the servant's optimism, did not pass the test.

If this story were dependent on the law of divination, Rebecca's part in it would have ended here – the servant would have continued on until he found a maiden who fulfilled his prediction using the exact formulation he established. Such a suggestion, for the sensitive reader, is unimaginable. True, Rebecca did not pass the test of the divination – but that was only due to the fact that she displayed *more* kindness than the servant surmised she might in the first place! Rebecca's actions deviate from the servant's prediction in two ways. Firstly, Rebecca only offered to water the camels after she had ensured that the servant drank his fill. Secondly, she offered to draw water for the camels, not just to "water" them. The distinction is profound. Watering the camels means allowing them to drink from the water in the trough, while Rebecca offered to fill the trough by drawing more water, as the verse

16. In marriage narratives or narratives with other sexual contexts, the beauty of the character is commonly described (David M. Gunn and Danna Nolan Fewell, *Narrative in the Hebrew Bible* [Oxford Bible Series: Oxford, 1993], 57). But the integration of the detail specifically in this place – before the servant runs toward the young woman – indicates that the Rebecca's beauty should also be viewed as an incentive for the servant's haste.

explains in detail: "She ran back to the well to draw, and she drew for all his camels" (Gen. 24:20).[17]

It is not only Rebecca's proactive magnanimity that is striking here. A heightened sense of urgency guides the scene as the text takes us through Rebecca's actions. "She *quickly* lowered her jar upon her hand and let him drink." "*Quickly* emptying her jar into the trough, she *ran* back to the well to draw, and she drew for all his camels" (Gen. 24:20).[18] The image of Rebecca running toward her guest, bringing him not only the water he requested but serving his camels, not resting until she is assured that he is satiated, happy, and content, conjures up another familiar image from a scene earlier in Genesis: Abraham's frenetic hospitality to the guests who arrived at his tent in Genesis 18. In that scene, Rebecca's future father-in-law was described using much of the same language. The combination of the verbs "*maher,*" "quickly," and "*vataratz,*" "and she ran," are reminiscent of Abraham's hospitality in Genesis 18,[19] these words being key in that chapter as well[20] (18:5–8), appearing alongside the verb "*vayaratz,*" "and he ran."[21] After running to greet his guests, Abraham initially offered them water: "Let *a little water* be brought" (18:4), and the servant, who ran to Rebecca, also asked for water: "Let me sip *a little water*" (24:17). The phrase "*me'at mayim,*" "a little water," appears only in these two instances in the entire Pentateuch. The text here makes a direct connection between the two characters and their intrinsic drive to do kindness by others. Rebecca may have failed the divination test, but she passed a far more important one – the test

17. Sternberg, *The Poetics of Biblical Narrative: Ideological Literature and the Drama of Reading*, 138–139. He also notes the wordplay in Rebecca's words: "I will also draw for your camels, until they finish (*kilu*) drinking," and her actions: "And she drew for all (*kol*) his camels."
18. Once again in the conclusion of the scene: "The maiden ran and told all this to her mother's household" (Gen. 24:28).
19. Sternberg, *The Poetics of Biblical Narrative: Ideological Literature and the Drama of Reading*, 138; Wenham, *Genesis 16–50*, 144; Hamilton, *The Book of Genesis, Chapters 18–50*, 147.
20. Gen. 18:5–8: "Abraham *hastened* into the tent to Sarah, and said, '*Quick*, three seahs of choice flour'... and gave it to a servant-boy, who *hastened* to prepare it..."
21. Gen. 18:2–7: "He ran from the entrance of the tent.... Then Abraham ran to the herd..."

of whether she is capable of carrying on the value system her future father-in-law dedicated his life to uphold.

The servant's moment of realization that Rebecca is, indeed, the maiden he sought, is deeply poetic. "The man, meanwhile, *mishta'eh* at her, silently wondering whether the Lord had made his errand successful or not" (Gen. 24:21). The verb is rare in biblical text, and has been translated as wonder,[22] amazement,[23] or "gazed."[24] I believe that the verb serves a literary purpose.[25] The verb seems to share the root SH-A-H with the word *shaon*, meaning "noise" – specifically the sound of waves crashing against the shore,[26] or the sound of the sea.[27] Verse 21 inundates the reader with the semantic field of sound, encouraging the wordplay between *mishta'eh* and the sound of water. The servant is simultaneously portrayed as *mishta'eh* and *maḥrish* ("silent"). The sound of the water splashing contrasts with the servant's silence as he watches the maiden work. The servant stands watching silently as Rebecca draws water from the well and pours it into the camel trough, over and over again. The silence of the servant is contrasted with the sound of the water. The servant, in requesting water, expected the maiden to offer him the water in her bucket, as per his predictive test. Rebecca quenches his thirst, then hastens back to the well to draw water for his ten camels – an incredible amount of water, certainly for one young girl to draw by herself. As Rebecca toils diligently – the bucket hitting the surface of the water, pulled up to her hands, the water poured into the trough, the bucket thrown back into the well – the servant looks on in awed silence. The scene is heavy with the splashes of Rebecca's

22. Kaddari, *A Dictionary of Biblical Hebrew*, 1039.
23. Yehoshua Steinberg, *A Dictionary of the Bible* (Tel Aviv, 1962), 815.
24. BDB, 981. Robert Gordis (*The Word and the Book: Studies in Biblical Language and Literature* [New York, 1976], 335) thinks the word *mishta'eh* is similar to the root SH-A-H, denoting "to destroy," which evolved into the word *hishtomem*, which can alternately mean "was destroyed" or "was amazed."
25. Note the wordplay between Rebecca's offer to the servant: "*sheteh*," "drink," and the servant's reaction: *mishta'eh*.
26. BDB, 981; Kaddari, *A Dictionary of Biblical Hebrew*, 1040.
27. Tzvi Raday and Chaim Rabin, *The New Bible Dictionary* (Jerusalem, 1989), 567.

kind actions, the amazement of the servant, and the slurps of his ten camels as they drink their fill.

As a reaction to Rebecca's actions, the servant offers her a gift of jewelry: "When the camels had finished drinking, the man took a gold nose-ring weighing a half-shekel, and two gold bands for her hands, ten shekels in weight" (Gen. 24:22).[28] Then, confident that he has found the maiden he searched for, the servant proceeds to the next step in his plan. He asks about her family, but before she has a chance to respond, he adds his request to come and stay at her house: "Whose daughter are you? Is there room in your father's house for us to spend the night?" (v. 23). The order of the questions reinforces the conclusion that the servant was sent to find a wife for Isaac from Abraham's land, but not necessarily from his family. The reader, who knows that Rebecca is related to the Abrahamic line, can sense the divine fortuitousness in the encounter, but the servant is oblivious to the familial connection. He makes his decision solely based on Rebecca's actions.

Rebecca willingly invites the stranger to the house of her parents: "There is plenty of straw and feed at home, and also room to spend the

28. The emphasis of the weight of the jewelry indicates unusually expensive jewelry. Later, the narrative will note that Laban noticed the jewelry. At the same time, the specific weight of the bracelets may hint to certain dialogue with the purification process of the high priestess ("NIN.DINGIR") at Emar. During the ritual, she is adorned with different jewelry, while at the same time, the priest-diviner's hands are laden with silver weighing *ten shekels*: "They put on her ears two gold earrings from her father's house,/put on her right hand the storm god's gold ring,/and wrap her head with a red wool headdress./They offer fragrant oil for the storm god./*They put in the diviner's hand a ten-shekel silver coil*" ("The Installation of the Storm God's High Priestess," trans. by Daniel E. Fleming, in *The Context of Scripture, vol 1: Canonical Compositions from the Biblical World,* ed. W. Hallo [Leiden: Brill, 2003], 429). For the role of this diviner, see Daniel E. Fleming, *The Installation of Baal's High Priestess at Emar: A Window on Ancient Syrian Religion* (Atlanta, 1992), 87–92.

This adornment seems to represent her transition to her new identity: "The rites surrounding her enthronement endow the new priestess with the essential accountrements of the NIN.DINGIR's office, and in receiving them she enters into her new identity" (Fleming, ibid., 182). If the servant's bestowal of jewelry upon Rebecca indeed alludes to this ceremony, comparing her betrothal to the priestess's communion with the gods, then this verse may be designed to raise connotations of festivity and exaltedness in the ancient reader's conscience.

night" (Gen. 24:25). Rebecca expresses concern for the stranger's camels by the well. Here, too, the servant had asked about himself and his people, "Is there room in your father's house for us to spend the night?" but Rebecca adds her concern for the camels, and prefaces her response with their food: "There is plenty of straw and feed at home." Rebecca's reaction is a comment on her family: she does not hesitate or feel the need to ask for permission before inviting a stranger to their home, indicating that this was common practice in the house of Bethuel. The man's wealth plays no role in Rebecca's invitation.

Rebecca neither refuses nor thanks the servant, and does not comment on the gift she was given. In fact, Rebecca does not react to the jewelry she was given at all. She is so indifferent to the gift that the servant is noted as the one to place the bracelets on her arms. Rebecca's focus is on her care for the stranger and his well-being, and the care for his camels. The lack of reaction is particularly apparent due to the emphasis of the narrative on the jewels, which are described in detail. Rebecca seems to view the jewels as secondary to the man's safety and comfort.

Rebecca's response to the question of her ancestry, "I am the daughter of Bethuel the son of Milcah, whom she bore to Nahor" (Gen. 24:24), is almost identical to the text's description of her ancestry when she appeared by the well: "Rebecca, who was born to Bethuel, the son of Milcah the wife of Abraham's brother Nahor" (v. 15). Rebecca does not limit herself to introducing her father's name; she adds her father's ancestry. Rebecca reveals the family relationship to Abraham's family, which was previously known only to the reader. The maiden's ancestry surprises the "man," and after he "bowed low to the Lord" he said a prayer of gratitude: "Blessed be the Lord, the God of my master Abraham, who has not withheld His steadfast faithfulness from my master; for I have been guided on my errand by the Lord, to the house of my master's kinsmen" (v. 27). As explained above, Abraham did not send his servant to find a woman from his family, but from his land. Therefore, the unexpected meeting with a family member is especially exciting. The servant had sought an appropriate local girl, but instead found a maiden of Abraham's own family, from the line of Terah. This revelation clinches the servant's surety that he has succeeded in his mission.

The servant's short prayer completes the literary frame for the well scene by mirroring the prayer he offered upon his arrival at the well in Haran. He had asked that God act graciously to his master (Gen. 24:12), and now thanks God for His kindness to his master (v. 27). The literary frame of a prayer about kindness links the concluding scene to the complex dialogue about divination. Divination in the ancient world has two categories: deciphering natural phenomena (astrology, bird flight, dreams, birth defects) and deciphering man-made phenomena.[29] The premise of the second category is that various techniques can be used to discover man's "destiny" and uncover the fate set by the gods. The servant points to God's kindness with Abraham; God's faithfulness to Abraham and guidance of his servant negates the premise of the deterministic world that is expressed by the belief in divination. The highlighting of the kindness in the prayers of the servant emphasizes the free will of God to repay Abraham's devotion. The narrative portrays God's actions as reliant on the actions of people; therefore, the servant does not use divination, but rather mocks the world of prediction. Rebecca's words stray from prophetic conduct, and the servant emphasizes God's kindness in arranging the meeting with Abraham's family.

Rebecca's Home

The next scene describes the servant's account of his tale to Rebecca's family. This scene takes place in the family house, but only after the characters are described moving from the well to the house.[30] In terms of plot structure, this discussion could be seen as a bridge.[31] We meet Rebecca's family for the first time, and there is some disagreement among

29. Mendelsohn, "Divination," *IDB*, vol. 1, 856. See also Burke O. Long, "The Effect of Divination upon Israelite Literature," *JBL* 92 (1973): 489–497.
30. In the previous verse (Gen. 24:28), Rebecca runs home and shares the story with her mother's household. Some claim that the bridging scene begins there, since the focus shifts to the maiden's home. Adele Berlin claims that the introduction of a new character – namely, Laban – is the opening of a new scene (Berlin, *Poetics and the Interpretation of Biblical Narrative*, 104). On opening a scene with a new character, see also Francis I. Andersen, *The Sentence in Biblical Hebrew,* Janua Linguarum, Series Practica 231 (The Hague, 1974), 79.
31. Sternberg, *The Poetics of Biblical Narrative: Ideological Literature and the Drama of Reading*, 143.

the commentators regarding what our first impression of them must be. In this scene, Laban, a character who, later in the Genesis narratives, will be perceived as quite wicked, is described as he goes out to greet the servant. The rest of Rebecca's family, too, act with grace and hospitality toward their guest. While Bethuel and his household's generosity are generally perceived at face value, there is some discussion as to whether Laban's motivations are pure.

The initial encounter with a character – or, in this case, a family – affects the continued evaluation and perception of that character. In contrast with Jacob, who identifies himself to Rachel at the well (Gen. 29:11–12), the servant keeps his identity silent, and only asks for a place to stay. Therefore, the maiden's story does not include the identity of the servant and the purpose of his arrival. Nonetheless, the family receives the stranger kindly and generously. One might say this behavior was influenced by his apparent wealth; this is reinforced by the verse describing Laban's motives: "When he saw the nose-ring and the bands on his sister's hands... he went up to the man."[32] However, the text does not seem to share in the negative evaluation of Laban, and at this stage of the narrative, Laban is painted in a positive light. First, just as Rebecca "runs" to water the camels, and then "runs" home to inform her family, Laban runs to receive the guest: "Laban ran out to the man at the spring." Additionally, haste contributes to the design of a character eager to receive guests. The text's attempts to "defend" Laban led to confusion in the order of the verses.[33] The parallel story of Jacob by the well (Gen. 29:13), in which Laban is portrayed more villainously, is delivered in the following order:

1. On hearing the news of his sister's son Jacob,
2. Laban ran to greet him.
3. He embraced him and kissed him
4. and took him into his house.

---

32. Emanueli, *Genesis – Commentary and Insights*, 324; Sternberg, *The Poetics of Biblical Narrative: Ideological Literature and the Drama of Reading*, 144; Wenham, *Genesis 16–50*, 146 and 153. Compare with Rashi on Gen. 24:29.

33. As a result some scholars viewed the order of the verses as a mistake requiring correction. Von Rad (*Genesis*, 252) views the sequence as "a rather awkward sequence of statements."

The structure of this sentence is logical: Laban hears that Jacob had come, he runs out to greet him, uncle and nephew meet, and finally, Laban brings Jacob to his home. In contrast, the order of the verses in Genesis 24:29–32 is illogical:

1. Laban ran out to the man at the spring.
2. When he saw the nose-ring and the bands on his sister's arms, and when he heard his sister Rebecca say, "Thus the man spoke to me,"
3. he went up to the man, who was still standing beside the camels at the spring.
4. He said, "Come in, O blessed of the Lord".... So the man entered the house.

Clearly the report uses standard formulations. Stages three and four appear in the same place in both narratives: Laban goes to greet the man waiting at the well, and brings him back to his home. But the order of the initial two components is changed. First Laban runs out to the man by the spring, and only then does he notice "the nose-ring and the bands on his sister's hands." The order of the Jacob narrative reads more clearly; the logical order of the present verse would have been, "When he saw the nose-ring and the bands on his sister's hands, and when he heard his sister Rebecca say, 'Thus the man spoke to me,' Laban ran out to the man at the spring/he went up to the man..." The change emphasizes that Laban did not act out of greediness, and ran to greet the man before he knew about the jewelry.

According to the reading which mocks Laban and paints him in a greedy light, Laban's flaws highlight Rebecca's positive character. Rebecca's willingness to go with the stranger should not be viewed as an accepted norm in Haran. Rebecca's unique personality is thus emphasized by Laban's crudeness.[34] According to the alternative reading, Laban is portrayed in a positive light in order to paint Rebecca's family as kind and hospitable toward strangers, so that Rebecca is placed in the

34. Sternberg, *The Poetics of Biblical Narrative: Ideological Literature and the Drama of Reading*, 144; Wenham, *Genesis 16–50*, 146.

context of a good family. Family culture is particularly significant in the context of marriage narratives, and praise of the family indicates praise for the bride. Since Rebecca "was born to Bethuel, the son of Milcah the wife of Abraham's brother Nahor" (Gen. 24:15), the family's kindness toward strangers is associated with Abraham as well. Apparently, hospitality is a unique family norm, which is prevalent throughout the various branches of the family, and that separates the family from other Canaanite and Mesopotamian families.

The food motif is emphasized in the narrative, befitting a narrative about hospitality. In contrast with the camels and the people in the servant's convoy, the servant refuses to eat until he has spoken (Gen. 24:33). In Genesis 18, when Abraham hosts the angels in his tent, the guests are fed before they speak. Here, the care for the stranger is interrupted by the desire of the servant to attend to his business. The interruption is a turning point from the family's perspective. Until this point, the family is unaware that the purpose of the journey of the rich merchant before them is to find a wife; they are unaware that he is no more than a servant and they are unaware of the familial relationship.[35] The interruption therefore corresponds with the exciting atmosphere of revelation and discovery of the servant's identity and the purpose of his journey.

The Servant's Recounting of the Story

Rebecca introduced herself to the servant in relation to her father: "I am the daughter of Bethuel" (Gen. 24:24), and the servant similarly introduces himself in relation to his master: "I am Abraham's servant" (v. 34).[36] Just as Rebecca's identity was a revolutionary discovery for the servant, the servant's identity is a revelation for the family, who is soon to discover that the man they believed to be a wealthy merchant is none other than the servant of their long-lost relative.

---

35. Note that the servant is called "the man" throughout the scene. Since the identity of the servant has not yet been revealed, according to the perception of Rebecca and her family, the servant is "a man." The narrative's titles identify with the prevalent viewpoint in any one of the given scenes.
36. Hamilton, *The Book of Genesis, Chapters 18–50*, 150n7.

The servant opens with a short but momentous statement that reveals his identity as servant, not master. An even more dramatic revelation from the family's perspective is that the servant is employed by the brother of their grandfather. The servant opens with a description of his master and God's blessings of wealth and a son and heir born in his old age. The purpose of the servant's journey is not revealed initially, and the family might be under the impression that the servant has come only to report Abraham's accomplishments. After impressing the family with Abraham's success, the servant reports the purpose of his journey: finding a wife for his master's son.

This leads the servant to embark on a long retelling of the story that led him to their home. Repetitions are common enough in the biblical narrative; however, Genesis 24 is a uniquely lengthy review of the entire chain of events.[37] In analyzing the servant's tale, we must focus on the differences between the plot and the tale the servant relates to Rebecca's family. In those nuanced divergences, the purpose of the repetition and the thematic motifs of the story as a whole will become clear. The servant sought to relate a story to Rebecca's family that would both flatter them and motivate them to agree to the match between Rebecca and Isaac. The servant adeptly changes a number of details in his tale in order to create a narrative that clearly achieves this purpose. He weaves a tale that portrays Bethuel and his family as the preferred future in-laws of Isaac, and places Rebecca at the center of a union that is destined to be.

The Retelling of the Narrative

As previously mentioned, the servant's account of the events requires interpretation. The approach that the repetition simply enriches the storytelling is difficult to accept.[38] The lengthy review is unusual, and seems like an odd choice for enrichment of the story. The servant begins his account by adulating Bethuel's family, enticing them with the benefits that would come from Rebecca and Isaac's union. Many commentators

37. Savran counts our story and the story of Judah (Gen. 44:18–34) as the two most salient biblical instances of a character's retelling of a story (Savran, "The Character as Narrator in Biblical Narrative," 1–17).

38. Jacob Licht, *Storytelling in the Bible* (Jerusalem, 1978), 76–77.

assume that the purpose of the servant's account is to flatter the family with Abraham's request. The subtle rhetoric is intended to convince the family to hand over Rebecca.[39] Below are three examples of changes in the retelling of the narrative, which can easily be interpreted as the servant's attempt to persuade the family to agree to the match:

- Abraham's wealth, which was briefly indicated at the start of the narrative – "The Lord had blessed Abraham in all things" (Gen. 24:1) – is described at length in the servant's account to Rebecca's family: "The Lord has greatly blessed my master, and he has become rich: He has given him sheep and cattle, silver and gold, male and female slaves, camels and asses" (v. 35). The purpose of the lengthy description of Abraham's wealth is to encourage the family's motivation to agree to the marriage. The servant adds that the wealth is to become the sole inheritance of Isaac: "And he has assigned to him everything he owns" (v. 36).[40]
- In the original narrative, Abraham encourages his servant by saying: "The Lord, the God of heaven, *who took me from my father's house and from my native land,* who promised me on oath, saying, 'I will assign this land to your offspring' – He will send His angel before you" (v. 7). In contrast, the servant changes the quote by his master and says: "The Lord, *whose ways I have followed,* will send His angel with you and make your errand successful"

39. See Abrabanel's commentary on Gen. 24; von Rad, *Genesis,* 253; Leibowitz, *Studies in Genesis,* 162–166; Hamilton, *The Book of Genesis, Chapters 18–50,* 153–155. Sometimes the repetition does not reflect the conscious aim of the speaker, but rather their point of view; e.g., Eve's words to the serpent in Gen. 3:2–3, or the repetitions integrated in the Joseph narrative (Jonathan Grossman, "The Story of Joseph's Brothers in Light of the 'Therapeutic Narrative' Theory," *Biblical Interpretation* 21 [2013]: 171–195). In the servant narrative, the repetitions seem deliberate, since the servant maintains continuity and coherence throughout the changes, as demonstrated below.
40. This phrase, which does not appear in the original narrative, will reappear in the description of Abraham's death: "Abraham willed all that he owned to Isaac" (Gen. 25:5). Apparently Abraham had already willed all that he owned to his son in his lifetime, and the servant was able to relate this fact to the family, but the text does not deliver the facts in order, and the information delivered by the servant might be viewed as foreshadowing for the next chapter.

(v. 40). The servant refrains from reminding the family about Abraham's abandonment, and therefore chooses a more general formulation.

- The options of refusal are also expressed with various formulations. The servant asks Abraham: "What if the woman does not consent to follow me to this land?" (v. 5), while the servant reformulated his question to the family: "What if the woman does not follow me?" (v. 39). The servant omits the maiden's free will as the determining factor, and replaces her desires with the family decision regarding her future.[41] For the sake of consistency, the servant replaces Abraham's response as well. Instead of "And *if the woman does not consent to follow you,* you shall then be clear of this oath to me" (v. 8), the servant quotes his master: "If, when you come to my kindred, they refuse you – only then shall you be freed from my adjuration" (v. 41). The servant wisely omits the alternative he had suggested to Abraham: "Shall I then take your son back to the land from which you came," since he prefers to omit the option of refusal from his discussion with the family.[42] Additionally, Abraham's vehement rejection of this option ("But do not take my son back there") might offend the family, and is left out of his retelling.[43] The servant changes Abraham's response, and omits Abraham's firm rejection.

Although the discrepancies above are easily understood, others cannot be explained on the basis of the positive impression the servant is trying to make. Such differences include:

- In the original narrative the servant mentions God's *ḥesed* ("kindness"/"graciousness"): twice in his prayer/attempted prediction (Gen. 24:12, 14), and once in his thanksgiving, as soon as he has discovered the identity of the maiden who had

41. Sternberg, *The Poetics of Biblical Narrative: Ideological Literature and the Drama of Reading*, 148.
42. Wenham, *Genesis 16–50*, 148.
43. Kiel, *Daat Mikra: Genesis*, 181.

given him water (v. 27). However, when the servant relates his prayers to Rebecca's family, he omits God's kindness. Instead, he uses the word *ḥesed* in reference to Rebecca's family: "And now, if you mean to treat my master with *true kindness* (*ḥesed ve'emet*), tell me; and if not, tell me also, that I may turn right or left" (v. 49). The words *ḥesed* and *emet* are combined in Abraham's prayer in relation to God's treatment of Abraham, and again in his request to the family, this time in relation to their treatment of his master.[44] In the original narrative, God showed kindness toward Abraham, while in the retelling the family was asked to do kindness with Abraham. The omission of God's kindness cannot be accidental, but the desire to attribute kindness to the family does not justify an omission of God's kindness. The exclusion of God's kindness therefore remains unclear.

- As noted above, Abraham did not ask his servant to seek a maiden specifically from his family, but from his land. The main distinction between the original telling and the retelling of the story is the emphasis on the family. This difference might be attributed to the servant's desire to portray Abraham as missing the family he had left and seeking to renew the relationship.[45] While flattery might be a good enough reason to change the retelling, such a central change might have a deeper purpose. The emphasis of the family in the servant's retelling (as opposed to Abraham's instructions) is expressed in the following elements:
- In the original telling, Abraham says: "He will send His angel before you, and you will get a wife for my son *from there*"

44. Mathews claims that there is wordplay between Laban's words to the servant before his speech: "He said, 'Speak, then'" (v. 33), and the servant's conclusion: "Tell me, and if not, tell me also" (v. 49) (Mathews, *Genesis*, 339). This wordplay, however, does not resonate in Hebrew, as two different verbs are used. Nonetheless, Mathews is correct in detecting some sort of *inclusio* in these two verses – at first, Laban invites the servant to speak, while at the end, the servant hands the microphone back to the family, so to speak, and awaits their response.
45. E.g., Kiel, *Daat Mikra: Genesis*, 181. Wenham (*Genesis 16–50*, 147) suggested that this would help the young maiden leave her family and join the servant.

(v. 7). The servant repeats Abraham's instruction by saying: "'The Lord... will send His angel with you and make your errand successful; and you will get a wife for my son *from my kindred, from my father's house*" (v. 40).

- Abraham promises his servant that in the event that his quest is unsuccessful, "you shall then be clear of this oath to me" (v. 8). Here, too, the servant portrays the conditions of the oath in relation to the family: "Thus only shall you be freed from my adjuration: if, *when you come to my kindred, they refuse you* – only then shall you be freed from my adjuration" (v. 41). Since the servant claims that Abraham had demanded a woman from his own kin, a consistent account necessitated a change in the order of the retelling. While in the narrative the servant offers the maiden jewelry before inquiring about her family (vv. 22–23), in the retelling, the servant changes the order of events, and only offers the gifts after inquiring about Rebecca's family (v. 47). In the original narrative, since the servant was not asked to seek a maiden from Abraham's family, he was able to offer the jewelry before knowing the identity of her family. In the retelling, he has to describe the events in correlation with seeking a maiden from Abraham's family.
- After discovering the identity of the maiden, the servant's prayer undergoes a minor change that is significant in this context:

Original Narrative (26–27)	**Retelling (48)**
The man bowed low in homage to the Lord	Then I bowed low in homage to the Lord
and said, "Blessed be the Lord, the God of my master Abraham	and blessed the Lord, the God of my master Abraham
who has not withheld His steadfast faithfulness (*ḥasdo ve'amito*) from my master	who led me on the right road (*bederekh emet*)
For I have been guided on my road by the Lord, to the house of my master's kinsmen."	to get the daughter of my master's brother for his son.

The servant blesses God for leading him "to the house of my master's kinsmen," noting the unexpected surprise of finding the maiden he sought and discovering that she was from Abraham's family. Although the "road" did not have to lead to Abraham's family in order for the errand to be successful, the servant feels more confident that Rebecca is the girl he seeks. The servant separates the guidance on his errand from the unexpected result of being led to his master's kin, since God could have guided him elsewhere for the success of his errand. In the retelling, the element of surprise is omitted from the blessing. The servant blesses God for leading him to the right place – as though the errand would not have been successful had the servant not arrived at Abraham's family. The "road" in each description is accompanied by a different atmosphere. The meaning of the word is identical – "to travel, to leave from one location."[46] However, the initial road is associated with a lack of confidence regarding the success of the mission. Therefore, the servant thanks God that although the road was unclear, God led him to his master's family, adding to his confidence that the right girl had been found. In the retelling, the servant mentions the fact that he was led by God before referencing the "road," and adds the adjective, "the right road." According to the retelling, the servant had sought Abraham's family from the outset, and God shortened his road to success by bringing Rebecca to him, while in the original narrative the road is unclear, and the right choice only becomes apparent through God's intervention.

- According to the narrative, after the servant sees Rebecca, he runs toward her (v. 17). The narrative had previously stated the reason that would make the servant run: "The maiden was very beautiful" (v. 16). In the servant's version, he omits the beauty factor – a remark previously made by the narrative – but also the fact that he had run. By omitting the running, the servant emphasizes the continuity between his prayer and his meeting with Rebecca, as though Rebecca had reached him on her own, without the need to run toward her.

46. Kaddari, *A Dictionary of Biblical Hebrew*, 196.

- Another difference relates to the depiction of Rebecca's action in correlation with the servant's prediction. Rebecca does not say the exact words the servant had anticipated. In addition to waiting for the servant to finish drinking before offering to water the camels, Rebecca also changes the phrase "*ashkeh,*" "I will water," with "*eshav,*" "I will draw [water]." These discrepancies would indicate that the divination was unsuccessful, and that Rebecca was not the right candidate for marriage with Isaac, while in truth Rebecca unequivocally proved her suitability to Abraham's family. When the servant repeats his story, he changes the order of events to correlate Rebecca's actions with his prediction: "She quickly lowered her jar and said, 'Drink, and I will also water your camels.' So I drank, and she also watered the camels" (v. 46). In addition to joining Rebecca's offer to water him with her offer to water the camels ("water," not "draw water"), he adds the fact that she lowered her jar earlier, so that the sentence she should have said based on his prediction could be complete.[47]

One common denominator in all the changes is the emphasis on prediction as an indisputable fate. The servant wanted to base his request for the maiden's hand on the prevalent Mesopotamian belief in divination. In the original narrative, the divination was de-emphasized, and emphasis was placed instead on the characters' attributes. When the servant retells the story, however, he emphasizes the divination instead

47. One difference remains between the servant's prediction and Rebecca's actions. According to the servant's account to the family, the maiden should have said, "You may *drink,* and I will also *draw* for your camels" (v. 44), while according to his account she said, "*Drink,* and I will also *water* your camels" (v. 46). The portrayal of Rebecca as "watering" rather than "drawing" continues throughout the servant's account: "So I *drank,* and she also *watered* the camels" (v. 46), in contrast with the original narrative that describes Rebecca drawing for all the camels: "Quickly emptying her jar into the trough, she ran back to the well to draw, and she drew for all his camels" (v. 20). The servant seems to minimize Rebecca's kindness in his account to her family, in order to emphasize the correlation of her actions with his prediction, while the narrative emphasizes Rebecca's kindness at the expense of the correlation of her actions with the servant's prediction.

of Rebecca's actions, assuming the family will be quicker to accept a match fated to happen.[48]

The distinctions above can easily be explained in light of this reading:

- The servant omits God's kindness, which indicates a personal relationship with God and emphasizes the reward of free will actions instead of fate and a preordained destiny. However, according to the common beliefs of the time, although man can discover what the gods have fated, human action has no impact on the outcome.
- The focus on the family contributes to the emphasis on divination. Introducing the family as the primary goal of the servant's journey flatters the family, which justifies his changing some facts and formulations; this portrayal also contributes dramatically to the success of the divination. The probability that the first girl approached by the servant will respond the way he had predicted, and that the girl is from Abraham's family, is virtually impossible if left to chance. If the purpose of the journey was to track down Abraham's family, the combination of the right girl and the correct response turns the meeting into fate, and conveys the sense that the gods have placed Rebecca in the servant's path.
- For obvious reasons, the servant omits any possible human intervention in the meeting between him and Rebecca. He omits the fact that he had run to her, creating the impression that Rebecca arrived without his interference. The chance meeting emphasizes the small probability of events unfolding the way they did, unless they were so fated.
- In order to convey the full extent of divination, the servant changes the order of Rebecca's actions, and has her formulate her words according to his prediction: "In Laban's eyes, no

48. Cf. Itamar Eldar, "The Servant and Rebecca Narrative," *Alon Shevut* 153 (1999): 137–149; Mathews, *Genesis*, 339.

> character test was involved, only the fulfillment of a magical sign."[49]

In parallel betrothal stories, the man must impress his future wife with displays of strength and might (such as Jacob in Gen. 29 and Moses in Ex. 2). As the servant is not interested in marrying Rebecca himself, he must persuade the family by other means.[50] The servant succeeds in convincing the family that the gods have spoken, as demonstrated by their reaction: "The matter was decreed by the Lord; we cannot speak to you bad or good. Here is Rebecca before you; take her and go, and let her be a wife to your master's son, as the Lord has spoken" (Gen. 24:50–51). The agreement of the family stems from their positive impression from the success of the divination. Their agreeability does not relate to the family relation or Abraham's wealth (although these factors may have had an inadvertent affect). The statement emphasizes the limitation of their free will in light of God's decision: "We cannot speak to you bad or good."

A Union of Fate

The servant shifts many details to contribute to the family's feeling of a seamless fate-driven encounter. As we mentioned, he omits the fact that he ran toward Rebecca, or that he noticed her beauty. These facts could point to his surprise upon noticing Rebecca, which of course would contradict the idea that their meeting was fateful. The servant also significantly edits the sequence of events in his divination, completely omitting the discrepancies between his prediction and Rebecca's response. While the servant surely recognizes the merit of Rebecca's extraordinary kindness, the message he wants to portray to the family is strict adherence to the prediction.

Rabbi Meir Simcha of Dvinsk makes a similar suggestion:

> And it is possible that Abraham did not tell him to go to his family, rather to the city where he was born, and from there he should

49. Leibowitz, *Studies in Genesis*, 247.

50. Savran, "The Character as Narrator in Biblical Narrative," 4.

> take a wife, regardless of whether she was of the family, just that she would be from the same city. And therefore he said that the girl who he saw was generous, who toiled to draw water for his camels, was worthy of marrying the son of Abraham, and certainly she and her father would be pleased for her to marry into Abraham's family, and there was no divination. Eliezer simply wanted to ensure and verify to the family that the entire episode was due to divine intervention (as it certainly was), and so he told the family that Abraham had asked him to find a wife who was from the family, from his father's house (perhaps he reasoned that this was implied in the phrase "from my homeland"); he set up the divination condition, and indeed the young woman was from the house of Abraham. For obvious reasons, the servant omitted any possible human intervention in the meeting between him and Rebecca. He omitted the fact that he had run to her, creating the impression that Rebecca arrived without his interference. The chance meeting emphasizes the small probability of events unfolding the way they did, unless they were so fated.[51]

In contrast with Rebecca's family, the reader feels ambivalent about the servant's divination. In light of all the changes that had to be made to turn the servant's prayer into a prediction, the original narrative seems far from a realization of the divination process. The retelling of the narrative encourages the reader's view of the incomplete process, thereby emphasizing the distinction between the prevalent belief in fate and divination, and the nature of God's relationship with Abraham. The former is a pagan belief that all events are predestined, while the latter is a living relationship that includes human action, prayer, and divine intervention. Rebecca is presented with an opportunity to leave behind the world of prediction and join a world where kind actions will affect the outcome. In light of Rebecca's actions by the well, she belongs in Abraham's family.

In response to the family's reaction, the servant bows down to God for the second time: "When Abraham's servant heard their

---

51. *Meshekh Ḥokhma* on *Ḥayei Sara.*

words, he bowed low to the ground before the Lord" (v. 52).[52] In the conclusion of the original narrative – when the servant discovered Rebecca's relationship to Abraham's family – he bowed down (v. 26), and at the culmination of his retelling of the narrative he bows again. However, while the first bow was in recognition of God's kindness for leading him to Rebecca, the second was in recognition of the family's kindness: "And now, if you mean to treat my master with true kindness, tell me; and if not, tell me also, that I may turn right or left" (v. 49). However, instead of bowing to the family in recognition of their kindness – just as he had bowed to God in recognition of His kindness – he bows, once again, to God. Abraham bowed low to the Hittites in the previous chapter, demonstrating that bowing to people is not unheard of. Perhaps the following verse, which describes the servant offering gifts to Rebecca's family, is an expression of his gratitude toward the family: "The servant brought out objects of silver and gold, and garments, and gave them to Rebecca; and he gave presents to her brother and her mother" (v. 53). According to this reading, the gifts parallel the prayer of thanksgiving to God, but the fact that the servant failed to bow to the family is further emphasized by this parallel. God's kindness is paralleled by the kindness of the family; the servant's prayer is paralleled by his gifts to the family, but the servant bows to God in recognition of His kindness, and then bows to God again, instead of to the family.

This incongruity relates to the delicate dialogue between God's decree and the free will of the characters in the narrative, as we saw above. The family has to agree to the match in order to realize God's kindness; therefore the servant recognizes God's kindness in the family's decision. Had the family (or Rebecca) objected, the fact that God had led to the meeting between the servant and Rebecca would have been futile. The narrative emphasizes the fact that God does not create, but rather enables, the reality; the kindness of the characters toward one another drives the plot to its final realization.

---

52. Hamilton (*The Book of Genesis, Chapters 18–50*, 158) writes that the servant worships God three times in the narrative. In vv. 12–14, the servant prays, but there is no prostration, which in the present narrative is linked with thanksgiving.

Rebecca's Choice

Rebecca's home and family are described in great detail in this narrative. The text weaves a vivid picture of the home in which Rebecca was raised – a place of unity and hospitality. Upon his arrival at Bethuel's doorstep, the servant – at this point a complete stranger, whose true purpose is unknown to the members of the household – is greeted with kindness and generosity. His visit in Bethuel's home is bursting with descriptions of the food and the household's preparations for their unexpected guest.

Just as Rebecca "runs" to water the camels, and then "runs" home to inform her family, Laban runs to receive the guest: "Laban ran out to the man at the spring." His haste paints a picture of a character eager to receive guests. As we mentioned previously, Laban can be seen here in both a positive and negative light. The positive perspective exists in the text in order to paint Rebecca's family as kind and hospitable toward strangers. Rebecca has grown up in the context of a good family. Family culture is particularly significant in the context of marriage narratives, and praise of the family indicates praise for the bride.

After the servant presented Rebecca and her family with gifts,[53] he ate, drank, and rested with the other members of his convoy. The servant had delayed eating until after he explained the purpose of his journey (Gen. 24:33), and finally the family is given the opportunity to host him properly. While the theme of hospitality seems to create continuity with the previous scene, the characters involved are replaced without warning. Whereas previously Laban and Bethuel interacted with the servant, suddenly the servant offers gifts to Rebecca's mother and brother, who take over the debate on Rebecca's future with the servant: "Let the maiden remain with us some ten days; then you may go" (v. 55).

Laban's attitude also seems to change between the two scenes. Until this point, Laban is mentioned by name ("Rebecca had a brother

53. Some viewed the gifts as a dowry (Speiser, *Genesis*, 182; Sarna, *Genesis* [JPS], 168; Wenham, *Genesis 16–50*, 149–50), while others viewed the gifts as independent of any legal connotations (Benno Jacob, *The First Book of the Bible: Genesis*, 161; Alexander Rofe, "The Betrothal of Rebecca [Genesis 24]," *Eshel Beer Sheva* 1 [1976]: 63–64; Westermann, *Genesis 12–36: A Continental Commentary*, 389).

whose name was Laban," "Laban ran out to the man at the spring," "Laban and Bethuel answered"), while in the following scene he is referred to as "the brother" ("And he gave presents to her brother and her mother," "But her brother and her mother said…"). The sudden replacement of Bethuel with Rebecca's mother seems intentional; Laban is paired with Bethuel, while "her mother" is accompanied by "her brother."[54]

The source of the changes is one and the same. The previous scene concludes with the family's consent to allow Rebecca to marry: "Here is Rebecca before you; take her and go, and let her be a wife to your master's son" (Gen. 24:51). According to the servant's account to Rebecca's family, this statement is the culmination of the servant's oath to Abraham: "Thus only shall you be freed from my adjuration: if, when you come to my kindred, they refuse you – only then shall you be freed from my adjuration" (v. 41). However, the reader is aware of the fact that the fulfillment of Abraham's oath is not dependent on the family, but on the choice of the maiden: "If the woman does not consent to follow you, you shall then be clear of this oath to me" (v. 8). This distinction is significant to the analogy between Rebecca and Abraham; the family's attempt to delay her departure makes room for Rebecca to decide her own future.

At this point in the narrative, the weight shifts to Rebecca. Previously, Bethuel and Laban played a significant role in the discussion – in the ancient world the father and brother would be the decision-makers regarding any marriage of a woman from their household. The rights to marry Rebecca were in their hands, and the scene was concluded with their agreement. In contrast, the second scene emphasizes Rebecca's choice. Here the father is eliminated, since according to prevalent norms the father should not ask his daughter what she desires (and compare with Laban's agreement to give his daughters to Jacob in Gen. 29:15–23). The mother is a more

54. It is noteworthy that the change in Laban's title was preserved in ancient translations, although the Septuagint reads "brothers" in plural in v. 55 ("*aḥeha*"), unlike the Masoretic text.

appropriate source of concern for the daughter's wishes.[55] In the initial scene, Bethuel and Laban are portrayed as independent characters, who determine Rebecca's future, but in the second scene, the role of the family is to make room for Rebecca's choice regarding her future. Father and brother are not the decision-makers, but rather components in Rebecca's decision.

The family does not object to the match, but does express a desire to delay it: "Let the maiden remain with us some ten days; then you may go" (Gen. 24:55). The servant is edgy; he does not wish to delay their departure lest further discussion lead to a change of heart. The disagreement culminates in placing the decision in Rebecca's hands: "Let us call the girl and ask for her reply" (v. 57). The servant probably shared the reader's concern that the maiden would refuse the offer to go with a stranger to an unknown place for an unknown purpose – or even for a known purpose of marriage to a man she has never met in a strange land, far from her family. While Isaac is apparently an unusually wealthy relative, leaving one's birthplace and homeland and disengaging from one's family is no small challenge. The family did not reject the offer of marriage, but only sought to delay the maiden's departure. From their perspective, there is no reason for haste, and Rebecca can leave when she is ready.

Despite the revelation of the servant's identity, the family refers to him as "man" in the formulation of their question to Rebecca: "Will you go with this man?" (Gen. 24:58). Apparently, Rebecca was not present in the discussion of her future, and she had to be "called in." Since Rebecca was not present throughout the servant's monologue,

55. Regarding the authority of the mother to marry off her son in the Ancient Near East (whether due to the absence of the father or along with the father), see Lea Jacobsen, *Aspects of the Legal Status of the Mother in the Ancient Near East and the Bible – A Comparative Study* (PhD diss., Bar Ilan University, 2011), 22–134. Some have claimed that alongside the parents' approval, it was customary in the Ancient Near East to ask the bride's permission, and some even use this story as proof. Others claim that in this story, the bride was only asked if she agrees to go to Canaan, not if she agrees to get married in itself. See this debate in Hennie J. Marsman, *Women in Ugarit and Israel: Their Social and Religious Position in the Context of the Ancient Near East* (*OTS* 49: Leiden and Boston, 2003), 70–71.

the family's question, "Will you go with this man?" seems to lack the necessary information for an informed decision. Does Rebecca know why she is following the man? Is she even aware that the purpose of her journey is marriage? Rebecca was not told that the servant was linked with Abraham, and has no way of knowing that going with the man is a good choice. The biblical narrative frequently leaves such gaps to be filled by the reader. The family probably explained the situation to Rebecca, even if the dialogue is not mentioned in the text. However, the failure to report to Rebecca is highlighted by the fact that the family asks whether she wants to go with "the man," without clarifying to what end.

The narrative design seems to leave Rebecca in the dark. The focus of the narrative surprisingly becomes Rebecca's willingness to go with the servant, instead of her suitability for Isaac. The servant's title in verse 61 sheds light on her decision in verse 58. Despite the fact that the servant's identity was revealed, he is referred to as a "man" in order to emphasize Rebecca's decision. The servant is referred to as "the servant" in relation to his mission to find Isaac a wife. He is referred to as "a man" in relation to Rebecca's personal decision to disengage from her land and family, and follow the man to her unknown future. In this regard, the servant does not represent Abraham or Isaac, but rather the stranger Rebecca chooses to follow. The servant achieves the independent status of "man" in the narrative to serve as the background character for Rebecca's decision. The choice Rebecca has to make at this point is not whether she wants to marry Isaac, but whether she is willing to go with the man. Simply put, Rebecca must choose to remain with her family, or to leave her home, the house of father, and her land, to go with a man she does not know.[56]

Rebecca responds quickly and succinctly: "I will go" (Gen. 24:58).[57]

The end of the narrative shifts the focus from the match to the question of Rebecca's free will. The word "go" is repeated several times

56. Menakhem Perry, "Literary Dynamics: How the Order of a Text Creates Its Meaning," *Poetics Today* 1 (1979): 196.

57. Teugels ("A Strong Woman, Who Can Find?" 98–99) notes that Rebecca is portrayed as one who wastes no words when she can take action.

in this exchange. Initially, the family uses the verb to delay Rebecca's departure: "Let the maiden remain with us some ten days; then you may *go*" (Gen. 24:55), to which the servant responds, "Give me leave that I may *go* to my lord" (v. 56). Finally, Rebecca decides "I will go" (v. 58).

Rebecca's simple declaration, "I will go," is reminiscent of Abraham's departure on the journey that began with the utterance, "Go forth." Rebecca's choice to venture into the unknown, unafraid and faithful, parallels and ultimately completes her father-in-law's journey. Whereas in the previous generation Abraham decided, of his own free will, to follow God's command, in the next generation Rebecca decided, of her own free will, to follow in Abraham's path, taking a leap of faith in going toward her unknown future in a foreign land.

While the presumption of Abraham and his servant was that the maiden would have the right to decide whether she is joining the journey (Gen. 24:5–8), the servant changes his tone when speaking to Rebecca's family, and presents the family as having the right to decide Rebecca's fate (v. 41). Ultimately, both decisions are necessary. Initially, the family agrees to the arrangement, conveying the sense of reunion of Abraham's family: Abraham's son will marry his brother Nahor's granddaughter, and the granddaughter of his niece Milcah, daughter of Haran. There is specific significance in the agreement of the family to this purpose, and Bethuel and Laban approve of the match that will reunite the family. However, the family seeks to delay the journey in order to give Rebecca room to voice her opinion. Rebecca decides that she is willing to disengage from the culture of Haran and Ur of the Chaldeans, and join the family of Abraham. The question of Rebecca's position does not focus on the match, but rather on the personal implications of leaving her past behind her.

The family sends Rebecca (with her nursemaid) and Abraham's servant (with his people), and they bless Rebecca: "O sister! May you grow into thousands of myriads; may your offspring seize the gates of their foes" (Gen. 24:60). The combined blessing of fertility and inheritance of the land is a distinct characteristic of God's blessings to the patriarchs. The unique use of the word *revava* ("thousands of myriads") links the blessing with Rebecca's name. The triple alliteration (*vayevarkhu – Rivka – revava*) indicates that Rebecca is deeply rooted in the blessing.[58] Additionally, the formulation of the family blessing is specifically linked with the blessing Abraham had received at the culmination of the binding narrative: "I will bestow My blessing upon you and make your descendants as numerous as the stars of heaven and the sands on the seashore; and your descendants shall seize the gates of their foes" (22:17). God blessed Isaac with fertility and the inheritance of the land; Rebecca's family blessed her with fertility and the inheritance of the land. The match seems to be surrounded by resonating blessings from all sides.[59]

The Lovers' First Meeting

Rebecca's departure from her home and the beginning of her journey with the servant is communicated twice, highlighting the dual aspects of her character's purpose: Rebecca chooses to leave her home, echoing the courageous first step of her father-in-law's journey from Haran. Rebecca is also "taken" by Abraham's servant to fill the role of Isaac's wife.

"Then Rebecca and her maids arose, mounted the camels, and followed the man. So the servant took Rebecca and went his way" (Gen. 24:62).

In the initial description, Rebecca is an active participant: she rises and mounts, and she follows the man. In the latter description, the servant takes Rebecca, and he is the one to go "on his way." The double reference presents a chiastic structure for the two courses of the narrative. In the "morning scene," Rebecca decides she would leave her land and birthplace and journey to the unknown. This scene is concluded in the initial statement of Rebecca's active decision to go with the servant. Rebecca is the subject of the sentence, and the servant is referred to as "the man." This title correlates with the morning scene, in which the servant became "a man" in order to emphasize Rebecca's journey from the house of her father to a strange place, independently of the groom

58. Similarly, Mathews, *Genesis*, 345.

59. Cf. Hamilton, *The Book of Genesis, Chapters 18–50*, 159, who believes Noah's blessing to Shem and Japheth in Gen. 9:26–27 was the background for the family blessing; Mathews, *Genesis*, 345.

waiting for her in the house of the servant's master. Rebecca's independent decision is highlighted by the fact that she is joined by her maids. The maids convey the sense of the journey of a central character, who is accompanied by servants. Rebecca becomes the focal point, and "the man" is no more than her guide. In contrast, the second description is the conclusion of the "evening scene."

In this scene, the family had agreed to marry Rebecca to the son of the servant's master. The maiden was not asked about her position on the matter, and therefore in the conclusion Rebecca is not the subject, but rather an object "taken" by the servant, to his master, for the purpose of marriage. Here, Abraham's servant is referred to as "the servant," since the verse describes the fulfillment of the mission he was sent on by Abraham. Appropriately, the details of the journey (camels, accompanying maids) are omitted. The details of the journey are insignificant from the goal-oriented perspective, which only includes the need to reach Canaan and offer Isaac his bride. When the servant began his journey, he "took ten of his master's camels and set out" (Gen. 24:10); for his return to Canaan he "took Rebecca and went his way." The appearance of the verb *lakaḥ* ("took") in the verse is the sixth appearance of the root over the course of the narrative. The initial five appearances denote marriage, in reference to the maiden who will be taken as a wife for Isaac (24:4, 7, 38, 40, and 48). But in Genesis 24:7, the verb is used in reference to God taking Abraham from the house of his father. "The Lord, the God of heaven, who *took* me from my father's house and from my native land.... He will send His angel before you, and you will *take* a wife for my son from there." The reader is expected to link taking the maiden with taking Abraham from his father's house and native land. In a way, Rebecca is Abraham's true successor: she exemplifies the qualities of hospitality and compassion, and she is willing to abandon her native land to journey to the land of Canaan.[60] Rebecca faces her destiny with her head held high.

The scene cuts from Rebecca and her entourage in the desert to a new character: "Isaac had just come back from the vicinity of

60. Also proposed by Savran, "The Character as Narrator in Biblical Narrative," 306; Eldar, "The Servant and Rebecca Narrative," 147.

Beer-lahai-roi, for he was settled in the region of the Negeb" (Gen. 24:62). Isaac's arrival is described with the unusual phrase, "*veYitzḥak ba mibo*," literally, "And Isaac came from coming." The Septuagint reads, "Isaac went through the wilderness by the seeing-well," indicating that the version before the translator was "*veYitzḥak ba bamidbar*."[61] According to both the Septuagint and the Masoretic versions the contribution of this detail remains unclear. Isaac is walking in the field when Rebecca arrives; the verse merely mentions that he had recently returned from another place. The significance of his recent journey remains unexplained in the text.

This description of Isaac's journey to Beer-lahai-roi reveals something of Isaac's character. We may envision Isaac as a spiritual man who journeys into the wilderness to meditate and awaits revelation. The significance of Isaac coming from Beer-lahai-roi seems to lie in the analogy that is created between Isaac and Rebecca. On the eve of their meeting, the narrative finds both Rebecca and Isaac by a well: Rebecca meets the servant by a well in Haran, while Isaac returns from Beer-lahai-roi – a well that is known as the place of revelation by angels. The relationship is expressed through the link. While the wells create a correlation between Isaac and Rebecca, the nature of the experience by the well is entirely different: Rebecca runs to show a stranger hospitality and kindness, while Isaac seeks the revelation of angels.[62] This stark contrast in their natures will shadow the couple throughout their marriage.

As Isaac returns from his meditation, Rebecca's entourage approaches the tent. The meeting between Isaac and Rebecca takes place outside, in the field, before the servant has had a chance to return to the house of Abraham. This detail offers a dual contribution to the narrative. First, just as Rebecca went out to draw water the moment the servant had completed his prayer (Gen. 24:15), Isaac and Rebecca "incidentally" meet just as Rebecca arrives in the field (24:63).[63] These

---

61. Zipor, *The Septuagint Version of the Book of Genesis*, 300. The Samaritan also translates it this way.
62. Later, their son Jacob will meet angels (Gen. 28) and a woman by a well (Gen. 29).
63. Cf. Mathews, *Genesis*, 347. Mathews views this as a general motif throughout the Abraham cycle, which he links to Hagar seeing the well in 21:19, and Abraham seeing the ram in 22:13. I believe the link above is more specific than a general motif.

"incidental" meetings correlate with the theology of the narrative. The obscured divine intervention in the timing of the meetings enables the characters to act freely once they have met. Additionally, the meeting with Isaac before the servant's arrival at the house of his master enables Isaac to replace Abraham as the protagonist of the narrative, as we will explain below.

Isaac sees the convoy coming toward him as he is "walking in the field (*lasuaḥ basadeh*)." The verb *lasuaḥ* is unusual, and has been interpreted in a variety of ways.[64] Some link the verb with the word *saḥ* ("to speak"), and in the context of the narrative believe that Isaac was praying to God (cf. Ps. 102:1).[65] Others believe the word denotes *siaḥ* ("a bush"), and Isaac was walking among the shrubbery, or planting and overseeing his field workers.[66] Gregory Vall supports the position that linked *lasuaḥ* with speech, but believes Isaac was engaged in a speech of bitterness, such as a eulogy, as in Psalms 77:4: "I call God to mind, I moan; I complain (*asiḥa*), my spirit fails," or Job 7:11–13: "I will complain (*asiḥa*) in the bitterness of my soul ... when I think my bed will comfort me, my couch will share in my sorrow (*besiḥi*)." According to Vall, Isaac went to the fields to mourn the death of his mother, and met Rebecca while he was grieving.[67] The suggestion is particularly interesting in light of the conclusion of the chapter, where, after marrying Rebecca, Isaac "found comfort after his mother's death" (Gen. 24:67).

The lovers' first glimpses of each other are vastly asymmetrical. While Isaac "went out walking in the field toward evening and *he raised his eyes and he saw* camels approaching" (Gen. 24:63), Rebecca "*raised her eyes, and she saw* Isaac; and she alighted from the camel" (v. 64).

64. This difficulty led NAB to ignore the verb altogether: "One day toward evening he went out [...] in the field."

65. Rashi on Gen. 24:63; Genesis Rabba 60:14. Gersonides interprets similarly, as did many of the ancient translations (Septuagint; Vulgate; Onkelos).

66. Westermann, *Genesis 12–36: A Continental Commentary*, 390, leans toward this possibility but continues to debate; Hans Peter Müller, "Die hebräische Wurzel שיח," *VT* 19 (1969): 368; Hamilton, *The Book of Genesis, Chapters 18–50*, 160. See also Ibn Ezra, Rashbam, and Radak on Gen. 24:63.

67. Vall ("What Was Isaac Doing in the Field [Genesis xxiv 63]?" *VT* 44 [1994]: 513–523) surveys twelve possible interpretations of the verb.

While Isaac raised his eyes to see the camels approaching, Rebecca raised her eyes to see Isaac. This could be explained by the logical sequence of events – Isaac saw a convoy approaching from afar, and the details of the convoy were indistinguishable at a distance, while Rebecca sees Isaac once the convoy comes a little closer. Moreover, the identity of the riders is difficult to determine in a large convoy, while Rebecca can only see one person. Nonetheless, the similar sentence structure creates a contrast between the two visions. Isaac has just returned from an introspective, spiritual retreat; Rebecca is at the end of an adventurous journey. Isaac arrives at the meeting from a well of revelation, while Rebecca comes from a well of kindness toward strangers. As characters, Isaac sees the bigger picture, while Rebecca processes details and is ready to spring into action: "And she alighted from the camel."[68] While Isaac's viewpoint leads to contemplation, Rebecca's viewpoint leads to action. Only from her perspective does the reader hear that Isaac also walks toward them: "Who is that man walking in the field toward us?" (v. 65). This difference will continue to characterize the couple throughout the Isaac narratives and the Jacob story cycle.

Rebecca's question about the identity of the approaching man is directed at "the servant" (Gen. 24:65). The servant regains his title as Abraham's servant when Rebecca finally meets Isaac, her betrothed, and the servant finishes his mission. The question indicates that Isaac began walking toward the convoy, even though he did not know the convoy's connection to him or his father. Nonetheless, Isaac inadvertently walks toward his betrothed, who approaches after a long journey from Aram-naharaim.[69]

The servant responds to Rebecca's question by stating: "That is my lord" (Gen. 24:65). In this utterance, the servant completes the purpose of his mission. The servant had named Abraham as his master several times in his dialogue with the family, and referred to Sarah as "the wife of my lord" and to the nameless Isaac as his master's son. The response to Rebecca's question should therefore presumably be, "He

68. Compare the image of Rebecca's descent from the camel with Judges 1:14 and I Sam. 25:23.

69. Cf. Gen. 46:29; Ex. 4:27; 18:7.

is my lord's son." In calling Isaac "master," the servant solidifies Isaac's new role as the protagonist of our story, and cedes the leadership of the Abrahamic line to him.

The definition of Isaac as the master and the conclusion of the entire narrative with a dialogue between the servant and Isaac without any additional mention of Abraham both serve as a delicate transition from father to son. Abraham sent the servant, but the servant returned to Isaac, who became his new master. Abraham steps aside to allow Isaac to become the new protagonist. Rebecca's arrival marks Isaac's transition from the son of Abraham to the inheritor of the covenant, the new patriarch, and Abraham's replacement.

When the servant identified Isaac as his master, Rebecca "took her veil and covered herself." While some interpreted this as an act of modesty, I believe Rebecca's inhibition in front of Isaac emphasizes the lack of communication between the betrothed throughout the scene. Rebecca asks the *servant* to identify the man and he responds (Gen. 24:65). The servant tells Isaac "all the things that he had done" (v. 66); but no dialogue passes between Isaac and Rebecca. Instead, she covers her face with a veil.

Rebecca and Isaac's story begins with a meeting between Rebecca and Abraham's servant. Isaac is absent from the initial encounter, and silent in the second. Isaac's world is one of revelation and introspection, Rebecca's of people and hospitality. The couple appropriately communicate through the servant, but not directly with one another, as the distance created by their separate worlds is too great to bridge. Throughout the Isaac narratives, the couple will rarely speak.[70] This fact does not indicate a lack of love or a faulty relationship. The following verses will, in fact, describe a deep emotional bond between husband and wife. Nonetheless, the inherent distance between husband and wife will accompany them throughout their joint lives. Isaac, the son who was sacrificed on the altar, will live out his days on a spiritual plane, perpetually caught in limbo between life and death. It is his wife,

70. When they do speak, only Rebecca's words are sounded, and the monologue hides more than it reveals (Gen. 27:46).

Rebecca, who will play the active role in advancing his legacy, and that of his father, Abraham.

The Marriage of Isaac and Rebecca

The marriage of Isaac to Rebecca is framed by the memory of Isaac's mother. Isaac brings Rebecca to his mother's tent, and after he finds he loves his new wife, he finds her a comfort for his mother's death. A psychologically based reading of this narrative may mistakenly view these details as a hint of seeking one's mother in the relationship with one's wife. However, in the concrete literary context of the narrative, the emphasis on Isaac's mother reveals only the deep emotional bond that Isaac felt toward Sarah. Sarah waited her whole life for a son, and the gift she was given at the end of her life would demand a unique relationship.

The fact that Isaac could only find comfort for his mother's death after his marriage has nothing to do with Isaac's close relationship with his mother, which stands on its own, but rather points to Rebecca's role as Sarah's replacement. Perhaps this is the reason Rebecca's name is only mentioned in the second statement, while the beginning of the verse only refers to her indirectly ("and he brought her"). The absence of a direct reference highlights the woman who is named explicitly: "his mother Sarah." This dovetails with the entire design of Isaac's character in the narrative. Isaac was not mentioned by name throughout the servant's account to Rebecca's family. One might conclude from the account that Rebecca was sent to marry a man whose name she did not know. The servant's admiration for his master is apparent, while Isaac's character remains vague. Isaac's wealth is an inheritance from his father (Gen. 24:36), and in response to Rebecca's question, "Who is that man walking in the field toward us?" the servant says simply, "That is my lord" (v. 65). Isaac's obscurity is reminiscent of the servant's anonymity, and they both seem to act only as representatives of Abraham's interests. However, while the servant is, in fact, no more than Abraham's emissary, the narrative centers around Isaac's intended marriage, which makes his portrayal as a non-protagonist more surprising. Some claim that this feature accompanies Isaac throughout the narrative in the following chapters as well, in contrast with his active wife, who takes over as the protagonist.[71] This definition of Isaac's character might correlate with his role throughout the patriarchal narratives.[72] Isaac was not selected by God to create a nation, but as the son of the chosen one. This detail has no effect on the evaluation of Isaac's character; it simply defines his role as the maintainer of the covenant between God and Abraham. Therefore, in the narrative describing Abraham's descent, Isaac is portrayed as "his son," and not as an independent personality. While Isaac became the "master" and Abraham's replacement in the final scene, his role culminates in maintaining Abraham's way, not in forging a new path. Parallel to Isaac, Rebecca is brought to Sarah's tent, and the new couple begins their journey, in the footsteps of the previous patriarch and matriarch.

The order of information is surprising. One would expect that with the death of his mother, Isaac would first undergo a process of mourning and comfort, then fall in love with a woman and take her as wife, and then, finally, he would bring the wife into his tent. The order of Isaac's actions is reversed. Initially he brings Rebecca to the tent, then he marries her, and after their marriage to each other, he falls in love with her. Finally, he is comforted for the death of his mother. The reversal is directly related to the sequence of events in the plot: Isaac did not select his own wife, who might even have been brought without his knowledge. He marries her, but only has the opportunity to fall in love after marriage. This model of marriage correlates with the position of the young couple as the successors of Abraham and Sarah. They enter an existing tent, which they are expected to maintain and expand, instead of creating their own. The Midrash describes this transition in the following way:

> As long as Sarah lived, a cloud would appear above the entrance of her tent; at her death the cloud ceased, but when Rebecca came, the cloud returned. As long as Sarah lived, her doors

71. Teugels, "A Strong Woman, Who Can Find?" 99.
72. Teugels (ibid.) emphasizes correctly that since Rebecca is the one joining the family, she has to "prove" herself through action, while Isaac, as the heir, is designed as a passive character.

> were wide open; at her death that openhandedness ceased; but when Rebecca came, it returned. As long as Sarah lived, there was a blessing on her dough, and the lamp used to burn from the evening of the Sabbath until the evening of the following Sabbath; when she died, these ceased; but when Rebecca came, they returned.[73]

Rebecca's actions revive Sarah's tent: the Tent of Sarah becomes the Tent of Sarah and Rebecca, and the sounds and energy of life live on through Rebecca. The union of Rebecca and Isaac seals the transition from one generation to the next.

73. Genesis Rabba 60:16.

The End of Abraham's Life (Gen. 25:1–18)

As Abraham's story draws to a close, the text offers a rare glimpse into our hero's personal life, while reiterating the importance of his national legacy. Abraham's narrative cycle concludes in three units: the birth and dismissal of the sons of Keturah (Gen. 25:1–6); the death and burial of Abraham (vv. 7–11); and the sons of Ishmael (vv. 12–18). As his life and journey wane, the text spotlights the legacy Abraham leaves behind, this time not only with Isaac at the forefront, but with a nod to all of Abraham's children and their fortunes.

The Sons of Keturah

Almost off-handedly, the text drops a shocking bombshell on the reader at the end of the narrative cycle – the fact that Abraham has taken another wife and has six additional sons comes as a complete surprise. The issue of Abraham's fertility is one of the established themes of the entire story cycle; the parenthetical mention of Abraham's apparently large family at the end of his life seems a jarring note. The text is vague about the sequence of events. If the verses are read in chronological order, Abraham remarried after Sarah's death and Isaac's marriage, supported by the caption, "Abraham went on to take another wife" (Gen: 25:1), and by the definition of Keturah as a wife and not a concubine. Alternatively, the reported event might have taken place before

Sarah's death, and perhaps even before Isaac's birth. This reading might be supported by the fact that Keturah had six sons, and Abraham was over 130 when Sarah died.[1]

If Abraham's marriage to Keturah is the report of an earlier event, the delay in exposing this information could be the result of one two different literary perspectives: (a) the need to eliminate the information from the appropriate chronological location, or (b) the need for this information in this location. Both possibilities seem plausible in the context of this narrative. The desire to portray Abraham and Sarah as a couple that is blessed by God, and the theme of Sarah's infertility and miraculous birth, sufficiently justify the omission of information regarding another wife who gave Abraham six sons. The detail is only offered at the conclusion of Abraham's life, so that it cannot accompany the reader throughout the cycle.[2] However, the information about Keturah at this junction plays a role in designing the reading consciousness of the present unit as well. The information is linked with the marriage of Isaac on the one side and the death of Abraham on the other. The purpose of mentioning Keturah's sons is to emphasize that they will not be Abraham's heirs; the appropriate place for the discussion of inheritance is on Abraham's deathbed.[3]

However, the report of Abraham's marriage to Keturah creates an interesting link between Abraham and his son: both Isaac and Abraham were married. Fourth-generation Babylonian *Amora* Rava was aware of this juxtaposition, as expressed in the following talmudic text:

> Rava asked Rabba bar Mari: What is the source of the saying recited by people, "Sixty pains afflict the teeth of him who hears the sound of his friend [eating], but does not eat"? He replied: It is written, "To me, your servant, and to Zaddok the priest and to Benayahu son of Yehoyada, he has not called" (I Kings 1:25–26).

1. See Sarna, *Genesis* (JPS), 172; Wenham, *Genesis 16–50*, 160; Hamilton, *The Book of Genesis, Chapters 18–50*, 165; Mathews, *Genesis*, 352. The caption *vayosef* (lit. "and he added another [wife]") indicates that the unit is based on the assumption that Abraham was already married to Sarah.
2. Cf. Jacob, *The First Book of the Bible: Genesis*, 164.
3. Wenham, *Genesis 16–50*, 161.

> He responded: You learn from there, but I learn from here: "Isaac then brought her into the tent of his mother Sarah, and he took Rebecca as his wife. Isaac loved her, and thus found comfort after his mother's death," followed by "Abraham went on to take another wife, whose name was Keturah."[4]

According to Rava, the juxtaposition of Abraham and Isaac taking wives demonstrates that when one sees a friend experiencing joy, the wise thing to do is emulate the friend and find one's own joy. Rava is noting a surprising literary model. While Isaac's character in Genesis 26 is designed based on Abraham's, here Abraham emulates Isaac's actions. The detail thereby contributes to the design of Isaac's character as Abraham's successor.

Based on the order of the text, Abraham marries Keturah after Sarah's death and Isaac's marriage, and lives with her for over thirty years. Thirty years is a significant amount of time from Abraham's perspective, but from the reader's point of view the time has no significance at all, since it passes uneventfully in any literary sense. The brief narrative and laconic report make Abraham and Keturah into a couple that does not contribute to the design of the literary cycle. The casual writing style correlates with the purpose of the information: the sons of Keturah are irrelevant to the development of the Abraham narrative. They do, however, play a part in the realization of the Covenant of Circumcision, where Abraham was promised that he would become the father of many nations.[5] Perhaps for this reason, it is noted that the sons of Dedan – Abraham's grandson – "were the Asshurim, the Letushim, and the Leummim" (Gen. 25:3). The noun form that turns "Ashur," "Letush," and "Leum" into nations[6] indicates that Keturah's sons fulfilled God's blessing to Abraham – "father of a multitude of nations" (17:5).[7]

4. Bava Kamma 92b.
5. Cf. Sarna, *Genesis* (JPS), 170–171; Wenham, *Genesis 16–50*, 161.
6. Regarding these tribes, see Frederick Victor Winnett, "The Arabian Genealogies in the Book of Genesis," in *Translating and Understanding the Old Testament: Essays in Honor of Herbert Gordon May*, ed. H. T. Frank and W. L. Reed (Nashville, 1970), 190–191.
7. Targum Pseudo-Jonathan translates the plural form of the names as adjectives, perhaps due to the word *hayu* ("were"), which creates the impression that the narrative

But the emphasis of the text is not on the multiplicity of nations that emerged from Keturah's sons, but rather on their expulsion. Immediately after the conclusion of the list of Keturah's offspring the text reports: "Abraham willed all that he owned to Isaac" (Gen: 25:5), while "to Abraham's sons by concubines Abraham gave gifts while he was still living, and he sent them away from his son Isaac eastward, to the land of the East" (v. 6). The main literary purpose of Keturah's sons is to clear the way for the one true heir: Isaac. This is not only apparent in the fact that they are sent away, but also in the definition of their inheritance: Abraham gave "all that he owned" to Isaac, while the sons of the concubines were only given "gifts." The chiastic structure of the two verses emphasizes the contrast between the sons:[8]

Abraham willed all that he owned	to Isaac
but to Abraham's sons by concubines	Abraham gave gifts

The text does not specify the "gifts" received by Keturah's sons; the structure indicates that Abraham's gifts are contrasted with "all that he owned." The gifts he bestows on the sons of Keturah are not an inheritance – in fact, they seem more of a parting gift given freely out of the kindness of Abraham's heart.

The purpose of this literary unit is the unequivocal statement that despite the fact that Abraham had several sons, Isaac is the one and only successor and legal heir. Some have claimed that Abraham's actions do not correspond with the law as stated in Deuteronomy 21:15–17. There, it describes laws of inheritance which prohibit choosing the younger son over the elder; even if the younger son is the son of the preferred wife, the elder son is always given "a double portion of all he possesses" (Deut. 21:15–16) as the chief heir. Yet, Abraham clearly prefers Isaac over any of his other children.[9] However, our narrative is not about a beloved

is explaining what they were, rather than introducing them by their first names. See the reservations of Nahmanides and Ibn Ezra (on Gen. 25:3) on this reading.

8. Cf. Mathews, *Genesis*, 355. Mathews notes correctly that the chiastic structure indicates that the letter *vav* ("and/but") at the start of the description of the concubines' sons indicates contrast ("but the sons of the concubines").
9. Bill T. Arnold, *Genesis* (NCBC: Cambridge, 2009), 226.

wife and a hated one, but rather about a wife and concubines. The law in Deuteronomy has no impact on this case, and in light of accepted Ancient Near East norms, the father has the right to determine whether the sons of his concubines will inherit like the sons of wives. The formulation of the narrative in Genesis 25 indicates that accepted legal norms play a part in the narrative, since the narrative emphasizes that Abraham sent the sons of his concubines "from his son Isaac / while he was still living" (v. 6). Both emphases are significant in the context of Ancient Near Eastern laws. As previously noted in the discussion on the expulsion of Ishmael, according to these norms the father decides whether the sons of the concubines are considered legitimate sons. The father acknowledges his sons by a positive statement – "You are my sons" – or denies them by sending them away. Clause 2 of the Laws of Lipit-Ishtar states that in the case of a master who has both a wife and a concubine who birth sons, and "the father granted freedom to the slave and her children, the children of the slave shall not divide the estate with the children of their (former) master."[10] The fact that the sons of the concubines are sent away "from his son Isaac" indicates that the act is one of pointing to the true heir. This formulation averts the claim that the sons of the concubines were sent away for the purpose of trading, marriage, broadening of the family borders, and so on. They are simply sent away to demonstrate the preference of the son of the wife. The second emphasis – "while he was still living" – proves that the heirs did not disperse as a result of a quarrel that Isaac won, but due to the father's decision while he was still alive. This is a significant legal issue, since according to the Hammurabi Code, "After the father has passed to his destiny the first wife's sons and the slave-girl's sons shall share out the treasures in the father's house equally."[11] The fact that the sons of the

10. ANET, 160. Regarding the link between this law and Abraham's treatment of Ishmael and the sons of the concubines, see Sarna, *Understanding Genesis*, 156; Grintz, *The Book of Genesis: Its Uniqueness and Antiquity*, 53–54; Fleishman, "The Expulsion of Ishmael," 151.

11. Richardson, *Hammurabi's Laws: Text, Translation and Glossary*, 94–95. The full law reads as follows: "If the first wife of a man has borne him sons and also his slave-girl has borne him sons, and during his lifetime the father has said to the sons the slave-girl bore him, 'My sons,' they shall reckon them together with the first wife's

concubines were sent away by their father prevents accusations that the concubines' sons were sent away without Abraham's knowledge, which would lead to doubts about Isaac's status as the sole heir.

The issue exceeds the matter of monetary inheritance. Abraham's legacy includes the inheritance of the land promised to his offspring, and is related to the fulfillment of the covenant. The inheritance of the land is indicated in the emphasis on the new location of the concubines' sons: "And he sent them away from his son Isaac eastward, to the land of the East." The rejected sons are sent to the east.[12] The word *kedem* ("east") is repeated twice ("*kedma, el eretz kedem*"), possibly as an indication of a direction (eastward) and the name of a place (the land of the East), or perhaps as a wordplay.[13] The emphasis on the east encourages the reader to contrast geographical locations, in addition to the question of ancestral status. Canaan is perceived as part of Abraham's inheritance (Gen. 15:7–8), and is passed along to his heir. As Abraham readies himself to leave this world, he prepares the path – spiritually and legally – for Isaac to take his place.

The Death and Burial of Abraham

Abraham lived 175 years. The standard age of death of the forefathers in Genesis is a whole number plus seven. Sarah lives to 127, Ishmael lives to 137, and Jacob lives to 147. Assuming the symbolism of numbers in the biblical narrative,[14] the age of death is not incidental but plays a role in the literary structure. Abraham departed for Canaan when he was seventy-five (Gen. 12:4) and died at 175 (25:7). Some suggested a chiastic structure for Abraham's life:[15]

---

sons. After the father has passed to his destiny the first wife's sons and the slave-girl's sons shall share out the treasures in the father's house equally."

12. Like other "rejected" people in Genesis: Adam (Gen. 3:24), Cain (4:16), Lot and his grandsons (13:11), and Esau (37:8).
13. See also Yisrael Efal, "*Kedem, Benei Kedem, Eretz Benei Kedem*," *Entziklopedya Mikra'it* 7:27; Westermann, *Genesis 12–36: A Continental Commentary*, 397.
14. Note the wordplay on the number *sheva* ("seven") in the description of Abraham's death: "*beseva tova, zaken vesave'a*," "dying at a good ripe age, old and contented."
15. Radday, "Chiasmus in Hebrew Biblical Narrative," 104.

Seventy-five initial years: Childless in Ur of the Chaldeans/ Haran
Twenty-five years: Childless in Canaan
Seventy-five final years: With Isaac in Canaan

According to this suggestion, Abraham lives with his son an equal number of years to the period before God's revelation. Abraham lived one hundred years after the revelation. Isaac was born when Abraham was one hundred years old. The number therefore has dual significance in the story cycle.

The report of Abraham's death includes a variety of complex descriptions: "And Abraham breathed his last, dying at a good ripe age, old and contented; and he was gathered to his kin." Some commentators felt the word for "contented," "*save'a*," is lacking, and should be completed, "*sava yamim,*" "content of days." This phrase is used in the death of Job (Job 42:17) and the death of David (I Chr. 23:1 and 29:28).[16] The death of Isaac is described in similar terms: "Isaac was one hundred and eighty years old when he breathed his last and died. He was gathered to his kin, old and content of days (*zaken useva yamim*), and he was buried by his sons Esau and Jacob" (Gen. 35:29). The full phrase is documented in ancient translations (Septuagint, Samaritan, Peshitta), and some believe this version was included in the original version of the Masoretic text.[17] However, there is a possibility that the text deliberately broke the common phrase.[18] The term *save'a* is broader than the more specific term *sava yamim*. The common phrase of "*sava yamim*" should be viewed as synonymous with the term "*zaken*," "old," but the more general *save'a* relates both to old age and to a general air of satisfaction. Abraham died satisfied and content on all accounts. Despite the trials and tribulations of his life, the conclusion of his days is portrayed as overflowing with

16. Cf. "Jehoiada reached a ripe old age (*vayizkan Yehoyada, vayisba yamim*) and died; he was one hundred and thirty years old at his death" (II Chr. 24:15).
17. E.g., Ball, *The Book of Genesis*, 79; von Rad, *Genesis*, 255; Westermann, *Genesis 12–36: A Continental Commentary*, 394; Wenham, *Genesis 16–50*, 155; Hamilton, *The Book of Genesis, Chapters 18–50*, 164.
18. For examples of this literary device, see Grossman, "Deliberate Misuse of Idioms in the Biblical Narrative," 23–44.

God's blessings. Abraham has finally arrived at his destination, and can watch his son and heir raise his own family.[19]

This might be the purpose of the lengthy description of Abraham's death; the usual description of death is considerably shorter.[20] This is apparent in the comparison of the deaths of Noah and Abraham:

The Death of Noah (Gen. 9:29)	**The Death of Abraham (25:7–8)**
And all the days of Noah	This was the total span of Abraham's life:
came to nine hundred and fifty years;	one hundred and seventy-five years.
then he died.	And Abraham breathed his last, dying at a good ripe age, old and contented; and he was gathered to his kin.

The number of Abraham's years is given a festive introduction, which is enhanced by breaking the common phrase *sava yamim* and leaving Abraham generally content. The phrase "*beseva tova*," "a good ripe age" echoes the fulfillment of God's promise to Abraham in the Covenant Between the Pieces: "You shall be buried at a ripe old age (*beseva tova*)" (Gen. 15:15).[21] The fulfillment of God's promise to Abraham as a private person confirms the fulfillment of all promises to his offspring.

Abraham's death is followed by a lengthy description of his burial place. "His sons Isaac and Ishmael buried him in the cave of Machpelah, in the field of Ephron son of Zohar the Hittite, facing Mamre, the field that Abraham had bought from the Hittites; there Abraham was buried, and Sarah his wife" (Gen. 25:9).

The burial itself is secondary to the emphasis of the location: in the cave of Machpelah. After identifying the location, the narrative repeats the exact location of the cave: "In the field of Ephron son of

19. Abraham died after the birth of Jacob and Esau. Even without this information, the fact that Abraham was able to will "all that he owned to Isaac" paints the verses in an uplifting light, and Abraham as one who merited continuous blessings to the day of his death and beyond.
20. Wenham, *Genesis 16–50*, 160.
21. This term is not used to describe any other biblical character in the Pentateuch. Two additional uses of the phrase appear in the biblical narrative: once regarding the death of Gideon (Judges 8:32), and in the death of David (I Chr. 29:28).

Zohar the Hittite, facing Mamre." Moreover, the narrative reiterates the fact that Abraham had purchased the field surrounding the cave as well: "The field that Abraham had bought from the Hittites." Finally, the narrative reviews the people buried in the cave to date: "There Abraham was buried, and Sarah his wife." While the extreme emphasis might relate to the significance of the cave of Machpelah, the purchase of the cave was Abraham's way of beginning to realize his right to the land of Canaan. Abraham's burial in the only location he formally purchased in Canaan creates the sense of the fulfillment of God's promises to Abraham. He lived to a ripe old age as God had promised, and was buried in the land that God had promised, in a plot that he had purchased and owned. This might be viewed as a sign that God's promises to Abraham's offspring will come to fruition as well.

The conclusion of Abraham's burial with a mention of Sarah creates another literary effect. The unit opened with the marriage of Abraham and Keturah, and concludes with Abraham's burial beside Sarah. Ishmael was banished along with his mother; Keturah, the mother of six of Abraham's sons, does not receive a special position. The last two words describing Abraham's final resting place report that Abraham is forever buried beside his wife Sarah.[22]

The departure from Abraham is moderated by the following information: "After the death of Abraham, God blessed his son Isaac. And Isaac settled near Beer-lahai-roi" (Gen. 25:11). The appropriate place for this verse would have been the end of Genesis 24, since once the servant returned to Canaan, Isaac replaced Abraham as the dominant character.[23] Had the information regarding Isaac's blessing been mentioned there as well, the generational transfer would have been complete. However, the contribution of relocating the information is obvious: Isaac's blessing softens the impact of Abraham's death. God Himself views Isaac as Abraham's successor, and His blessing continues to accompany Isaac

22. Skinner (*A Critical and Exegetical Commentary on Genesis*, 352) claims that the phrase "there Abraham was buried, and Sarah his wife" is out of place. There is no justification for such a claim, but he surmised that special effort was made in order to integrate the information in the conclusion of Abraham's burial.

23. Van Seters, *Abraham in History and Tradition*, 248.

once Abraham is gone. Since the blessing is such a central motif in the cycle, the integration of this formulation should not be perceived as incidental; from the time of Abraham's death, his blessings will accompany his son Isaac.

The surprising detail in the description of Isaac – Abraham's successor – is the fact that he settles in Beer-lahai-roi. The location was previously linked with Isaac's character in the introduction to his meeting with Rebecca: "Isaac had just come back from the vicinity of Beer-lahai-roi, for he was settled in the region of the Negeb" (Gen. 24:62). As previously noted, Isaac's travels to Beer-lahai-roi design his character as one who seeks divine revelation, and Hagar's revelation might have led to the development of a pilgrimage to that location for those who seek divine encounters. But while Isaac's journey to the well played a part in the contrast between Isaac and Rebecca, the contribution of Beer-lahai-roi in this context is difficult to determine.

The location might be viewed in two contexts. First, Isaac settling near a well (the very location in which Hagar was given the blessing of fertility) can be seen as a contrast to Abraham's death and burial in the cave of Machpelah. This is a portrayal of the passing of generations: one generation dies, while the next draws water. The fertility and vitality that are symbolized by the well correlate with the earlier statement of God's blessing accompanying Isaac. Isaac settles near a well, and begins the process of fulfilling the covenant and promises received by the previous generation.

Second, the well creates a surprising connection between Isaac and Ishmael. Hagar was given tidings of Ishmael's birth by Beer-lahai-roi, and was told to name her child Ishmael (Gen. 16:11). There is, therefore, no location better identified with Ishmael. For some unexplained reason, that very same place becomes Isaac's home. This information correlates with the burial of Abraham by both of his sons: "His sons Isaac and Ishmael buried him in the cave of Machpelah" (25:9).[24] Reading

24. Von Rad (*Genesis*, 275) wonders whether P was unfamiliar with the tradition regarding Ishmael's expulsion, and therefore has both sons bury Abraham together. But Isaac is also buried by his two sons, Jacob and Esau (Gen. 35:29), despite Esau's separation from Jacob and journey to settle in Seir.

the narrative cycle in sequence generates the impression that despite Ishmael's expulsion from Abraham's home, and despite his marriage to an Egyptian, the next generation renews their relationship; in fact Isaac seeks out Ishmael, and makes his home in the place that is most identified with his older brother. The surprising link relates to the wordplay that had accompanied the expulsion narrative, regarding Ishmael's "playfulness" – *metzaḥek* (21:9), while Sarah's son had received a name that stems from the same root – "Isaac" – *yitzḥak* (21:3).[25] The wordplay indicates that Isaac and Ishmael are two sides of the same coin: they are both rooted in laughter, and they are both of a world of breaking boundaries. As long as the issue of inheritance remained in question, Sarah and Hagar were at war, but once the question is resolved and the identity of Abraham's successor clarified, Isaac can explore Ishmael's world at Beer-lahai-roi, and Isaac and Ishmael can come together to bury their father, side-by-side.[26]

The overt reference to Ishmael in the burial of Abraham and the reference to Ishmael through Isaac's choice of home both link this unit with the line of Ishmael.

The Line of Ishmael

Ishmael is described at length: "This is the line of Ishmael, Abraham's son, whom Hagar the Egyptian, Sarah's slave, bore to Abraham" (Gen. 25:2). The lengthiness serves an additional purpose several verses later, at the start of the Jacob cycle: "This is the story of Isaac, son of Abraham; Abraham begot Isaac" (25:19). The juxtaposition of the two characters contrasts the son of "Hagar the Egyptian, Sarah's slave" with Abraham's true son. Although the text devotes several verses to Ishmael's descendants, the narrative emphasizes that he is not "the next protagonist" of the book of Genesis, but only a supplement to the previous story cycle.

---

25. The verb form *metzaḥek* is only used again in reference to Isaac. "Looking out the window, he saw Isaac fooling around (*metzaḥek*) with his wife Rebecca" (Gen. 26:8).
26. For a discussion of the complex dialogue between the brothers, see Jonathan Grossman, "The Notions of 'Savage' and 'Cultured' in Genesis and in The Epic of Gilgamesh: A Structural Analysis," in *Lilkot Shoshanim: LeZikhrah shel Shoshana Kind*, ed. G. Kind (Jerusalem: Revava, 2007), 349–368.

Nonetheless, the reference to the line of Ishmael differentiates him from the status of the sons of the concubines who are discussed at the start of the unit. Ishmael's status is therefore somewhat ambivalent. The use of the plural "*hapilageshim*," "concubines," may be a hint that Hagar and Ishmael were sent away by Abraham along with Keturah's sons (Gen. 25:6). Even if this is correct, the omission of a direct reference to Ishmael is not accidental. Unlike the sons of the concubine, Ishmael buries his father along with Isaac, and he is referred to as the "son" of Abraham in that context: "His sons Isaac and Ishmael buried him in the cave of Machpelah" (v. 9). This complexity accompanies the reader in the reference to the descendants of "Sarah's Egyptian servant."

The significance and success of Ishmael's sons is emphasized in two ways. Firstly, by the framing of the list with two captions: "These are the names of the sons of Ishmael, by their names, in the order of their birth" (Gen. 25:13), and, "These are the sons of Ishmael and these are their names by their villages and by their palaces" (v. 15). While the frame itself lends a festive tone to the list, the opening and closing remarks include a variation. Whereas the opening remark uses the phrase "*bishemotam letoldotam*," "by their names in the order of their birth," the conclusion adds "*beḥatzrehem uvetirotam*," "by their villages and by their palaces." The use of a two-word phrase to describe the descendants lends a similar rhythm to the beginning and end, while the lack of symmetry emphasizes unique information regarding Ishmael's sons: they settled in villages and palaces. "Villages" are open cities, without walls, a term that relates to the lifestyle of nomadic tribes,[27] while "palaces" denote lavish accommodations,[28] or at the very least "a camp protected by a stone wall."[29] This information is not provided in other lists, and seems

27. This is reflected in the words of the prophet: "Let the desert and its towns cry aloud, the villages where Kedar dwells (Is. 42:11). See Van Seters, *Abraham in History and Tradition*, 18; Abraham Malamat ("'Haserim' in the Bible and Mari," *Yediot Bahaqirat Eretz-Israel Weatiqoteha* 27 [1963]: 181) writes, "The term *ḥatzer* ('village') is the method of settlement by nomads, known from archeology"; Westermann, *Genesis 12–36: A Continental Commentary*, 399.

28. Ibn Ezra on Gen. 25:16.

29. Westermann, *Genesis 12–36: A Continental Commentary*, 399; however, see also BDB, 377 ("encampment, esp. of circular encampment of nomad tribes").

to indicate unique success: Ishmael's sons merited their own land – not only nomad villages, but permanent palaces as well.

Secondly, the number of sons is a reminder of the realization of God's blessing to Ishmael in the Covenant of Circumcision: "I will make him fertile and exceedingly numerous. He shall be the father of twelve chieftains, and I will make of him a great nation" (Gen. 17:20). God fulfilled His promise to Abraham and made a great nation of Ishmael, having granted him twelve sons. But not only is the Covenant of Circumcision alluded to here. The description of their land is a realization of the angel's blessing of Hagar: "They dwelt from Havilah, by Shur, which is close to Egypt, all the way to Asshur; he camped (*nafal*) alongside all his kinsmen" (25:18). The reference to Shur, on the border of Egypt, is reminiscent of the location of Hagar's revelation: "An angel of the Lord found her by a spring of water in the wilderness, the spring on the road to Shur" (16:7), while the report "they camped alongside all their kinsmen" is a direct fulfillment of the angel's prophecy: "He shall dwell alongside of all his kinsmen" (16:12).[30] Speiser translates "And each made forays against his various kinsmen," interpreting the verb *nafal* as an offensive act.[31] However, in light of the angel's tidings in the flight narrative, and Judges 7:12, the word *nafal* seems to indicate "to spread out," or in the present context – "camped alongside all of his kinsmen," as in the translation above.[32] The beginning of the verse, which describes the realization of the blessing, mentions the verb "dwell" (*vayishkenu*), and parallels the formulation of the promise (compare to Num. 34:3).[33] However, perhaps the phrase *vayishkenu* ("and they dwelled") was deliberately substituted for *nafal* ("they camped") in order to hint at the alternative meaning of the verb that relates to war stories.[34] Nonetheless, Hagar's prophecy is realized in these verses, even at the cost of battles and quarrels with surrounding desert tribes.

30. Cf. Sarna, *Genesis* (JPS), 171. The fact that this unit creates a dialogue both with the Covenant of Circumcision (commonly attributed to P) and with Hagar's flight (associated with J) demonstrates that the story cycle is unified and cohesive.
31. Speiser, *Genesis*, 187–188.
32. BDB, 657; *HAL*, 710.
33. See also Horst Seebass, "נפל," *TDOT* 9:488–497.
34. BDB, 657; *HAL*, 710.

In these three units, Abraham's story reaches its resolution. The father of sons and of nations sees his progeny advance to claim their legacies: Isaac, the true heir and leader of the Israelite nation; Ishmael, the scorned but legitimate son; and the children of Keturah, whose only link to their father remains a handful of gifts. As the curtain closes on his story and reopens on a new scene, the text once again reminds us of the complexity of the protagonist's life. In his death, as in the narrative of his life, we see Abraham living on two separate planes – the individual and the national. Abraham, the father, acknowledges and affects each of his children as they are. Abraham the leader must ensure the continuation of his nation.

Conclusion

As I mentioned in the introduction, the Abraham narrative is arranged in a concentric structure, with the Covenant of Circumcision and the protagonist's name change at its center:

- **A:** The line of Terah: Abram, Nahor, and Haran (11:27–32).
  - **B:** Abram's separation from his father's house: "Go forth…to the land" (11:27–32).
    - **C:** Abram journeys through the land and invokes the name of God (12:1–5).
      - **D:** Abram's separation from family members: Sarah is taken by Pharaoh, but returned to Abram (12:10–20); Lot departs for Sodom and does not return (13:1–18).
        - **E:** Lot is rescued from captivity (14:1–24).
          - **F:** The promise of offspring and land (15:1–21). Abram complains (15:2: "What can You give me") and the word *tzedaka* ("righteousness") is used in the context of his belief in God (15:6).
            - **G:** The angel's tidings to Hagar regarding the birth of Ishmael (16:1–16).
              - **H:** The Covenant of Circumcision: Abram and Sarai's names are changed (17:1–27).

G': The angel's tidings to Sarah regarding the birth of Isaac (18:1–15).

F': Debate over the destruction of the land (18:16–33). Abraham complains (18:25: "Far be it from You to do such a thing!") and the word *tzedaka* is used in the context of God's decision to reveal his plan to Abraham (18:19).

E': Lot is rescued from Sodom's destruction (19:1–37).

D': Abraham's separation from family members: Sarah is taken by Abimelech but returned to Abraham (20:1–18); Ishmael is expelled to the desert of Paran, and does not return (21:1–21).

C': The covenant of Abraham and Abimelech: Abraham invokes the name of God (21:22–34).

B': Abraham's separation from his son: "Go forth to the land of Moriah" (22:1–19).

A': The line of Nahor (22:20–24).

Transitional Narratives and Conclusion (22:23–25).

Before we delve into the larger discussion of the two halves of the narrative, I would like to justify the frame of D and D'. According to this structure, we should include the story of Abram and Sarai in Egypt (Gen. 12) and the separation from Lot (ch. 13) under the same caption (D'); in parallel, the story of Abraham and Sarah in Gerar (ch. 20) and the story of Isaac's birth and Ishmael's expulsion should be in the same caption (D'). In our analysis of Genesis 12 and 13, we demonstrated the bold literary link between the story of Abram and Sarai's descent to Egypt and their subsequent separation from Lot. Although each of these stories stands on its own, they are also brazenly linked to one another.[1] It is far more surprising to link the stories of Abraham and Sarah in Gerar with the story of Isaac and Ishmael. Indeed, it is not my intention to claim that these two stories comprise a single narrative. That said, from the perspective of the stories' order in the narrative cycle, the common theme which arises from these two narrative pairs deals with Abraham's

1. Wenham, *Genesis 1–15*, 263.

separation from members of his extended family. Sarah is captured by a foreign king, actively throwing an obstacle in the way of God fulfilling His promise to the couple to provide them with an heir. Immediately upon Sarah's return – when the possibility of siring a son through her once again becomes a reality – Abraham banishes Ishmael, who stands as a likely alternative to Abraham and Sarah's progeny, and who would have been eligible to receive the blessings God promised Abraham in the covenants (chs. 17 and 18). Lot, the nephew, could have stood as a viable heir for Abraham should Sarah not succeed in conceiving. However, he chooses to separate from Abraham and therefore relinquish any claim to his uncle's legacy. Reading the two pairs of stories in this way reveals an additional underlying theme that is not apparent when the stories are read individually. Both "separation narrative" duos end in the same way: Sarah is taken from Abraham, and when she returns, the likely contender for Abraham's legacy is sent away, making room for Isaac.

This reading also sheds new light on the apparently untidy order of the stories from both a chronological and literary view. The order in which the stories are told – Sarah kidnapped and Ishmael expelled to the wilderness – seems jumbled. First, we hear about Sarah's capture by Abimelech (Gen. 20), then the story of Isaac's birth and Ishmael's separation from Abraham (ch. 21), and then the text returns us, perplexingly, to the relationship between Abraham and Abimelech (end of ch. 21). As we mentioned earlier, the story of the treaty with Abimelech in Beersheba (21:22–34) is the direct continuation of the story of Abraham and Sarah in Abimelech's home in Genesis 20. In fact, the treaty relies on Abimelech's response to Abraham after returning his wife: "Just as I have treated you with kindness, deal with me and with the land in which you have sojourned" (21:23). Juxtaposing the story of Ishmael's expulsion to Sarah's kidnapping by Abimelech creates a clear literary link between the narratives.

The main challenge with the literary structure of the narrative is understanding the relationship between the two halves in the cycle. Does the literary frame point to an essential development that takes place throughout the individual stories? Can we identify a significant change in the characters of Abram and Sarai between the first seven stories and the second seven? In order to analyze these questions, let us first examine the links between the two halves of the narrative cycle, as well as the differences that arise between them.

B–B′: Abraham's Separation from His Past, into His Future: "Go forth"

Many commentators have discussed the similarities between these two tests – Abram's first directive to leave his father's house (B), and the command that opens the unspeakable journey of the binding of his son (B'). The two tests share far more than the essential order, "*Lekh lekha*," "Go forth." Both narratives convey a similar divine demand to "go forth" to an unknown place – a place that will become holy to the future generations of Abram's progeny. In the first part, Abram is commanded to leave behind his native land and the house of his father to go to Canaan. In the second part, Abraham is commanded to go to an unknown hilltop in the land of Moriah and sacrifice his son there. Despite the similarity between the two tests, each is accompanied by a different atmosphere. The initial test demands the resilience involved in leaving behind what is familiar and facing a new human culture. Abram is expected to go to a "land"; it is a geographical place, with political borders. There, he must cope with the political significance of emigrating to that land. In his final test, Abraham is asked to go to the "land of Moriah." Here the significance of geographical place pales in comparison to the emotional and spiritual road Abraham is required to travel. The significance of Abraham's initial journey is to arrive in physical Canaan, while the purpose of his final journey is to come to the point of willingness to sacrifice his future to God.

C–C′: Abraham Builds Altars and Invokes the Name of God

In the two halves of his journey, Abram invokes the name of God by the altar he had built near Bethel (Gen. 12:13–4), while Abraham invokes the name of God by a tamarisk he had planted in Beersheba (21:33). The two narratives create a geographical frame – from the northern city of Bethel to the southern city of Beersheba.[2] When God's name is invoked in Beersheba, He is referred to by the unique title "Everlasting God" (21:33). Planting the tamarisk (and later creating a pact

2. Cf. Amos 5:5.

with Abimelech) is symbolic of Abraham's belief in the permanence of his relationship with the land. Abraham's God is therefore given a title that expresses His ability to maintain Abraham's permanent ownership of the land.

D–D′: Abraham's Separation from Family Members

The distinction between the two halves of the Abraham cycle is particularly apparent in the two narratives describing Abraham's separation from various family members. In four different narratives Abram/Abraham is required to separate from a close family member: Sarai/Sarah is taken from him twice, although he is reunited with her at the conclusion of both narratives. Additionally, Abram is separated from Lot, his adopted nephew (D), and from Ishmael, son of Hagar (D'). Comparing the separation stories from Lot and from Ishmael sheds new light on the significance of Abram's separation from his nephew. Emotionally, Abraham's relationship with Lot is compared to the relationship with a son. The ramifications on the narrative cycle are profound, since in view of Sarah's infertility Lot – like Ishmael – might have been perceived by Abraham as a possible heir. The separation from Lot challenges Abraham's security in an existing – albeit not a biological – heir, while the separation from Ishmael denies him the hope of an existing heir.

Water plays an important role in both the Ishmael and Lot narratives. Lot separates from Abraham when he sees the fertility of the Transjordan: "Lot looked about him, and saw how well watered (*mashkeh*) was all the plain of Jordan, all of it" (Gen. 13:10), while Ishmael is saved from death after his mother was shown a well: "Then God opened her eyes and she saw a well of water. She went and filled the skin with water, and let the boy drink (*vatashk*)" (21:19). Water, which enables life, serves an opposing function in each of the narratives. In the Lot narrative, water represents "riches hoarded by their owner, to his misfortune" (Eccl. 5:12). The permanent fertility of the land leads to the corruption of the people of Sodom, who become overconfident and uncompassionate. In the Ishmael narrative the water symbolizes giving new life and growth. While Ishmael is reborn in the desert, Lot settles in a place whose inhabitants are "very wicked sinners against the Lord" (Gen. 13:13).

The changing image of God is noteworthy in the context of the story cycle, and particularly in the separation narratives. God's affliction of Pharaoh is negligible compared with His involvement in the Abimelech narrative. God reveals Himself to Abimelech and commands him, in addition to physically restraining him from touching Sarah and punishing his household. While Lot's separation from Abraham does not involve God, God encourages Abraham to follow his wife's instructions and send Ishmael away. That said, God also accompanies Ishmael on his new path. Ishmael's rebirth portrays God as an alternative to the parents who had abandoned him.

E–E': Lot Is Rescued from Sodom

The similarity between the two Lot narratives is obvious. Although Genesis 14 differs in nature and style from the other narratives in the cycle, the chapter finds its place in the concentric structure of the cycle, and is paralleled by Lot's rescue from the people of Sodom. Here, too, God's involvement is infinitely greater in the second part of the cycle. In Genesis 14, Abram rescues Lot without God's command or involvement. In fact, God is absent from the narrative altogether, and Abram's unlikely success is not attributed to God's assistance. In the parallel narrative, Lot is rescued by God and His angels. While Abraham is involved in the theoretical debate regarding the fate of Sodom, he is not actively involved in the destruction of Sodom or in Lot's rescue from the city. That decision was left in the hands of God.

F–F': The Promised Land and the Destruction of the Promised Land

The Covenant Between the Pieces (Gen. 15) and the discussion of the destruction of Sodom (ch. 18) might at first seem unrelated, but both episodes demonstrate Abraham's role as a partner with God in relation to the future of the Promised Land. In response to Abraham's question, "How shall I know that I am to possess it?" (15:8), God confides His plans about the inheritance of the land by Abram's descendants. In the parallel narrative, God reveals His plan to destroy an area of the land that was promised to Abraham. The debate between God and Abraham on the fate of Sodom should not be viewed as

"Abraham's prayer,"[3] but rather as a legal debate on the parameters of what is "charitable and just." The design of the narrative emphasizes the partnership between God and Abraham in the decision to destroy Sodom; Abraham seems to have the right to be heard in the matter of a decision that will affect the land he was promised on the merits of charity and justice.

Genesis 15 and 18 include the only two instances in the cycle in which Abraham complains before God, and is perhaps even critical of His ways (15:2–3 and 18:22–25). Interestingly, these are the only two narratives in which the word *tzedaka* ("justice/charity") is mentioned as justification for the selection of Abraham (15:6 and 18:19).[4] But in this instance as well, the interaction between God and Abraham is much more involved in the second part of the narrative cycle. While a covenant expresses a degree of partnership, the covenant between man and God cannot be viewed as an agreement between equals.[5] In the Covenant Between the Pieces, Abraham is a passive participant – in fact, he is asleep throughout the ceremony! He is told of God's plans and terms without the ability to influence the agreement. In contrast, the debate on the destruction of Sodom gives Abraham the opportunity to express his position, and God's edict is affected by Abraham's involvement. This is a dramatic change from the first part of the narrative cycle to the second – Abraham transforms from the passive object of God's decrees to a seemingly "equal" partner, with the ability to change the outcome of God's judgments!

G–G′: Tidings of the Birth of Abraham's Son

The plot points in the two narratives in Genesis 16 and 18 are comparable. In both, an angel appears to announce that Abram's wife will

---

3. As indicated by the caption offered by Skinner (*A Critical and Exegetical Commentary on Genesis*, 304).
4. On the importance of this phrase, see Olivier Artus, "La mise en oeuvre du droit et de la justice par les figures exemplaires de l'Ancien Testament: Abraham, David, Salomon, Josias," in *Loi et justice dans la littérature du Proche-Orient ancien*, ed. O. Artus (Wiesbaden, 2013), 225–233.
5. Weinfeld, "The Covenant of Grant in the Old Testament and in the Ancient Near East."

bear a son. In addition to the plot, the narratives are linked by a similar ethical theology: the birth of the son is a reward or compensation for human action. Hagar's son is a compensation for her unjust suffering at the hands of Sarah, while Sarah merits a son for her hospitality. The personal reward to each of the wives is the reason the tidings are not delivered to Abraham, and the reason for a direct and intimate meeting with God's angel.

Most noteworthy is the difference between how each mother receives the news of her pregnancy. An angel appears to Hagar "by a spring of water in the wilderness" (Gen. 16:7), far from the home in which she had conceived the child. Hagar has disengaged from Abram and his household, and meets the angel on her way to Egypt. Therefore, the angel's message can only be attributed to Hagar's merit, not to Abram's influence. In contrast, the visit of the angels to Abraham's tent – immediately after the Covenant of Circumcision and Abraham's name change – expresses God's closeness to Abraham in the second part of the cycle. God descends to Abraham's tent to discuss the fate of Sodom, and promises Abraham and Sarah a son as a reward for their hospitality. This intimacy of the Divine descending upon Abraham and Sarah's home, entering their tent to deliver the message about their son, is an introduction to the atmosphere that will accompany the Abraham narratives throughout the second part of the cycle.

H: The Covenant of Circumcision and Changing Abraham's Name

The eighth story, which is the central axis of the cycle, centers on the Covenant of Circumcision. God demands of Abraham: "Walk in My ways and be blameless" (Gen. 17:1), and in return promises: "I will maintain My covenant between Me and you, and your offspring to come, as an everlasting covenant throughout the ages, to be God to you and to your offspring to come" (v. 7). This verse embodies the essence of the transition from the first part of the cycle to the second. In the Covenant of Circumcision, Abraham commits to "walk in God's ways," while God promises to "be Abraham's God." The parameters set by the Covenant of Circumcision enable a uniquely intimate relationship between God and Abraham. God's personal visit to Abraham's tent (G') is appropriately positioned after this covenant, followed by Abraham's "partnership" with God, which is expressed by the discussion on the destruction of Sodom (F') – which is absent from the first part of the cycle.

This essential change in the relationship sheds light on the differences between other parallel narratives in the concentric structure. The change is expressed in Abraham's character, but also in a greater degree of initiation and intervention by God in the second half of the cycle.

God commands Abraham to "go forth" in both parts (B–B'), but while Abraham follows God's command both times, his actions in the second part seem to express an unusual closeness to God, who acknowledges that "now I know that you fear God" (Gen. 22:12). In the first part of the cycle Abraham was told, "Up, walk about the land, through its length and its breadth" (13:17); the Covenant of Circumcision replaces this demand with the expectation that Abraham "walk in My ways and be blameless" (17:1). The new expectation is tested in the final test of Abraham, when he is told to go to the land of Moriah and sacrifice his son to God. The new significance of Abraham's "going" or "walking" in the second half of the cycle sheds light on the physical journey to the binding of Isaac – which is a realization of walking in God's ways.

In conclusion, the first part of the cycle describes Abram's acceptance of God's authority, while the second part portrays the close interaction between God and Abraham and the strengthening of Abraham's loyalty to God. God becomes more heavily involved in every aspect of Abraham's life. He consults with Abraham regarding the fate of Sodom, He intervenes in Abraham's personal relationship with Ishmael, and Abraham's faith in God is tested and proved time and time again. This idea was previously expressed by the Sages in the following midrash:

> Abraham said: Before I was circumcised passers-by would come to me; perhaps now that I am circumcised they will cease from coming? The Holy One, blessed be He, said to him: Before you were circumcised people would come and visit with you, now I come and reveal Myself to you in all My glory, as it is written, "And the Lord appeared to him by the terebinths of Mamre."[6]

6. Genesis Rabba 47:10. Another version reads: "He said, 'Before I was circumcised passers-by would come to me.' God said to him, 'Before you were circumcised the

The midrash portrays Abraham's ongoing relationship with "passers-by" before his circumcision, while after he was circumcised Abraham was visited by God Himself. This idea is indicated in the Covenant of Circumcision, and is reflected in the literary structure of the story cycle. It is by no means the obvious literary structure; it would be just as logical to portray God throughout the narrative cycle as a divine power, commanding absolute obedience, with Abraham's personal journey being one of self-deprecation, learning to push aside his personal feelings for the sake of his loyalty to God, as he did in the binding of Isaac. However, this literary journey finds Abraham and God growing closer. Once Abraham has proven his blind loyalty, he is given a platform to debate God in issues of charity and justice.

A general overview of the Abraham cycle cannot be limited to an exploration of the process that the characters undergo in light of the narrative's structure. Besides arranging the story into two mirroring halves, we must consider the broader themes of the story as a whole. Two major themes bind the story cycle. One is the theme of national blessing. Thus, the tidings of Isaac's birth in the Covenant of Circumcision (Gen. 17), the expulsion of Hagar (ch. 21), and Lot's rescue in merit of Abraham (ch. 14). The other is the theme of moral blessing. Thus, the tidings of Isaac's birth in Abraham's tent (ch. 18), Hagar's flight (ch. 16), and Lot's rescue in merit of his hospitality (19:1–28). These themes express the essential duality of the story cycle. Abraham is portrayed as a complex character who successfully established a nation committed to a covenant with God, while maintaining moral sensitivity by instructing his children and his descendants to keep the way of the Lord by doing what is charitable and just.

These parallels between the comparable stories in the Abraham narrative cycle are part of a larger literary motif throughout Genesis and the patriarchal narratives, which all utilize the devices of mirroring and analogous narratives in their storytelling. The lives of these characters in Genesis take place on two levels, both of which are essential to

uncircumcised would come, now I appear before you with My host,' as it is written: 'Looking up, he saw three men standing near him'; 'he saw' the presence of God; 'he saw' the angels" (Genesis Rabba 48:9).

their development. The forefathers were chosen to establish a nation, and their actions represent an implementation of a divine plan (following the destruction of the world in the Great Flood). However, the characters also play out their stories in the contexts of their own inner worlds, their personal ethics, and the ramifications of their own decisions. God responds to their actions, and judges them according to a well-established and consistent structure of justice. This is rare in the ancient world, where gods and divine beings are generally described as self-serving, and even when their actions benefit humanity, there always seems to be an underlying personal agenda. Divine or human action stemming from an ethical and moral decision is almost unheard of in ancient mythological literature. The combination of the concept of divine ethics with the description of the characters' choice to exercise free will in following God in Genesis represents a complete revolution in the way these narratives had been told previously. Not only is Abraham the founder of a new nation, bound by a covenant with God, but he lived according to an ethical creed. He would invite three weary strangers to rest and eat in his home, and when the time came to pass on his legacy, the message was clear: the covenant with God is to walk in His ways by performing acts of justice and charity for all.

Abraham's actions embedded an essential value in Judaism that lives on until today – the concept of choice. Before the Great Flood, all of humanity were "loyal" to God, and the demand for ethical norms was spread evenly across all people. After the Flood and the dispersion of peoples throughout the world (Gen. 10–11), one man and his progeny were chosen to be the protagonists to continue the biblical narrative. As we saw in our analysis, God's purpose in choosing a new hero was still to propagate blessing and ethics among all peoples (A–A'). The only change is the tactics to create a better world. From now on, the expectation to walk in God's ways falls only on those who were bound by His covenant with Abraham.

Surprisingly, the one man chosen as the vessel of the world's blessing did not benefit from them so easily. Sarah's infertility is described throughout the narrative cycle as a painful and perplexing contradiction to God's promises that the couple would be fruitful and bear entire nations. This ongoing spiritual test Abraham finds himself in is the root of the challenges of faith. How does one continue to believe that God's promise will come to pass, when everything about reality seems to point to the opposite? Abraham and Sarah's final act sees one of God's promises overcoming the harsh reality they faced, solidifying the veracity of their faith. However, they must keep faith that four generations later, their great-grandchildren will settle and inherit the land promised to them by God, that their progeny will number as the stars in the sky and the sands on the shore, even though they will never see these promises fulfilled with their own eyes. They were blessed to purchase a piece of land to be buried in, and to plant a tree in Beersheba, but they don't live to see the destinies they were promised being fulfilled. Some may call this a tragedy, but in truth it is the paving of a path that delineates a faith in the promises of the future, even when the current reality seems to make their fulfillment impossible. Abraham and Sarah's legacy of faith challenges us to walk the long path, believing in the resolution, even if it is not yet apparent.

List of Abbreviations

Abbreviations used in footnotes and bibliography:

AB – Anchor Bible
ABD – Anchor Bible Dictionary
ABR – Australian Biblical Review
AnBib – Analecta Biblica
ANET – Ancient Near Eastern Texts
ASV – American Standard Version
AUSS – Andrews University Seminary Studies
BA – The Biblical Archaeologist
BASOR – Bulletin of the American Schools of Oriental Research
BBB – Bonner biblische Beiträge
BDB – Brown-Driver-Briggs (Hebrew and English Lexicon)
BJS – Brown Judaic Studies
BTB – Biblical Theology Bulletin
BWAT – Beiträge zur Wissenschaft vom Alten Testament
BZ – Biblische Zeitschrift
BZAW – Beihefte zur Zeitschrift für die alttestamentliche Wissenschaft
CAD – Chicago Assyrian Dictionary
CBC – Cambridge Bible Commentary
CBQ – Catholic Bible Quarterly
Fertil and Steril (Fertility and Sterility)
FOTL – Forms of Old Testament Literature Series
HALOT – Hebrew and Aramaic Lexicon of the Old Testament
HAR – Hebrew Annual Review
HUCA – Hebrew Union College Annual
ICC – International Critical Commentary

IDB – *Interpreter's Dictionary of the Bible*
JANES – *Journal of Ancient Near Eastern Studies*
JAOS – *Journal of the American Oriental Society*
JBL – *Journal of Biblical Literature*
JBQ – *Jewish Bible Quarterly*
JFSR – *Journal of Feminist Studies in Religion*
JHS – *Journal of Hebrew Scriptures*
JJS – *Journal of Jewish Studies*
JNES – *Journal of Near Eastern Studies*
JPS – Jewish Publication Society
JSOT – *Journal for the Study of the Old Testament*
JSOTSup – *Journal for the Study of the Old Testament, Supplement*
JSS – *Journal of Semitic Studies*
JTS – *Journal of Theological Studies*
KAT – Kommentar zum Alten Testament
KJV – King James Version
NAB – New American Bible
NAC – New American Catholic Bible
NAS – New American Standard Bible
NCBC – New Cambridge Bible Commentary
NIB – New Interpreter's Bible
NICOT – New International Commentary on the Old Testament
NIDOTTE – *New International Dictionary of Old Testament Theology and Exegesis*
NIV – New International Version
NJPS – New Jewish Publication Society
NKJV – New King James Version
NRSV – New Revised Standard Version
OBO – Orbis Biblicus et Orientalis
OTG – Old Testament Guides
OTL – Old Testament Library Commentary Series
OTS – *Oudtestamentische Studiën*
PEQ – *Palestine Exploration Quarterly*
RB – *Révue Biblique*
RSV – Revised Standard Version
SBL – Society of Biblical Literature
SBLSS – Society of Biblical Literature Symposium Series
SEÅ – *Svensk Exegetisk Årsbok*
SJT – *Scottish Journal of Theology*
TDOT – *Theological Dictionary of the Old Testament*

TOTC – Tyndale Old Testament Commentaries
UF – *Ugarit-Forschungen*
VT – *Vetus Testamentum*
VTSup – Vetus Testamentum, Supplements
WBC – Word Biblical Commentary
WMANT – Wissenschaftliche Monographien zum Alten und Neuen Testament
WTJ – *Westminster Theological Journal*
ZA – *Zeitschrift für Assyriologie und Vorderasiatische Archäologie*
ZAW – *Zeitschrift für die alttestamentliche Wissenschaft*
ZDMG – *Zeitschrift der Deutschen Morganländischen Gesellschaft*

Bibliography

Abela, Anthony. "Difficulties for Exegesis and Translation: The Inversion of Genesis 18:7a." *Bible Translator* 60 (2009): 1–4.

Achituv, Shmuel. "Shechem." *Entziklopedya Mikra'it* 7:662–670 (Hebrew).

Aharoni, Reuben. "Three Similar Stories in Genesis." *Beit Mikra* 24 (1979): 213–223 (Hebrew).

Ahuvia, Avraham. "The Expressions '*Shakhav Im*' and '*Shakhav Et*' in the Bible." *Beit Mikra* 40 (1995): 276–278 (Hebrew).

Ahuvia, Avraham. "An Angel of the Lord Found Her by a Spring of Water in the Wilderness." *Beit Mikra* 39 (1994): 71–75 (Hebrew).

Albright, William Foxwell. "Abram the Hebrew: A New Archaeological Interpretation." *BASOR* 163 (1961): 36–54.

Albright, William Foxwell. "The Names Shaddai and Abram." *JBL* 54 (1935): 173–204.

Alexander, Thomas Desmond. *From Paradise to the Promise Land: An Introduction to the Main Themes of the Pentateuch*. Grand Rapids, MI, 1998.

Alexander, Thomas Desmond. "Abraham Re-Assessed Theologically." In *He Swore an Oath: Biblical Themes from Genesis 12–50*, edited by R. S. Hess, G. J. Wenham, and P. E. Satterthwaite, 7–28. 2nd ed. Carlisle, UK, 1994.

Alexander, Thomas Desmond. "Lot's Hospitality: A Clue to His Righteousness." *JBL* 104 (1985): 289–291.

Alexander, Thomas Desmond. "The Hagar Traditions in Genesis 16 and 21." In *Studies in the Pentateuch*, edited by J. A. Emerton, 131–148. VTSup 41. Leiden, 1990.

Alexander, Thomas Desmond. "A Literary Analysis of the Abraham Narrative in Genesis." PhD diss., The Queen's University of Belfast, 1982.

Alexander, Thomas Desmond. *Abraham in the Negev: A Source-Critical Investigation of Genesis 20:1–22:19*. Carlisle, UK, 1997.

Alfrink, Bern. "L'expression נאסף אל עמיו." *OTS* 5 (1948): 118–131.

Alter, Robert. *Genesis – Translation and Commentary*. New York, 1996.

Alter, Robert. *The Art of Biblical Narrative*. New York, 1981.

Alter, Robert. *The Five Books of Moses*. New York and London, 2004.

Amit, Yairah. "Elisha and the Great Woman of Shunem: A Prophet Tested." *Zmanim* 77 (2001): 4–11 (Hebrew).

Amit, Yairah. "Progression as a Rhetorical Device in Biblical Literature." *JSOT* 28 (2003): 3–32.

Amit, Yairah. "The Place of Jerusalem in the Pentateuch." *Studies in the Bible and Exegesis* 5 (2000): 41–57 (Hebrew).

Amit, Yairah. *Reading Biblical Narratives: Literary Criticism and the Hebrew Bible*. Minneapolis, 2001.

Anbar, Moshe. "Abrahamic Convenant – Genesis 15." *Shnaton* 3 (1979): 34–52 (Hebrew).

Andersen, Francis I. *The Sentence in Biblical Hebrew*. Janua Linguarum, Series Practica 231. The Hague, 1974.

Angel, Hayyim. "Learning Faith from the Text, or Text from Faith: The Challenges of Teaching (and Learning) the Avraham Narrative and Commentary." In *Wisdom From All My Teachers,* edited by J. Saks and S. Handelman, 192–212. Jerusalem and New York, 2003.

Angel, Hayyim. "The Chosen People: An Ethical Challenge." *Conversations* 8 (2010): 52–60.

Ararat, Nisan. *Emet VeḤesed BaMikra*. Jerusalem, 1993 (Hebrew).

Arnold, Bill T. *Genesis*. NCBC. Cambridge, 2009.

Artus, Olivier. "La mise en oeuvre du droit et de la justice par les figures exemplaires de l'Ancien Testament: Abraham, David, Salomon, Josias." In *Loi et justice dans la littérature du Proche-Orient ancien,* edited by O. Artus, 225–233. Wiesbaden, 2013.

Assis, Elie. "The Alphabetic Acrostic in the Book of Lamentations." *CBQ* 69 (4) (2007): 710–724.

Astour, Michael C. "Political and Cosmic Symbolism in Genesis 14 and in Its Babylonian Sources." In *Biblical Motifs: Origins and Transformations,* edited by A. Altmann, 65–112. Cambridge, MA, 1966.

Avishur, Yitzhak. "The Angels' Visit with Abraham (Gen. 18:1–16) and Its Parallels in Ugaritic Literature." *Beit Mikra* 32 (1986): 168–177 (Hebrew).

Avishur, Yitzhak. "The Narratives of the Binding of Isaac and Abraham's Exodus from Haran – Structure, Style and Language." In *Studies in the Archaeology and History of Ancient Israel,* edited by M. Heltzer, A. Segal, and D Kaufman, 91–106. Haifa, 1993 (Hebrew).

Awabdy, Mark A. "Babel, Suspense, and the Introduction to the Terah-Abram Narrative." *JSOT* 35 (2010): 3–29.

Bader, Mary Anna. *Sexual Violation in the Hebrew Bible: A Multi-Methodological Study of Genesis 34 and 2 Samuel 13*. SBL 87. New York, 2006.

Bailey, Lloyd R. "Israelite 'Ēl Šadday and Amorite Bêl Šadê." *JBL* 87 (1968): 434–438.

Ball, Charles James. *The Book of Genesis: Critical Edition of the Hebrew Text*. Leipzig: J. C. Hinrichs, 1896.

Baltzer, Klaus. "Jerusalem in den Erzväter-Geschichten der Genesis? Traditionsgeschichtliche Erwägungen zu Gen 14 und 22." In *Die Hebräische Bibel und Ihre Zweifache Nachgeschichte: Festschrift fur Rolf Rendtorff zum 65. Geburtstag*, edited by E. Blum, C. Macholz, and E. W. Stegemann, 3–12. Neukirchen-Vluyn, 1990.

Baly, Denis, and A. Douglas Tushingham. *Atlas of the Biblical World*. New York, 1971.

Bartelmus, Rüdiger. "פתח." *TDOT* 7:173–191.

Batscha, Zvi, and Avraham Yassour. *The Great Modern Political Theories*. Vol. 1. Jerusalem and Tel Aviv, 1975 (Hebrew).

Bauer, Hans. "Die hebräischen Eigennamen als sprachliche Erkenntnisquelle." *ZAW* 48 (1930): 73–80.

Baumgart, Norbert Clemens. "Gottesbild, Schöpfungstheologie und die Völker in der Genesis." In *Schöpfung, Monotheismus und fremde Religionen* (BTS 95), edited by L. Borman, 63–98. Neukirchen-Vluyn, 2008.

Baumgärtel, Friedrich J. *Elohim außerhalb des Pentateuch: Grundlegung zu einer Untersuchung über die Gottesnamen im Pentateuch*. BWAT 19. Leipzig, 1914.

Bechtel, Lyn M. "A Feminist Reading of Genesis 19:1–11." In *A Feminist Companion to Genesis*, edited by A. Brenner, 108–128. Sheffield, 1993.

Bechtel, Lyn M. "What If Dinah Is Not Raped." *JSOT* 62 (1994): 19–36.

Becking, Bob. "Abram in Exile: Remarks on Genesis 12, 10–20." In *Die Erzväter in der Biblischen Tradition: Festschrift für Matthias Köckert*, edited by A. C. Hagedorn, and H. Pfeiffer, 35–47. BZAW 400. Berlin and New York, 2009.

Ben Zvi, Ehud. "The Dialogue between Abraham and Yahweh in Gen 18.23–32: A Historical-Critical Analysis." *JSOT* 53 (1992): 27–46.

Benzinger, Immanuel. "Zur Quellenscheidung in Gen. 14." In *Vom Alten Testament. Festschrift fur K. Marti*, edited by K. Budde, 21–27. BZAW 41. Giessen, 1925.

Bergen, Robert D. "The Role of Genesis 22:1–19 in the Abraham Cycle: A Computer-Assisted Textual Interpretation." *Criswell Theological Review* 4 (1990): 313–326.

Bergen, Wesley J. *Elisha and the End of Prophetism*. JSOTSup 286. Sheffield, 1999.

Bergey, Ronald L. *The Book of Esther: Its Place in the Linguistic Milieu of Post-Exilic Biblical Hebrew Prose*. PhD diss., Dropsie College, Philadelphia, 1983.

Berlin, Adele. *Poetics and the Interpretation of Biblical Narrative.* Bible and Literature Series. Sheffield, 1983.

Berlin, Adele. *The Dynamics of Biblical Parallelism.* Rev. ed. Grand Rapids, MI, 2008.

Berlyn, Patricia. "The Journey of Terah: To Ur-Kasdim or Urkesh?" *JBQ* 33 (2005): 73–80.

Bimson, John J. "Archaeological Data and the Dating of the Patriarchs." In *Essays on the Patriarchal Narratives,* edited by A. R. Millard and D. J. Wiseman, 59–92. Leicester, 1980.

Bin-Nun, Yechiel. *Erez HaMoria: Pirkei Mikra VeLashon*, edited by Yo'el Bin-Nun. Alon Shevut, 1996 (Hebrew).

Bin-Nun, Yoel. *Chapters of the Fathers: Studies in Narratives of the Patriarchs in the Book of Genesis,* edited by H. Navon. Alon Shevut, 2003 .

Blenkinsopp, Joseph. "Abraham and the Righteous of Sodom." *JJS* 33 (1982): 119–132.

Blenkinsopp, Joseph. *Ezra-Nehemiah.* OTL. Philadelphia, 1988.

Block, Daniel I. "Nations/Nationality." *NIDOTTE* 4:966–972.

Block, Daniel I. *Judges, Ruth.* NAC. Nashville, 1999.

Blum, Erhard. "Der vermeintliche Gottesname 'Elohim.'" In *Gott Nennen: Gottes Namen und Gott als Name,* edited by I. U. Dalferth and Ph. Stoellger, 97–119. Tübingen, 2008.

Blum, Erhard. *Die Komposition der Vätergeschichte.* WMANT 57. Neukirchen-Vluyn, 1984.

Boda, Mark J. *Praying the Tradition: The Origin and Use of Tradition in Nehemiah 9*. Berlin, 1999.

Boehm, Omri. "The Binding of Isaac: An Inner-Biblical Polemic on the Question of 'Disobeying' a Manifestly Illegal Order." *VT* 52 (2002): 1–12.

Boehm, Omri. *The Binding of Isaac: A Religious Model of Disobedience.* New York, 2007.

Brawer, Abraham J. "Am HaAretz KiFeshuto BaMikra." *Beit Mikra* 15 (1970): 202–206 (Hebrew).

Brawer, Abraham J. "The Negotiations for Purchasing a Tomb in Hebron." *Beit Mikra* 4 (1966): 92–94 (Hebrew).

Brenner, Athalya. "On Incest." In *A Feminist Companion to Exodus to Deuteronomy,* edited by A. Brenner, 113–138. Sheffield, 1994.

Brenner, Athalya. "On the Semantic Field of Humor, Laughter, and the Comic in the Old Testament." In *On Humour and the Comic in the Hebrew Bible,* edited by Y. T. Radday and A. Brenner, 39–58. JSOTSup 92. Sheffield, 1990.

Breuer, Mordechai. *Pirkei Bereshit,* edited by Y. Ofer. 2 vols. Alon Shevut, 1999.

Briggs, Charles Augustus, and Emilie Grace Briggs. *A Critical and Exegetical Commentary on the Book of Psalms.* ICC. Edinburgh, 1907.

Bright, John. *A History of Israel.* 2nd ed. Philadelphia, 1972.

Brilmayer, Lea. "The Moral Significance of Nationalism." *Notre Dame Law Review* 71 (1995): 7–33.

Brodie, Thomas L. *Genesis as Dialogue: A Literary, Historical, and Theological Commentary*, New York, 2001.

Brodsky, Harold. "Bethel." *ABD* 1:710–712.

Bronner, Leila Leah. *The Stories of Elijah and Elisha as Polemics Against Baal Worship*. Leiden, 1968.

Brown-Driver-Briggs (BDB). *A Hebrew and English Lexicon of the Old Testament*. Oxford, 1906.

Brueggemann, Walter. "A Shape for Old Testament Theology, 1: Structure Legitimation." *CBQ* 47 (1985): 28–46.

Buber, Martin. *Darko shel Mikra*. Jerusalem, 1997 (Hebrew).

Callaway, Joseph. "Ai." *ABD* 1:125–130.

Canney, Maurice A. "Contribution and Comments: Shaddai." *The Expository Times* 34 (1923): 329–333.

Caquot, André. "L'alliance avec Abram (Genèse 15)." *Semitica* 12 (1962): 51–66.

Carmichael, Calum M. *Law, Legend, and Incest in the Bible: Leviticus 18–20*. Ithaca, 1997.

Carmy, Shalom. "A Room with a View, but a Room of Our Own." *Tradition* 28 (1994): 39–69.

Carr, David M. "'Biblos Geneseos' Revisited: A Synchronic Analysis of Patterns in Genesis as Part of the Torah." *ZAW* 110, 2 (1998): 159–172; 3: 327–347.

Carr, David M. *Reading the Fractures of Genesis: Historical and Literary Approaches*. Louisville, 1996.

Carroll R., M. Daniel. "Blessing of the Nations: Towards a Biblical Theology of Mission from Genesis." *Bulletin for Biblical Research* 10 (2000): 17–34.

Cassuto, Umberto. "Abraham." *Entziklopedya Mikra'it* 1:61–67 (Hebrew).

Cassuto, Umberto. "Bethel." *Entziklopedya Mikra'it* 2:61–67 (Hebrew).

Cassuto, Umberto. "Jacob." *Entziklopedya Mikra'it* 3:716–722 (Hebrew).

Cassuto, Umberto. *A Commentary on The Book of Genesis: From Adam to Noah*. Translated by Israel Abrahams. Magnes Press: Hebrew University, 1961.

Cassuto, Umberto. *A Commentary on the Book of Genesis: From Noah to Abraham*. Translated by Israel Abrahams. Magnes Press: Hebrew University, 1964.

Cassuto, Umberto. *Biblical and Canaanite Literatures: Studies on the Bible and Ancient Orient*. 2 vols. Jerusalem, 1979 (Hebrew).

Cassuto, Umberto. *The "Quaestio" of the Book of Genesis*. Translated by M. E. Hartom. Jerusalem, 1990 (Hebrew).

Chandler, Tertius. "When Was Abraham?" *Bibbia e Oriente* 50 (2008): 95–101.

Childs, Brevard S. *Old Testament Theology in a Canonical Context*. Philadelphia, 1986.

Chisholm, Robert B. "הפך." *NIDOTTE* 1:1048–1050.

Clements, Ronald E. "גוי." *TDOT* 2:426–433.
Clements, Ronald E. *In Spirit and in Truth: Insight from Biblical Prayers*. Atlanta, 1985.
Clines, David J.A. *What Does Eve Do to Help?: And Other Readerly Questions to the Old Testament*. JSOTSup 94. Sheffield, 1990.
Coats, George W. "Lot: A Foil in the Abraham Saga." In *Understanding the Word*, edited by J. T. Butler et al., 113–132. JSOTSup 37. Sheffield, 1985.
Coats, George W. *Genesis*. FOTL. Grand Rapids, MI, 1983.
Cody, Aelred. "When Is the Chosen People Called a *Goy*?" *VT* 14 (1964): 1–6.
Cogan, Mordechai. "'The City that I Chose' – The Deuteronomistic View of Jerusalem." *Tarbitz* 55 (1986): 301–309 (Hebrew).
Cohen, Hezi. "Abraham's Separation from Lot (Genesis 13)." *Megadim* 52 (2011): 9–22 (Hebrew).
Connor, Walker. "Nation-Building or Nation-Destroying?" *World Politics* 24 (1972): 319–355.
Cotter, David W. *Genesis*. Collegeville, MN: Berit Olam, 2003.
Craigie, Peter C. *Psalms 1–50*. WBC. Dallas, Texas, 1998.
Crenshaw, James L. *A Whirlpool of Torment: Israelite Traditions of God as an Oppressive Presence*. Overtures to Biblical Theology 12. Philadelphia, 1984.
Cross, Frank Moore. "אל." *TDOT* 1:242–261.
Cross, Frank Moore. *Canaanite Myth and Hebrew Epic: Essays in the History of the Religion of Israel*. Cambridge, 1973.
Crotty, Robert. "The Literary Structure of the Binding of Isaac in Genesis 22." *ABR* 53 (2005): 31–41.
Culley, Robert C. *Studies in the Structure of Hebrew Narrative*. Philadelphia, 1976.
Dahood, Mitchell. *Psalms*. AB. Garden City, NY, 1970.
Daube, David. "Rechtsgedanken in den Erzählungen des Pentateuchs." In *Von Ugarit nach Qumran: Beiträge zur alttestamentlichen und altorientalischen Forschung*, edited by O. Eissfeldt, 32–41. *ZAW* 77. Berlin, 1958.
Davidson, Robert. *Genesis 12–50*. CBC. Cambridge, 1979.
De Vaux, Roland. *Ancient Israel: Its Life and Institutions*. Translated by J. McHugh. 2nd ed. London, 1965.
Delitzsch, Franz. *Neuer Commentar über die Genesis*. Leipzig, 1887.
Dhorme, Edouard P. "Abraham dans le Cadre de l'Histoire." *RB* 37 (1928): 367–386.
Dillmann, August. *Genesis, Critically and Exegetically Expounded*. Translated by William Baron Stevenson. 2 vols. Edinburgh, 1897.
Dore, Joseph. "La rencontre Abraham-Melchisedech et le probleme de I'unite litteraire du Genese 14." In *De la Torah au Messie*, edited by M. Carrez, J. Dore, and P. Grelot, 75–95. Paris, 1981.

Douglas, Mary. *Thinking in Circles: An Essay on Ring Composition*. New Haven, CT, and London, 2007.

Doukhan, Jacques B. "The Center of the Aqedah: A Study of the Literary Structure of Genesis 22:1–19." *AUSS* 31 (1993): 17–28.

Doyle, Brian. "'Knock, Knock, Knockin' on Sodom's Door': The Function of פתח/דלת in Genesis 18–19." *JSOT* 28 (2004): 431–448.

Dozeman, Thomas B. "The Wilderness and Salvation History in the Hagar Story." *JBL* 117 (1998): 23–43.

Drey, Philip R. "The Role of Hagar in Genesis 16." *AUSS* 40 (2002): 179–195.

Driver, Samuel Rolles. "On Some Alleged Linguistic Affinities of the Elohist." *The Journal of Philology* 11 (1882): 201–236.

Driver, Samuel Rolles. *The Book of Genesis*. Westminster Commentaries (10th ed.). London, 1916.

Dvir, Jehuda. *Biblical Proper Names and Their Mission*. Tel Aviv, 1969 (Hebrew).

Efal, Yisrael. "*Kedem, Benei Kedem, Eretz Benei Kedem*." *Entziklopedya Mikra'it* 7:26–29 (Hebrew).

Ehrlich, Arnold B. *Mikra KiFeshuto: The Bible According to Its Literal Meaning*. Edited by H. M. Orlinsky. 3 vols. New York, 1969 (Hebrew).

Eichler, Barry L. "On Reading Genesis 12:10–20." In *Tehillah le-Moshe: Biblical and Judaic Studies in Honor of Moshe Greenberg*, edited by M. Cogan, B. L. Eichler, and J. H. Tigay, 23–38. Winona Lake, IN, 1997.

Eichler, Barry L. "'Say That You Are My Sister': Nuzi and Biblical Studies." *Shnaton: An Annual for Biblical and Ancient Near Eastern Studies* 3 (1978): 108–115 (Hebrew).

Eichrodt, Walther. *Theology of the Old Testament*. Translated by J. A. Baker. Vol. 1. OTL. Philadelphia, 1961.

Eldar, Itamar. "The Servant and Rebecca Narrative." *Alon Shevut* 153 (1999): 137–149.

Elgavish, David. "The Encounter of Abram and Melchizedek King of Salem: A Covenant Establishing Ceremony." In *Studies in the Book of Genesis; Literature, Redaction and History*, edited by A. Wénin, 495–508. Leuven, 2001.

Elitzur, Yehuda. "Key Words as Indicators of Hidden Meaning in Biblical Passages and the Question of *Mimoḥorat HaShabbat*." *Megadim* 38 (2003): 33–42 (Hebrew).

Elmslie, W. A. L. "Ethics." In *Record and Revelation*, edited by H. Wheeler Robinson, 275–302. Oxford, 1938.

Emanueli, Yitzhak Moshe. *Genesis – Commentary and Insights*. Tel Aviv, 1978 (Hebrew)

Emerton, John A. "A Consideration of Some Alleged Meanings of *yd'* in Hebrew." *JSS* 15 (1970): 145–180.

Emerton, John A. "The Riddle of Genesis xiv." *VT* 21 (1971): 403–439.
Etshalom, Yitzchak. *Between the Lines of the Bible: Genesis: Recapturing the Full Meaning of the Biblical Text.* Jerusalem and New York, 2015.
Exum, J. Cheryl. "Desire Distorted and Exhibited: Lot and His Daughters in Psychoanalysis, Painting, and Film." In *"A Wise and Discerning Mind": Essays in Honor of Burke O. Long.* Edited by S. M. Olyan and R. C. Culley, 83–108. Providence, RI, 2000.
Exum, J. Cheryl. "Who's Afraid of the 'Endangered Ancestress'?" In *The New Literary Criticism and the Hebrew Bible.* Edited by D. J. A. Clines and J. C. Exum, 91–113. JSOTSup 143. Sheffield, 1993.
Exum, J. Cheryl, and J. William Whedbee. "Isaac, Samson, and Saul: Reflections on the Comic and Tragic Visions." In *On Humour and the Comic in the Hebrew Bible,* edited by Y. T. Radday and A. Brenner, 117–160. JSOTSup 92. Sheffield, 1990.
Feldman, Louis H. *Flavius Josephus: Translation and Commentary. Volume 3 – Judean Antiquities 1–4.* Leiden: Brill, 2000.
Fensham, F. Charles. "The Son of a Handmaid in Northwest Semitic." *VT* 19 (1969): 312–321.
Fidler, Ruth. "Abimelech's Dream in the Context of the 'Matriarch in Danger' Genre." *Turra* 2 (1991): 19–38 (Hebrew).
Fidler, Ruth. *"Dreams Speak Falsely?" Dream Theophanies in the Bible: Their Place in Ancient Israelite Faith and Traditions.* Jerusalem, 2005 (Hebrew).
Fidler, Ruth. "Genesis XV: Sequence and Unity." *VT* 57 (2007): 162–180.
Finkelstein, Israel, and Thomas Römer. "Comments on the Historical Background of the Abraham Narrative: Between 'Realia' and 'Exegetica,'" *Hebrew Bible and Ancient Israel* 3 (2014): 3–23.
Finkelstein, Jacob Joel. "*Mishpat, HaMishpat BaMizraḥ HaKadmon.*" *Entziklopedya Mikra'it* 5:588–614 (Hebrew).
Finlay, Timothy D. *The Birth Report Genre in the Hebrew Bible.* Tübingen, 2005.
Fisch, Harold. *The Holy Scriptures.* Jerusalem, 1977.
Fisch, Harold. "Ruth and the Structure of Covenant History." *VT* 32 (1982): 423–437.
Fishbane, Michael. "The Treaty Background of Amos 1:11 and Related Matters." *JBL* 89 (1970): 313–318.
Fisher, Loren R. "Abraham and His Priest-King." *JBL* 81 (1962): 264–270.
Fleishman, Joseph. "Name Change and Circumcision in Genesis 17." *Beit Mikra* 46 (2001): 310–321 (Hebrew).
Fleishman, Joseph. "The Expulsion of Ishmael." *Beit Mikra* 44 (1999): 146–162 (Hebrew).
Fleming, Daniel E. *The Installation of Baal's High Priestess at Emar: A Window on Ancient Syrian Religion.* Atlanta, 1992.

Fokkelman, Jan P. *Reading Biblical Narrative: An Introductory Guide*. Translated by I. Smit. Louisville, 1999.

Fox, Michael V. "Sign of the Covenant: Circumcision in the Light of the Priestly 'ot Etiologies." *RB* 81 (1974): 537–596.

Frankel, Jonathan. *The Damascus Affair: 'Ritual Murder,' Politics, and the Jews in 1840*. Cambridge, 1997.

Frayne, Douglas. "In Abraham's Footsteps." In vol. 1 of *The World of the Aramaeans: Studies in Honour of Paul-Eugène Dion*, edited by P. M. M. Daviau, J. Wevers, and M. Weigl, 216–236. Sheffield, 2001.

Frazer, James George. *Totemism and Exogamy: A Treatise on Certain Early Forms of Superstition and Society*. 4 vols. London, 1910.

Freedman, David Noel. "The Real Formal Full Personal Name of the God of Israel." In *Sacred History, Sacred Literature: Essays on Ancient Israel, the Bible, and Religion in Honor of R. E. Friedman on His 60th Birthday*, edited by S. Dolansky, 81–89. Winona Lake, IN, 2008.

Fretheim, Terrence E. "ידע." *NIDOTTE* 2:411.

Fretheim, Terrence E. "The Book of Genesis: Introduction, Commentary, and Reflections." In *The New Interpreter's Bible*, edited by L. E. Keck et al., 319–674. Nashville, 1994.

Friedler, Shevach (et al.). "The Effect of Medical Clowning on Pregnancy Rates after In Vitro Fertilization and Embryo Transfer." *Fertil and Steril* 95 (2011): 2127–2130.

Frisch, Amos. "SH-M-A and R-E-H as a Pair of Leitwörter." *Proceeding of the Twelfth World Congress of Jewish Studies* Division A (1999): 89–98 (Hebrew).

Frymer-Kensky, Tikva. "Virginity in the Bible." In *Gender and Law in the Hebrew Bible and the Ancient Near East*, edited by Victor H. Matthews, Bernard M. Levinson, and Tikva Frymer-Kensky, 79–96. Sheffield, 1998.

Garsiel, Moshe. *Biblical Names: A Literary Study of Midrashic Derivations and Puns*. Translated by Phyllis Hacket. Ramat Gan, 1991.

Garsiel, Moshe. *The First Book of Samuel: A Literary Study of Comparative Structures, Analogies and Parallels*. Ramat Gan, 1983 (Hebrew).

Gelander, Shamai. "Defus Sifruti VeHistorya." In *Haim M. I. Gevaryahu: Memorial Volume*, edited by J. Adler, 48–56. Jerusalem, 1990 (Hebrew).

Gelander, Shamai. *Art and Idea in Biblical Narrative*. Tel Aviv: Hakibbutz Hameuchad, 1997 (Hebrew).

Gelander, Shamai. *Studies in the Book of Genesis*. 2 vols. Ra'anana: The Open University of Israel, 2009 (Hebrew).

Gerleman, Gillis. "Nutzrecht und Wohnrecht: Zur Bedeutung von אחזה und נחלה." *ZAW* 89 (1977): 313–325.

Gevirtz, Stanley. "Of Patriarchs and Puns: Joseph at the Fountain, Jacob at the Ford." *HUCA* 46 (1975): 33–54.

Giesebrecht, Friedrich. "Zum Hexateuchkritik: Der Sprachgebrauch des Hexateuchischen Elohisten." *ZAW* 1 (1881): 177–276.

Gilad, Chaim. "Hine Hu Lakh Kesut Einayim." *Beit Mikra* 22 (1977): 43–45 (Hebrew).

Ginzberg, Louis. *Legends of the Jews*. Translated by H. Szold. Vol. 1. Philadelphia, 1961.

Gitay, Yehoshua. "Geography and Theology in the Biblical Narrative: The Question of Genesis 2–12." In *Prophets and Paradigms: Essays in Honor of Gene M. Tucker*, edited by S. B. Reid, 205–216. JSOTSup 229. Sheffield, 1996.

Goldingay, John. "The Place of Ishmael." In *The World of Genesis; Persons, Places, Perspectives*, edited by P. R. Davies and D. J. A. Clines, 146–149. Sheffield, 1998.

Goldingay, John. "The Significance of Circumcision." *JSOT* 88 (2000): 3–18.

Gordis, Daniel. "The Tower of Babel and the Birth of Nationhood." *Azure* 40 (2010): 19–36.

Gordis, Robert. *The Word and the Book: Studies in Biblical Language and Literature*. New York, 1976.

Gordon, Cyrus H. "Biblical Customs and the Nuzu Tablets." *BA* 3, no. 1 (1940): 1–12.

Gossai, Hemchand. *Power and Marginality in the Abraham Narrative*. Lanham, MD, 1995.

Gray, John. *Joshua, Judges, and Ruth*. New Century Bible Commentary. London, 1986.

Grayson, Albert Kirk, and John van Seters. "The Childless Wife in Assyrian and the Stories of Genesis." *Orientalia* 44 (1975): 486–485.

Greenberg, Moshe. *Ezekiel 21–37*. AB. New York, 1997.

Greengus, Samuel. "Sisterhood Adoption at Nuzi and the 'Wife-Sister' in Genesis." *HUCA* 46 (1975): 5–31.

Greenstein, Edward L. "Reading Pragmatically: The Binding of Isaac." In *Words, Ideas, Worlds: Biblical Essays in Honour of Yairah Amit*, edited by A. Brenner and F. Polak, 102–132. Sheffield, 2012.

Grintz, Yehoshua M. *The Book of Genesis: Its Uniqueness and Antiquity*. Jerusalem, 1983 (Hebrew).

Grönbäk, Jakob H. "Juda und Amalek – Uberlieferungsgeschichtliche Erwägungen zu Exodus 17, 8–16." *Studia Theologica* 18 (1964): 26–45.

Grossman, Avraham. *Rashi*. Jerusalem: Zalman Shazar Center, 2006 (Hebrew).

Grossman, Jonathan. "Abrabanel's Stance towards the Existence of Ambiguous Expressions in the Bible." *Beit Mikra* 52 (2007): 126–138 (Hebrew).

Grossman, Jonathan. *Ambiguity in the Biblical Narrative and Its Contribution to the Literary Formation*. PhD diss., Bar Ilan University, 2006 (Hebrew).

Grossman, Jonathan. "Deliberate Misuse of Idioms in the Biblical Narrative." *Tarbitz* 77 (2008): 23–44 (Hebrew).

Grossman, Jonathan. "Dynamic Analogies in the Book of Esther." *VT* 59 (2009): 394–414.

Grossman, Jonathan. *Esther: The Outer Narrative and the Hidden Reading.* Siphrut: Literature and Theology of the Hebrew Scriptures 6. Winona Lake, IN, 2011.

Grossman, Jonathan. "Hagar's Characterization in Genesis and the Explanation of Ishmael's Blessing." *Beit Mikra* 63 (2018): 249–286 (Hebrew).

Grossman, Jonathan. *Joseph: A Tale of Dreams.* Rishon LeZion, 2021.

Grossman, Jonathan, and Sara Daniel. "'Like Arrows in the Hand of the Warrior, So Are Youths': Reading Ishmael's Expulsion in Genesis 21 in Light of Hermann Hesse's 'Siddhartha.'" *Hebrew Studies* 57 (2016): 73–91.

Grossman, Jonathan. *Text and Subtext: On Exploring Biblical Narrative Design.* Tel Aviv, 2015 (Hebrew).

Grossman, Jonathan. "The Binding of Isaac and the Sinai Covenant." In *The Sacrifice of Isaac in Israeli Eyes: Memorial Volume to Yitzhak Hirschberg,* edited by I. Rosenson and B. Lau, 355–364. Tel Aviv, 2003 (Hebrew).

Grossman, Jonathan. "The Expulsion of Ishmael Narrative – Boundaries, Structure and Meaning." In *Doubling and Duplicating in the Book of Genesis: Literary and Stylistic Approaches to the Text,* edited by Elizabeth R. Hayes and Karolien Vermeulen, 27–37. Winona Lake, IN, 2016.

Grossman, Jonathan. "The Notions of 'Savage' and 'Cultured' in Genesis and in The Epic of Gilgamesh: A Structural Analysis." In *Lilkot Shoshanim: LeZikhrah shel Shoshana Kind,* edited by G. Kind, 349–368. Jerusalem: Revava, 2007 (Hebrew).

Grossman, Jonathan. "The Story of Joseph's Brothers in Light of the 'Therapeutic Narrative' Theory." *Biblical Interpretation* 21 (2013): 171–195.

Grossman, Jonathan. "The Use of Ambiguity in Biblical Narratives of Misleading and Deceit." *Tarbitz* 73 (2004): 483–515 (Hebrew).

Grossman, Jonathan. "The Vanishing Character in Biblical Narrative: The Role of Hathach in Esther 4." *VT* 62 (2012): 561–571.

Grossman, Jonathan. "Two 'Doubled' Narratives in Genesis: Hagar's Departure (16; 21) and the Announcement of Isaac's Birth (17–18)." *Megadim* 29 (1998): 9–30 (Hebrew).

Grossman, Jonathan. "'What You Vow, Fulfill': The Meaning of Jacob's Struggle with the Angel." *Megadim* 26 (1996): 9–26 (Hebrew).

Gruber, Mayer I. "A Re-Examination of the Charges Against Shechem Son of Hamor." *Beit Mikra* 157 (1999): 119–127 (Hebrew).

Gunkel, Hermann. *Genesis – Translated and Interpreted.* Translated by M. E. Biddle. Macon, GA, 1997.

Gunn, David M., and Danna Nolan Fewell. *Narrative in the Hebrew Bible*. Oxford Bible Series. Oxford, 1993.

Guttman, Yehoshua. "Aram." *Entziklopedya Mikra'it* 1:573–577 (Hebrew).

Ha, John. *Genesis 15: A Theological Compendium of Pentateuchal History*. BZAW 181. Berlin and New York, 1989.

Habel, Norman C. "The Form and Significance of the Call Narrative." *ZAW* 77 (1965): 297–323.

Halevy, Joseph. *Recherches Bibliques*. 5 vols. Paris, 1895.

Hall, Robert G. "Circumcision." *ABD* 1:1025–1031.

Hallo, William W. "Biblical History in Its Near Eastern Setting: The Contextual Approach." In *Scripture in Context: Essays on the Comparative Method*, edited by C. D. Evans, 1–26. Pittsburg, 1980.

Hals, Ronald M. *The Theology of the Book of Ruth*. Philadelphia, 1969.

Hamilton, Victor P. "מלח." *NIDOTTE* 2:947–949.

Hamilton, Victor P. *The Book of Genesis, Chapters 1–17*. NICOT. Grand Rapids, MI, 1990.

Hamilton, Victor P. *The Book of Genesis, Chapters 18–50*. NICOT. Grand Rapids, MI, 1995.

Harland, James Penrose. "The Destruction of the Cites of the Plain." *BA* 6 (1943): 41–52.

Harland, James Penrose. "The Location of the Cities of the Plain." *BA* 5 (1942): 17–32.

Hartom, Elia S. "Covenant." *Entziklopedya Mikra'it* 2:347–351 (Hebrew).

Harvey, Bruce J. *Yhwh Elohim: A Survey of Occurrences in the Leningrad Codex and Their Corresponding Septuagintal Renderings*. New York and London, 2011.

Harvey, John E. *Retelling the Torah: The Deuternonmistic Historian's Use of Tetrateuchal Narratives*. JSOTSup 403. London, 2004.

Hasel, Gerhard F. "The Meaning of the Chronogenealogies of Genesis 5 and 11." *Origins* 7 (1980): 53–70.

Hawk, Lewis Daniel. *Every Promise Fulfilled: Contesting Plots in Joshua*. Literary Currents in Biblical Interpretation. Louisville, 1991.

Heard, R. Christopher. *Dynamics of Diselection: Ambiguity in Genesis 12–36 and Ethnic Boundaries in Post-Exilic Judah*. SBLSS 39. Atlanta, 2001.

Hegel, Georg Wilhelm Friedrich. "Grundlinien der Philosophie des Rechts." In *Werke in zwanzig Bänden*, edited by E. Moldenhauer and K. M. Michel. Vol. 3. Frankfurt am Main: Suhrkamp Verlag, 1970.

Heinemann, Isaac. *The Methods of the Aggada*. 2nd ed. Jerusalem, 1954 (Hebrew).

Helfgot, Nathaniel. *Mikra and Meaning: Studies in Bible and Its Interpretation*. Jerusalem, 2012.

Helyer, Larry Randall. "The Separation of Abram and Lot: Its Significance in the Patriarchal Narratives." *JSOT* 26 (1983): 77–88.

Herrmann, Siegfried. *A History of Israel in the Old Testament Times*. Translated by J. Bowden. Philadelphia, 1975.

Hertz, Joseph H. *The Pentateuch and Haftorahs*. London, 1952.

Herzog, Ze'ev. "Fortifications (Levant)." *ABD* 2:844–852.

Hess, Richard. "שער." *NIDOTTE* 4:208–211.

Hiebert, Theodore. "The Tower of Babel and the Origin of the World's Cultures." *JBL* 126 (2007): 29–58.

Ho, Craig Y. S. "The Stories of the Family Troubles of Judah and David: A Study of Their Literary Links." *VT* 49 (1999): 514–531.

Hoffman, A. "Between Absolutism and Revolution: Rousseau and the 'Social Contract' in Historical Context." In *Jean-Jacques Rousseau's The Social Contract*, translated by Ido Bassok. Tel Aviv, 2006 (Hebrew).

Hoffner Jr., Harry Angier. *The Laws of the Hittites: A Critical Edition*. Leiden, 1997.

Hoftijzer, Jacob. *Die Verheißungen an die drei Erzväter*. Leiden, 1956.

Horsley, Greg H. R. "Names, Double." *Anchor Bible Dictionary*. Vol. 4. Edited by David N. Freedman et al., 1011–1017. New York, 1992.

Huffmon, Herbert B. "The Treaty Background of Hebrew Yāda." *BASOR* 191 (1966): 31–37.

Hutchinson, John, and Anthony Smith. *Nationalism*. New York: Oxford University Press, 1994.

Irwin, William A. "The Hebrews." In *The Intellectual Adventure of Ancient Man: An Essay of Speculative Thought in the Ancient Near East*, edited by H. Frankfort et al., 223–360. Chicago, 1946.

Isaac, Eric. "Circumcision as Covenant Rite." *Anthropos* 59 (1965): 444–456.

Jacob, Benno. *The First Book of the Bible: Genesis*. Translated by E. I. Jacob and W. Jacob. New York, 1974.

Jacobs, Jonathan. "Willing Obedience with Doubts: Abraham at the Binding of Isaac." *VT* 60 (2010): 546–559.

Jacobs, Jonathan. *Measure for Measure in the Storytelling Bible*. Alon Shevut, 2006 (Hebrew).

Jacobsen, Lea. *Aspects of the Legal Status of the Mother in the Ancient Near East and the Bible – A Comparative Study*. PhD diss., Bar Ilan University, 2011 (Hebrew).

Jeansonne, Sharon Pace. "The Characterization of Lot in Genesis." *BTB* 18 (1988): 123–129.

Jenkins, Allan K. "A Great Name: Genesis 12:2 and the Editing of the Pentateuch." *JSOT* 10 (1978): 41–57.

Jenks, Alan W. "Eating and Drinking in the Old Testament." *ABD*, 2: 252–253.

Kaddari, Menahem Zevi. *A Dictionary of Biblical Hebrew*. Ramat Gan, 2006 (Hebrew).

Kahana, Avraham. *Bible Series with Scientific Commentary*. Zhitomir, 1903 (Hebrew).

Kalimi, Isaac. "The Land of Moriah, Mount Moriah and the Site of Solomon's Temple in Biblical Historiography." *Shnaton* 11 (1997): 180–194 (Hebrew).

Kallai, Zekharyah. "The Wandering-Traditions from Kadesh-Barnea to Canaan: A Study in Biblical Historiography." *JJS* 33 (1982): 175–184.

Kalumba, Bertin. "L'emploi programmatique du nom divin YHWH: Ex 6,3 et son context." *Estudios Bíblicos* 67 (2009): 537–581.

Kant, Immanuel. *Religion and Rational Theology*. Edited and translated by A. W. Wood and G. Di Giovanni. Cambridge, 1996.

Kant, Immanuel. *The Conflict of the Faculties (Der Streit der Fakultaten)*. Translated by Mary J. Gregor. New York: Abaris Books, 1979.

Kaplan, Aryeh. *The Living Torah*. 5 vols. New York and Jerusalem, 1981.

Kasher, Menachem Mendel. *Torah Shelema*. 45 vols. Jerusalem, 1992 (Hebrew).

Kasher, Rimon. "Jehoshaphat's Victory: Proportions, Parallels, and Significance." *Beit Mikra* 31 (1986): 242–51 (Hebrew).

Kaufmann, Yehezkel. *The Religion of Israel*. 8 vols. Jerusalem, 1953 (Hebrew).

Kedourie, Elie. *Nationalism*. Oxford and Cambridge, MA, 1993.

Keil, Karl Friedrich, and Franz Delitzsch. *Biblical Commentary on the Old Testament: Volume I: The Pentateuch*. Translated by J. Martin. Grand Rapids, MI, 1980.

Kidner, Derek. *Genesis*. TOTC. London, 1967.

Kiel, Yehuda. *Daat Mikra: Genesis*. Vol. 1. Jerusalem, 1997 (Hebrew).

Kiel, Yehuda. *Daat Mikra: Genesis*. Vol. 2. Jerusalem, 2000 (Hebrew).

Kilian, Rudolf. "Zur Uberlieferungsgeschichte Lots." *BZ* 14 (1970): 23–37.

Kilian, Rudolf. *Die Vorpriesterlichen Abrahams-Überlieferungen, Literarkritisch und Traditionsgeschichtlich Untersucht*. BBB 24. Bonn, 1966.

Kitchen, Kenneth A. "Genesis 12–50 in the Near Eastern World." In *He Swore an Oath: Biblical Themes from Genesis 12–50*, edited by R. S. Hess, G. J. Wenham, and P. E. Satterthwaite, 67–92. 2nd edition. Carlisle, UK, 1994.

Klitsner, Judy. *Subversive Sequels in the Bible: How Biblical Stories Mine and Undermine Each Other*. Jerusalem, 2011.

Knauf, Ernst Axel. *Ismael: Untersuchungen zur Geschichte Palästinas und Nordarabiens im 1. Jahrtausend v. Chr*. Wiesbaden, 1985.

Koch, Klaus. "Die Toledot-Formeln als Strukturprinzip des Buches Genesis." In *Recht und Ethos im Alten Testament – Gestalt und Wirkung*, edited by S. Beyerle, G. Mayer, and H. Strauss, 183–191. Neukirchen-Vluyn, 1999.

Koch, Klaus. "*Pahad jishaq*: eine Gottesbezeichnung?" In *Werden und Wirken des Allen Testaments: Festschrift für Claus Westermann*, edited by R. Albertz et al., 107–115. Göttingen, 1980.

Köckert, Matthias. "'Glaube' und 'Gerechtigkeit' in Gen 15,6." *Zeitschrift für Theologie und Kirche* 109 (2012): 415–444.

Koehler, Ludwig, and Walter Baumgartner. *Lexicon in Veteris Testamenti Libros*. Leiden, 1953.

Kogut, Simcha. *Syntax and Exegesis: Studies in Biblical Syntax as Reflected in Traditional Jewish Exegesis*. Jerusalem, 2002 (Hebrew).

Kohn, Hans. *The Idea of Nationalism*. New York, 1944.

Kohn, Hans. *Nationalism: Its Meaning and History*. Malabar, FL, 1982, 1965.

Aaron Koller, *Unbinding Isaac: The Significance of the Akedah for Modern Jewish Thought*. Philadelphia and Lincoln, 2020.

Konkel, August H. "זעק." *NIDOTTE* 1:1131.

Koschaker, Paul. "Fratriarchat, Hausgemeinschaft, und Mutterrecht in Keilschriftrechten." *ZA* 41 (1933): 1–89.

Kremnitzer, Mordechai. "The Jewish State Bill: A Danger for Zionist Enterprise." *Makor Rishon*, May 9, 2014.

Kruger, Paul. "פלא." *NIDOTTE* 3:616.

Kutsch, Ernst. "Gesetz und Gnade: Probleme des alttestamentlichen Bundesbegriffs." *ZAW* 79 (1967): 18–35.

Langlame, François. "Josué II et les traditions de l'Héxateuque." *RB* 78 (1971): 5–17, 161–183, 321–354.

Lasine, Stuart. "Guest and Host in Judges 19: Lot's Hospitality in an Inverted World." *JSOT* 29 (1984): 35–59.

Leech, Geoffrey. *Semantics*. Harmondsworth, 1974.

Lehmann, Manfred R. "Abraham's Purchase of Machpelah and Hittite Law." *BASOR* 129 (1953): 15–18.

Leibowitz, Nechama. "How to Read a Chapter of the Bible." *Reflections on the Bible* 1 (1973): 129–138 (Hebrew).

Leibowitz, Nechama. *Studies in Genesis*. Jerusalem: World Zionist Organization, 1966 (Hebrew).

Lemaire, Andre. "La Haute Mésopotamie et l'origine des Benê Jacob." *VT* 34 (1984): 95–101.

Letellier, Robert Ignatius. *Day in Mamre, Night in Sodom: Abraham and Lot in Genesis 18 and 19*. Biblical Interpretation Series 10. Leiden, 1995.

Levenson, Jon D. *The Death and Resurrection of the Beloved Son*. New Haven, CT, 1993.

Levenson, Jon D. "Abusing Abraham: Traditions, Religious Histories, and Modern Misinterpretations." *Judaism* 47 (1998): 259–277.

Levenson, Jon D. *Inheriting Abraham: The Legacy of the Patriarch in Judaism, Christianity and Islam*. Princeton and Oxford, 2012.

Levi-Strauss, Claude. *The Elementary Structures of Kinship*. Translated by J. H. Bell, J. R. von Sturmer, and R. Needham. Boston, 1969.

Lev-Ran, Yitzhak. *Narrative Modes for Presenting Complexity of Inner Life of Biblical Characters*. PhD. diss., Bar Ilan University, 2009 (Hebrew).

Licht, Jacob. *Testing in the Hebrew Scriptures and in Post-Biblical Judaism*. Jerusalem, 1973 (Hebrew).

Licht, Jacob. "*Am*." *Entziklopedya Mikra'it* 4:235–239 (Hebrew).

Licht, Jacob. *Storytelling in the Bible*. Jerusalem, 1978.

Lipiński, Edward. "עם." *TDOT* 11:163–177.

Lipka, Hilary B. *Sexual Transgression in the Hebrew Bible*. Sheffield, 2006.

Lipton, Diana. *Revisions of the Night: Politics and Promises in the Patriarchal Dreams of Genesis*. JSOTSup 288. Sheffield, 1999.

Loader, James Alfred. "The Sin of Sodom in the Talmud and Midrash." *Old Testament Essays* 3 (1990): 231–245.

Loewenstamm, Samuel E. "*Yerusha*." *Entziklopedya Mikra'it* 3:788–791 (Hebrew).

Loewenstamm, Samuel E. "Moriah, the Land of Moriah." *Entziklopedya Mikra'it* 5:458–460 (Hebrew).

Lohfink, Norbert. "ירש." *TDOT* 6:368–396.

Long, Burke O. "The Effect of Divination upon Israelite Literature." *JBL* 92 (1973): 489–497.

Low, Katherine B. "The Sexual Abuse of Lot's Daughters: Reconceptualizing Kinship for the Sake of Our Daughters." *JFSR* 26 (2010): 37–54.

Lubetski, Meir. "Lot's Choice: Paradise or Purgatory." *Jewish Studies at the Turn of the Century* 1 (1999): 164–172.

Lundbom, Jack R. "Parataxis, Rhetorical Structure and the Dialogue over Sodom in Genesis 18." In *The World of Genesis: Persons, Places, Perspectives*, edited by P. R. Davies and D. J. A. Clines, 136–145. JSOTSup 257. Sheffield, 1998.

Luzzatto, Samuel David. *The Book of Genesis*. Translated by Daniel A. Klein. Northvale, NJ, 1998.

Lyons, William John. *Canon and Exegesis: Canonical Praxis and the Sodom Narrative*. JSOTSup 352. London, 2002.

MacDonald, Nathan. "Listening to Abraham – Listening to Yhwh: Divine Justice and Mercy in Genesis 18:16–33." *CBQ* 66 (2004): 25–43.

MacDonald, Nathan. "Driving a Hard Bargain? Genesis 23 and Models of Economic Exchange." In *Anthropology and Biblical Studies: The Way Forward*, edited by M. I. Aguilar and L. J. Lawrence, 79–96. Leiden, 2004.

Machinist, Peter. "Outsiders and Insiders: The Biblical View of Emergent Israel and Its Contexts." In *The Other in Jewish Thought and History: Constructions of Jewish Culture and Identity*, edited by L. J. Silberstein and R. L. Cohn, 35–60. New York, 1994.

Mackay, Cameron. "Salem." *PEQ* 80–81 (1948/9): 121–130.

Mafico, Temba L. J. "The Divine Compound Name Yhwh Elohim and Israel's Monotheistic Polytheism." *Journal of Northwest Semitic Languages* 22 (1996): 155–173.

Malach, Assaf. "The Bases for the Legitimacy of a Jewish Nation-state in a Post-modern Era." Diss., Bar Ilan University, 2009.

Malamat, Abraham. "'Haserim' in the Bible and Mari." *Yediot Bahaqirat Eretz-Israel Weatiqoteha* 27 (1963): 181–184 (Hebrew).

Malamat, Abraham. "On the Study of the Israelite Pre-History of the People of Israel." In *The Controversy over the Historicity of the Bible*, edited by L. Levine and A. Mazar, 112–123. Jerusalem: Yad Itzhak Ben Zvi, 2001 (Hebrew).

Malul, Meir. "The Origins of Israelite Self-Perception – the Motif of the Other and the Foundling." *Zion* 67 (2002): 5–18 (Hebrew).

Malul, Meir. *Law Collections and Other Legal Compilations from the Ancient Near East*. Haifa, 2000 (Hebrew).

Mann, Thomas W. "'All the Families of the Earth': The Theological Unity of Genesis." *Interpretation* 45 (1991): 341–353.

Marcus, Yosef. "The Role of the Prophet in Israel – The Figure of the Shunammite Woman as a Case Study." *Megadim* 51 (2010): 31–40 (Hebrew).

Marsman, Hennie J. *Women in Ugarit and Israel: Their Social and Religious Position in the Context of the Ancient Near East*. *OTS* 49. Leiden and Boston, 2003.

Mathews, Kenneth A. *Genesis*. 2 vols. NAC. Nashville, 2005.

Matthews, Victor H. "Hospitality and Hostility in Genesis 19 and Judges 19." *BTB* 22 (1992): 3–11.

McCarter, P. Kyle Jr. "The Historical Abraham." *Interpretation* 42 (1988): 341–352.

McCarthy, Carmel. *The Tiqqune Sopherim and Other Theological Corrections in the Masoretic Text of the Old Testament*. OBO 36. Freiburg and Göttingen: Universitaetsverlag, 1981.

McCarthy, Dennis J. *Treaty and Covenant: A Study in Form in the Ancient Oriental Documents and in the Old Testament*. AnBib 21. Rome, 1978.

McComiskey, Thomas Edward. "The Religion of the Patriarchs: An Analysis of The God of the Fathers by Albrecht Alt." In *The Law and the Prophets*, edited by J. H. Skilton, 195–206. Nutley, NJ, 1974.

McComiskey, Thomas Edward. *The Covenants of Promise: A Theology of the Old Testament Covenants*. Grand Rapids, MI, 1985.

McConville, J. Gordon. "Abraham and Melhizedek: Horizons in Genesis 14." In *He Swore an Oath: Biblical Themes from Genesis 12–50*, edited by R. S. Hess, G. J. Wenham, and P. E. Satterthwaite, 93–118. 2nd ed. Carlisle, UK, 1994.

McConville, J. Gordon. "ברית." *NIDOTTE* 1:747–755.

McEvenue, Sean E. "The Elohist at Work." *ZAW* 96 (1984): 315–332.

McEvenue, Sean E. *The Narrative Style of the Priestly Writer*. AnBib 50. Rome, 1971.

Meacham, Tirzah. "The Missing Daughter: Leviticus 18 and 20." *ZAW* 109 (1997): 254–259.

Medan, Rabbi Yaakov, *The Word Is Very Near – Bereshit*. Tel Aviv, 2014.

Meier, Samuel A. *Speaking of Speaking: Marking Direct Discourse in the Hebrew Bible*. VTSup 46. Leiden, NY, and Köln: E. J. Brill, 1992.

Melamed, Ezra Zion. "Purchase of the Cave of Machpelah." *Tarbitz* 14 (1942), 11–18.

Mendelsohn, Isaac. "Divination." *IDB*, vol. 1, 856–858.

Mendenhall, George E. "Covenant Forms in Israelite Tradition." *BA* 17 (1954): 50–76.

Milgrom, Jacob. *Cult and Conscience: The Asham and the Priestly Doctrine of Repentance*. Leiden, 1976.

Moberly, Robert Walter L. "The Earliest Commentary on the Akedah." *VT* 38 (1988): 302–323.

Moberly, Robert Walter L. *Genesis 12–50*. OTG. Sheffield, 1995.

Montgomery, James A. "The *hemzah-h* in the Semitic." *JBL* 46 (1927): 144–146.

Moran, William L. "The Scandal of the 'Great Sin' at Ugarit." *JNES* 18 (1959): 280–281.

Morgenstern, Julian. *The Book of Genesis: A Jewish Interpretation*. New York, 1965.

Morschauser, Scott N. "Hospitality, Hostiles and Hostages: On the Legal Background to Genesis 19.1–9." *JSOT* 27 (2003): 461–485.

Muffs, Yochanan. "Abraham the Noble Warrior: Patriarchal Politics and Laws of War in Ancient Israel." *JJS* 33 (1982): 81–107.

Müller, Hans Peter. "Die hebräische Wurzel שיח." *VT* 19 (1969): 361–371.

Muraoka, Takamitsu. "On the So-Called Dativus Ethicus in Hebrew." *JTS* 29 (1978): 495–498.

Naveh, Joseph. *Early History of the Alphabet*. Jerusalem, 1997.

Ne'eman, Nadav. "Israel in the Canaanite Era: Middle Bronze Age and Late Bronze Age." In vol. 1 of *The History of the Land of Israel*, edited by Yisrael Efal, 131–213. Jerusalem, 1992 (Hebrew).

Nelson, Richard D. *Joshua*. OTL. Louisville, 1997.

Nicholson, Ernest W. "The Meaning of the Expression *am hā'āres* in the Old Testament." *JSS* 10 (1965): 59–66.

Noble, Paul R. "A 'Balanced' Reading of the Rape of Dinah: Some Exegetical and Methodological Observations." *Biblical Interpretation* 4 (1996): 173–203.

Noble, Paul R. "Esau, Tamar, and Joseph: Criteria for Identifying Inner-Biblical Allusion." *VT* 43 (2002): 219–252.

Noegel, Scott B. "A Crux and a Taunt: Night-Time Then Sunset in Genesis 15." In *The World of Genesis: Persons, Places, Perspectives,* edited by P. R. Davies and D. J. A. Clines, 128–135. JSOTSup 257. Sheffield, 1998.

Noort, Ed. "Abraham and the Nations." In *Abraham, the Nations, and the Hagarites: Jewish, Christian, and Islamic Perspectives on Kinship with Abraham,* edited by M. Goodman, et al., 3–31. Leiden, 2010.

Noort, Ed. "Created in the Image of the Son: Ishmael and Hagar." In *Abraham, the Nations, and the Hagarites: Jewish, Christian, and Islamic Perspectives on Kinship with Abraham,* edited by M. Goodman, G. H. van Kooten, and J. van Ruiten, 33–44. Leiden, 2010.

Noth, Martin. "Old Testament Covenant-Making in the Light of a Text from Mari." In *The Laws in the Pentateuch and Other Essays,* 108–117. Edinburgh, 1966.

Noth, Martin. *A History of Pentateuchal Traditions.* Translated by B. W. Anderson. Englewood Cliffs, NJ, 1972.

Novick, Tzvi. "'Almost, at Times, the Fool': Abimelekh and Genesis 20." *Prooftexts* 24 (2004): 277–290.

O'Connell, Robert H. "שתה." *NIDOTTE* 4:260–262.

Oded, Bustenay. "*Ammon.*" *Entziklopedya Mikra'it* 6:254–271 (Hebrew).

Orlinsky, Harry M. "The Hebrew Root ŜKB." *JBL* 63 (1944): 19–44.

Oswalt, John N. *The Book of Isaiah, Chapters 1–39.* NICOT. Grand Rapids, MI, 1986.

Otto, Eckart. "Abraham zwischen JHWH und Elohim. Zur narrativen Logik des Wechsels der Gottesbezeichnungen in den Abrahamerzählungen." In *Die Erzväter in der biblischen Tradition, Festschrift für Matthias Köckert,* edited by A. C. Hagedorn and H. Pfeiffer, 49–65. Berlin and New York, 2009.

Ouellette, Jean. "More on 'Êl Šadday and Bêl Šadê." *JBL* 88 (1969): 470–471.

Ozkirimli, Umut. *Theories of Nationalism: A Critical Introduction.* New York, 2000.

Pagolu, Augustine. *The Religion of the Patriarchs.* Sheffield, 1998.

Parrot, André. *Abraham and His Times.* Translated by James H. Farley. Philadelphia, 1968.

Pascal, Blaise. *Pensées.* Translated by W. F. Trotter. New York, 1910.

Peleg, Yitzhak. "Was the Ancestress of Israel in Danger?" *ZAW* 118 (2006): 197–208.

Perry, Menakhem. "Literary Dynamics: How the Order of a Text Creates Its Meaning." *Poetics Today* 1 (1979): 35–64, 311–361.

Peter, Michal. "Wer sprach den Segen nach Genesis xiv 19 über Abraham aus?" *VT* 29 (1979): 114–120.

Poirier, Jean-Michel. "'De Campement en campement. Abram alla au Négev' (Gen 12, 9): Le thème de la marche dans le cycle d'Abraham." In *Bible et Terre Sainte: Mélanges Marcel Beaudry,* edited by E. Aguilar Chiu, 31–45. New York, 2008.

Polak, Frank H. *Biblical Narrative Aspects of Art and Design.* 2nd ed. Jerusalem, 1999 (Hebrew).

Polak, Frank H. "Divine Names, Sociolinguistics and the Pragmatics of Pentateuchal Narrative." In *Words, Ideas, Worlds: Biblical Essays in Honour of Yairah Amit*, edited by A. Brenner and F. Polak, 159–178. Sheffield, 2012.

Polak, Frank H. "Epic Formulae in Biblical Narrative and the Origins of Ancient Hebrew Prose." *Te'uda* 7 (1991): 9–53 (Hebrew).

Pratt, Richard L. "Pictures, Windows, and Mirrors in Old Testament Exegesis." *WTJ* 45 (1983): 156–67.

Procksch, Otto. *Die Genesis*. KAT. Leipzig, 1913.

Pushkin, Alexander. *Eugene Onegin*. Translated by Babette Deutsch. Baltimore: Penguin Books, 1964.

Rabinowitz, Jacob J. "The 'Great Sin' in Ancient Egyptian Marriage Contracts." *JNES* 18 (1959): 73.

Rabinowitz, Peter J. "Showing vs. Telling." In *The Routledge Encyclopedia of Narrative Theory*, edited by D. Herman et al., 530–531. London, 2005.

Raday, Tzvi, and Chaim Rabin. *The New Bible Dictionary*. Jerusalem, 1989 (Hebrew).

Radday, Yehuda T. "Chiasmus in Hebrew Biblical Narrative." In *Chiasmus in Antiquity*, edited by J. Welch, 50–115. Hildesheim, 1981.

Rahman, Yossefa. "The Embarrassment Effect in the Sodom and Gomorrah Narrative (Gen. 18–19)." In *A Light for Jacob*, edited by Y. Hoffman and Frank H. Polak, 185–197. Jerusalem, 1997 (Hebrew).

Reimer, David J. "צדק." *NIDOTTE* 3:744–769.

Rank, Otto. *The Incest Theme in Literature and Legend: Fundamentals of a Psychology of Literary Creation*. Translated by G. C. Richter. Baltimore, 1992.

Rashkow, Ilona N. "Daddy-Dearest and the 'Invisible Spirit of Wine.'" In *Genesis: The Feminist Companion to the Bible*, edited by A. Brenner, 82–107. Sheffield, 1998.

Rashkow, Ilona N. "Sexuality in the Hebrew Bible: Freud's Lens." In *Psychology and the Bible: A New Way to Read the Scriptures: From Freud to Kohut*, edited by J. H. Ellens and W. G. Rollins, 33–74. Westport and London, 2004.

Reich, Rachel. *The Woman Whom Thou Gavest to Be with Me*. Tel Aviv, 2005.

Reis, Pamela Tamarkin. "Hagar Requited." *JSOT* 87 (2000): 75–109.

Rendsburg, Gary A. "Notes on Genesis XV." *VT* 42 (1992): 266–268.

Rendsburg, Gary A. *The Redaction of Genesis*. Winona Lake, IN, 1986.

Rendtorff, Rolf. *Das Uberlieferungsgeschichtliche Problem des Pentateuch*. BZAW 147. Berlin and New York, 1977.

Retief, C. Wynand. "When Interpretation Traditions Speak Too Loud for Ethical Dilemmas to Be Heard: On the Untimely Death of Haran (Genesis 11:28)." *Old Testament Essays* 23 (2010): 788–803.

Richardson, Mervyn Edwin John. *Hammurabi's Laws: Text, Translation and Glossary*. Sheffield, 2000.

Rofe, Alexander. "The Betrothal of Rebecca (Genesis 24)." *Eshel Beer Sheva* 1 (1976): 42–67 (Hebrew).

Römer, Thomas C. "The Exodus in the Book of Genesis." *SEÅ* 75 (2010): 1–20.

Römer, Thomas C. "Recherches actuelles sur le cycle d'Abraham." In *Studies in the Book of Genesis: Literature, Redaction and History*, edited by A. Wénin, 179–211. Leuven, 2001.

Roning, John. "The Naming of Isaac: The Role of the Wife/Sister Episodes in the Redaction of Genesis." *WTJ* 53 (1991): 1–27.

Roshwald, Mordecai. "A Dialogue between Man and God." *SJT* 42 (1989): 145–165.

Ross, Allen P. *Creation and Blessing: A Guide to the Study and Exposition of Genesis*. Grand Rapids, MI, 1988.

Rost, Leonhard. "Die Bezeichnungen fur Land und Volk im Alten Testament." In *Das kleine Credo und andere Studien zum Alten Testament*, 76–101. Heidelberg, 1965.

Rost, Leonhard. "Fragen zum Scheidungsgerecht in Gen 12, 10–20." In *Gottes Wort und Gottes Land: Hans-Wilhelm Hertzberg zum 70*, edited by H. G. Reventlow, 186–92. Göttingen, 1965.

Rousseau, Jean-Jacques. *The Social Contract*. Jonathan Bennett edition, 2010.

Rudin-O'Brasky, Talia. *The Patriarch in Hebron and Sodom (Genesis 18–19)*. Jerusalem, 1982.

Sabato, Mordechai. "The Story of the Shunammite Woman." *Megadim* 15 (1992): 45–52 (Hebrew).

Sacks, Robert D. *A Commentary on the Book of Genesis*. Adelaide, 1990.

Samet, Elchanan. *Studies in the Weekly Parasha: First Series*. 2 vols. Maaleh Adumim, 2002 (Hebrew).

Samet, Elchanan. *Studies in the Weekly Parasha: Second Series*. 2 vols. Maaleh Adumim, 2004 (Hebrew).

Šanda, Albert. *Moses und der Pentateuch*. Münster: Aschendorffsche Verlagsbuchhandlung, 1924.

Sarna, Nahum M. "The Anticipatory Use of Information as a Literary Feature of the Genesis Narratives." In *The Creation of Sacred Literature: Composition and Redaction of the Biblical Text*, edited by R. E. Friedman, 76–84. Berkeley, 1982.

Sarna, Nahum M. "Genesis 21:33: A Study in the Development of a Biblical Text and Its Rabbinic Transformation." In *From Ancient Israel to Modern Judaism: Intellect in Quest of Understanding: Essays in Honor of Marvin Fox*, edited by J. Neusner, E. S. Frerichs, and N. M. Sarna, vol. 1, 69–75. BJS 159. Atlanta, 1989.

Sarna, Nahum M. *Genesis*. JPS Torah Commentary. Philadelphia, New York, and Jerusalem: JPS, 1989.

Sarna, Nahum M. *Understanding Genesis*. New York, 1966.

Sasson, Gilad, and Jonathan Grossman. "On Implicit Biblical Analogies in Midrashim of the Sages." *Megadim* 46 (2007): 17–42 (Hebrew).

Sasson, Jack M. "Circumcision in the Ancient Near East." *JBL* 85 (1966): 473–476.

Savran, George. "The Character as Narrator in Biblical Narrative." *Prooftexts* 5 (1985): 1–17.

Schlossberg, Eliezer. "There Is Not a Man on Earth to Consort with Us in the Way of All the World." *Sinai* 111 (1993): 146–161 (Hebrew).

Schmid, Konrad. *Erzväter und Exodus: Untersuchungen zur doppelten Begründung der Ursprünge Israels innerhalb der Geschichtsbücher des Alten Testaments*. Neukirchen-Vluyn, 1999.

Schmidt, Ludwig. *"De Deo": Studien zur Literakritik und Theologie des Buches Jona, des Gesprächs zwischen Abraham und Jahwe in Gen 18, 22ff und von Hiob 1*. Berlin and New York, 1976.

Schmitt, Götz. "El Berit-Mitra." *ZAW* 76 (1964): 325–327.

Schökel, Louis Alonso. *A Manual of Hebrew Poetics*. Subsidia Biblica 11. Roma, 2000.

Scholz, Susanne. *Rape Plots: A Feminist Cultural Study of Genesis 34*. New York, 2000.

Schweid, Eliezer. *The Philosophy of the Bible as Foundation of Jewish Culture*. Translated by L. Levin. Boston, 2009.

Seebass, Horst. "נפל." *TDOT* 9:488–497.

Seebass, Horst. *Genesis II. Vätergeschichte I (11, 27–22, 24)*. Neukirchen-Vluyn, 1997.

Seeligman, Isaac Leo. *Studies in Biblical Literature*, edited by A. Hurvitz, S. Japhet, and E. Tov. Jerusalem, 1992 (Hebrew).

Seifert, Elke. "Lot und seine Töchter: Eine Hermeneutik des Verdachts." In *Feministische Hermeneutik und Erstes Testament: Analysen und Interpretationen*, edited by H. Jahnow, 48–66. Stuttgart, 1994.

Seymour, Michel, Jocelyn Couture, and Kai Nielsen. "Introduction: Questioning the Ethnic/Civic Dichotomy." In *Rethinking Nationalism*, edited by J. Couture et al., 7–28. Calgary, 1996.

Shama, Avraham. "Processes of Formulation and Changes in Ramban's Critical Attitude Towards Abram's Descent to Egypt (Genesis 12)." *Megadim* 50 (2009): 199–220 (Hebrew).

Shanks, Herschel. "Illuminations: Abraham Cut off from His Past and Future by the Awkward Divine Command 'Go You!'" *Bible Review* 3 (1987): 8–9.

Shapira, Amnon. "He Shall Be a Wild Ass of a Man." *Beit Mikra* 41 (1996): 101–127 (Hebrew).

Shemesh, Yael. "Biblical Stories of Rape: Common Traits and Unique Features." *Studies in Bible and Exegesis* 6 (2002): 315–344 (Hebrew).

Shemesh, Yael. "Lies by Prophets and Other Lies in the Hebrew Bible." *JANES* 29 (2002): 81–95.

Shiloach, Meir. "And He Said ... and He Said." In *Sefer Korngreen*, edited by A. Weiser and B. Z. Luria, 251–267. Tel Aviv, 1964 (Hebrew).

Shimon, Zvi. *Contrast in Biblical Narrative: The Literary Device and the Drama of Choice*. PhD diss., Bar Ilan University, 2009 (Hebrew).

Simon, Uriel. "Biblical Abraham: The Blessing of Contrasts." In *The Faith of Abraham: In the Light of Interpretation Throughout the Ages*, edited by M. Hallamish, H. Kasher, and Y. Silman, 41–46. Ramat Gan, 2002 (Hebrew).

Simon, Uriel. "Notes on the Binding of Isaac." *Hagut BaMikra* 1 (1973): 163–170 (Hebrew).

Simon, Uriel. *Reading Prophetic Narratives*. The Biblical Encyclopedia Library and Bialik Institute. Jerusalem, 1997 (Hebrew).

Simons, Jan Jozef. *The Geographical and Topographical Texts of the Old Testament*. Leiden, 1959.

Singer, Itamar. *The Hittites and Their Civilization*. Jerusalem, 2009 (Hebrew).

Sivan, Abraham. "The Negotiations over the Cave of Machpelah." In *The Book of Sivan – A Collection of Studies in Memory of Shalom Sivan*, edited by Abraham Even-Shoshan et al., 207–215. Jerusalem: Kiryat Sepher, 1979.

Ska, Jean Louis. "Gn 18,1–15 alla prova dell'esegesi classica e dell'esegesi narrative." *Asprenas* 40 (1993): 5–22.

Skinner, John. *A Critical and Exegetical Commentary on Genesis*, 2nd edition. ICC. Edinburgh, 1930.

Smith, Anthony D. *The Nation in History: Historiographical Debates about Ethnicity and Nationalism*. Hanover, 2000.

Smith, Cheryl Hogue. "Challenged by the Text: Interpreting Two Stories of Incest in the Hebrew Bible." In *A Feminist Companion to Reading the Bible: Approaches, Methods and Strategies*, edited by A. Brenner and C. Fontaine, 114–135. Sheffield, 1997.

Smith, Robert Houston. "Abram and Melchizedek (Genesis 14, 18–20)." *ZAW* 77 (1965): 129–153.

Smith, Ralph L. *Micah-Malachi*. WBC. Dallas, Texas, 1998.

Sonek, Krzysztof. *Truth, Beauty, and Goodness in Biblical Narratives: A Hermeneutical Study of Genesis 21:1–21*. BZAW 395. Berlin and New York, 2009.

Sorman, Guy. "Where Nationalism Still Matters: Asia's Simmering Political Tensions Defy Conventional Wisdom." *City Journal*, August 20, 2012.

Speiser, Ephraim A. "'Coming' and 'Going' at the City Gate." *BASOR* 144 (1956): 20–23.

Speiser, Ephraim A. "'People' and 'Nation' of Israel." *JBL* 79 (1960): 157–163.

Speiser, Ephraim A. *Genesis*. AB. Garden City, NY, 1964.

Speiser, Ephraim A. "The Wife-Sister Motif in the Patriarchal Narratives." In *Biblical and Other Studies*, edited by Alexander H. Altmann, 15–28. Cambridge, MA: Harvard University Press, 1963.

Spiro-Applebaum, Devorah. "Between Isaac's Ascent (to the Altar) and Elijah's Ascent (to Heaven)." *Megadim* 45 (2007): 9–19 (Hebrew).

Stade, Bernhard. *Geschichte des Volkes Israel*. 2 vols. Berlin, 1887–1888.

Stanzel, Franz K. *Theorie des Erzählens*. Göttingen 1979.

Stav, Shira. "Fathers and Daughters: The Incest Trap." *Theory and Criticism* 37 (2010): 69–95 (Hebrew).

Steinberg, Yehoshua. *A Dictionary of the Bible*. Tel Aviv, 1962.

Steinmetz, Devora. *From Father to Son: Kinship, Conflict, and Continuity in Genesis*. Louisville, 1991.

Sternberg, Meir. "Delicate Balance in the Story of the Rape of Dinah: Biblical Narratives and the Rhetoric of the Narrative Text." *Hasifrut* 4 (1973): 193–231 (Hebrew).

Sternberg, Meir. "The Structure of Repetition in Biblical Narratives: Strategies of Informational Redundancy." *Hasifrut* 25 (1977): 109–150 (Hebrew).

Sternberg, Meir. *The Poetics of Biblical Narrative: Ideological Literature and the Drama of Reading*. Bloomington, 1985.

Sternberg, Meir. "Double Cave, Double Talk: The Indirections of Biblical Dialogue." In *Not in Heaven*, edited by J. P. Rosenblatt and J. C. Sitterson, 28–57. Philadelphia and Bloomington, 1991.

Stigers, Harold G. *A Commentary on Genesis*. Grand Rapids, MI, 1976.

Suomala, Karla R. *Moses and God in Dialogue: Exodus 32–34 in Postbiblical Literature*. New York, 2004.

Sutherland, Dixon. "The Organization of the Abraham Promise Narratives." *ZAW* 95 (1983): 337–343.

Sutskover, Talia. "Lot and His Daughters (Gen. 19:30–30): Further Literary and Stylistic Examinations." *JHS* 11 (2011): 2–11.

Talmon, Shmaryahu. *Darkhei HaSippur BaMikra*. Edited by G. Gil. Jerusalem, 1965 (Hebrew).

Terrien, Samuel L. *The Elusive Presence: Toward a New Biblical Theology*. San Francisco, 1978.

Teugels, Lieve M. "'A Strong Woman, Who Can Find?' A Study of Characterization in Genesis 24, with Some Perspectives on the General Presentation of Isaac and Rebecca in the Genesis Narratives." *JSOT* 63 (1994): 88–104.

Thames, John Tracy. "A New Discussion of the Meaning of the Phrase *'am hāāreṣ* in the Hebrew Bible." *JBL* 130 (2011): 109–125.

Thomas, D. Winton. "Julius Furst and the Hebrew Root ידע," *JTS* 42 (1941): 64–65.

Thompson, Thomas L. *The Historicity of the Patriarchal Narrative: The Quest for Historical Abraham*. BZAW 133. Berlin and New York, 1974.

Thompson, Thomas L. *The Origin Tradition of Ancient Israel: The Literary Formation of Genesis and Exodus 1–23*. JSOTSup 55. Sheffield, 1987.

Tomasino, Antholy. "עולם." *NIDOTTE* 3:345–351.

Tonson, Paul. "Mercy without Covenant: A Literary Analysis of Genesis 19." *JSOT* 95 (2001): 95–116.

Toombs, Lawrence. "Shechem." *ABD* 5:1174–1186.

Trible, Phyllis. "Genesis 22: The Sacrifice of Sarah." In *"Not in Heaven": Coherence and Complexity in Biblical Narrative,* edited by J. P. Rosenblatt and J. C. Sitterson, Jr, 170–191. Bloomington, 1991.

Trible, Phyllis. *Texts of Terror: Literary-Feminist Readings of Biblical Narratives.* London, 1984.

Tsamudi, Yosef. *A Second Look at the Bible.* Tel Aviv, 1997 (Hebrew).

Tucker, Gene M. "The Legal Background of Genesis 23." *JBL* 85 (1966): 77–84.

Tucker, JoAnne, and Susan Freeman. *Torah in Motion: Creating Dance Midrash.* Denver, 1990.

Turner, Laurence A. "Lot as Jekyll and Hyde: A Reading of Genesis 18–19." In *The Bible in Three Dimensions: Essays in Celebration of Forty Years of Biblical Studies in the University of Sheffield,* edited by D. J. A. Clines et al., 59–98. JSOTSup 87. Sheffield, 1990.

Tzohar, Yael. *The Exposition in the Biblical Narrative.* PhD diss., Bar Ilan University, 2005.

Uspensky, Boris. *A Poetics of Composition: The Structure of the Artistic Text and Typology of a Compositional Form.* Translated by V. Zavarin and S. Wittig. Berkeley and Los Angeles, 1973.

Van den Berg, Evert. "Van elohim tot JHWH: het boek Job als zoektocht naar het monotheïsme." *Nederlands Theologisch Tijdschrift* 66 (2012): 266–282.

Vall, Gregory. "What Was Isaac Doing in the Field (Genesis xxiv 63)?" *VT* 44 (1994): 513–523.

Van Dijk-Hemmes, Fokkeilen. "Sarai's Exile: A Gender-Motivated Reading of Genesis 12.10–13.2." In *A Feminist Companion to Genesis,* edited by A. Brenner, 222–234. Sheffield, 1993.

Van Ruiten, Jacques. "Lot versus Abraham: The Interpretation of Genesis 18:1–19:38 in *Jubilees* 16:1–9." In *Sodom's Sin: Genesis 18–19 and Its Interpretations,* edited by E. Noort and E. Tigchelaar, 29–46. Leiden, 2004.

Van Seters, John. "The Problem of Childlessness in Near Eastern Law and the Patriarchs of Israel." *JBL* 87 (1968), 401–408.

Van Seters, John. *Abraham in History and Tradition.* New Haven, CT, 1975.

Van Uchelen, Nico Adriaan. *Abraham De Hebreeër: Een literair en historisch-kritische studie naar aanleiding van Genesis 14:13.* Assen, 1964.

Vaughn, Andrew G. "'And Lot Went with Him': Abraham's Disobedience in Genesis 12:1–4a." In *David and Zion: Biblical Studies in Honor of J. J. M. Roberts,* edited by B. F. Batto and K. L. Roberts, 111–123. Winona Lake, IN, 2004.

Vawter, Bruce. *On Genesis: A New Reading.* Garden City, NY, 1977.

Vogels, Walter. "Lot in His Honor Restored: A Structural Analysis of Gen 13:2–18." *Eglise et Théologie* 10 (1979): 5–12.

Vogels, Walter. *Abraham et sa legend: Genèse 12.1–25.11.* Lire la Bible 110. Paris, 1996.

Von Rad, Gerhard. *Genesis.* OTL. Translated by J. H. Marks. 2nd ed. London, 1963.

Von Rad, Gerhard. *Das erste Buch Mose: Genesis.* Göttingen: Vandenhoeck und Ruprecht, 1958.

von Soden, Wolfram. *The Ancient Orient: An Introduction to the Study of the Ancient Near East.* Grand Rapids, MI, 1994.

Walsh, Jerome T. *Style and Structure in Biblical Hebrew Narrative.* Collegeville, MN, 2001.

Walters, Stanley D. "Wood, Sand and Stars: Structure and Theology in Genesis 22:1–19." *Toronto Journal of Theology* 3 (1987): 301–330.

Waltke, Bruce K., and Cathi J. Fredricks. *Genesis: A Commentary.* Grand Rapids, MI, 2001.

Warner, Megan E. "Keeping the Way of YHWH: Righteousness and Justice in Genesis 18–19." In *Universalism and Particularism at Sodom and Gomorrah,* edited by Z. Garber and R. Libowitz, 113–128. Atlanta, 2012.

Weinfeld, Moshe. "The Covenant of Grant in the Old Testament and in the Ancient Near East." *JAOS* 90 (1970): 184–203.

Weinfeld, Moshe. "ברית." *TDOT* 2:253–279.

Weinfeld, Moshe. *Deuteronomy and the Deuteronomic School.* Oxford, 1972.

Weinfeld, Moshe. *From Joshua to Josiah: Turning Points in the History of Israel from the Conquest of the Land Until the Fall of Judah.* Jerusalem, 1992.

Weippert, Manfred. "Erwägungen zur Etymologie des Gottesnames 'El Ŝaddaj." *ZDMG* 111 (1961): 42–62.

Weiser, Asher. "Egypt in the Bible." *Mahanaim* 105 (1961): 16–24 (Hebrew).

Weisman, Zeev. *From Jacob to Israel: The Cycle of Jacob's Stories and Its Incorporation within the History of the Patriarchs.* Jerusalem, 1986 (Hebrew).

Weiss, Meir. *Scriptures in Their Own Light: Collected Essays.* Jerusalem, 1987 (Hebrew).

Weissbluth, Shlomo. "'Abraham Planted a Tamarisk at Beersheba, and Invoked There the Name of the Lord, the Everlasting God' (Gen. 21:33)." *Beit Mikra* 36 (1990): 11–19 (Hebrew).

Wellhausen, Julius. *Prolegomena to the History of Israel.* Atlanta, 1994.

Wenham, Gordon J. "The Symbolism of the Animal Rite in Genesis 15." *JSOT* 22 (1982): 134–137.

Wenham, Gordon J. *Genesis 1–15.* WBC. Waco, Texas, 1987.

Wenham, Gordon J. *Genesis 16–50.* WBC. Waco, Texas, 1994.

Westbrook, Raymond. "Purchase of the Cave of Machpelah (Gen. 23)." *Israel Law Review* 6 (1971): 29–38.

Westermann, Claus. *Genesis 1–11: A Continental Commentary.* Translated by J. J. Scullion. Minneapolis, 1994.

Westermann, Claus. *Genesis 12–36: A Continental Commentary.* Translated by J. J. Scullion. Minneapolis, 1995.

Westermarck, Edward. *Three Essays on Sex and Marriage.* London, 1934.

Wheaton, Byron. "Focus and Structure in the Abraham Narratives." *Trinity Journal* 27 (2006): 143–162.

Williamson, Paul R. *Abraham, Israel and the Nations: The Patriarchal Promise and Its Covenantal Development in Genesis.* JSOTSup 315. Sheffield, 2001.

Willi-Plein, Ina. "Power or Inheritance: A Constructive Comparison of Genesis 16 and Genesis 21." In *Genesis, Isaiah and Psalms: A Festschrift to Honour Professor John Emerton for his Eightieth Birthday,* edited by K. J. Dell, G. Davies, and Y. Von Koh, 33–44. VTSup 135. Leiden, 2010.

Winnett, Frederick Victor. "The Arabian Genealogies in the Book of Genesis." In *Translating and Understanding the Old Testament: Essays in Honor of Herbert Gordon May,* edited by H. T. Frank and W. L. Reed, 171–196. Nashville, 1970.

Wyatt, Nick. "Circumcision and Circumstance: Male Genital Mutilation in Ancient Israel and Ugarit." *JSOT* 33 (2009): 405–431.

Wyatt, Nick. "The Story of Dinah and Shechem." *UF* 22 (1990): 433–458.

Yeivin, Shemuel. "Patriarchs in the Land." In *The History of the People of Israel: The Patriarchs and the Judges,* edited by Benjamin Mazar, 103–110. Jerusalem, 1967 (Hebrew).

Yona, Shamir. "Stylistic and Syntactic Variants in Repeated Texts in the Bible." In *Yitzhak Avishur Festschrift,* edited by Michael Heltzer and Meir Malul, 225–232. Tel Aviv: Archaeological Center Publications, 2004.

Zakovitch, Yair. "Explicit and Implicit Name-Derivations." *HAR* 4 (1980): 167–181.

Zakovitch, Yair. "Foreshadowing in Biblical Narrative." *Beer Sheva* 2 (1985): 85–105 (Hebrew).

Zakovitch, Yair. *"I Will Express Riddles of Old": Riddles and Dream-Riddles in Biblical Narrative.* Tel Aviv, 2005 (Hebrew).

Zakovitch, Yair. *"Man Sees Only What Is Visible But the Lord Sees into the Heart": Disguise and Retribution in Biblical Narrative.* Jerusalem, 1998 (Hebrew).

Zakovitch, Yair. "The Exodus from Egypt in Genesis." *Al Haperek* 3 (1987): 25–34 (Hebrew).

Zakovitch, Yair. "The Exodus from Ur of the Chaldeans: A Chapter in Literary Archaeology." In *Ki Baruch Hu: Ancient Near Eastern, Biblical and Judaic Studies in Honor of Baruch A. Levine,* edited by R. Chazan, W. W. Hallo, and L. H. Schiffman, 429–439. Winona Lake, IN, 1999.

Zakovitch, Yair. *"I Will Express Riddles of Old": Riddles and Dream-Riddles in Biblical Narrative.* Tel Aviv: Am Oved, 2005 (Hebrew).

Zakovitch, Yair. *Introduction to Inner-Biblical Interpretation.* Kadima, 1992 (Hebrew).

Zakovitch, Yair, and Avigdor Shinan. *That's Not What the Good Book Says.* Tel Aviv, 2004 (Hebrew).

Zakovitch, Yair. *Through the Looking Glass: Reflection Stories in the Bible.* Tel Aviv, 1995 (Hebrew).

Zakovitch, Yair, and Avigdor Shinan. *Abram and Sarai in Egypt.* Jerusalem, 1983 (Hebrew).

Zevit, Ziony. "Expressing Denial in Biblical Hebrew and Mishnaic Hebrew, and in Amos." *VT* 29 (1979): 505–509.

Zimmerli, Walther. "Abraham und Melchisedek." In *Das nahe und dasferne Wort,* edited by F. Maass, 255–264. BZAW 105. Berlin, 1967.

Zipor, Moshe A. *The Septuagint Version of the Book of Genesis.* Ramat Gan, 2005 (Hebrew).

Other books in the *Maggid Tanakh Companions* series

To This Very Day: Fundamental Questions in Bible Study
Amnon Bazak

Textual Tapestries: Explorations of the Five Megillot
Gabriel H. Cohn

Places in the Parasha: Biblical Geography and Its Meaning
Yoel Elitzur

Creation: The Story of Beginnings
Jonathan Grossman

Subversive Sequels in the Bible: How Biblical Stories Mine and Undermine Each Other
Judy Klitsner

Tribal Blueprints: Twelve Brothers and the Destiny of Israel
Nechama Price

Great Biblical Commentators
Biographies, Methodologies, and Contributions
Avigail Rock

Elijah
Elhanan Samet

The fonts used in this book are from the Arno family

Maggid Books
The best of contemporary Jewish thought from
Koren Publishers Jerusalem Ltd.